CW00685498

The Mosaics of Roman Crete

This book examines the rich corpus of mosaics created in Crete during the Roman and Late Antique eras. It provides essential information on the style, iconography and chronology of the material, as well as discussion of the craftspeople who created them and the technologies they used. The contextualized mosaic evidence also reveals a new understanding of Roman and Late Antique Crete. It helps shed light on the processes by which Crete became part of the Roman Empire, its subsequent Christianization and the pivotal role the island played in the Mediterranean network of societies during these periods. This book provides an original approach to the study of mosaics and an innovative method of presenting a diachronic view of provincial Cretan society.

Rebecca J. Sweetman is Senior Lecturer in Ancient History and Archaeology at the School of Classics, University of St. Andrews. She has published widely on Roman and Late Antique Greece, including articles in the *American Journal of Archaeology*, the *Annual of the British School at Athens* and the *Journal of Late Antiquity*, and is the editor of *Roman Colonies in the First Century of Their Foundation* (2011). A former Assistant Director of the British School at Athens she has run and participated in excavations around Greece including Sparta, Melos, Corinth and Knossos.

THE MOSAICS OF ROMAN CRETE

Art, Archaeology and Social Change

Rebecca J. Sweetman

University of St. Andrews

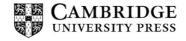
CAMBRIDGE
UNIVERSITY PRESS

CAMBRIDGE UNIVERSITY PRESS
Cambridge, New York, Melbourne, Madrid, Cape Town,
Singapore, São Paulo, Delhi, Mexico City

Cambridge University Press
32 Avenue of the Americas, New York, NY 10013-2473, USA

www.cambridge.org
Information on this title: www.cambridge.org/9781107018402

© Rebecca J. Sweetman 2013

This publication is in copyright. Subject to statutory exception
and to the provisions of relevant collective licensing agreements,
no reproduction of any part may take place without the written
permission of Cambridge University Press.

First published 2013

Printed in the United States of America

A catalog record for this publication is available from the British Library.

Library of Congress Cataloging in Publication data
Sweetman, Rebecca J.
The mosaics of Roman Crete : art, archaeology and social change /
Rebecca J. Sweetman, University of St. Andrews.
p.   cm.
Includes bibliographical references and index.
ISBN 978-1-107-01840-2 (hardback)
1. Mosaics, Roman – Greece – Crete.   2. Crete (Greece) – Civilization.   I. Title.
NA3770.S94   2012
738.50939′18–dc23   2012002644

ISBN 978-1-107-01840-2 Hardback

Cambridge University Press has no responsibility for the persistence or accuracy of URLs
for external or third-party Internet Web sites referred to in this publication and does not
guarantee that any content on such Web sites is, or will remain, accurate or appropriate.

To my families in Ireland, Canada and Scotland

CONTENTS

CONTENTS

CONTENTS

ILLUSTRATIONS

LIST OF ILLUSTRATIONS

FIGURES

PREFACE

An impressive series of corpora of mosaics now exists for nearly every province of the Roman world with the notable exception of Crete. The corpora range from those that cover wide geographical areas such as Dunbabin's (1978b) *Mosaics of Roman North Africa* to the series of monographs recording the mosaics of Gaul (*Recueil général des mosaïques de la Gaule*) to those which deal with specific sites within a province such as Campbell's (1991) *Mosaics of Aphrodisias in Caria*. The considerable evidence has been approached in different ways, such as by focusing on a particular period (e.g., Alföldi-Rosenbaum and Ward-Perkins's (1980) *Justinianic Mosaic Pavements in Cyrenaican Churches*) or on an identifiable style or technique such as Clarke's (1979) *Roman Black-and-White Figural Mosaics* or on a specific element of iconography such as Parrish's (1984) *The Seasons Mosaics of Roman North Africa*. Balmelle's (1985 & 2002) edited collections of geometric elements have made a significant contribution in allowing scholars to use a standardized terminology for mosaic descriptions. In more recent years, mosaic studies have fuelled some of the more enlightening debates on issues of craftspeople and use of architectural space (such as Kondoleon's (1995) *Domestic and Divine: Roman Mosaics in the House of Dionysos* and Muth's (1998) *Erleben von Raum, Leben im Raum: Zur Funktion mythologischer Mosaikbilder in der römisch-kaiserzeitlichen Wohnarchitektur*) but without the publication of the basic corpus such analysis and interpretation is not possible.

In 1982, Sanders's pivotal publication *Roman Crete* allowed scholars access to an area of Roman studies which had been sadly neglected. This work was an indispensable record of the Roman and Late Antique archaeology and history of Crete, but the author's untimely death meant that the contextual analysis of the material was limited. In recent years, an increase in archaeological surveys and excavations has provided new primary material, and current research on aspects of Roman and Late Antique Crete is leading to a contrary and more nuanced view than that of Sanders. In this context, it is clear that a diachronic analysis of the island from a range of perspectives (local and centre) is needed to reverse the creeping determinism[1] that has propagated the idea of Roman and Late Antique Crete as a provincial dead end. As such it is apparent that alternative means of assessing the nature of Crete within the context of the Roman Empire must be pursued and that mosaics, as a body of material common throughout the island and the empire across both the Roman and Late Antique periods, should be used to provide the core evidence.

This work represents the first corpus of the Roman and Late Antique mosaics of central and eastern Crete.[2] As a corpus, the mosaics of Crete are not well known; the material published thus far has appeared either in Greek excavation reports such as *Αρχαιολογικόν Δελτίον*, in journals such as *Κρητική Εστία* or in local newspaper reports. In some cases, records of the mosaics exist only in archives and have yet to be published at all. In more recent mosaic studies, the published Knossos mosaics are being used in comparative analysis and this highlights the urgent need for the publication of the corpus. This monograph uses an archaeological approach to the interpretation of mosaics (Chapter 2) while providing essential information on their iconography (Chapter 3). Together these chapters allow a new interpretation of the evidence concerning their date and distribution (Chapter 4), the urban and architectural contexts in which they were found (Chapter 5) and the technology involved in their creation (Chapter 6). Ultimately, this approach affords a fresh view on the mosaics within various theoretical frameworks (Chapter 7). In the analytical discussion, full consideration is given all the mosaics of the island, evidence that contributes to a new diachronic study of Roman and Late Antique Crete. It is my contention that the mosaics of Crete do not simply belong in either a Western or an Eastern koine and that a careful analysis of their iconography, date and distribution will show that the fluctuating styles, locations and density of mosaics indicate subtle changes in the nature of the society of Roman Crete.

The inclusion of the Late Antique mosaics emphasizes the importance of Crete during the period and contradicts the common perception of decline. Not only do these mosaics indicate that the island was booming, but the evidence of itinerant mosaicists suggests that the island played a crucial role in the communication network of the Eastern Empire.

Through an interpretative archaeological approach to the Roman and Late Antique mosaics this monograph will offer a comprehensive and enlightened view of the nature of society in Crete from the first century B.C.E. to the seventh century C.E. In doing so, this work will make two major contributions to Roman Mediterranean archaeology: it will be the first publication of the corpus of mosaics of Crete, and it will present a new perspective on the long-term continuity and change of Roman and Late Antique Crete.

ACKNOWLEDGEMENTS

This work was undertaken with the generous support of a number of people and institutions. I have been extremely fortunate to have met so many who have been more than willing to help me in a variety of ways, ultimately leading to my completion of this work.

I started this work during a research leave supported by the School of Classics, University St Andrews, and I have benefited greatly from an AHRC Research Leave award. A Cotton Fellowship ensured me four months of invaluable research at the British School in Athens, and my fieldwork in 2008 was generously funded by the Carnegie Trust.

I am grateful for the significant help given to me by many Ephores, Ephorea staff and colleagues in Greece, particularly those in the Athens Archaeological Society (especially Mrs Ninou), Professor Platon, Dr Karetsou, Professor Themelis, Dr Hadzi-Vallianou and the late Professor Bourboudakis and the French and Italian Schools. I would especially like to thank Ms Stavroula Markoulaki for her help and useful discussions on the Roman mosaics of Crete, and also Dr Panajota Assimakopoulou-Atzaka and Dr Anastasia Panagiotopoulou for their enlightening discussions on mosaics in general, and to thank all for sharing their material.

The library, office and archive staff at the British School at Athens has, as always, been extremely supportive and helpful with material and permits. I would like to thank all my good friends there – Helen Clark, Vicki Tzavara, Maria Papaconstantinou and Tania Gerousi – for their help in securing permits as well as for giving me access to material and publication rights. The librarians and the archivists of the British School are remarkable. Penny Wilson, Sandra Pepelasis and Amalia Kakissis searched for and acquired books, permissions and material on my behalf with patience and good humour, and they are always helpful with matters inside and outside the library. As well as these staff members, the British School's director, Cathy Morgan; assistant director, Robert Pit; and Knossos curator, Don Evely helped create a superb working environment for much of this research. I am particularly grateful to the director and all the staff for their kindnesses during my visit in spring 2008.

I am very grateful to Ben Millis for his generous help with my incessant questions about the mosaic inscriptions. Michael Boyd was particularly encouraging with the work for my thesis. Guy Sanders provided me with endless help and encouragement in discussions of this and other work. I am grateful to him for the invaluable opportunity to spend time working in Corinth.

I owe a huge debt of gratitude to Sara Paton. She gave me the opportunity to work on the Villa Dionysus mosaics and has generously allowed me to reproduce some of her photographs from the Villa Dionysus and Myrtos. She has encouraged me throughout my career, and I have benefited greatly from her extensive knowledge of and contagious enthusiasm for Roman Crete. I would especially like to thank her for her kindness on my trip to Chania.

Dr Liz Waywell kindly gave me access to her thesis, as well as much encouragement and many helpful insights on the material. Dr Demetrios Michaelides was also very helpful, particularly with information on the Cyrenaican mosaics. Professor Katherine Dunbabin, Dr Ruth Westgate and Dr Janet Huskinson provided encouragement and advice.

Permission for the reproduction of images has kindly been given by the following: S. Paton (Pls. 1–7, 13, Fig. 18); BSA Archives (Pls. 8, 9, 12, 23, 24, Fig. 12); K. Wardle (Pl. 10); A. Karetsou (Pl. 14); D. Hadzi Vallianou (Pl. 16, Fig. 19); Italian School of Archaeology (Pls. 17–19); Archaeological Society at Athens (Pls. 21, 27, 37); 13th Byzantine Ephorea (Pls. 25, 26, 28–30, 38); P. Themelis (Pl. 31); 28th Byzantine Ephorea (Pls. 32–6, 45–9); KE Ephorea of Prehistoric and Classical Antiquities (Pls. 39–44) and the Κρητικά Χρονικά © Society of Cretan Historical Studies (Pl. 50). The inclusion of colour illustrations would not have been possible without the generous support of ASPROM, The Association for the Study and Preservation of Roman Mosaics.

Particular thanks to James Stewart for his timely editing work and to Clare Lewis for all her help and her mad dash to the post office on the 14th of November. I have enjoyed years of fieldwork and happy discussions of Crete in preparation for this manuscript and the thesis before. Early fieldwork was undertaken with the help of Michael Boyd, Johnny Gogan, Amanda Kelly and Kevin Sullivan. I was ably assisted in the most recent fieldwork by Brad MacKay, David Sweetman, Rosanne Meenan, and Barry and Kae Anne MacKay. Each went beyond the call of duty in their help on this project, and I am very pleased that they all *enjoyed* traipsing around Crete. I would like to thank my godparents, James Nugent and Mary Murnane, for their encouragement. My parents have always been particularly encouraging of this work, and their delight in it is inspiring. I am very grateful to Katie Sweetman, who skilfully and patiently produced the line drawings, and to Margarita Lianou, who checked my Greek. I would also like to acknowledge my colleagues in the School of Classics for their encouragement and for creating a happy working environment. The work of the three external readers was of enormous help to me in getting the book into shape, and I am very grateful for their thorough comments. I would also like to thank everyone at Cambridge University Press who worked hard to see this through.

Finally, I would like to thank Brad, Conor and Aidan, mostly for allowing me to hijack their holidays but also Conor and Aidan for holding on just long enough. Brad has been incredibly encouraging in this project and now knows significantly more than he ever expected to about Roman and Late Antique Crete.

ABBREVIATIONS

AAA	*Athens Annals of Archaeology*
ABSA	*Annual of the British School at Athens*
A.Delt.	*Αρχαιολογικόν Δελτίον*
AE	*Αρχαιολογική Εφημερίς*
AJA	*American Journal of Archaeology*
AMP	Levi, D. 1947. *Antioch Mosaic Pavements*. Vols. I and II (Princeton)
AR	*Archaeological Reports*, 'Archaeology in Greece', *JHS*
ASAtene	*Annuario della scuola archeologica di Atene e delle missioni Italiane in oriente*
BCH	*Bulletin de correspondance hellénique*
BICS	*Bulletin of the Institute of Classical Studies*
Byz Corp I	Pelekanidis, S., and P. Atzaka, 1988. *Σύνταγμα των παλαιοχριστιανικών ψηφιδωτών δαπέδων της Ελλάδος I; Νησιωτική Ελλάς* (*Κέντρον Βυζαντινών Ερευνών Θεσσαλονίκη*) (Thessaloniki)
Byz Corp II	Assimakopoulou-Atzaka, P. 1987. *Σύνταγμα των παλαιοχριστιανικών ψηφιδωτών δαπέδων της Ελλάδος II: Πελοπόννησος – Στερεά Ελλάδα* (*Κέντρον Βυζαντινών Ερευνών Θεσσαλονίκη*) (Thessaloniki)
Décor	Balmelle, C., et al. 1985. *Le Décor géometrique de la mosaïque gréco-romaine* (Paris)
DOP	*Dunbarton Oaks Papers*
IC	Guarducci, M. 1935. *Inscriptiones Creticae Opera et Consilio Frederici Halbherr Collectae*. Rome. Vols. I, II, III, IV
IG	*Inscriptiones Graecae*

ILN   *Illustrated London News*
JHS   *Journal of Hellenic Studies*
JRA   *Journal of Roman Archaeology*
JRS   *Journal of Roman Studies*
K.Estia   *Κρητική Εστία*
K.Khron   *Κρητικά Χρονικά*
KS   Hood, S., and D. Smyth. 1981. *Archaeological Survey of the Knossos Area*. BSA Suppl. Vol. 14 (London)
LIMC   *Lexicon iconographicum mythologiae classicae*
MAAR   *Memoirs of the American Academy at Rome*
OCD   *Oxford Classical Dictionary* (3rd ed.). 1996. Edited by S. Hornblower and A. Spawforth (Oxford)
PAE   *Πρακτικά της Αρχαιολογικής Εταιρείας*
PBSR   *Papers of the British School at Rome*
R   The letter **R** with a number after it indicates the number of the geometric motif in *Le Décor géométrique de la mosaïque romaine* (C. Balmelle, et al., 1985, Paris)
RPGR   Reinach, S. 1922. *Répertoire de peintures grecques et romaines* (Paris)
Sanders   Sanders, I. F. 1982. *Roman Crete* (Warminister)
SEG   *Supplementum Epigraphicum Graecum*
Volanakis   Volanakis, I. H. 1987. ΄Τα παλαιοχριστιανικά μνημεία της Κρήτης' *K.Khron*, ΚΖ, 235–61

@@ @@ @@ @@

ONE

INTRODUCTION

1.1 A Study of the Roman and Late Antique Mosaics of Crete

Until the latter part of the twentieth century, the archaeology of Roman and Late Antique[1] Crete was commonly seen as an inconvenient stepping stone to reaching the more tantalizing levels of Minoan occupation. Recently, a significant change in approach has been exemplified by the increase in research excavations which focus specifically on post-Minoan levels[2] and through progressions in survey methods.[3] The resulting data have partly been the motivation for the now buoyant interest in synthetic analysis and publication on a range of material and issues concerning Roman and Late Antique Crete.[4] In view of the enlightened perspective, this work attends to two key topics. It contributes to mosaic research agendas, and it uses the material to provide an up-to-date interpretation of Roman and Late Antique Crete. Altogether, this study applies a contemporary theoretical approach to a once poorly published body of evidence. Traditional studies of provincial mosaic corpora supply essential discussion of iconography, techniques and style, but tend not to apply the analysis to comment on the socio-economic nature of the provinces in question.[5] An archaeological approach to the study of the Cretan mosaics enables a wide-ranging view of contexts and associated material. This demands a reassessment of long-established views, for example, assumptions concerning absolute cultural change when Crete became part of the Roman Empire, the rise and decline of the island's settlements and the impact of earthquakes. All of this can be achieved through the acknowledgement of such psychological biases as creeping determinism and hindsight bias that shape our interpretation of the past (see Chapter 3).[6] In turn, the application of theoretical methodologies such

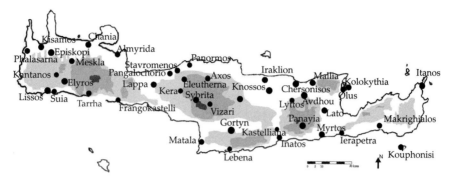

Fig. 1 Map of Crete showing location of mosaics.

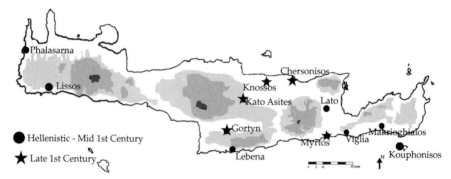

Fig. 2 Map of Crete showing Hellenistic and first-century C.E. mosaics.

as spatial analysis, globalization and Christianization[7] facilitates insights from multiple perspectives (e.g., Cretan and Roman, and craftspeople and patrons). Diachronic diversity between cities and between the urban and rural landscapes is reflected in the analysis of mosaics. For example, the distribution of mosaics (Figs. 1–6) illustrates the diversity of urban occupation in the first century after the island became part of the empire; they demonstrate that by the second century Crete has become firmly part of the koine of the Eastern Empire, and together with other evidence, they provide indications of how and why this happened. The resulting diachronic study from Hellenistic to Late Antique will present a much-needed insight into the transformations within Cretan society, when the island became part of the empire and when Christianity became the state religion. It will ultimately illustrate how Crete played a pivotal role as part of the Roman network society, with the mosaics and other material reflecting its character and success.

1.2 MOSAICS AS MATERIAL CULTURE

Mosaics are an ubiquitous element of the Roman and Late Antique periods and are found in a range of contexts. Their durability is such that they are often the

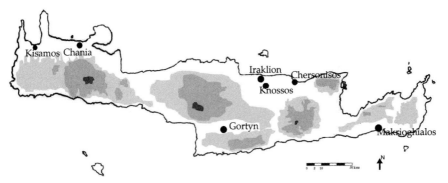

Fig. 3 Map of Crete showing second-century mosaics.

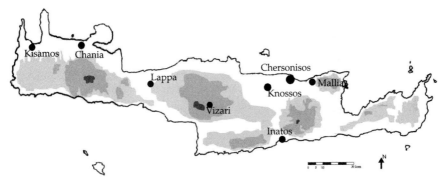

Fig. 4 Map of Crete showing third-century mosaics.

sole surviving representative of an entire context or feature in terms of archaeological evidence. Consequently, when in context, mosaics are often essential dating evidence for otherwise poorly preserved domestic, public or religious remains and associated artefacts. Furthermore, mosaic studies have provided the archaeologist with iconographic dating options, however reliable given the inherent subjectivity. Given the increasing number of rescue excavations, a dependence on using mosaics as the crux on which to build the interpretation of the site has become more common, and often subjective iconographic interpretations are accepted as 'fact'. Mosaics are commonly a case in which the art is primary, but the human agency is rarely explored.

Mosaics studies are generally more concerned with issues of iconography, style and influence than with interpretations of context.[8] The use of terms such as 'style' and 'influence' are dismissive when mosaic studies can be applied with significant results. If mosaics are described as Western or Eastern 'in style', an indication of social designation is often implicit.[9] Although mosaics may have identifiable Western or Eastern elements, this should not automatically mean that they are indicative of the origins of the craftspeople who laid them or the patrons who commissioned them. The term 'influence' presents another problem as it suggests passive rather than active processes. As Baxandall notes,[10]

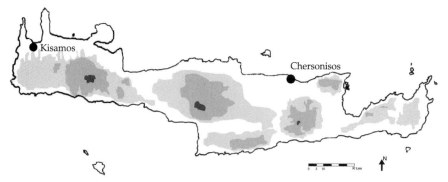

Fig. 5 Map of Crete showing fourth-century mosaics.

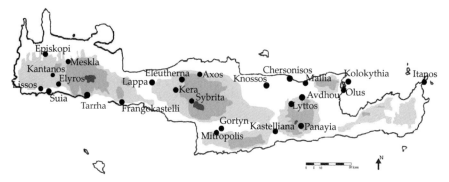

Fig. 6 Map of Crete showing Late Antique mosaics.

influence has been used too often as a short-cut phrase which does not provide detailed explanation for the complexity of processes involved in the contact between populations and the exchange of ideas. Mosaics are neither the results of passive influence nor solely indicative of specific cultural groups. They are the product of cognitive choices made for a multitude of reasons relating in part to the socio-political context.[11]

In the early twentieth century, the removal of a mosaic (or more commonly of figured sections) from its context, often without recording full details, for a prestige acquisition in a museum could be considered an act of its time, as was the case of the Antioch excavations.[12] But even as archaeological practice developed, the treatment of mosaics as typological studies intensified and the importance of context was marginalized. Mosaics, much like archaic and classical painted pottery, began to suffer the ravages of connoisseurship; they were viewed as superior ancient art and divorced from their archaeological contexts. The connoisseurship of mosaic studies is perpetuated by the way in which figured mosaics are more valued over geometric in museums and in publications. In museum environments mosaics are commonly displayed on walls, which further divorces them from their contexts.

Whereas pottery research has moved on significantly,[13] mosaic studies are still somewhat focused on the minutiae of iconography and style. This is not to suggest that iconographic studies are redundant. Moreover, they provide crucial data, such as identification of the scene, the date and the possible hand, but that should not overshadow application of further detail. Iconographic studies can be quite subjective, but to balance the bias scholars should be open about the methods used and through visual aids bring the realms of connoisseurship into discourse while still accepting the inherent subjectivity in the study. It is not unusual to discuss processes of cultural change while using mosaics as indicative. Millet's work on Romanization in fact reflects a commonly held view that mosaics can be used as evidence for provincials' adopting elements or for symbols of Roman power.[14] Dunbabin[15] also suggests that Western mosaics can be seen as 'one index of Romanisation: immigrant settlers and elements of the indigenous population adopted the Roman way of life, expressed through public building and a certain style of housing, complete with its comforts and ornament'. A more nuanced approach is one already taken by Papaioannou on domestic architecture in Roman Achaea. Rather than focusing on ideas of indiscriminate Western or Eastern influence, or ascribing indices of change, individual elements of the form and iconography of mosaics can be examined to identify the variety of socio-political, historical and geographical reasons for their occurrence.[16]

Studies of both figured and geometric decoration can provide a wealth of information concerning craftspeople and workshops. This information should be developed to further our knowledge of Greek and Roman society, allowing a range of informative contributions to be made pertaining to Crete: chronologies and distribution; different levels of communication within and between the island and other parts of the empire; identification of the function and use of areas and architecture; everyday life and significant events; knowledge of different groups across the island; access to a diachronic view of the island, from Hellenistic to Roman to Late Antique periods and, importantly, the diverse nature of Crete in the eastern Roman Empire.

To date, Romano-Cretan society can be understood through a variety of archaeological data; for example, mortuary evidence reveals broad patterns of settlement, chronologies and changes in religious practice, but generally the osteological data is limited. Epigraphic and numismatic sources[17] commonly provide closer insights on communities and their populations. Architecture can be a more revealing element of material culture which allows access to both the cognitive and personal elements of society. As Marx noted, what separates 'the most incompetent architect from the best of bees, is that the architect has built a cell in his head before he constructs it in wax'.[18] Ingold stated that the creation of art, artefact or architecture is a reflection of both natural and cultural developments allowing access to the routine as well as to extraordinary events.[19] Substantial evidence has been lacking for the Romano-Cretan culture and its subsequent transition in the Late Antique period, but an archaeological approach to the study of the mosaics of Crete provides some significant data to redress this issue.

1.3 Chronology

The focus of this study is on the period between the first century B.C.E. and seventh century C.E.,[20] starting with the fall of Crete to the Romans in 67 B.C.E. For this work the chronological range of the Late Antique period is from the early fifth century to the Arab invasions of 827. The Christianization of Crete occurred slowly from the second century onwards, and by the late fourth century the religion had been centralized.[21] Although there is little transformation in secular material in Crete, the start of the Late Antique period is marked by the mass construction of the Christian churches.

1.4 Geographical Focus

The primary focus in the catalogue of mosaics is on the Cretan *nomoi* of Iraklion, Rethymnon and Lasithi (central and eastern Crete) (Fig. 1). The reason for this focus is one of practicality: the mosaics of western Crete are currently being published by Stavroula Markoulaki of the KE′ Prehistorical and Classical Ephorea. Notwithstanding, the published mosaics of western Crete will be drawn upon to provide as complete a picture as possible. These mosaics are given a separate set of catalogue numbers, starting with the supplementary number S200. The material presented has been collated from a range of sources, and the latest archaeological reports that were consulted are *Αρχαιολογικόν Δελτίον* 1999, no. 54 Β′2, 844–80; *Annuario della Scuola Archeologica di Atene* 2008, 86; *Κρητική Εστία* 12 2007–8, *Αρχαιολογικές Ειδήσεις*, 233–345; and *Archaeological Reports* 2008–9, no. 53, 1–121.

1.5 Crete: Landscape and Historical Contexts

1.5.1 Historical Context

Sanders's analysis of literary sources remains the foundation for the study of Roman Crete.[22] The majority of the surviving literary evidence is confined to the period of Rome's early intervention in Crete. By any standard this is inadequate, but the limitations are most pronounced for the Late Antique period.[23] This dearth of sources has meant that scholars are dependent on a narrow range, and consequently only partial views, for the occupation of Crete and its role in the empire.[24]

1.5.2 The Hellenistic Background

From literary sources such as Livy, Dio and Diodorus there are two key traditional (if not overtly propagandist) beliefs: that the inclusion of Crete in the Roman Empire was necessary so that the Mediterranean would be free from pirates, and that the Romans brought peace and prosperity to the warring islanders of Crete. The most common perception of Hellenistic Crete is that it was an island which rarely saw a prolonged period of peace.[25] This view is over-simplified, and it is increasingly apparent that all of Hellenistic Crete was not as under-developed and economically restrained as once believed. Recent historical analysis and excavation have led to a reappraisal of Crete's piracy and its war-worn state.[26] Three Hellenistic mosaics are certainly known (66, 76, 142)[27] and two possible examples (67, 77–9). Several Hellenistic cities[28] have been investigated, and for the most part buildings and other architecture suggest that these cities were no less developed than were other parts of the Hellenistic world.[29] However, Chaniotis has argued that although Crete shows similarities with other parts of the Hellenistic world in terms of ceramic and terracotta production, there were key economic differences, such as Crete's lack of long-distance trade or participation in the network society, craft specialization and, to an extent, conspicuous consumption.[30] Westgate's discussion of the evidence of domestic architecture from Classical and Hellenistic Crete highlights the diversity and uniqueness of the style rather than the old view of residences inferior to those in the rest of Greece. She also notes the bias on the evidence created by a lack of systematic excavation.[31] There is little evidence of island-wide cooperation, and Chaniotis argues that it was the lack of a predominant manager or even leader within a collection of self-contained states that emphasized the island's communal organization.[32] When the island came under Roman control, Rome filled the vacant position of communal organizer and as such enabled the more visible wider scale projects to be realized.[33] De Souza goes further and suggests that Crete's prosperity was what attracted Roman attention and, in the Late Republic, Rome's determination to seize the island.[34] Regarding the historical source explanations for Rome's intervention, it is fair to say that Crete prospered by its inclusion in the empire. However, the extent of Cretan piracy in the Mediterranean and the urgent need for an external arbitrator to quell the inner state conflicts are likely to have been over-emphasized excuses for the Roman invasion of the island.[35] The main attraction of Crete for Rome is likely to have been its location and as such its potential as an economic resource.

From 195 B.C.E. the Romans were conservatively involved in Cretan affairs, apparently under the guise of bringing peace to the Cretan states. There was no serious attempt to take the island until 71 B.C.E., when many Cretan cities openly supported Mithridates VI and the island was accused of piracy or harbouring pirates.[36] Although this attempt by Marcus Antonius failed, the timing

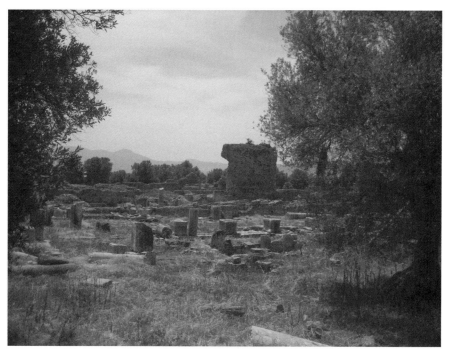

Fig. 7 Gortyn, Gymnasium.

clearly indicates that Roman interest in Crete was more likely to have been part of the general expansion of the empire in the east – a need for harbours and ready resources – than revenge for a serious transgression.[37] That support for Mithridates was a veiled excuse is further emphasized by Rome's restrained involvement in Crete up to this point, even over the issue of the return of Roman prisoners.[38] In 69 B.C.E. Q. Caecilius Metellus landed on the island with three legions. The first part of the island to be seized was Kydonia (around Chania) in the west (Fig. 1). Metellus was then quick to take Knossos, central Crete and the southeast. With the fall of Lappa, the three-year battle was over and the island finally succumbed in 67 B.C.E.[39] Gortyn (Fig. 7), the one city which surrendered, was made the provincial capital, and despite its initial resistance to the Roman invasion, Knossos was chosen as the site of the only colony, Colonia Julia Nobilis Cnosus, in the province.[40] The date of the foundation of the colony is contentious, but both Paton (1994, 142) and Sanders (14) suggest that it must have been around 27 B.C.E. Moreover, the status of the colony, whether military or civilian, is still not certain but the weight of evidence points to a civilian establishment. Baldwin Bowsky argues that although there may have been some evidence for military colonization in Crete after the conquest, the new population would have been a commercial one, particularly after the fall of Delos.[41] Under Augustan administration, the Senate combined the government of Crete and Cyrene, making it a joint praetorian province.[42] It was not until 295–7 C.E.

that Crete was separated from Cyrene and made into a single province under an equestrian *praeses* in the Diocese of Moesia.[43]

The dearth of historical accounts of Roman Crete is an indication of the peace the island experienced under Roman rule: contemporary writers were more likely to have been interested in sensational accounts rather than tales of tranquil life. Only one reference to a potential city war is known, between Kisamos and Polyrrhenia, which was quickly brought under control through Roman intervention.[44] The Roman system of installing a governor to supervise the pre-existing city-state organization was successful and as with most areas of the empire, as long as taxes were paid and the infrastructure was in place to allow this, there was little intervention.[45] Epigraphic remains evince 55 governing proconsuls. The majority of evidence accounts for the first-century governors, with 15 in the second century and 4 in the third; after the split from Cyrene only one governor is known of.[46] Seventeen quaestors and four procurators are also known.[47] The Provincial Council officiated over the imperial cult and over the games held every five years and issued coins until at least the second century.[48] The significant contribution that Cretans made in official administrative and political positions, often with commercial connections, is clear from inscriptions.[49] Whereas Rome called upon many of its provinces to assist in its internal and external struggles, the Cretans were only occasionally called upon to help. For example, Cretan archers were used in Gaul under Caesar, and supplies of corn and archers from Crete were also raised by Pompey during the civil war with Caesar.[50]

1.5.3 Late Antique Crete

Although evidence of Christian populations is found at sites such as Mount Ida,[51] Eleutherna[52] and Knossos,[53] the visual impact of the monumentalization of the cities and countryside through churches does not begin until the fifth century. Written sources for Late Antique Crete consist primarily of a collection of episcopal letters (dating between the sixth and seventh centuries), accounts of the lives of saints (which date from the sixth century onwards) and the sixth-century *Synekdemos* of Hierokles (an account of the 64 Byzantine provinces and their some 900 cities).[54] It is known that St. Paul organized the first Christian church on Crete, and Titus is credited with its subsequent development.[55] The paucity of evidence for domestic occupation, even from well-excavated cities such as Gortyn, Knossos, Itanos and Eleutherna,[56] dictates a reliance on religious architecture and burials. Epigraphic sources, ranging from religious dedicatory to civil inscriptions, often provide indirect evidence for the nature of the administration on the island. A fourth- to fifth-century inscription from the area of Mount Ida indicates that some of the clergy were being brought into the church from the upper social classes (as was common in other areas of the empire).[57]

Spyridakis suggests that the first monasteries of Crete were likely located in the Mesara to exploit the fertile land of the plain.[58]

In terms of political and administrative changes, Constantine I (324–37) upgraded the island to a senatorial province under a *consularis* in the Diocese of Macedonia in the Prefecture of Illyricum and this arrangement lasted until the seventh century.[59] Other than Justinian's promotion of the governorship from *consularis* to proconsul[60] there appear to have been few administrative changes between the fifth and seventh centuries. Politically, Crete was administered by the Eastern Empire, but as part of Illyricum it came under the ecclesiastical jurisdiction of the West and remained under papal control until the first half of the eighth century.[61] Crete suffered a series of unsettling events from the fifth century to the eighth, such as Vandal attacks in 457[62] and Slavic raids in 623.[63] The almost incessant threats to the imperial security from the Avars, Moors and Persians and, during the sixth and seventh centuries, the problem of plague had an adverse economic impact on the empire. Yet Crete appears to have remained prosperous and reasonably secure, as marked by the construction of a church at Vizari and possibly one at Fodele in the eighth century. The Arabs made their first concerted raid on the island in 674, and from then on the island was continuously threatened by raids and suffered economically, until it was finally taken in 827–8.

1.6 Topography of Crete

Crete is an island some 240 km long and 48 km wide at its maximum width. Located in the middle of the eastern Mediterranean, it was an essential communication hub and as such was always a pivotal trading point. The topography of Crete delineates regions which are separated by mountains: the Dictaean range divides the eastern part of the island from the central, the White Mountains separate the west from the centre and the Idean range in the middle creates a divide between the north and the south central area (Fig. 1).[64] Though largely mountainous, the island has two fertile plains, Lasithi in the east and the Mesara in the central south part. Survey evidence in recent years suggests that both these areas have always been heavily exploited agriculturally (see later discussion). Key land routes through the plains between the mountains are found between Ierapetra and Mirabello Bay, Gortyn (Matala) and Knossos (Iraklion), Agia Galini and Rethymnon and possibly Inatos and Chersonisos. The route between Ierapetra and Mirabello Bay is the shortest across the island, at *c.*15 km, while one of the longest is between Gortyn (Matala) and Knossos (Iraklion) at *c.* 65 km, and both routes were well exploited. The island is sufficiently watered in the winter, with a network of rivers originating in the mountains. The majority of these rivers dry up in the summer months.

1.7 SETTLEMENT, ECONOMY AND SOCIETY

Crete's landscape is the primary dictate on settlement patterns, which means that when changes occur they are more commonly a result of external factors (such as shifts in trade focus).[65] There were key urban centres from at least the Hellenistic period onwards, including Knossos, Gortyn, Lissos, Chersonisos, Myrtos, Ierapetra, Chania and Kisamos (Fig. 1). Better evidence for Hellenistic houses is now available, with increasing archaeological work indicating a broad spread of occupation but also a diversity of styles of architecture.[66]

Sanders notes that there was little evidence for Hellenistic farmsteads but that there was a small growth in the number of rural sites in the first century, with examples from Koleni Kamara in the west and Pachyammos and other parts of the Vrokastro in the east.[67] Although rural sites are notoriously difficult to define, a survey suggests that Sanders was likely correct in his assessment, although the reason may have been a change in economic focus rather than a desire for increased levels of security.[68] According to Haggis, settlement choice was based on the location of valuable fertile ground or important route ways which took precedence over any other factor (such as security or religion).[69] Hayden's Vrokastro survey has indicated occupation of the hills and ridges above the fertile area used for agriculture or timber processing. Further to this, the survey located settlements along key communication routes.[70] Raab's work on the Akrotiri Peninsula supports this picture of lively rural occupation, but she argues that this had already been the pattern in the late Hellenistic period.[71]

Evidence from the Vrokastro and Galatas surveys underscores Roman occupation of the rural landscape in the third century, with a possible villa at Elleniko[72] and third-century rural farmsteads and hamlets in the Galatas area.[73] As in some other areas of the Roman Empire (such as North Africa and Dalmatia), large-scale villa sites are not in evidence until the fifth century in Crete and churches remain the key source for settlement patterns.[74] The location of the churches indicates that the primary occupation of the coast and the edges of fertile plains or around other natural resources continued until the eighth century. At this time, settlement patterns in Crete, like those in the rest of the empire, shifted from the large urban centres to small, fortified settlements.[75] As yet, there is no archaeological evidence for Roman military settlement on the island. These kinds of settlements and Roman villas may still be found, but given the large area covered by intensive fieldwalking thus far, the number of military settlements likely to be discovered is minimal.[76]

All evidence points to economic stability in Crete throughout the Roman and Late Antique periods. Furthermore, the variety in architecture, imports and luxury items attests to a good level of economic comfort.[77] Crete derived its wealth in part from agriculture, with an emphasis on wine production (as a producer and exporter).[78] Moreover, the disproportionally high levels of imports (including luxury items) for an agricultural economy indicate that the island must have generated some considerable income from an external source. One of the key results of this study is to show how Crete was able to generate an income surplus through its role as a trade facilitator.

The nature and extent of farming in Roman Crete is, however, unclear; if large-scale farms were in operation, they must have been confined to the plains. Raab's study of the Akrotiri Peninsula[79] suggests that, unlike in much of the rest of Crete, agricultural estate practices revolving around a central villa residence did occur in this area. Olives, grapes, wheat, barley, vegetables and fruit were produced, and Sanders[80] notes more specific archaeological evidence for agriculture (such as wine and olive presses).[81] The Sphakia survey has produced good evidence for beekeeping in southern Crete.[82] Beehives are also found in urban spaces such as Knossos.[83] As Pompey supposedly was able to raise corn supplies, it is possible to add this indirect evidence to the known data.[84] In terms of resources Crete had fertile plains and a long exploitable coast, and it was densely wooded. Cretan exports probably included timber and salt, but these products likely made only a small contribution to the overall trade and were not significant sources of income, according to Tsougarakis.[85]

Sanders suggests that Cretan industries such as glass (Tarrha), ore smelting (Kantanos), tile production (Zakros), fish farming (Chersonisos) and lamp production (Knossos) must have functioned for local rather than export consumption.[86] Moreover, Bekker-Nielsen has shown that fish processing is likely to have been more of a lucrative market than previously believed.[87] Amphorae were produced in some of the key port cities such as Kisamos and Chersonisos.[88] Numerous ceramic workshops have been identified on Crete, and one of the most recent is that from the southern port town of Matala.[89] However, in terms of ceramic material, only lamps were exported.[90] Small-scale or home industries were also evident from the excavations of the Unexplored Mansion in Knossos.[91] When manufactured goods were needed they were imported from the nearest available source.[92] In addition to the necessary resources, luxury items such as marble[93] and glass were also imported. The ceramic imports come from a variety of places, such as North Africa, Egypt and the East. Pottery from Italy and the West is also found and was most popular in the first century but decreased by the end of that century. Raab notes the importance of Cretan herbs for medicinal use across the empire (harvested, for example, at Lyttos) and draws on the epigraphic evidence for Crete's position on the grain routes as noted by Baldwin Bowsky.[94]

It is likely that Crete functioned as an entrepôt. The prevailing winds circulating in the Mediterranean meant that one usually had to land on Crete at some point when travelling east or west.[95] Crete was positioned on the north–south trade links (between Egypt, Cyrenaica and other areas of the Mediterranean) as well as on the east–west link, between Syria, Greece and the western provinces.[96] A range of good harbours from Suia to Ierapetra on the island's south coast offered shelter, re-fuelling points and an opportunity to off-load and take on trade goods (Fig. 1). On the return journey, a slightly less direct route along the east and then the south coast of Crete was taken, primarily because of a lack of safe harbours on the north. However, a study of the mosaics and other archaeology clearly indicates a change by the end of the first century when the south no longer dominates trade. At this time, the coastal towns of the north begin to flourish as a result of what must have been a concerted effort to maximize the trade potential of the island's location.

With the exception of the changing trade foci, the overall economy of Crete does not appear to have varied greatly throughout the Roman and Late Antique periods. The reliance on the production of agricultural goods for home consumption continued until the eighth century. Crete remained on the lucrative grain route, even when it was transferred from Egypt to Constantinople.[97]

Sanders suggested that Crete suffered an economic decline in the third to fifth centuries.[98] He based his analysis primarily on the evidence of the Roman Empire as a whole and may have assumed more of an economic decline than there are actually data for. Indications of a slight waning of inland settlements such as Knossos and Eleutherna may be attributed in part to the immediate outcome of the 365/367 earthquake, but given the extent of Late Antique occupation such a decline was likely to have been short lived.[99] The recent archaeology of the coastal settlements, particularly those on the north coast such as Kisamos, Chania, Chersonisos (Fig. 8) and Itanos, indicates that they were, contrary to Sanders's view, flourishing in the fourth century.[100] More than 45 Christian basilicas are securely identified in Crete and a further 45 tentatively identified,[101] and evidence suggests that the majority of these buildings were built between the fifth and sixth centuries.[102] In the Peloponnese, roughly three times the size of Crete, there are only 130 known basilicas from a similar period. The degree to which one can gauge the wealth of a population based on the number and quality of basilicas is debatable,[103] but the extent of the building in Crete does imply that the population of the island throughout the Late Antique period was financially stable. By the seventh century the number of churches constructed declines significantly. This possibly reflects both the direct and indirect threats to the island's security.[104] The increased threats from the Slavs, Persians and Arabs against the Eastern Empire during the seventh century would have caused a significant disruption to trade and economic stability.[105] Furthermore, the 718 earthquake would have added to the destabilization of Crete and the empire. The church building patterns reflect this on Crete, and with the possible

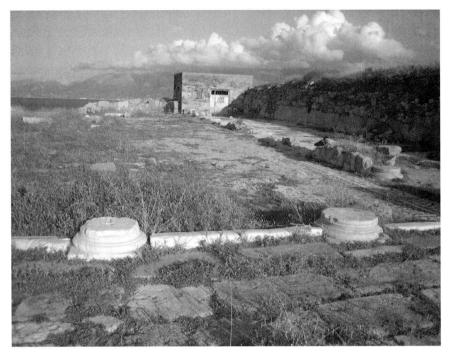

Fig. 8 Chersonisos, Basilica B and north coast of Crete.

exception of Vizari[106] and Fodele, there is no evidence for church construction in the eighth century.

1.8 ROMAN AND LATE ANTIQUE CRETE: THE CURRENT EVIDENCE

Sanders's 1982 *Roman Crete* is an indispensable record of the archaeology and history of Crete and set a new agenda for its study; however, the contextual analysis of the material was limited. Since then, research on post-Minoan Crete has increased and the amount of excavation and survey material has been greatly augmented, in part due to the rapid development which has taken place on the island. Harrison's 1993 work synthesized much of the new archaeology with the historical evidence. Baldwin Bowsky's prosopography studies are highlighting the regional diversity within the island with Crete's inclusion in the empire.[107] Forster's work on the ceramic assemblages is leading to a revision of chronologies.[108] More recent analysis of Knossos has illustrated that the city, despite its status as a colony, does not exhibit any significant changes in the archaeological record until 100 years after its foundation.[109] Raab's 2001 analysis of the survey evidence for the Akrotiri Peninsula and Hayden's 2004 work on Vrokastro highlight the value of survey data, particularly for an understanding of rural occupation, economy, industry and trade.

1.8.1 Approaches

Survey data have provided general information about urban and rural space in areas such as Sphakia, Lasithi, Vrokastro and the Akrotiri Peninsula and in the more recent Galatas survey.[110] More detailed information is known from urban sites as a result of research and rescue excavations. The inconsistencies of data are further complicated by a lack of precise dating evidence, which makes a nuanced view of the whole island over eight centuries difficult. Archaeologists have commonly dated Roman and Late Antique material, constructions and destructions to events such as invasion, plague or earthquakes attested in the sources. Increasingly, seismologists such as Ambraseys argue against the long-term effect of an earthquake, suggesting that populations return to their dwellings quite quickly, even after a serious event.[111] Furthermore, Stiros and Papageorgiou[112] argue that in fact the west and north of the island were relatively free of earthquakes and that for the whole island there were really only two major earthquakes, one sometime between 46–66 and the other in 365, in the Roman and Late Antique periods. Arguably, the construction of the archaeological record around historical chronologies is not a poorly judged methodology, but is rather the effect of a subconscious psychological bias (normally hindsight bias or creeping determinism).[113] In analysing and presenting their material archaeologists seek all evidence to explain changes in the archaeological data. The historical record often provides fixed dates, though sometimes incorrect ones, and hindsight bias is where scholars may perceive changes in their material culture that are not actual changes but would fit with a pattern according to the historical event. Once this scenario is presented, it may become an accepted 'fact' because it fits neatly with the story, and consequently, it remains unquestioned (creeping determinism). An example of this can be seen in some archaeological publications concerning Knossos, where a change in material culture is alleged to fit with the 69 B.C.E. creation of the province of Crete and Cyrene, which is well attested in the historical sources. Furthermore, a theory of fourth-century abandonment of the city following an earthquake had been accepted primarily on the basis of negative evidence.[114] The attribution of abandonment as a result of an earthquake is in many respects a convenient way of constructing the story.[115] A successful area with such potential would likely have been resettled quickly even if there had been disastrous earthquakes.[116] These examples highlight two misconceptions pertinent to this study: that there was a significant widespread cultural change with the inclusion of Crete into the Roman Empire and that the 365 earthquake compounds the perceived cultural differences between the Roman and Late Antique periods.

It is now accepted that Crete can no longer be considered a provincial outpost, and current research is questioning long-held assumptions about the island.[117] Additionally, studies of Roman Crete have tended to be couched in terms of the

'Romans Romanizing' rather than in terms of the local perspective. As such, a commonly held view of Crete is one which suggests that the Romans facilitated seven centuries of peace and prosperity until the Arab invasions; crucially, the diversity of the island's economy, society and relationship with Rome and the empire is often overlooked.

By focusing on the perspective of the local population of Crete rather than on the top-down view from Rome, it is possible to achieve a comprehensive understanding of an area and its relationship with Rome and the empire over a period of seven centuries. Comparative analysis of the archaeology supports the new thesis of long-term continuity and change in Roman and Late Antique Crete. The application of globalization and Christianization theories to all the evidence allows a diachronic view of the cities and states of Crete and of the island's role in the empire: from reluctant participant to critical player.

1.8.2 Globalization

It is generally accepted that the Romans had something of a laissez-faire attitude when it came to the running of the Eastern provinces. As long as the provinces were peaceful enough and had the infrastructure to allow for payment of taxes, the Romans tended to insert governors into pre-existing provincial administrative and political arrangements. With the exception of Christianity, they were flexible when it came to religious expression. Cities such as Aphrodisias, Palmyra and Damascus blossomed under Roman rule, and by the first century even more obstreperous cities such as Corinth, Ephesus and Knossos appeared to be toeing the line and benefiting from their inclusion in the empire. By the time of Hadrian, many of the Eastern provinces had been part of the empire for nearly two centuries and had settled into their roles after the initial administrative and political change.

The development of an Eastern koine by the second century masks the extent of diversity throughout the Eastern Empire in the first century B.C.E. and first century C.E. as indicated by the archaeological evidence. Many provinces and cities were quite strongly opposed to the threat of Roman rule, in contrast to some that willingly gave themselves (or others) up to become part of the Roman dream. In the East, there was a sharp distinction in the reasons why provinces became part of the empire and a difference in their willingness to do so. Within the provinces themselves, the same contrasts existed between cities, between urban and rural areas and between populations.

The diversity of the East and the benefits of being part of the empire are topics which are often sidelined in the equalizing theory of Romanization.[118] Although definitions of Romanization may be adapted to fit with established models of how provinces may have behaved and they may include a range of perspectives, more commonly the imperial view is taken, which does not always allow for the possibility that cities and populations made choices about the extent to which they wanted to become involved in the empire. Nor does it allow for obvious differences between people of different statuses to be clear.[119] The inclusion of Crete within the Roman Empire certainly led to numerous changes, but not as a homogenous alteration affecting the whole island, and not always within the timescale that we would expect to find them.[120] The extent to which there was a conscious systematic cultural change is highly debatable, and significant issues still remain, including where and why such developments took place if at all. By applying globalization theory it is possible to explore the diversity of Roman Crete in the context of the empire. For the purposes of this work, Waters's definition of globalization is used: 'A social process in which the constraints of geography on social and cultural arrangements recede and in which people become increasingly aware that they are receding.'[121] With these perceptions of globalization in mind, it is possible to approach the study of Crete in a more nuanced way, that is, that Crete was an important economic part of the Roman Empire but that there was a strong desire to maintain the cultural identity within.[122] Furthermore, cultural developments in Crete can be viewed as relative to Rome and the empire, rather than as falling under a subsuming process of Roman acculturation.[123] Within this characterization, diversity within a region is possible; for example, although Gortyn may have actively desired Roman attention, Knossos originally did not. Globalization theory can account for elements of intentional change such as Rome's establishment of a colony in Knossos and, at the same time, for the unintentional on the part of the Knossians. Ultimately, as in the case of Crete, diversity prospers and regional identities become stronger in the globalized world.

1.8.3 Christianization

When Christianity became the state religion it became the main conduit of power in the Roman Empire at a range of levels from the imperial court to the provincial countryside.[124] Whereas in the earlier period power was maintained in part through military control, popular support and the collection of taxes, the Christian emperors used the church. There were clearly political, social and economic changes, but local populations had a certain amount of choice in what they accepted. Any transformations may not necessarily have concerned the entire population either equally or at the same time. During the Late Antique period, Christianity was heavily promoted across the empire, in part because it became a central conduit for power. It is argued here that rather than forcing the population to adopt the religion wholesale, the Christians took a more sensitive approach so as not to drive the population away.[125] Processes of Christianization encourage adoption of the religion by providing links with community memories and familiar elements of pre-Christian religions (through art and architecture),[126] by tantalizing the population with impressive monumental buildings and secret ceremonies and through the promise of redemption and everlasting life. While Christianity and pre-Christian religions were maintained alongside each other for some time, it was necessary in terms of security of power for Christianity to become the dominant and sole religion.[127] In this respect, active processes of de-memorization of the earlier lives and creation of new memories and symbols can be seen in many urban and rural landscapes.[128]

1.9 CONTRIBUTION TO SCHOLARSHIP: CRETE AND MOSAICS

This volume offers an original approach to the study of mosaics and an innovative method of presenting a diachronic view of provincial society in the East. Current research on globalization theory and its application to studies of the Roman Empire are facilitating an innovative approach to the question of the nature of provincial society in the empire. As has been shown in recent publications such as those by Hingley and also Hitchner,[129] among others, the application of globalization theory to the Roman Empire works well in principle and has been successfully applied to a study of Knossos.[130] The mosaic analysis will provide the archaeological evidence, and this work takes the application of the theory further in examining one part of the joint province of Crete and Cyrene, as well as by extending the chronological range to include the Christianization of the island.

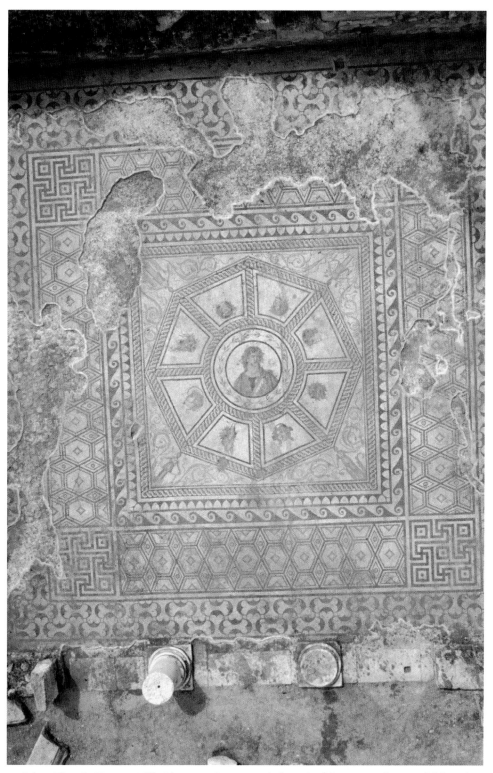

Colour Plate 1. Knossos, Villa Dionysus, Oecus mosaic (Mosaic 1) (courtesy of S. Paton) (Plate 1)

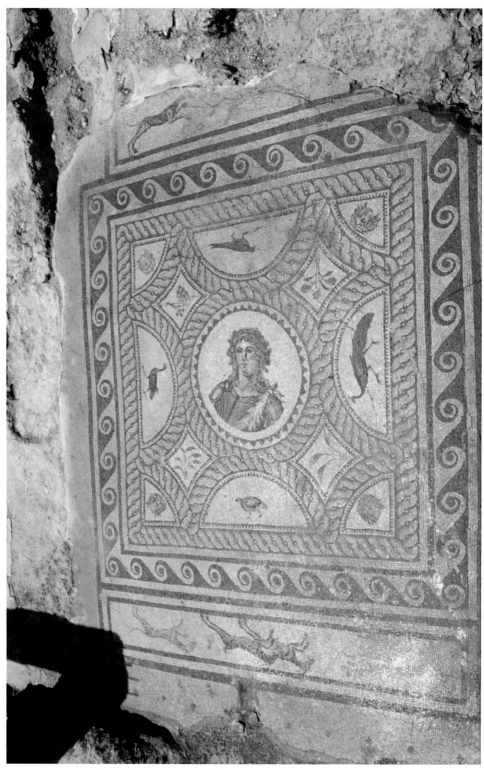

Colour Plate 2. Knossos, Villa Dionysus, Seasons mosaic (Mosaic 3)
(courtesy of S. Paton) (Plate 3)

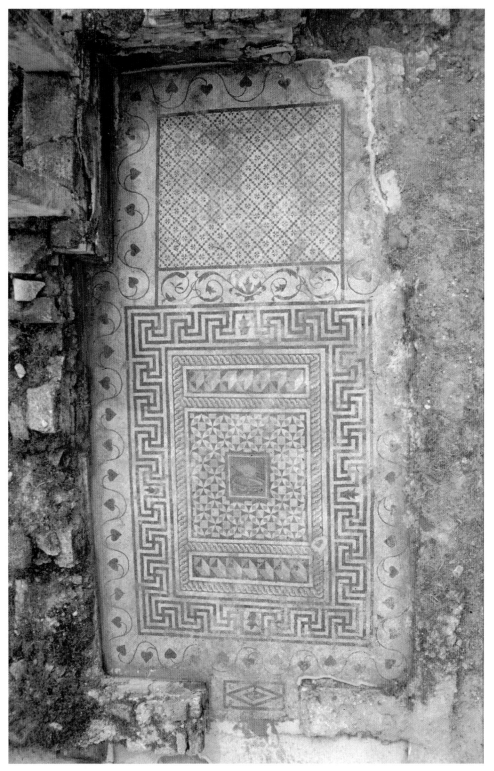

Colour Plate 3. Knossos, Villa Dionysus, Three-Part mosaic (Mosaic 8)
(courtesy of S. Paton) (Plate 7)

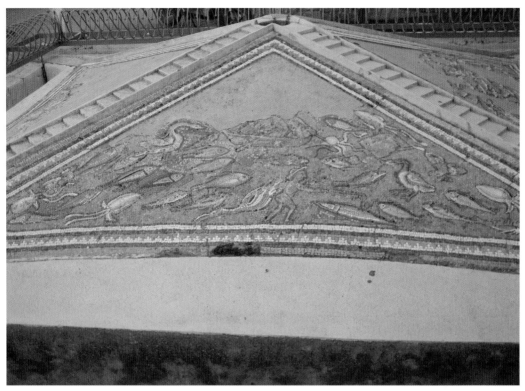

Colour Plate 4. Chersonisos, Fountain mosaic, northwest panel (Mosaic 38) (Plate 15)

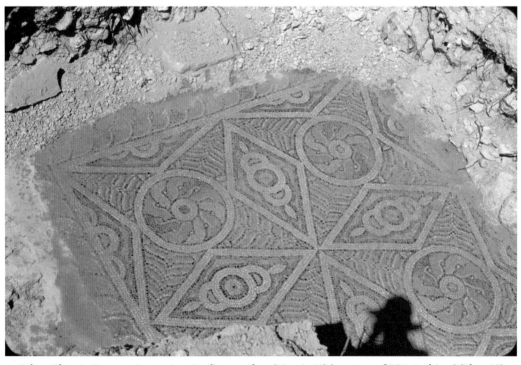

Colour Plate 5. Knossos, Sanatorium Basilica, narthex (Mosaic 88) (courtesy of BSA Archives) (Plate 23)

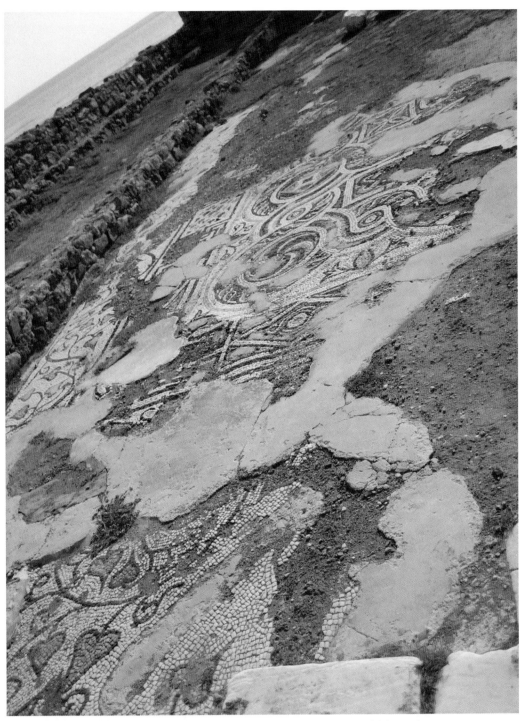

Colour Plate 6. Chersonisos, Basilica A, nave (Mosaic 93) (Plate 26)

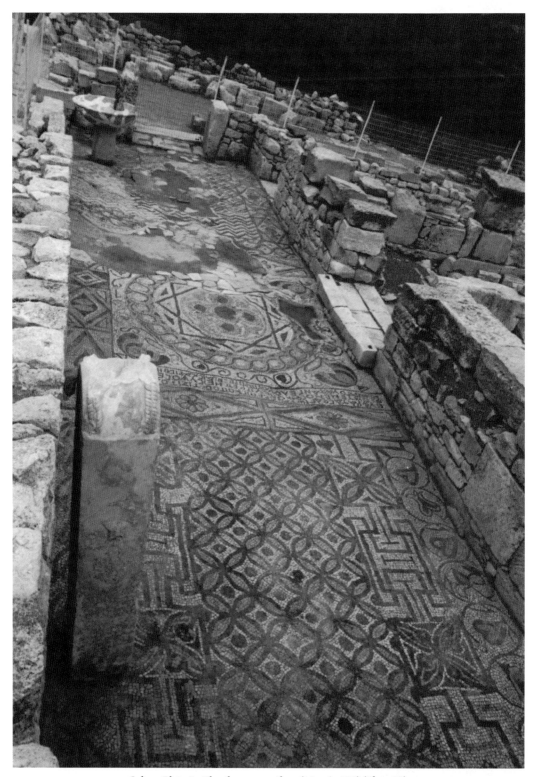

Colour Plate 7. Eleutherna, narthex (Mosaic 111) (Plate 32)

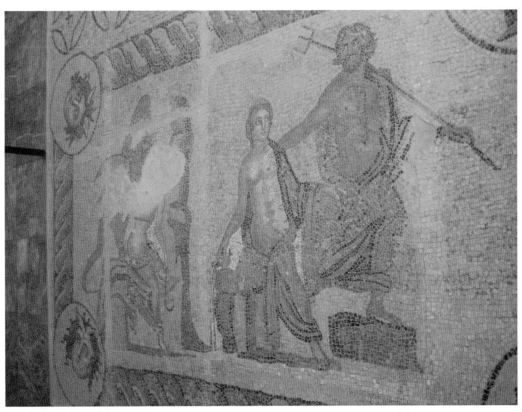

Colour Plate 8. Chania, Poseidon and Amymone mosaic (Mosaic 129) (Plate 39)

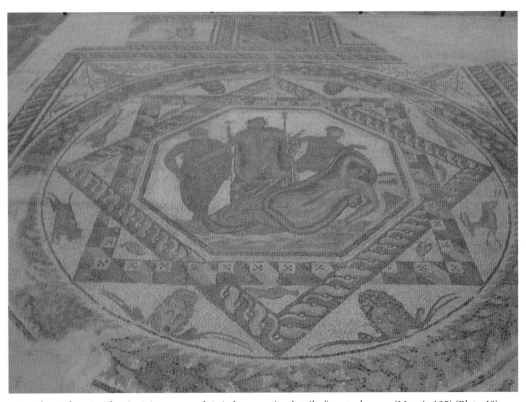

Colour Plate 9. Chania, Dionysus and Ariadne mosaic, detail of central scene (Mosaic 135) (Plate 40)

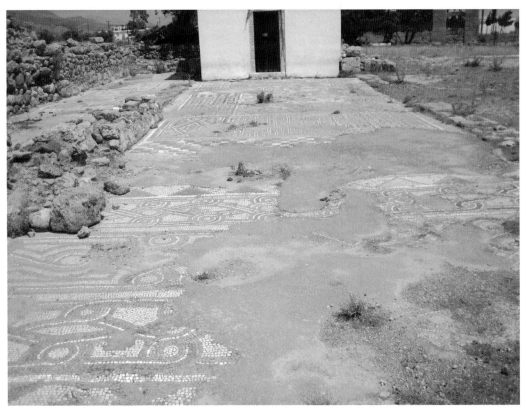

Colour Plate 10. Agios Niketas (Mosaics 143–6) (Plate 45)

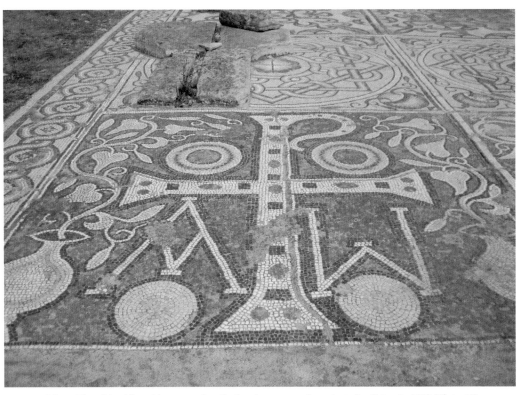

Colour Plate 11. Almyrida, nave, detail of web, cross and semi-circles (Mosaic 150) (Plate 48)

ஒ ஒ ஒ ஒ ஒ ஒ

TWO

THE ARCHAEOLOGY OF CRETE

2.1 INTRODUCTION

The archaeological landscape of Roman and Late Antique Crete changes annually through the extensive numbers of rescue excavations, in particular in urban areas, and through survey projects, especially in rural areas (see site catalogue in Appendix 4). Nearly 30 years on from Sanders's *Roman Crete*, many of his conclusions, particularly concerning the rural occupation of the island from the first century B.C.E. to the seventh century are proving to be correct.[1] Ultimately, the increase in new primary material and recent research on aspects of Roman and Late Antique Crete is leading to a more nuanced view of the island and has reversed the idea of the island as having been a quiet bystander in the bustle of the Roman world.

2.2 MOSAICS IN CONTEXT

Traditionally, mosaics are rarely placed within their broader archaeological frameworks although the focus has changed in more recent years as typified by the work of scholars such as Kondoleon and Muth.[2] To incorporate a significant range of archaeological evidence, the discussion here will focus on the contribution of material culture to an examination of the diversity of the island across a diachronic range. The study is based on the material in Appendix 4, which is a summary of the reports of rescue and research excavations from 1980;[3] evidence from Sanders's 1982 *Roman Crete*;[4] survey publications;[5] and an analysis of the rescue excavations in key urban centres as presented in Chapter 5. The new material produced since 1980 will be contextualized and discussed in terms of settlement patterns, mortuary evidence, religion, art and architecture, pottery, industry, agriculture and harbours to form a new diachronic view of Cretan society from the Roman to Late Antique periods.

2.3 ARCHAEOLOGY OF CRETE: SOCIETY

2.3.1 Settlement Patterns

A significant advantage of archaeological survey is the broad information over a wide geographical area that it can provide. Surveys can give evidence for long-term continuity and change and for intra-site relationships, communications and movement. Without testing the results of a survey through excavation, caution must be taken with the results. There are both practical and interpretative issues that may bias the evidence. For example, coarsewares survive in the greatest quantity on the surface and in significantly higher amounts than diagnostic finewares. The problem with a higher visibility of coarsewares is that they are much slower to change, in terms of development, technique and style, than are finewares, making refined chronologies elusive.[6] Consequently, a broad date range, commonly Classical/Hellenistic or Hellenistic/Roman, is often ascribed. Furthermore, subtle changes or periodization may not be identifiable, as frequently the latest occupation phase will be the best represented on the surface. Even taking these issues into account, ceramic evidence remains the core basis for chronologies and information on economy for areas of Crete.[7] Overall, the benefits of surface survey are enormous in terms of identifying sites, indicating a broad chronology and function especially for rural areas.

The recent survey data have supported Sanders's theories of changing settlement patterns through the Roman period as well as provided new data on the organization and function of the sites. The increased and broader distribution of settlement is evidenced on the north coast by the Vrokastro and Kavousi surveys with a range of new coastal sites,[8] as well as by the revived occupation of the islands of Mochlos and Pseira in the Roman and Late Antique periods.[9] Hilltop occupation, which was so common in the Hellenistic period, broadens to occupation of the slopes and even of the valley floors as shown in the northern Schinauria Plateau,[10] as well as in the southern site of Katelionas.[11] On the south coast, Blackman and Branigan identified a range of new settlements in the Agiofarango Valley, including a new settlement at Gavaliana, and in some areas, such as Kaloi Limenes, there was no visible evidence of occupation any earlier than the Roman period.[12] They noted that part of the reason for the new settlements in this area may be due to the increased focus on fertile land, surpassing the earlier concentration on locations around cult sites. Eleven individual farmsteads were identified in the area, and many of them were of a type consisting of a rectangular building with a small internal courtyard. The change in focus away from rural cults seems also to be mirrored in the Mesara, where shrines such as Kamilari and Agia Triadha go out of use in the Roman period.[13] Nine Roman settlements (possibly farmsteads) were identified on the edge of the plain, and continued occupation of many of the Hellenistic settlements in this area is also seen.[14] The same pattern of occupation around the plain also occurs at Lasithi.[15] Overall, the widespread evidence of rural occupation indicates a range of dwellings in terms of size and function, but many of them (such as Gavdos and Smarion Pediadha) also display evidence for small-scale industrial use, as well as some with reasonable storage facilities.[16]

Further evidence for the organization of the rural community indicates an increase in dispersed rather than nucleated settlement.[17] Although clusters of dwellings are often found (as shown in the Galatas survey),[18] they tend to be more independent complexes. This is seen in surveys in the north and south of the island (e.g., the Ziros survey).[19] Blackman and Branigan suggest that this indicates the absence of a local landlord system.[20] Haggis originally believed it to be evidence of a more confident occupation of the countryside, although he may now argue that it was likely due to economic conditions.[21] As the economic and settlement focus changed, the once-thriving settlement of Praisos decreased in size, possibly because of its proximity to the dominant city of Ierapetra or even in favour of the less well-known settlements of Lamnoni and Katelionas.[22] Changes are also seen in the Sphakia region, where, for example, the port of Tarrha appears to decline in favour of nearby Loutro (Phoenix).[23]

The broad range of survey data has provided evidence for the economic importance of settlement location rather than other factors such as issues of security as suggested by Sanders.[24] A clear pattern of sites clustering around the route between Ierapetra and the north coast was identified during the Vrokastro survey.[25] The power and economic function of this route and its importance to Ierapetra in the Roman period is supported by the epigraphic study undertaken by Baldwin Bowsky.[26] Ierapetra not only took advantage of its southerly location in the path of the prevailing winds that impacted east–west Mediterranean trade, but it also extended its perview to take advantage of its location at one end of the shortest land route across the island. Use of this route increased during the Roman period. This is in part indicated by the growing importance of the northern terminal of the land route, the port of Tholos. The first settlement appears here in the first century B.C.E., followed by steady growth to the second century and unbroken occupation until the seventh century.[27] To date, significant warehouses have been identified at Pachyammos, Tholos[28] and Sta Lenika at the northern end of the shortest land route and at other ports on the south (Lissos and Lasaia).[29] These may have been used as re-distribution centres for local consumption or temporary storage facilities for exported and imported goods, particularly if the north-coast ports functioned as entrepôts. Small storage areas were recognized in many of the Cretan farmhouses (such as at Smarion), which may have negated the need for a centralized re-distribution point.

The data from the larger and already well-known cities such as Chania, Chersonisos, Knossos and Kisamos are discussed in Chapter 5. Excavation of any type can provide more detailed pictures of occupation or identify periods of occupation not previously well known. For example, during the excavations on the Minoan site of Kephala at Thronos Sybrita, the public area of the Roman city was investigated on the south plateau.[30]

The north-coast area around Rethymnon, once poorly understood in terms of Roman evidence, is emerging. Excavations are helping to define this area as well-occupied and perhaps even as a Roman seaside resort. At Stavromenos, previously defined by a cemetery and the remains of a concrete building,[31] a large Roman bath complex in use at least until the fifth century has been excavated.[32] The site at Sphakaki Pangalachori was also known by Sanders because of finds of sherds and a statue,[33] and in the 1990s, a Roman seaside house with mosaic floors was revealed.[34] At Panormous, apart from a Late Antique church, very little of the town has been revealed.[35] However, a recently exposed Roman building in poor condition has the remains of a mosaic floor preserved.[36]

Although Sanders[37] argued for a decline from the late third century in Crete, more recent archaeological evidence is indicating otherwise. During the Late Antique period, both on the north and south coasts, occupation appears to be consistent well into the seventh century, as noted during the Vrokastro and Agiofarango surveys.[38] At some sites, for example, Suia and Gavdos, there is a revival of occupation at this period.[39] Blackman and Branigan also identified new Late Antique occupation on Nisis Trafos, where little Roman evidence has been found.[40] Further west, the Sphakia survey's initial indications are that the Frangokastelli plain becomes much more densely occupied in the Late Antique period than it had been in the Roman (Fig. 9).[41] For some areas of the north, a different view is possible. Haggis[42] argues that the Kavousi evidence points to an increased nucleation in the later Roman period with five main settlements, Tholos, Sta Lenika, Kambos, Chrodakia and Petras, regularly spaced with smaller dwellings dependent on them. Raab suggests that there was some decline in the number of sites and nucleation around villages on the Akrotiri Peninsula.[43] Two more recent surveys, Mallia and Moni Odigitrias, have revealed limited evidence for Roman but good indications of Late Antique occupation of these areas.[44] At Mallia, after the Minoan period, occupation was not revived until the fourth to sixth century.[45] Tsipopoulou suggests that a 'country house' was found during the Agia Photia survey,[46] and as Sanders noted, the first real evidence for rural villas is found in the Late Antique period.[47] The locations of the Late Antique burials in Knossos, Gortyn and Chania show that the urban space appears to contract somewhat and in tandem with this contraction, the wider occupation of the island, particularly in terms of renewed interest in upland and rural occupation, is seen.[48]

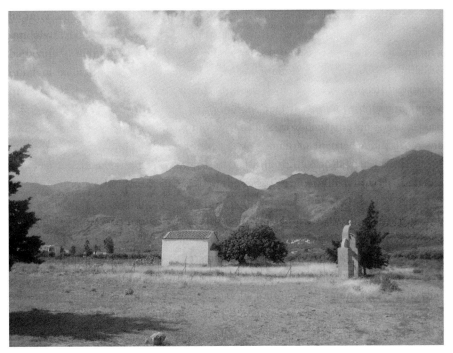

Fig. 9 Frangokastelli plain and Agios Niketas Basilica.

Research excavations at Eleutherna and Itanos have also looked at Late Antique secular evidence as well as church architecture. Roads and houses have been revealed at Itanos,[49] and at Eleutherna, the bath house and domestic complex have now been excavated.[50] In addition to isolated finds such as that of the Late Antique rock-cut water tank in Minoa Akroteriou,[51] rescue excavations have revealed fourth-century and Late Antique houses in Elounda, Ierapetra and Maleme.[52] Chersonisos and Kisamos appear to have particularly flourished, with evidence of mosaics (e.g., nos. 39 & 47), houses and workshops (Fig. 5).[53] One of the few examples of seventh-century domestic evidence was found in the form of two domestic complexes at Agia Galini.[54] The full publication of all these domestic complexes will be an important contribution to studies of Late Antique Crete where once the only architectural evidence was that of the churches.

2.3.2 Mortuary Evidence

A range of burial types found in the cities of Crete is presented in Chapter 5; this section contextualizes the types of burials and highlights some recent discoveries. Sanders[55] identified a variety of mortuary practices across the island: hypogeion (found exclusively in Chania), cist graves, tile graves and rock-cut chamber tombs. The latter are found most famously in Matala, but also in other

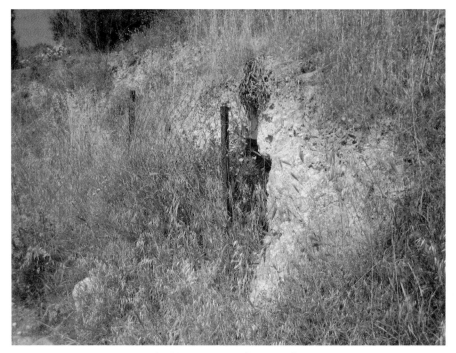

Fig. 10 Knossos, rock-cut tombs.

areas such as Knossos (Fig. 10), and now they have been identified for the first time in the western Mesara.[56] New tomb types, hut-shaped or tent-tombs, have also been discovered, particularly in cities.[57] Freestanding mausolea have been found only in Late Antique Knossos.[58] Excavations of the Venizelio cemetery, in the area of Monastiraki Kephala, Knossos, have extended the date range of these built tombs to the first and second centuries (the implications of these finds are discussed in more detail in Chapter 5).[59]

The free-standing barrel-vaulted tombs which dominate the slopes of Lissos (Fig. 11) are found only on the south coast of the island. These types appear in the Isola Sacra cemetery in Ostia, and they are also found in Cilicia. It is not possible to link them with a specific population group,[60] but their presence on the south coast may be indicative of the early contact that the south had with the West (and possibly with the East) through trade routes. More recent work at the Lissos cemetery has focused on classifying the tombs. They are mostly of the single-vault type with internal niches, and there are three examples of two-storied tombs as well (Fig. 11).[61] Evidence of cemetery burial or even of single burial is rarely found during surveys, and in cases where it is, precise dating is difficult. Blackman and Branigan noted further examples of the barrel-vault tombs on the edge of the city of Lasaia. [62]

Different burial groups have been found, commonly single inhumations but also possibly family burials.[63] Both single and collective burials occur in the

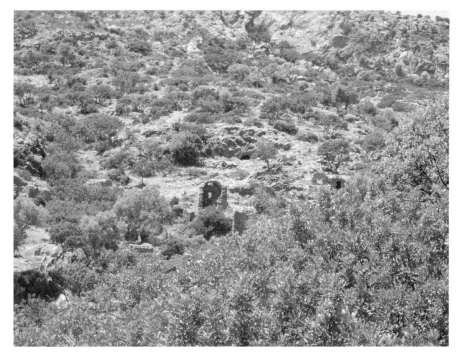

Fig. 11 Lissos, tombs.

same cemeteries, as do different types of tombs (from the mausoleum to tile to shaft graves) as evidenced by excavations of the Agii Deka cemetery of Gortyn.[64] Inscriptions have been found identifying the occupants of the tombs,[65] but as Wardle and Wardle note for Knossos, little in the evidence allows different communities to be distinguished.[66]

In the Late Antique period new burial types occur, such as the box-like tombs from Chersonisos,[67] and whereas some burial forms continue, such as cist and slab graves, in Christian contexts they are orientated east–west. Associated grave goods are limited, often to personal items that may have been on the body, or occasionally coins. Ossuaries are more common in the period, and monumental tombs are sometimes found in or immediately outside churches.[68] As the location of many of the Cretan Late Antique cities change, many of the Christian cemeteries encroach on previously secular domestic space, as noted in Chapter 3 (e.g., in Knossos).[69] In this respect a diachronic view of the material provides a more up-to-date understanding of the changing topography of the city from Roman to Late Antique.

Although small finds were commonly pillaged during tomb robbing,[70] some material, such as single lamps,[71] glass vessels, bronze items[72] and jewellery, survives.[73] There are also more unusual finds, such as the silver pyxis from the Venizelio excavations at Knossos[74] or the theatre mask from the first-century Potamou cemetery.[75] Although coins[76] and lamps[77] can be used to date the burials if the context is sealed, a broad date range is more commonly provided. For example, the Axos cemetery and the Mirabello one at Agios Nikolaos continued in use from the Hellenistic to the Roman period,[78] and the Matala rock-cut tombs certainly continued to be used in the Late Antique period.[79] The presence of tombs may often be the main evidence for Roman occupation of an area, for example, the second- to fourth-century cemetery at Sphakaki Pankalochoriou (Rethymnon) or the first- to second-century cemetery at Ierapetra.[80]

2.3.3 Religion

According to Sanders, local caves and rural shrines are in abundance, but the monumentalization of the religious rural landscape was not so obvious.[81] Very few Roman-period temples are known to have survived, particularly outside the major urban centres. Some exceptions to this are the Asclepius sanctuaries at Lissos and Roman renovations at Lebena (Pl. 20). With the increased attention to Roman Crete in recent years, more evidence for the religious architectural landscape of the cities, and to some extent the countryside, has been forthcoming.

Sanders attributed much of the popularity of certain cults in Crete such as those of Isis and Serapis to patterns of trade contact.[82] He noted particular concentrations of these newer cults in established ports such as Chersonisos and Olus, and in some of the larger cities such as Gortyn and possibly Knossos.[83] More commonly, epigraphic rather than architectural evidence helps identify indications of a cult. Cults of Apollo, Artemis, Asclepius and Demeter, commonly found on Crete, belong to the standard repertoire of empire-wide cult practice. Epigraphic evidence also points to the association of new deities with older or more familiar ones, for example, Serapis with Zeus,[84] and, as recently suggested, Isis with Demeter at Knossos. In the same study, Baldwin Bowsky also identified the cult of Castor and Pollux at the Glaukos shrine.[85] The cult of Diktynna, argued by Sanders to be the most prosperous on Crete, is a particularly local Cretan cult and not commonly found outside the island.[86]

Evidence for the imperial cult at Gortyn was noted by Sanders in the form of a temple to Augustus and Roma as identified by a fragmentary inscription. The imperial cult continued to be popular here, with epigraphic records indicating Trajanic and Severan involvement.[87] At Knossos, Sanders argued that epigraphic references to the deified Claudius and evidence of the elite priesthood indicate the presence of the imperial cult, but a location for it has yet to be identified.[88] Numerous statues of the imperial families have been found across the island, and particularly common is the figure of Hadrian with the cuirass depicting Athena standing on the back of the wolf who is nursing Romulus and Remus. This is found in Knossos, Kisamos, Iraklion, Agios

Nikolaos and Ierapetra so far.[89] It is likely, in the case of the Greek provinces, that the imperial cult was more often established by the local population, in a sense carrying on the traditions of a ruler cult already established in the Hellenistic period.

Religion in the City

A variety of new temples, which may otherwise not be known, has been tentatively identified during archaeological surveys. For example, a Roman podium temple (one of the few in Crete) was identified in Lasaia on the south coast.[90] Other examples are not so straightforward: architectural remains found north of Priniatikos Pyrgos on the north coast may belong to a temple or a house.[91] Excavations often prove to be more instructive, with examples of a hero cult shrine at Aptera and new temples at Kouphonisi and Chersonisos.[92] In Gortyn, one of the most significant finds has been that of the so-called Temple of the Augusti, which is likely to have been constructed during the reign of Marcus Aurelius.[93] A number of striking features, including the crocodile-head spout and the stepped monumental altar (attributed to Tiberius) which the excavators suggest was used for night-time rituals, initially indicate a possible dedication to Egyptian gods. There was some re-working of the temple after the 365 earthquake, and it is unusual in that it survived until the sixth century; Byzantine tombs were constructed on it later.

Sanders's catalogue of Late Antique buildings is comprehensive, but a few new buildings have been revealed in recent years. For example, at Syme Viannos a small, one-roomed church with a later church constructed within was discovered dating to between the fourth and sixth centuries.[94] This may be one of the earliest churches found on the island. Rescue excavations in Kisamos and Chersonisos have indicated the presence of churches in the main square and a possible one in the Papadakis Plot, respectively.[95]

Religion in the Rural Context

A number of investigations have revealed supporting evidence for Sanders' claim that local shrines and caves used for cult were in abundance in the Roman period.[96] For example, a first- to third-century shrine at the site of Agios Nikolaos in the Samarian gorge was excavated and it is likely that it was dedicated to Apollo or Artemis Britomartis (a local cult).[97] Sanctuaries to Hermes have been identified at Kato Syme and Patsos.[98] Recently, evidence for the use of the multi-period Skotino cave in the Roman period was identified in the form of votive offerings and a Roman phase of the Tsiskiana Selinou shrine was also identified at Epanochori.[99]

2.3.4 Sculpture and Other Material Culture

Few wall paintings have been discovered in Crete, and those that have are often badly damaged. The paintings from the House of the Diamond Frescos at Knossos are some of the better preserved, and they consist of broad geometric blocks of colour.[100] The range of new discussions on Roman or Late Antique portable material culture from Crete, other than numismatics, ceramics and epigraphy, has remained somewhat limited.[101] Publications of sculpture are on the increase, but still, material from jewellery to architecture remains under-studied outside of presentations in conferences.[102] Although the precise context is often difficult to ascertain, the material still merits attention and can often be key to providing dates or indications of occupation not previously known.[103] For example, a considerable amount of statuary has been and continues to be discovered in Ierapetra and Iraklion, even though much of the Roman architecture is still elusive.[104] Such finds broaden the scope of topographic understanding; for example, in Knossos, the Venizelio excavations have produced finds of statues (such as a herm) and in the Vlachakis Plot, Bougada Metochi, a bronze miniature of Artemis was identified along with some architectural fragments in a Roman building.[105]

2.4 TRADE, ECONOMY AND INDUSTRIES

Sanders concluded generally that Crete relied on agriculture for its own use and to a degree for export for its financial security.[106] In addition to analysis of the settlement patterns, recent studies and fieldwork enable a significantly more detailed view of the economic horizon of diverse areas of the island at different times.[107]

2.4.1 Ceramic Evidence

Sanders established a sequence of the finewares imported to Crete.[108] In the first century B.C.E., Eastern sigillata A (ESA) was the most common import, with some Eastern sigillata B (ESB). From the end of the first century B.C.E. to the first century C.E. Arretine ware dominated; it gave way to a preference for Çandarli in the second century. During the fourth century and Late Antique period, Late Roman C and African Red Slip (ARS) were the most prevalent imports to Crete, with some Cypriot imports towards the end of the period.[109] Less common imports included Western types such as Aco beakers, Gaulish Samian and Pompeian Red Ware, as well as material from the East, such as Koan and Cypriot sigillata. Although some Italian amphora types were present, the most common forms were Koan, Knidian and Rhodian.[110] A more refined picture of the variety and preference for both imported ceramics and local production is now emerging. Stratified excavations at Knossos have shown a continuation of Hellenistic types into the first century[111] with a high proportion of local wares.[112] Although some Italian wares made a marked appearance in the mid-first century, they were quickly replaced by the imports from Asia Minor, particularly ESA by the end of the first century.[113] Baldwin Bowsky suggests that Italian sigillata may be an indicator of trade contacts rather than of Italian settlers on Crete.[114]

Survey evidence from areas of Crete's north (Kavousi and Gournia), south (Agiofarango and Sphakia), west (Akrotiri) and centre (Mesara) indicate different patterns of ceramic production and import across the island. In addition to local productions in the northeast of the island (particularly in the Mirabello Bay area), ESA and ESB, Phoenician Red Slip and Late Roman cooking wares have also been located.[115] Phoenician Red Slip (as well as ARS) was also found during the Vrokastro survey, but it is not commonly seen in other areas of the island.[116] Within these broad areas some sites have more evidence for imports than do others; for example, more imports have been found at Tholos than at Priniatikos Pyrgos, which favoured local products.[117]

The data from the Akrotiri Peninsula indicates a preference for locally produced coarsewares and finewares with a limited quantity of imports such as Italian sigillata, ESA and ESB and Çandarli.[118] Blackman and Branigan[119] identified local production from the southeast, as well as a range of imports such as Arretine, Cypriot sigillata (in particular from Lasaia), ARS and Late Roman C (LRC). The lack of Italian sigillata, ESA or ESB is peculiar; however, it may be explained by an archaeological bias such as its survival rate rather than by a dearth of first-century imported pottery. Watrous's work on the Mesara survey has shown evidence for an increased and more varied trade from the first century.[120] Broad trade contacts are indicated by imports like Phoenician and Cypriot Red Slips and, in smaller quantities, ESA, Çandarli, Rhodian and Campanian amphorae. Early contact with the West is also indicated by the evidence of the Italian sigillata.[121] In the less accessible Sphakia area to the southwest, surveys show that following some early imports of Italian terra sigillata and Campanian amphorae, the majority of material from the Roman and Late Antique periods was locally produced.[122] In the fifth to seventh centuries, clusters of pottery such as ARS and Phoenician Red Slip appear at some Late Antique sites such as Tarrha and Frangokastelli (Fig. 9).[123] This is consistent with the settlement patterns as discussed earlier where the indications are of a prosperous first-century occupation that levels off until a re-invigorated interest in the harbours in the Late Antique period.

A significant number of Roman and Late Antique ceramic manufacture centres have newly been identified across Crete. The study of the Roman pottery from the Gournia project has presented strong evidence of a local ceramic production centre. This finding is supported by the survey evidence from Vrokastro and Kavousi.[124] New kilns were excavated in Chersonisos[125] and in Knossos (which was already well known as a centre of ceramic production).[126] Excavations at

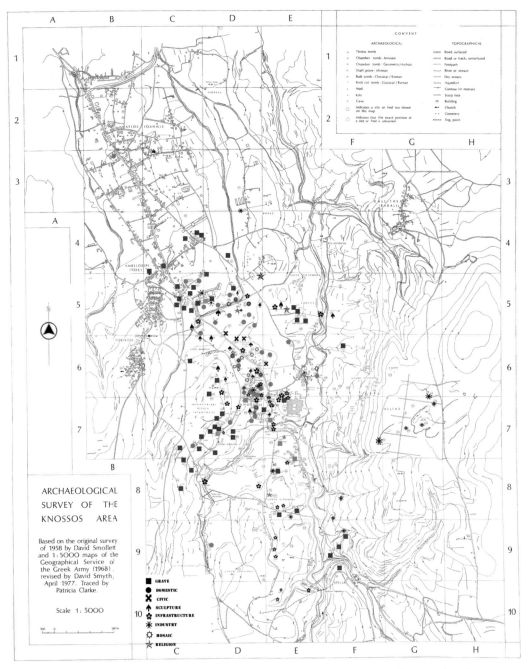

Fig. 12 Plan of the Knossos Valley (after Hood & Smyth 1981, courtesy of BSA Archives).

Bougada Metochi (Knossos village) produced the Hellenistic/Roman remains of a clay potter's wheel, a plaster pit, clay stands and unbaked pottery (Fig. 12, Grid squares D6–7).[127] Although no kiln was discovered (perhaps due to the limitations of the excavation area), this is one of the best examples of a potter's workshop on Crete. The pottery, consisting of amphorae, cooking pots and imitation terra sigillata A and N Italian Grey ware, ranged in date from the first century B.C.E. to the first century C.E.[128]

At the western edge of Chania's Roman city, two first- to second-century kilns were revealed. The find of amphora type AC1a in the kilns indicates another production site of this Cretan amphora already known from Kisamos (the Health Centre) (S207),[129] Knossos and Eleutherna.[130] In Kisamos, workshop installations which included kilns and iron slag were identified in the Paterakis Plot and dated between the third and fourth centuries.[131] In the south of the island, an extensive complex of 25 rooms including a potter's workshop was excavated in Matala.[132] Late Antique kilns in Gortyn[133] and Kisamos[134] have extended the evidence of industrial areas for the period on the island. Both are likely to have functioned primarily for local production.

2.4.2 Small-Scale Industries

Sanders noted that the industries known from Roman Crete, such as copper and gold mining, and lamp, terracotta, pottery and glass production, were all for the local market.[135] Whetstones may have been quarried and exported from Olus, but there is little secure evidence for this. Small-scale industries and agricultural processing are in evidence in cities such as Knossos, where, in areas around the Unexplored Mansion and the Stratigraphic Museum, evidence for bone- and metal-working as well as for pottery production has been revealed.[136] Dye works and olive oil production have also been discovered.[137] Workshop installations identified by kilns and iron slag were found at the Paterakis Plot, Kisamos.[138] Other areas investigated revealed evidence for fine moulds[139] and evidence for glass production.[140] A number of workshops have been recently identified in Chania[141] and in Ierapetra.[142] As can be seen from the plans of the major urban centres (Figs. 12–16), several different industries appear to be grouped together to form well-defined industrial areas in Roman Cretan towns.

At Xerokambos, Lasithi,[143] new evidence of the rock-salt cuttings was revealed supporting Pliny's claim for salt production on the island, which had not been known in Sanders's time.[144] Haggis suggested murex, fishing rights, the slave trade and textiles as important elements of the east Cretan economy,[145] and excavations at Kouphonisi revealed evidence for the large-scale extraction of purple from murex shells as well as evidence for the area's fishing industry.[146]

2.4.3 Agriculture

As few farms have been excavated, there is a reliance on survey evidence and on extrapolation from other data like ceramics to establish general farming practices. In addition to pastoralism and crop production, small diversified industries

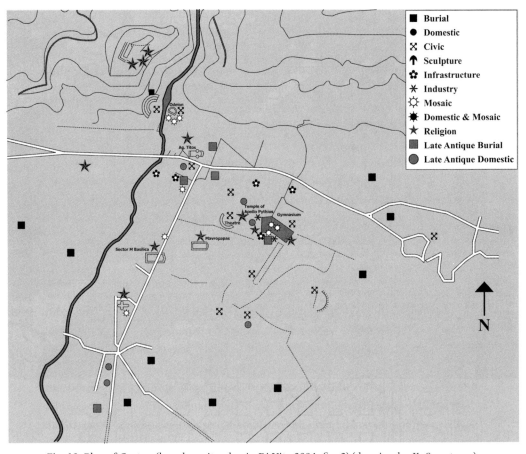

Fig. 13 Plan of Gortyn (based on site plan in Di Vita 2004, fig. 2) (drawing by K. Sweetman).

such as milling, textile production (dyeing and weaving), beekeeping[147] and oil and wine production are in evidence. The extensive study of a Roman farmstead on Gavdos is an invaluable contribution to an understanding of farming practices in rural Greece. Work here has revealed, like at other farmsteads, small-scale industrial functions (e.g., olive processing).[148] In the Kampos area, the Kavousi survey identified a small-scale industrial farmstead with evidence of olive industry.[149] The survey directors likened the arrangement of the site to that of Khoriodhakia, identified by Sanders, which contained a limekiln and a cistern.[150] In the less well-known east of the island, two surveys, the Itanos and Ziros projects, have recognized a similar pattern of occupation in the rural landscape of combined farmstead and small industry; for example, at Lamnoni[151] and at Travouni (in the north).[152] At Smarion in Pediadha, work on a Roman farmstead revealed a large wine press, an olive press and storage areas.[153] The large pithoi which contained the remains of resin indicate storage of wine for the local rather than the export market.[154] Many of the farmsteads had further purposes, such as serving as centres for storage and possibly re-distribution. At

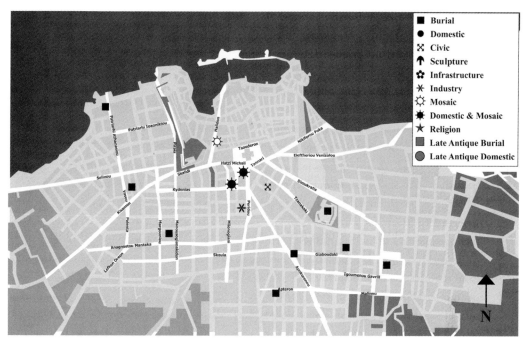

Fig. 14 Plan of Chania (drawing by K. Sweetman).

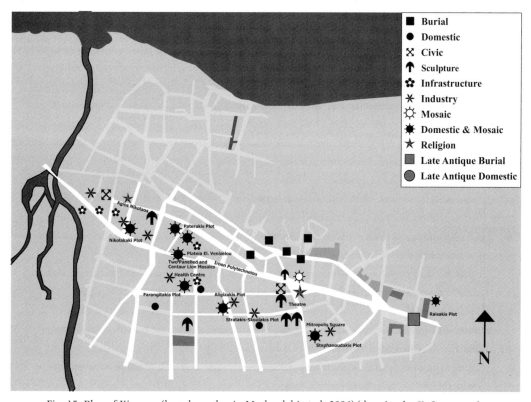

Fig. 15 Plan of Kisamos (based on plan in Markoulaki et al. 2004) (drawing by K. Sweetman).

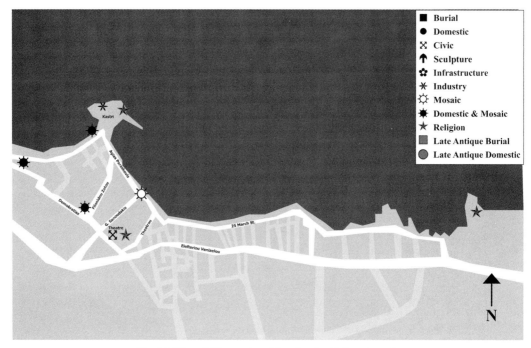

Fig. 16 Plan of Chersonisos (drawing by K. Sweetman).

Sta Lenika, for example, a series of warehouses was found during the Kavousi survey, good evidence for storage and re-distribution.[155] The Pachyammos 'Villa' may be a warehouse or an industrial area of the house.[156] It shares some similarities with the Tholos building in its long narrow corridors suggesting storage, while a complex of cisterns and a water system on the east side indicate an industrial use.

2.4.4 Harbours

Several new Roman harbours have been identified (Pseira, Sitia, Astale)[157] or confirmed (Navarchos Nearchos Road in Chersonisos)[158] since Sanders's work.[159] The Vrokastro survey identified a number of harbours at Ioannimiti and the continued use of early harbours such as Priniatikos Pyrgos and Nisi Pandeleimon in the Roman period.[160] Moreover, some focused investigations are contributing significantly to an overall understanding of trade across the island. Haggis's convincing study of Tholos showed its growing importance as a port in the Roman period in part because of its likely function as a *horreum* on the Mediterranean grain route.[161] The lack of evidence of agricultural processing equipment and facilities and the fact that the storage capacity was disproportionate to the agricultural potential of the area allow this theory.[162] Haggis argued that Tholos would have been used as a 'contingency' port if ships from Alexandria and the

East were caught out by the northwesterly winds and had to land on northeast Crete for safety.[163] The shipment would then be transported south to Ierapetra to continue its journey to Rome. However, an alternative scenario is more likely; Tholos was part of a well-organized and profitable overland shipping system which benefited from investment in the mid to late first century to make it so. Goods may have been taken overland (on the 15 km route) from the southern port of Ierapetra for re-distribution to the Aegean.[164] Equally possible is that goods were shipped from Rhodes or Knidos (along the grain route) south to Tholos and then brought overland to be shipped out again at Ierapetra.

From the south coast, a number of harbour towns were recorded during surveys. At Lasaia, the survey found that the town was equipped with warehouses and a breakwater as well as with an aqueduct.[165] Mineral deposits of copper and a good source of stone would have helped the town prosper.[166] At Lissos, the ancillary buildings located close to the harbour have also been investigated as part of a re-study of the site.[167]

The evidence of the new sites and material and the diversity of foci across the island indicate that Crete played a much more active economic role in the Roman Empire than Sanders's survey could have shown.

2.5 CONCLUSION: SETTLEMENT PATTERNS

While the evidence for Roman settlement patterns is growing to include new types such as seaside resorts, the primary reason for the establishment and growth of most sites still appears to have been economic: agricultural development, exploitation of the natural resources or proximity to one of the major north–south communication links for participation in the trade network. Sites are rarely seen to have expanded significantly because of the presence of a cult as they had in the earlier pre-Roman periods (e.g., see the site of Agia Kyriaki in the Agiofarango Valley, which declined when the Asclepius cult site was abandoned in the first century B.C.E.).[168] Further evidence for the intense economic focus across the island is seen in the spread of imported pottery, even on small rural sites, other than in the east (discussed in Chapter 7). This indicates a generation of surplus wealth from all elements of economic investment in the island. But this is not to say that there was a uniformity of development on the island. There are differences in land management; for example, Sanders argues for absentee landlords in the Mesara, whereas they are clearly not in evidence in the Agiofarango Valley. A larger social range is seen in urban spaces than in rural ones, and chronological distinctions in the occupation of different areas for diverse reasons are also clear. Additionally, a variety of communication links are seen at a range of periods and between distinct areas of the island as typified by the character of the ceramic imports and, as will be seen, by the mosaics.

ණ ණ ණ ණ ණ ණ

THREE

ICONOGRAPHY OF CRETAN MOSAICS

3.1 INTRODUCTION

As a corpus, Cretan mosaics demonstrate enough variety in iconography over a period of 700 years to allow a diachronic view of society: for example, from the preference for black-and-white mosaics in the first century in the south to the dominance of the multi-panel[1] polychrome mosaics primarily in the north between the second and fourth centuries to the prevalence of carpet-style geometric polychrome mosaics in the Late Antique period. Rather than detailing each element of geometric and figured decoration on each mosaic from central and eastern Crete, the discussion will draw upon the examples in the catalogue (Appendix 1) to illustrate issues that particularly concern the date and distribution of mosaics, their spatial context, the craftspeople responsible for them and the communication links they suggest (Chapters 4–7).

3.2 GEOMETRIC ELEMENTS ON CRETAN MOSAICS

The Cretan corpus presents a wealth of geometric decoration displayed in frameworks, borders or filler decoration. Although most geometric elements and schemes are reasonably conventional, there are a few uniquely Cretan geometric elements, positions and combinations and some distributions of specific geometric designs that can lead to the identification of common craftspeople and communication links. Although this may be an argument for the use of pattern books, common traits in geometric designs indicate that there was at least the movement of ideas through craftspeople or patrons.[2] Such theories in all cases need further iconographic and contextual support to strengthen the argument.

The use of a particular compositional type and the setting of the viewpoints may indicate the function or the layout or both of a specific room, and the identification of geometric borders can help determine the size of a room. Variations in the use of space, such as that designated for the family or for visitors or, in a church context, as being more sacred, may be indicated through layout and geometric décor. Finally, the preferred progression of movement throughout a space may be indicated through subtle designs, particularly through geometric borders. When describing the geometric pattern, the Balmelle **R** number (*Décor*)[3] will be provided. A catalogue of these images with their full descriptions is found in Plate 52.

3.2.1 Cretan Geometric Frameworks (Roman and Late Antique)

The majority of Roman Cretan mosaics are composed of multiple panels within frameworks, which were customarily used throughout the Roman Empire. The carpet-type popular in the Roman West is not widespread on Crete until the Late Antique period. As such, geometric frames are a quintessential element of Cretan mosaics. The use of a framework gives the artist a means to provide an architectural setting, tell different stories or display different themes in a single mosaic. While providing a means for orientating the scene or emphasizing a theme, the framework could also act as both a division of and a link between figured themes (such as Dionysus and theatre elements). Late Antique floor space was not always conducive to the incorporation of frameworks as there was less of a focus on expressing complex figured themes. Even so, frameworks are found in small versions within elements of larger swathes of decoration, for example, the central panel of the lion and deer in the narthex of Basilica A at Chersonisos (Mosaic 92) (Pl. 25).[4]

A range of different frameworks may be incorporated in a single mosaic, and four main categories of frames are used in the Roman and Late Antique mosaics of Crete.[5] They are as follows:

(i) Circle/octagon set within a square (Pl. 1) (which includes spoked-wheel and hexagon arrangements)
(ii) Nine-panel arrangement (Pl. 44)
(iii) Vault pattern (Pl. 3)
(iv) Two rectangular panels on either side of a square

Circle/Octagon Set within a Square

Octagon set within a square:

(a) Mosaic 1. Bust of Dionysus in a circle, Knossos, Villa Dionysus, 2nd c. (Pl. 1)

(b) Mosaic 9. Apollinaris mosaic, Knossos, North City, 2nd half 1st c. to early 2nd c. (Pl. 8)

There are no Late Antique examples.

Circle set within a square (Pl. 2) (including published examples from west Crete):

(a) Mosaic 2. Dionysiac followers, Knossos, Villa Dionysus, 2nd c. (Pl. 2)
(b) Mosaic 5. Medusa and the Four Seasons, Knossos, Villa Dionysus, 2nd c. (Pl. 5)
(c) Mosaic 6. Geometric designs, Knossos, Villa Dionysus, 2nd c. (Pl. 6)
(d) Mosaic 17. Hutchinson's mosaic, 3rd c. (Pl. 12)
(e) Mosaic 33. Iraklion mosaic 2, 2nd c. (Pl. 14)
(f) Mosaic 34. Iraklion mosaic 3, 2nd c. (Pl. 14)
(g) Mosaic 42. Kypriotakis Plot, Chersonisos, 4th c.[6]
(h) Mosaic 70. Vizari, 3rd c. (Pl. 21)
(i) Mosaic 84. Geometric mosaic, Myrtos, 1st c. (Pl. 22)
(j) Mosaic 135. Dionysus and Ariadne, Chania, 3rd c. (Pl. 40)
(k) Mosaic 139. Two-Panelled mosaic, Kisamos, 3rd c.

Late Antique examples (including published examples from west Crete):

(a) Mosaics 94–100. Chersonisos (Pl. 27)
(b) Mosaic 126. Olus, 5th c. (Pl. 38)
(c) Mosaics 148–51. Almyrida, 5th c. (Pl. 47)
(d) Mosaics 161–2. Episkopi, 5th–6th c.
(e) Mosaics 156–8. Suia Basilica A, 6th c. (Pl. 50)

The circle or octagon set within a square is by far the most common of the frameworks in Cretan mosaics, and the majority are circles rather than octagons (the two octagon examples come from Knossos). Complex borders often surround the square, and the spandrels are filled with decorative elements. In three of the Cretan examples the spandrels contain busts or full-length figures: Mosaics 1 and 5 (Pls. 1 & 5), from Knossos, and Mosaic 135 from Chania (Pl. 40). The spandrels of Mosaic 139, Kisamos, contain kantharoi.

These composition types are appropriate in rooms where circulation is expected and the division of the framework allows for emphasis on a central scene with surrounding panels of associated themes, for example, in Mosaic 9 (Poseidon and subsidiary panels of the marine thiasos) or Mosaic 135 (connecting the central Dionysiac theme with theatrical masks occupying the space between the octagon and the circle) (Pls. 8 & 40). The associations between the subjects or themes, for example, between Medusa and the Seasons in Mosaic 5 (Pl. 5), are not always so obvious. Although there are no direct links between these mythological figures, one can assume that the association is due to the prophylactic powers of both Medusa and the Seasons.[7] Eight-, 12- or 16-spoked wheels are used to further delineate panels within circle- or hexagon-in-a-square compositions. Mosaics 1 and 9 have 8- and

16-spoked wheels contained within octagons, and Mosaic 139 has a 12-spoked wheel within the main circle framework. This form may be used to both place emphasis on a central figure as seen from a doorway and encourage circulation within a room, for example, Mosaic 1.

The circle or octagon within a square was popular across the Roman Empire; in the West it was particularly common in the first century B.C.E. and first century C.E. and in the East from the late first to the fourth century.[8] The variations on how the frameworks were used are vast, and there may be commonality in the frameworks selected, yet the choice of subject matter portrayed was often entirely different. The Cretan preference was to use the framework to display as many elements of a particular figured theme as possible without over-cluttering the scheme. Mosaic 17 is thus far the only Cretan example of the use of the circle or octagon in a square framework to divide up a geometric scheme, a common pattern in other areas of the empire, including Greece. Figured schemes have been found at Argos (fourth century)[9] and Corinth (Hadrianic or Antonine period).[10] A close example of some of the Cretan varieties (such as Mosaic 135) is found in the House of the Calendar, Antioch, dated to the second century.[11] Outside Crete, the design of the circle within the square is used within panels of carpet-type schemes rather than as a structure for the overall mosaic theme. This is seen in the Late Antique period in Crete, but in some areas, such as Antioch, the examples range in date from the second century to the fifth century (e.g., DH 24-S and the Baths of Apolausis).[12]

The spoked wheel was popular in all areas of the empire, particularly in the Antonine period in mainland Greece. Examples are that of Apollo and the months from Elis and the Poseidon and marine thiasos mosaic from the baths at Olympia (similar to Mosaic 9).[13] A more complex fourth-century version from Room 1 of the Constantinian Villa in Antioch demonstrates the growing popularity in the East of free-form narrative figured scenes while retaining the overall frame.[14] This example is also notable because usually single mythological figures are depicted within the panels rather than narrative scenes. Examples from other areas of the Roman Empire also tend to have a late date, such as two fourth-century mosaics from Horkstow and Winterton.[15] Crete's late first- and second-century examples of the spoked wheel are of the earliest known in the East, which may point to the island as the origin for its use in the eastern Mediterranean.

Nine-Panel Arrangement

The nine-panel format[16] is thus far found only in west Crete:

(a) Mosaic 140. Centaur and Lion, Kisamos, *c.* 2nd c.
(b) Mosaic 141. Paterakis Plot, Kisamos, *c.* 2nd c. (Pl. 44)
(c) Mosaic 137. Lissos mosaic, 1st c. (which may be considered a variation)[17]

There are no Late Antique examples from Crete.

While dividing up geometric or figured schemes, this framework can allow a focus on a central figured scene and make a thematic connection with the surrounding panels clear. In the Cretan examples, the main panels are orientated so that only a single viewpoint is provided. Two examples come from *triclinia* (Mosaics 139 & 141), and the figures in each panel are orientated to face the doorway (Pl. 44). In Mosaics 140 and 141, only single viewpoints are provided by the central panel of the centaur and lion, and the panels of the Horae and seasons, respectively. It is the reverse for Lissos (Mosaic 137) in which each figure faces away from the door of the temple in which the mosaic is situated. This would imply that there was some significance of the figures for the god rather than the temple visitors. The room in which Mosaic 17 was found has not been identified and the panels are of geometric décor.

The Cretan examples date to a period between the first and second century. The use of a swastika meander to link panels (as in Mosaic 137) is common in the earlier part of the range. Five-, seven- and nine-panelled arrangements are found in Italy and the West from the mid-second century onwards (e.g., the second-century Dionysus and Ariadne from Italica), with repeated panels in registers common in carpet-swathe mosaics (e.g., the second- to third-century Dionysus and Seasons mosaic from the SW quarter excavations at El Djem). A more complex variation of the grid of uniform hexagons is found in the Zodiac mosaic found in the vicinity of Zaghouan dated to the third century that is now in the Bardo Museum, Tunisia.

Waywell argues that the development of use of several different panels with multiple viewpoints did not occur until the first century in Greece.[18] The arrangement of panels around a central panel became popular in the second century in Greece, in particular, the nine-panelled arrangement.[19] Variations of the grid of uniform panels are found in Antioch and Cyprus, where multiple large panels are laid normally in a line or a register rather than in a grid. This can be seen, among others, in the House of Porticoes and the House of Dionysus and Ariadne, Antioch (both dated to the Severan period), and the nine-panel arrangement in the House of Dionysus in Paphos, Cyprus.[20]

Vault Pattern

Vault pattern is found on the following mosaics:

(a) Mosaic 3. Dionysus and the Seasons, Villa Dionysus, Knossos 2nd c. (Pl. 3)
(b) Mosaic 73. Bath House mosaic, Lappa, 3rd c.

There are no Late Antique examples.

In both Cretan examples, bands of guilloche are used to create the vault design, consisting of a central circle, four semi-circles, four rounded triangles (quadrants) and four concave squares. In the Knossos example, vault pattern links the central figure of Dionysus to the subsidiary panels of the Seasons represented by birds and plants (Pl. 3). The panels in Mosaic 73 contain geometric décor and stylized plants.

Vault pattern is considered to be one of several compositions which derived from ceiling decoration and was originally found in black-and-white Pompeian mosaics such as the mosaic from Casa del Poeta.[21] This format remained popular in Italy and the West throughout the Roman period, with a second-century example from Ostia[22] and a fourth-century example from Hinton St. Mary's.[23] Several developed examples are found in Tunisia, where the framework becomes less prominent (e.g., the mid-second-century La Chebba Triumph of Neptune mosaic in the Bardo). Mosaic 3 shares a number of common features with an example from Korone, Greece, particularly the framework, the figured theme of Dionysus and animals as seasons, dated to the second half of the second century.[24]

Hellenkemper Salies stresses that the vault pattern was a common scheme throughout the Roman Empire and that the mid-second-century Knossos example (Mosaic 3) is likely to be early in the development.[25] The framework is not often found in the eastern provinces, and neither Levi nor Campbell records mosaics with vault patterns from either Antioch or Daphne.[26] However, as already noted, it is found in the second century in the West and North Africa. The early use of the vault pattern at Knossos is indicative of the multiple sources for mosaics recognizable on the island while also noting an early use of a style in the East.

Two Rectangular Panels on Either Side of a Square

The framework of rectangular panels on either side of a square is found in:

(a) Mosaic 8. Three-Part mosaic, Villa Dionysus, Knossos 2nd c. (Pl. 7)
(b) Mosaic 34. Iraklion mosaic 3, 2nd c. (Pl. 14)
(c) Mosaic 55. Room XI, Odeion, Gortyn 2nd c. (Pl. 18)[27]
(d) Mosaic 84. Geometric mosaic, Myrtos, 1st c. (Pl. 22)

Mosaic 66, the Lebena Hippocamp mosaic (Pl. 20), also belongs in this classification.

There are no Late Antique examples.

The layout of this basic framework consists of a single central square which is bordered on two opposite sides by a rectangular panel. All three panels are usually enclosed and joined by a border of geometric decoration; the layout gives rise to a single viewpoint only and is suited to smaller rooms or even corridor spaces. Numerous examples of this grid are found in Greece and Antioch, including in Athens,[28] and the Medusa mosaic from the House of the Red Pavement dated to the second century.[29] This form is particularly popular in Italy at the end of the first century B.C.E. through to the early second century,[30] and it is likely that the Myrtos example (Mosaic 84) belongs to this particular period of fashion. As a fairly basic form, it is not surprising that it has a wide geographic and date distribution, with examples found in Spain,[31] Switzerland, Germany and North Africa.[32]

Other mosaics with definable borders, such as those in the list that follows, do not employ a specific framework to present the scene.

(a) Knossos: Mosaics 4 & 12
(b) Iraklion: Mosaics 32, 35, 36, 37
(c) Chersonisos: Mosaics 38, 39, 41, 49
(d) Gortyn: Mosaics 53, 57, 58, 60, 61

Published examples from western Crete are:

(e) Chania: Mosaics 129, 134
(f) Lissos: Mosaic 137

3.2.2 Geometric Borders

Given the number of grids on Cretan mosaics it is not surprising that a wide array of borders are found in the island's repertoire. Unlike frameworks, geometric borders are not commonly period or context specific, although some patterns are discernable in Crete. This kind of study can provide corroborative evidence for attribution of mosaics and craftspeople.[33] Some 40 different types of borders are found on the 159 known Cretan mosaics.[34] Twenty-four border types occur only once, and 8 of these, that is, one-third, occur in the Agios Niketas mosaic (143–6) (Pls. 45–6).

The three most common borders on the Roman and Late Antique mosaics of Crete are

(i) **R** 70–**R** 75. Guilloche and guilloche variations
(ii) **R** 101. Wave pattern and variations
(iii) **R** 64. Leaf scrolls and variations

R 70–R 75. Guilloche and Guilloche Variations

There are 11 different types of guilloche (Pl. 52) found on 27 Roman and Late Antique mosaics. Guilloche was one of the most common geometric elements used in mosaics across the Roman Empire, and some types are more frequently found at certain periods. For example, **R** 74h and **R** 75a (double guilloches) are thus far found in Crete primarily on Late Antique mosaics[35] such as the fourth-century Kypriotakis Plot mosaic (42) from Chersonisos.[36] The occurrence of **R** 74f on the third-century Lappa mosaic (73) is unusual in Crete with its early date. **R** 75a is also found on Hutchinson's mosaic (17), Knossos, but there is no secure date as yet. On present evidence, **R** 71a and **R** 72c would appear to have been forms of guilloche used primarily in the Late Antique period. Of note is the occurrence of thick guilloche on two early third-century mosaics in western Crete, Mosaic 136 (Pl. 42) from Chania and the Medusa and Masks mosaic (S207d) from Kisamos (discussed in more detail in Chapter 6).

R 101. Wave Pattern and Variations

Two different types of wave scroll (Pl. 52) (**R** 101b & **R** 101a) are found on a total of 16 Roman and Late Antique mosaics in Crete. As with guilloche, wave scroll is found on mosaics all over the Roman Empire across the full chronological span. Type **R** 101b is used in part to identify workshop connections between the Knossos-Iraklion groups (see Chapter 6). It is possible to infer that the design began to decline in popularity in the Late Antique period because it was less suited to the long carpet-style mosaic fitting for churches.[37]

R 64. Leaf Scrolls and Variations

Four types of leaf scrolls (Pl. 52) occur as borders on 20 different Roman and Late Antique mosaics in Crete. The main distinction between their uses in these periods is context: in the church, scrolls may be symbolic of Christ or paradise. The scroll borders of the Roman period tend to be more stylized than the realistic (often inhabited) Late Antique examples. For example, compare the scrolls of Mosaic 8 (Pl. 6) and Mosaics 111–14 (Pl. 31). Scroll borders can help to identify common workshop activity. Thus the occurrence of **R** 64d helps in the identification of the Knossos-Iraklion group. The leaf scroll at Agios Niketas (Mosaic 144) (Pl. 45) is unparalleled in Crete with the large-sized leaves which alternate with buds. This is in keeping with the other elements of this particular mosaic as discussed later.

Other Border Types

Twenty-four other border types are found on 36 Cretan mosaics, and the **R** 10g serrated saw-tooth pattern (Pl. 52) is the next most common type, though it provides little period- or location-specific evidence. Intersecting semi-circles (**R** 49a), swastika meander (**R** 35d & f), intersecting circles (**R** 237b) and linked circles (**R** 68–9) (Pl. 52) are the next most common borders found on the mosaics of Crete. Other borders include rows of cubes in perspective (**R** 99e & f) and rows of thorns and ogives (**R** 49h) (Pl. 52). With one exception, these borders are found on both Roman and Late Antique mosaics in every part of the empire. Intersecting semi-circles (**R** 49a) are found only on Late Antique mosaics in Crete, with a total of six examples at Chersonisos Basilica B, Tarrha, Suia and Episkopi (Mosaics 94–100, 147, 156–8 & 161–2) (Pls. 27 & 50). This type is especially well suited as a border to large swaths of geometric patterns rather than smaller square panels. Intersecting semi-circles are not commonly found in mainland Greece in either Roman or Late Antique mosaics. Variations are found in North African provinces, for example in El Alia (Nilotic mosaic) and the Beasts of the Amphitheatre mosaic from Carthage,[38] as well as in areas of the East such as Syria. The presence of some of these geometric elements in Crete but not in mainland Greece shows that Crete was open to a range of different sources for mosaic inspiration.

Late Antique Mosaic Borders

The Late Antique mosaics of Crete use one of three possible border types: intersecting semi-circles, variations of different scroll designs and variations of intersecting circles. With the exception of Almyrida (Mosaics 148–51) (Pls. 47–9), intersecting circles and scrolls are usually not used as borders within a single mosaic. Chersonisos Basilica B (Mosaics 94–100) (Pl. 27), Tarrha (Mosaic 147), Suia (Mosaics 156–8) (Pl. 51) and Episkopi (Mosaics 161–2) all use intersecting circles in their borders; Olus (Mosaic 126) (Pl. 38), Chersonisos Basilica A (Mosaics 92–3) (Pl. 26), Mallia (Mosaics 102–3) and Eleutherna (Mosaics 111–14) (Pl. 31) all use scroll patterns as borders; and Kolokythia (Mosaic 127), Gortyn Sector M (Mosaic 109) (Pl. 28) and Sybrita (Mosaics 116–17) (Pl. 34) all use horizontal intersecting circles. The remainder have either simple guilloche borders, as in Knossos (Mosaics 88–90) (Pls. 23–4) and Kera (Mosaics 122–5) (Pl. 35), or else have no visible borders. It is possible that the use of horizontal intersecting circles is of a period around the mid-fifth century, and it is certainly earlier than all the other Late Antique mosaics in Crete.

3.2.3 Geometric Compositions and Elements of Roman and Late Antique Mosaics

There are many different geometric elements used in a variety of different positions on Cretan mosaics of both the Roman and Late Antique periods. The issues will be discussed as follows:

(i) Use of specific geometric patterns exclusively in the Roman period
(ii) Use of specific geometric patterns exclusively in the Late Antique period
(iii) Comparative evidence

Use of Specific Geometric Patterns Exclusively in the Roman Period

Many of the less common geometric designs used in the Roman period disappeared from the Late Antique repertoire likely owing to the change in context.

Furnishing large expanses of space meant that geometric elements such as dentilled simple fillet (**R** 2d) and running saltires (**R** 4e) (Pl. 52) declined in use in the Late Antique period. Combinations of standard geometric elements such as squares, diamonds and triangles, common in the Roman period, would have been eclipsed in the long-aisled church spaces (e.g., **R** 213a in Mosaic 1 (Pl. 1) or **R** 161a in Mosaic 137 (Pl. 52)).

Use of Specific Geometric Patterns Exclusively in the Late Antique Period

Variations of borders of intersecting circles and semi-circles and double guilloche are prevalent in the Late Antique Cretan repertoire examples such as **R** 68b and **R** 69f (Pl. 52). Fields of geometric décor are found on seven different Late Antique mosaics in Crete, including scale patterns like **R** 215b and **R** 217c (Pl. 52). Furthermore, specific combinations of geometric patterns are found exclusively in the Late Antique period in Crete. One example comes from the basilica at Kera (Mosaics 122–5) (Pls. 35–6), which uses the three elements to give the effect of Maltese crosses and hexagons. A second combination consisting of stars and octagons, **R** 186b (Pl. 52), is found in Almyrida (Mosaics 148–51) (Pls. 47–9).[39] While the preceding examples are exclusively Late Antique in Crete, similar patterns can be found in Roman mosaics in other parts of the empire.

Some Late Antique-only designs such as zigzags like **R** 199b (Pl. 52) are used abundantly (particularly as filler decoration) on Crete and have the same time scale of use as other areas, including mainland Greece (e.g., Epidauros dated to the fifth century).[40] Another example is a combination of a circle surrounded by squares and rectangles as found in Chersonisos Basilica A and Kera and also in Syria (e.g., Deire Sharqi).[41] This combination indicates that, at least in the Eastern Empire, there were some period-specific geometric elements. The field of intersecting bands creating circles and bobbins or mat of circles and squares (**R** 144e) (Pl. 52) is a distinguishable geometric design found only in Late Antique mosaics in Crete; in combination with other type-specific elements, it can be used as workshop evidence (see Chapter 6) for sites within both Crete and the Eastern Empire. A second element, the knot design (Pls. 23 & 36), is also found exclusively in the Late Antique period and can also be used to identify common craftspeople working in Crete and the East.

Comparative Evidence

Crete has evidence for 7 of the 30 compositions types defined by Hellenkemper Salies.[42] Most of the types that Hellenkemper Salies identified, such as the system of octagons types 1, 2 and 6, occur so commonly that they cannot provide much conclusive dating or craftspeople evidence; however, two elements are worth noting. Rautensternsystem I (which is a system of lozenge and squares similar to **R** 173b) (Pl. 52) is found in Crete in second-century mosaics (e.g., Gortyn Mosaic 60 and several mosaics from Kisamos), but those found in the majority in mainland Greece date to the third century.[43] The earliest example in mainland Greece is from Eleusis, dated to the Severan period, and the earliest in Africa is Late Antonine, from El Djem.[44] Regarding the system of circles (Type 4) (Kreissystem IV), Crete fits in with Hellenkemper Salies's suggestion that the scheme is rare in the East with the exception of Late Antique mosaics (the single example of this type coming from Chersonisos Basilica A (Mosaics 92–3)) (Pl. 26).[45]

The Agios Niketas mosaics (143–6) remain anomalous in the Late Antique Cretan repertoire (Pls. 45–6). Precise parallels have not been located from either the Eastern or Western Empire, but the abundance of intersecting squares suggests more of a Jordanian, Syrian or even Cyrenaican style. Elements can be paralleled; for example, the eye design which is found in Athens and **R** 68b is also common in areas other than Crete.[46] The distinctive mosaic is perhaps an example of the work of an experimental artist, a patron with innovative ideas, an inexperienced craftsperson or a combination thereof. Such individual elements may be ascribed to artistic whim, and although craftspeople may be identifiable through their originality (or in the case of the exo-narthex, their inexperience), these occurrences are too few or too different in date to ascribe workshop indications.

3.3 FIGURED MOSAICS

As shown earlier, discussions of craftspeople, use of space and changing communication links over time are enhanced by a study of geometric décor. Examination of the figured iconography builds upon those three elements and enables discussions on the social application of the evidence: why certain scenes were fashionable in Crete, how mosaics helped to promote the patron and how the use of mosaics changed in Christian structures.

Much of the figured decoration of Roman Cretan mosaics is typical of that from across the empire. To provide a contextual focus, the comparative discussion will draw primarily on material from the Eastern provinces, in particular, material from Greece, including all the other islands (and which from now on will be called Greece), Antioch, Cyprus and the Mediterranean more broadly.

Categories of figured scenes:

(i) Mythology (which includes personifications)
(ii) Genre
(iii) Animals

3.3.1 Mythological Scenes

Mythological scenes are the most common figured theme found on Cretan mosaics, making up nearly 20 per cent of all known pre-Christian figured examples. As was the case across the Roman Empire, the most popular theme in Cretan mosaics was Dionysus (50%). In Crete, this was followed by Poseidon and personifications of the seasons.

The mythological scenes discussed in this section are:

(i) Dionysus and the Dionysiac thiasos
(ii) Poseidon
(iii) Medusa
(iv) The Four Seasons
(v) The Horae
(vi) Other Scenes

Dionysus

Four different subjects involving Dionysus or his attributes are found on published Cretan mosaics: the rescue of Ariadne by Dionysus (Mosaic 135) (Pl. 40); vintaging scenes (Mosaics 136 & S211) (Pl. 43); and scenes without a narrative episode (Mosaics 1, 2, 3 & S207e) (Pls. 1–3).[47] Scenes from the theatre are discussed in the section on genre scenes.[48] The unpublished Mosaic S207f from Kisamos depicts a scene of the Wedding of Dionysus. One mosaic (S216) illustrating the Triumph of Dionysus has been discovered in Kisamos and is on display in the museum there. The Triumph of Dionysus is a popular North African theme,[49] and the frame and decoration of the Kisamos example is very close to the North African style with the use of vine scroll to create a framework.[50]

(a) Dionysus and Ariadne

Mosaic 135 from Chania (mid-third century), depicting the rescue of Ariadne at Naxos, is one of the best preserved mosaics on Crete (Pl. 40). It is likely that the room in which it was discovered functioned as an *oecus,* or a main reception room, as evidenced by the grid and iconography. Distinctive Dionysiac paraphernalia such as theatre masks are included, and the bordering panels are scenes from Menander comedies. The main scene and the filler decoration are commonly found across the empire. The precise scene of Dionysus and Ariadne is found in a range of media such as painting and sculpture and on sarcophagi.[51] Regarding mosaics, it is a particularly favoured scene in the areas of mainland Greece and Antioch.[52] Each illustration of this scene is depicted in the same basic format with deviations. Dionysus and various followers approach the sleeping Ariadne, and a figure lifts her cloak. The examples range in proficiency too; thus the somewhat haphazard late fourth-century example from Merida in Spain, which contains all the standard figures (Pan is included revealing the sleeping Ariadne), may be contrasted with that from Socrates Street, Thessaloniki.[53] This scene is one of the strongest pieces of evidence for the existence of types or formulas for both mosaics and wall paintings (discussed further in Chapter 6).

A precise parallel for the Chania example is not yet known. Mosaics from Thessaloniki and Antioch are different in the nature of the background scenery.[54] A close parallel in the arrangement of the figures comes from Apollonia, but little in the portrayal of the characters is comparable.[55] Many mosaics from areas such as Cyprus and North Africa portray scenes of the myth concerning Ariadne, Theseus and Dionysus.[56]

(b) Vintaging Scenes

The figures are not clearly visible in Mosaic 136 because of damage, but the remains indicate a scene of Dionysus on a leopard amid a background of vine leaves.[57] It was discovered in the *triclinium* of the mid-third-century House of Dionysus (Pl. 43), which also contained the Dionysus and Ariadne mosaic. Included in the scene may also have been figures of Pan (the legs are present) and a maenad (Pl. 43).[58] The inscription which runs along the top of the scene (Pl. 43) is discussed in detail in Chapter 6, but it has raised some speculation that the mosaicist came from Antioch.

The four subsidiary panels depict theatre masks (discussed later), and of the remaining two, one is damaged, but there appears to be a tambourine in a preserved fragment (Pl. 42). The final panel comprises Dionysus, leaning on a pillar, with Pan standing just behind him. In the right-hand corner is either a seated figure or a boat, with the scene possibly representing the rescue of Ariadne at Naxos (Pl. 42). A similar example from Room 3 of the House of the Boat of Psyches in Antioch has a satyr replacing the figure of Dionysus in the same arrangement.[59]

Another mosaic from the west, S211 from Kisamos, is more certainly a scene of *putti* vintaging.[60] The triumph mosaic in the Kisamos museum is surrounded by panels of scenes of *putti* stomping the grapes (S216) as well as of the hunt and ritual celebrations.

Neither vintaging scenes nor triumph scenes are common in the eastern provinces: they are much more familiar in the North African repertoire.[61] Those vintaging scenes found in the Greek mosaics tend to be secondary to the main scene and are commonly found in the depiction of Autumn or the autumn months.[62] That the only examples of such North African-themed mosaics are found in the west of the island may be indicative of certain communication links there in the third century.

(c) Non-narrative Dionysus Scenes

Two examples of busts of Dionysus (Mosaics 1 & 3) (Pls. 1 & 3) and a further example containing busts of the followers of Dionysus (Mosaic 2) (Pl. 2) are among the Villa Dionysus mosaics. All three mosaics have been dated to the mid-second century.

Mosaic 1 from the *oecus* shows a central bust of Dionysus surrounded by the heads of his followers in subsidiary panels (Pl. 1). The image of the regal Dionysus is perfected through his depiction with long hair and heavy clothes and in the extensive use of glass. As with the detail of the god, particularly in the face, a great deal of time has also been spent in the portrayal of the followers of Dionysus, all of whose individual characteristics are in evidence.

Mosaic 3 also depicts Dionysus as a portrait. It is possible that this room functioned as a *cubiculum* (see Chapter 5). Dionysus is readily recognizable through the attribute of the crown of vine leaves (Pl. 3). The garland and the pose of the god are so similar to those of Mosaic 1 that although the treatment of the two Dionysus figures is not exactly the same, the likenesses in portrayal, style and date suggest that both figures were the work of the same group of craftspeople, if not the same craftsperson.[63] Mosaic 2 has a central panel of a figure with pointed ears who despite his central position is likely to be just a member of the thiasos rather than Dionysus (Pl. 2). The grid types and the portrayal of busts may be regular in the East,[64] but the sober bust figure of Dionysus in Mosaic 1 appears to be unique. In the West and North Africa, non-narrative Dionysiac scenes are uncommon.[65]

Poseidon

Two Cretan mosaics depict scenes concerning Poseidon. One is a narrative scene from Chania (Pl. 39) depicting the myth of Poseidon and the nymph Amymone at Lerna Spring (Mosaic 129). The other is a generic scene of the god in his chariot from Knossos (Mosaic 9) (Pl. 8). Both scenes are common representations of Poseidon on Roman mosaics.

(a) Poseidon and Amymone

The myth of Poseidon and Amymone is illustrated in two scenes on the third-century mosaic (129). The first contains Amymone's search for water and the approach of the satyr, and the second illustrates her rescue by Poseidon and the creation of the spring (Pl. 39).[66] The identification of the room as either a small *triclinium* or a *cubiculum* is discussed in Chapter 5.

Parallels for the myth are found across the Mediterranean: Neapolis, Tunisia,[67] Italy,[68] Amphipolis, Greece[69] and Cyprus.[70] As these show, it was more common to depict a single scene of Amymone being rescued by Poseidon and often with a cupid. The second- to third-century single-panelled scene from Paphos has some parallels with the mosaics from Amphipolis and Chania, but craftspeople connections are unlikely.[71] The Amphipolis mosaic has two panels, but only the first is from the Poseidon and Amymone myth; the second depicts Hylas and the Nymphs.[72] Kankeleit argues that it is unique in Greece to depict the Poseidon and Amymone myth in two panels; yet it is found in two panels in areas such as Syria, Spain and North Africa.[73]

The four faces depicted in the subsidiary panels may represent winds indicating Poseidon's realm covering the four corners of the earth and the control the god had over the winds and the sea. Kankeleit suggests that they are Medusas.[74] The small doormat panel of fighting cocks may represent a fertility symbol. Darmon suggests, after Bruneau, that the cocks may be a symbol of victory.[75]

(b) Poseidon in His Chariot

The Apollinaris mosaic (9), Knossos, is dated to the second half of the first to early second century (Pl. 8). The function of this room is undetermined. A central scene of Poseidon riding the waves being drawn by sea horses (but without a clear chariot) is surrounded by panels depicting images of tritons being chased by dolphins (Pl. 9).[76] An example found at Sousse dated to the late second to early third century is a good parallel.[77] It is noteworthy that both mosaics encompass Poseidon in frontal position and that the depiction of the horses to the side is also the same. The gap of a century between the mosaics makes any workshop connections impossible but does not preclude the possibility of pattern-book circulation. The Poseidon theme was popular across the Roman Empire with many variations, including the free-form action-filled, black-and-white examples from Italy.[78] On others, found in Greece and North Africa, the central scene may be reserved for static images and the action depicted on subsidiary panels.[79] Other variations include Amphitrite in the chariot (e.g., the fourth-century floor from Constantine, North Africa).[80]

Parallels have already been drawn between the framework of Mosaic 9 and the Poseidon mosaic from the Alpheos Baths, Olympia, which is Antonine in date.[81] Despite the damage it is possible to reconstruct a central scene of Poseidon on the remains of a wheel and horses' legs, and the subsidiary panels also depict scenes of dolphins and other sea creatures. The difference in date rules out any direct craftsperson connection between the two mosaics.

Mosaics were the most common media for the popular scene of Poseidon, with variations found in paintings and sculpture.[82] In all these instances the scene is of one of two standard types: crowded with many members of the marine thiasos, or depicting Poseidon with his cloak billowing out behind as he rides in a chariot. The myth of Poseidon and Amymone is not common in media other than mosaics.

Medusa

Three Cretan mosaics display Medusa themes, and as with most Medusa mosaic representations, none displays a narrative scene.[83]

The second-century Mosaic 5, Villa Dionysus, Knossos (Pl. 5), comes from a room of unknown function. The central panel has been severely damaged, but the fragments of snake heads and the surrounding shield of scales (the most common of the Medusa portrayals) identify this clearly as a Medusa mosaic. The four seasons are depicted as fillers in the corners of the space left over from where the square surrounds the circle.[84] A similar well-preserved Medusa mosaic (42) from Chersonisos encompasses a quarto-chrome shield of scales with the Medusa head quite visible (save for a section of wall sitting on top).[85] The knotted snakes at the neck are of the standard form and are likely to have been present in the Knossos mosaic (Pl. 5). In this fourth-century example, pairs of opposed dolphins occupy the spaces between the circle and square. The other Cretan example, dated to the early third century from Kisamos, is Mosaic S207d and depicts a central panel of Medusa surrounded by panels of masks and followers of Dionysus.[86] The Medusa head (along with snakes) is depicted as sitting directly on the shield of scales, all of which is contained in a concave square.

Both Daszewski and Dunbabin note that the popular Hellenistic and Roman portrayal of the head of Medusa on its own could be considered apotropaic.[87] The black and white triangles surrounding the central Medusa are arranged to induce a feeling of dizziness in the observer and were repeatedly used in connection with the portrayal of Medusa all over the empire, from Bulgaria to North Africa.[88] This idea relates to the myth that to gaze upon the face of Medusa would mesmerize the spectator, enabling her to stun her victims long enough to turn them into stone. This geometric décor is also found with Dionysus where the dizziness may be associated with feelings of drunkenness, as seen in Corinth.[89]

Scenes of Medusa are common across the empire, and many display a combination of upward-staring eyes, a pair of wings on her forehead and snakes. One of the better preserved examples is from Piraeus dating to the end of the first century. Two variations from Sparta include one from the property of Paraskevopoulou (third century)[90] with a shield design which uses semicircular shapes rather than triangular ones. The second, from the property of Alexopoulou (third century), does not have the shield design surrounding the mosaic, but the basic features of this Medusa are still the same.[91] Examples from Antioch include one from the House of the Red Pavement (Room 5).[92] Although the shield of scales effect is not the same, the central emblem of Medusa is very similar in design to the mainland Greek examples. The Medusa in a shield of scales is also popular on North African mosaics, in particular, in mosaics from Tunisia,[93] Dar Zmela, Sousse[94] and Egypt.[95] From Cyrenaica, examples include one from Palazzo delle Colonne in Ptolemais[96] where Medusa's head is contained in a circular panel surrounded by elongated scales and is quite different from the scales used in the Medusa mosaic in the Villa Dionysus.

The Four Seasons

Four Cretan mosaics depict the four seasons; they are Mosaics 3, 5, 135 and 141 (Pls. 3, 5, 40 & 44). Another floor, Mosaic 13, is now lost.

Seasons are among the most common motifs used on Roman mosaics across the empire. They occur both as main motifs and in secondary design, and their number means they are a good motif to use in areas such as spandrels or in other four-part framework arrangements. Parrish noted that seasons depicted in private contexts, as is the case with those of Crete, had general overtones of being symbols of good fortune and prosperity.[97] Of Parrish's three categories of seasons, personifications (men or women, with or without wings) and plants and animals are found on Crete, but images of seasonal activity are not.[98] According to Parrish, the full-figure depiction lasts from the mid-second to mid-third century, and the busts date from the mid-second to the end of the fourth century.[99] Regional preferences for different representations of the seasons are clear.

The Seasons Mosaics of Crete

(a) Mosaic 3. Dionysus and the Four Seasons

Dionysus and the Four Seasons (Mosaic 3) (Pl. 3), mid-second century, contains panels of plants and birds representing the seasons surrounding the main panel of Dionysus. Dionysus was commonly associated with the seasons because of the symbolism of growth, decay, death and re-birth.[100] Each semi-circle encloses a bird: a partridge representing Summer and the harvest, a peacock representing Spring and renewal, a parrot or other small bird representing Autumn and a waterbird representing Winter (Pl. 3).[101] Each concave square contains a different plant positioned so that each season is represented on the same side by a plant and a bird. They are not oriented to be seen together, as the correct plant is situated to the right of each bird. Here the peacock is associated with the rose symbolizing both beauty and Spring. The panel to the right of the waterbird displays a small bunch of reeds (Pl. 3), a symbol of the rain and dampness of Winter. To the right of the partridge, is a panel showing a small bundle of grain symbolizing the Summer harvest. Finally, to the right of the small bird is a small vine cutting with a bunch of grapes which signifies Autumn. A face is depicted in each of the four corners of the outer border (Pl. 3). There are no clear attributes to define the heads as winds, although their tousled hair and associations with the seasons suggest it. For example Varro associated Spring with Zephyrus, Summer with Notus, Autumn with Eurus and Winter with Boreas.[102]

Although rare in Greece, a few mosaics depict animals considered to be representations of the seasons. It is possible that the second-century mosaic from Korone depicts seasons in the form of the lion, the bull and another cat representing Spring, Summer and Autumn, respectively.[103] That each creature is portrayed in a hunt scene casts some doubt on the identification of the animals as seasons, but the date and overall form of the mosaic compares well with Mosaic 3.

(b) Mosaic 5. The Medusa Mosaic

The four seasons that appear in bust form on the Medusa mosaic (mid-second century) occur as fillers in the spandrels (Pl. 5). From the southeast corner moving clockwise: Winter is recognized by her heavy clothes and the dead twigs in her hair; Spring is illustrated wearing a loose mantle with flowers in her hair; Summer has wheat or corn in its hair, with one bare shoulder representing the heat of the season; and though largely destroyed, Autumn can be identified by the bunches of grapes in the dark hair of the figure. Here the seasons are depicted with wings, giving them more of a supernatural characteristic and emphasizing the sense of fortune and goodwill that they were intended to represent (Pl. 5).

(c) Mosaic 135. Dionysus and Ariadne, Chania

The third-century Mosaic 135 was discovered in what likely had been the *oecus* of a private house. Surrounding the main panel of Dionysus and Ariadne is a series of panels depicting scenes from Menander comedies with personifications of the seasons in between (Pl. 41). The seasons' position, in the middle on each side, is peculiar in that they break up the panels of the play.[104] Only two seasons, Autumn and Summer, have been preserved, and they are male busts.[105] Summer is typically bare shouldered, with a sickle at his right shoulder and a crown of summer flowers in his hair. Autumn wears a light garment gathered at his chest and a crown of vine leaves. An implement, like a grape cutter may also have been at his shoulder, but the panel is too damaged to be certain.

(d) Mosaic 141. The Paterakis Plot, Kisamos

Mosaic 141 (second half of the second century) (Pl. 44) is divided into two main sections. The lower consists of five panels within a grid of swastika meander. The central panel contains the Horae dancing (Pl. 44), and each of the four surrounding panels contains a bust of a female Season. In a clockwise manner, Summer appears in the top right-hand corner, Spring below her, Winter to Spring's left and Autumn above Winter (Pl. 44). Summer is lightly dressed with a crown of corn ears on her head and is accompanied by a sickle. Spring is depicted in dark clothes and has a wreath of spring flowers in her hair. She does not carry any other kind of seasonal attribute. Winter (probably female) is almost completely covered in a red cloak with a wreath of dead twigs around her head. Autumn is not identifiable by any of her usual attributes, and the only recognizable feature is the wreath of vine leaves in her hair. Her attire, like Summer's, is almost transparent.

Given such variety in both the seasonal mosaics of Crete and those in all other places of the empire, it is hardly surprising that exact parallels indicating common craftspeople are difficult to establish.[106] According to Parrish, the most common rooms in which to find seasons mosaics are *oeci* and *triclinia* and the second most common places are *cubicula*.[107] Of the four examples found in Crete, one came from a room of unidentified function (the Medusa mosaic) and the remaining three occur, in *oeci* and *triclinia*.

The Horae

As with representations of the four seasons, it was common to find in Greece and other parts of the Roman Empire mosaics depicting the Horae (the hours). Thus far, only one example is known from Crete, Mosaic 141 from Kisamos (Pl. 44) (second half of the second century), and it is remarkable because the Horae depicted in it are dressed quite heavily. The Horae were the goddesses of the seasons, and they were connected with the Charites, identifiable as a dancing trio, who symbolize the creation of beauty in humans. In the case of Mosaic 141, given their mythological connotations, it is appropriate to have the panel of the Charites central to those depicting the Seasons. Here, the three barefoot females hold hands as they dance around a low central pillar. All three wear a large expanse of drapery which falls and folds heavily around their bodies. It is common to have the clothes falling off the figures as they dance, as is seen with one of the women on the Cretan example (Pl. 44). This may also be paralleled with an example in the museum at Patras where one of the three is almost naked with just a cloth floating off her left shoulder.

A Severan mosaic from Lixus in North Africa displays a similar arrangement of panels with the Horae (or possibly the Charites) central to four surrounding panels of the Seasons.[108] The difference in the iconography is quite marked, ruling out direct connections between the two areas.

Other Scenes

Recently discovered mosaics, particularly in Kisamos and the west, are broadening the known Cretan repertoire of mythological scenes. For example, a range of new mosaics from Kisamos depict the following: a scene of Orpheus and the Animals

(Mosaic S212);[109] large panels of tritons (Mosaic S213); a scene of Leda and the Swan (Mosaic S215); and two scenes that have already been mentioned, the Wedding of Dionysus (Mosaic S207f) and the Triumph of Dionysus (Mosaic S216).[110]

3.3.2 Genre Scenes on Figured Mosaics

Unlike other areas of the Roman Empire, genre scenes are not common on Cretan mosaics and represent only around 8 per cent of the total of the Roman-period examples. Only the Lappa mosaic (121) depicts hunt scenes in the main field, and the three other examples are in subsidiary fields.[111] To date, no mosaics depicting arena, circus or pastoral scenes have been found. Mosaic S216 from Kisamos is a rare example of Greek mosaic depicting a ritual scene comprising the hunt gathering at an altar. The majority of genre scenes in Crete depict views of or allusions to the theatre; Mosaic 12, however, portrays an athletic scene.

Athletic Scenes

Throughout the ancient world, athletic scenes were depicted in a range of media, including pottery, wall paintings and sculpture, but during the Roman period, scenes from the gymnasium and athletics declined and were limited to mosaics and, in particular, to sculpture.[112] Mosaics with athletic scenes were most common in bath house contexts and are rarely found in domestic spheres. They do appear in specific public spaces such as the South Stoa, Agonotheteion, in Corinth, and in the Odeon at Gafsa, Tunisia, but in both these cases the context was likely to have been prize-giving ceremonies.[113] When athletic scenes were portrayed in Roman times their scope was largely limited to wrestling and boxing; field events such as running and discus throwing were rarely shown (although the Athlete and Theatre mosaic from Psila Alonia Square in Patras, now in the Patras museum, does show a range of different athletes and victors).[114]

It is likely that the two figures portrayed in Mosaic 12 are boxers (Pl. 10). Both are standing upright and wearing gloves.[115] The suggested date is the late second to the mid-third century, and the context is a small bath house. The damaged inscription (No. 2) above the heads of the figures probably gives their names ... ΚΛΟΣ ΣΑΤΟΡΝΙΛ ... (see Chapter 6). One of the most detailed gymnastic mosaics in the Eastern Empire comes from Psilalonia Square in Patras.[116] This mosaic depicts athletic activities, including discus and javelin throwing, but it mostly illustrates boxing and wrestling bouts.[117]

Hunt Scenes

Hunt scenes involving humans and animals, mythological hunts or animals alone are found primarily in subsidiary panels on Cretan mosaics.

(a) Humans Hunting Animals

Mosaic 121 from Lappa (end of fourth to beginning of fifth century) is the only Cretan mosaic completely devoted to the hunt and displays the scenes in several panels.[118] From the published photographs, it is possible to identify a number of the figures and their various activities: one panel shows a figure commanding two dogs on the right to attack a wild boar (?); a second has a man holding what appears to be a hunting knife (if so, a rather large one) with dogs pursuing a deer; another illustrates a deer running away; and in the final published example, a man holds onto his dog.[119] There are no convincing parallels to Mosaic 121 where the figures of the hunt are in silhouette. Both the date of the mosaic and the context (a Christian church) in which it was found are questionable.

Mosaic S207c, from a *triclinium* in the Health Centre, Kisamos (late second to early third century), contains a hunt scene in a subsidiary panel. This is of a standard type where a couple of men with dogs and possibly horses chase deer into a net. The scene is similar to a section of the small hunt mosaic in Piazza Armerina.[120] Mosaic S216 contains a range of subsidiary panels displaying hunt scenes of a Western or North African variety. The scenes include images of *putti* hunting, as well as panels of animals hunting each other.

Scenes of humans hunting were most popular on North African mosaics from the second century on, particularly in private villas and baths.[121] Dunbabin notes that hunt and amphitheatre scenes reached a new popularity in areas other than North Africa at the end of the third century to the beginning of the fourth century.[122] Few Roman mosaics in Crete are dated any later than the end of the third century, which may explain in part why there is such a lack of these otherwise common themes. Unlike in North Africa and the West, mosaics of the Eastern Empire favoured scenes of hunting in either single panels or uncluttered friezes, as borders or as mythological themes.[123] Waywell notes the paucity of hunt scenes in Greece; therefore, Crete fits in with the Eastern preference.[124]

(b) Mythological Hunt Scenes

Two Cretan mosaics depict scenes of the Lion and the Centaur, both from Kisamos. One is in black-and-white (Mosaic 140) (second century).[125] The other (S207a), from the Health Centre, has the entire field given over to the figured scene with the centaur confronting the lion in an aggressive manner.[126]

The hunt occurs in a central panel amid a swathe of geometric design in Mosaic 140. The scene is of a standard format seen commonly in mosaics where a lion leaps from behind a tree to attack a centaur. The centaur is shown rearing with his arm back and ready to throw a spear at the lion. Somewhat similar to the Cretan mosaic is a poorly preserved example from Room 11 of the 'Villa' in Ptolemais.[127] It is possible to identify a small black-and-white panel with the legs of an animal raised over some vegetation in a similar position to the centaur in the Kisamos mosaic.

(c) Animals Alone (Chase Scene)

Two of the three scenes of animals hunting are found as borders. The second-century Mosaic 3 from Knossos (Pl. 3) has a border depicting a simple chase scene on either side of the main field, each featuring two dogs chasing an agrimi.[128] Mosaic 141 from Kisamos (late second century) also has a subsidiary panel of a hunt scene of a leopard pursuing a stag. Here the motion in the mosaic is expressed mainly through the shadowing beneath the feet of the leopard and the stag.[129] One of the two main panels in the second-century Mosaic 139 from Kisamos is very badly damaged but it shows a dog chasing a goat.[130] The dog's shadow is included to give the effect that the dog is jumping to attack.

Scenes from the Theatre

Scenes from the theatre on Cretan mosaics are either from specific plays or depict generic theatre elements such as groups of actors or masks. Particular plays are often identifiable through inscriptions or specific elements within the scene, such as the Menander play scenes from Mytilene.[131] Mosaic 135 (Pl. 41) from Chania and Mosaic S207e from Kisamos both contain scenes from Menander plays. It has been postulated that a theatre mosaic from Patras may also have represented a Menander comedy.[132] Mosaic 136 (Pl. 42) and Mosaics S207d, S207e and S207f are the only other mosaics which have depictions representing the theatre, and these all display masks.

(a) Specific Plays

Mosaic 135 (second half of the third century) contains scenes from the lost Menander play *Plokion* (*The Necklace*) in subsidiary panels (Pl. 41), four of which are preserved.[133] One of the panels, bearing the ΠΛΟ ΚΙΟ Ν inscription, includes three figures, one standing on either side of a seated figure. The figure standing on the left holds a rod in his hand, and the other two figures both point at him. Another panel illustrates a standing naked figure holding a rod and stretching out an object to a seated figure. There are two other, badly damaged, panels. In one, a standing figure wears a cloak, and in the other, a standing figure wears a red cloak over a blue robe. These figures are all shown wearing masks.

Comparing the Mytilene mosaic with the Chania mosaic it is possible to see certain similarities, which helps to confirm the identification of the Chania scenes despite the damage. In the Mytilene mosaic, the inclusion of the characters' names identifies them as Moschion, Laches and Krobyle. The scene (from Act 2 of the Menander play), depicts Laches who is angry with his wife, Krobyle, for arranging a marriage between their son, Moschion, and a woman in whom the youth is not interested. These figures in the Chania example can be identified by their positioning; it is likely that the figure holding the stick is Laches (on the left), the seated figure is Moschion (as he is the one who is under discussion) and the figure standing on the far right is Krobyle. Although the panels of the two mosaics are not exactly the same, there are similarities between the dress, the masks and the stances of the figures. Judging from the different artistic standards of these two mosaics, their mosaicists cannot be connected. It is plausible that both artists derived the scene from a common source, either an illustrated manuscript of the play or a pattern book or an existing artistic image, be it mosaic or wall painting or other.

The other Cretan Menander mosaic (207e), from the Health Centre in Kisamos, contains scenes of the plays *Sikyonian(s)* and *Theophoroumene* with a central figure of Menander (?).

(b) Elements of the Theatre: Masks

Mosaics 135, 136, S207d, S207e and S207f contain depictions of masks (Pls. 40 & 42).[134] Recognizable styles of masks denoted different characters; for example, there were particular masks for slaves and for old women and within those groups there were variations of the main theme. Because variety was so important in theatre few masks are exactly the same.[135]

Four masks are used as decorative fillers in Mosaic 135 (Pl. 40). They are liberal representations of standard theatre masks, and in this case their origin or inspiration may lie in Webster's mask 38, The Full Grown Hetaerae.[136] The preserved remains of Mosaic 136 (Pl. 42) indicate that there would have been a pair of masks in each of two panels that also contained other pieces of theatre paraphernalia, such as a ribbon and part of a robe.[137]

Mosaic S207d from the Health Centre originally contained seven masks, and two have been published, one male and one female.[138] Their association with Medusa is not clear. In the other two examples (S207e and S207f), the masks are included in the Dionysiac mosaics as filler décor.[139]

The rendering of the masks in the subsidiary panels of the *triclinium* of the House of Dionysus mosaic (136), Chania, and of those in medallions in the Medusa mosaic (S207d), Kisamos, are so similar (mouths, eyes and noses) that they must have been made by the same workshop or even craftsperson. The fact that these mosaics also have the rare thick guilloche in common (see earlier in this chapter) gives weight to this notion. This will be discussed in detail in Chapter 6.

Fishing Scenes

Only one mosaic, from Chersonisos, contains a fishing scene of the type which is so common in areas outside Crete, in particular, in North Africa and Spain. Originally, all four sides of the fountain at Chersonisos (Mosaic 38) (Pl. 15) would have had a fishing scene, each with slight variations from the others. The best-preserved panel has a huge variety of sea creatures (squid, eels, octopuses, etc.) of every size and shape. There are also two fishermen in the scene. The other three panels are badly damaged, yet it is likely that they depicted similar arrangements. The gills, eyes and tails of the fish have all been carefully detailed, and many of them have their dorsal fins depicted.

3.3.3 Animals

As elsewhere, animals on Cretan mosaics make up a huge portion of iconographic material. They occur in borders, as parts of friezes, as filling motifs, in panels or as part of the central scene. The groups of animals discussed here are birds, fish, quadrupeds and mythological animals.

The mosaics on which the animals occur are as follows:

Mosaic 2. Dionysiac followers: cocks, peacocks, parakeet, white birds and fish (Pl. 2)

Mosaic 3. Bust of Dionysus in a circle: dogs, goats, partridge, waterbird, peacock and pheasant (?) (Pl. 3)

Mosaic 8. Three-Part mosaic: parrot (?) (Pl. 7)

Mosaic 9. Apollinaris mosaic: dolphins, tritons, hippocamps and a duck (Pl. 8)

Mosaic 17. Hutchinson mosaic: dolphins (Pl. 12)

Mosaic 30. Hippocamp (Pl. 13)

Mosaic 35. Iraklion mosaic 4: bird (Pl. 14)

Mosaic 38. Chersonisos, Fountain mosaic (Pl. 15)

Mosaic 39. Perakis Plot: birds (Pl. 16)

Mosaic 42. Kypriotakis mosaic: birds and dolphins[140]

Mosaic 66. Lebena, Hippocamp mosaic: hippocamp (Pl. 20)

Mosaic 129. Chania, Poseidon and Amymone: cocks

Mosaic 132. Chania, Cathedral Square, Plateia Mitropolis: triton[141]

Mosaic 135. Chania, Dionysus and Ariadne: lion, bull, stag and big cat (Pl. 40)

Mosaic 136. Chania, *triclinium* of the House of Dionysus mosaic: leopard (Pl. 43)

Mosaic 137. Lissos, black and white with coloured figures: pig, cock and a possible dove or duck[142]

Mosaic 139. Kisamos, Two-Panelled mosaic: birds, dog, cat and goat[143]

Mosaic 140. Kisamos, Centaur and Lion mosaic: lion and centaur[144]

Mosaic 141. Kisamos, Paterakis Plot: leopard, stag, partridges, hens and other birds[145]

Birds, Fish and Dolphins

Birds are by far the most frequently portrayed animals on Cretan mosaics and occur in borders, in subsidiary panels and as filler motifs. The birds that are most commonly portrayed are cocks and peacocks, which have symbolic meaning both in other media and in mosaics of later periods. The peacock is often included as a symbol of Spring, and when this happens its role is clearly understood. In the Cretan mosaic, cocks are either fertility symbols (Mosaic 129) or represent an element of sacrifice to Asclepius (Mosaic 137); in the case of the Paterakis Plot mosaic (141), the sitting hens represent *xenia* scenes.[146] Birds may also be found in *triclinia* and could be indicative of elements of the feast, either for eating or entertainment. Paton has identified the parakeet in Mosaic 2 as an Indian red-necked parakeet.[147] Pliny notes in the *Natural Histories* (10.117) that this was a favourite 'pet bird' kept in the Roman period for entertainment, and it was apparently even more amusing when the birds got drunk.[148] The scene of doves drinking is a common one in Hellenistic and Roman mosaics and is found on Mosaics 2 and 8 from the same *domus*.[149] Ducks are often used to indicate marine scenes (as in Mosaics 9 & 38). The birds surrounding the main panel of the Medusa mosaic (42) from the Kypriotakis Plot in Chersonisos have also been identified as *xenia* scenes because of the inclusion of the kantharoi.[150] The small birds in Mosaic 141 are indicative of *xenia* scenes or scenes to encourage a good appetite for dining.[151] Fish are found in *xenia* scenes or other scenes conducive to dining, and Mosaic 2 has a pair of fish on a platter (Pl. 2). In the Late Antique period, fish are symbolic of Christ. Arrangements of pairs of opposing dolphins are found in three Cretan mosaics. In both Hutchinson's mosaic (17) and the Kypriotakis Plot mosaic (42),[152] the dolphins function as filler motifs in the space left over between the circle and the squares. In the third example, from Iraklion mosaic 5 (36), the dolphins are used in a doormat panel (Pl. 14). Each of the eight rectangular subsidiary panels of Mosaic 9 (Pl. 8) has a depiction of a triton, with a dolphin following close behind.

Quadrupeds

As noted earlier, the majority of quadrupeds occurring on Cretan mosaics are in either hunt or chase scenes. There are five examples of this: Mosaics 3, 121, 139, 140 and 141 (each has already been described in the section on hunt scenes). Mosaic 137 depicts the only representation of a pig on Cretan mosaics and is likely to have indicated a particular animal suitable as a sacrifice to Asclepius. Filling motifs of mammals are found in Mosaic 135; a stag (or gazelle), a lioness, a bull and a lion fill the space between the main scene and subsidiary panels. The animals are arranged so that it looks as though the lioness is chasing the stag and the lion is chasing the bull (Pl. 40).

Mythological Animals

In this section I refer only to those animals which cannot be considered natural. Besides the centaurs of Mosaic 140 (already discussed), four other mosaics contain mythological animals: Mosaics 9, 39, 66 and 132 show scenes from marine mythology. The Apollinaris mosaic (9) (already discussed) displays eight tritons in subsidiary panels (Pl. 8). Some of the tritons (all are in motion) hold tridents and others clubs, and some hold nothing despite having their arms raised. Only a fragment of Mosaic 132 has been preserved, and it consists of a tiny triton blowing a conch in the corner of the mosaic.[153] It was found in a bath house so the choice of figures, at least in the part preserved, fits with the use of the building.

Only a small amount of Mosaic 30 from Knossos has been excavated, yet it is clear that the scene involves an embellished hippocamp (Pl. 13). Mosaic 66 (Lebena) portrays a hippocamp in the main field (Pl. 20).

As with the other animal scenes, representations of mythological creatures were not limited to any particular area of the mosaic, and they are used in many different ways, as subsidiary panels, as main features and as central emblems within a surround of many other features.

3.3.4 Peopled Scrolls

Three Cretan mosaics contain peopled scrolls.[154] The earliest example is from Knossos (Mosaic 1) and dates to the mid–second century (Pl. 1). The other two come from the west: Chania (Mosaic 135) (Pl. 40) and Kisamos (Mosaic S207f), both dated to the mid-third century.[155] All three mosaics have Dionysiac depictions (this is likely to be a coincidence rather than a connection with Dionysus) as the main theme in a geometric grid of a circle contained within a square. In these cases, the peopled scrolls occupy each of the corners in the remaining space (Pl. 1). The peopled scroll is further evidence for a clear workshop connection between the Chania and Kisamos examples, but it is implausible for the Knossos example to be a product of the same workshop (see Chapter 6).

3.4 ICONOGRAPHY OF LATE ANTIQUE CRETAN MOSAICS

Even in the period before iconoclasm there were certain rules to which artists, in particular floor mosaicists, had to conform, and as a result, there is more uniformity in the iconography of Late Antique (church) mosaics than there had been during the Roman period.[156] For example, to ensure that the image of Christ would not be trampled on, the law of Theodosius II and Valentinian III, which was passed in C.E. 427, forbade artists from using it on the ground.[157] In early church decoration, a careful balance had to be struck so that the art would be recognizable but not overtly polytheistic.[158] As emphasized by Gough, during the Late Antique period both artists and patrons were moving towards a preference for the more extraordinary, resulting in somewhat peculiar creations showing a mixture of Greco-Roman realism and Christian fantasia.[159] One of the best examples of this is the mosaic from Osios David in Thessaloniki, where the naturalistic portrayal of the figures against an unreal background is striking.[160] According to Dauphin, by the Late Antique period the mosaicist had reached the point where mosaic making was well recognized as an art of quality and skill.[161] The shape of churches, with their simply furnished naves, aisles and narthexes, offered space for large swathes of geometric patterns. Pre-Christian scenes could be adapted to suit Christian themes, and scenes of flora and fauna were easily converted.[162] Even quite simple depictions of birds had new meaning in the context of church architecture. For example, peacocks, which were often images of Spring in the Roman period, became symbolic of re-birth and everlasting life in the context of the Christian church.

The Late Antique mosaics of Crete do not differ greatly from this general characterization of floor mosaics. They primarily depict geometric panels (see, e.g., Pls. 23, 26, 32 & 45); no humans are portrayed on Cretan floor mosaics.[163] The animals are often treated as part of the geometric decoration and are regularly highly stylized (Pls. 47 & 51). Their inclusion is commonly intended to relay a message to or be a symbol of the religion for the worshipper, as in the example of an image of paradise as in the Gortyn Sector M mosaic (109). The layout of floor mosaics was well thought out and often utilitarian. A carpet mosaic may include different designs and elements, mostly in panels, which are commonly unified by at least one main border (Pl. 27). This arrangement would have given visitors within the space a little more detail for consideration at the same time as the decorative scheme provided indications of a route (Pl. 50) or of areas of particular sanctity (Pls. 32, 47 & 51) (see Chapter 5). As such, Late Antique church mosaics are particularly helpful for casting light on the otherwise shadowy discussion of the function of different types of churches and their liturgy.

Given space restrictions and issues of ideology concerning the Late Antique mosaics it is not surprising that the fundamentals of commonality in iconography between different provinces increase from the Roman period. Moreover, where there are recognizably different geometric elements they can often be used with some confidence to discuss evidence of communication and common workshops. In the Late Antique period, iconographic regionality is being broken down, and, ironically, in some respects this makes it easier to identify common workshop evidence.

As discussed earlier, in the Late Antique period, multiple panels in frameworks are rare, some favoured designs disappear and new designs become more popular.[164] Often elements that became popular only in the Late Antique period in Crete are found earlier in other areas. This may be indicative of a wider or different circulation of craftspeople or of pattern books from outside the island.[165] Dauphin argued that the limitations of designs meant that forgotten elements would re-emerge, but so far this is not in evidence in the Late Antique mosaics of Crete.[166] As with the Roman repertoire, the choice of iconography and its placement is often quite deliberate. The discussion that follows focuses on elements such as the location of the figure on the mosaic and the symbolism of each figure or combination of figures portrayed. Interpretation of such images may be considered subjective, and thus the readings provided here should be considered working suggestions for the number of possible perceptions of the images.

3.4.1 Animals

In terms of figured iconography on mosaics, animals are most frequently depicted; birds are among the more popular and of these, peacocks are by far the most prevalent.

Small Birds

Multiple birds in leafy scrolls in Eleutherna (Mosaics 111–14) and Gortyn Sector M (Mosaic 109) or in large spreads of foliage as in Mitropolis (Mosaic 108) were common features in Late Antique church mosaics and are often symbols of paradise, that is, either the paradise of the church or that of life after death. Identification of the type of bird is not always necessary to understand the symbolism. As in the Roman period, images of birds in Christian art were associated with the transferral of the souls of the dead.[167] Waterbirds, including ducks and waders through their association with water, are representative of the water of life and baptism.[168]

Of the surviving birds of the Sybrita mosaic (116–17) only one is identifiable, a duck in a vine scroll in the western end of the preserved part of the mosaic (Pl. 34). The alternating panels of circles and squares which surround the area of main decoration in Mosaic 109 (Gortyn Sector M) depict birds, fish and leopards (Pl. 28). This could be taken to represent the three orders of living which make up the creation of the earth: the birds of the air, the fish of the sea and the animals of the land. A similar arrangement of birds in interlocking circles and squares is found in the north and south aisles at Eleutherna (111–14) (Pl. 31). In the north aisle, panels of squares and octagons contain geometric patterns, birds, a stylized tree and flowers, which together are a symbol of paradise.

A small stylized black-and-white bird is found on Mosaic 126 (Olus), and also preserved in the same panel are stylized plants and a peacock (Pl. 38). Smaller birds appear in the deer-and-kantharos panel in Suia (Mosaics 156–8): one of the birds within the panel can be identified as a peacock by its crown and long tail, but it is difficult to identify the other (Pl. 51). Two small ducks occur on a geometric panel in the nave of the Agios Niketas Basilica (Mosaic 145).[169]

Peacocks

Of the 34 Late Antique mosaics in Crete, 7 have depictions of peacocks.[170] The peacock is an emblem of immortality, and it is thought to be a symbol of re-birth (from the legendary belief that its flesh does not decay and because its feathers are renewed every spring).[171] It is also rendered on mosaics to convey the idea of paradise. The peacock motif is found in many different parts of the church, but when it is in a doorway, either leading into the narthex or into the nave, it has the power to ward off evil and is, in this respect, an apotropaic symbol. In this position it can also be considered a means of directing people into the realms of the holy area (paradise). Peacocks are located in doorways from the narthex to the nave on Mosaics 92–3 (Pl. 26),[172] Mosaics 148–51 (Pl. 47) and possibly Mosaics 156–8 (Pl. 50). Only the tail of the peacock is preserved in the narthex at the southern entrance to the nave of Almyrida (Mosaics 148–51) (Pl. 47). Like the rest of the mosaic it has been exquisitely executed; the colours blue, red and white are the same as those used to depict the leafy scroll surrounding the peacock. In the case of Suia (Mosaics 156–8), the remains in the narthex do not indicate definitively if the peacock marks the location of the entrance to the nave (Pl. 50). In other mosaics, peacocks are found standing on either side of a kantharos, which can be taken as a symbol of the cup that holds the water of life because of the immortality of the peacocks, for example, at Suia Basilica A (156–8) (Pl. 51)[173] and in Mosaic 109, Sector M, Gortyn (Pl. 29). As in the case of Suia, these images are often found in the most holy area of the church, such as the bema. Only the bottom of the stylized tail of the Olus (Mosaic 126) peacock, which has been rendered in red and black, survives (Pl. 38). It seems that the peacock was intended to be depicted as standing among foliage. In Mosaic 109, the head of a peacock is clearly recognizable by its crown, and in this case the bird occurs in a border decoration of a series of circles. According to Sanders, there was a peacock panel at Avdhou (Mosaic 104), but because the mosaic is no longer *in situ* the exact nature of the peacock or its position cannot be determined.[174] The same is true for the mosaic at Elyros (Mosaic 155).[175]

That the depictions of the birds and other animals are positioned in main or subsidiary panels or in scrolls does not detract from their symbolism. For example, even with the weight of religious meaning, the peacock was used interchangeably as a main panel (as in Suia (Mosaics 156–8) (Pl. 51)), a smaller subsidiary panel (as in Olus (Mosaic 126) (Pl. 38)) or as part of a leafy scroll (Mosaic 109).

Fish and Dolphins

Fish are one of the more common symbols in Late Antique art. Its most frequent use was as a symbol of Christ. This is because the five Greek letters forming the word 'fish', ΙΧΘΥΣ, are the initial letters of the five words Ἰησοῦς Χριστὸς Θεοῦ Υἱὸς Σωτήρ (Jesus Christ God's Son, Saviour). As with the waterbirds, fish symbolize the water of life and baptism. They are also emblems of the miracles of multiplication.[176] They occur in geometric borders and in their own panels. It is common to find fish and dolphins (symbolizing resurrection and salvation) together, for example, in the two main figural panels of the Olus mosaic (126) (Pl. 37) and in the frieze around the border of the narthex in Almyrida (Mosaics 148–51) (Pl. 47) (as well as the kantharoi panels). In the Olus example, the dolphins and fish are haphazardly placed within the panels, except for one panel where it looks as if the dolphin is carrying a fish in its mouth (Pl. 38); perhaps this scene represents the dolphin carrying the soul (the fish) to the afterlife. In the Almyrida example, the dolphins and fish are neatly arranged around the border, the fish in pairs facing each other (Pl. 47). Furthermore, in the same mosaic there are two panels of kantharoi and scrolls which have fish and dolphins on either side of them (Pl. 47).

Several examples of fish are found in Mosaic 109 at Gortyn Sector in the borders of circles and in the outer border of alternating circles and squares (Pl. 28). They have also been used as filler designs around the kantharos. Dolphins and fish occupy the area between the looped circle and the square. The loops of the circle contain leopards. This panel has been damaged, and it is possible that there may have been birds in this area too (together symbolizing the order of the world). The use of the geometric design links the symbolism of the kantharos (the Eucharist), the earth (the leopards in the loops), baptism and Christ (the fish) and the resurrection (the dolphins). A similar use of fish as subsidiary designs is found on Mosaic 161, Episkopi. In this case, the panel has been damaged, but it is possible to identify two fish facing each other in the area between the intersecting squares and the outer circle. Also within the panel is a kantharos with vine leaves spilling from its mouth. The squares enclose a looped circle which could be representative of God's everlasting love for his people. The association of this geometric design with the fish recalls the positioning of the fish and kantharos panels at Almyrida (148–51) (Pl. 47) symbolizing the Eucharist, the body and blood of Christ. Here the two panels are on either side of a geometric panel which contains a looped circle within intersecting squares. In this case, the fish and kantharoi panels flank the geometric panel thereby indicating the importance of its symbolism. At the same time the geometric panel is centred at the point of entrance into the nave and acts as an indicator of the way into the holy area of the basilica. A similar panel in Episkopi is also positioned in the doorway into the main area of the church.

At Suia Basilica A, a small panel to the south of the altar depicting a single fish (Pl. 50) is mirrored by a panel on the north showing a cross in a circle (Pl. 51). A small fraction of a fish panel survives in the nave of Basilica B at Chersonisos (Mosaics 94–100) (Pl. 27). Its opposing panel is almost completely destroyed, but a small fragment of vine scroll survives and it may be that it would have originally contained a peacock.

Deer

In Late Antique art deer were often depicted standing on either side of a kantharos or alternatively on either side of a tree. Occasionally, the two images were combined where the deer stand on either side of a kantharos which contains a tree (symbolizing the tree of life). Deer may also be depicted drinking at a stream which is indicative of the rites of baptism, echoing imagery found in Psalm 42:1: 'As the hart panteth after the water brooks, so panteth my soul after thee, O God'. The connection can be confirmed with the mosaic of the nave of the Basilica of Chrysopolitissa in Cyprus, which has a panel of a deer drinking with the psalm inscribed above it.[177]

A variation of the kantharos type comes from Suia Basilica A (Mosaic 158) (Pl. 51), which shows a single deer amid the vines emanating from the kantharos. A deer occupies a large panel in the north aisle of the Agios Niketas mosaic (146).[178] The deer is stylized (as are the leaves and plants in which it is intertwined), and it is not anatomically accurate. A deer in its own panel in the narthex mosaic of Basilica A, Chersonisos (Mosaics 92–3), is depicted together with a lion (Pl. 25). This is likely to be a symbol of utopia similar to the prediction of paradise in Isaiah 11:6–7 (see next section) when wild beasts will lie with the meek. In the case of the Cretan basilica, the deer can easily be considered as representing the same form of meek animal as the lamb. A similar example but one no longer in evidence may be from Suia; it is described by Pendlebury as having a motif of a lion chasing a deer.[179] Deer were also noted by Sanders on the Elyros mosaic (155), and images of deer occur as filler décor (such as in the knotted circle motif) in the basilica in Sector M, Gortyn (Mosaic 109).

Other Animals

Other animals which occur on Christian mosaics in Crete are the lion and the leopard, both already mentioned. The lion is found on Mosaics 92–3 (Pl. 25) and the leopard is found in the bordering panels of the Gortyn Sector M Mosaic 109. Michaelides notes that a range of different animals (often within scrolls) is indicative of the idea of paradise as described in the Peaceable Kingdom of Isaiah 11:6–7: 'The wolf also shall dwell with the lamb, and the leopard shall lie down with the kid; and the calf and the young lion and the fatling together;

and a little child shall lead them. And the cow and the bear shall feed; their young ones shall lie down together: and the lion shall eat straw like the ox'. This is surely the explanation for the variety of animals found in the scrolls around the mosaics of the basilica in Sector M, Gortyn (Mosaic 109), Almyrida (Mosaics 148–51) and Sybrita (Mosaics 116–17).

3.4.2 Plants

Many varieties of plants are depicted on Late Antique mosaics, and in Crete the ivy and vine occur most frequently. From earliest times, ivy was identified with death and immortality, and because of its constant greenness it was a symbol of fidelity and eternal life. The vine is representative of the relationship between God and his people, God being the one who looks after the vines (his people).[180] In the mosaic of the nave of the Basilica of Chrysopolitissa in Cyprus, the panel of the vine and the ram is accompanied by the inscription from John 15:1: 'I am the true vine'.[181]

The vine and the ivy used on mosaics as secondary decoration, as fillers and as borders always retain their symbolism.[182] Ivy leaves are found as scrolls and individual panels in the mosaic at Almyrida (Mosaics 148–51) (Pl. 47). The most common depiction of vine leaves or other leaves is as they emerge from kantharoi, often with peacocks or deer shown amongst the tendrils (Pls. 28 & 50).[183] Panels of scrolls are found at Almyrida, Chersonisos Basilica A, and Olus with peacocks contained within (Mosaics 148–51, 92–3 & 126, respectively) (Pls. 47, 26 & 38).[184] Gortyn Sector M (Mosaic 109) has a panel of simple vine scroll (Pl. 28), and the same occurs in the narthex and the south aisle of the basilica at Eleutherna (Mosaics 111–14) (Pl. 31). It is possible to recognize part of a damaged panel of vine leaves in the nave of Basilica B at Chersonisos (Mosaics 94–100) (Pl. 27). There were also panels of vine leaves in the poorly preserved mosaic in Episkopi (Mosaics 161–2) on either side of the central guilloche border.

The presence of vine or ivy scrolls can help to define geometric elements as meaningful, such as, for example, at Almyrida (Mosaics 148–51) (around the intersecting squares panel) (Pl. 48), Eleutherna (Mosaics 111–14) (around the intersecting squares) (Pl. 32) and Episkopi (Mosaics 161–2) (in the looped circle).

The mosaic at Olus (Mosaic 126) displays a variety of different flowers; many of them are so stylized they cannot be identified (Pl. 37). The variety of flowers in the central panel of the Mitropolis mosaic (108) is considered a symbol of paradise. Other floral designs include possible clematis from the basilica at Kastelliana (Mosaic 107).[185] Filler decoration in the form of stylized plants is found in the nave and exo-narthex of the basilica at Agios Niketas (Mosaics 143–6) (Pls. 45–6). One element may represent a pomegranate, which could be taken as a symbol of immortality and resurrection.

Only a small number of Late Antique Cretan mosaics do not have some form of floral decoration incorporated into the overall design; in fact, the majority of these are only fragments which may have originally had floral decoration in them. These are Kolokythia (Mosaic 127), Knossos (Mosaics 88–90), Lappa (Mosaic 121) and Tarrha (Mosaic 147). With the exception of the stylized four-petalled flower arrangements which act as fillers in the narthex mosaic of Kera (Mosaics 122–5), nothing suggests that there would have been other floral decoration in the basilica.[186]

3.4.3 Symbols

Crosses

The nave mosaic from the basilica at Almyrida is the only definite example of a cross in Late Antique mosaics in Crete. The cross is of a monogrammatic type, and it is created in white tesserae with different colours used within to give the impression that it is jewelled (Pl. 48). There are parallels for this type in other media within Crete, both for the cross itself and for the arrangement of the alpha and omega on either side of it, for example, on a late seventh- to eighth-century sepulchral inscription on a rimmed disk from Kisamos, and on another sepulchral inscription from Kisamos.[187] A similar design to the Almyrida monogram is that from Itanos, which is dated to the end of the fifth or beginning of the sixth century.[188]

The Octagon

Intersecting circles could represent God, Christ and the Holy Spirit, and intersecting squares form an eight-pointed star. The number eight was important in Late Antique iconography as regeneration, salvation and resurrection; the world started on the eighth day after creation began, and Christ rose from the dead on the eighth day of the Passion.[189] Milburn also associates the number eight with the resurrection and new creation. Evidence of Late Antique recognition of a symbolic meaning comes from St. Ambrose's writings regarding the octagonal baptistery close to the church of St. Thecla, Milan.[190] Intersecting squares are used to form eight-pointed stars as on Mosaics 111–14, 148–51 and 161–2 (Eleutherna, Almyrida & Episkopi) (Pls. 32 & 48). Notably, these designs are located in doorways.

The arrangement of the iconography and its symbolism in Late Antique mosaics is particularly beneficial for a study of the function of the church at this period. A number of points can be made concerning the layout of the mosaics (e.g., at Eleutherna and Knossos) in terms of the nature of the liturgy and the indications given to the visitor about the sanctity of the space. The position of these elements is discussed in greater detail in Chapter 5.

3.5 INSCRIPTIONS

Of the 98 published Roman mosaics in Crete, 6 (6.2%) have inscriptions; of the 34 published Late Antique mosaics, 5 (15%) have inscriptions (see Appendix 2). In mainland Greece, out of *c*. 200 Roman mosaics, 14 have inscriptions (7%), a percentage which is very close to the figure for Crete.[191] When compared to other areas, such as Cyprus, Antioch and North Africa, these are very low numbers.[192]

3.5.1 Categories of Inscriptions on Cretan Mosaics

The inscriptions found on Cretan mosaics can be identified as labels for figures or scenes, apotropaic and message inscriptions, donor inscriptions and signature of the artist (discussed in Chapter 6).

Of the inscriptions in the surviving Roman mosaics on Crete, three are signatures of craftspeople, two are labels for scenes, two are apotropaic and one is unclear.[193] Of the Late Antique examples, all are donor panels with the exception of the information panel from Eleutherna (Inscription 12). The AΩ from Almyrida (Mosaics 148–51) (Pl. 48) is simply a religious symbol which refers to Christ's being the beginning and the end. Parallel examples are found carved on stone from the basilica at Itanos (late fifth to sixth century) and on a sepulchral plaque from the region of Mount Ida.[194] In a similar vein, the Chi-Rho symbol found on the Kisamos grave mosaic (S218)[195] is more symbolic than inscriptional.

The majority of mosaic inscriptions from areas outside Crete and Greece are labels for characters in, or titles for, depicted scenes. In Crete, only two examples of a 'label' are known, and in mainland Greece, of the 200 mosaics in Ramsden's (1971) corpus, only 5 contain the names of the personifications or mythological characters. When compared with the Cypriot corpus, where there are at least 10 label inscriptions out of a much smaller number of published Roman mosaics, the difference is remarkable. It is possible to use inscriptions as a dating tool, but they are a more reliable method when used in conjunction with other evidence.[196] Furthermore, inscriptions can on occasion help to identify the subject matter of the mosaic. One example is in Mosaic 135, where the inscription identifies the otherwise lost Menander play *Plokion* (Pl. 41).

3.5.2 Labels for Figures or Scenes

Two Cretan mosaics bear inscriptions which label the scene being illustrated. The first, the Athlete mosaic from Knossos (Inscription 2), names one of the figures in the scene (Pl. 10), and the second, the Dionysus and Ariadne mosaic from Chania (Mosaic 135), provides the name of the play being depicted (Inscription 4) (Pl. 41). A third inscription (no. 6) from Ierapetra (Mosaic 85) includes the label Εἰσίων. It occurs within the central medallion which once held a figured scene, now destroyed. Reconstruction is difficult as it is unclear how much of this inscription has survived; it may be the name of a craftsperson or a label for the scene, but most likely it is a general address to the viewer (e.g., to go in and enjoy or something similar).

Inscription 2 is a personal inscription, suggesting that the patron may have had a particular connection with the athletes (Pl. 10).[197] Or it may simply be that the patron was commemorating a famous event without necessarily having a direct connection with the athletes.

The single example from Crete where the identification label for a play survives is the Dionysus and Ariadne mosaic, Chania (Mosaic 135) (Inscription 4) (Pl. 41). With the exception of the four panels that depicted the Seasons, the remaining subsidiary panels around the main scene of Dionysus and Ariadne portray scenes from a Menander play known as ΠΛΟΚΙΟΝ (*The Necklace*). The inscription reads *Plokion* (the name of the play) and is rather squashed between two figures, one seated and one standing, in three lines: PLO | KIO | N (Pl. 41). One of the closest parallels for this mosaic comes from Mytilene,[198] which depicts the same Menander play, and in which the characters are named. Inscription 4 was located on a mosaic from the same house as contained Inscription 5 (Mosaic 136), which suggests that the artist (or patron) may have had either an ability or propensity for inscriptions (see Pls. 41 & 43).

Scene and figure labels occur most frequently on mosaics in the East, in particular, Syria, Turkey and Cyprus. But as Kondoleon notes, the reason for the prevalence of inscribed titles here is difficult to establish.[199] Although she states that such inscriptions were more popular from the fourth century, she discounts the possibility that this was because the scenes would otherwise be unrecognizable. It may simply have been a case of fashion and perhaps such an inscription added value to the work (particularly if literacy was seen as a status element). In the North African corpora, mythological characters are occasionally named, but other, more personal labelling is uncommon. Examples include that from Khanguet-el-Hadjaj, where in an amphitheatre scene the *venator* (gladiator) is named *Lampadius*;[200] another is from Maison à Trifolium, Dougga, where two pairs of racehorses are named[201] as well as a gazelle (*Bodala*). From mainland Greece a Late Antique mosaic from Andania has four panels surrounding a central hunt scene, each depicting a charioteer. At least one of the panels names the character as ΙΕΡѠΝΑΣ, whereas the other labels like εὐήνιος (easy to manage) or εὐνοῦδα (easy to rule) may describe particular talents of the charioteer or the animals.[202]

3.5.3 Apotropaic and Message Inscriptions

The ΛΑ (λοῦσαι ἀσφαλῶς) (bathe safely), inscribed in the straps of a pair of sandals which are depicted on Mosaic 133 (Inscription 3)[203] from Chania could be interpreted as providing a welcoming message as well as a warning to wear sandals.[204] The inscription is located at the entrance to one of the rooms of the bath suite. Such inscriptions are common in bath houses of all periods, and on a range of media from sculpture to mosaic to plaques.[205] They range from dedications to the gods to warnings about slippery floors to dedications by patrons. The greeting or warning of Inscription 3 is one of the more common types. Dunbabin provides a range of examples of footprints occurring in mosaics, both in bath houses[206] and in other contexts, for example, in the mosaic from the sanctuary of Demeter and Kore.[207] Parallels for both the sandals and the inscription are found,[208] but the inscription in the form of the sandal straps as in Chania is so far unique.

From a Late Antique context, although incomplete, Inscription 12 in the north entrance of the Eleutherna church (Mosaics 111–14) urges visitors to be pious and reinforces the sanctity of the place they are visiting.[209]

Found in the so-called House of Pheidias as part of the Health Centre excavations, another welcoming inscription may be that from Kisamos, located in what may be a corridor of or entrance to the house (Mosaic S207b).[210] The mosaic itself consists of a field of geometric decoration and a large panel depicting a leopard and a centaur. The inscription was created on a square panel made from black tesserae which has a triangle on either side. The design panel gives the effect of the inscription having been written on a plaque, a common technique in both mosaics and painting.[211] ΕΥΧΗΣΗ]ΤΥΧΗΤΗ*ΣΑΙ]ΚΙΝ·ΙΣ ΕΛΒΕΝ] ΦΙΟΙΟΥ (Good luck fortune, to be on Pheidias) seems to be the reading of the inscription, but some letters are difficult to decipher. The first part clearly asks for the fortune of Pheidias to prosper; this inscription may therefore be honouring the patron or a family member. Parallels for inscriptions wishing good luck are found all over the Roman Empire. A pebble mosaic from Olynthus[212] reads ΕΥΤΥΧΙΑ ΚΑΛΗ (εὐτυχία καλή) (Good luck is good). At the threshold of the entrance into Room 2 of the House of Dionysos in Paphos is a panel which bears the inscription ΧΑΙΡΕΙ (χαίρει) (Welcome) on one side and ΚΑΙ ϹΥ (καὶ σύ) (and you) on the other.[213] The centre of the room contains the mosaic of the Youth and the Seasons. Dedicatory inscriptions to the patron of a house or establishment are found, for example, in the baths of a house at Uzitta 'O LEO· PRAE·SVMSISTI· EXPEDISTI· DEDICASTI' (O Leo, you anticipated, you arranged, you dedicated).[214]

3.6 CONCLUSIONS

3.6.1 The Cretan Repertoire

The range of Cretan mosaics is vast: from the retro styles of the *impluvium* mosaics in Kisamos (Mosaic S213) to the traditional Dionysiac multiple panels in grid compositions of the Villa Dionysus (Mosaics 1–3) to the only definitive example of a North African-style mosaic in Crete (Mosaic S216). Cretan mosaics commonly display different traits, even within the same mosaic or group of mosaics, that are attributable to different regions. For example, some mosaics may incorporate characteristically western geometric elements within an eastern framework form. Having established the overall mosaic repertoire, one needs to to understand it by comparing the trends of the corpora from a variety of areas of the empire. For consistency, and to limit inherent subjectivity, the comparative analysis that follows is based on a single scholar's study of provincial mosaics.[215]

Northern Provinces

Dunbabin notes the preference in Britain and other northern provinces for geometric rather than figured decoration.[216] Furthermore, in the northern provinces when figured scenes occur they are often in small panels as part of the large swathe of an overall geometric scheme.[217] The preference in these cases is often for images of daily life rather than mythological scenes.[218] Britain differs somewhat from this trend in that by the fourth century, figured scenes and pseudo-emblem style come into fashion.[219] Although grids are common in the northern provinces, they are more often used to break up geometric schemes; only one such example is known from Crete thus far, that from Lappa (Mosaic 73).

Iberian Peninsula

The mosaics of the Iberian Peninsula display a mêlée of traditions from across the Roman Empire but retain a strong preference for the Italian types. Moreover, the black-and-white mosaics showing strong first-century Italian characteristics, such as the silhouette and free-form figures, continue well into the fourth century (e.g., at the House of Neptune, Italica).[220] Combinations of black-and-white mosaics with polychrome elements in a single mosaic occur in the late first to early second century, and examples of this are found in Crete, including the Apollinaris mosaic (9) (Pl. 8) and the Lissos Temple of Asclepius mosaic (137). During the second century, polychrome mosaics, such as the Cosmological mosaic from the Mithreaum House in Merida, are found more frequently.[221] Some mosaics, such as examples from Italica, use the same kinds of grids as those seen in the Villa Dionysus (Mosaics 1–3); examples include the field of seven hexagons seen in the House of the Planetarium mosaic of the planetary deities.[222] Dunbabin describes examples of emblemata mosaics as being unusual imports, and they may reflect some individual, perhaps even experimental, choice on the part of the patron or craftsperson.[223]

North Africa

The mosaics of North Africa stand out as the largest surviving corpora of mosaics in the Roman Empire and are found in the largest range of contexts. Like those in the western areas of the empire, the first-century mosaics share many common elements with contemporary Italian mosaics. By the second century, polychrome mosaics predominate, and across North Africa lavish designs of floral swathes creating compartments for figured scenes become popular.[224] Dunbabin states that the free-form type, which was common in Italy in black-and-white mosaics (e.g., in vast quantities in Ostia, Herculaneum and Pompeii), is more often used in the third and fourth centuries in North Africa.[225] One factor defining the North African koine is the clear preference for certain types of figured scenes. Scenes of the hunt and the amphitheatre are particularly popular.[226] Regional characteristics are common; for example, Dunbabin has noted the 'multiple-décor' types of Tripolitania.[227] In the Late Antique period, hunt scenes continue to be very popular and mosaics generally become more schematic with the use of registers and panels.[228]

Eastern Provinces

Even allowing for individual choice in design and skill in layout, the mosaics of the eastern provinces display diverse characteristics over time, and, depending on their contexts, many of them are identifiable as from or peculiar to that region. It has already been shown, for example, that labels for figures are common; yet mosaicists rarely signed their work in areas of Syria or Asia Minor, although they did in Cyprus, Greece and Crete (see Chapter 6). In addition to the stylistic preference for displaying panels within complex borders or frameworks, figured scenes, commonly from the standard mythological repertoire, dramatically outnumber genre scenes in the East. Within this broad characterization, regional differences are strong, and Dunbabin provides the example of Syria, where from the third century onwards, a marked fashion for depicting the personification of abstract ideas in addition to philosophy and allegory is seen in the mosaics of Antioch and Apamea.[229] The preference for the use of architectural elements, perspective and colour to produce three-dimensional effects has also been noted.[230] This is seen in northern Greece[231] and some of the East Aegean Islands; however, it is not found in the Peloponnese or in Crete.[232] Within Syria, the Antioch mosaics are one of the better-known groups of mosaics, and in the second and third centuries the preference was for figured panels (commonly of mythological scenes) in geometric borders. Furthermore, in the northern part of Syria, for example, in Shahba-Philippopolis, mosaic panels are generally more ostentatious and larger than those of Antioch.[233] The Palmyra mosaics are likened to the Antioch examples, whereas the mosaics from Edessa in the northeast are quite different, mostly because of the funerary context in which they were found.[234] Furthermore, Dunbabin[235] notes that the mosaics from Palestine differ quite notably from mosaics from other areas of the East because of their predominantly religious contexts, be it Jewish, Islamic or Christian. Here, the material is focused on geometric, floral and animal figures rather than on the repertoire of mythological and genre scenes so common elsewhere.

The current evidence for mosaics in western Asia Minor is still somewhat limited, in part because of the emphasis on the excavation of public rather than domestic buildings. Here, Late Antique evidence is abundant because of, among other reasons, the number of churches with paved floors and the use of carpet-style swathes.[236] As can be seen with the peristyle mosaics of the Great Palace in Constantinople, the mosaics are not limited to religious contexts.[237]

A feature common to many of the late third- and fourth-century mosaics of the East is the framework that breaks up a series of scenes rather than separates a scene into a series of elements.[238] In the Late Antique period in the East (including Crete) the demand for mosaics in churches meant that carpet-style geometric swathes dominate the period, and also, as Dunbabin has noted, an increasing preference for particular geometric elements such as rainbow patterns (as seen in Mosaics 143–6, Pl. 45).[239] Unlike many other areas of the empire, the Syria-Palestine regions have a high proportion of secular mosaics from the Late Antique period, in particular from Antioch.[240] Figured scenes are found more commonly (though not exclusively) in domestic contexts, and when they occur, scenes of the hunt or personifications are favoured.[241]

The extensive mosaic floors of Cyprus are particularly fine examples, and while they display an Eastern tradition with a preference for multiple panels in grid layout, elements of the Western tradition are also found in the figured compositions, such as the use of long friezes of figured scenes from the hunt or amphitheatres. Unlike in other areas of Asia Minor, artists commonly signed their work in Cyprus. Kondoleon's assessment of the Cypriot mosaics indicates contact with Asia Minor and also the possibility of direct contact with Rome through the communities of Roman traders known to have resided on the island.[242] Michaelides argues that the strongest parallels for the Roman and Late Antique Cypriot mosaics come from Syria, Lebanon, Israel and in particular Antioch.[243] The Late Antique mosaics are richly varied and retain a strong use of the multiple panel in grid format in addition to rich, complex geometric designs.[244]

Mainland Greece

The majority of mainland Greek mosaics favour polychrome panels in grid compositions, yet some black-and-white Italian style mosaics survive, particularly from the first century (e.g., in Isthmia and in Olympia).[245] The themes follow the Eastern traditional preference for mythological repertoire, with significantly fewer hunt or amphitheatre scenes than in North Africa or even the East. Syrian elements are seen in both the Greek and Cypriot mosaics, according to Dunbabin and Kondoleon, respectively, but they cannot be definitively identified in Crete.[246] For example, the persistent use of frameworks in Crete is quite unlike that of the Syrian mosaics and few of the architectural or three-dimensional elements are found in the Cretan repertoire. Dunbabin sees a strong Western influence in Greek cities such as Patras and Corinth that she perceives as having more Roman contact,[247] whereas I would argue that in some respects this is a case of creeping determinism, in which the archaeological evidence is adapted around an analysis of the historical evidence where a certain level of Roman-ness is presumed.[248]

The Cretan Corpus

The Cretan repertoire follows some empire-wide patterns in its breadth of iconography, but unique geometric elements help to formulate evidence of workshops and craftspeople.[249] With the favoured mythological scenes (in particular, Dionysus, the Seasons, *xenia* and the theatre), the Cretan mosaics do not stray far from the paradigm across the empire. Some general points are clearly observable: a broad preference for frameworks and multiple panels until the Late Antique period; a lack of amphitheatre, circus or hunt scenes in favour of mythological scenes; and an average number of signatures and labels. These general points might indicate a favourable comparison with the mainland Greek and Cypriot corpora, but with close examination, it is clear that Cretan mosaics do not slavishly follow a mainland Greek or even an Eastern tradition and that they also feature a number of Western elements. It is better to examine the Cretan mosaics on an individual, contextual or chronological level rather than to attempt to attribute one particular style to the entire island or even to different parts of the island at different times.

The first-century mosaics (Myrtos (84), Kouphonisi (81–2) and Lissos (137)), with their black-and-white formats and Western geometric designs, are indicative of the Italian type. That a number of black-and-white mosaics are found on the island in the first century is entirely in keeping with other areas of the East, such as mainland Greece, as well as the West. Divergences between Crete and the West are seen, a key point being when the preference for the black-and-white mosaics peters out in Crete and the East by the beginning of the second century but in Italy continues well into that century.[250] The main geometric field within the circle of the Myrtos mosaic (84) is found only in Western contexts, such as the geometric mosaic from the House of the Planets in Italica and Italy.[251] Other contacts with the West, be they through craftspeople, patrons, visitors or pattern books, are evidenced by a number of other elements which are found earlier in Crete than in other areas of the East or even North Africa. One of the earliest examples of the use of the spoked-wheel design in the East is in the Apollinaris mosaic (9), suggesting a Western connection for this design.[252] The circle-within-the-square framework is found in Crete before it is on the Greek mainland. More widespread and slightly later contact with the West can be read in the occurrence of examples of the vault pattern at Knossos and Lappa (Mosaics 3 & 73). This may reflect the increased focus on the north coast from the mid-first century (Fig. 8). The vault pattern is rarely found in Antioch or Cyprus. The arrangement of squares and lozenges (**R** 173b) is found on three Kisamos mosaics dating to the early second century, almost a century before it is found in mainland Greece (in the Severan period). Its first recorded use in North Africa is likely to be Antonine. Overall, the early date suggests that perhaps there was a Cretan source for the use of the design in the East.

From the second century onwards Cretan mosaics display a mêlée of elements found in many areas of the Roman Empire. Frameworks such as the field of hexagons and uniform panels are found in the West and central provinces such as Germany, Hungary, Belgium, France and Switzerland, but here the preference is for complex geometric mosaics rather than complex figured ones.[253] The frameworks found on the Cretan mosaics share some parallels with those from Asia Minor and Egypt, but mosaics from Syria (with the exception of Antioch) tend to employ simple borders around single panels rather than complex frames to break up the composition.[254] When frameworks are used in North African examples, such as the Seasons mosaic from Sousse,[255] they are inclined to be more complex than the Cretan examples, particularly with the use of elaborate scrolls. But there are less complex grids that could be considered closer to the Cretan ones, such as the Apollo and Diana and the Year and Seasons mosaics from El Djem.[256] Furthermore, the few connections identifiable between the figured iconography of North African mosaics (other than the Kisamos example) may indicate a lack of direct communication links with the region, or, in part, the later date of the mosaic (mid-third century), when such North African styles were becoming more common around the empire.

Late Antique Cretan mosaics share geometric and figurative designs, both among themselves and with mosaics of the same period outside Crete. This is unsurprising given their uniformity of architectural contexts, restrictions on depictions and common patronage (from the church or affluent individuals). Despite this new standardization, key similarities in these mosaics provide clear evidence for workshop production in the Late Antique period within Crete (discussed in Chapter 6). This evidence can also be linked with mosaics outside Crete to provide convincing indications that there were at least two workshops of mosaicists working both within and outside Crete.

In some respects, what is clear from the contextualization of the Cretan mosaics, particularly the early occurrence of some formats, is that often the choice of grid type is dictated by the choice of figured scene or the type of room to be floored rather than by a regional style as such. Parallels between areas of the empire may therefore be indicative not necessarily of direct contact links, but of a common desire to portray themes such as Dionysus and his followers, or the Seasons, where a set number of characters needs to be portrayed. In areas where the preferences for scenes such as those depicting fishing or the amphitheatre are strong, the use of frameworks is limited and not so comparable to Crete. Cyrenaica is a good example of an area where frameworks are not necessary for the composition because of the genre of the scene or because black-and-white geometric designs are popular.[257] Closer parallels can be drawn between Roman Cyrenaican mosaics and Late Antique Cretan ones. For instance, the mosaic of the west portico of the 'Villa' in Ptolemais is the same as that found in the nave of Basilica B, Chersonisos (Mosaics 94–100) (Pl. 27), and the north aisle of the basilica at Knossos (Mosaic 90) (Pl. 24).[258] Given the chronological difference, the suggestion of common workshops is unlikely, with the Late Antique examples' being drawn from a more general mosaic repertoire as the more likely scenario.[259]

Frameworks, Iconography and Architectural Context

The use of frameworks gave the mosaicist or patron more scope to display different themes suitable for different room functions or types of visitors (Chapter 5). While square panels give rise to a single and therefore a stationary experience, mixed viewpoints are achieved mostly through more complex frames, such as the vault pattern (Mosaic 3), spoked wheel (Mosaic 1) or circle within a square (Mosaic 2), that encourage circulation. Perspective, as evident from framework, emphasizes the importance of creating a good impression either from the doorway or within the room depending on the context, level of privacy or desire of the patron. A temple may have the mosaic figures orientated so that they can be seen most appropriately by the god (e.g., the Asclepion at Lissos, Mosaic 137).[260] A dining room may have figures orientated towards the door or for a viewer in the room (Mosaic 129). That some mosaics have multiple perspectives (Mosaic 2) may be indiciative of the intention to have varying levels of privacy depending on the use of the room at any given time. Breaking up a theme into different connected units would normally have been complex enough to encourage the visitor to want to stay and consider the piece, and to provide talking points. The ability to present such a multifaceted design might emphasize the patron's knowledge and cultural awareness. When the filler decoration or subsidiary panels are not directly related to the central theme, they can usually be related to the function of the room. For example, the filler decoration of birds and fish in Mosaic 2 relates to the room as a *triclinium* rather than to the mosaic's Dionysiac figures (Pl. 2).[261] Figures in a secondary position may still create a strong impact; the Seasons are a good example of this where they are intended to suggest welcome and benevolence (Mosaics 5 & 141).

As would be expected given Crete's location in the Mediterranean, the Cretan mosaic repertoire benefited from the direct contact the island had with many different areas of the empire through its use as an entrepôt and a stopping-off point. Nonetheless, evidence for its own innovative elements, such as 'thick guilloche', is clear. That Crete can often be directly linked with the West or with Syria and the East without having a connection to mainland Greece suggests that at times its northern points of communication were not as strong as its west-east ones. The occurrence of some geometric elements (such as the vault pattern and eight-spoked wheel) earlier in Crete than in mainland Greece or the East suggests that the island may have played a key role in circulating artistic ideas.[262]

FOUR

DATE AND DISTRIBUTION

4.1 Introduction

The high survival rate for mosaics and the connoisseurship of mosaic studies have provided the archaeologist with an essential (though not necessarily a completely reliable) tool of iconographic dating. Valuable contributions to a diachronic study of Cretan society can be made based on the date and distribution of the mosaics. To analyse the material, the established chronologies and locations of the corpus of Cretan mosaics are tabulated and the results from both are combined. To reduce bias, the methods of dating and the reliability of the proposed date are included in Appendix 3 (Tables A3.1 and A3.2). While little can be done about bias in the circumstances of the excavation, it can be acknowledged. The focus here is on the *nomoi* of Iraklion, Lasithi and Rethymnon, with the published mosaic data from the west of the island included to allow as complete a view as possible.[1] Dates for the earliest and latest mosaics, as well as particular periods of concentration, are established. Geographical concentrations are highlighted: urban or rural; coastal or inland; north, south, east or west of the island. Together with the iconographic evidence, the date-distribution analysis reveals how the Cretan mosaics can be used to illuminate social issues such as settlement patterns, the practices of craftspeople, communications and the economy.[2] Furthermore, differences in settlement patterns based on mosaic distribution between two key periods, the first century B.C.E. to C.E. and the fourth and fifth centuries, will provide pivotal evidence for the discussion of globalization and Christianization. Finally, the analysis will be placed in the broader context to illustrate how Crete's role in the Roman Empire changed over time and how some of the wider socio-political machinations may have shaped the island.

4.2 DATING METHODOLOGY

As can be seen from Tables A3.1 and A3.2, the mosaics of Crete have been dated through a range of means including stratigraphy, iconography and inscriptions, with the most reliable being a combination of these methods. Even with the emphasis on the full recording of the entire strata, contextual problems continue because the majority of Cretan mosaics are found as a result of rescue excavations. An inherent bias is present as the majority of Roman Cretan mosaics are located in urban space and when they occur in rural space in the Late Antique period they are normally in churches.

4.2.1 Stratigraphy and Associated Material Culture

As floor contexts, mosaics can ideally be dated through investigation of the sealed strata below the floor, thereby establishing a *terminus post quem*. For a variety of reasons, such opportunities are not commonly taken although strata below some of the Health Centre mosaics in Kisamos were investigated (Mosaic S207).[3] In the case of the Cretan corpora, many mosaics, once uncovered, are either removed or covered over too quickly to allow excavation of the level beneath. In other instances, they have been left in their findspots without testing below the floor. In earlier excavations, records sometimes were not kept at all for either the mosaic or its context. With continued progress in archaeological excavation and a reduction in the consideration of mosaics as prestige art objects, it has become increasingly important to establish the full stratigraphic record associated with a mosaic.[4] Sometimes a *terminus ante quem* can be established, as in Basilica B, Chersonisos (Mosaics 94–100), where the pottery in the pastophorion tombs is dated to the late sixth century. Other issues with mosaic chronologies are with those that are 'lost', have been removed from their contexts without being recorded (Mosaic 121) or remain unpublished. Some mosaics are mentioned only in brief reports without photographs (Mosaic 47). Whereas the date of the building in which a mosaic is located is commonly postulated, often the relationship between the mosaic and various phases of the structure cannot be well established.

Mosaics are commonly dated iconographically, although the subjectivity can be counterbalanced with contextual dating.[5] Good context dating is often difficult because of problems with determining assured relationships between archaeological elements or establishing how long a mosaic may have lain exposed before the context became sealed. Even when mosaics are dated through architecture, architectural fragments, coins or ceramics they cannot be used as an exclusive dating tool. As with the establishment of any chronology through material culture, the archaeologist must be aware of the possibilities of reuse of material from earlier phases, and allow for the portability of the object and the

length of time it may have been in circulation. There are circumstances where
secure dating is not possible, and in these cases a best estimate using a variety of means should be provided. For example, the mosaic at the martyrium at
Mitropolis (Mosaic 108) has no Cretan parallels for either its decoration or architectural context and little dating evidence was uncovered during excavation.
The triconch element of the architecture is found at the KMF Basilica (Mosaic
91), dated to the early fifth century, and the martyrium at Corinth, dated to the
late fifth century.[6] But owing to this chronological range further evidence is
required, and the mosaic has been dated by the architectural fragments to the
end of the fifth century.[7] As long as direct associations can be established, coins
and architectural fragments may be useful dating tools. Architectural fragments
such as capitals or columns frequently have definite time spans for their use.[8]
Although a great deal of work has been carried out in ceramic studies,[9] the chronology for Roman and Late Antique pottery is constantly being refined and in
some areas of Crete it has yet to be firmly established.[10] Cretan amphorae have
been quite securely dated,[11] but more so for the Roman period than for the Late
Antique. Lamps too are often used to date contexts, but their chronologies are
being reviewed.[12] Epigraphic evidence (separate from inscriptions found on the
mosaics themselves) is rarely used to date Roman mosaics in Crete, but it can be
used for Late Antique ones.

4.2.2 Inscriptions on the Mosaics

Eleven[13] Roman and Late Antique Cretan mosaics carry inscriptions (see
Appendix 2). More commonly, the substance of the inscription (mention of a
date, event or individual) rather than the type of lettering helps to establish a
date for the mosaic. For example, in Mosaics 109 and 111–14 (Inscriptions 9 &
11) (Pls. 29 & 33) the archbishops mentioned in each can be identified. Attempts
have been made to date individual letter types, but there is little substantial
evidence to support the validity of this process.[14] Sanders has dated the Olus
mosaic (Mosaic 126) (Pl. 38) to the fourth century on the basis of the lettering
of the inscription.[15] This supports the fourth-century date he proposes for the
style of the Corinthian capitals, but neither can really substantiate a fourth-
century date for the mosaic.

4.2.3 Iconography of the Mosaics

The majority of Cretan mosaics are dated using a combination of techniques, the
most common among them being iconographic scrutiny. Such analysis is based
on comparing both the geometric and the figured elements of Cretan mosaic
decoration with mosaics outside Crete. Comparative analysis is subjective, and
primary among the range of associated problems is establishing whether the

similar mosaic or group of mosaics have themselves been dated reliably. To attempt a secure chronology at least one mosaic in the analysis must be dated through stratigraphic means. Furthermore, a range of similar constituents in one or more reliably dated mosaics should be analysed rather than just a single element in common.[16] Many geometric elements or figured themes are so widespread that identifiable resemblances may be meaningless. Another pitfall is that floors are often visible for a considerable time and so may be copied decades after they were originally laid. The possible existence of pattern books may similarly skew the date.[17] Comparative analysis does not always allow for the unexpected, such as a retrospective or traditional look that some patrons may choose. For example, an *impluvium* in Kisamos has trichrome mosaics (S213) around its edges which use the first-century Western element of floating silhouetted figures, but the house itself is dated to the mid-second century.[18] In some cases, iconographic dating may be the only possible means of establishing a date. Mosaic 38 from Chersonisos (Pl. 15) has been dated based on its iconography alone. When the fountain was discovered, no associated archaeological finds or architectural remains were recorded. As there are no parallels for this mosaic's style, technique, figures or theme within Crete, comparative evidence from outside Crete was sought to establish a date. This effort was unsuccessful, even from areas where the fishing theme is common, particularly in North Africa and the West. Sanders deduced that enough similarities exist between a group of fountain mosaics from Utica and the Chersonisos example to date the Fountain mosaic there to the second century.[19] While the contexts and themes of the Utica and the Chersonisos mosaics are similar, there are few other details in common. Consequently, a second-century date has been proposed, but cannot be regarded as secure. Where clear-cut parallels are not found, a broad date range is a more satisfactory proposition than a narrow but potentially incorrect date.

4.2.4 Late Antique Mosaics

The majority of Christian churches in Crete have been dated to the late fifth to early sixth century and so have their mosaics.[20] The same dating cluster of the late fifth/early sixth century occurs for Peloponnesian churches.[21] The problems of Late Antique chronologies in Crete are common to the rest of Greece and are partly due to a dearth of historical sources and a lack of domestic evidence. In some cases, mortuary evidence (as a sealed context) may provide a date for a particular phase of the church, but it is not always easy to then connect the burial(s) with the laying of the mosaic (as in Chersonisos Basilica A (Mosaics 92–3)). Although a number of fourth-century mosaics have been revealed in domestic contexts,[22] mosaics of the fifth and sixth centuries are found primarily in churches.

In most cases, the proposed dates in this study are formed based on a combination of sources and the incorporation of securely dated parallel evidence. The small number of mosaics on the island, particularly when viewed over six centuries, makes a study of their iconographic development of minor value. But, in combination with date and distribution analysis, a significantly more detailed picture emerges. In terms of date distribution, only the published mosaics are included because of the uncertainty of the chronologies and archaeological contexts of the unpublished mosaics (see the Supplementary Catalogue). For the distribution analysis, all known mosaics are included to give as wide a view as possible.

4.3 CHRONOLOGY

Table A3.1 provides a chronology for 93 of the published Cretan mosaics and also includes the dating methods and their degrees of security. A further 22 mosaics have been ascribed to a wide date range of around a century (Table A3.2). Forty-nine mosaics cannot be dated. This covers the total of 164 mosaics in the Catalogue, Parts 1 and 2.[23] The analysis of the chronological data will highlight densities of mosaics by period and then by location, and the diachronic range will in turn allow for suggestions as to the meaning of such concentrations.

The evidence of Graph 1 indicates that 4 mosaics date to the first century, 3 to the late first/early second century, 33 to the second century, 4 to the late second/ early third century, 5 to the third century, 2 to the fourth century, 3 to the late fourth/early fifth century, 14 to the fifth century, 18 to the late fifth/early sixth century and 7 to the sixth century (see also Figs. 1–6). Two concentrations – in the mid-second century and the late fifth/early sixth century – are clear.

The earliest known Hellenistic mosaic in Crete was found on the south coast of the island (Fig. 2). The Lebena Hippocamp mosaic (66), situated in a sanctuary to Asclepius, is dated to the late third or early second century B.C.E. (Pl. 20). Undecorated pebble floors which may be called mosaics are found in the Prytaneion at Lato (Mosaic 76) in the east and in the tower at Phalasarna (Mosaic 142) in the west. For the first century of Roman rule (late first century B.C.E. to late first century C.E.), stretching into the early second century, the number of mosaics steadily grows, evidenced by the early examples on the south coast at Lebena (Mosaic 67), Makrigialos (Mosaics 77–9) and Kouphonisi (Mosaics 81–2) (dated either to the Hellenistic or Early Roman period). The focus on the south coast continues in the first half of the first century, with examples at Myrtos and Lissos (Mosaics 84 & 137) and Gortyn (Mosaics 55, 63 & 64). These mosaics are predominantly of black-and-white tesserae, some with cut pebbles, and are mostly geometric, but they have some stylized figured elements. Mosaic 137 contains a mixture of tesserae and pebbles; the geometric decoration is in black and white and the figured decoration is in colour.[24] The earliest mosaics found

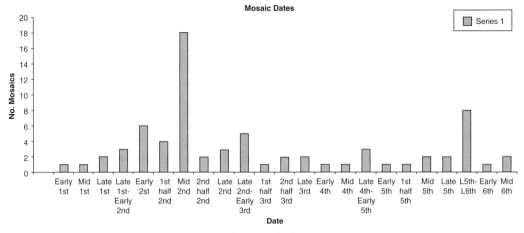

Graph 1 Mosaic dates.

on the north coast were located at Knossos (Mosaics 9 & 28) and Chersonisos (Mosaics 43a & 45). The dates for the Chersonisos mosaics are not yet secured, but it seems that they and the Knossos mosaic belong in the second half of the first century. As yet, there are no published first-century mosaics from the west of the island.

The late second-century boom in mosaic production is primarily represented by rich polychrome tessellated mosaics found in the cities of the northern half of the island. Outstanding among them are the mosaics of Chania and Kisamos for their quality and themes (Fig. 3). Knossos also has fine mosaics from this period, and more evidence is emerging from Chersonisos. During the third century, Kisamos becomes the area with the largest concentration of mosaics, and there is a sharp decline in numbers at Knossos (Fig. 4).[25] At the same time, Chersonisos on the north coast has increasing evidence for mosaics (Fig. 8). Chersonisos (Mosaics 39, 40 & 42) and Kisamos (from the Kakaournakis Plot) (Mosaic S210) and the Hartzoulakis Plot (Mosaic S208) have the latest pre-Christian mosaics, which indicates their importance as harbour towns in the fourth century (Fig. 5). Thus far, all the fourth-century mosaics are geometric, but the description of the Kakaournakis mosaics is limited and there are no published photographs. Only the matrices of the Hartzoulakis Plot mosaics survive. Of the Chersonisos mosaics, Mosaics 39 and 42 have elements familiar to both the Roman and Late Antique Cretan repertoires. The double guilloche (**R** 74h) of Mosaic 42 is more common in the Late Antique period in Crete, even if it is found earlier outside the island. From the mid- to late fourth century there is a significant drop in mosaics, only to be reversed from the early fifth century owing to the extensive church-building programme. The number of mosaics builds to a peak in the late fifth to early sixth century and then declines in the mid-sixth century (Fig. 6).

The recent finds of mosaics in Chersonisos (Mosaics 40 & 43) and Kisamos are extending the knowledge of Late Antique Crete, as domestic contexts dating to the late fourth to fifth century are increasingly revealed. From Kisamos, the unpublished Theodosakis Plot mosaic (Mosaic S220) may come from a secular building but contextual detail is not yet available.[26] The only other possible Late Antique domestic mosaic is Mosaic 121, but when it was 'excavated' in 1918 little contextual information was recorded. The proposed church context is unsupported, and scenes of the hunt, which are more commonly found in domestic contexts in this period, are unlikely themes for a religious mosaic. The earliest church mosaic is possibly that of Olus (Mosaic 126) (Pl. 37). The mosaic is stylistically unique, which makes it extremely difficult to date (see earlier). The fragmentary early fifth-century wall mosaics from the KMF Basilica, Knossos (Mosaic 91), are remarkable; not only are they one of the two sets of Late Antique wall mosaics in Crete (the other being from the Gortyn Sector M Basilica), but they are also one of the few examples known in Greece.[27] The majority of Late Antique mosaics are dated to the late fifth or early sixth century and, as discussed earlier, there are issues with the accuracy of this chronology. The latest known mosaics on the island come from Suia (Mosaics 156–8) and Elyros (Mosaic 155), with a mid-sixth-century date. The latest known church, Vizari, did not contain mosaics.

4.4 LOCATION AND DISTRIBUTION

Following the creation of the province, the location and distribution of the mosaics suggest a diversity of change across Crete, one which is not necessarily 'in response' to the Romans, as was previously thought, and one which varies significantly from the alleged patterns of cultural change.

4.5 THE EVIDENCE

Graphs 2 and 3[28] illustrate the main concentration of mosaics in the urban sphere, in particular, Knossos followed by Kisamos, Chersonisos, Gortyn and Chania. The graph highlights such central issues as the significant concentrations of mosaics in some cities and unexpected lack of mosaics in others (Agios Nikolaos and Aptera) in the Roman period, and for the Late Antique period, the date and extent of occupation of both rural and urban areas. Many of the Late Antique sites are marked by a single mosaic context, normally one church (e.g., Olus), but there are also some sites such as Knossos and Chersonisos that have many different churches, each with mosaic floors. The reasons why certain areas had multiple churches often in use at the same time will be addressed.

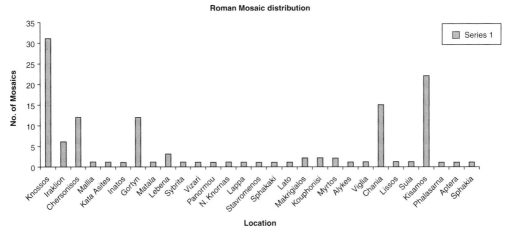

Graph 2 Roman mosaic distribution.

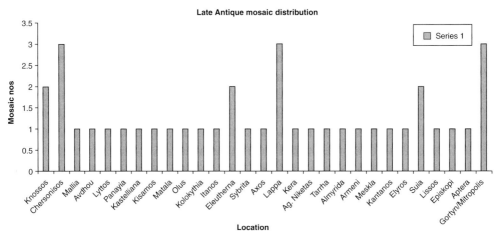

Graph 3 Late Antique mosaic distribution.

4.5.1 Issues with the Evidence

When analysing the material, the circumstances of the recovery should be taken into account. The vast majority of Roman mosaics are found in urban contexts as a result of rescue excavations, which in part explains the urban bias in the evidence. Those of the Late Antique period are more widespread across the island since monumental architecture (churches) is often the focus of excavation. As discussed in Chapter 2, survey data have contributed significantly to the knowledge of settlement patterns, but without excavation, mosaics are not often found[29] and close chronological scrutiny can produce at best broad date ranges. Furthermore, evidence for rural sites is notoriously difficult to closely define based on survey data. There is also an archaeological bias in the evidence between urban spheres. For example, Knossos clearly has the highest concentration of mosaics, but it has not suffered from modern urban encroachment, whereas Chania has. Because of the weight of interest in the Bronze Age material and the need for rescue excavations, quite a significant portion of the valley has been surveyed and investigated. In Gortyn, the public rather than the private area of the city has been the focus of investigation.

4.5.2 Implications of Mosaic Concentrations

Even taking account of the bias in archaeological recovery, the mosaic date distribution indicates significant differences in the occupation of urban and rural areas, as well as among the cities of Crete. Out of the 48 sites in Crete that have either Roman or Late Antique mosaics or both, 24 have coastal locations (Fig. 1). The distribution widens significantly in the Late Antique period; the earliest mosaics of this period appear at inland sites with a slow expansion to include coastal sites. Notably, the lack of activity in the east of the island continues from the Roman period. These mosaic concentrations are a result of social and economic factors, and their analysis is crucial for a diachronic view of Cretan society in the Roman and Late Antique periods.

Coastal Focus and Lack of Mosaics in Rural Regions

The strong coastal focus of the mosaics is indicative of the importance of trade and the location of the main urban spaces (which took advantage of one of the island's key resources as a trade facilitator). On the basis of the survey evidence, there are several farms but no definite rural villa sites, indicating that this is a real trend rather than an archaeological bias.[30] Furthermore, for some areas, it is believed that farms were managed more commonly by slaves or tenants, with the landlords presumably more attracted to urban coastal living. Thus the lack of mosaics in inland rural space and the focus on the coastal urban areas reflect a more cosmopolitan population of traders and politicians, among others, living in the governmental seat, the *colonia*, and in the busy trading towns. Moreover, as can be seen by the evidence of the imports and exports it is likely that the Cretans were not going to become wealthy on their agriculture alone. There was little room (literally, owing to the mountains) on the island for agricultural expansion, and the economy of trade must have appeared a more attractive option in the Roman period.

Lack of Mosaics in the East

The mosaic distribution maps (Figs. 1–6) indicate that there was very little activity in the east of the island during either the Roman or the Late Antique period.

With the exception of Itanos, or even Sitia, it may be that the poor quality harbour facilities of the northeast coast resulted in a lack of their use for trade and therefore a lack of their attraction for a sizeable segment of the working Cretan population. A possible land route across the island may have been in place from Kalo Nero or Makrigialos on the south to Sitia, but survey evidence has not picked up the kind of occupation or imports along this route that might be expected of a busy thoroughfare. Given that the route was relatively mountainous and some 30 km longer than the Ierapetra–Mirabello Bay route, it is unlikely that it would have been exploited heavily.

Late Antique Mosaics

The Late Antique mosaics cover a much broader distribution than do the Roman (Graphs 2 and 3; Fig. 1). Of the 95 known[31] Christian churches on Crete, 40 are paved with or have evidence for mosaic floors, and another one has wall mosaics (the Knossos KMF Basilica) (42.1%). The mosaics are spread quite evenly across the island with a ratio of distribution similar to that of the total number of churches. In the *nomos* of Chania, 16 out of 27 churches have mosaics; for Rethymnon, 9 out of 19 churches have mosaics; for Iraklion 13 out of 36 churches have mosaics; and finally, for Lasithi, 4 out of 12 churches have mosaics.

The change in mosaic distribution in the Late Antique period is in part because the majority of these mosaics are found in churches which were newly constructed to be accessible to a wide swathe of the population for purposes of Christianization. The construction and maintenance of churches in the rural and inland landscape would have helped generate economic opportunities, further strengthening new or renewed communities. The wider distribution of mosaics, therefore, initially reflects the spread of Christianity, and it quickly comes to reflect the settlement patterns too.[32]

While the main Roman urban centres such as Gortyn and Knossos continue, some inland and some acropolis sites which had diminished in the Roman period appear to be revitalized in the Late Antique, such as Eleutherna, Kera, Almyrida, Lappa, Avdhou, Tarrha, Frangokastelli (Fig. 9), Mallia and Sybrita. Significant harbour towns such as Chersonisos and Suia continue to be important, possibly because of their trade facilities, and this is marked in part by their multiple churches (at least three in each town). In the fifth and sixth centuries, new coastal settlements are also established, for example, at Almyrida on the north coast and Agios Niketas on the south (Fig. 9). Together with the evidence of other flourishing ports, such as Olus, Lissos and Itanos, it is clear that the island continued to focus on its trading resources. The sites of Kisamos and Chania are peculiar in that they were both once-flourishing Roman towns, and until recently there was little evidence for Christian churches.[33] Regarding domestic occupation, by the sixth to seventh century villages with associated outlying farmsteads vastly outnumber the villas of the fifth to sixth century.[34] As in most other areas of the Roman Empire, until the mid-seventh century urban areas were probably the focus point, with smaller settlements, such as villages and farmsteads, partially dependent on them. The lack of mosaics and churches (with the exception of Vizari and Fodele) from the late sixth century onwards may be physical evidence of what is already known in the sources to be the decreasing levels of security and changes in economic stability.[35] With the fall of North Africa to the Arabs in the mid-seventh century, Crete was pushed to the borders of the empire, thereby increasing the need for fortified sites along its coastline. The changing military situation was possibly responsible for the ultimate decline of the southern coastal cities (e.g., Suia and Lissos) which faced the North African coast. Despite problems in the south, the northern coastal cities such as Chania and Elounda continued to function as important port towns until the C.E. 827 Arab invasion. The only real evidence for construction during the seventh and eighth centuries comes from the inland sites of Vizari, Fodele and Piskopiano, which would have had a stronger element of security than the coast.

4.6 Conclusion

Contrary to Sanders's pessimistic view of what it is possible to ascertain about the economy of Crete without knowledge of its manufacturing or exports, the date distribution not only provides a diachronic view of Cretan mosaics over seven centuries but also accounts for the broad economic range of the island within the wider context of the Roman Empire. The diachronic perspective has allowed a view of the reasons some areas are occupied at some times and others are not. There are clear differences across time and space: the first-century preference for the south coast and a few select cities on the north; the clear coastal preference, certainly until the fourth century; the relative dearth of mosaics in the east; the urban focus until the Late Antique period; the flourishing of rural inland sites in the Late Antique period; and finally, the spread of occupation to the urbanized coastlines.

༼༽ ༼༽ ༼༽ ༼༽

FIVE

URBAN AND ARCHITECTURAL CONTEXTS

5.1 INTRODUCTION

Detailed hypotheses on routine or mundane actions of the Roman and Late Antique Cretans have been difficult to achieve, particularly as other key sources such as historical and literary accounts rarely devote discussion to anything other than the exciting but unusual events.[1] To achieve an understanding of a broad range of Cretan society, in terms of both the ordinary and the extraordinary, as well as across social levels, it is necessary to examine a body of material made and used by a variety of people. Since the work of social anthropologists such as Bourdieu,[2] a clear relationship between spatial organization and society is accepted and consequently allows archaeologists to access the society through the nodes around which people physically structure their lives. Further advances have been made, particularly regarding space both as a stage for and a shaper of society. For example, Maca,[3] in his studies of the Maya at Copan in Honduras, noted that routine actions may be part of the space but that as the actions change and progress, the development is mirrored in the changing spatial organization. The extent to which scholars can apply the evidence of this social theory has been played out in a range of social studies concerning space, occupation, status, gender and so on, which are all based around organizational rules.[4] Understanding this allows scholars to reconstruct routine actions from social and spatial organization. Bourdieu's work on the relationships between spatial boundaries and social organization led to later developments, particularly in the categorizing of space, by scholars such as Hodder in 1989 and Stark in 1998.[5] In turn, other scholars have refined the focus to concentrate on architectural space and also interior décor.[6]

Analyses of the layout of space and architecture provide a means of defining areas as public or private space, identifying the function of architecture (such as domestic or religious) and ascertaining the activities undertaken within various rooms. Once the space is recognized, further investigation of the roles of its users, occupants and visitors can be postulated.[7] Such reinvestigation is in part because architecture and the organization of space are conceived and used both consciously and subconsciously.[8] Moreover, architecture and organized space provide a stage for social actions and interactions (conscious) and help to dictate the way in which these actions are played out (subconscious).[9] Consequently, an examination of how space is used allows the archaeologist to reconstruct routine actions and their development over time, as well as cognitive elements that are not necessarily recorded otherwise.[10] Bourdieu emphasized that the observers must always try to provide an objective analysis of society and divorce themselves from the interpretation of practice; they cannot allow either themselves or their experiences to be introduced into the study.[11] The two central aims of the current analysis are to apply the evidence of mosaics to further inform our understanding of the layout and function of space in Roman and Late Antique towns and countryside and, subsequently, to discuss the implications of mosaic choice and location for an understanding of Cretan society.

In terms of the occupation of space, different spatial units should be considered. The broadest unit of space, the island of Crete, has already been examined in Chapters 2 and 4, and this provides the overall context. In this section and in Chapter 6, the focus narrows to the cities, the neighbourhoods within and the buildings and, finally, individuals. These units are delineated by boundaries – natural (e.g., the sea or mountains (Fig. 9)), physical (e.g., a line of burials) and conceptual (e.g., the delineation of a territory through its occupation by one definable community as opposed to another) – and are recognized at the conscious level. These boundaries are further defined through people's actions, such as ritual performance or the erection of specific architecture, and through memories, as well as through everyday use. Furthermore, actions played out in one space will have an impact on all other units.[12]

5.1.1 Methods

Ideally, when formulating a definition of space, the full range of associated material culture within a building should be included. Until recently, the nature of archaeological processes in Crete had in many respects resulted in a dearth of Roman and Late Antique architecture and associated material culture pertinent to a study of use of space. Consequently, in many situations mosaics survive as the only evidence by which to define architectural space (see Chapter 1). Notwithstanding, mosaics are a valuable source of information as they are found in such a broad range of contexts: domestic to civic, private to public, and religious to leisure. Mosaics can be fundamental in revealing critical evidence, such as the function of the immediate (room) and of the broader space (building and urban zone), identification of civic and domestic space, and insight into the occupants and users of the space (as outlined in Chapter 3). More precise details can be ascertained, for example, the mosaics in the Forum of the Corporations at Ostia. Here, with their images of exotic goods and animals and the names of the ports, the mosaics provide a starting point for a broader discussion about levels of literacy, extent of trade, supply and demand, markets and competition.[13] In some contexts, particularly domestic ones, mosaics may allow considerable personal access to the occupants of a building, especially through the mosaics' preconceived cognitive elements. The choice of a mosaic's material, colour, décor and theme, as well as of its location, can help in determining the function of the room, building and area in which it is found.[14] A mosaic may also provide subtle guidance (e.g., for circulation within or contemplation of a space), good wishes (for a pleasant bath, for example) and clear warnings (such as the well-known example of *Cave Canem* from the House of the Tragic Poet at Pompeii).[15] Thus the use of mosaics to guide visitors, signal privacy or a change of space, entertain guests, or project certain qualities onto the patron provides unique access to an aspect of society that was not necessarily deemed worthy of description in the written sources.

5.1.2 Issues Concerning Architectural Analysis

Although mosaics are an invaluable resource for spatial analysis, there are limitations; some, such as the scarcity of rural mosaics, have already been highlighted. Furthermore, mosaics are not ubiquitous. For example, they are rarely found in industrial quarters or in poorer areas of a town. Thus mosaic studies and architectural analysis cannot always directly illuminate elements of society that are traditionally sidelined, for example, the presence and roles of slaves or the definition of gender roles.[16] Space provisions for slaves seem to have varied considerably, as some slaves had their own quarters while others just slept outside the door to the master's rooms.[17] The focus on mosaics here is not intended to result in a concentration on elite housing or to contribute to Romanization studies as de Haan has argued for.[18] By widening the discussion to include non-domestic space, as well as how a range of different types of space function, a broader perspective can be achieved. As spatial analysis involves so many inter-related levels, from the island itself to its domestic residences, issues such as spatial boundaries, social divisions and the functions of space are revealed. It is often assumed that prominent members of society will be more visible in such an analysis, yet, as Maca points out, it is not always a foregone conclusion that the quantity and quality of architectural remains relate directly to status.[19]

5.2 ANALYSIS OF URBAN SPACE

The date distribution of the mosaics across Crete (Chapter 4) has shown that the largest concentrations of mosaics are found in urban, and often coastal, locations until the Late Antique period. Using the evidence presented in Appendix 4 and starting with Knossos, as the island's colony, a range of towns with different numbers, chronologies and degree of preservation of mosaics will be discussed to formulate a diachronic understanding of the topography of the urban space.

5.2.1 Urban Evidence

Knossos

Knossos (Fig. 12) became the Colonia Julia Nobilis Cnosus around 27 B.C.E.[20] With this status, that it had a high concentration of mosaics is not surprising given the regular investment to make the city attractive so that it could thrive.[21] Furthermore, the Knossos Valley is extremely fertile and, with an established port nearby at Iraklion, the city maintained a stable, if not a flourishing, economy. An unexpected issue is that the concentration of mosaics in Knossos occurs much later (second century) than would be expected of a first-century B.C.E. colony. Traditionally, such a colony would have a comparatively high quota of Roman officials and a newly established population (of whatever size) comprising either retired soldiers or transplanted Italians.[22] There are few mosaics known from the late third century and the fourth, and a general lack of evidence in the valley at this point has led to a theory of abandonment after two possible earthquakes.[23] However, this theory has been refuted and the explanation for the third- to fourth-century dearth may simply be archaeological bias. It is hoped that the current Knossos survey will help to fill in the gap in evidence.[24]

The paucity of literary data for Roman Knossos means that we rely primarily on archaeological evidence for an understanding of the city over six centuries.[25] The excavation focus thus far has primarily been on the Minoan levels, yet there have been notable intensive Roman and Late Antique excavations, for example, at the Unexplored Mansion, the Stratigraphic Museum extension, the Villa Dionysus, the Sanatorium Basilica, the Knossos 2000 excavations and the KMF excavations.[26] The lack of modern urban encroachment has been invaluable to the preservation of material. Hood and Smyth recorded the standing remains in the 1981 Knossos survey.[27] Additionally, the number of rescue excavations undertaken throughout the valley affords a means to reconstruct the outline of urban topography, particularly the domestic and industrial space, as well as areas of the road network and infrastructural elements such as the aqueduct and cisterns (Fig. 12).[28] The Demeter Sanctuary, on the southern edge of the town, is located at the distance it should be from the nucleus of the settlement as recommended by Vitruvius.[29] Other cults, such as that of Isis at the Demeter Sanctuary and Castor and Pollux at the Glaukos shrine, have been identified through epigraphic evidence.[30] A small temple at the east end of the Makritikhos wall may be a Temple of Asclepius.[31] The public area of the Roman and Late Antique city is not well known and has been identified primarily by the remains of substantial Roman walls (e.g., the Civil Basilica).

The Unexplored Mansion excavations revealed significant evidence for small-scale industrial activity.[32] The evidence for industry has expanded both north and south with the discovery of kilns in the Venizelio area[33] and the evidence of wasters and cisterns indicating pottery workshops in Knossos village.[34] Other activities include agricultural processing, as well as a possible dye works on the edge of the urban space.[35] The city did not change significantly in size from the Hellenistic to the Roman period, with the cemeteries in the surrounding hills marking the city limits (Fig. 10). The northern edge of the city is marked by a Roman cemetery located in the area of the KMF Basilica (Fig. 12, Grid square C5). The southern extent is at least at the river Vlikhia, just south of the village of Knossos. In the Late Antique period, the surviving remains indicate that the central focus shifted northwards.[36] This is particularly distinguished by the location of the two fine Christian basilicas, as well as by the increasing evidence for Late Antique houses uncovered during rescue excavations.[37] The shift northwards is further defined by the location of Christian graves in what was once the southern part of the Roman residential area in the modern Knossos village.[38] The extent of architecture, epigraphic and numismatic evidence, statuary, pottery, glass, marbles and other archaeology representative of the fraction of the city that has been excavated is good supporting evidence for what the mosaics already indicate, namely, the presence of a flourishing and important city in the Roman and Late Antique periods. The mosaics further refine the nature of occupation in the valley.

The Roman mosaics are distributed in a north-south spread (from the Apollinaris mosaic (9) *KS* 91 to *KS* 206) with an east-west spread of no more than around 500 m. With few exceptions, the mosaics are either figured or complex geometric designs, indicative of the contexts (domestic) in which they were discovered. Other than a possible public bath house containing Mosaic 10, few civic buildings have been investigated in detail.

Of the four significant concentrations of mosaics in Knossos, the most northerly indicates the location of the Late Antique centre of the town as the two Christian churches there contain mosaics. Just to the south is a second concentration which represents the earliest evidence for mosaics in Knossos. This group contains Mosaics 9 and 15 which are black and white, although the Apollinaris mosaic (9) has a polychrome panel. Both date to the late first century. The marine iconography of the Apollinaris mosaic (Poseidon and the hippocamps) points to a possible bath house context. It is postulated that these Western-type mosaics may actually be evidence for the location of Campanian settlers who are otherwise known only from the epigraphic data which record a land dispute between them and the local residents.[39] Recent publication of the Venizelio cemetery excavations has provided tentative evidence of Italian settlers in Knossos with the find of a monumental first-century tomb which includes the names CLUATIUS and CLUATIUS C.f.CONINUS along the south side.[40] More evidence is needed to support the excavator's theory that the cemetery may have been an exclusive one for prominent Knossian families. On Crete, these tombs are found only in Knossos, indicating to the excavator that their form must have originated in the Via Laurentina cemetery in Ostia, thus supporting the suggestion of early Western settlers in the colony.[41] While this is possible and it is tempting to associate the early black-and-white mosaics with such settlers, it is difficult to be precise about their origins and status.[42]

The third concentration of mosaics is around the Villa Dionysus and the so-called Civil Basilica. Here the mosaics are a mix of the lavish Villa Dionysus mosaics (1–8), the figured bath house mosaic (12), and others, such as Mosaics 10, 11, 13, 16 and 17. The discovery of a section of a large wave-scroll mosaic (10), which would have occupied a substantial room, may be part of the hypothesized civic baths. The location of these mosaics in the area of the theatre, the Civil Basilica and the large baths helps to further define the area as the civic centre bounded by the residences of presumably the local elite or government officials (on the west and southeast, at least).

The final concentration of mosaics is in the area of the modern village of Knossos and intermittently north towards the Villa Dionysus. The village concentration can be explained by the focus of rescue excavations here. Given the sporadic finds of mosaics in the undeveloped areas between here and the Villa Dionysus, it can be confidently postulated that this was a residential area. An industrial zone lay to the east of this concentration and is also marked by the lack of mosaics, despite excavations there.[43] These hypotheses are supported by the finds of statue fragments, coins and inscriptions and Roman concrete ruins which have yet to be investigated throughout the valley.[44]

Gortyn

Partly in recognition of its support during the Battle of Actium, Octavian established Gortyn (Fig. 13) as the capital, the administrative centre for the koine of Cretans and seat of the proconsul of the joint province in 27 B.C.E.[45] Epigraphic evidence indicates a substantial population of Greek and Western merchants.[46] Given the status of Knossos, a concentration of mosaics would be expected, and the excavations thus far support this expectation.[47] Like Knossos, the Roman and Late Antique city has had little or no modern encroachment. Gortyn has also benefited from a long-term programme of research excavations, but the focus has been primarily in the civic rather than domestic realm of the city, that is to say, in the area of the Odeion,[48] the Gymnasium (once the so-called Praetorium) (Fig. 7)[49] and the Acropolis.[50] As with other parts of Crete and the empire, the pinnacle of Gortyn's opulence was in the second century, and to the existing Odeion and Greek theatre were added two new theatres, the amphitheatre and the circus (Fig. 13). In more recent years the Roman Forum has been located in the southeast sector of the town, close to a substantial bath house.[51] The southern, western and eastern extents of the city are marked by the circle of Roman cemeteries which lie just to the west of the river Mitropolianos, south just below the village of Mitropolis and east at Agii Deka (Fig. 13).[52] The northwestern extent is at the Acropolis. Within this area are numerous fountains and nymphaea, three bath houses, sections of the aqueduct (Roman and Late Antique) and the Roman and Late Antique road system.[53] The settlement evidence, certainly from the Hellenistic period through to the Late Antique, is to the west of the Agora, primarily along the road toward ancient Lebena.[54] A range of religious buildings, including Apollo Pythios, Isis and Serapis, Demeter and Kore, and more recently the so-called Temple of Divus Augustus[55] have been investigated.

Recent excavations and topographic survey emphasize how the layout of the city changed during the Justinianic period. Excavations in the Agora have shown that Late Antique settlement encroached on previously civic space with a significant concentration in the area between the Temple of Pythian Apollo and the Gymnasium.[56] Renewed excavations have revealed a significant portion of the Late Antique city which lay to the south of Agios Titos.[57] A substantial public building was located in the eastern part of the Pythion residential area.[58] Here also sixth- and seventh-century houses have been excavated, including evidence of a kitchen equipped with ovens and a raised hearth.[59] That Gortyn flourished throughout the Late Antique period is evidenced by the construction of at least eight Christian basilicas and the triconch Martyrium at Mitropolis and the tetraconch building at the agricultural school.[60] Epigraphic indications are that by the middle of the sixth century Gortyn had become the Mitropolis of Crete and the basilica in Sector M (109) may well have been the episcopal seat.[61] It is the largest Christian basilica known in Crete, and in addition to the floor mosaics, traces of wall mosaics are also evident. The church was destroyed by an earthquake in the seventh century, and as the mosaic inscription indicates, both the mosaics and the church were repaired only to be destroyed again by another earthquake.[62] These destruction horizons are also seen in the latest excavations of the Pythian theatre.[63] After the early seventh-century earthquake, the emperor Heraclius had a number of infrastructural elements (such as the water supply) restored. Recent excavations have revealed different Late Antique buildings in the area south of the Gymnasium, including an apsidal building, a large two-storeyed building (seventh century) and parts of the Byzantine aqueduct which was built on the collapsed remains of the apsidal building.[64] Continuing excavations in the Byzantine quarter have revealed smaller buildings in the Late Antique period and the excavators postulate a greater focus on independent rural living and seasonal work in the city.[65] Indications are that the area was abandoned in the seventh century with evidence only for burials until the ninth-century Arab invasions.[66]

For the periods between the first and fifth centuries in Gortyn the mosaics are of simple design, largely in black and white. The bath houses in the Gymnasium area have been the focus of much work, and many of the town's mosaics have been located here.[67] Fine Late Antique mosaics have been recovered, and an excavation in the area of the Gymnasium revealed a Late Antique workshop producing glass tesserae.[68]

Thus far, only two domestic mosaics have been identified in Gortyn, both from different first-century houses in the same residential area to the west of the Agora: a plain white mosaic (63), and the *Opus signinum* mosaic (64). The remainder of the mosaics were found in two civic locations, the area of the Odeion (53–5) and the area of the Gymnasium (56–62), as well as in churches (108 & 109). The Odeion mosaics (53–5) are of complex geometric designs, whereas the mosaics from the Gymnasium area (56–62) are plain black and white with the most basic geometric decoration. It is likely that both sets of mosaics from Sectors B and C come from bath houses and that the mosaics from the west baths (Sector B) are a little more detailed than those from the Gymnasium baths. The Odeion as entertainment space would have been an inviting and quite lavish building, whereas the public bath buildings were likely a little more functional and used by a broader segment of the population. Therefore, for the more functional buildings here, the plainer and possibly cheaper mosaics are the most suitable floor type. The degree of complexity of mosaics within bath houses varies, which may also indicate a further delineation of space, as discussed later in this chapter.

Chania and Kisamos

The concentration of mosaics in Chania and Kisamos is likely to be a result of a combination of factors stemming from the location of these cities on the north coast, which gave both of them prime trading advantages.[69] The mosaics found so far in both towns are primarily from either private residential contexts or public baths. Little of the public areas of both Roman cities have been investigated in detail. Unlike Knossos and Gortyn, Chania and Kisamos have been continuously occupied, and, as a result, most excavations have been carried out under rescue conditions, making the complete topography of the Roman and Late Antique towns difficult to establish. Furthermore, it is only in recent years that material from the Late Antique period is being found.

Chania

Chania (Fig. 14) was one of the two freed cities of Crete, giving it privileges valuable to its economy,[70] and the city, with its excellent harbour, thrived. Although Chania is mentioned among the 22 most important cities in Crete in the sixth-century *Document of Ieroklis*, the material evidence for this is limited to the remains of what is presumed to be a Christian church near the Venetian Cathedral.

Chania is a good example of a location where mosaics are some of the few surviving signs of the Roman city. The cemeteries marking the extent of the town have been found in a semi-circle some 500 m from the exterior of the Venetian walls (Fig. 14).[71] On the east side, a number of Roman graves along the modern Demokratias Street may mark part of the boundary of the town.[72] The tomb types are cist form, *hypogaea*, tile graves and simple pits. Sanders is likely to be correct that the finds of mosaics (129–36) in the area immediately to the south and west (e.g., the Mayrigiannakis Plot (Mosaic S204)) of the Venetian walls represent the central residences of the political or upper echelons of society.[73] Sanders's designation is further emphasized by the location of the Roman public building, religious buildings and a possible theatre here.[74] The concentration of mosaics (Fig. 14) at present suggests that the domestic part of the town would have been located around the area of the modern market square. Baths, part of the Agora (identified by the stoa, rooms and fluted columns) and streets have also been revealed during rescue excavations.[75] Excavations to the west of Tzanaki Street have also uncovered what may have been a small industrial workshop,[76] and small-scale industries may have been concentrated in the west of the city. A spectacular amount of material culture has been recovered which clearly supports the evidence of the mosaics' indicating that Chania became a popular centre in the first century and continued to be so until the fourth century, whereas Kisamos thrived from the late second to third centuries onwards.

Kisamos

As with Chania, the nature of the rescue excavation in Kisamos (Fig. 15) has meant that sections of the domestic areas (and the cemeteries) of the city have been the key revelations.[77] Parts of the civic area of Kisamos may be identified around the the Amphitheatre (Fig. 15). The Agora is suggested to be located in the northwest of the town, not too far from the port, and a stoa and theatre have been identified in the east of the town.[78] In the same area, the remains of a temple, possibly to Dionysus, have been revealed, and this would make it one of the only temples known in Kisamos. At the Mylonaki Plot, substantial remains of a large building with a paved court may be indicative of a late third- to fourth-century civic building.[79] The road network, including the *decumanus maximus* uncovered during 1991 excavations, has been revealed in various plots (Fig. 15).[80] This road was flagged, and wheel ruts were visible.[81] Part of the *cardo maximus* was exposed in 1970 in the central square of the town.[82] The extent of the road system is reflected in the evidence found during the 1993 excavations of the Raisakis Plot,[83] and the Orpheus mosaic (S212) was found here. The remains of an aqueduct were uncovered by the edge of what is presumed to be the residential area of town. Small-scale industrial areas may also be identified at the Paterakis Plot on the east side of the town where kilns and iron slag were identified.[84] Another metallurgical installation was uncovered in the south of the town, which also included a number of water features.[85] In the Stratake and Skoulake Plot evidence for a glass-production workshop was revealed. Here, a circular structure divided into rooms was found with vast quantities of glass and faience and other features indicating a workshop.[86] A 'Late Roman' water-mill which could not be well dated owing to a lack of material culture was found at the Moraitakis Plot in Kisamos.[87]

Remains of bath houses have been found at the Farangitakis Plot marked by the hypocaust (Mosaic S209), at the Stimadorakis Plot and for the southeast baths and the western baths south of the church of Agios Nikolaos.[88] A further possible example was identified in the Apostolaki Plot by the remains of water tanks and storage areas.[89] More than 30 houses have been identified, and mosaics have been recovered from more than 15 plots scattered throughout the modern town, from the northern section marked by the Nikolakis Plot with its two mosaics (S214) to the south with its early second-century Triton mosaics (S213). In the centre of the residential area, excavations revealed the Paterakis Plot's second-century mosaics of the Seasons, and nearby was the mosaic of the Grape-Picking Scene (Mosaic S211).[90] The substantial third-century houses, one of which had two storeys, found during the Health Centre excavations contained six stunning mosaics *in situ* (Mosaic S207), in addition to the bedding of some which had fallen from the floors above.[91] Also in this plot, the remains of a first-century amphorae workshop were revealed.[92] In addition to the extensive kitchens, the *domus* had its own private bath suite. Some of the cemeteries dating between the first and third centuries were located just to the north of the modern town, and some of the Late Antique cemeteries have been excavated to the east of the town.[93] The remains of at least one Christian basilica, with geometric mosaic floors made from pebbles, have been revealed close to the Museum Plateia during 1986 rescue excavations.[94] Markoulaki et al. note that after the fourth-century earthquake the nature of the town changed and the Late Antique settlement shifts location somewhat, as evidenced by the construction of graves on space once occupied by Roman buildings with mosaic floors.[95]

Chersonisos

The vast majority of mosaics located in Chersonisos (Fig. 16) have been found in the 1990s, during the peak of urban development and consequently of the rescue excavations there.[96] Two of the Christian basilicas are on either end of the urban sprawl which has helped protect them. A possible third church was located at the Spanoudakis Plot (Mosaic 101). Bath houses, residences and mosaics have been found throughout the town, and it is notable that they favour a third- to fourth-century date. The fourth-century house with mosaics on the Kypriotakis Plot (Mosaic 42) was located just to the southeast of Kastri, and the fourth-century buildings of the Yiakoumis Plot (Mosaic 43) were found in the area of the Roman moles (by the east beach). In the same area, a house with two phases, including a floor of the first century, was excavated at the Moudatsakis Plot (Mosaic 44). Two hundred metres southwest of the north beach, an apsidal building with a mosaic was found.[97] The evidence of other rescue excavations in the north, such as the Perakis and Papadakis Plots (Mosaic 39)[98] and the Papageorgiou Plot, and the bath house excavations on Demokratias Street, indicate that it was a well-populated part of town. The only definite Roman public building known so far is the theatre, which lies in the southwest of the modern town.[99] Another Roman building identified in the Apostolaki Plot may be a temple, with which a marble statue of Trajan was associated.[100] The area of the Agora is presumed close to the theatre (Fig. 16), and although streets and houses have been uncovered here, definitive evidence for the Agora is not yet forthcoming.[101] In the same area, the remains of a bath house have been uncovered.[102] Cisterns have been found throughout the town,[103] and remains of the aqueduct can be seen on the Chersonisos-Kastelli Pediados road (Fig. 17). Roman fish tanks were identified on the western side of the town (below Chersonisos Basilica B) (Fig. 8). The Fountain mosaic was found on the east end of the port (Pl. 15).

In terms of the development of the town, a parallel may be that of Kisamos. The fishing industry must have helped Chersonisos to grow, and the current evidence suggests that it began to flourish later than the second century.[104] Ninety ostraca from Chersonisos, spanning a period from the first century to the third century, record a series of transactions pertaining to slaves and shopkeepers and to the larger business of imports and wholesale, indicating the town's role as a port and exploitation of its anchorage.[105] It is possible that these ostraca can be related to the increased attention on Crete's north coast after the first century (discussed later). By the Late Antique period, Chersonisos had grown to be an important town, marked in part by its two basilicas, and it was the episcopal centre of Pediada until the sixth century when the administration was transferred inland to Piskopiano.[106]

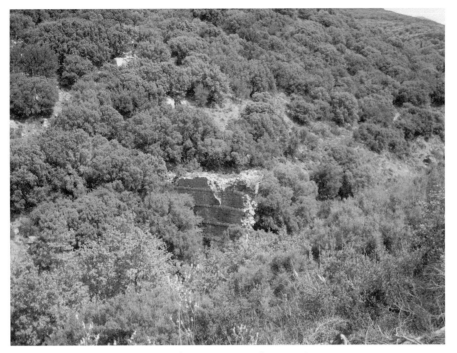

Fig. 17 Chersonisos, aqueduct remains.

Ierapetra and Agios Nikolaos

Ierapetra and Agios Nikolaos are notable for their dearth of mosaics thus far.[107] Historically and archaeologically, one would expect to find mosaic concentrations similar to those of Chania and Kisamos (see Graph 2), particularly during the first century given the evidence for an early Roman focus on the south coast.[108] The likelihood that Ierapetra controlled a north–south overland trade corridor also makes it a good candidate for a bustling city.[109] Epigraphic evidence reveals the fundamental role the city played and Rome's early interest in its maintenance.[110] The explanation for the dearth of mosaics may be an excavation bias or because later remains obscure the earlier. Ierapetra has evidence for a number of public buildings such as theatres, baths and temples, and as illustrated in Gortyn, such buildings are not usually heavily laden with mosaics.[111] Finds of Roman sculpture, coins and sarcophagi are abundant, and more evidence for houses has been coming to light.[112] Rescue excavations in the suburbs of Ierapetra (such as Alykes and Viglia) have increased our knowledge of the city with finds of material from the first century B.C.E. to the Late Antique period.[113] Once published, the rescue excavation finds of houses, streets and water systems can be collated to give a good understanding of the city's topography.[114]

At Agios Nikolaos, Roman buildings have been revealed in the area of Kitroplateia and Mylos which appear to be of domestic function and date from at least the first century.[115] A large complex of 15 rooms was revealed in the area of Kastelli, and it was in use with two phases between the first and fifth centuries.[116] In Lyttos, among other Cretan towns, one would expect a high proportion of mosaics given its unusually high number of Roman citizens, but only a small area of the site has been excavated.[117] These excavations have identified shops, workshops and possibly two public buildings.[118] In Rethymnon, excavations have revealed evidence of Roman houses, but not as yet evidence for mosaic floors.[119] Many other Roman Cretan towns have little or no evidence for mosaics.

5.2.2 Discussion

The diversity among Cretan towns is clear, but there are some similarities in the urban topography. In most cases it is likely that cemeteries delineated the extent of urban space. They represent the conceptual limits while helping to reinforce a shared identity partly through common ancestral memory.[120] To date, only a single mosaic has been found directly associated with a burial (Mosaic S218).

In many respects, civic space (the Agora or the Forum and buildings within like a stoa or basilica) is central to defining the identity of a community, but other than in baths, few Cretan mosaics are found here. The political and administrative buildings, as well as the array of inscriptions and dedications, help to distinguish the character of a community through both shared past memories and associations with the landscape and with present function.[121] As Aguilar defines the contribution social memory makes to group identity, 'Collective memories contribute to the process of imagining a subject, thus creating myths of nationalism and belonging, while social memories use social discontinuities that in turn produce social cohesion through an acknowledgment of social diversity and social difference (alterity).'[122] Furthermore, the choice of religious focus and architecture further emphasizes the individuality of the social group. The repeated actions of visiting this space evoke collective memories, bind the community together and continue to promote it in its own eyes as well as in the eyes of others. And if the necessity of markets and administration were not enough, entertainment and leisure buildings like baths or odeia further attract the population to circulate in civic space. Within the civic area, different social performances in economic, religious, political and leisure realms are played out. Civic space is a forum for public activities in everyday life, and the space is often well delineated through architecture.[123] The attractions it offers, necessary and discretionary, make it a space with the potential for allowing different cultures, as well as urban, suburban and rural populations, to mix.

The civic centres of Knossos, Chania, Kisamos and Chersonisos have tentatively been identified also by the location of buildings and mosaics.[124] In these sectors, concentrations of richly decorated polychrome mosaics are found adjacent to the proposed civic areas of the town. This perhaps indicates that the elite were living and working in the same areas. Other levels of accommodation are seen in the industrial parts of the towns, where there is a paucity of mosaics. The medium level of dwellings can be identified by mosaic concentrations which may be representative of commercial classes or similarly of wealthy residents. Knossos appears to be a special case where different populations may be definable, such as the possible early Western population in the north of the valley. In the cases of Gortyn, Knossos and Chania, it is evident that the extents and layouts of the Late Antique cities change, which may indicate a conscious de-memorization of the earlier pre-Christian space.[125]

5.3 Analysis of Architectural Space

The urban analysis has shown how mosaics can help define the diachronic topography of Cretan cities. Additional identification of the type of space enables access to the individuals who worked in, lived in or visited that space. Sessa's work has helped to further refine what is meant by the term 'domestic space' in the Late Antique period.[126] As she notes, the domestic sphere was not just the location of family life, it also reflected the aspirations of the household. The size and decoration of the house may not have directly indicated the resources available to the home's residents, but they did project the way in which the residents wished to be viewed.[127] Within the household there were areas of both public and private space, but in many respects the function of space was fluid and areas could be both private and public. Riggsby has argued that ideas of public and private space would not have had the same resonance earlier as they do today and are therefore less useful when discussing domestic space. More useful classifications of users might be insiders/outsiders or perhaps residents/visitors.[128] In this study, domestic space describes residential spaces, including small-scale industrial areas. Mosaics are most frequently found in domestic space above all other types.

5.4 Mosaics and the Identification and Classification of Space

Wallace-Hadrill argued the importance of an analysis of the use of space and its decoration in order to say more about how society functioned in Roman houses.[129] Others such as Locock and Scott have widened the discussion.[130] Some have countered that Wallace-Hadrill carried the analysis too far, that in fact the study of the décor of a Roman house is limited in what it can reveal.[131] Allison believed that the choice in décor, both as to mosaics and wall painting, is far too subjective to be taken to the extreme of creating a model on which to base other conclusions. In contrast, Scott maintained that a great deal can be said about the society on the basis of the mosaics and wall paintings of a Roman house, for example, by looking at them as symbols of power.[132]

Geometric patterns or vegetal/floral scrolls may have served as guides to visitors by indicating the circulation or accessibility of rooms within the *domus*. The reception room set the standard so that the first glimpse of the owner's abode was both imposing and lasting. Welcoming or powerful images like those of the Seasons or Orpheus would have left a striking impression which was reflected onto the architecture and the patron. Complex themes for contemplation may have been used in rooms where guests were expected to linger. In some instances, threshold panels indicated a change in space and perhaps a different level of privacy. The iconography, layout and shape of the mosaics often helped to mark a function of a room (most easily identifiable are *triclinia* or *cubicula*) or emphasize a particular quality of the patron or residents. Commonly, plainer mosaics are found in rooms that are not normally seen by visitors, such as inside or residents' space; sometimes they are found in corridors where a less time-consuming and less expensive version of the mosaic floor can be laid.[133] A range of floor types may indicate different levels of visitors and the multiple functions of a *domus*, which may also help reveal the role of the patron.

Such an analysis is not without its problems. The choice of mosaic may demonstrate how the patron wants to be perceived by society rather than the patron's actual financial, social or political status. Moreover, the extent to which the skill of the craftsperson selected to do the work dictated the mosaic's iconography is difficult to assess. These factors bring into question the extent to which the final choice of design was consciously intended to project a particular significance. Yet despite such issues, the analysis of interior decoration in Roman houses can go some way to defining the function of a room, particularly when supporting evidence is available, such as the architecture itself or other associated material culture. Vitruvius stressed the importance of the choice of decoration for a Roman room, and that the room's function should play a significant role in the selection of the specific décor.[134] Ideally, a combination of the evidence of wall paintings and other interior décor would provide a strong data set; however, only a few scraps of wall paintings survive from Roman Cretan contexts, for example, those of the Villa Dionysus and the House of the Diamond Frescos, Knossos.[135]

5.5 Architecture in Crete: Evidence of Mosaics

5.5.1 Domestic Space

A range of houses have been identified on Crete, through surveys and rescue excavations, providing good representation of both urban and rural dwelling practices. Altamore's recent study includes a variety of dwelling types from seaside villas to working farmsteads.[136] The number of known seaside residences is rising (see Chapter 2) and to examples such as Minoa in Kydonia, with its small bath suite, can be added that of the recently excavated residence at Sphakaki Pangalachori in the area of Rethymnon.[137] The Makrigialos house and baths may also have been a substantial luxury seaside residence offering quality views of the Libyan sea from its cliff-top location. It is difficult to establish whether the buildings on Kouphonisi were intended to be domestic seaside retreats or working houses in the form of *villae rusticae*.[138] The remains of the complex at Pachyammos may indicate the location of an agricultural residence, but the exposed rooms thus far suggest storage and industrial functions and show little evidence for habitation.[139]

Most of the urban houses in Crete are of the circulatory form, such as the peristyle type typical of the eastern provinces, like the Villa Dionysus in Knossos and House 1 in Eleutherna, or the atrium type of the House of Dionysus in Chania.[140] Markoulaki argued that the destroyed Iraklion house was of a peristyle or atrium type and that the main rooms with the mosaics were orientated around the best available views (both internally and externally).[141] The application of the *fauces-atrium-tablinum* arrangement indicates the location of the *oecus* or *tablinum* in the house, and the mosaics help to define the functions of other rooms as will be discussed.[142] The current extent of the Villa Dionysus at Knossos does not allow a reconstruction of the same kind of *fauces-atrium-tablinum* axis, but the possibility cannot be ruled out (Fig. 18).

The earlier form of the inclusion of the *impluvium* is also found on Crete and is particularly common in the southern part of the island in the first and very early second centuries. The Makrigialos house is a good example where its early date, Western-style mosaics and architecture point to its having been constructed either by early Italian settlers or by persons who had significant contact with Italy.[143] The Kisamos house in which the Mosaic of the Tritons was found had an *impluvium* (Mosaic S213). However, this is likely to be an example of retrospective architectural style, since the house is dated to the third century and the use of *impluvium* was quite out of fashion at that point.[144] Altamore suggested that the Papadakis Plot building in Chersonisos (Mosaic 39) had an *impluvium*.[145] The function of the Papadakis Plot building is unclear because of the nature of the rescue excavation, and it has been variously suggested as a bath house, a basilica or a house.[146] If the Chersonisos example really does contain an *impluvium*, given the late date of the fourth century this may also be an example of retrospective fashion.

Cretan mosaics have been found in *triclinia*, *cubicula* and *oecii*; around an *impluvium*; and in other unidentified rooms.[147] A good example of the multi-functionality of Roman space is with the *oecus* or *tablinum*, which could be business rooms as well as entertainment rooms.[148] Although it is not always

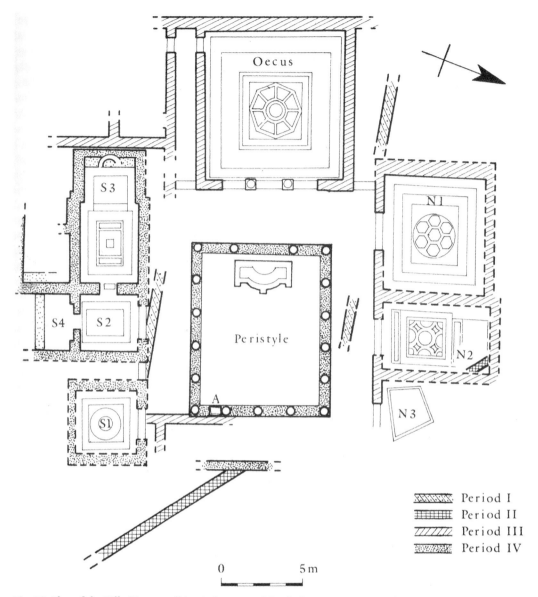

Fig. 18 Plan of the Villa Dionysus (Mosaic 1 = *oecus*; Mosaic 2 = Room N1; Mosaic 3 = Room N2; Mosaic 4 = Room N3; Mosaic 5 = Room S1; Mosaic 6 = Room S2; Mosaic 7 = Room S4; Mosaic 8 = Room S3) (courtesy of S. Paton).

possible to define the function of space and motifs, there are instances where the weight of evidence indicates a high probability for identifying a function or a range of functions.[149]

The Villa Dionysus, Knossos, is one of the key buildings in Crete in which analysis of the mosaics can shed light on the function of space (Fig. 18).[150] While the location of the original entranceway is not clear, the rooms surrounding the peristyle are likely to have been the ones most visible to the visitor, and it is these rooms therefore that the patron would have been able to most efficiently use to articulate the view of his status he wanted to promote. On entering the peristyle, the first room on the left (Room S1) would have set the tone for the visit. The theme of Medusa and the Seasons (Mosaic 5), particularly the Seasons as a symbol of bounty, would have given a welcoming aura, with Medusa's being an apotropaic symbol. Few of the remaining rooms of the south wing would have been visible from the peristyle and so would have provided only limited distraction for one of the key destinations, the *oecus*. The shape and design of Mosaic 8 (Room S3) clearly indicates the use of this room as a *cubiculum*. It was not as accessible as were the other *cubicula* on the north wing as one would have to pass through two doorways to get to this room from the peristyle, indicating its resident rather than visitor use. It may be that it was used as a reception room for preferred visitors.[151] The lavish geometric decoration and the central panel of the bird on the bowl provide little evidence to further elucidate the room's use (Mosaic 8). The location of the *oecus* and its double-columned entranceway clearly denote this as one of the most accessible rooms to visitors and more than likely the room where the patron would see his clients. The mosaic of the rather regal Dionysus (Mosaic 1) orientated to be seen from outside the room is fitting for a patron who may want to have a noble yet bountiful impression projected onto him. The Dionysiac-themed mosaic (2) in Room N1, directly accessible from the peristyle, clearly belonged in a dining room. Even without an obvious *triclinium* shape, the room's filler decoration of food, such as fish on a platter, partridge and so on, and the Dionysiac and entertainment themes (the ring-necked parquets) are typical dining-room décor.[152] The number of wide borders allowing space for couches and the orientation of the subsidiary designs facilitated for multiple viewpoints make this an ideal dining-room mosaic. Room N2 is likely to have been another *cubiculum* as is clear from the shape of the mosaic with the large geometric mat panel (Mosaic 3). The welcoming images of birds and plants as Seasons and the direct access from the peristyle indicate that this bedroom may have been for visitor use. For all of these rooms on the west and north, frameworks and subsidiary panels enable multiple perspectives that allow views from the peristyle, as well as encourage circulation around the individual rooms when permitted.[153]

Different levels of access for a variety of visitors would in itself have been an impressive feature and a signal of the power of the patron. With the Villa Dionysus it is possible to identify the interface between the visitor, or different levels of visitors, and the residents. This feature is exemplified by the contrast in accessibility to the two known *cubicula* in the house. Most visitors would have been able to circulate around the peristyle, thereby viewing the welcoming Medusa and Seasons mosaic as they entered and moved by the south wing. The lack of visibility of the remaining rooms along the south range suggests that these may be the rooms of either the family or close visitors, indicating a boundary between the more private and the public space. This unapproach-ability would have signalled exclusivity and perhaps may have motivated visi-tors who wanted to become part of the inner circle of friends. Neither Room S3 nor S4 was accessible from the main courtyard; entry to these rooms was via Room S2 (Fig. 18). This layout makes Rooms S3 and S4 the most private around the peristyle. As Room S2 mediated access to S3 and S4 it was quite public (it contained a mosaic of intersecting circles) (Pl. 6). Room S4 had a rough white tessellated floor, and two strong-boxes were discovered in it. A suite of private rooms would have been located behind the south wing of the house, which was accessible by a small corridor to the south of the *oecus*.[154] With its monumental wide doorway, the *oecus*, the focus of a visit, would have been open to all lev-els of visitor, from clients to friends. And although not quite as open from the peristyle, the visibility of Room N1 *triclinium* would have impressed all visitors to the house, but perhaps only a close selection was allowed to actually enter the room. The orientation of the mosaics (discussed in Chapter 3) and the range of accessibility of the rooms give a good indication of the multi-functionality of the Villa Dionysus and the complexity of the impression that the patron wished to make on a range of visitors.

Although the precise loci of associated finds in many of the domestic sites in Crete are difficult to reconstruct, a few observations and conjectures may be made. As with the Villa Dionysus, in all cases the rooms identified in the bal-ance of this section may well have been multi-functional. Domestic sites where more than a single room with mosaics has been excavated are the Iraklion town house (Mosaics 32–7); the House of Dionysus in Chania (Mosaics 135–6); and from Kisamos, the House with the Two-Panelled mosaic (Mosaics 139–40), the Paterakis Plot (Mosaic 141) and the Health Centre Plot (Mosaic S207). For the Iraklion house, Markoulaki has postulated a similar layout to the Villa Dionysus at Knossos where a north and south wing can be identified on either side of an *oecus* (containing Mosaic 1) in the west.[155] Iraklion 5 (Mosaic 36) contains an off-centre doormat panel which may indicate a *triclinium* (Pl. 14). Little in the mosaic décor refutes or supports this. Extensive re-modelling and later build-ings have meant that very little of the Iraklion mosaics' associated architecture has survived. Furthermore, the geometric designs and plain rectangular shapes of the mosaics make it difficult to use them to define the space any further. Similarly, little information regarding the function of the three rooms of the Makrigialos house is decipherable from the mosaics (77–9), although one of the rooms (H1) may lead directly off a large reception room (D1), suggesting the pos-sibility that it was more a visitor than a family space.[156] The shape and theme of the *triclinium* of the house of Dionysus mosaic (136), the Paterakis Plot mosaic (141) and the Two-Panelled mosaic (139) point to three second-century exam-ples of houses with T-shaped *triclinia* and mosaics appropriately themed with *xenia*, hunt and Seasons scenes.[157] Markoulaki also noted that the north–south orientation of the *triclinium*, which contains the Seasons mosaic (Mosaic 141) in Kisamos, is such that it allows good sea views, and that the mosaics are orientated to be best seen from the south, although the room entrance seems to be from the north (Pl. 44).[158] This layout emphasizes the importance of the views for the diners within the room, rather than the impact of the mosaic on a person entering the room (similar to the Poseidon and Amymone (Mosaic 129)). Another mosaic (135) from the House of Dionysus may have belonged in an *oecus* or another *triclinium*, or both, but certainly in a room that was intended to be seen by many visitors. The orientation of the subsidiary panels would have allowed multiple views, suggesting circulation as well as dining. The plan of the Health Centre Plot buildings is particularly informative, with evidence for the later Roman preference for the apsed *triclinium*.[159] A second *triclinium* in the same Kastelli house as Mosaic 139 may be identified on the surviving shape of the mosaic (140). Here, the extra border of individual chevrons may indicate space for couches. The mosaic of Poseidon and Amymone (Mosaic 129) (Pl. 39) would have come from either a *cubiculum* or a small dining room, with the offset door panel's allowing for an odd number of couches suggesting the latter possibility.[160] Furthermore, the orientation of the scene suggests a very private use since the panels were all orientated towards people in the room rather than towards people who may be on the outside looking in. Even if it is difficult to establish the function of the Perakis Plot building in Chersonisos (Mosaic 39), it is possible that it may also be a large-apsed *triclinium* (Fig. 19).

The only Fountain mosaic (38) in Crete is that from Chersonisos, and it depicts an appropriate aquatic theme of fishing (Pl. 15). Given the amount of glass tesserae, the fountain is more than likely to have been ornamental and whether it belonged in a domestic or a civic context is difficult to ascertain.[161]

5.5.2 Non-domestic Space

Mosaics were a practical floor type for the watery functions of baths. Nielsen notes that marble was the decoration of choice for the more lavish baths from the first century, where mosaics and wall paintings were the everyday option.[162] Mosaics variously covered the floors, the walls and sometimes the vaults, and were often repaired a number of times.[163] Commonly, mosaics in bath houses had marine-themed iconography, such as tritons, Poseidon or the marine thiasos.[164] The marine thiasos was the most common; images of bath-related activities, such as scenes from the gymnasium, or even of baths themselves were less frequent.[165] Instructions in a mosaic inscription are often presented as symbols or possibly as a greeting or a warning.[166] Images of sandals or footwear are found in a number of baths, often at the doorway, as an indication that bathers should remove their outer footwear (e.g., at Kerkounae).[167] Mosaic 133, Chania, depicts a pair of sandals incorporating a greeting, ΛΑ, either as a welcoming sign (Λοῦσαι

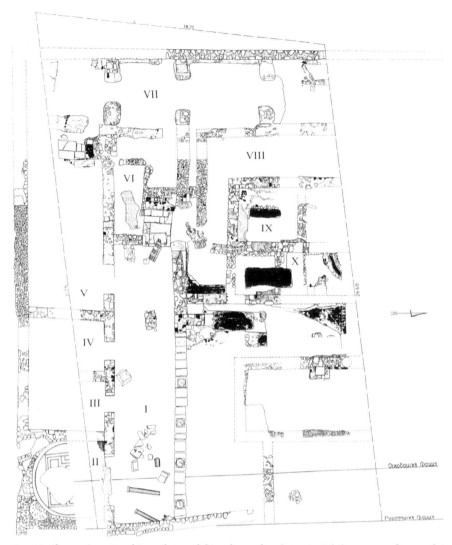

Fig. 19 Chersonisos, Perakis and Papadakis Plots, plan (Mosaic 39) (courtesy of D. Hadzi Vallianou).

Ἀσφαλῶς) or as a reminder to wear sandals.[168] Both possibilities are supported by the location of the sandals at the entrance to Room 2 of the bath suite and the position of the inscription on the sandal straps. Farrington suggests that there were 'Romanizing baths' in the first century B.C.E. in Greece, and while I would dispute that such buildings were intended to play that role, he does point out that the type of bath-only complex found in Roman Greece was less common than the combination of palestra and baths found in other areas.[169] The connection between athletes and bathing is seen in Mosaic 12 (Pl. 10),[170] and the room in which the Athlete mosaic was found may have been the *apodyterium* of the building. Its small size makes it more likely to have been a private bath house, and the use of the less common figured theme, potentially a more personal depiction, gives weight to this theory.[171] A second example may be the Vizari mosaic (Mosaic 70), which contains images of helmets and greaves (Pl. 21).

The majority of Cretan bath-house mosaics are geometric, such as those from Makrigialos (Mosaic 80) and Kouphonisi (Mosaic 83). New examples have been found in Neos Kournas (Kavros) (Mosaic 72) and in a well-preserved complex geometric one in Lappa (Mosaic 73). Several excavated bath houses do not contain mosaics at all. The iconography of the Apollinaris mosaic (9) suggests that the building in which it was found was actually a bath house. Rooms in bath houses commonly follow a standard range, but where the architecture may not be so obvious or where only one or two rooms remain, it is possible to postulate the function of the room from the mosaics on a general level. For example, some bath houses may provide the more impressive mosaics at the entranceway or in the *apodyterium*, whereas others may be found in areas where people tend to linger more, such as the *tepidarium*. The Kladeos baths at Olympia have a range of mosaics found in different parts and show that areas such as the *tepidarium* and the circulating room contain complex geometric mosaics, whereas the atrium and the *apodyterium* are covered with *opus sectile*.[172] In Cretan examples, the Gymnasium baths in Sector C at Gortyn have mosaics of black-and-white geometric decoration, with the more complex example found in the *apodyterium* (Mosaic 57) and the plain example found in the area of the latrines (Mosaic 58). Geometric mosaics have been found in the entrance halls of bath houses in Chersonisos (Mosaic 41) and Kato Asites (Mosaic 51), but in both cases only limited amounts of the mosaics survive. The geometric mosaic from Myrtos (Mosaic 84) is in the *tepidarium*; the Triton mosaic, Chania (Mosaic 132), is in the hypocaust room; and the Scroll Panel mosaic, Chania (Mosaic 134), is from a corridor. In each of these three examples, the function of the room has been determined by the excavator on the basis of the architecture.

Other than those in religious contexts, the only certain non-domestic Roman mosaics are found in the Odeion at Gortyn (Mosaics 54–5).[173] Entertainment space was used not simply to embellish a city and benefit the occupants but also to draw people into specific parts of the city, and mosaics would have helped in this as a visual lure.[174] Figured scenes of myths and other narratives would not necessarily have been appropriate for the space, with the Odeion mosaic in Argos – a mosaic of context-specific scenes concerning prize giving – as an example.[175] Mosaics in odeia are therefore more commonly found in corridors, atria and smaller rooms. As such, the Gortyn complex geometric mosaics are typical of those found in Greek odeia. Unlike in other areas of Greece, in Crete no Roman mosaics have been found as yet in areas such as stoas or in commercial spaces or theatres.[176]

5.5.3 Religious Space

There are two examples of Roman mosaic in Cretan temples. At Lebena, the fragmentary black-and-white mosaic covered the *cella* floor but only small sections of geometric décor remain (Mosaic 67),[177] and in Lissos, the mosaic (137) covers the small *cella* floor.[178] The temple was dedicated to Asclepius, and three surviving polychrome images of the cock, the goose and the pig as offerings appropriate to Asclepius (in particular, the cock, which was sacred to Apollo, Leto and Asclepius) can be identified.[179] The figured décor is orientated to be seen not from the temple entrance, but from the statue base, possibly indicating the role of the décor as an offering to the god. The occurrence of mosaics in temples is not particularly common either for the Roman or the Hellenistic period.[180] On mainland Greece, the Temple of Zeus at Olympia and the Temple of Despoina at Lycosura both have mosaics.[181]

5.5.4 Christian Churches

Little is currently known about the nature of the liturgy and the function of space within the church, so mosaics and architecture are essential to proposing hypotheses on the use of religious space. In turn, the role of the church (in terms of its use by the community and also its functions within the community) contributes to evidence of Crete's Late Antique community. This is crucial because the domestic evidence is limited to a small number of houses in Gortyn and Chersonisos, and to some survey results indicating the existence of other houses scattered in Lasithi and the Mesara.[182]

Church location has been discussed in Chapter 4, and to understand the role and functioning of the building it is also beneficial to examine the variety of architectural forms that the churches with mosaics take. Clark has detailed three types of experiences that can occur in a church as a result of different types of architecture: spaciousness may help the participant think about the wider context of involvement, openness encourages a desire to seek shelter, and complexity leads to the sensation of being excited by the unexpected.[183] The most common architectural form is the standard triple-aisle type with a single central apse at the east and the narthex acting as the main entrance point in the west. The basilicas at Olus, Knossos Sanatorium, Eleutherna, Kera, Agios Niketas and Suia A are typical. Variations on the standard type are seen throughout Crete through the presence and locations of annexes; the existence of a *tribelon* or atrium, of high or low stylobates, of relics, foundation offerings or martyria; the location of the ambo (pulpit); and the presence of baptisteries. Chersonisos A and Chersonisos B are variations with the addition of the exo-narthexes, an additional north aisle in Chersonisos B and the atrium on Chersonisos A. Another type found in both Crete and Epirus, but not as commonly as elsewhere in Greece, is the triple-aisled, tripartite transept church.[184] The churches at Kolokythia, Panormos and Almyrida are good examples where the sanctuary space, the diakonikon and the prothesis project outwards past the width of the north and south aisles.[185] The KMF Basilica, with its trefoil sanctuary, is arguably a transitional type of church with martyrium functions.[186] The triconch building at Mitropolis is likely to have been a martyrium rather than a church for regular practice. The surviving central domed remains of the Episkopi Basilica largely date to the tenth century: however, Sanders argues that the original design may have been of a round building and certainly the remains of the mosaic would support this.[187] Often the remains of a baptistery indicate another key function of churches, and examples are found in Mallia, Lebena, Suia Basilica A and Loutro.[188] The presence of a synthronon (bishop's throne or seating space) may indicate a function as the episcopal church, for example, in Itanos Basilica A, Kera, Olus, Suia, Gortyn Basilica in Sector M and Panormos.[189] A new episcopal church has been recently identified at Ini.[190]

Chersonisos Basilica B, Almyrida and Gortyn Basilica in Sector M all have the combination of a *tribelon* and an ambo. The size of the nave, the complexity of the interrupted views and the location of the ambo in the centre of the space suggest that there was a strong focus on the processional elements of the liturgy, as these elements are all highly suitable for the function of these basilicas as the episcopal seats.[191] In all three cases, the mosaics occur exclusively in the nave and narthex where the focus of attention would have been. There would have been no need for mosaics in the aisles since that is where the congregation would have been standing. The presence of mosaics in the narthex would have established the lavish tone on entry to the church, and the monumental doorway between the narthex and nave indicates that the clergy would have processed from this point through the nave. A similar situation can be read in the Gortyn Sector M Basilica (Mosaic 109).

In other examples, a platform from the sanctuary would have extended into the nave. Examples include Suia, Eleutherna (Pl. 31), Olus, Vizari and, judging by the evidence of the mosaics, Chersonisos Basilica A. Here, the border scroll in the nave makes a return, marking the end of the nave in the east. In these instances, the lack of complex views and a *tribelon* suggest an absence of processional features.[192] Crucially, these churches are all shorter by some distance than the examples that indicate processional function. For example, from the narthex to nave, Gortyn Sector M Basilica is 63 m long and Chersonisos Basilica B is 60 m long, whereas Vizari is 30 m long and Suia Basilica A is 25 m long. The evidence of mosaics in the aisles and narthex of Knossos Sanatorium and Eleutherna raise engaging issues.[193] That they both have sanctuaries projecting into the nave suggests less of a focus on procession, a notion supported by the absence of mosaics in the nave too. Whereas other churches in Crete favour the less visually obstructive use of low stylobates and columns, both the Knossos Sanatorium and Eleutherna have high stylobates and low visibility between the aisles and nave. By its location, the sanctuary is still the focus, but the lack of direct views to the rites being undertaken in the sanctuary heightens the mystery of the liturgy.[194] This and the absence of mosaics may indicate a focus of much more secretive elements of the liturgy taking place in the nave.[195]

5.5.5 Late Antique Church Mosaics

Agios Titos was probably one of the principal churches of Crete and even if it was not paved with mosaic floors it is the most architecturally complex of the churches on Crete. This is a salient reminder that the presence or lack of mosaics in a church cannot be indicative of the wealth or status of the church and community.[196] Long-term use of the churches can also be seen by the construction of elements on top of mosaics (such as the tomb and ambo in Chersonisos Basilica A or the synthronon in Kolokythia), as well as by the patching of mosaics (such as in Chersonisos Basilica B) (Pl. 27).

The most common location for mosaics in Cretan churches is in the nave and the narthex. The exceptions to this are the Knossos Sanatorium Basilica and Eleutherna; in both cases the naves are paved with slabstones, which suggests a different use of space and liturgical practice from those of other Cretan churches. As noted in Chapter 3, the locations of specific images in the church indicate areas of sacred or more sacred space, for example, the placement of the peacock panel in the doorways into the naves of Almyrida (Mosaics 148–51) and Chersonisos (Mosaics 92–3) (Pls. 47 & 26). In Almyrida this change in space is further emphasized by the central panel of the eight-pointed star and the adjacent panels of dolphins and fish on either side of a kantharos in the narthex (Pl. 47). The eight-pointed star is also used in a similar fashion at the entrance to the nave in the Eleutherna church (Mosaic 111) (Pl. 32). Panels of vines and kantharoi are found in both the bema and nave of Suia Basilica A (Mosaics 156–8), but peacocks are included in the scene in the bema, defining it as being more sacred than the nave (Pl. 50).

Some church mosaics (particularly in the Levant) have been specifically laid to indicate the direction of movement throughout the church, often by using inhabited scrolls.[197] There would appear to be no such clear-cut examples of this in Crete. However, mosaics do point to areas of different levels of space according to their use by clergy, baptised or catechumens. The infrequent occurrence of mosaics in the bema is evidence of their function as inspiring elements for the congregation, rather than for the benefit of the clergy or God. Although catechumens may not have been permitted to enter the more sacred space of the nave and aisles, the mosaics visible there would have heightened the church's positive impression on them. In the Late Antique period, the locations of mosaics and donor panels indicate that visitors to the church were the primary concern in terms of viewing orientation. This fits well with the proposal that a key function of the church was to impress the population in its Christianization role.

5.6 CONCLUSION

In addition to the identification of individual rooms, some edifices are complex enough to allow one to test the hypothesis of use of space and to reconstruct how and why space was used overall. At all levels the value of architecture and mosaics for projecting an identity, individual or communal, is clear and can be seen particularly from the Villa Dionysus, Knossos, where the patron used the lavish rooms to highlight his high standing within the community.

Dunbabin suggested that there are no special rules about the distribution of mosaics within a house.[198] Furthermore, one cannot just examine the quality of the décor and make assumptions either about the room or about the wealth of the patron of the house.[199] Identifying the function of a room based on the evidence of decoration requires both objectivity and further supporting evidence.[200] There are many reasons why the identification of rooms cannot be grounded solely on a study of mosaics. The function of the room may change over time without any change in the mosaics the room contains. There are also more benign determinants, such as the limitations of the architect or the craftsperson carrying out the decorative work.[201] The role of the patron is also important, in the respect of how much say he had in choosing the designs. Dunbabin favours the idea of the patron's having the most influence in the choice of subjects portrayed on mosaics, naturally within the bounds of the mosaicist's capabilities.[202] In most cases, the choice of whether to lay a mosaic, as well as the mosaic's style, allows us insight into social interactions, such as those between a patron and visitors; social complexities, such as elite or non-elite status or baptised and catechumens; and subconscious social etiquette, such as access options in houses or in churches. More mundane evidence is forthcoming, including the cost of a donation and trends in fashion. In broader terms, the mosaics reveal multiple levels of the use of space and have enough variety to suggest that there was little repression or social control, certainly before the Late Antique period.[203] The analysis of the epigraphic and craftspeople evidence will broaden our understanding of Roman and Late Antique society in Crete.

SIX

MOSAICS OF CRETE

CRAFTSPEOPLE, TECHNOLOGY AND WORKSHOPS

6.1 INTRODUCTION

Given the time and expense involved in laying a mosaic, these floors in context are often seen as a means of accessing evidence about the upper echelons of Roman society. Moreover, a study of the mosaic itself – its materials, bedding, production technique, level of skill and choice of design – can give insight into the working practices of the craftspeople who made it, as well as into the role of the patron. Evidence for the workshop activity, extent of travel and communication links between craftspeople across the empire may be forthcoming. The inclusion of both Roman and Late Antique mosaics in this study means that it is possible to see whether materials and procedures change over time and whether they vary according to the different social contexts.

6.2 IDENTIFICATION OF CRAFTSPEOPLE

The identification of individual craftspeople through their methods, styles or even signatures is fundamental to the recognition of the broader organizational and communication links within Crete and the Roman Empire. Unlike artists such as painters, mosaicists are seldom identified in the sources. The most direct route to identifying individual craftspersons is through their signatures on pavements.[1] Because only a small number of mosaicists' signatures survive, it is necessary to identify craftspeople or the workshops of mosaicists through their work. A reasonable variety of inscriptions survive from the Cretan corpora, and before focusing on the evidence of the artists' work, the inscriptions can be examined to help identify craftspeople and to gain insight into the nature of the patrons or donors, particularly in the Late Antique period.[2]

6.2.1 Signature of Artist or Patron

The catalogue of Cretan inscriptions is compiled in Appendix 2, and those inscriptions that label figures, convey messages or are apotropaic are discussed in Chapter 3. In this chapter, the signatures of the artists and donor inscriptions are discussed. It is not easy to establish whether the craftsperson or the patron decided the content of a mosaic. Only rarely is direct evidence forthcoming, such as happened with Fayum Papyrus, which reveals the extent of the patron's input through his detailed instructions, down to the dimensions of the borders, for the mosaics to be laid in his bath houses.[3] Not all patrons may have had such input, but it gives an indication of the range possible in terms of choice.[4] A number of different formulae indicate the signature of the artist or patron on a mosaic. These include the verbs ἐποίει (made this) or ἐψηφοθέτησα (placed the tesserae),[5] or other terms, such as ψηφιῶται (person who worked the mosaic), κυβευταί (person who made the cubes), or τεχνῖται (craftsperson). In Latin, signatures may include the words *musearius*, probably referring specifically to a worker on wall mosaics, or *tesserarius*, a worker on tessellated floors.[6] Different terms may refer to aspects of laying a pavement, but it is not always certain which term applies to which task. Dunbabin adduces some informative examples such as that of the Uzitta mosaic where the craftsperson has specified through the phrase '*abumbr(avit) et alb(icavit)*' that he did the work of filling in the black-and-white parts.[7] Another example is that of the difference between the designer (*pictor*) and the person who did the setting (indicated through the use of the verbs *tessellarius* or *pavimentarius*), with the implication that the *pictor* was the more skilled of the two.[8] During the Imperial period, the meaning of ἐποίει changed from indicating only the artist (as it had in the Classical period) to indicating either the artist or the patron, and in the late fourth century ἐποίει came to mean the patron only.[9] In some cases just a name appears, as on a mosaic from Argos, where 'Nikoletesis' is found without the verb.[10] This name could refer to the patron, but as it is a single name, it is commonly assumed to be that of the mosaicist. Some secure examples of the patron's name are found, such as on a mosaic from Pissonas which records that Nikephoros in fulfilment of a vow decorated the exedra with mosaic.[11] Donors' names are more commonly found on mosaics in the Late Antique period, particularly in church contexts. The patron is most easily identified in an inscription if he is named as making a donation, identified by the verb ἔδωκεν (donated or gave). In the Late Antique period, donor panels commonly provide more information about what exactly was paid for and whether the donor chose the design; salient details of the life of the donor are also sometimes provided.[12]

6.2.2 Origins and Organization

Names on mainland Greek mosaics are commonly written in Latin, whereas in Crete they are all written in Greek.[13] From the three signatures found on Crete, it seems that the craftspeople were Greek speakers, and it is unlikely, given that only single names are provided, that they were of elite status.[14] The signatures appear on the Apollinaris mosaic (Inscription 1) (Pl. 9), the *triclinium* of the House of Dionysus mosaic (Inscription 5) (Pl. 43) and the Wedding of Dionysus mosaic (S207f).[15] The last of these has not yet been published in detail, and the *triclinium* of the House of Dionysus inscription is damaged, which has given rise to a debate about the meaning of the inscription. In the case of Inscription 1, the signature is within the central hexagon containing the main polychrome figured panel (Pl. 9). The example is straightforward: (Ἀπολλινάρις ἐποίει) the imperfect tense of the verb 'to make' and the name Apollinaris. The use of the single name means that it likely refers to the mosaicist, who was probably not a Roman citizen.[16] The name Apollinaris does not occur on any other mosaic inscription, nor is it found in any other context in Crete. It is not common in Greece but appears at least four times in areas such as Athens and Thasos; its occurrence in the late first or early second century in Crete is one of the earliest examples in Greece.[17] The name arises more frequently in Campanian inscriptions, with at least 11 examples recorded from this area.[18] This may give weight to the suggestion that many of the settlers in the *colonia* of Knossos were originally Campanian (see Chapter 5).[19] Kankeleit argues that an Italian craftsperson was responsible for the Apollinaris mosaic on the basis of the inscription and 'style' of the mosaic.[20] Donderer proposes that Apollinaris is a Latin name that has been Hellenized and therefore suggests that the mosaicist may have been an Italian immigrant.[21] This would be in keeping with the black-and-white style of the mosaic and the possibility that there had been a new group of Italian settlers in the north of the city.[22]

Mosaic S207f contains the inscription ΜΕΡΟΠΑΣ ΕΨΗΦΟΘΕΤΗΣΑ (Μέροπας ἐψηφοθέτησα) (I, Meropas, placed the tesserae) within the central Dionysiac panel over the heads of the figures. Because of the use of the aorist here, it is possible that in this case Meropas is the patron and not the artist. There are no references to this name in the masculine form in the *Lexicon of Greek Personal Names* although the feminine form, ΜΕΡΟΠΗ, is occasionally found.[23]

The signature in Inscription 5 is in a thin black border surrounding the main figured panel (Pl. 43). The inscription reads [– -]ΔΑΦΝΗΝ ΕΠΟΙΕΙ (Δάφνην ἐποίει) (from Daphne made it), and it is damaged on both sides, particularly on the left. The small amount of letter preserved before the Δ has led some to suggest a sigma before the ΔΑΦΝΗΝ, which would support the possibility that there was a πρὸς before the ΔΑΦΝΗΝ (Pl. 43).[24] Given the form of the noun it is unlikely that the ΔΑΦΝΗΝ refers to the name of the artist, and Donderer suggests that ΔΑΦΝΗΝ refers to the region of Daphne (near Antioch) and that the full inscription would read that *person from Daphne made it*.[25] The accusative of the ΔΑΦΝΗΝ would be explained as a qualifier of the ethnikon of Antioch, and as such Donderer suggests that the following should be restored: [Ἀντιοχεὺς τὸν πρὸς] Δάφνην ἐποίει᾽ (… from Daphne in Antioch made it). Earlier examples of this formula from Olympia and Delphi support Donderer's interpretation.[26] Kankeleit maintains that the inscription refers exactly to the place where the artist came from without further details being necessary, as Donderer and Markoulaki suggest.[27] Kankeleit also argues that similarities in the border style and floral decoration with mosaics from Antioch support the possibility that the mosaicist was from Daphne.[28] This view is quite subjective, and it is arguable that the style of the mosaic itself is closer to a mainland Greek or even a Cretan genre. Crucially, if the artist was from Daphne, he chose to advertise his name on a work found in Crete despite having come from a tradition of artists' not signing their work.[29] This may indicate an attempt to fit in with a local tradition of signing work rather than adhere to the artist's own which favoured the labelling of figures but not the signing of mosaics. Although it is now generally accepted that the artist for this mosaic came from Daphne in Antioch, other interpretations cannot be entirely ruled out, such as a misspelling or a reference to an element within the mosaic.

Caution must be taken when attributing the creation of an entire mosaic to one craftsperson. Examples of mosaics outside Crete demonstrate that several craftspeople may have worked on a single mosaic, and in some mosaics it is possible to read evidence of both a master craftsperson and an apprentice.[30] The difference in money earned by the *musearius* and the *tessellarius* is distinct in Diocletian's late third-century price edict, although how their tasks differed is unknown.[31] An example from Thebes, discussed later, records two craftspeople as having two different jobs, one as the designer and the other as the mosaicist.[32] Through inscriptions, evidence for the product of an established mosaic workshop may be given with the words *ex officina* (from the workshop of). Examples can be seen on a mosaic from Tossa near Gerona, which bears the inscription '*ex officina* Felicis', and one from Thuburbo in Tunisia, which gives '*ex officina* Nicenti', but there are not yet any examples from Crete.[33] Signatures without *ex officina* (such as Ἀπολλινάρις ἐποίει) do not exclusively indicate the work of an itinerant craftsperson, but could just as easily denote a workshop.

6.2.3 Late Antique Inscriptions: Donors, Patrons, Clergy

Three Christian basilicas contain mosaic inscriptions: Olus (Mosaic 126) (Inscriptions 7i, 7ii & 8) (Pl. 38); Gortyn Sector M (Mosaic 109) (Inscriptions 9 & 10) (Pls. 29 & 30); and Eleutherna (Mosaic 111) (Inscription 11) (Pl. 33).

Of the two inscriptions from the Olus basilica, the first (Inscriptions 7i & 7ii) occurs in the nave in a circular panel (Pl. 37)[34] that has lines of tesserae running across as guidelines for where the letters should be written. The panel is divided into two: on one side is a commemoration to one individual, and on the other side is a commemoration to another person. The second Olus inscription (Inscription 8) is also found in the nave and is laid quite clumsily above one of the dolphin panels. Both inscribed panels are orientated to be visible from the narthex and read as one enters the nave; the first to be seen would be the inscription above the dolphin panel.

Inscription 7i. Olus

In the Olus panels, semis (semissis) is a monetary unit which is half an as (one-fortieth the value of gold). The question of whether Θεόδουλος refers to a name, Theodoulos, or as 'servant of the Lord' has been discussed (*IC*.1 65), and Bandy, Fraser and Matthews all suggest that it is a proper name.[35] The wording implies that Theodoulos is paying for the work, and Epiphanes may be the mosaicist, as suggested by Bandy.[36] According to Bandy, the name Ἐπιφάνις occurs frequently in Christian Greek inscriptions, and the absence of the omikron of Ἐπιφάνιος is seen often in Cretan inscriptions.[37] A close parallel is found on an inscription from the Christian basilica on Ploutarchou in Thebes, which records the name of the two artists on the mosaic: Demetrius, who credits himself as the designer, and Epiphanes, who is credited as being the mosaicist (Δημήτριος Ἐπιφάνης τε τὸ μουσῖον ποεῖ / Δημήτριος μὲν ἐννοήσας τὴν γραφὴν ταύτης δ' ὑπουργὸς Ἐπιφάνης εὐνούστατ(ος) / Παῦλος δὲ πάντων αἴτιος τῶν εὐπρεπ(ῶν) / ἱερεύς τε καὶ θείων λόγων διδάσκαλ(ος)).[38]

Inscription 7ii. Olus

The second half of the Olus inscription reads: 'Antaxios for his own salvation and of all his own household gave one semis'. The name Antaxios is found in Athens.[39]

Inscription 8. Olus

The second Olus inscription is also straightforward. It translates as 'Heliodoros for his own salvation gave one semis'. Bandy notes that the name Heliodorus was also a common one in Latin inscriptions.[40]

Inscriptions 9 and 10. Gortyn Sector M

Both Inscriptions 9 and 10 are donor panels found in the mosaic on the south side of the solea in the nave of the Gortyn Sector M church, orientated and visible from the narthex, with the smaller panel found closest to the narthex. It is possible that there were equivalent panels on the north side of the solea, though the mosaic is too damaged to ascertain this. The larger of the two is significantly better preserved than the more westerly one and can be read with confidence.[41] Inscription 9 (Pl. 29) records that the mosaic was restored (or made new) in the reign of Bishop Vetranios, who is not found in the Gortyn catalogue of bishops.[42] Farioli Campanati argues that this is the same bishop whose monograms appear on the capitals at Agios Titos,[43] and the suggested date for this is 553–97.[44] Inscription 10 (Pl. 30) is poorly preserved,[45] but based on the formula in Inscription 9, the excavators suggest the following reconstruction:

Ἐπὶ Θ[εοδώρου τοῦ ἀγιωτά]του [καὶ μακαριωτάτου ἡμῶν ἀρχι]επι[σκόπου – -](In the reign of Theodoros, our most holy and most blessed archbishop)

This would be a convenient fit, particularly if the reconstruction of the name of the bishop is correct as Archbishop Theodoros of Gortyn is recorded as having participated in the Council of Constantinople in 536 and 553.[46] When this donor panel was lifted, a tomb of Imperial date was revealed below the bedding. The number of tombs across the site indicates that this is more likely a coincidence rather than a deliberate demarcation of one of the tombs.[47] The visible repair in the mosaic indicates either that the basilica was in use over a long time and retained its importance or that the mosaic sustained some damage and was quickly repaired. Given the similarities in the style of the new panel and the rest of the mosaic it may be that the latter scenario is more likely. If the interpretations of the inscriptions are correct, it is possible that there was a significant event that warranted the repair of the mosaics in the sixth century (or perhaps two events in quick succession). If Farioli Campanati's suggestion that the same Bishop Vetranios is responsible for both the Agios Titos capitals and the repair or laying of Mosaic 109, then he may have been present between the years 553 and 597. As Bishop Theodoros attended the ecumenical councils in 536 and 553, the year in common between the two bishops is 553. There are copious problems in ascribing earthquake damage to 'known' earthquakes in antiquity; however, in this case it may be too much to dismiss the evidence of the recorded earthquake in 552.[48] This is particularly emphasized through the wording of the inscription, which specifically indicates that the existing mosaic was restored. If the 552 earthquake caused damage to the basilica, then 553 may well be an appropriate year for the mosaics to have been repaired.

Inscriptions 11 and 12. Eleutherna

There were originally two inscriptions in the narthex mosaic from Eleutherna.[49] The first, discussed in Chapter 3, is situated near the north entrance and although damaged it is possible to see that it provided a reminder to the visitor of the sanctity of the space. The second inscription in the narthex mosaic is just to the south of the entrance to the central aisle (Pl. 33). It is orientated to be seen by those entering the church from the north doorway in the narthex. It reveals the name of the founder, the first bishop of Eleutherna, Euphratas, and also that the church is dedicated to the archangel Michael. It is recorded in Hierokles's *Synekdemos* that the first bishop of Eleutherna attended the Fourth Ecumenical Council in Chalcedon in 451.[50] This indicates a foundation date in and around 451 for the church.

6.2.4 Chronology of Late Antique Cretan Mosaic Inscriptions

Where donor panels are present in the nave (such as in Olus and Gortyn) they are orientated to be seen on entry to the nave as one looks towards the bema. The majority of the inscriptions found in church mosaics of the Late Antique period are quite formulaic in that they mostly record the name of the patron who paid for the work, and this is the case for all the Cretan mosaics except Inscription 12. Although the Cretan donor panels are informative, there are examples from other areas that provide even more information. Dunbabin notes the Nikopolis Basilica A example where the donor is named as 'archpriest Dometios', and a description of the mosaic scene is also provided so that the full meaning is not lost.[51]

Lettering style can provide chronologies but is by no means a secure way of dating inscriptions, as frequently letterforms from early periods continue to be used much later.[52] Furthermore, the material used would often have dictated the type of lettering chosen to inscribe the mosaic. The substance of the inscription is more likely to provide reasonable dating evidence, as is certainly the case with Eleutherna (Mosaic 111), and possibly with Gortyn Sector M (Mosaic 109). Bandy also stresses the role of the artist's whim and of how much the artist may have decorated the letterforms to embellish the work. In some cases it may be possible to use such personal traits as workshop evidence, but the differences in the Cretan letterforms do not indicate that any of the mosaic inscriptions shared craftspeople. Even in Mosaic 109, the few letterforms in common between the two inscriptions (such as the E, C, and Π) are different enough to denote the work of different craftspeople. Although there may be similarities in a few of the letters, such as the use of the X without serifs in Olus and Eleutherna (Pls. 38 & 33), there is enough variation, such as the squared C (sigma) in Eleutherna but the rounded one in Olus, to nullify any suggestion of common craftspeople.

Despite the rather small number, the inscriptions on Cretan mosaics represent a wide range of types and functions, and in many cases provide evidence for chronology, patrons and craftspeople. For example, the inscription on Mosaic 136 raises some pertinent questions, such as the possibility that a craftsperson from Syria would work on Cretan mosaics (as the inscription suggestions) and adapt to local fashion (in the fact that there is an inscription). With the exception of the named bishops, the names of the other patrons and craftspeople in the Cretan repertoire do not reveal their owners' origins or statuses, although Roman citizen names do not occur frequently on mosaics.

While the Cretan mosaic inscriptions provide some good insights on society during the Roman period and Late Antiquity, they belong to a fairly standard repertoire. The Cretan evidence of the artists' signatures is paralleled in a Greek and even a Cypriot fashion, though not in other areas of the East.[53] The Eastern partiality for labelling personalities or for personification is not so common in Crete or Greece. In the West, labels and signed mosaics are widespread, but the particular combination in Crete and Greece is indicative of its own preferences. To provide more detail on craftspeople and society it is necessary to turn to the evidence of the iconography and technology of the mosaics.

6.3 CRAFTSPEOPLE: TECHNIQUES, ICONOGRAPHY AND COMMUNICATION

6.3.1 Analysis

At each point in the production of a mosaic floor, either the craftsperson or the patron (or both) had to make decisions. The results of these decisions provide the material for the study of choice, which in turn allows access to the people behind the results. The preferences for geometric or figured decoration, schemes and combinations, in addition to the technology of the mosaic in terms of colours, dimensions, material, bedding and form, are diverse throughout both Crete and the empire. In recent years, scientific analysis on the technology and methods of laying mosaics and their beddings has been undertaken. This kind of work is not always possible on mosaics still *in situ*, although the scientific work of the Worcester Art Museum of Massachusetts on some of the Antioch pavements has been exemplary.[54] The staff re-examined the excavation notebooks to establish the methods of laying the tesserae in the bedding. Furthermore, some of the mosaics revealed the presence of a small break between the figured panel and the geometric, indicating that distinct elements were laid at different times and the figured section probably after the geometric. In the Judgement of Paris mosaic, the differences in the thickness of the bedding indicated that only small areas of tesserae were laid at a time. The authors note that the variation is less likely to indicate a pre-fabricated manufacture of the figured panel and more likely simply to show the order in which the mosaic was laid.[55] Studies on glass tesserae using spectrophotometry and ED-XRF and EPMA analyses, with an emphasis on the chemical composition of the glass, can provide information on the tesserae's source and colourants.[56] The Worcester museum's work on the glass tesserae, using scanning electron microscopy and X-ray spectrometry, focused on evidence for technology.[57] The museum's study of the stone tesserae focused on material source and dating, and a firm conclusion from this work was that stones from the same source were generally used throughout the creation of a pavement.[58] The only imported material identified was obsidian.[59] Isotope analysis indicated that the quarry would have been in use from about 125 to 540.[60] Ideally, such scientific studies should be carried out on at least a representative number of the Cretan mosaics, but as many of the mosaics have not been lifted, and those that have were lifted under rather intense rescue excavation conditions, the opportunity for such studies rarely arises. For the present, discussion of the materials used in Cretan mosaics is limited to those that can be identified in the field.[61]

6.3.2 Materials

The basic materials used in Roman and Late Antique Cretan mosaics consist of stones of white (marble), black (likely limestone) and red (limestone, igneous rock or, commonly, terracotta). Yellows are often used; they may be a yellow limestone or, more likely, a sandstone found in east Crete. Some metamorphic rocks are also found in east Crete, and the plain grey sometimes found as tesserae may be from this area. The limestone sources on the island are numerous, as are soft stones such as steatite and serpentinite, and some blue and green tesserae may have come from such rock.[62] Given the diversity of the geological makeup of the island a pressing need to import many of the necessary materials for tesserae was unlikely. Glass tesserae would have allowed for a greater diversity of colour, and a glass-making workshop has been excavated in Gortyn in the Byzantine quarter between the Temple of Apollo Pythios and the Gymnasium complex.[63] In the floor mosaics of Crete, glass tesserae are used sparingly, as is to be expected in part to avoid cutting people's feet and in part because of the expense, and normally just in areas of design detail such as hair or clothes (Mosaic 1). Glass tesserae are found only in wall mosaic remains of the KMF Basilica and not at all in Crete's Late Antique floor mosaics.[64] More marble is used in the Late Antique mosaics. Large quantities of marble would have been obtainable from Roman spolia. Furthermore, the marble imported to adorn the basilicas with columns and screens would have provided many more chips and fragments than were available before. Another difference between the Roman and the Late Antique floor mosaics is the more limited range of colours in the Late Antique period. Between three and five colours (black, white, red, yellow and grey/blue) are normal in Late Antique mosaics, whereas a significantly wider colour palette is seen in the polychrome Roman examples.[65] The size of tesserae also varies somewhat, for example, between geometric and figured décor, and between mosaics of different periods and areas. The tesserae in Roman mosaics are often smaller and sometimes more neatly cut than they are in Late Antique examples: con-trast, for example, the tesserae in Olus (Mosaic 126) and Kera (Mosaics 122–5), which average 32–5 tesserae per 10 x 10 cm area, with some Roman examples, such as the Lappa bath house (Mosaic 73) and Chersonisos Fountain (Mosaic 38), where the average is 38–42 tesserae per 10 x 10 cm area. This difference in size is in part because of the nature of the iconography: generally, the figured scenes of Roman mosaics require more detailed work and therefore smaller tesserae, but the swathes of geometric patterns in the Late Antique mosaics need less subtle toning. The same type of variation can be seen in a single mosaic; for example, in Suia Basilica A (Mosaics 156–8) the border panel and other geometric elem-ents have *c.* 35 tesserae per 10 x 10 cm area, whereas the figured panels contain 42 tesserae per 10 x 10 cm area. A similar difference is found in the Lissos mosaic (137), which is also remarkable for the tiny size of the tesserae: there are *c.* 80 tesserae per 20 x 20 cm area in the geometric panels, and the figured panels con-tain 154 tesserae per 20 x 20 cm area.

6.3.3 Techniques

Only in a small number of cases has it been possible to study the bedding of the Cretan mosaics. At Myrtos, because the mosaic had more or less vanished owing to severe erosion, the bedding was visible, consisting of a 4-cm thick mix of clay and pinkish mortar on a 7-cm thick bed of cobbles. The same bedding was found in the mosaics at Makrigialos in areas that were exposed because of damage. It is reported that the bedding of the mosaics from the upper storeys of the House of Pheidias at the Health Centre excavations in Kisamos consisted of large pebbles (cobbles?) and mortar with a 1 cm band of lime. Below this was a mixture of plaster and sherds.[66] From the same house, the bedding of Mosaic S207e was examined. It consisted of several layers of loose shingle and a mortar base.[67] The variety in bedding types must reflect trends, available materials and the craftspersons' prerogatives. That the Myrtos and Makrigialos beddings are so similar likely shows the proximity of the sites and their comparable chronol-ogies. In terms of the techniques for laying the floor, there is little clear evidence for either guidelines or inserted panels in the Cretan repertoire, and during the Villa Dionysus conservation project these were specifically elements of evidence that were sought.[68]

In a recent survey of the Cretan mosaics, those at Frangokastelli (Mosaics 143–6) were the only examples that contained definite evidence for multiple hands in a single context (Pls. 45–6).[69] The exo-narthex mosaic uses the same materials, but is of a poorer quality design and manufacture than the rest of the mosaics. Whether this was contemporary with the other mosaics or a later addi-tion, the same craftsperson could not have been responsible for all. Although unusual in their iconography, with a unique range of decorative elements, the surviving mosaics in the narthex, nave and north aisle are neat and confident. In contrast, the mosaic of the exo-narthex does not fit the space provided, there is patching in one area (Pl. 46), the shield of scales is a mess, and the floral panel around the looped diamond in the north has been badly executed (Pl. 46). There are elements of design in the exo-narthex that are similar to those in the nave, which suggests that at some point the same group of craftspeople were working on both areas, and it may be that some of the patching was a later addition. It also appears that there may have been an apprentice at work at some point as the filler décor around the looped diamond in the exo-narthex exhibits a range of errors that are not seen around the looped diamond in the nave (Pl. 45). Furthermore, it may be that the north aisle mosaic was laid at a different time, or by a different set of craftspeople, as the only common element between the north aisle mosaic and any other part of the mosaic is the use of the same colours.

6.3.4 Iconography and Workshops

Given the lack of scientific evidence from the Cretan repertoire, it is necessary to examine the iconography (both figured and geometric) of Cretan mosaics in the first instance for the identification of common workshops. In addition to evidence for the working practices of craftspeople, workshop indications can help with defining chronologies, thereby placing the Cretan mosaics within the broader context of the Roman Empire and providing a diachronic view of changing communication links in Crete.

Craftspeople and Organization

A number of studies deal with the identification of groups of mosaics and, by inference, the organization of the craftspeople behind them: in permanent workshops (atelier), in mobile workshops or as itinerant workers.[70] Before a more detailed discussion of how one can identify the product of a group or a single craftsperson, the terms of reference should be defined. For the purposes of this discussion the term 'workshop' is used instead of 'School'.[71] A workshop can be understood as an organization where mosaicists could train and where a recognized team of craftspeople could be connected through a range of skills and a body of work and, perhaps, through the sharing of particular pattern books. A workshop could be either mobile or permanent. A mobile workshop could move from place to place, wherever the skills of its members were in demand. Membership in a workshop may not have been fixed, with craftspeople drifting away or returning in response to the demand for their services. A permanent workshop, although none has been identified in the archaeological record, may be termed an atelier, where tools and a working area and other facilities could be situated. Evidence for the off-site manufacture of entire mosaics or of parts of them, possibly in the environs of an atelier, is seen in locations other than Crete, such as North Africa. Experienced craftspeople and apprentices could work together as part of a workshop, either in the field or in the atelier itself.

To assign mosaics to a single workshop a number of factors must be evident. Mosaic organizations can be identified on the basis of either common elements or peculiar combinations of elements, where these elements are sufficiently characteristic to make them appear exclusive to that particular grouping. The elements can be figural (such as characteristic quirks in the rendering of the eyes and nose) or geometric (such as an unusual geometric filler or grid type) or a combination of several elements (such as the Iraklion and Villa Dionysus mosaics discussed later). The interpretation of any perceived grouping of mosaics centres on a linkage with the organization of the craftspeople responsible. Both the repeated patterns and the quality of the mosaics contribute to this interpretation.

Pattern Books

It is sometimes clear that elements of mosaics were made in ateliers and inserted into the floor at a later point either before or after other decoration was included.[72] However, there is no evidence for such separation in the Cretan material. As was true for sculpture, it is likely that original mosaics seen by patrons or craftspeople were often the inspiration for copies. Issues concerning pattern books and their existence have fuelled many academic discussions, and the frequency with which certain geometric grids and elements occur, as well as mistaken interpretations of figured scenes, suggests that there must have been at least some pattern books or variations of the type in circulation.[73] Simply put, the commonality of some mosaic iconography over long periods of time and over vast areas cannot be attributed solely to the travels of either patrons or craftspeople.[74] Furthermore, the significant chronological difference between similar depictions, such as that of the musicians on the mosaic from the Villa of Cicero, Pompeii (late second to first century B.C.E.), and that of the musicians from the *Theophorumene* play on the wall painting from Stabiae (mid-first century),[75] strongly argues for the existence of pattern books.[76] Themes and compositions could also have circulated through illustrated texts. Pliny describes this phenomenon with reference to *Imagines*, in which Varro wrote about various characters and the several portraits that accompanied the descriptions.[77] Westgate notes the evidence of a papyrus now in Berlin which appears to be an artist's pattern book.[78] There were other means by which images and ideas were circulated, such as terracotta figurines and plaster casts of well-known statues.[79] Pattern books may well have served different media such as painting and relief sculpture. They would have functioned as a guide for the mosaicist. They also provided patrons and artists with design choices for geometric panels, figurative scenes, grids and layouts.[80] There is little evidence that artists slavishly followed set patterns, and craftspeople may well have adapted the originals to suit their patrons, the media or just their own whims. Not all mosaicists would have needed to use pattern books all the time. But because so many mosaics have striking similarities in their scenes, details and layouts some kind of archetype or precedent is probable, and most likely it was found in a pattern book. For example, the scene of the rescue of Ariadne by Dionysus seen in Mosaic 135 (Pl. 40) occurs frequently in mainland Greece (Thessaloniki),[81] Syria[82] and Antioch,[83] as well as in wall paintings (e.g., from Herculaneum).[84] The characters may differ, yet similar arrangements of the scene are found, such as, for example, in the painting from the Domus Aurea which depicts Silvia and Mars. The sleeping figure of Silvia is in the same pose as that of the sleeping Ariadne.[85] The variations of the scene of Dionysus and Ariadne are probably the artists' or patrons' interpretations of a standard form. The use of the prototype for other figures, such as Hermaphroditus and Silvia, would also support the idea of blueprints for scenes being available in a pattern book. A sarcophagus, once from Rome but now lost, illustrated a similar arrangement of the scene of the sleeping Ariadne, arm stretched over her head, with a cupid figure lifting her cloak to reveal the sleeping figure to Dionysus.[86] Artistic interpretation is clear here in that all of the figures are children. The same Dionysus and Ariadne scene is also found in free-standing sculpture, for example, in a piece in the museum in Chania. Standard figure groups may also have been adapted to suit different contexts; this is particularly true of the adoption of secular images into the Christian repertoire, for example, the transmutation of the scene of Orpheus and the animals into that of Christ the Good Shepherd.[87]

6.3.5 Identification of Common Craftspeople

Little indication of workshop activity is found in literary sources. Although Vitruvius 7.1 mentions the best method of laying a mosaic pavement, there are few indications of how craftspeople may have organized themselves, and the range of possibilities in the division of labour is already seen in the earlier section on mosaic inscriptions.[88] In terms of archaeological evidence, sometimes the tools of the mosaicist survive, for example, in the Avenches archaeological museum, and there are occasional depictions of the craftspeople at their work, for example, the depiction on the stele fragment from Ostia of the manufacture of tesserae.[89] But because of the limitations imposed by the scarcity of archaeological and historical evidence, a workshop of mosaicists is better described and identified in terms of the work which it produces (or, where possible, through epigraphic evidence as discussed previously).

A possible method of identifying the work of travelling craftspeople is to distinguish a mosaic pavement which is different from others in a particular area where the regional style is strong. This pavement would have the design, style and characteristics of a mosaic from another, clearly identifiable, region. Identification of a workshop may also be possible through the recognition of a 'signature', that is, a favourite combination of patterns or variations on a standard motif.[90] A good example of the use of a combination of motifs is found in France, where Lavange cites a mosaic pavement executed in the style of Syrian mosaics.[91] The evidence of a possible Syrian craftsperson working in Chania has led scholars to classify the Mosaic 136 as Syrian in style (see the discussion of Inscription 5 in Section 6.2 for details). Conversely, the iconography and the unique example of a Syrian mosaicist's signing his work strongly suggest that the artist is following local fashion. Whether this was because the artist was working in a Cretan workshop organization or because the design, iconography and inscription were the consequence of a patron's choice is impossible to ascertain. Inscriptions in this matter can be ambiguous, but there are several groups of mosaics from Crete which can be identified as the product of the same craftsperson or craftspeople. Whether these craftspeople were free to move around or were part of an atelier is impossible to tell, hence the advantage of understanding a workshop as a collective of people rather than a fixed space.

6.3.6 Evidence of Common Craftspeople (Workshops and Itinerant Craftspeople)

The primary way of determining whether different mosaics are the product of a single craftsperson or of a group of craftspeople (workshop) is through basic comparative analysis, and for the Cretan mosaics this has been presented in Chapter 3. Two or more mosaics can be identified on a range of levels as the output of a single craftsperson or organization. The most basic criterion is that the mosaics have the same general constituents; whether they are polychrome or black and white does not matter as long as they are made from the same materials depending on the region, and that they are found in the same architectural context. If convincing similarities are seen, the evidence of commonality may be supplemented by the other evidence of iconography: first, geometric decoration, and second, elements of figured iconography. Once general likenesses and common elements have been distinguished, such as a particular grid type, design or geometric element, it is possible to begin looking at smaller details of both the geometric and the figured decoration. The Villa Dionysus and Iraklion mosaics (1–8 & 32–7) are examples. Some flexibility is necessary; the grid type and geometric décor chosen may differ between the mosaics as long as there are enough identifiable and exclusive similarities.[92] To illustrate, the resemblances in the overall scheme for and the use of individual panels is striking in the Villa Dionysus mosaics (1, 2 & 3), yet the choice of grid type is different in each mosaic. Moreover, it is clear from the construction and small details of the depiction of the figures that the three mosaics were the product of the same workshop (Pls. 1, 2 & 3). However, the identification of a common workshop based on parallels of figural style alone is highly subjective. For example, scholars cannot agree on how many or which craftsperson(s) may have been responsible for the work of each mosaic in Piazza Armerina.[93]

Contextualizing the evidence may reveal the work of itinerant or semi-permanent workshops. For example, Wilson's suggestion that North African craftspeople laid the mosaics of Piazza Armerina is supported by Gentili's claim that the tesserae were made mostly from African stones.[94] But this is a subjective opinion based on criteria of 'style'. It is equally possible that the patron encouraged a North African theme and that the tesserae were imported, or that the craftspeople were using pattern books. As will be discussed shortly, Late Antique examples from Crete show particularly good evidence for peripatetic craftspeople.

Several external factors can support or undermine an argument for mosaics' being the product of the same workshop. The most prominent of these factors are the mosaics' chronology and distribution. Clarke's criteria for identifying common workshop activity, based on his study of the Pompeii and Ostia mosaics,[95] can usefully be applied to studies in other parts of the empire. His criteria are the external dating evidence, the correspondence of motifs and the manner of laying tesserae, but these three criteria cannot be used in isolation. Regarding chronology, Clarke suggests that for mosaics to have come from the same workshop they should all have been laid within a period of 20 years.[96] Although Pompeii and Ostia may be special cases, 20 years seems a very short and restrictive period, and it is more plausible that groups of craftspeople or workshops existed for generations. This would allow for apprenticeship practices and for changes or improvements to diffuse over time as the workshop's repertoire and skill increased.

In areas like Britain,[97] Antioch,[98] Cyprus,[99] Egypt,[100] Italy[101] and North Africa,[102] where mosaics studies have been a focus, research indicates that organizations of craftspeople were established. However, in other areas, such as Greece, little attention has been paid to these topics until more recent times. On Crete, three groups of mosaics can be attributed to a common craftsperson or craftspeople on the basis of the mosaics' similar themes, geometric decoration and dates.

The first of these mosaic groups consists of the three Villa Dionysus mosaics dating to the mid-second century which depict Dionysiac themes (Mosaics 1, 2 & 3) (Pls. 1, 2 & 3). As well as their common context and theme, they all use an emblem-type layout and have characteristic style elements, such as the rendering of the noses and chins of the figures portrayed.[103] Mosaic 6 is likely to belong to this group based on the use of a stylized flower (Pl. 6).[104] The poor preservation of the mosaic does not allow more certain connections. What makes the connections of these mosaics more obvious is their lack of shared elements with other mosaics in the Knossos Valley (such as the earlier Apollinaris mosaic (9) (Pl. 8) or the later Athlete mosaic (12) (Pl. 10)). The Medusa mosaic (5) (Pl. 5) possibly belongs with this early Villa Dionysus group, but the style of its figured elements is quite different. Mosaic 1 and Mosaic 5, may have come from the same group of craftspeople, particularly if a number of them were working on the house at the same time. The connections that exist between the mosaics of the Villa Dionysus and the Iraklion *domus* mosaics would support this analysis. Furthermore, Hutchinson's mosaic (17) may also belong to the Villa Dionysus group, particularly in its use of a large outer border as seen in Mosaic 1 and a simple dentilled fillet to outline the geometric décor and arrangement of hexagons in a circle as seen in Mosaic 2. Unfortunately, because this mosaic is no longer visible this point cannot be verified.[105]

Clearly related to some of the Villa Dionysus mosaics is the group of mosaics from Iraklion (Mosaics 32–7) (Pl. 14).[106] Iraklion mosaic 1 (32) contains a vine scroll identical to that of the Three-Part mosaic (8) of the Villa Dionysus. Furthermore, the Iraklion mosaic and Mosaic 4 from the Villa Dionysus both contain a field of **R 184b** (Pl. 52), a combination of lozenges and squares forming four-pointed stars. Of particular note is the fact that in both mosaics the diamonds and squares bear crosslets terminating in chevrons. These mosaics show enough quirks of style to have been the product of the same organization.

Iraklion mosaic 2 (33) uses the circle-in-the-square grid, and the more convincing evidence of commonality is the inclusion of miniature crosses as an exterior border which is also seen with slight variations in the *triclinium* and Seasons mosaics (2 & 3) from the Villa Dionysus. Such an uncommon style quirk must be indicative of a link between these mosaics.

Iraklion mosaic 3 (34) shares elements with the Villa Dionysus mosaics through the use of the shield of triangles in contrasting colours and the grids of the circle within the square. The acanthus scroll is very slightly different from that in Mosaic 8 (the Three-Part mosaic).

Iraklion mosaic 6 (37) bears a design of hexagons and semi-hexagons which is a variation of the border of hexagons and diamonds surrounding Mosaic 1. The inclusion of the chevron border and the stylized-flower filler is also reminiscent of the idiosyncrasies of the Villa Dionysus mosaics. Although damaged, the stylized-flower filler of Mosaic 6 may well have been a close parallel, and it may also be linked with the Hutchinson's mosaic (17) through the presence of the stylized flower within its border.

Iraklion mosaic 4 (35) uses the same swastika-meander border as that of the Three-Part mosaic (8), but the definitive evidence of common workshop production is the inclusion of the stylized acanthus bud within the meander of both. The use of stepped triangles and dentilled fillets is also seen in the Mosaics 1 and 3 and in the Hutchinson's mosaic (17). The mosaic's serrated squares in blues and red-yellow are reminiscent of the serrated red-yellow squares and blue circles used in Mosaic 1. Iraklion mosaic 5 (36) incorporates a doormat panel of a dolphin on either side of an anchor. The doormat panel in Mosaic 8 is one of the few other examples of its use in the Cretan repertoire. Furthermore, the net pattern used in both mosaics is similar.

The most convincing points of comparison are found between Mosaic 8 and Iraklion mosaics 32 and 35. Based on these points of commonality, in particular, the shared occurrence of idiosyncratic elements (such as the stylized acanthus in the swastika meander), this group has strong evidence for the same crafts-people for shared worked production. Individually, the elements in common between Mosaics 1–5 from the Villa Dionysus and Hutchinson's mosaic (17) and the Iraklion group (Mosaics 32–7) do not amount to much, but taken together, they are sufficiently strong to serve as evidence of workshop production, as well as providing a link between these mosaics and Mosaic 8. Overall, Markoulaki dates the Iraklion mosaics to the first half of the second century primarily on stylistic analysis pending the ceramic analysis.[107] If the date differences are correct within the group of Villa Dionysus mosaics (see Appendix 1), it may well be the case that the Iraklion and Villa Dionysus mosaics represent two generations of the same workshop. If the dating evidence is incorrect, the differences between the groups of mosaics may be indicative of the stylistic ranges of the same workshop.

The Two-Panelled mosaic (139) and the Centaur and Lion mosaic (140) have been dated to the late second century.[108] Hellenkemper Salies[109] argues for an Italian 'influence' in both of them. The geometric decoration, particularly the grid type and the use of black and white, may make this possible; however, the figures do not attest to an Italian origin. This group is of note as it may have connections with the Villa Dionysus–Iraklion group based on a number of factors: the circle-in-the-square and hexagon grid type of the Two-Panelled mosaic, the similarity between the birds in the subsidiary panels in this mosaic and on Iraklion mosaic 4 (35) and the extra borders of rows of stepped squares or chevrons as found in the Villa Dionysus–Iraklion group. Further points of comparison lie primarily in the use of stylized flowers, as seen in Mosaic 17 (Pl. 12), which appears to have its origins in the acanthus flower and is found specifically in Mosaic 6 (Villa Dionysus) and Mosaic 140 with a slight variation in Mosaic 35 (Iraklion).[110]

A clear third group of 'workshop' mosaics is from Chania. It is likely that the mosaics of Dionysus and Ariadne (Mosaic 135) (Pl. 40) and of the *triclinium* of the House of Dionysus (Mosaic 136) (Pl. 43) were products of the same workshop on the basis of their common theme and depictions of the figures (note in particular the rendering of the torso of the Dionysus figure and the folds of the clothes in each one). Mosaic 129 of Poseidon and Amymone (Pl. 39) shares notable similarities with Mosaic 135, in particular in the rendering of the cloaks, eyes and noses of all the figures. All three mosaics have been dated to the third century. The geometric decoration differs markedly among these three, although the discrepancy may be accounted for if different craftspeople were responsible for the geometric elements. To the Chania group can be added with more certainty Mosaics S207d and S207f from Kisamos. Given the strikingly similar grid (intersecting squares within a circle), theme (Dionysiac) and smaller elements of decoration (such as peopled scrolls, the depiction of wings on these figures and faces (or masks) in the angles of the intersecting squares), it is likely that Mosaics S207f and 135 are products of the same workshop. This conclusion has further implications in that the date of the Dionysus and Ariadne mosaic is likely to be earlier than the late third century which had previously been attributed to it.[111] The second mosaic from Kisamos Health Centre is Mosaic S207d, which is of the same phase as S207f and has two matching elements with the Chania Mosaic 136 (Pl. 42). The first element is that the masks in both are very similar, and minor details such as noses and eyes are almost identical.[112] The second and actually the point of confirmation of common craftspeople is that both use a particular type of guilloche (thick guilloche) which is not found on any other mosaic either on the island or in the empire.[113] This guilloche, used exclusively in Crete, is on its own fairly convincing evidence that there was a school of mosaicists in operation in the Chania-Kisamos region in the mid third century. The added evidence of the similarities in the depictions of the figures, and the similarities between the other mosaics, 135 and S207f, in the two buildings, makes it almost conclusive (see discussion in Inscription 5 (Section 6.2) for the origins of the craftsperson).

It is more difficult to attribute possible origins or inspirations for single occurrences of mosaics around Crete. For example, the mosaic of the fishing scene from Chersonisos (Mosaic 38) (Pl. 15) has no parallel within or outside Crete; the same is also true of the Lissos mosaic (137). Elements such as the theme or the geometric decoration are found in other areas of the empire, but it is the execution and the combination of geometric elements that respectively make these examples unique.

6.3.7 Evidence for Workshops in the Late Antique Mosaics

Because of the uniformity of space within church buildings and the limitations imposed by the religious context on the iconography of the mosaics, common craftspeople are easier to identify for Late Antique mosaics than for Roman-period mosaics. Of the Cretan corpus, several mosaics can be attributed to common workshops, and many of these have clear associations with mainland

Table 1. Sites Arranged According to Common Elements

Basilica	Circles and Squares (**R** 144e)	Knot Design	Circles and Diamonds (variation of **R** 184b)	Zigzags	Squares and Diamonds (**R** 184b)
Knossos	Yes	Yes	Yes	Yes	No
Elis	Yes	Yes	Yes	Yes	No
Gytheion	No	Yes	Yes	Yes	No
Istanbul	No	Yes	No	Yes	Yes
Kera	No	Yes	No	No	Yes
Chersonisos A	No	Yes (similar)	No	No	Yes
Sardis	Yes	No	No	No	No
Chersonisos B	Yes	No	No	No	No
Eresos	Yes	No	No	No	No
Suia A	Yes	No	No	No	No

Note: For each of the designs, see Pl. 52.

Greece and Asia Minor. Campbell and Sodini have already pointed out the likely links between the mosaics at Knossos (Mosaics 88–90), Elis, Istanbul and Sardis on the basis of the geometric designs, and a second group at Sardis, Knossos and Eresos (on Mytilene) (Pls. 23 & 24).[114] To this group it is possible to add further Cretan examples such as Kera (Mosaics 122–5) (Pl. 35), Chersonisos Basilica A (Mosaics 92–3) (Pls. 25–6), Chersonisos Basilica B (Mosaics 94–100) (Pl. 27) and Suia Basilica A (Mosaics 156–8) (Pl. 50). Also included in this group are the mosaics at Gytheion (Table 1).

Similarities of design as displayed in Table 1 are based on the fact that there are repetitions of entire panels of geometric forms and that there are also three other basic elements in common which do not occur on other mosaics known thus far from Greece and Asia Minor. The table clearly shows that Knossos and Elis have all of the elements except the mat of squares and diamonds. Moreover, where the mat of squares and diamonds occurs, the mat of circles and diamonds (variation of **R** 184b) is absent.

With Table 1 in mind it is possible that there are two connected groups of mosaicists, and it may be that these groups were a generation or two apart. The first group is represented by the mosaics from Knossos (Mosaics 88–90), Elis,[115] Gytheion,[116] Istanbul,[117] Chersonisos Basilica A (Mosaics 92–3) and Kera (Mosaics 122–5) (Pls. 23, 24, 25 & 35). The second group comprises mosaics from Sardis,[118] Eresos,[119] Chersonisos Basilica B (Mosaics 94–100) and Suia Basilica A (Mosaics 156–8) (Pls. 27 & 50). Although the two groups have elements in common, namely, the mat of circles and squares (**R** 144e) (Pls. 24 & 52), there are very important elements in the first group which make it distinct from the latter.

The mosaics in the first group all have the knot design (Pls. 23, 25 & 36) or, as in the case of the Elis example, the 'developed' knot design,[120] and this is the most important common denominator. Within this group, two sub-groups can be identified, but all are linked by the knot design. The first sub-group is defined by the mat of circles and diamonds which create tangent four-pointed stars. The arms of the stars are filled with a chevron design (Pl. 23). Each star contains a circle which contains a guilloche band. Each of the diamonds contains the central circle flanked by the semi-circle with the hooks on either side (knot design), as at Knossos, Elis and Gytheion (Pl. 23). The second sub-group is represented by the mat of squares and diamonds, as at Istanbul, Kera and Chersonisos Basilica A (Pls. 25 & 35), which replaces the circles and diamonds. Undoubtedly, with this combination of elements a single workshop was involved in the making of these mosaics.

The second group is defined by the mat of circles and squares (**R** 144e) (Pl. 52): Chersonisos Basilica B, Eresos, Sardis and Suia Basilica A (Pls. 27 & 50). The Cretan examples are closer to one another, with the combined elements of the double guilloche and the border of intersecting circles used in the Suia Basilica A and Chersonisos Basilica B examples. The Knossos and Elis examples pose something of a problem. They clearly belong with the first group, but their mats of circles and squares connect them to the second group (Pl. 24). They lack the Cretan criteria of having borders of intersecting circles **R** 49a and double guilloche **R** 75a. It is possible that there are two different groups which are connected by the craftspeople themselves, or simply that in the case of the Knossos example two different workshops were involved in the laying of the pavements. As the Knossos mosaics are no longer *in situ*, it is not possible to identify distinct methods or techniques in the laying of the pavement. In terms of chronology, a range of dates has been proposed for these mosaics: Knossos, mid-fifth century; Elis, second half of the fifth century; Gytheion, first half of the sixth century; Istanbul, mid-fifth century; Kera, late fifth to early sixth century; and Chersonisos Basilica A, late fifth or early sixth century. The second group has the following dates: Sardis, mid-fifth century; Eresos, mid-fifth century; Chersonisos Basilica B, early sixth century; and Suia, first half of the sixth century. The range of dates may suggest more evidence for a single pattern book than for common craftspeople but for the fact that Late Antique churches are notoriously difficult to date and few of the preceding examples other than Sardis and Istanbul are based on stratigraphic evidence.

The mosaics of Sybrita (Mosaics 116–17) and Eleutherna (Mosaics 111–14) may also have common workshop connections as indicated through the use of inhabited scrolls and over-sized buds and leaves, as well as circles in diamonds. However, the Sybrita mosaic is not well enough preserved to provide conclusive evidence.

6.4 CONCLUSION

The epigraphic, technical and iconographic evidence of the Cretan mosaics indicates that there was a lively demand for quality mosaics, enough to have established a number of mosaic workshops on the island. Patching in the Late Antique mosaics such as Chersonisos Basilica B (Mosaics 94–100) and Gortyn Sector M (Mosaic 109) suggests both the value of the mosaic and the length of time the church was in use. The lack of repair work on the Roman mosaics is indicative of the shorter length of time the mosaics were in use and the less wear they got because of the private nature of the space. House owners may have been more inclined to change their interior décor to suit their own tastes. Late Antique donor panels indicate something of the value of a donation and their orientation for maximum and instant visibility reveals their fundamental role in highlighting the donor. In this respect, mosaics continue as a way to impress visitors and reflect positively on the patrons in the Late Antique period as they had in the Roman.

Mosaic studies provide both direct and indirect data on craftspeople and patrons in the Roman and Late Antique periods. The mosaic signatures primarily indicate Eastern or local craftspeople. The occurrence of signatures and labels on mosaics is clearly a Cretan and Greek preference and quite different from the East and West. The possibility that a Syrian craftsperson was working in Crete but signing his work demonstrates the strength of either the local tradition or a patron's preference. The Knossos and Iraklion mosaics show overwhelming evidence for a common workshop, and another workshop from the Chania-Kisamos region in the third century is also clear. Even if there were foreign craftspeople working on the island there is certainly no clear evidence for an external regional character in their work. The indications are that the Roman-period workshops were quite regionalized and local to Crete. Conversely, the evidence of the Late Antique mosaics provides clear connections with workshops of the East. This may reflect a change in communication links from the Roman to the Late Antique period and more development of an Eastern koine by the fifth century, to a certain extent defined by not being part of the Western church. In many respects, the evidence of the craftspeople reflects a picture similar to the one being established in terms of iconographic and contextual evidence: that the Cretan mosaics cannot be directly attributed to either a Western or an Eastern or even a Greek influence, and that much more obvious communication links with the East are in evidence by the Late Antique period.

SEVEN

THE PROVINCIAL VIEW, GLOBALIZATION AND CHRISTIANIZATION

7.1 INTRODUCTION

The supposition that the mosaics of Crete can simply be defined as belonging to a Western tradition fits well with the inaccurate but common belief that Crete (and in particular Knossos and Gortyn) took on all the trappings of Roman culture once it became part of the empire.[1] A renewed contextual look at the mosaics within the theoretical framework of globalization and Christianization provides a more nuanced diachronic view of the island from the first century B.C.E. to the seventh century C.E. and shows how Crete benefited from and contributed to the Roman network society.

7.2 THE MOSAICS OF CRETE

The Cretan repertoire displays great diversity between the north and south of the island and between different periods. By comparing the Cretan mosaics with those of other areas of the Roman Empire (Chapter 3), a better understanding of the range of communications emerges. The mosaics demonstrate that the earliest persistent connection Crete had with the West was through its southern harbours, probably by using the trade routes or the early traders who may have settled on the island as a conduit.[2] When Crete became part of the Roman Empire, the first places to experience the consequences would naturally have been the parts of the island that were already well known to the Romans (Kouphonisi, Myrtos and Makrigialos), and the location of the earliest evidence of black-and-white mosaics on the island shows this. The earliest northern mosaics are found some 50 years later, and are of black-and-white form, but they use the multiple panel in grid format (such as the Apollinaris mosaic (9) and Mosaics

139–40 from Kisamos). These mosaics may be indicative of early Roman settlers or local patrons who were inclined towards Western styles. The small number of black-and-white mosaics in the early years of Roman rule in Chania may also be a result of its trade contacts with the West, and, in the case of Knossos, it may be the result of there having been Italian settlers in the valley when the city became a colony. By the mid-second century, however, only polychrome mosaics (primarily multiple panel in grid compositions) are found in the towns of the north, and this is also where the majority of mosaics are located. Thus far, the only second-century mosaics on the south coast are located in Gortyn.

The high density of mosaics in the north throughout the second and third centuries reflects the changing focus and the possible rise in importance of the harbours and towns on Crete's northern coast (Fig. 8). The abundance of mosaics is also indicative of the stability and prosperity of the empire at this time.[3] Across the island, the number of mosaics decreases in the third century. But at this point, the mosaic densities show that the towns of Kisamos and Chersonisos are clearly favoured; there is very little southern coastal activity. This may indicate a preference for northern ports for re-fuelling and re-stocking on the Mediterranean trade routes. Undoubtedly, the mosaics of western Crete, from Chania and Kisamos, are outstanding in the middle period (late second to late third century) for their quantity, quality and themes. The latest pre-Christian mosaics which are found in Kisamos and Chersonisos in particular share some elements of decoration common to the Late Antique church mosaics. Although there is a cluster of mosaics in the late fifth to early sixth century, the span of Late Antique mosaics runs from the early fifth century to the mid-sixth century. By this time, mosaics are reasonably equally distributed across the island, with the southern ports becoming popular again, and an even spread of occupation, as suggested by the mosaics in rural areas. Alcock suggests that increased interest in agriculture helped with demographic growth, which may explain why there is a return to some of the inland sites occupied in the Hellenistic period but abandoned in the Roman.[4] Overall, the mosaics reflect the great variety of the contact the population of Crete had through craftspeople, traders and patrons with areas across the Roman Empire. As will be seen from the following discussion, the evidence of other archaeological material supports this conclusion.

7.3 Roman Crete: A Diachronic View

The conventional view is that once Crete became part of the Roman Empire an immediate and equal socio-political change occurred throughout the island.[5] Yet from the mosaics and material culture analysed, it is clear that this is not the case. The south coast is quite different from the north, and there is almost a century's difference in when cities begin to display elements of change from the Hellenistic norm on Crete, such as new mosaics and buildings or different import profiles. By the time this happens, it could reasonably be argued that this was part of the overall developments occurring in the Eastern Empire. As demonstrated, the mosaics and material culture show that different levels of transformations occur not just between regions within the island but within smaller units of space too such as urban areas. There is little evidence of systematic or forced cultural change, and to understand the processes involved possibly a more effective approach would be to apply globalization theory. Furthermore, the locations of mosaics, their styles and the evidence of workshops suggest that quite a large amount can be postulated regarding the Christianization of the area.

7.3.1 The Conquest of Crete

According to Baldwin Bowsky, Knossos and Gortyn in the 80s B.C.E. were part of a pro-Rome group.[6] When Knossos defected and gave its support to Mithridates this must have triggered an aspiration for Cretan subjugation. Gortyn showed early support for Metellus, as evidenced by a coin minted by Metellus sometime in the 60s B.C.E. But Baldwin Bowsky suggests that it was Gortyn's support for Octavian that made it the capital of the province, whereas Knossos chose to back Antony.[7] The south coast had already been popular with Romans and other foreigners because until the end of the first century it was the safest place to re-stock, rest or shelter along the west–east grain route.[8] Southern ports from Lissos to Ierapetra exploited their positions from the Hellenistic period. Consequently, it is not surprising that these ports display early and increasingly intense contact with Rome from the first century B.C.E. to the first century C.E., as evidenced by the concentration of black-and-white mosaics, Western-style *impluvium*-type houses and barrel-vaulted tombs at sites such as Lissos, Myrtos and Kouphonisi. That there is little evidence for this kind of material on the north side of the island in the late Hellenistic or early Roman period adds weight to the assessment. The storage facilities and other provisions, such as temples, at southern ports such as Lissos and Lasaia indicate not merely a stop-over point but that some kind of commercial activity or exchange of goods was also undertaken there. Increasingly, evidence for merchants and traders and commercial activity is being found; for example, an inscription from Gortyn records the substantial population of *cives Romani qui Gortinae negotiantur* (Roman and Italic merchants).[9] Baldwin Bowsky has also discussed the evidence for commercial classes among the Roman citizens in Crete, particularly in Gortyn in the first century B.C.E. and later.[10] The preponderance of names in an economic rather than a political or military context is indicative of the key reason why Crete, like many other provinces, became part of the empire: financial interests. That such names continue to be prevalent within the onomastic evidence is a further indication that there was generally a relaxed attitude when it came to the political and military control of the island. Onomastics are also useful for identifying the presence of a Roman citizen population across the island, particularly from graves and dedicatory inscriptions. It is unsurprising that Gortyn, as the capital, provides evidence for a wide range of names from governors to priests to merchants to donors.[11] Although Knossos as a colony should have a similar quantity and range of Roman citizen names in the first century, it does not, and when they are found they are limited in variety and number.[12]

By the end of the first century C.E., the north coast was fast becoming a competitive player in the island's function as an entrepôt.[13] As Rackham and Moody note, the ports of Iraklion and nearby Amnisos were not physically the best harbours but their location close to the sheltered island of Dia just to the north meant that ships could stay there until favourable weather allowed them to land on Crete.[14] The colony at Knossos may have been founded in part because of its attractive mythical and historical past, but it was also founded because it was a potential flashpoint for rebellion and, more importantly, because of the value of the trade corridor between Gortyn and Knossos.[15] Although there were certainly Roman citizens at Knossos, in part seeded from within the island itself, they did not have much of an impact on the existing population.[16] Baldwin Bowsky notes that as was the case in Gortyn, the majority of names in Knossos are connected with commerce and banking rather than with the military or politics.[17] All signs point to a continuation of Hellenistic life in Knossos until the second half of the first century, with pockets of evidence in the form of mosaics, epigraphy and graves for citizen or Italian settlers in the north of the valley (Fig. 12).[18] The recent excavations at the Venizelio cemetery which have uncovered unique, possibly Western-style tombs, have also provided epigraphic evidence for some citizens buried there.[19] In other areas of the north coast the same continuation of occupation can be seen from the Hellenistic period in both urban and rural sites.[20]

7.3.2 First Century B.C.E.–First Century C.E. Mortuary and Religious Evidence

A clear difference between the north coast and the south coast is seen in the mortuary data. Sites such as Lissos, Lasaia and Suia all have the first-century barrel-vaulted tombs seen in both Italy and Turkey, but there are no such sites on the north coast of Crete. The broad chronology of these tombs makes it difficult to ascertain whether they are indicative of a particular group or of a fashion started by visitors to or travellers from one of the southern towns, or whether they are a combination of both. Further external contact exclusive to the southern towns of Crete is evidenced by the location of first-century temples, many of them podium style, as, for example, at Lebena,[21] Lissos, Lasaia and Kouphonisi.[22] Although Gortyn is not on the coast, it controlled many of the ports and its status would have attracted early investment, as can be seen with the Temple of Isis and Serapis, whose dedication was provided by Flavia Philyra in C.E. 1 or 2.[23] On the north coast, many Classical and Hellenistic temples continued in use, and current evidence suggests that any new temples were not completed before the end of the first century, and then, only in cities such as Aptera, Knossos[24] and Chersonisos.[25] Sanders argues that new cult probably spread through trade, as is evidenced by the concentration of inscriptions in harbour towns.[26] If this is the case for Crete, it is not surprising that the south of the island sees the first concentration of new cult buildings in the first century.

The paucity of evidence for new public buildings (religious, entertainment, political or administrative) also points to a minimal impact caused by the island becoming part of the empire on the north coast. Furthermore, although an increase in imported pottery is evidenced on the north from survey work and particularly from the excavations at Knossos, the Hellenistic types overwhelmingly continue.[27] Epigraphic data in Knossos is surprising in having far fewer Latin inscriptions than one would expect from a colony (58.5% Latin v. 41.5% Greek).[28] Baldwin Bowsky suggests that although Latin may have been the official language, it was not the everyday language.[29]

7.3.3 First-Century Change

In the first half of the first century C.E., pockets of change become visible in the north and even here there are variations in the extent of transformation. Notable is the area around Mirabello Bay which marks the shortest route between the south and north of the island. Thus far much of the evidence from sites with storage areas and from inscriptions comes from survey work and epigraphic data, both of which show an unmistakeable commercial network within Ierapetra's area of control.[30] It is possible that the harbours at Tholos and Priniatikos Pyrgos were among the first on the north coast to benefit from the use of the island as an entrepôt. Modifications at this point are evidenced in cities such as Chania and Chersonisos. At Knossos too changes are indicted by mosaics and the new cemetery in the northern half.[31] Baldwin Bowsky has identified an early first-century funerary inscription, possibly commemorating a member of the Ancharii family (a colonist, or descendent of one), found at Knossos.[32] She also notes that the number of Roman citizen names in Gortyn decreases slightly from the first century B.C.E. to the first century C.E., which she believes may be partly due to migration to Knossos.[33]

By the latter half of the first century changes in the archaeology of the north coast are widespread. As just noted, mosaics are found for the first time during this period in areas like Chania and Knossos. The ports of Tholos and Bali are expanded, and new cemeteries, public buildings and houses are found in, for example, Knossos, Rethymnon and Chania.

From the archaeological material discussed in Chapter 2, it is possible to sur-
mise that the south coast had a greater range of imports than did the north
in the first century, with Arretine, African and Cypriot Red Slipped appear-
ing in quantities and fewer examples of Çandarli and Italian sigillata. By the
end of the first century, ESB appears to dominate the imports across the island.
By the second century, the diversity of locally made, imitation and imported
(including amphorae types) pottery indicates the wide range of contacts that
the island had while not being particularly dependent on any one area to fill
its ceramic need. Across Crete, strong evidence for local ceramic production is
seen through the Roman and Late Antique periods, even in large centres such
as Knossos and Gortyn. In some areas it seems that specialized vessels, such as
amphorae, may have been produced solely for the export market.[34] Other locally
produced pottery that has been identified is that which imitates foreign types,
such as the local production of terra sigillata A types at Knossos.[35] Based on the
Vrokastro evidence, Hayden suggests that the second-century boom in locally
produced imitation wares was a result of increased local competition with the
import market, which may also be an indication of the high levels of prosperity
at this time.[36] Whereas most areas appear to fit with Sanders's general outline
of the diachronic range of imported ceramics, there are areas that have different profiles. For example, the northeast part of the island has evidence for more
Phoenician Red Slipped wares, which may point to a particular type of trade
between that part of Crete and the eastern Mediterranean. That Italian sigillata is found at sites scattered across the island, most commonly in Gortyn and
Knossos, suggests the roles that these cities played in terms of trade routes and
in controlling the island, rather than simply being indicative of Italian settlers.

7.3.4 Second-Century Crete

Although Gortyn in particular, but also Ierapetra, saw investment from the first
to the second century in public buildings such as temples, theatres and baths,
the cities on the north coast did not begin to benefit until the second century,
as demonstrated by the construction at this time of the basilica at Knossos,
as well as of theatres there and in Chersonisos. The same building expansion
can be seen in cities of the north such as Chania and Kisamos. The epigraphic
record indicates a broad continuation of investment, with dedications and hon-
orific inscriptions ranging from the infrastructural development of Ierapetra to
the dedicatory inscriptions of Eleutherna to the honouring of athletes in the
Gymnasium at Gortyn.[37] By the second century, the mosaics across the island
are predominantly polychrome multiple panel in grid compositions, and on current evidence it is noticeable that the majority are found in the northern half
of the island. Although this may in part be attributable to the nature of the
recovery of the material, the dearth of mosaics from the late second to the fourth

century coincides with the scant evidence of a sustained building programme in the south.[38] It may be that after the initial focus on the southern coast for trade reasons, the northern ports, with their new potential for Aegean trade, now commanded attention. By the beginning of the second century, all the cities of Crete share common traits, such as industry, a successful economy, a range of dwellings from lavish to basic with interior décors to match, substantial public buildings and more Greek than Latin inscriptions. The freedom to allow cultural diversity finally develops into cultural commonality.

7.3.5 Diversity on Crete

By and large, the interpretation of settlement patterns across Crete (Chapter 2) fits with mosaic date and distribution analysis (Chapters 4–5). Although there may be general trends there are also clear exceptions. For example, unlike most of the island which left valley floors free for agricultural exploitation the Mesara plain, for example, at Vounos, had some domestic occupation, and Watrous suggests that this was due to the introduction of drainage technology by the Romans.[39] Further diversity can be seen with Lasithi, where the peak of population seems to have been in the fourth century, particularly with the substantial settlement of Kardamoutsa.[40] At this point, the unsettled nature of the Roman Empire may have encouraged populations to turn to more secure income sources like agriculture rather than trade. If in the fourth century there is a greater occupation of rural areas, as suggested by Sanders, the decline in the numbers of mosaics in the fourth century may be explained in part by an archaeological focus on urban landscapes.[41] The lack of evidence for Roman occupation and limited ceramic imports in the east of the island may be partially an archaeological bias. But even where surveys have been undertaken, such as that of Praisos, the evidence for Roman occupation remains somewhat limited.[42] Itanos is the exception to this, likely because of its geographical position and therefore its role in the trade network.

7.4 CRETE IN THE EMPIRE: GLOBALIZATION

Archaeological evidence points to trade and economic potential as primary among Rome's reasons to include Crete in its empire. With consideration, there was no pressing need for enforced change. Although a key player in the wine trade, the island did not have precious resources nor was it a rebellious flashpoint.[43] Nothing denotes oppression: there is little evidence of Foucault's monitored society or of the holding back of information that one might witness of the oppressed, there are no known military establishments, and there are no visible indications of the enforcement of imperial control.[44] As outlined by Kokkinia, evidence for the multitude of ways a governor could deal with a province, or for the ways local control could be exercised through language or even sham-ing, are absent from Crete.[45] The island's main value and possible threat lay in its geographical potential as an entrepôt of some strategic importance.[46] The fact that the earliest non-Cretan occupiers appear to have been traders or financially motivated is further indication of this. Cretans would have benefited greatly from the commercial interest in the island, as can be seen on the south coast and then on the north coast. Thus by the late first century, Crete can be seen as part of the globalized Roman Empire, as a place where investments are made if the returns (be they strategic or material) are viable, yet at the same time as someplace where cultural diversity is allowed to prosper.[47] Crete was valuable to Rome as an economic resource, and the same can be said of the value of Rome to Crete. In this respect, as outlined in Chapter 1, a symbiotic affiliation between Crete and Rome can be understood, resulting in little need to impose elements of cultural change in order to make the relationship work. Thus we can under-stand processes of globalization rather than traditional ideas of Romanization. For Crete, it is more useful to conceive a relationship with Rome and the East which had the momentum to have cultural consequences primarily when they were mutually beneficial. Crete's key role as part of the Roman economic network (discussed later) meant not only that the island benefited but also that Rome had to pay attention to Crete in order to maintain its own economic viability.

7.5 CRETE IN LATE ANTIQUITY: CHRISTIANIZATION

7.5.1 Late Antique Crete

Compared with the quantities of mosaic evidence from the second century, the identifiable material in Crete from the second half of the third century through the fourth century is less apparent. Certain cities continue to flourish, and some such as Kisamos and Chersonisos appear to have reached their zenith during this period, as indicated by mosaics, dwellings and public buildings. In other centres, such as Chania, Gortyn and Knossos, few mosaics and buildings (if any) can be dated to the second half of the third or to the fourth century until the highly visible and strategically placed Christian churches are constructed. That is not to suggest that the cities went into decline; the cemeteries remained in use, and the evidence of other material culture, such as pottery, indicates con-tinued occupation of these cities.[48]

Although the catalyst for social change may have been the island's embrace of Christianity, the adjustment is also remarkable in other ways. Along with a new religious practice, distinct alterations are seen in the art, architecture and iconography of the island, and the evidence of the churches and cemeteries suggests that settlement patterns may also have changed. The distribution of Late Antique mosaics and churches in Crete indicates a wider occupation of the countryside than in the preceding period. Scott has argued that the arena for conspicuous consumption shifts from urban to rural space, which may mean that the more overt material indicators may be absent from the urban archaeological record.[49] Nevertheless, as discussed in Chapter 2, rescue excavations have been producing more evidence for Late Antique urban domestic occupation from Viglia (Ierapetra) in the southeast to Olus in the northeast to Kisamos in the northwest and Agia Galini in the southwest. Much of the occupation remains consistent in some areas,[50] but new or re-occupied settlements are also known from some of the southern islands such as Gavdos and Nisis Trafos and from areas of the north such as Mallia. The characteristics of occupation varied from the earlier period, with evidence for more nucleated settlement in some places (such as Kavousi), as well as for the emergence of the rural villa.[51] Although more refined work needs to be completed, the preponderance of early churches and mosaics (particularly in Knossos and Olus) on the north coast may indicate that this was the first area of the island to be Christianized.[52] The innovative architecture of the KMF Basilica, which owes its origins in part to a Western form, appears to have set the trend for architectural styles further south and east to regions like Egypt.[53] Hierokles refers to Gortyn as a Cretan metropolis by the middle of the sixth century, and this is supported by epigraphic evidence.[54] The continued importance of major urban centres such as Gortyn, Knossos and Chersonisos was marked by the construction of multiple churches, and on this basis, coastal centres such as Itanos and Suia also remained popular ports. Whereas once large Roman urban hubs, often with coastal locations, dominated the economy of the island, in the Late Antique period, church distribution indicates a more widespread distribution of settlement, including the renewed occupation of the hilltops and slopes. Notable is the fact that the threat of Arab invasion did not appear to hamper the construction of churches until the late sixth century when there was a marked decline in mosaics too. At this point the decline in church building is seen first on the south coast, and then on the north followed by inland areas, with the latest known Late Antique churches constructed in Vizari and possibly in Fodele in the eighth century.

Christianization

It is arguable that a definitive programme of Christianization of the urban sphere began in the fifth century and is marked not just by the construction of churches but also through the topographic layout of some cities. Mortuary evidence in places such as Gortyn, Chania and Knossos indicates that the perimeters of the old towns were not adhered to and that Late Antique graves were placed in what had been residential and domestic areas (see Chapter 2 for discussion). There may have been multiple phases to the Christianization of the Cretan city, but the Late Antique data here are such that a close chronology is not yet achievable.

Whereas many of the earliest churches were likely constructed on land donated to the church, or in areas where new cemeteries would not pollute domestic space, the location of the church, often on the urban fringes, provided a new focus for the town. The move into the area of the Roman cemeteries as seen in Gortyn and Knossos may have in part been due to the need for space for the structure, but it was also because some churches were built on top of martyr graves. The new locations had the advantage of creating a fresh architectural landscape and focus, thus actively diminishing the memories of the pre-Christian space.[55] This point can be illustrated in Knossos. Here, two monumental churches were constructed in the valley, at least 500 m north of the civic centre. The KMF Basilica is likely to date to the early fifth century and the Sanatorium Basilica to the early sixth century. Although evidence for housing, wells and other domestic structures is limited, the location of the Christian cemeteries helps to define the layout of the Late Antique city.[56] With the construction of the KMF Basilica in the north, the city seems to have contracted somewhat; graves occur along the valley floor rather than on the slopes of the surrounding hills, and most notably in what used to be domestic areas in the southern part of the city. The whole focus of the city appears to shift northwards (Fig. 12). Without any sign of a dramatic end to the old way of life, the centre has moved although still retaining such elements familiar to the population as a monumental building and regular community use of the space in ceremonial and private forms. The church's architecture, interior decoration and ceremonies would have served to impress, inspire and encourage the congregation and converts. In addition, the cemeteries and martyr graves (some associated with the churches) would have provided another focal point for the population, and regular visits to these sites would have reinforced the sense of community ownership of the city.[57]

Late Antique Distribution

The same situation can be read across the island. Large churches are commonly placed in striking, visible locations: on hill tops (such as Lyttos), promontories (Chersonisos Basilica B), coasts (Almyrida) and places of natural beauty (Episkopi). These locations do not just mark the presence of a Christian population; they indicate a Christianization of the landscape, be it through the visual impact of the church itself or through the pilgrimage that would be taken to get to the church. The Late Antique churches are widespread across the island. In both urban and rural contexts, the majority of churches[58] are of the simple, triple-aisled, single-apse type, such as seen in Eleutherna (Pl. 31)[59] or Kera (as discussed in Chapter 5).[60] Variations on the standard can be seen in the tripartite-transept types like the basilica in Almyrida,[61] or in the use of the triple apse as in Agios Titos (Gortyn)[62] or in the triconch form of the KMF Basilica (Knossos).[63] As yet, no common pattern between architectural style and location has been identified.[64] The presence of multiple churches may reflect donations or the size of the community or the community's administrative or ecclesiastical status or even its piety. If so, the provision of several churches may indicate demand for a range of church functions within the community, including serving as martyria or episcopal, mortuary or private family churches.[65] As Crete's Roman capital and Christian metropolis, Gortyn, with ten examples, has the largest concentration of Late Antique churches on the island. Multiple churches make strong visual statements, and in Crete they are found at Gortyn, Chersonisos, Itanos and Suia.[66] With the exception of Gortyn, these sites are all in coastal locations, and each may have been an episcopal seat. The coastal locations may suggest a desire to impress visitors as well as the local population, but it also indicates a certain sense of security on the island between the fifth and sixth centuries. Rarely in Crete are earlier temples converted into churches, the only possible example being the Temple of Apollo Pythios at Gortyn.[67] Churches are found more commonly near earlier cult sites (such as in Lissos and Lebena), but this may be more to do with the gradual Christianization of the area and with making use of an already popular site rather than forcing a decisive end to a pre-Christian sanctuary.[68] Although Sanders attempts to classify the origins for some of the Christian churches on Crete as either Eastern or Western, it is more likely that the type of liturgical practice shaped the architecture rather than the other way round.[69] Even though Crete, as part of Illyricum, came under the ecclesiastical jurisdiction of the West until the first half of the eighth century, the architecture of many of the churches (including Chersonisos Basilica B and Gortyn Sector M) indicate primarily Eastern liturgical practices, particularly in the processional elements. Some of the early churches, such as the KMF Basilica in Knossos, with its unusual sanctuary, or Eleutherna and Knossos Sanatorium, with their focus on revelation, may incorporate Western elements too.[70]

Although the iconography of the Cretan mosaics changes from Roman to Late Antique, it is not a total transformation and many geometric elements continue to be used. For the most part, little distinguishes the floors in either church or secular contexts in the Late Antique period and this is seen universally across the Mediterranean.[71] The Late Antique mosaics of Crete are distinguishable as a corpus by the absence of personifications and of other figured designs except as overtly Christian symbols (such as the peacock or fish) or as filler décor in geometric contexts. Late Antique mosaics in other parts of the Roman Empire do incorporate figures, for example, the hunting scenes in the Argos mosaic.[72] The number and quality of mosaics constructed during the period is indicative of the continued prosperity of the island, quite different from the picture of decline proposed by Sanders and others.[73] Sanders postulated that Crete would have suffered badly from a series of earthquakes during the period, but the evidence of the mosaics, particularly those that have been repaired, shows that even if earthquakes did disrupt the population, they seem to have recovered quickly (see Chapter 4 on the attribution of decline to seismic events).

7.6 CRETE AND ITS ROLE IN THE EMPIRE

Crete's strongest economic asset was its location on the Rome-Alexandria grain route, and this is probably the reason the island was included in the empire.[74] The southern harbours of Crete would have been passed in both directions along the grain route. Vessels following the route westwards would also have stopped along the Lebanese coast (at Tyre, for example), at Cyprus, along the south coast of Asia Minor and at Rhodes and/or Knidos.[75] After a ship left Rhodes to head west to Rome, the south coast of Crete would be the last safe stop until Malta.[76] The north coast of Crete was originally not set up to facilitate large-scale Roman trade; it was believed to be too dangerous in terms of prevailing winds. As a result, the Aegean was bypassed in favour of a safer route that took shipments directly to the east coast of Crete. The development in the cities and harbours of the north coast of Crete in the mid-first century likely reflects a focused investment in and new use of the area for trade. In the first instance, the northern ports may have been used to re-distribute to the Aegean goods which originated from the southern ports on the route from Rome to Alexandria. This would be a more efficient way of exporting the goods than doing so on the way back from Rhodes or Knidos. The key land routes would have been the ones between mountain ranges: Ierapetra to Mirabello Bay (Tholos) being the shortest, Matala (Gortyn) to Iraklion (Knossos) and Agia Galini to Rethymnon. A route between Inatos and Chersonisos and others may also have been used. Certainly, the route between Ierapetra and Mirabello Bay, populated by clusters of settlement, would have been a faster way to the Aegean than sailing around the island, particularly when the prevailing winds are taken into account. Horden and Purcell and others have postulated the role of Crete as a centre of re-distribution in this manner, with a key focus on trade to the Cyclades.[77] The likely scenario is that the northern towns then became profitable and successful ports in their own right as opposed to simply being re-distribution points. The southern ports are also likely to have been used extensively for further shipment of goods to Cyrenaica; however, it should be noted that little in the material culture of either Crete or Cyrene suggests significant and sustained contact.

That imports can be traced from coastal to inland areas as well as between coasts suggests an active exploitation of all that the trade routes could offer. Although Crete played an important role in the wine trade,[78] its other exports may have been limited to the mundane, such as timber and whetstones; however, Crete's imports, of sarcophagi, glass and marble, were altogether more luxurious, which is certainly indicative of the profits the island made through trade.[79] The various elements of economic evidence when taken together with the evidence of settlement patterns provide a significant clue as to the nature of Crete's financial status as well as to the reasons the Romans were interested in the island. The evidence of the locally produced pottery across the island, in addition to the quantity of fertile land, indicates that Crete had the potential to be a self-sufficient economy. As Marangou notes, while Cretan wine was certainly valued it was not until after the first century that production became intensive and was aimed more at the export than the home market.[80] The archaeological evidence, particularly in terms of the non-local ceramic material as well as luxuries such as marble, indicates a relatively strong import market.[81] To be in a position to import goods of the quality and in the quantity that Crete was importing necessitated some form of external currency coming onto the island. Although wine may have created some profit, it is likely that significant revenues would have had to come from Crete's provision of a service industry, in this case shipping. Crete profited as a facilitator in cutting the costs of shipping across the Mediterranean by offering overland transport in addition to providing harbour amenities. Such a role would also have endowed the island with greater means and better access to a broad range of goods for purchase. This is seen in the regular occurrence of imported ceramic material on rural sites. Although some of the shipments may not ultimately have been intended for a Cretan market, they may well have been made accessible for purchase as they made their way across the island from coast to coast.[82] While more work needs to be done on sites along the other inland routes, intensive survey evidence in Ierapetra's territory and around Mirabello Bay is supporting this theory. Furthermore, the east of the island, even where there have been archaeological surveys, may be seen in contrast to the finds of mosaics, marbles and other luxuries in rural areas which may have been part of the overland Cretan trade network. In the east, the mountainous and difficult terrain would have made any kind of north-south overland route slow and difficult.

7.7 CRETE: FROM RELUCTANT PARTICIPANT TO CRITICAL PLAYER

The location of Crete in the Mediterranean means that the island is at the centre of a range of routes and networks. The mosaics and other material culture echo this as they represent active elements of choice. The presence of the mosaics is a starting point for further discussion of the people responsible for their existence. In terms of the southern mosaics, some may well have belonged to Italian merchants who may have either settled or sojourned on Crete. It could also be that the mosaics (of both the north and south) are indicative of trends in the movement of craftspeople or patrons, as is clearly indicated by the increase in similarities in the Late Antique mosaics. Like the mosaics, the surviving buildings of Roman Crete contain elements identifiable from both sides of the empire, as well as the island's own strong interpretation of the art. For example, theatres in Crete may be Western in construction (often because they are original constructions rather than Roman reconstructions of earlier Classical or Hellenistic theatres) but may retain many Eastern elements in their design. According to Sanders, some bath houses in Crete, such as the trilobite building at Kato Asites, are of identifiably Western types.[83] Sanders concluded in his section on the architecture of Crete that the island was notably different from other areas of the empire as it lacked evidence of temples but had quite a large number of amphitheatres in comparison to other Greek provinces.[84] He also noted a number of outstanding buildings, such as the bath house at Lappa and the new temple at Lebena. These structures indicate that innovative as well as experienced quality architects were working on the island.

Before the Roman occupation, Crete was relatively isolated, which probably allowed the stories of its harbouring of pirates or its warring city-states to be perpetuated. Throughout the Civil Wars diverse areas within seem to have provided various levels of support for different sides, such as Brutus or Antony or Octavian.[85] What the Romans did for Crete was provide the island with the ability to fit into their expanding empire, in part through globalization; in doing so, they made Crete part of the Roman network society. In contemporary scholarship, the network society is based on the sharing of information and communication, making a whole new economic world available. The mosaics of Crete reflect the island's increasing involvement in the broader network; in turn, its new routes of communication contributed to bursts of creativity which may be seen by the late first century. Its southern communication links may already have been well opened, but the increasing confidence and development of its northern ports in the first century would have led to wider and more frequent communication links. A consequence of being part of a network society is that it would have absolved the residents from a certain level of responsibility and, as Castells argues, widened the gap between the residents and politics.[86] With Rome at the head of the globalized Mediterranean, the individual would have had less power to act; different provinces could provide different resources (natural or labour), and a shared market economy would have meant more open communication links. Ironically, this does not necessarily lead to a diluting of provincial identity. Castells argues that being part of a network society leads to strong national or regional identities. As such, rather than see the mosaics of Crete as having to fit into the koine of the globalized Roman world, they can be seen as strongly retaining their own form, certainly from the second century and well into the Late Antique period. In a network society, information and communication are central to success. Individuals can mediate between different societies that are often unequal in power, and in the case of Crete, it appears that these individuals were the merchants. During the Roman period, information flow was faster and more available than ever before, and there is certainly no sense that there were any attempts to stifle it. As has been argued here, it is likely that Crete functioned as an entrepôt, using its southern ports to connect to the west–east traffic and its overland routes and northern ports to distribute material to the mainland and the Cyclades. Crete was not only part of the network, but it also provided the links between various networks. As argued by Castells, this is an important element of power in the network society, more powerful than simply belonging to it. During the Roman and Late Antique periods, the mosaics of Crete indicate a diversity of fashion and of communications links befitting an island that was making the most of its fortuitous location.

APPENDIX 1

CATALOGUE OF MOSAICS

A1.1 INTRODUCTION

In compiling the corpus of Cretan mosaics, a range of different sources were used: periodicals, newspapers, archives, site publications and personal contacts. Intensive fieldwork was undertaken at all findspots, whether the mosaics were visible or *in situ*, to record the mosaics and their contexts. This corpus records essential information on iconography, chronology and technology. The inclusion of a detailed section on context allows for more analytical discussion on distribution, architecture, patrons and craftspeople.

The catalogue is first divided into Roman and Late Antique periods. If the period is in doubt, the mosaic is listed under the Roman section. Each section is then organized according to geographical area covering the four *nomoi* of Crete, starting with Iraklion followed by Rethymnon and then Lasithi. Because the mosaics of west Crete (the Chania *nomos*) are not the focus of this study, they are presented at the end, followed by a brief list of hitherto unpublished mosaics. As some of the unpublished mosaics are referred to in the discussion but not used in the statistical analysis, they are provided with a separate set of catalogue numbers starting with S200 to distinguish them from the main corpus.

The known Hellenistic mosaics from Crete are included in the corpus. The most securely dated is that of the Hippocamp mosaic from Lebena (Mosaic 66). A second Hellenistic floor from Lato is also included but it bears no decoration, just a pebble floor. The entry for each mosaic in the catalogue is organized as follows:

Plate: Refers to the plate number in the publication.

Location and discovery: Gives the current location and date of discovery of the mosaic.

Dimensions: Records the surviving dimensions of the mosaic.

Context: In excavation reports, the type of building in which a mosaic was discovered is usually recorded. Because of the nature of preliminary reports, however, the exact function of the room in which a mosaic was found is seldom suggested. It is important to treat each of the mosaics not as an isolated find but as a part of a broader archaeological (and consequently, social) context. Where information is unavailable, a reconstructed context has been suggested.

Description: All mosaics are tessellated unless otherwise stated here or in the materials section. Details of colour and a basic account of the type of frame and the geometric and figural elements are given. Where possible, the standard description as defined in Balmelle et al.'s catalogues of geometric decoration is provided.[1] This takes the form (**R** + number) and the standard description can be found with the image in Plate 52. Any inscriptions contained within the mosaics are noted by their Inscription number and the translation and details are found in Appendix 2 (discussed in Chapters 3 & 6).

Materials: Included only when the types of materials, such as stone, glass or terracotta, are definitely known either from site visits or excavation reports.

Date: Notes how the mosaic has been dated and discusses methodology and problems of dating.

Bibliography: Provides a bibliography for each mosaic and a plate reference. These references relate to primary sources where the mosaic in question is considered in detail.

A1.2 Catalogue: Part 1. Roman Mosaic Corpus

Prefecture of Iraklion

Knossos

THE VILLA DIONYSUS MOSAICS

The Villa Dionysus is the largest excavated *domus* in the Knossos Valley (Fig. 12, Grid square D6).[2] Several other areas in the valley have revealed mosaics with a variety of dates (Fig. 12), as will be discussed in detail later.[3] The excavations of the Villa Dionysus were begun before the Second World War in the 1930s by Richard Hutchinson; a plan was made by Arthur Raleigh Radford; and between 1957 and 1961, and then in 1971, work was continued by Michael Gough.[4] Under the directorship of Sara Paton work on the Villa Dionysus began again in 1997. The

excavated remains consist of the peristyle and the series of rooms arranged around its north, west and south (Fig. 18). The rooms are the so-called *Oecus*, N1, N2, N3, S1, S2, S3 and S4. The area directly surrounding these rooms has yet to be investigated; therefore the full extent of the *domus* is not yet known. All of the eight rooms so far excavated are paved with mosaic.

By the time Gough's excavations began, the *oecus* (originally called the atrium) and northern range and their mosaic floors had been exposed, and it was at this stage that modern roofs were built over the mosaics (later replaced as part of the Paton conservation programme) (Paton 2004b & *AR* 1996–7, 106–8). Gough had four campaigns, in 1957, 1958, 1961 and 1971.

A small excavation in the southwest corner (S3) revealed a brick niche which was at the time suggested to be a receptacle for a statue and the site of a small household shrine. This led the excavator to term this room the 'shrine room'.

In 1958 the work continued, and according to the brief report, pottery discovered in that season of excavation dated the villa to the second century. There was evidence to suggest that the walls of S3 had been covered in fresco on top of a marble dado. During this excavation S3 (Fig. 18) was fully excavated, and the 'Three-Part Mosaic' (8) was discovered.

In 1961 Gough virtually finished his excavations: the *oecus* (Fig. 18) was further cleared and was found to have some of its marble dado *in situ* on the walls. The excavation of a small area to the north of this room with two phases (late first century B.C.E. and second century) also took place.

In 1971 Gough decided to go back for another campaign in an attempt to uncover the rooms to the south of the *oecus*. It was then that he determined that the villa had been used as a cult area.[5]

S3 had a window which at one point would have had a clear view to the south. In the third century, however, it was blocked up by the wall of a new house 'itself well built and sumptuously decorated' (*AR* 1971–2, 22). Owing to Gough's untimely death, the 1971 season was his last at the Villa Dionysus. At that point, the S3 and the *Oecus* mosaic were fully covered with plastic and sand. There has been a small amount of work carried out on the villa since then; David Smyth re-erected the columns around the peristyle in the early 1980s, and John Hayes (1983, 97–169) published some of the pottery. It was not until April 1997 that work began again in earnest. A team led by Paton began the work of uncovering the mosaics and assessing the amount of conservation that would be needed on the mosaics to uncover them and keep them open to the public. During this process a new mosaic (30) separate from the Villa Dionysus groups was discovered. The following year the excavations (also by Paton) began to prepare the ground for the new mosaic shelters. The shelters have now been erected, and the mosaics, with the exception of the Geometric mosaic (4), are all currently under plastic as they await further conservation.

DATING OF THE VILLA DIONYSUS

Based on Paton's 1998 chronology, the *domus* was built in the first century. It was altered and re-decorated at least twice in the second century (mid-second century and late second century). Finally, it was destroyed by an earthquake around 200. The only evidence for the use of the house after this was in the *oecus*; here the damaged mosaic suggests that there had been a squatters' fire. Little work has been undertaken on the earliest phase

(late first century) of the house. As part of the second-century renovations, the peristyle was re-modelled and enlarged; the original south wing was dismantled to accommodate the new, larger peristyle; and the *oecus* and Rooms N1 and N2 were re-styled. This date is reasonably secure based on the finding of a coin sealed by one of the columns on the south, a sestertius of Faustina II with the legend FAUSTINA AUGUSTA. The enlargement has to be after 1 December 147, when the empress was given that title after the birth of her first child (Paton 1998).

With this refurbishment, it is likely that all three rooms were paved with mosaic floor (Pls. 1–3) and there is no doubt that they are the product of the same craftspeople. It is possible that the mosaic of S1 (Mosaic 5) (Pl. 5) also fits into this period, but this remains uncertain. Rooms S3 and S4 may have been rebuilt and may also have had mosaic floors at this period. A wall built over part of the mosaic in S4 is likely to date to the late second-century reconstruction of the south wing. In the case of S3, the mosaic currently in this room may belong to the slightly later phase of re-decorating in the late second century.

After the earthquake a house of early third-century date was built up against the window of S3. The mosaics of the Villa Dionysus share clear workshop connections with the Iraklion mosaics 32–7 and possibly with the Hutchinson's mosaic (17) (Chapter 6).

1. *Knossos: Villa Dionysus*, Oecus *Mosaic*
Plate: 1.

Location and discovery: Covered *in situ*. Discovered during the Gough excavations, it is in good condition.

Dimensions: 8.5 x 8.5 m. Geometric décor: tesserae *c*. 1 x 1 cm. Figured décor: tesserae *c*. 0.75 x 0.75 cm.

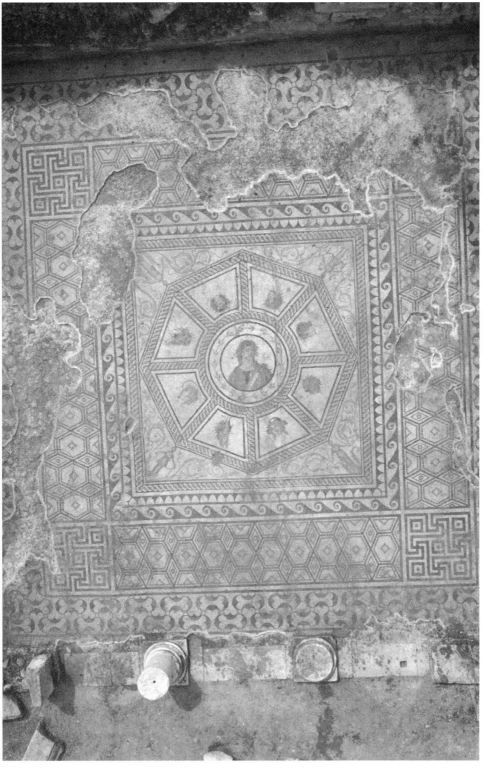

Plate 1 Knossos, Villa Dionysus, *Oecus* mosaic (Mosaic 1) (courtesy of S. Paton).

Context: This mosaic was found in the largest room in the *domus,* which looks directly onto the central portico (Fig. 18). The room was originally called the *oecus,* but its exact function has not yet been defined.

Description: Mosaic 1 is made of polychrome tesserae and some glass in the figures. Within a series of square borders is an octagon divided into eight panels surrounding a central circular medallion (Pl. 1).

The central medallion of Dionysus is bordered by a circular garland of flowers; the design is similar to a laurel garland (**R** 88g), without the stem and the berries. This is set within a circular border of guilloche in brown, light brown and white (**R** 70j). Dionysus is illustrated as a youngish man with a thoughtful expression, gazing to his left. On his brown curly hair is set a crown of vine leaves. He wears a blue robe with a vertical black band down its centre. Across his left shoulder is a cluster of coloured wreaths (blue, orange, green and white) which fall across his chest and are tied in a knot on his shoulder. Blue and green glass tesserae are extensively used for the depiction of the drapery and the crown.

Each of the eight panels of the octagon contains an elaborate depiction of Dionysus's followers, including Silenus and the maenads and other characters from the Dionysiac thiasos such as satyrs and Pan. Only the head of each is portrayed and elaborately executed. The maenads have very detailed hair with ribbons, and their facial features have been delicately rendered. Equal care has been taken over the heads of Pan and the satyrs.

Outside the octagon, in the four corners of the square, female figures emerge from leaves (Pl. 1). The eight panels of the octagon are divided by eight connecting spokes of guilloche (**R** 70j) radiating from the central circle.

The same form of guilloche band is used to create the overall grid and acts as an inner border of the main square. On the inside of the outermost band of guilloche is a small band of dentilled simple fillet (**R** 2d). This fillet also borders the outside of the band of guilloche which creates the octagon. Outside this is a row of ogives and thorns (**R** 49h). The thorns are dark and the ogives are light. The outer border of the square panel is decorated with a wave pattern (**R** 101a). Beyond this central design with its three different geometric borders is a further two borders which are much larger than the three inner ones. The two large outer borders could be considered as separate panels.

The inner border of the two contains two different geometric designs in eight panels (Pl. 1). There are four corner panels (all the same) and a further four panels which occupy the same length of each side of the wave-scroll border. The four side panels consist of a design of hexagons, diamonds and semi-hexagons. This design is similar to a field of hexagons and lozenges (**R** 213a). In each of the hexagons a small square is set at a point and each of the diamonds contains a smaller diamond with a central small circle. A grid of swastika meander (**R** 38c), contained in a square is at each corner. The final border enclosing the entire mosaic consists of a running peltae (**R** 222d).

Materials: Glass, stone (local limestone), terracotta and marble tesserae.

Date: The *oecus* itself may date to the early second century, but the mosaic was probably laid during re-modelling in the mid-second century.

Bibliography: Hutchinson 1934–35, 5; *AR* 1958, 24; id. *AR* 1959, 22; *AR* 1961, 29–30; *AR* 1971–1972, 22; Michaud 1972, 802; Sanders, 51–3 & 69; Paton 1998; Paton 2000, 553–62; Sweetman 2003.

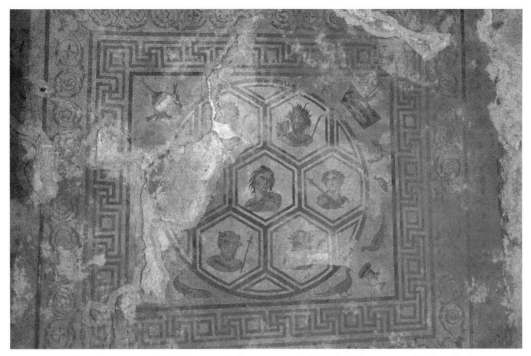

Plate 2 Knossos, Villa Dionysus, Followers mosaic (Mosaic 2) (courtesy of S. Paton).

2. *Knossos: Villa Dionysus, Followers of Dionysus*

Plate: 2.

Location and discovery: Covered *in situ*. Discovered during the Hutchinson excavations, the mosaic is in a delicate state following exposure to the elements for more than 40 years.

Dimensions: *c.* 7 x 6.5 m. Geometric décor: tesserae *c.* 1 x 1 cm. Figured décor: tesserae *c.* 0.75 x 0.75 cm.

Context: Room N1, the most westerly room in the north range of the Villa Dionysus (Fig. 18).

Description: The mosaic is made from polychrome tesserae. A square frame encloses a circle which itself contains a central hexagon surrounded by six others (Pl. 2).

The central hexagon depicts a wild-looking Dionysiac follower with pointed ears. Other attendants of Dionysus are excellently rendered in the remaining six hexagons. In a clockwise direction, from the top right-hand corner: Pan with pipes, a maenad with a thyrsus, a figure with pointed ears accompanied by a *pedum*, Silenus with a thyrsus – the next panel is too damaged to identify – and finally another figure with a *pedum* (Pl. 2). The central figure is distinguished from the others by the inclusion of his hands in which he holds an *aulos*. Blue and green glass is used extensively in the figures, and yellow occurs in their garments to a lesser degree. The great many colours used intensifies the vibrant appearance of the mosaic, making the representation of the Dionysiac thiasos more effective.

The spaces at the four corners, between the circle and the enclosing square, are filled either with birds, including cocks and peacocks, or with fish (as in the northeast corner). These fish are depicted on a wooden platter or a table with a single leg. To the right of the fish panel is a crab. In the north-west corner, two blue birds stand on either side of a bowl. To the right of these is another blue bird, which could be part of the bowl scene. In the southwest corner, a peacock and a small fragment of a kantharos survive; the head and crown of a second peacock can be identified facing the first on the other side of the vessel. This theme is repeated again in the southeast corner of the mosaic where two parrots face each other on either side of a kantharos (Pl. 2). Between this corner and the northeast corner motif, a cock and a partridge face each other. Different shades of blue-glass tesserae as well as green and yellow glass are used extensively in the rendering of these birds and fish.

The outer square is formed by a band of swastika meander (**R** 38c); the mosaic is then bordered by an elaborate leafy scroll similar to acanthus scroll (**R** 64e). In the Knossos example, however, there are four-petalled flowers, buds and bichrome-coloured flowers, all complex and all with different centres; this contrasts with the alternating flowers and buds in the décor example. The centre of the scroll is pink, and the main part is black (Pl. 2). Each corner contains a large bushy acanthus, and it is from its calyx that the scroll around the mosaic grows. This scroll is one of the finest and best-executed on any Roman mosaic in Greece. Finally, the whole mosaic is bordered by a triple row of chevrons arranged in fours and touching at their points, rendered in black on a white background. A wide black band separates each of the borders.

Materials: Glass, stone, terracotta tesserae.

Date: Like Mosaic 1, this mosaic is probably from the mid-second-century re-modelling of the villa, although the room (N1) in which this mosaic was laid dates to the early second century.

Bibliography: *AR* 1935, 164; *AR* 1961, 29–30; Sanders, 51–3; Paton 1998; Paton 2000, 553–62; Sweetman 2003.

3. *Knossos: Villa Dionysus, Dionysus and the Four Seasons*

Plate: 3.

Location and discovery: Covered *in situ*. Discovered during the Hutchinson excavations, the larger figured panel has survived well, but the smaller northern panel of geometric decoration is largely destroyed.

Dimensions: 3.25 x 4.5 m (excluding small panel at the northern end). Geometric décor: tesserae *c*. 1 x 1 cm. Figured décor: tesserae *c*. 0.75–0.50 x 0.75–0.50 cm.

Context: This mosaic is located in Room N2 in the northern wing of the villa complex (Fig. 18). From the shape of the mosaic, a large rectangular panel adjoining a smaller geometric panel, N2 probably functioned as a *cubiculum*. The size of this panel (1.90 x 2.5 m) would be appropriate.

Description: The main figured area of the mosaic is framed by a vault pattern contained within a square grid (Pl. 3). The outer border consists of a band of guilloche (**R** 70j) and an enclosing band of wave pattern (**R** 101b). A broad black band five tesserae wide further encloses this.

A central circle, defined by a guilloche band and a band of a monochrome, serrated saw-tooth pattern (**R** 10g) contains a bust of Dionysus (Pl. 3) in sombre mood. Dionysus wears a garland, running from his left shoulder across his chest and bunched at his left shoulder, in a similar way to Dionysus in Mosaic 1. There are also vine leaves in his hair. As with Mosaic 1, blue and green glass tesserae are used in the crown and drapery.

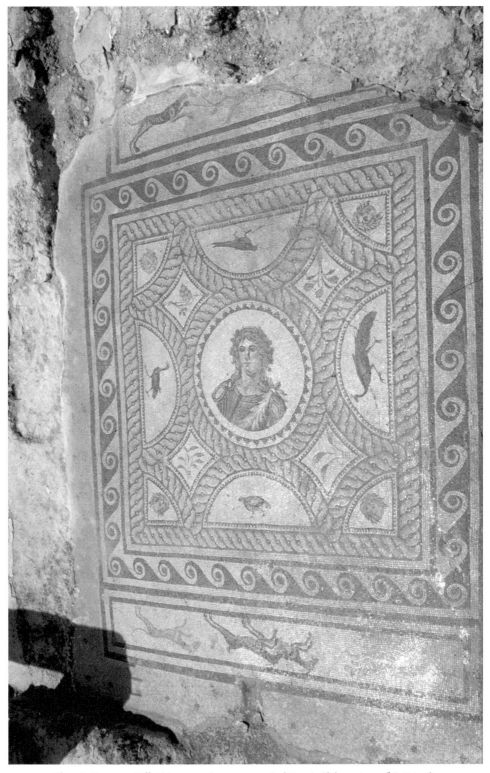

Plate 3 Knossos, Villa Dionysus, Seasons mosaic (Mosaic 3) (courtesy of S. Paton).

The overall design of the mosaic, with the continuous movement of the guilloche (**R** 70j) border, consists of intermeshing semi-circles and tangents in a vault pattern. This creates rounded triangles and concave squares, which are filled with various still-life scenes. Birds are placed in the semi-circles, including a peacock (Pl. 3), and what appear to be a partridge, a waterbird and a small bird of some kind, possibly a parrot. The four concave squares surrounding the central medallion contain plants: a rose, some kind of grain, a vine branch and reeds. These probably represent the seasons (Pl. 3) (see discussion in Chapter 3) and the association of each plant with a bird strengthens the connection – for example, the small bird is associated with the vine, and the peacock with a rose bush. If the birds and plants do represent the four seasons, then the following suggestion is likely:

Spring = peacock and rose (beauty)
Winter = wader and reed or olive (rain and damp)
Summer = partridge and grain (harvest)
Autumn = parrot (?) and vine (harvest)

As with Mosaic 2, blue and green and occasionally red glass is used in the depiction of the birds and plants.

There are four rounded triangles in the corners of the outer border, each enclosing a face (Pl. 3). Given that they are four in number, the faces could be representations of the winds, but they have no characteristic features. A small border of dentilled simple fillet (**R** 2d) surrounds each of these figures.

On the north side, outside the border, is a frieze of a black dog chasing a goat, and even though the mosaic is badly damaged, there are traces of another dog approaching the goat from behind. On the south side is a second frieze depicting two red dogs chasing two black goats (Pl. 3).

A large border surrounds the main figured field. A very wide band of white tesserae *c.* 40 cm wide containing rows of black stepped squares (**R** 5a) appears to be more like a space filler.

A subsidiary panel of peltae (**R** 222d) is connected to the main figure. This geometric panel at the back likely marks the position for the bed.

Materials: Glass, stone, terracotta tesserae.

Date: Like the *oecus* and Room N1, Room N2 is likely to date to the early second century, but the mosaic is probably contemporary with the re-modelling of the *domus* in the mid-second century.

Bibliography: Hutchinson 1934–5, 5; *AR* 1961, 29–30; Sanders, 51–3; Paton 1998; Paton 2000, 553–62; Sweetman 2003.

4. *Knossos: Villa Dionysus, Geometric Mosaic*

Plate: 4.

Location and discovery: Exposed *in situ*. The excavations of Hutchinson (for the eastern part) and then Gough revealed this mosaic. Sections are missing and consolidation work has kept the surviving 70 percent together.

Dimensions: The preserved part of the mosaic measures *c.* 2.5 x 2.5 m. Tesserae *c.* 1.2 x 1.2 cm.

Context: Room N3 on the north side of the *domus*. No evidence for the function of the room has been unearthed and the walls are not preserved; however, Fig. 18 shows clearly the peculiar orientation of the room.

Description: This geometric mosaic in black and white has a black border six tesserae wide (Pl. 4). All the other renderings are two tesserae in width.

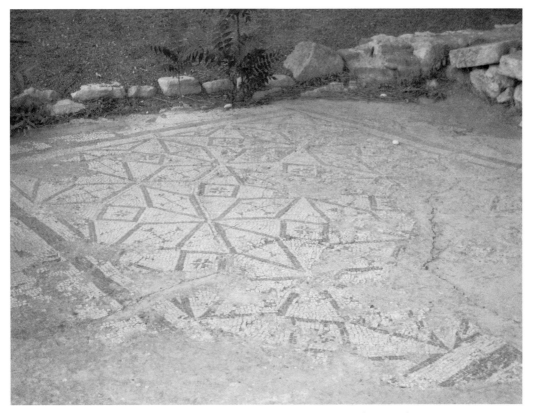

Plate 4 Knossos, Villa Dionysus, Geometric mosaic (Mosaic 4).

The design is a mat of four-pointed stars forming lozenges (**R** 184b), here with the stars bearing an axially inscribed square. Each square contains four chevrons joined together at the outer angles. Each of the diamonds contains a crosslet design consisting of intersecting rows of squares terminating in the chevron (**R** 4e). A band of blank triangles surround the inner edge of the border.

Materials: Stone tesserae.

Date: As yet no stratigraphic information is available, and therefore the mosaic must be dated from a combination of architectural and stylistic evidence. The orientation of the mosaic suggests that it might not be contemporary with the other two mosaics of the north wing, but comparisons with the Iraklion-Knossos workshop suggest otherwise. Recent excavation indicates that this room may have been in line with the peristyle before the refurbishment of the villa; further excavation will be needed to confirm this.[6] At best we can say that the mosaic is likely to date to before the mid-second century.

Bibliography: Paton 1998; Sweetman 2003.

5. *Knossos: Villa Dionysus, Medusa and the Four Seasons Mosaic*

Plate: 5.

Location and discovery: Covered *in situ*. Exposed during the Gough excavations. Despite the destruction of the central figured panel, the remainder is in good condition.

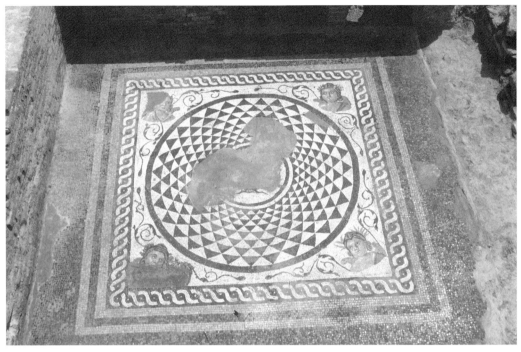

Plate 5 Knossos, Villa Dionysus, Medusa mosaic (Mosaic 5) (courtesy of S. Paton).

Dimensions: 3.75 x 3.75 m. Geometric décor: tesserae *c.* 1 x 1 cm. Figured décor: tesserae *c.* 0.75 x 0.75 cm.

Context: Southeast room of the Villa Dionysus, Room S1 (Fig. 18).

Description: The central scene is set within a square which is bordered by guilloche (**R** 70d). The only part of the central area remaining is a small section of a motif, possibly knotted snakes (Pl. 5). This is surrounded by a circular design of a chessboard pattern of triangles (**R** 327b) which, by getting progressively larger from the inside out, creates a swirling pattern. This design is enclosed by a wide black circular band.

The outer border is created by two white bands on a black background. In each corner, just within the outer border, a figure represents one of the four seasons. All the figures have wings, and this was a more common feature in the East from the mid-second century onwards (Pl. 5). The figure in the southeast corner can be identified as Winter. Dead twigs can be seen in its hair, symbols of death and decay. Moving clockwise from the southeast corner, the figures follow each other according to the order of the seasons. The figure in the southwest corner is Spring as a female wearing a wreath of spring flowers in her hair. In the northwest corner is Summer, also a female, wearing a crown of wheat in her hair, a symbol of the summer growth and harvest. Finally, the female figure in the northeast corner represents Autumn, the season of the grape harvest. The figure is badly damaged, though grapes and vine leaves are still visible in her hair. Red, yellow and to a lesser degree green and blue glass tesserae are used in the drapery and wreaths of the figures. Extending out from either side of each of the figures is a length of acanthus scroll (**R** 64e). Each of the scrolls is slightly different, which indicates either that there was no set pattern or that the artist was following a specific design for the scrolls.

Materials: Glass, stone, terracotta tesserae.

Date: The south range in which the mosaic lies dates to the mid-second century. The mosaic has some features in common with the other mosaics in this range: a similar scroll pattern is found in Mosaics 2, 5 and 6; in Mosaics 1, 3 and 5 the figures are rendered in a similar way. It is possible therefore that Mosaic 5 can be ascribed to the same workshop as Mosaics 1, 2, 3 and 6. This supports a date of the mid-second century for the mosaic.

Bibliography: Hutchinson 1934–5, 5; Sanders, 51–3; Paton 1998; Paton 2000, 553–62; Sweetman 2003.

6. *Knossos: Villa Dionysus, Geometric Designs S2*

Plate: 6.

Location and discovery: Covered *in situ*. The mosaic was badly damaged and only partially survived when uncovered in the 1970s excavations.

Dimensions: Only a small amount of the mosaic is preserved. The room measures 3.2 x 3.2 m. The tesserae are between 1.00 and 1.20 cm.

Context: The function of Room S2 in which this mosaic is found is difficult to discern (Fig. 18). There were two or three doorways into the room so it may have been a small hall. Paton (1998, 126) notes that when first excavated it was clear that the room had been richly decorated.

Description: The mosaic is rectangular in plan with an outer border of guilloche (**R** 70e). Within the border a further rectangle is outlined. Within this, the remaining mosaic fragments indicate either one of two designs.

The first possibility is of two intersecting circles as shown in Pl. 6. The second is of one circle containing shields divided up into triangles similar to the central circle of Mosaic 2. In two of the corners, in the space left over between the circle and the rectangle, there are two circular-type designs, perhaps flowers, similar to the stylized flowers within the scroll border of Mosaic 2. The fact that they are black on white though, and with longer petals, suggests a closer similarity with those in Mosaics 17 and 37. A small section of wave scroll is also in the northern part of the mosaic, but it is difficult to identify as only a small fragment is undamaged.

Materials: Stone tesserae.

Date: Paton (1998, 126) notes that a new range of rooms (S2, S3 and S4, incorporating Mosaics 6–8, respectively) was laid out on the south side of the villa during the mid-second-century re-modelling. Further support for this date is offered by a stylistic comparison between Mosaic 6 and Mosaics 1–3. The subsidiary design of the stylized plant in Mosaic 6 (Room S2) is almost the same as that in Mosaic 2 (mid- to late second century). As the same craftspeople are likely to have been responsible for Mosaics 1, 2, 3 and 6, it probably dates to the mid-second century.

Bibliography: Paton 1998; Paton 2000, 553–62; Sweetman 2003.

Note: It is likely that Mosaic 6 and the northern panel of Mosaic 7 were originally one mosaic, similar in layout to that of Mosaic 3, indicating that the original function of the room may have been a *cubiculum*.

7. *Knossos: Villa Dionysus, Geometric Designs S4*

Plate: 6.

Location and discovery: Covered *in situ*. Discovered during excavations in the 1970s,

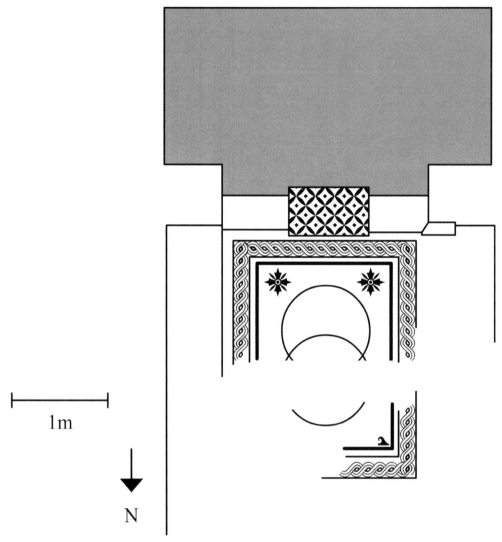

Plate 6 Knossos, Villa Dionysus, schematic plan of S2 and S4 (Mosaics 6 and 7)
(drawing by K. Sweetman).

and despite damage on the southern side, it is quite well preserved.

Dimensions: 3.2 x 1.6 m. Tesserae are uneven. Black tesserae are *c.* 1.75 x 1.75 cm, and the spindles on white are rendered in 1.4 x 1.4 cm.

Context: Room S4. It is linked to Room S2 by a doorway, and this appears to have been the only access. The remains of a strong-box were discovered in Room S4, and given the small dimensions of the room (*c.* 3.2 x 1.6 m) it could hardly have functioned as anything other than a storage area (Fig. 18).

Description: The mosaic consists of two main fields. The most northerly contains a simple design of circles creating concave squares and spindles (**R** 238b). The second field, of plain black with occasional white tesserae, covers most of the floor (*c.* 3.2 x 1.1 m). No border separates the two fields.

Materials: Stone tesserae.

Date: The partition dividing Rooms S2 and S4 is constructed on top of Mosaic 7 in Room S4. So a mid-second century date is likely.

Bibliography: Paton 1998; Paton 2000, 553–62; Sweetman 2003.

8. *Knossos: Villa Dionysus, Three-Part Mosaic*

Plate: 7.

Location and discovery: Covered *in situ*. It was in a notably fine state of preservation when discovered in 1958, and when uncovered again in 1997 it was still well preserved.

Dimensions: 3.75 x 2.80 m. Geometric décor: tesserae *c.* 1 x 1 cm. Figured décor: tesserae *c.* 0.75 x 0.75 cm.

Context: Room S3. Likely a *cubiculum* (Fig. 18).

Description: A large band of ivy scroll (**R** 64d) surrounds the mosaic. The main area enclosed by the scroll is divided into two unequal parts (Pl. 7). The simple section consists of a net pattern with each compartment enclosing a chevron rendered in black on a white background (**R** 124a). This panel is joined to the larger one by a smaller section of acanthus scroll (**R** 64e). The larger area is bordered by a swastika meander (**R** 35d). At the midpoint of this meander is a highly stylized acanthus flower. An alternative interpretation is that it is a 'trifid' like those in **R** 84d. A single trifid is located in the middle of each side of the meander (Pl. 7).

Inside this border, a smaller guilloche border (**R** 70f) occurs and within this there are three central panels, divided by bands of the same guilloche. The central panel depicts a bird drinking. A 'mat' of intersecting circles forming spindles (containing a poised square) and concave squares (**R** 239a) surrounds the bird. Each yellow spindle contains a dark

orange square, and each circle encloses a larger square, also orange in colour. The whole design is set against a black background. This panel is enclosed above and below by panels made up of a row of tangent cuboids (**R** 99e). The sides of the blocks are coloured brown and at the top of each are two side-by-side triangles, one blue and one black, forming a square. The two rows are both oriented inwards towards the central medallion, which gives an overall unified feeling to the three central panels. In the same area, to the east of the main Three-Part Mosaic, a small panel acts as a threshold panel for the room (Pl. 7). This consists of a rectangle outlined in black with a diamond inside, the points of which touch each side of the rectangle. In the centre of the black diamond, a small motif consists of two small triangles facing each other. Another small motif, possibly a circle, is contained in each of the four corners of the space between the diamond and the outer rectangle.

Materials: Glass, stone, terracotta tesserae.

Date: Paton notes that a phase of re-modelling in this room took place in the late second century, just before the destruction of the *domus* was undertaken. The mosaic may date to this period, but the workshop connections that this mosaic has with the Iraklion mosaics make it possible that all the mosaics belong to the same phase in the mid-second century.

Bibliography: *AR* 1959 22; *AR* 1961, 29–30; Sanders, 51–3; Paton 1998; Paton 2000, 553–62; Sweetman 2003.

9. *Knossos: Apollinaris Mosaic*

Plate: 8–9.

Location and discovery: On display in the Iraklion museum, the mosaic is roughly square and in fairly good condition except

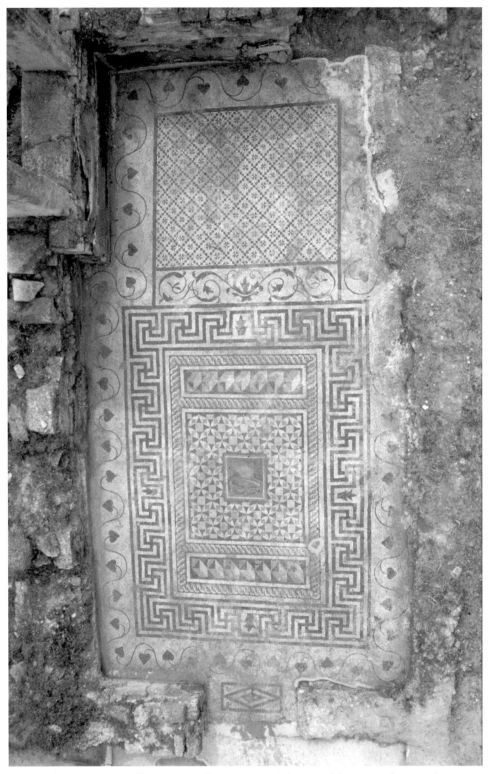

Plate 7 Knossos, Villa Dionysus, Three-Part mosaic (Mosaic 8) (courtesy of S. Paton).

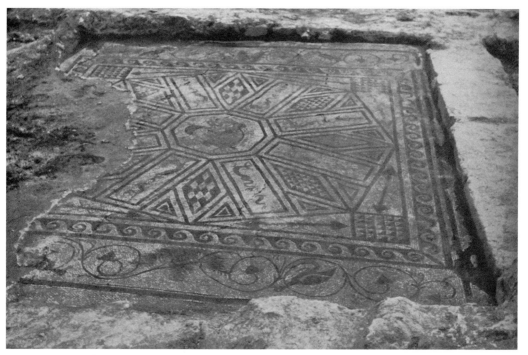

Plate 8 Knossos, Apollinaris mosaic (Mosaic 9) (courtesy of BSA Archives).

that a corner on the left-hand side has been slightly damaged. The mosaic was uncovered in 1951 while workers were diverting a stream.

Dimensions: 3.50 x 2.85 m

Context: Discovered in the northern part of the Roman city of Knossos in the same area as Mosaics 15, 23 and 24 (Fig. 12, Grid square D5). The exact context was not recorded in *KS* 91, but the mosaic was believed to have come from a *domus*. The mosaic's aquatic theme suggests that it may actually come from a bath house. Dunbabin (1999, 211) notes that its limited polychrome style is primarily, but not exclusively, found in baths, but it is also possible that the mosaic came from a room in the *domus* that had water features or a focus on activities involving water.

Description: The mosaic is mostly of black-and-white geometric design with a polychrome central emblem of Poseidon in his chariot drawn by hippocamps (Pl. 8). Its most outstanding feature is the signature of the artist (Ἀπολλινάρις ἐποίει) (Inscription 1) discussed in Chapter 6.

The mosaic consists of a large octagon set within a square. Within this, a smaller octagon frames Poseidon in a rather stylized non-narrative scene (Pl. 8). Poseidon is in his chariot; his left leg and right arm are outstretched. In his left hand he holds a trident and the reins of the seahorses. As he stands on two seahorses (the structure of the chariot is not depicted) his cloak, which falls around his right leg, billows out behind his shoulders. This gives the impression of speed.

Radiating out from the inner octagon are alternate lozenges and rectangles (eight of each) which reach the edges of the outer octagon. The rectangles contain images of sea centaurs and dolphins, each portrayed

ॐ   171

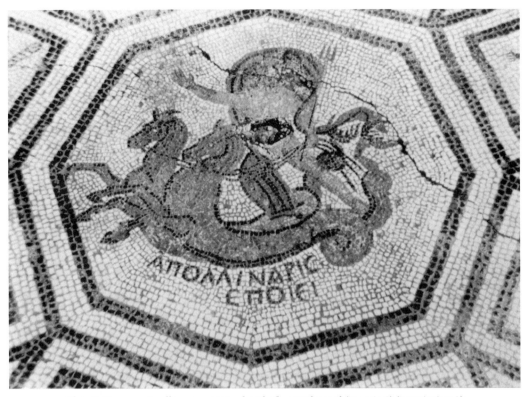

Plate 9 Knossos, Apollinaris mosaic, detail of central panel (Mosaic 9) (Inscription 1)
(courtesy of BSA Archives).

in a different manner; for example, one sea centaur carries a conch, and another, a club. The lozenges are further divided into two right-angled triangles and a central lozenge. The lozenges contain fields of a chessboard pattern of equilateral triangles (**R** 198e) and a chessboard pattern of lozenges (**R** 202a). The triangles on either side of the lozenges are filled with smaller triangles.

Each of the four corners of the square surrounding the octagon contains a smaller square which touches the edge of the octagon. Each square is filled with a chessboard pattern of right-angled isosceles triangles (**R** 197a). There are eight right-angled triangles in the space between the octagon and the square, and each triangle contains a thyrsus.[7] Running through the centre of the line is a cross with a small circle at the point where all the lines intersect (Pl. 8).

An inner wave-pattern border (**R** 101b) directly surrounds the main square. At each of the four corners the wave pattern extends into a point and the scroll changes orientation, so that the direction of the wave alternates around the four sides of the panel. The wave pattern is bordered on two sides by an elaborate ivy scroll (**R** 64d). On the south side a duck and a leafy fern are entwined in the scroll. A final border of a plain white band surrounds the mosaic.

Materials: Stone tesserae.

Date: First century to early second century. In the absence of surviving stratigraphy and recorded contexts, this date is based on the iconography. The design of the mosaic (the octagon within the square) and the scroll (with triangular leaves) leads Sanders to propose an early second-century date. Waywell, however, suggests that the mosaic could be dated a century earlier, based on the evolution of peopled scrolls and the birds within them. The marine creatures depicted on this mosaic can be compared with others from the first century, particularly in mosaics from Pompeii and Ostia (Blake 1930, 121 & Becatti 1961, 42–4). Dunbabin (1999, 111) notes that the black-and-white style or limited polychrome types are found early in the Roman period in Greece, when mosaics became fashionable again and developed under strong Italian influence. As the Apollinaris mosaic fits this description, this gives further support to a late first- or early second-century date.

Bibliography: *KS* 91; Platon 1951, 439; *AR* 1951, 45; Waywell 1979, 311; Sanders, 53; Dunbabin 1999, 211; Sweetman 2003.

10. *Knossos: Wave-Scroll Fragment*

Plate: http://artsweb.bham.ac.uk/aha/kaw/ Knossos/MOSAIC.html

Location and discovery: Covered *in situ*. The mosaic was mostly destroyed when uncovered during the 1993 season of the K2K[8] research excavations, and only a few fragments survive.

Dimensions: *c.* 70 cm surviving width. Tesserae *c.* 1.1 x 1.1 cm.

Context: This mosaic was discovered around 25 m to the southeast of the Villa Dionysus (Area H of the Roman Knossos excavations) and to the west of the Civil Basilica. It belongs to the largest concentration of mosaics in the Knossos Valley (Fig. 12, Grid square 6). The fragment was found at the foot of a wall which was preserved to a height of 6 m and a length of 20 m. The wall was faced with large dressed blocks, and Wardle suggests that

it may have belonged to a two-storey public building (*AR* 1993–4, 75). The 1995 excavations proved that the wall continued for more than 30 m and also revealed a semi-circular brick-lined niche at the southern end of the wall and a tile arch at floor level, which is probably a drain or conduit (*AR* 1994–5, 96). On the basis of these features and the great size of the wall, Wardle has proposed that the building may have been a large public bath house. Its location in the centre of the city, opposite the Civil Basilica, supports this premise, but there are insufficient data to establish this securely.

Description: The largest fragment consists of a wave-crest border rendered in black and white tesserae. The outer part of the border (closest to the surviving wall) is a black band, *c.* 25 cm wide. On the interior, a small fragment of a white band *c.* 10 cm wide survives. The actual wave crest is quite wide (*c.* 28 cm), and its size in combination with the surviving architecture may indicate that this mosaic covered a large floor space. Wardle identifies the Wave-Scroll fragment with Mosaic 13, which was discovered and then re-buried by Halbherr at the turn of the century. However, the surviving sketch by Halbherr does not show a wave-scroll border and his mosaic is located closer than Mosaic 10 (Scuola Archeologica Italiana di Atene 1984, fig. 21) to the Civil Basilica. Further work on Halbherr's Knossos excavations has recently been undertaken by Morgan and Whitelaw (Morgan 2009).

Materials: Stone tesserae.

Date: According to the preliminary reports a date of late second or early third century is suggested.

Bibliography: *AR* 1992–3, 21–2; *AR* 1993–4, 75; *AR* 1994–5, 20; *AR* 1995–6, 42; Wardle 1998; Sweetman 2003.

11. *Knossos: Net-Pattern Mosaic*

Plate: http://artsweb.bham.ac.uk/aha/kaw/Knossos/AreaCroom3.html

Location: Covered *in situ*. The mosaic was badly damaged when uncovered during the 1990s and only a third of it survives.

Dimensions: *c.* 300 x 100 cm (surviving).

Context: Area C of the K2K excavations. The six-room complex in which this mosaic is found is located around 150 m southwest of the Villa Dionysus (Fig. 12, Grid square D6). Within the complex the remains of a bath house have been brought to light. On the basis of its small size the excavators suggest that the bath suite was associated with a *domus*, thus identifying it as a private complex (*AR* 1993–4, 75). There is as yet no substantial evidence to support the existence of a *domus*. Mosaic 11 was found in the largest room (Room 3) (7 x 7 m), which is located south of the courtyard and east of the cistern. The complex also contains both the remains of a rough pebble floor in Room 2 and the Athlete mosaic (12).

Description: The remains are a net pattern of black tesserae on a white background (R 124a) (the compartment here enclosing a parallel serrated square). Within each of the squares of the net there is a single, black, serrated square.

Materials: Glass, stone, terracotta tesserae.

Date: According to the excavators, the complex appears to have been constructed in the late second century and to have fallen out of use by the mid third century (*AR* 1995–6, 42). The walls were heavily robbed out, and in the late third or early fourth century a dry-stone walled building was constructed on the site on the same alignment. It is reasonable therefore to date the mosaic to the late second or early third century.

Bibliography: *AR* 1992–3, 21–2; *AR* 1993–4, 75; *AR* 1994–5, 20; *AR* 1995–6, 42; Wardle 1998; Sweetman 2003.

12. *Knossos: The Athlete Mosaic*

Plate: 10.

Location and discovery: Covered *in situ*. It was very badly damaged when excavated in 1995 – only the westernmost section of the mosaic survives, no more than a quarter of the original.

Dimensions: The mosaic survives to a length of 2 m and is roughly 1.75 m at its greatest width.

Context: Area C of the K2K excavations (Fig. 12). Found in the same complex as Mosaic 11, in Room 10, to the east of the plunge bath and to the north of the hypocaust in the bath house. There is little evidence for doorways because the associated walls were badly robbed.

Description: The surviving portion of the mosaic is polychrome and depicts the upper parts of two figures. Both have their arms raised and appear to be wearing gloves. The gloves indicate that they might be boxers, and the stance suggests that they are involved in a contest. The names of the figures are inscribed over their heads: ([– – –]κλος Σατορνῖλος) (Inscription 2) (Pl. 10) (discussed in Chapter 3).

Materials: Stone tesserae.

Date: The context has been dated to the late second to mid-third century.

Bibliography: *AR* 1992–3, 21–2; *AR* 1993–4, 75; *AR* 1994–5, 20; *AR* 1995–6, 42; Wardle 1998; Sweetman 2003.

13. *Knossos: The Four Seasons Mosaic*

Plate: Scuola Archeologica Italiana di Atene 1984, fig. 21.

Location and discovery: The current location of the mosaic is unknown. Found in 1885 by Halbherr, he recorded few details.

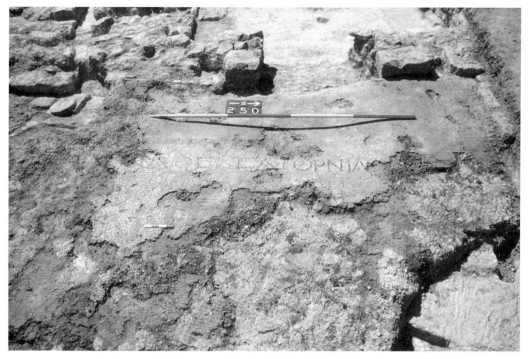

Plate 10 Knossos, Athlete mosaic (Mosaic 12) (Inscription 2) (courtesy of K. Wardle).

Dimensions: 2 x 2 m (according to Morgan).

Context: It is difficult to reconstruct the exact context of this mosaic as Halbherr merely produced a sketch of the location (Scuola Archeologica Italiana di Atene 1984, fig. 21) and stated that he had found a well-preserved pavement with representations of the four seasons (Halbherr 1893, 110–12). The sketch locates the mosaic just to the west of a large Roman building. This may possibly be part of the Civil Basilica, but the orientation is incorrect (Fig. 12) (See *Scuola Archeologica Italiana di Atene 1984*, 61).[9] It is unlikely that the mosaic was directly associated with the large Roman building (*KS* 112) because it is not aligned with any of the nearby walls, but it may be linked to the Roman Concrete Building noted by Carington Smith (*KS* 111). However, this is difficult to confirm, as only a small section of the building was uncovered during a rescue excavation (KN Logbook 75).[10]

In his brief report, Halbherr (1893, 110–12) mentions that close to the large Roman public building he 'disinterred' a group of Roman houses which were near the remains of a further large edifice decorated with columns and fragments of statues. It would be tempting to suggest that the latter were the remains of the Villa Dionysus; however, it is not possible to verify this hypothesis. Morgan's recent study (2009), which draws upon the excavation notebook, suggests that this is not the case, but the description of the mosaic is so close to that of Mosaic 5 that the possibility cannot be ruled out.

Description: The only recorded details note a circle which had a central panel containing Medusa. The circle was enclosed in a square and there were heads in the spandrels.

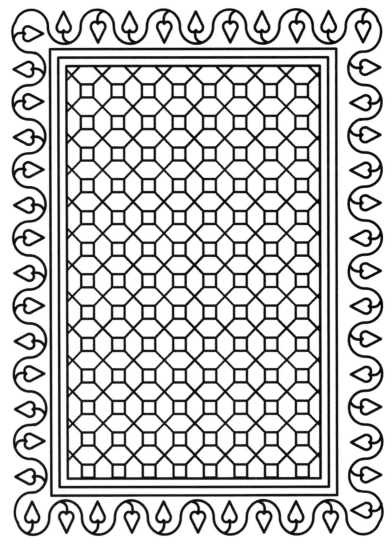

Plate 11 Knossos, Theodosius mosaic (Mosaic 14) (drawing by K. Sweetman).

It would be reasonable to suggest that each season would have occupied a corner of the mosaic. The description is strikingly similar to that of Mosaic 5, and although Morgan (2009) clearly indicates that they cannot be the same mosaic, based on the evidence of the sketch plans, the chances of having two such similar mosaics so close by are not common.

Date: No date is available.

Bibliography: Halbherr 1893, 110–12; Sanders, 53; *KS* 111 & 112; KN Logbook 75; Scuola Archeologica Italiana di Atene 1984; Sweetman 2003; Morgan 2009.

14. *Knossos: Theodosius Mosaic*
Plate: 11.

Location and discovery: This mosaic was drawn and removed shortly after discovery in 1950. The KN Logbook record notes the mosaic was in good condition when discovered.

Dimensions: Not known.

Context: Found just to the east of the Roman Civil Basilica (Fig. 12, Grid square D6) when a vineyard was being planted. Two other floors are briefly noted in the KN Logbook. One is described simply as a marble floor and the other as a 'mosaic' made from broken red tile. Also found with the mosaic, but not necessarily directly associated with it, were a number of architectural remains, including a marble half-column and a Roman capital.

Description: Geometric panel bordered by an ivy scroll (**R** 64d) (Pl. 11). The basic geometric pattern was executed in red and blue against a cream background, and the main design was composed of small squares (2 x 2 cm) which were surrounded by hexagons measuring 3 x 2 x 4 cm (one on each of the four sides) (**R** 169a). The horizontal hexagons were rendered in blue and the vertical ones in red.

Date: A bronze coin of Theodosius was discovered on top of the mosaic floor along with a piece of a glass bowl and a fragment of a bronze mirror. The coin can be dated 379–95 but does not help provide a date for the mosaic. The hexagon pattern is similar to examples found on mainland Greece, such as that from the Brick Building, Kenchreai, dated to the first half of the second century (Waywell 1979, cat. 29, Pl. 48). Sanders (53) suggested some commonality between Mosaics 14 and Mosaic 55 (from Gortyn), dated to the late second century, but while they both use hexagons, there are few other similarities.

Parallels can also be drawn within Crete on the basis of the type of scroll used, for example, with that in Mosaic 8 (second half second century). The ivy-scroll border is similar to a form found in Greece in the second to third century, for example, at the Baths of Olympian Zeus (Waywell 1979, pl. 50). A date of late second century to early third century is likely.

Bibliography: KN Logbook, 21 January 1950, 10; *KS* 119; Sanders, 52; Sweetman 2003.

15. *Knossos: Paterakis Building Plot*

Plate: None available.

Location and discovery: Destroyed; it was in poor condition when originally excavated in 1976 by Paton.

Dimensions: Unknown.

Context: Located nearby the Apollinaris mosaic (9) in the north of the Roman city (Fig. 12, Grid square D5). The mosaic overlay an earlier limestone slab floor (Paton in Catling 1976–7, 21), and the latter was laid over a fill containing Hellenistic sherds. There were two building phases, and the earlier structure was levelled in order to erect the building with the mosaic floor. Paton noted that the buildings were probably too large to be classed as domestic, but that they could not have been public buildings of great significance either (ibid.).

Description: The mosaic was laid using mostly white limestone tesserae with the occasional use of black. There is no further description of the mosaic.

Materials: Stone tesserae

Date: Paton (in Catling 1976–7, 21) suggests that the mosaic must be later than the first century, on the basis of the date of the material on which the mosaic lay.

Bibliography: Catling 1976–7, 21; KN Logbook, 21 July 1976; *KS* 92; Sweetman 2003.

16. *Knossos: Semi-circular Mosaic*

Plate: Not available.

Location and discovery: Current location and condition of the mosaic when first

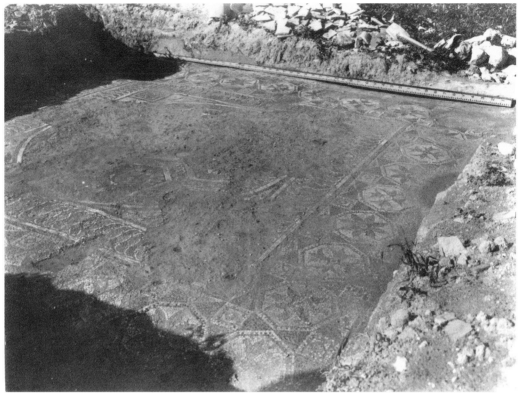

Plate 12 Knossos, Hutchinson's mosaic (Mosaic 17) (courtesy of BSA Archives).

excavated (end of nineteenth century) are unknown.

Dimensions: Unknown.

Context: Found southwest of the basilica (Fig. 12). It was recorded in Fyfe's plan of 1900, which is published with Hogarth's analysis (1899–1900). The mosaic also appears on Evans's plan of Knossos, where it is described as a 'Roman mosaic, perhaps baths' (Evans 1928, opp. 547). Hood (*KS* 115) suggests that the mosaic may be associated with 'a stretch of concrete wall running parallel with the road immediately south of KS 114'.

Description: Fyfe's plan indicates that the mosaic was semi-circular, but Hogarth does not discuss it in his article. Sanders (53) suggests that this is actually Halbherr's mosaic

(13), but it is clear from Halbherr's plan that his mosaic was not semi-circular (Scuola Archeologica Italiana di Atene 1984, fig. 21).

Date: Unknown.

Bibliography: Hogarth 1899–1900, 70–85, esp. pl. xii; Evans 1928, opp. 547; *KS* 115; Sweetman 2003.

17. *Knossos: Hutchinson's Mosaic*

Plate: 12.

Location and discovery: The mosaic was in good condition when first excavated by Hutchinson in 1938 and is covered *in situ* (Hutchinson's diary of unpublished finds, 1938–40, 23).[11]

Dimensions: From the surviving photographs the mosaic appears to be at least 5.5 x 5.5 m.

Context: Located to the southeast of the Civil Basilica (Hutchinson 1938–40, 19). It is unclear from Hutchinson's plan whether the mosaic was associated with any architecture. However, Hutchinson includes a sketch of some Roman walls just to the east of the mosaic.

Description: A large portion of the main field was damaged at the time of excavation, but it consisted of a circle-within-a-square design (Pl. 12). A guilloche band bordered the circle and divided the main field of the circle into hexagons. Originally there were probably six hexagons arranged around a central one. Only one survives intact and it contains a stylized flower. The remaining hexagons probably contained a similar motif. The design of the hexagons in the main field is reminiscent of that of Mosaic 2, but there are not enough data to support a common workshop. The central hexagon was destroyed. In each of the spandrels is a small square containing a single Solomon's knot. In the remaining space, on either side of the small square, is a single, stylized dolphin (Pl. 12). The central field is defined by a border of double guilloche (**R** 75a). An outer border of tangent octagons (**R** 27e) surrounds three sides of the main field. Each of the octagons contains a bordering row of dentilled simple fillet (**R** 2d). Within this there is a simple floral design in black on a white background.[12] This design alternates from one octagon to another: in one, it is an eight-petalled flower, in the other, a four-petalled flower with acanthus heads as petals. The arrangement of the octagons creates squares and triangles along both sides of the border. A band of dentilled simple fillet outlines the triangles and forms the inner border of the squares and each of these squares contains a single poised serrated square.

The border on the fourth side[13] consists of an orthogonal pattern of octagons, squares and rectangles (**R** 176f). In this case the rectangles alternate between enclosing a single pelta in black on a white ground or a single short knot of guilloche (Pl. 12). The poised small squares alternate between containing a single Solomon's knot and a poised stepped square.

Date: Hutchinson excavated small test pits around the mosaic, but he did not investigate directly below the mosaic level. From his description, it seems that at least one of the walls enclosing the mosaic was constructed directly on top of a Hellenistic level. Hood (*KS* 117) suggests a date of the second century, but there is no secure proof of this date. Stylistic matters can help to date the mosaic in the absence of recorded stratigraphy. There are parallels between this and the third-century mosaic (73) from Lappa. Both mosaics use flowers as the main filling motif and both use double guilloche. Although the evidence is insufficient to suggest a common workshop, it might indicate that the two are contemporary. Moreover, double guilloche rarely occurs in Crete before the Late Antique period, and Mosaic 73 contains the earliest example in Crete, dating to the third century. This does not provide a firm indication of the date of Mosaic 17 as forms of double guilloche occur elsewhere as early as the third century B.C.E. (e.g., in Egypt (Daszewski 1985, cat. 38)). While a date of the third century for Hutchinson's mosaic is reasonable, an earlier date in the second century is also feasible based on the use of the stylized flower fillers as seen in Villa Dionysus Mosaics 1 and 6 (see discussion Chapter 6).

Bibliography: *KS* 117; Hutchinson's diary of unpublished finds, 1938–40, 19; Hutchinson 1934–5, 5–7; Sweetman 2003.

18. *Knossos: Taverna Mosaic*

Plate: Sweetman 2003, pl. 88a.

Location and discovery: Discovered in 1933, it is possible that the remains of this mosaic are those fragments which have been set into the footpaths around the Taverna. Nothing is known about the condition of the mosaic when it was first excavated.

Dimensions: Unknown.

Context: This mosaic was uncovered during a rescue excavation under the steps leading to the roof of the Taverna (*KS* 128). Few details were recorded but it may be associated with the Roman buildings which lie below the Taverna.

Description: Even if Mosaic 18 is related to these fragments they merely tell us that it was polychrome.

Date: Unknown.

Bibliography: *KS* 128; Sweetman 2003.

19. *Knossos: Mosaic Pavement*

Plate: Sweetman 2003, pl. 88b.

Location and discovery: Recovered in 1971 during a rescue excavation by Hayes recorded in the Telegraph Pole Hole (TPH) Notebook, 12.[14] Hayes noted that four floor fragments were found, but he mentioned only one actual mosaic, whereas Sanders mentioned two.[15] Only a single fragment survives, and it is stored in the Stratigraphic Museum, Knossos.

Dimensions: The surviving fragment measures 35 x 21 cm. It is impossible to reconstruct the original floor dimensions. Tesserae *c*. 0.75 x 0.75 cm.

Context: Located north of the Villa Ariadne (Fig. 12, Grid square D6), it was found during the digging of a new drainage system for the Villa Ariadne (KN Logbook, 39). The mosaic had a thin bedding layer on top of loose fill. Below the loose fill was an earlier pink cement floor which was bisected by a wall. The wall may have been a foundation for an earlier phase because the mosaic lies directly on top of it. Hayes argues that the mosaic was associated with a second wall that was covered with marble veneer.

The location (Fig. 12) in the residential area of the valley and the presence of marble veneer in the room indicate that the mosaic came from a well-appointed space. It may be connected with the semi-circular Mosaic 20 which is located *c*. 10 m away.

Description: From what remains, the mosaic depicted a six-petalled flower with alternating pink and blue petals on a circular black background. Surrounding this is a thin white band, two tesserae wide, and then an outer black band also two tesserae wide. A small amount of a second black band survives, but its position suggests that it did not enclose the central section and that it probably is the start of another pattern rather than an additional border. The mosaic could be reconstructed in a number of ways. The stylized flower motif may have been the central design and the small fragment of black band at an angle might represent a shield of scales surrounding it.

Materials: Glass and stone tesserae.

Date: Waywell (1973, 295–6) dated a bust found during the excavation as Trajanic. According to Hayes, this predates the mosaic and therefore the mosaic is probably mid-second century or later. An exact date is difficult to establish because the meagre pieces of pottery collected with the mosaic contained some third-century Çandarli and ARS and some second-century material (Sweetman 2010b).[16] The tesserae are tightly packed (*c*. 8 tesserae per 5 x 5 cm) and reminiscent of the form of the Dionysiac mosaics from the Villa Dionysus. However, not enough of the mosaic remains to date it accurately on the basis of either its design or construction.

Bibliography: *KS* 130; KN Logbook, August 1971, 39; TPH Notebook, 1971, 9–14; Sanders, 153; Sweetman 2003.

20. *Knossos: Semi-circular Mosaic*

Plate: None available.

Location and discovery: Location is unknown. The mosaic was discovered by a local resident before 1957 during the construction of the garden of the Villa Ariadne.

Dimensions: Unknown.

Context: It is apparently located in the northwest corner of the garden of the Villa Ariadne (Fig. 12).

Description: There is very little information on the mosaic: no traces of it remain and no description is provided in the KN Logbook.

Date: Unknown

Bibliography: *KS* 131; Sweetman 2003.

21–2. *Knossos: Two Mosaic Pavements*

Plate: None available.

Location and discovery: Location is unknown. The mosaics were found by local residents around 1936, but the nature of their discovery is otherwise unknown.

Dimensions: Unknown.

Context: Found in a field 100 m north of the Villa Ariadne, near some Roman concrete ruins. According to Hood, one mosaic was found 10 m south of these ruins and the other 20 m west of them (Fig. 12, Grid square D6). It is unsurprising to find mosaics in this area as it is as close to the centre of the Roman city. These mosaics may be connected to Mosaics 11 and 12, which were found in the nearby Roman bath house.

Description: None given.

Date: Unknown.

Bibliography: *KS* 135; Sweetman 2003.

23. *Knossos: Possible Wall Mosaic*

Plate: None available.

Location and discovery: The existence of the tesserae was noted in the 1950s. Current location is unknown.

Dimensions: Unknown.

Context: The mosaic was associated with the remains of a Roman building located 300 m north of the Roman basilica and 150 m south of *KS* 92 (Mosaic 15) (Fig. 12, Grid square D5).

Description: There is nothing left of the mosaic except many blue and white tesserae; some of these are glass.

Materials: Stone and glass tesserae.

Date: Unknown.

Bibliography: *KS* 94; Sweetman 2003.

24. *Knossos: Mosaic Pavement*

Plate: None available.

Location and discovery: Current location is unknown, and the mosaic is said to have been exposed in 1936.

Dimensions: Unknown.

Context: It was located just west of the gully and north of the basilica (Fig. 12).

Description: No traces of the mosaic remain.

Date: Unknown.

Bibliography: *KS* 100; Sweetman 2003.

25. *Knossos: Small Mosaic Pavement*

Plate: Lembesis 1972, 624, pl. 584a.

Location and discovery: Unknown location. The mosaic was exposed while opening a cesspit in 1971 in the house of Maria Kastoveli.

Dimensions: 0.75 x 1.68 m.

Context: Uncovered in the southern part of the village of Knossos (Fig. 12, Grid square D7).

Description: From the published photograph it is possible to distinguish an outer border of spaced saltires of tassels (**R** 4j) (black on white). Within this is a plain dark band. A small geometric design in light (white) on dark tesserae is just about visible. The rest of the mosaic cannot be seen at all.

Date: Two lamps from the second century were found associated with the mosaic floor.

Bibliography: *KS* 195; Lembesis 1972, 624, pl. 584a; Sweetman 2003.

26. *Knossos: Mosaic Pavement*

Plate: None available.

Location and discovery: Unknown location. It was noted in 1957 at the bottom of a modern water channel.

Dimensions: Unknown.

Context: No description is available, but it is the easternmost mosaic known from the Knossos Valley (Fig. 12, Grid square E6). There was some exploratory work undertaken in this area between the basilica and the village of Makritikhos by Halbherr and Hogarth, but they do not provide detailed accounts of their work, noting only that they 'cleared' some Roman houses. It is possible that the mosaic may have been associated with a residential area.

Description: None given.

Date: Unknown.

Bibliography: *KS* 234; Sweetman 2003.

27. *Kambourakis Plot, Bougada Metochi*

Plate: Sweetman 2003, pl. 88c.

Location and discovery: Destroyed. The floor was very fragmentary when first excavated at the KKE[17] plot in 1980.

Dimensions: Not known. Two fragments of this mosaic survive, one in the northeastern section of the trench and the other in the southwestern. Tesserae size: *c.* 0.90 x 0.90 cm.

Context: The mosaic was excavated as part of a rescue excavation in the modern village of Knossos in an area some 250 m south of the Unexplored Mansion (Fig. 12, Grid square D7). The excavator reports that the tesserae of the floor must have been removed or destroyed in antiquity. He also notes that there was a badly worn 'stucco' floor which bordered the mosaic on the eastern side. He describes it as pink gravel mixed with medium-sized stones, which suggests that it was mosaic bedding rather than the remains of another floor. Directly below the mosaic floor was a pit which contained material dating to the Classical or Hellenistic period.

There were no walls associated with the floor, making it difficult to suggest a function for the building in which the mosaic was found. The broken roof tiles lying on the floor may have been deliberately placed there and are therefore unlikely to represent a destruction level.

Description: Very little of the floor survives, but there is enough to distinguish most of the overall design. An outer guilloche border (**R** 70f) is made up of alternating shades of blue and pink/orange. In each strand the colour gets gradually darker, from white to blue to dark blue, and from white to light pink to dark pink. Contained within the border is a field of intersecting circles forming spindles and concave squares (**R** 237a). Within this field there appears to be a second internal panel which is surrounded by a band of serrated saw-tooth pattern (**R** 10g). This encloses a further field of intersecting circles forming spindles (containing a poised square) and concave squares (**R** 239a).

Materials: Stone and terracotta tesserae.

Date: According to the unpublished excavation report, the mosaic dates to the Hadrianic period, but this is not supported by clear evidence. The excavator draws a parallel between this mosaic and those of the Villa Dionysus. In particular, Mosaic 8 is quite a close match as both the form of the spindles and the layout are quite similar (Pl. 7). This would suggest the mosaic dated to the late second century.

Bibliography: *KKE* excavation notebook, housed in the BSA Archives; Sweetman 2003.

28. *The Road Trial Fragments*

Plate: Sweetman 2003, pl. 89a.

Location and discovery: Stored in the Stratigraphic Museum, Knossos. These four small mosaic fragments were recovered from the Road Trial rescue excavations (1959–60).

Dimensions: The original dimensions cannot be reconstructed. Tesserae: *c.* 0.90 x 0.90 cm.

Context: These are the most southerly mosaics of the Knossos Valley. According to the publication, the fragments were found in an early Roman house (Hayes 1971, 248–75). Hayes notes that a blue-glass tessera was discovered nearby.

Description: The four pieces are so fragmentary that it is impossible to describe the design of the floor with confidence.

Fragment i is made up of nine tesserae which are light pink and loosely packed. It is just possible to make out some sort of diamond design with four central tesserae.

Fragment ii consists of a chunk of mosaic bedding containing a single blue tessera and the impressions of a number of others. It does not further our understanding of the mosaic.

Fragments iii and iv are clearly connected to Fragment i. However, they too consist only of tesserae held together by the mosaic bedding. The limited colour variance of blue and white suggests that they may belong to a band of dentilled simple fillet (**R** 2d).

Materials: Stone tesserae.

Date: Some of the finds from the excavation have been published (Hayes 1971), but the mosaic fragments are not specifically referred to, and their exact stratigraphic location is difficult to verify. Apparently the fragments came from the upper levels, which had been disturbed by later walls, and the contexts were not very clear. Hayes notes that many of the finds from the upper levels were similar to those of the lower layers. The latter were dated to the end of the first century B.C.E. and beginning of the first century. There were also some finds of later Roman date in the upper levels. Therefore, at best a date of the first century can be postulated for the mosaic in this case because the mosaics are too fragmentary to date stylistically.

Bibliography: Hayes, 1971, 270–2; pers. comm. Sinclair Hood; Sweetman 2003.

29. *The Unexplored Mansion Fragment*

Plate: Sweetman 2003, 89b.

Location and discovery: Stored in the Stratigraphic Museum, Knossos, since its excavation in 1970.

Dimensions: It is impossible to reconstruct the full dimensions of the mosaic, which measures 8 x 8 cm. Tesserae: *c.* 0.90 x 0.90 cm.

Context: The fragment was found during the Unexplored Mansion excavations (Fig. 12), during the removal of a baulk located on the east side of the site (near Hutchinson's well), so the precise context was not recovered. Sackett (1992, 457) notes that 18 glass tesserae were found during the excavation but that no mosaics were associated with them. The location in which the mosaic fragment was discovered is one of the known residential areas of the Roman city, possibly in an area of home industries (ibid.).

Description: Three colours are used: white, pink and blue. Enough remains to deduce that the fragment belonged to either

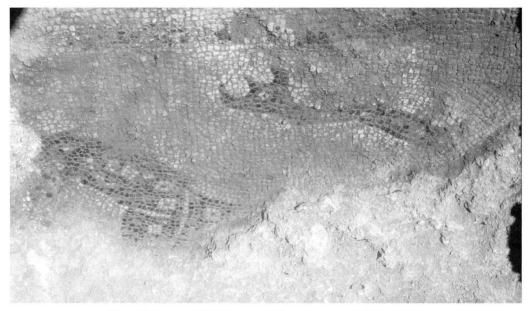

Plate 13 Knossos, Villa Dionysus, Hippocamp mosaic (Mosaic 30).

a floral or a geometric design (possibly even to part of a guilloche). The preserved section consists of a central white tessera surrounded by a circular band of blue glass, one tessera wide. This is further enclosed by a band of pink and finally by a band of white, each row one tessera wide.

Materials: Stone and glass tesserae.

Date: On the evidence of the baulk levels, the fragment has two possible dates: either pre mid-third century or pre first half of the second century.

Bibliography: Unexplored Mansion Daybooks Book 27, p. 16; Sweetman 2003.

30. *The Hippocamp Mosaic*

Plate: 13.

Location and discovery: Covered *in situ*. The mosaic was found during preparations for roofing the Villa Dionysus in 1998. The mosaic section that was uncovered was well preserved.

Dimensions: Not yet fully uncovered; the extent of the section exposed is just over 1 m x 25 cm. Tesserae *c.* 1 x 1 cm.

Context: It was found in an area located some 3 m above the Villa Dionysus (Fig. 12). It is unclear whether this mosaic belongs to an upper storey of the villa or a dwelling located on the terrace just above it.

Description: The exposed part of the mosaic is a thin border of blue tesserae, enclosing small fragments of a figured design (Pl. 13). These consist of the tail of a sea creature and the head of a horse. They probably come from a single figure, a hippocamp. The hippocamp is depicted in blue with diamond designs of white and red (made of out glass) along its neck. Some internal features, such as the curve of the neck, have been outlined in white. The blue tail has a few white diamond shapes for decoration and terminates in a W-shaped fin.

Materials: Stone, glass, terracotta tesserae.

Date: Not yet ascertained

Bibliography: Personal observation; pers. comm. Sara Paton; *AR* 1998–9, 115; Sweetman 2003.

31. *The Bougada Mosaic*

Plate: None available.

Location and discovery: Found during rescue excavations in the 1990s; current state unknown. The mosaic was very badly damaged.

Dimensions: None available.

Context: Found in the northern part of the valley, in Bougada Metochi, in the Babouraki Plot, where a Roman drainage system was discovered. The mosaic was located to the south of the drainage system.

Description: The only description is that it was a plain white tessellated mosaic with tile elements.

Date: Not yet ascertained.

Bibliography: *AR* 1997–8, 114; Grammatikaki 1992, 558.

Note: Many loose tesserae have been found throughout the valley, and Sinclair Hood has been kind enough to send me information regarding some of them. These include tesserae from the Middle Minoan round tomb on lower Gypsadhes (LG1) (*KS* 308), excavated in 1957, and three tesserae from the Royal Road (*KS* 214 & 215) excavations.

Iraklion

THE IRAKLION *DOMUS*

In advance of construction work, a rescue excavation was undertaken in the centre of Iraklion in 1995, near the archaeological museum. The remains of a substantial *domus* were revealed, yet the precise function of the building is uncertain (Pl. 14). Five rooms of the complex and substantial portions of the building such as two large arches and a complex drainage system were preserved. Wall paintings were recovered. Initial reports suggested that the *domus* dates to the end of the first century; however, recent work suggests a

later date of the second century (pers. comm. Stavroula Markoulaki). The immediate area appears to have been occupied from the middle of the second century to the medieval period, with finds including coins, Roman lamps, decorated incised bone, ceramics from Italy and pottery such as scraffito. All the pavements have now been lifted for conservation.

32. *Iraklion: Mosaic Pavement 1*

Plate: 14.

Location and discovery: Rescue excavation in 1995. Mosaic removed for conservation.

Dimensions: 4.03 x 2.95 m (surviving).

Context: North wing of a substantial *domus*. As with most of the floors in this house, this had been partly obscured by later rebuilding, though half of it was still visible.

Description: Black-and-white geometric mosaic. An ivy scroll (**R** 64d) encloses a rectangular field consisting of a geometric pattern of four-pointed stars forming lozenges (**R** 184b). Within each of the lozenges there is a small crosslet terminating in a chevron. The ivy scroll is similar to that of Mosaic 8 and the geometric field is similar to that of Mosaic 4.[18]

Materials: Stone tesserae.

Date: End of the first century or mid-second century. Based on its workshop connections with the Villa Dionysus mosaics, I would argue for a mid-second-century date.

Bibliography: *Η Καθημερινή* 30 November 1995; *AR* 1998–9, 114 & *AR* 2001–2, 107; Ioannidou-Karetsou et al. 2008, 75–95; Markoulaki in Ioannidou-Karetsou et al. 2008, 109–47.

33. *Iraklion: Mosaic Pavement 2*

Plate: 14.

Location and discovery: Rescue excavation in 1995. The mosaic had sustained quite

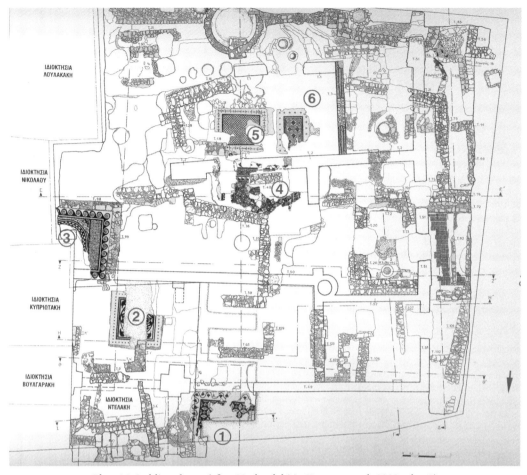

Plate 14 Iraklion *domus* (after Markoulaki in Karetsou et al. 2008, plan 1)
(Mosaic 32 = 1; Mosaic 33 = 2; Mosaic 34 = 3; Mosaic 35 = 4; Mosaic 36 = 5; Mosaic 37 = 6)
(courtesy of A. Karetsou).

considerable damage through the central section and has now been lifted.

Dimensions: 3.30 x 3.30 m.

Context: North wing of a substantial *domus*.

Description: A black-and-white geometric mosaic. An outer sequence of chevrons encloses a central field consisting of a circle within a square. A single black pelta occupies each spandrel. The area within the circle has been damaged, but the reconstructions (see Markoulaki in Ioannidou-Karetsou et al. 2008, 116) illustrate a geometric design of a central square (bearing an eight-petalled flower), the square being surrounded by four hexagons. Each hexagon bears a six-pointed diamond enclosing another hexagon which bears a six-petalled flower. Between each of the outer hexagons is a scheme of three triangles forming a square. The chevron border is similar to that surrounding Mosaic 2.

Materials: Stone tesserae.

Date: End of the first century or mid-second century. Based on its workshop connections with the Villa Dionysus mosaics, I would argue for a mid-second-century date.

Bibliography: *Η Καθημερινή* 30 November 1995; *AR* 1998–9, 114 & *AR* 2001–2, 107; Ioannidou-Karetsou et al. 2008, 75–95; Markoulaki in Ioannidou-Karetsou et al. 2008, 109–47.

34. *Iraklion: Mosaic Pavement 3*

Plate: 14.

Location and discovery: Rescue excavation in 1995. The mosaic had been damaged by later building and not all of it was recovered from below the modern road.

Dimensions: 4.20 x 3.74 m.

Context: East wing of a substantial *domus*. Markoulaki suggests that the mosaic may have occupied either the *oecus* or *tablinum*.

Description: A black-and-white mosaic. Three panels are contained within a wave-scroll border (**R** 101b). The central panel shows a circle contained within a square. A design of a chessboard pattern of triangles in quarto-chrome is similar to **R** 198e, which by getting progressively larger from the inside out creates a swirling pattern in the circle.[19] Not enough of the mosaic has been preserved to tell if there had been a central figure within the design. An acanthus scroll occupies each of the spandrels. The two secondary panels on either side of the central one contain a complex geometric design of four-pointed stars forming lozenges (**R** 184b). Within each of the lozenges is a small crosslet. The central panel consists of a circle within a square.

Materials: Stone tesserae.

Date: End of the first century or mid-second century. Based on its workshop connections with the Villa Dionysus mosaics, I would argue for a mid-second-century date.

Bibliography: *Η Καθημερινή* 30 November 1995; *AR* 1998–9, 114 & *AR* 2001–2, 107; Ioannidou-Karetsou et al. 2008, 75–95;

Markoulaki in Ioannidou-Karetsou et al. 2008, 109–47.

35. *Iraklion: Mosaic Pavement 4*

Plate: 14.

Location and discovery: Rescue excavation in 1995. The areas of mosaic that had not been built over were quite well preserved.

Dimensions: 4.5 x 6.5 m.

Context: South wing of a substantial *domus*. One hundred sixty-six copper coins of a variety of dates were found overlying this mosaic floor.

Description: Polychrome mosaic with a central square panel depicting a bird on a branch. The central panel is surrounded by a bichrome border of serrated triangles. Although not enough is preserved to be certain either way, it is just possible that the scene depicts one of Zeus and Ganymede, particularly given the spread of the brown wing of the bird. Surrounding the central panel is a composition of squares and diamonds rendered in white (**R** 161a). Each of the squares contains a serrated poised square in red and yellow colours, and each of the diamonds contains a serrated poised square in blue. This is enclosed by an inner border consisting of a wave scroll (**R** 101b). An outer border of poised stylized flowers encloses a large border of plain swastika meander (**R** 35d) which bears an acanthus flower the same as that in Mosaic 8.

Materials: Stone and glass tesserae.

Date: End of the first century or mid-second century. Based on its workshop connections with the Villa Dionysus mosaics, I would argue for a mid-second-century date.

Bibliography: *Η Καθημερινή* 30 November 1995; *AR* 1998–9, 114 & *AR* 2001–2, 107; Ioannidou-Karetsou et al. 2008, 75–95; Markoulaki in Ioannidou-Karetsou et al. 2008, 109–47.

36. *Iraklion: Mosaic Pavement 5*

Plate: 14.

Location and discovery: Rescue excavation in 1995. This was one of the better-preserved mosaics.

Dimensions: 3.30 x 2.60 m.

Context: South wing of a substantial *domus*.

Description: A black-and-white geometric mosaic. A plain outer border of a row of opposing stylized flowers (formed of chevrons) separated by a double chevron encloses a rectangular field of black-and-white net pattern (**R** 124a*)*. A doormat panel is located off centre on the north side and contains a pair of dolphins situated one on either side of an anchor. The net-pattern design is similar to that of Mosaic 8.

Materials: Stone tesserae.

Date: End of the first century or mid-second century. Based on its workshop connections with the Villa Dionysus mosaics, I would argue for a mid-second-century date.

Bibliography: *H Καθημερινή* 30 November 1995; *AR* 1998–9, 114 & *AR* 2001–2, 107; Ioannidou-Karetsou et al. 2008, 75–95; Markoulaki in Ioannidou-Karetsou et al. 2008, 109–47.

37. *Iraklion: Mosaic Pavement 6*

Plate: 14.

Location and discovery: Rescue excavation in 1995. Well preserved despite the later building. Mosaic removed for conservation.

Dimensions: 2.70 x 2.10 m.

Context: South wing of a substantial *domus*, directly to the west of Mosaic 36.

Description: A black-and-white geometric mosaic. An outer sequence of chevrons encloses a central field consisting of octagons and semi-octagons, each of which contains a stylized flower and half a stylized flower, respectively. The stylized-flower filler is similar to that used in Hutchinson's mosaic (17) and to those in the corners between the circle and square in Mosaic 6.

Materials: Stone tesserae.

Date: End of the first century or mid-second century. Based on its workshop connections with the Villa Dionysus mosaics, I would argue for a mid-second-century date.

Bibliography: *H Καθημερινή* 30 November 1995; *AR* 1998–9, 114 & *AR* 2001–2, 107; Ioannidou-Karetsou et al. 2008, 75–95; Markoulaki in Ioannidou-Karetsou et al. 2008, 109–47.

Chersonisos

38. *Chersonisos: The Fountain Mosaic*

Plate: 15.

Location and discovery: This mosaic was restored by Platon in 1954 (Pl. 15) and is visible at the harbour in Chersonisos. Two panels are damaged but reasonably well preserved, while two others have only small fragments of the field preserved.

Dimensions: *c.* 0.75 x 2.50 m. Tesserae: *c.* 38–40 tesserae per 10 x 10 cm area.

Context: The mosaic appeared on four sides of a fountain, and little of the architectural context survives or is ascertainable. The fountain was located west of the Roman quay in Chersonisos and southeast of a Roman apse. Because of the iconography, Sanders (51) suggests that this fountain was used for washing fish. This is an unlikely scenario. The glass content and the quality of the mosaic indicate a more decorative aspect, and Hood (Hood & Leatham 1958–9) is likely correct in arguing that the fountain was part of a large *domus*. This suggestion is further supported by Sanders's own note that when the fountain was being restored it was found to be

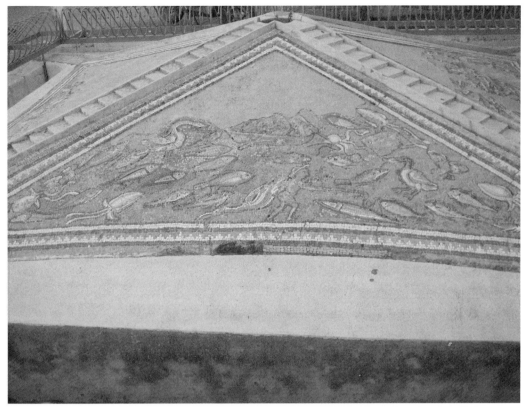

Plate 15 Chersonisos, Fountain mosaic, northwest panel (Mosaic 38).

situated in the courtyard of a large building of unknown function.

Description: The mosaic is made up of four separate triangular panels, each occupying a side of a low pyramidal fountain (Pl. 15). Each panel has the same border of a red band within which is a black band; inside this is a band of saw-tooth (**R** 10g) made up of brown and white, and inside this are three bands of red, white and black.

Two panels are sufficiently well preserved to define the marine scenes, and it is likely that the remaining panels were of the same theme.

The northwest panel has a background of blue/grey, which represents the sea. There appears to be no strict logic as to the order of creatures depicted in the scene. In the 'sea' there are, along with numerous fish and a squid, a goose and a duck. In the middle of the sea is a man in a boat who appears to be hauling up a large octopus. At the base of the scene (on the shore?) another fisherman has cast a line out into the sea. Both fishermen are outlined in dark black, as are the fish and other aquatic creatures. The fisherman on the 'shore' is depicted in profile, quite skilfully rendered, suggesting the work of a mosaicist of moderate ability. There is also an attempt at perspective, with the fishermen depicted as much smaller than the animals (Pl. 15).

The southwest panel is quite badly damaged, but two men at the bottom of the scene are defined by black outlines. Conceivably, one of the men is spearing something. As

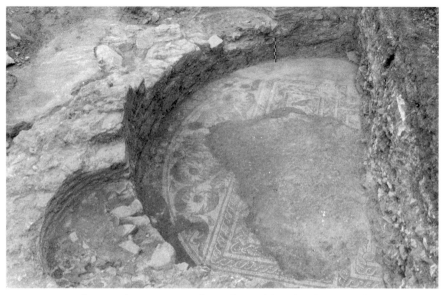

Plate 16 Chersonisos, Perakis and Papadakis Plots (Mosaic 39)
(courtesy of D. Hadzi Vallianou).

with the first panel, the 'sea' is filled with a range of different fish.

In the southeast panel it is possible to make out a man who is holding something over his head, and this is possibly some kind of animal. As for the north-east panel, this is the most damaged of the four but it is just possible to detect a man at the bottom of the scene bending down to pick up something.

All the scenes are very colourful with extensive use of glass, particularly in areas such as the fishes' eyes.

Materials: Glass, stone, terracotta tesserae.

Date: The earliest reports of this mosaic offer a date of 'Roman' for the mosaic (Xanthoudidis 1918). Since then no reasonable chronology has been put forward for it on the basis of any excavations carried out in the area of the town of Chersonisos. In this situation we are forced to rely on stylistic criteria from comparative dated material for a possible date for the mosaic.

There is no exact parallel for the scene, but there is a group of mosaics found in Utica which were specifically used on fountains and these date to the second–third century (Alexander & Ennaifer 1973). Sanders particularly takes note of mosaics on a rectangular fountain in the Maison de la Cascade at Utica (Alexander & Ennaifer 1973, no. 28 in Insula II, pl. IX) dated to the second century (Sanders, 51). While the scenes and contexts of the Utica mosaics are similar, alone they are not enough to compare with the Chersonisos mosaic and to give it a secure date.

Bibliography: Xanthoudidis 1918; Platon 1956, 419; Hood & Leatham 1958–9; *AR* 1973–4, 17; Sanders, 51; Harrison 1993, 195–6.

39. *Chersonisos: Perakis and Papadakis Plots*

Plate: 16; Fig. 19.

Location and discovery: This mosaic was found in a 1985 rescue excavation close to the Creta Maris Hotel undertaken by the

Byzantine Ephorea.[20] Its current location is possibly in the Historical Museum of Crete.

Dimensions: None available.

Context: Room II of a building (Fig. 19) which was part of a residential complex located east of Chersonisos (Fig. 16). Terra sigillata was also found in the same context as the mosaic but has not been published. The building from which the mosaic came was apparently a substantial one, with a colonnade as well as an apse (*AR* 1991–2, 59). The apse in which the mosaic occurs also contains two semi-circular niches located around 0.45 m above the floor level. From the excavation plan it appears that they were part of the original construction. The *xenia*-type scenes would indicate a room with an entertainment function, possibly even a *triclinium*. But the presence of the semi-circular niches is comparable to plans of bath houses, making this also a possibility, as suggested by Touchais (1989, 688). A good parallel for this arrangement is that of the Nymphaeum and the entrance of the baths at the Temple of Olympian Zeus. Another possibility is that it is a basilica, and a good comparison for the apse and colonnade arrangement is that of the basilica in the Gymnasium (see Tommaso, in Di Vita (ed.) 2000, fig. 61).

Description: The remains of this polychrome mosaic consist of an outer guilloche border which encloses a semi-circle bearing a lush pomegranate scroll and a rectangular field bearing a grid of panels of birds (Pl. 16). The outer open guilloche border is similar to **R** 68d. The semi-circular panel of pomegranate scroll contains numerous pomegranates and vegetation similar to acanthus leaves. The main field is bordered by a guilloche band which continues within the field to create individual square panels in a Greek key formation. The guilloche is similar to

R 70j. Surrounding the square panels, the guilloche is more similar to **R** 72c, which is a three-strand variation. Only one of the figured panels is preserved well enough to describe, and the remains suggest that there would have been at least five more in the exposed area. The preserved panel is of a bird (possibly a thrush) standing on a branch with a branch emerging from the top right corner (Pl. 48). The panel is surrounded by a border of serrated triangles. There is also a tiny part of a plain white mosaic found in the northwest corner of the room.

Material: Stone, terracotta and glass. The colours used are white, black, grey and various reds from pink to brown.

Date: According to the excavation report, the mosaic can be dated to the third quarter of the fourth century. This is based on a date for the ceramics given by Hayes. It has been suggested for the area in which the mosaic occurs that the building was first constructed in the Roman period and expanded in the Late Antique (Hadzi-Vallianou 1990, 412). The evidence from the colonnade and the rooms around it suggests that these areas were abandoned after the 365 earthquake and not rebuilt.

Bibliography: Hadzi-Vallianou 1990, 409–15; Rethemiotakis 1984, 296; *Η Καθημερινή* 19 August 1988; Touchais 1989, 688; *AR* 1991–2, 59; Harrison 1993, 195–6.

Note: This mosaic is described in Chaniotaki-Starida and Mari 2004, 294, as the Apostolidi Plot, which was actually located across the road from the Perakis and Papadakis Plots.

40. *Chersonisos: The Bath House Floor*

Plate: None available.

Location and discovery: The remains of a paved floor were found in what appears to be a late Roman bath house on Demokratias Street in Chersonisos.

Dimensions: None available.

Context: The floor occurs over the hypocaust of the bath house. An inscription has been reused from elsewhere in part of the wall of the adjoining room. There also appears to be reuse of large Hellenistic stone blocks. The pottery lying around the site appears to be late Roman in date, and there are many fragments of early Byzantine combed ware.

Description: The remains of the floor consist of large, coloured, irregularly cut marble tiles which are not very well preserved.

Materials: Marble tiles.

Date: Fourth to fifth century?

Bibliography: Unpublished.

41. *Chersonisos: Geometric Mosaic*

Plate: None available.

Location and discovery: Rescue excavations. The mosaic was quite damaged, in part due to Late Antique interventions.

Dimensions: 2.80 x 1.50 m (patches of the mosaic cover this area).

Context: A bath house. Within the multiple phases of use there is clear evidence for a third-century addition of a new set of bathing suites. The mosaic was found in the northern section of the complex, to the west of what appears to be the main courtyard. The location of the mosaic, to the north of a threshold block, led the excavators to assume that this may have formed the main entrance to the building.

Description: The remains show that it was a black-and-white geometric mosaic. A plain border of black band (4–5 tesserae in width) encloses a field of outlined swastikas (in a latchkey pattern) and lozenges in the interior spaces.

Materials: Stone tesserae.

Date: This particular pattern is not commonly found in mosaic décor. It does however have two parallels from Corinth, both of which date to the third century (Sweetman & Sanders 2005, 361). The building may have an earlier foundation date, and it is possible that the mosaic dates to a period of reconstruction in the third century.

Bibliography: Pers. comm. Dimitris Grigoropoulos.

42. *Chersonisos: Kypriotakis Plot*

Plate: Chaniotaki-Starida & Mari 2004, 290–2 & fig. 4.

Location and discovery: Located a little distance southeast of the Kastri hill on the northern part of the beach. The mosaic was found in good condition in rescue excavations between 1983 and 1985.

Dimensions: Not known.

Context: The house in which the mosaic was found had three phases of use: Roman with a destruction phase, the fourth century and the seventh century.

Description: The rich polychrome mosaic floor has a central scene of Medusa in a medallion surrounded by a circular design of a chessboard pattern of triangles which by getting progressively larger from the inside out creates a swirling pattern (**R** 327b). In this case the rows alternate their colours. The circle is set within a square, and each spandrel contains a pair of opposing dolphins (Chaniotaki-Starida & Mari 2004, fig. 4). The square is surrounded by a border of double guilloche similar to **R** 74h and a further border consisting of a row of tangent cuboids (**R** 99e). The sides of the blocks are coloured, and at the top of each there are is a chevron (?).[21] The central field is surrounded by panels of trichrome intersecting circles forming spindles and concave squares (**R** 238a); in the centre of each concave square is a poised square. The fourth side is made up of five figured panels depicting scenes of birds and kantharoi, possibly *xenia* scenes (see Markoulaki in Ioannidou-Karetsou et al. 2008, fig. 32), and according to Chaniotaki-Starida and Mari 2004, 292, also scenes from the animal kingdom.

Date: The excavators date the mosaic to the fourth century; much of the associated material culture such as lamps, coins and pottery date to the same period. The excavators suggest that the technique of the mosaic is similar to parts of the Chersonisos Basilica A and B mosaics. Although the overall style may be somewhat similar to Chersonisos Basilica B (i.e., particularly with the large size of the geometric forms), there are no specific elements of comparison to support any suggestion of a workshop or craftspeople in common.

Bibliography: Chaniotaki-Starida & Mari 2004, 290–2 & fig. 4; Markoulaki in Ioannidou-Karetsou et al. 2008, figs. 19 & 32.

43a & 43b. *Chersonisos: Yiakoumis Plot*
Plate: None available.

Location and discovery: Rescue excavations in 1985 at the eastern part of the beach near the Roman moles.

Dimensions: Not known.

Context: A large Roman house. Mosaics date to the first century as well as to the Late Antique period.

Description: The first-century mosaic is made from blue tesserae on a white background. The Late Antique mosaics were polychrome and of geometric designs of intersecting circles and semi-circles using large size geometric forms (as in Basilica B), but they were not as fine as the mosaics from the Kypriotakis Plot.

Materials: Stone tesserae.
Date: First century. The Late Antique mosaics date from the end of the fourth to the beginning of the fifth century.
Bibliography: Chaniotaki-Starida & Mari 2004, 292.

44. *Chersonisos: Moudatsakis Plot*
Plate: Chaniotaki-Starida & Mari 2004, fig. 6.

Location and discovery: Rescue excavations on Filonidou Zotou Street about 100 m to the west of the port.

Dimensions: Not known.

Context: A Late Antique house was discovered under a layer of sand.

Description: A pebble floor with dolphin and floral designs.

Materials: Pebbles.
Date: The date of the floor is unclear.
Bibliography: Chaniotaki-Starida & Mari 2004, 293–4.

45. *Chersonisos: Papageorgiou Plot*
Plate: Chaniotaki-Starida & Mari 2004, fig. 11.

Location and discovery: Rescue excavation a short distance from the Apostolidis Plot.

Dimensions: Not known.

Context: A large house with several different rooms. The large rectangular room (A) in the south and east had a floor of limestone slabs. There were three further rooms (B) in the west of the site, and in these rooms were found first-century mosaics. Rooms with plaque floors were uncovered to the north of rectangular room (A). Also found was a Roman bath house associated with the complex.

Description: From the published image (Chaniotaki-Starida & Mari 2004, fig. 11), it is clear that one of the mosaics consists of a series of squares of different designs of geometric compositions and stylized floral fillers. One, for example, is of a net pattern, at the centre of which is a square containing a stylized flower. Another consists of a poised square within the outer square; in the space between the two are stylized plants and at the centre of the square is a five-petalled flower.

Date: First century?

Bibliography: Chaniotaki-Starida & Mari 2004, 296–9.

46. *Chersonisos: Sfakianakis Plot*

Plate: Not available.

Dimensions: Not known.

Context: Not known.

Location and discovery: Rescue excavations.

Description: Traces of cement and pebble floors in a Late Antique building.

Materials: Pebbles.

Date: Unknown.

Bibliography: *AR* 1997–8, 112.

47. *Chersonisos: Davakis-Koukovas Plot*

Plate: None available.

Location and discovery: Rescue excavations.

Dimensions: Not known.

Context: Dwelling?

Description: A house with two third- to fourth-century mosaics was uncovered.

Date: Third–fourth century.

Bibliography: *AR* 2000–1, 126; *Ergon Work of the Archaeological Service* 3, 1999, 159.

48. *Chersonisos: Danellakis Plot*

Plate: None available.

Location and discovery: Rescue excavations.

Dimensions: Not known.

Context: Dwelling?

Description: A Roman building with floors of stone and pebbles (and two Hellenistic graves).

Materials: Pebbles.

Date: Unknown.

Bibliography: *AR* 2000–1, 126; *Ergon Work of the Archaeological Service* 3, 1999, 159.

49. *Chersonisos: Kassabetis Plot*

Plate: Markoulaki in Ioannidou-Karetsou et al. 2008, fig. 6.

Location and discovery: Rescue excavation close to the port.

Dimensions: Not known.

Context: Not known.

Description: The remains of this geometric mosaic consisted of an outer ivy-scroll border within which was a band of **R** 237a (intersecting circles forming spindles and concave squares, the concave squares containing crosslets). At each corner there was a square in which was a circle containing a stylized four-petalled flower. A further border of wave scroll enclosed the main field of running peltae (similar to **R** 222d).

Date: Second century.

Bibliography: Markoulaki in Ioannidou-Karetsou et al. 2008, fig. 6, n. 27.

Mallia

50. *Mallia Bath House*

Plate: None available.

Location and discovery: The bath house is situated at the west end of the Minoan palace.

Dimensions: Not known.

Context: Bath house. Its location in an area of Roman and Late Antique activity may indicate the presence of a residential complex. The bath house is built into the natural rock and has an *opus signinum* floor. The floor lies on top of a cistern.

Description: *Opus signinum* floor.

Date: The bath house is considered to date to the end of the third century.

Bibliography: Sanders, 147.

Kato Asites

51. *Kato Asites: Bath House Pavement*
Plate: None available.

Location and discovery: Reported in the 1960s, but the current location of the mosaic is unclear.

Dimensions: The dimensions of the floor of the hall in which the mosaic occurred are 5.80 x 10.30 m. It is unclear how much of this the mosaic actually covered.

Context: The mosaic was situated in a trilobate bath house which survived up to roof height. The area in which the mosaic occurred was the main rectangular entrance hall, the first room one reached upon entering through the doorway in the west wall. During the fifth century the bath house was used as a church dedicated to St. Catherine.

Description: Geometric polychrome mosaic using blue, white and red marble tesserae. A guilloche border encloses the main geometric field.

Materials: Stone and marble tesserae.

Date: The dates of both the bath house and the mosaic are unclear, yet Sanders indicates a date earlier rather than later in the Roman period.

Bibliography: Alexiou 1964, 444; Sanders, 70.

Inatos

52. *Inatos: Vlastos Plot*
Plate: Mandalaki 1997, pl. 378.

Location and discovery: Found in rescue excavations on the coastal road of the modern town of Tsoutsouros (ancient Inatos) near to the Roman cemetery. The current location of the mosaic is unclear.

Dimensions: 0.90 x 0.80 m (surviving).

Context: A third-century six-roomed Roman house. The mosaic had been repaired in the fourth century, and in the Late Antique period the area was used as a cemetery. A large pithos was found in one of the rooms used in the fourth century. This may indicate the room's use in small-scale industries or for storing olive oil.

Description: A tessellated mosaic which was not well-preserved; only a small area of it was uncovered (there was a Late Antique cemetery on top).

Date: Third century?

Bibliography: Mandalaki 1997, 995–8; *AR* 2003–4, 80.

Gortyn

THE ODEION

Three different mosaics were discovered during the excavations of the multi-period Odeion in the northern section of Gortyn (Fig. 13). The Odeion itself was constructed in the first century B.C.E. on top of an earlier Hellenistic building whose superstructure provided parts that were reused in the Odeion. A first-century rebuilding followed. In either the late second or the third century some auxiliary rooms were added. The site eventually was used as a cemetery in the Late Antique period.

53. *Gortyn: The Odeion Area*
Plate: 17.

Location and discovery: Found during Pernier's 1920 excavations. Current location is unclear. Only small fragments were left of these mosaics at the time of their discovery.

Dimensions: Only a small fragment survived.

Context: West of the *pulpitum* in the passage close to the entrance to the Odeion. The mosaic was located in a range of rooms

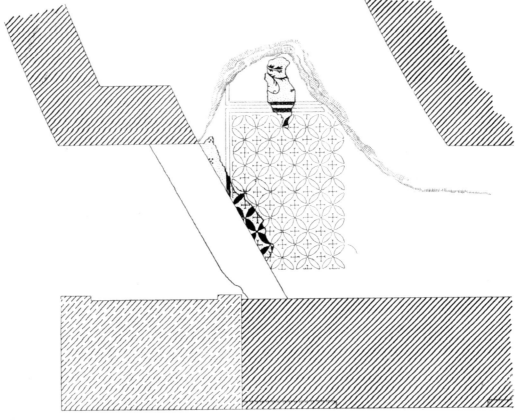

Plate 17 Gortyn, Odeion mosaic (Mosaic 53) (after Pernier 1925–6, fig. 37) (reproduced with permission from the Scuola Archeologica Italiana di Atene).

for which the function and date are unclear although Sanders (66) suggests a bath suite.

Description: The remains of two panels of a black-and-white geometric mosaic are each bordered by a plain black band. Exterior to the black-band border is a large outer border of rows of poised squares rendered with five tesserae. One panel contains a field of intersecting circles forming spindles and concave squares (R 237a) which contained equal-armed crosses terminating in chevrons. The second panel contains a fragment of a floral scroll (possibly acanthus) (Pl. 17). The outer border of poised squares is the same as that occurring around Mosaic 2, but alone this cannot indicate firm workshop connections.

Materials: Stone tesserae.

Date: Trajanic (Sanders, 53).

Bibliography: Sanders, 53, 66; Pernier 1925–6, 42; Lippolis 2005, 173–89.

54. *Gortyn: The Odeion Doorway*
Plate: Pernier 1925–6, fig. 44.

Location and discovery: Found during the 1920 excavations by Pernier. Current location is unclear.

Dimensions: Only a small fragment survived.

Context: Doorway in the west side of the Odeion.

Description: Only a small fragment of a border survived, consisting of a row of diamonds all touching each other, each containing a small square.

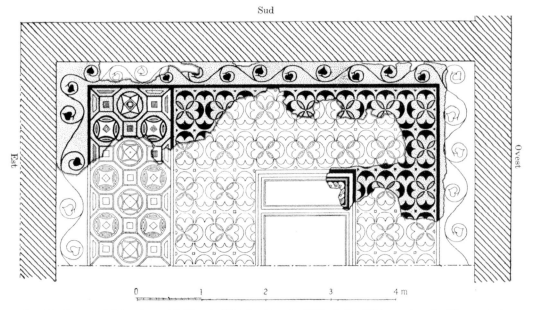

Plate 18 Gortyn, Odeion Room XI (Mosaic 55) (after Pernier 1925–6, fig. 62) (reproduced with permission from the Scuola Archeologica Italiana di Atene).

Date: Trajanic construction of the Odeion.

Bibliography: Sanders, 53, 66; Pernier 1925–6, 42; Lippolis 2005, 173–89.

55. *Gortyn: The Odeion, Room XI*

Plate: 18.

Location and discovery: Only fragments were found during Pernier's 1920 excavations. Current location is unclear.

Dimensions: 3.25 x 6.5 m.

Context: Room XI of the range west of the Odeion. This room appears to be secondary to the main structure.

Description: A border of a black-and-white ivy scroll (**R** 64d) surrounds two central polychrome panels (Pl. 18). The first panel had a mat design of octagons and squares, with the octagons arranged in groups of four surrounding a square. Each of the octagons contains a circle, and these circles are then further divided into four spindles arranged so that they form a concave square. Other circles are

filled with a central square surrounded by four triangles. The second panel has a small fragment of a border consisting of a black band and an interior band of trichrome guilloche. The main field is made up of peltae and four-petalled crosses which are distinguished from each other by their different colours. This arrangement is comparable to **R** 229a.

Date: The mosaic itself sealed a coin which is dated to the first century B.C.E. and gives the mosaic a *terminus post quem*. Several floor levels were excavated, and the report states that the mosaic comes from the earliest floor-level (Pernier 1925–6, 65). Although it is difficult to date the mosaic, the excavators indicate that the mosaic dates to the foundation of Gortyn as the provincial capital, and the black-and-white style of the mosaic would support a date of the early first century.

There is no exact match in Greece for the particular type of design for Panel 2, but variations of the peltae form date to the first century, for example, the Kladeos baths in Olympia (Waywell 1979, cat. 31, pl. 49). In all, a date of the early first century is reasonable.

Bibliography: Sanders, 53–4; Ramsden 1971, 145; Pernier 1925–6, 65–7; Lippolis 2005, 173–89.

SO-CALLED PRAETORIUM, NOW KNOWN AS GYMNASIUM

The excavations in the southeast sector of the Roman town revealed a number of paved streets and a substantial Gymnasium complex which included the start of the stadium, a bathing suite and a temple to the *Divus Augustus* (Figs. 7 & 13). The area until recently had been erroneously identified as the Praetorium.

56. *Gortyn: Gymnasium Mosaic (a)*
Plate: Lippolis 2000, fig. 31 (mosaic 256).
Location and discovery: *In situ*. Located during research excavation.
Dimensions: Unknown.
Context: The mosaic of oblong pebbles (possibly a bedding) paves the portico of the bath house (Area 80) in the Gymnasium.
Description: A plain, tightly packed cobble bedding.
Materials: Pebbles.
Date: Found in an early second-century context of the baths.
Bibliography: Lippolis 2000, 389–513.

57. *Gortyn: Gymnasium Mosaic (b)*
Plate: Lippolis 2000, figs. 33–5 (mosaic 254).
Location and discovery: *In situ*. Located during research excavation.
Dimensions: Reconstructed dimensions *c.* 4.5 x 10 m. The sub-rectangular tesserae measure between 1 and 2 cm.
Context: The mosaic comes from the *apodyterium* of the second- to third-century baths in the Gymnasium (Plan 3). The rather

simple style of the mosaic is typical for public areas such as baths.
Description: This black-and-white tessellated mosaic consists of a field of thin bands of black creating large triangles and rectangles.
Date: Originally the mosaic was dated by Di Vita (1990–1, 458) to the late second to early third century. Recent excavations indicate an early second-century date (Lippolis 2000, 412–19).
Bibliography: Di Vita 1990–1, 432–86; Lippolis 2000, 389–513.

58. *Gortyn: Gymnasium Mosaic (c)*
Plate: Lippolis 2000, figs. 43–6 (mosaics 418, 1309, 1316).
Location and discovery: *In situ*. Located during research excavation.
Dimensions: None available. The tesserae are mostly 1 x 1 cm, but some are as big as 2 cm.
Context: Area 47. The fragments occur in the area of the latrines.
Description: White tessellated mosaic with black geometric décor. The geometric design consists of a field of rhomboids and possibly other elements, but only small fragments survive.
Date: The successive building makes a date difficult to establish, but the mosaics are likely to belong to the late second- to early third-century phase of the baths (Lippolis 2000, 441).
Bibliography: Lippolis 2000, 389–513.

59. *Gortyn: Gymnasium Mosaic (d)*
Plate: Lippolis 2000, fig. 45 (mosaic 1296).
Location and discovery: *In situ*. Located during research excavation.
Dimensions: None available. The tesserae are around 1 x 1 cm in area.
Context: Area 47.

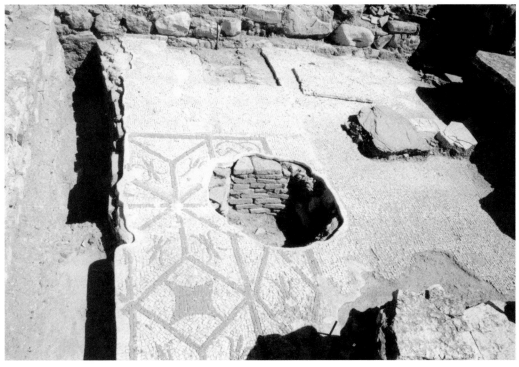

Plate 19 Gortyn, Gymnasium mosaic (e) (Mosaic 60).

Description: Plain white tessellated mosaic.

Date: The mosaics belong to the early second-century phase of the baths.

Bibliography: Lippolis 2000, 389–513.

60. *Gortyn: Gymnasium Mosaic (e)*
Plate: 19; Tommaso 2000, figs. 15, 32, 33 & 34 (mosaic 1046).

Location and discovery: *In situ*. Located during research excavation.

Dimensions: 2.70 x 1.50 m (surviving). The tesserae measure c. 1 x 1 cm.

Context: Area 64. Located by the central area, which was converted into the west baths after the first century destruction in the southwest of the Gymnasium. The mosaic is constructed on top of a bedding of large river pebbles. A limestone floor was constructed on the mosaic in the third century. In the later period, the mosaic is cut into by an encasement for a pithos for the oil-making industry of the later monastery.

Description: Black-and-white mosaic (Pl. 19). Consists of a plain black band which borders a field of triangles and diamonds. The diamonds form eight-pointed stars, and between the rows of stars there are squares. In at least one of the squares there is a Solomon's knot and in the other, a concave square. Each of the diamonds contains a vegetal motif. The arrangement of diamonds and squares is similar to that of the Stephanoudakis Plot, which also contains the same vegetal design (Papapostolou 1975, 347).

Date: The mosaic is dated stratigraphically to the late Hadrianic period (Di Vita 1990–1, 444).

Bibliography: Di Vita 1990–1, 432–86 (mosaic 1046); Tommaso 2000, 284–383.

61. *Gortyn: Gymnasium Mosaic (f)*

Plate: Tommaso 2000, fig. 34 (mosaic 885).

Location and discovery: *In situ*. Partially excavated during research excavation.

Dimensions: Unknown.

Context: Located to the south of Mosaic 60.

Description: Small fragment of black-and-white mosaic which may consist of a field of squares and hexagons containing elements of geometric décor including Solomon's knots and stylized flowers.

Date: Not known.

Bibliography: Tommaso 2000, 284–383.

62. *Gortyn: Gymnasium Mosaic (g)*

Plate: Di Vita 2000c., fig. 5 (mosaic 1977).

Location and discovery: *In situ*. Located during research excavation.

Dimensions: None available.

Context: Areas 52 and 50 of the west baths.

Description: White tessellated mosaic with black geometric décor.

Date: Second to fourth century.

Bibliography: Di Vita 2000c, 767–81.

63. *Gortyn: Plain White Mosaic*

Plate: None available.

Location and discovery: West of the main road in the main cemetery area (Area L) (Fig. 13). The mosaic has now been conserved.

Dimensions: None available.

Context: Discovered during the excavation of a Roman house in a residential area of the suburbs of the Roman city. A bath house is located nearby.

Description: A plain white floor, bound in plain white cement. There was a stratum of a pink floor that was preserved to 1 cm in thickness underlying the mosaic.

Date: It is thought that the houses date to the first century (Orlandos 1975, 197), and some of the other houses did continue on in use until the sixth century. It is most likely that this particular floor is as early as the first century, as suggested by Rendini (1988, 317). Rendini argues that the irregularity of form makes one think of a period later in the first century.

Bibliography: Lembesis 1971, 292; Alexiou 1973, 474; Orlandos 1975, 197; Sanders, 158; Rendini 1988, 317, 317–19 (mosaic 333).

64. *Gortyn:* Opus Signinum

Plate: None available.

Location and discovery: Discovered in the same area as Mosaic 63 (Plan 3).

Dimensions: None available.

Context: Discovered during the excavation of a Roman house in a residential area of the suburbs of the Roman city. A bath house is located nearby.

Description: Grey, green and white tesserae. The type of cement that the tesserae are laid in (with its crushed-up pieces of terracotta) is similar to a cement type that Dunbabin (1978b, 172–4) terms IIIc and which is found in Africa at the beginning of the first century.

Materials: Stone and terracotta.

Date: Because of its similarities to the North African IIIc *opus signinum*, it is possible that the Gortyn mosaic is also dated to the first century (Rendini 1988, 317).

Bibliography: Rendini 1988, 317–19; Dunbabin 1978b, 172–4.

Note: During excavations in an area of the Praetorium, some Late Antique houses were excavated and 293 kg of glass tesserae were recovered. The excavators postulated that the tesserae were intended to be laid as wall mosaics (*AR* 1998–9, 113–14).

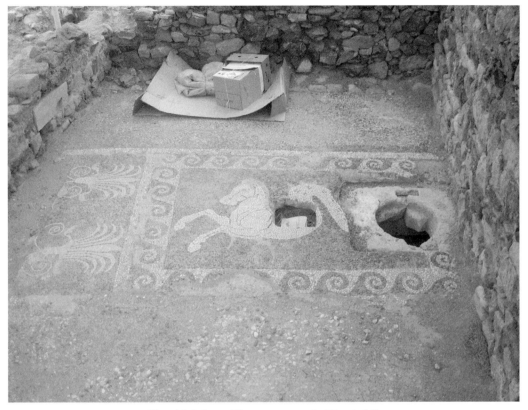

Plate 20 Lebena, Hippocamp mosaic (Mosaic 66).

Matala

65. *Matala: Possible Mosaic Fragment*

Plate: None available.

Location and discovery: The mosaic was noted by the mid-nineteenth century traveller Falkener. Current location is unknown.

Dimensions: Unknown.

Context: It is claimed by Platon (Sanders, 114) that the local church of Panagia is situated on the site of an earlier church and that the mosaic may have been associated with the earlier church.

Description: None available.

Date: Sanders (114) notes that Falkener had recorded an inscription which had been associated with the mosaic but that the content is unknown.

Bibliography: Falkener 1860, 283. Sanders, 114; *Byz Corp I.*

Lebena

66. *Lebena: Hippocamp Mosaic*

Plate: 20.

Location and discovery: Earliest record of the mosaic is from the nineteenth-century traveller Falkener. The mosaic is currently exposed *in situ*. It was damaged in the second century when the tail was cut off by the sinking of a circular hole. Later, a more crudely cut hole was dug through the body of the sea horse (Pl. 20).

Dimensions: 4.20 x 2.20 m

Context: A fourth-century B.C.E. sanctuary to Asclepius,[22] the mosaic was discovered in the Treasury, located in the southern part of the west stoa (Pl. 20). The mosaic is contemporary with the first phase of building; there were two late construction phases, in the first century and the second–third century.

Description: A black-and-white pebble mosaic which depicts a white sea horse on a black background (Pl. 20). Red pebbles are used for décor, for example, in the mane of the horse. Detail is rendered using thin black pebbles, for example, for the eyes and the mouth and the front of the horse. The sea horse is set within a rectangle bordered by a thick band of wave pattern (**R** 101b). To the east of this is another panel which shares the border of the wave pattern on one side only. Within the panel are two large palmettes, similar to **R** 92h, only in this case they are single and do not occur in a band. Each is contained in a pot; the palmette springs from an Ionic volute arrangement with two opposed spirals coming out of the bottoms. The palmettes are rendered in white on a black background and are similar in design to a pebble mosaic discovered in Corinth and the fourth-century B.C.E. in date (*AR* 1979–80, 23–4). Much of this area of the Lebena mosaic has been damaged, but from one surviving side we can see that it was bordered by a thick white band. Around the outside of the wave-pattern border of the mosaic is a large area of small pebbles which have been laid in such a way that subtle swirls are identifiable.

Uncut pebbles are used with the exception of the rendering of the sea horse and the palmettes, which contain cut pebbles.

Materials: The white used in the mosaic is marble. There is also red terracotta, black and white pebbles and very roughly cut black and white tesserae.

Date: Sanders suggests that the mosaic can be dated from the early part of the Hellenistic phase. Salzmann dates the mosaic to the second half of the third century B.C.E. The western wall of the later Roman stoa (early first century) was built on top of the mosaic, and this gives a *terminus ante quem* of the early first century. Hadzi-Vallianou argues strongly for a late Hellenistic date, based on the date of the stoa. The mosaic probably dates to the third century B.C.E., if not the early second century B.C.E.

Bibliography: Falkener 1854, 25; Sanders, 55; Salzmann, D 1982, 117; Hadzi-Vallianou, 1989.

67. *Lebena: The Sanctuary of Asclepius*
Plate: Melfi 2004, fig. 3; Melfi 2007, figs. 25, 32, 33.

Location and discovery: Fragments of the mosaic are preserved *in situ*.

Dimensions: Unknown.

Context: Temple of the Sanctuary of Asclepius. The surviving patches of mosaic are found just behind the statue base erected by Xenion in the second/third century (Melfi 2007, fig. 33) and in the northwest corner of the *cella* (Melfi 2007, fig 32). It may have originally covered the whole floor of the temple.

Description: Two fragments of black-and-white tessellated geometric mosaic remain. A large black square and the rounded lines may have formed part of an intersecting circle and spindle design. A second small fragment of mosaic is situated beside the brick wall (the original wall was in rough-cut stone, which during the Roman period was faced with brick) to the west of the stoa. Hadzi-Vallianou (1989, 16) suggests that the mosaic framed a paved floor of marble slabs (see also Melfi 2007, fig. 35, for the remainder of the guidelines for the pavement).

Materials: Stone tesserae.

Date: The mosaic is laid in the sanctuary temple which was built at the end of the Hellenistic period. As the temple had a number of building phases, it is difficult to date the mosaic with any certainty to either the Late Hellenistic period or the second or third century.

Bibliography: Sanders, 81; Hadzi-Vallianou, 1989; Melfi 2004, 515–30; Melfi 2007.

68. *Lebena: The Domestic Area*

Plate: None available.

Location and discovery: Discovered during rescue excavations in the late 1980s.

Dimensions: None available.

Context: The mosaic was found in a domestic area of the Sanctuary of Asclepius, apparently in a central chamber or hall.

Description: Following an excavation in 1988 there were reports that a polychrome mosaic was found in a large building with a central hall, but there are no descriptions of the mosaic. From the published photograph a border can be made out.

Marble paving is preserved in the area, but its relationship to the mosaic is unknown.

Date: Unknown.

Bibliography: Vasilakis 1989–90, 286.

Prefecture of Rethymnon

Sybrita

69. *Sybrita: Ta Marmara Mosaic*

Plate: Matz 1951, pl. 119.4.

Location and discovery: The mosaic was found by Russian sailors and later excavated by a German team. Location is unknown.

Dimensions: Unknown.

Context: Unknown.

Description: A polychrome mosaic depicting red, blue and white shells and apparently now lost.

Date: Unknown. Sanders suggests third–fourth century but without explanation. Volanakis suggests that it is of Late Antique date.

Bibliography: Matz 1951, 145 & 149; Sanders, 54; Volanakis, 45; *Byz Corp I*, no. 98.

Vizari

70. *Vizari: Black-and-White Mosaic*

Plate: 21.

Location and discovery: Current location unknown.

Dimensions: 3.35 x 5 m.

Context: The fact that the mosaic is no longer visible makes it difficult to define its precise context. Sanders (54) claims that the mosaic was found in a possible bath house. Kalokyris (158) states that it was actually located near to the eighth-century triple-aisled basilica. Hood, Warren and Cadogan (77) suggest that there were two mosaics, one which occurred in the bath house and the other in the basilica.[23] They note that the 'traces of occupation, including remains of concrete walling and mosaic pavements, cover an area of perhaps 300 m' (ibid.) and that Sanders's mosaic was situated about 100 m southeast of the basilica. I have had an opportunity to check the archives of the Archaeological Society, and the Black-and-White mosaic clearly comes from a context outside the basilica but within an apsed room. Although the only major structure currently visible on site is the basilica, it is clear from the archives that the basilica excavations did not produce any mosaics.

Description: Black-and-white tessellated mosaic. A border surrounding two panels is formed of a double row of evenly spaced black squares (Pl. 21). Each of the panels is bordered by a thin black line. The first panel shows remains of a border of an elaborate

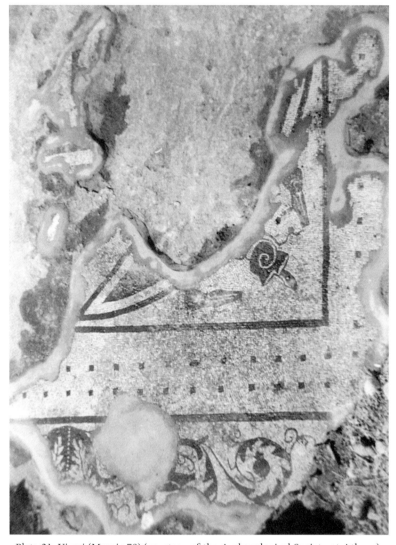

Plate 21 Vizari (Mosaic 70) (courtesy of the Archaeological Society at Athens).

inhabited acanthus scroll (**R** 64e) containing a pomegranate and a bird. The second panel was badly preserved, but evidence for a jagged scroll bordering the panel is clear. The main field consists of a circle within a square. The circle contains a shield design, possibly with a central emblem. There is a unique motif in the spandrels (Pl. 21). Sanders is certainly correct in his suggestion that this is a helmet flanked by two greaves (confirmed by the study of the archival material). The helmet

and greaves may indicate that Sanders is also correct that the mosaic originally came from a bath house.

Date: Sanders (54) suggests that because of the particular shield design and the fact that the jagged scroll is similar to some examples at Nea Paphos in Cyprus, a third-century date could be inferred.

Bibliography: Platon 1956, 33; Kalokyris 1956, 258–9; Hood, Warren & Cadogan 1964, 50–99; Sanders, 54.

Panormou

71. *Panormou Port: E. X. Drandakis Plot*

Plate: None available.

Location and discovery: Rescue excavations. Location is unknown. There was little coherent *in situ*.

Dimensions: None available.

Context: House.

Description: Fragments of the mosaics and the tesserae were found in the dirt.

Date: Unknown.

Bibliography: Andreadaki-Vlazaki, 2000–1a, 315; *AR* 2003–4, 92.

Kavros

72. *Neos Kournas (Kavros): Mosaics*

Plate: None available.

Location and discovery: Rescue excavations. Location is unknown. Fragments only.

Dimensions: None available.

Context: Fragments found in the largest room of a four-roomed bath house and also in the apse. Other rooms and the staircase were also decorated.

Description: The largest room had a mosaic bedding made of white cement. Wall painting and marble fragments were also found here, and the apse also contained fresco fragments.

Date: The building has a range of phases from the first century with the final one dating between the third and fourth centuries. The mosaics date to between the first and second centuries.

Bibliography: Karamalaki 2002, 259–61.

Lappa

73. *Lappa: Polychrome Mosaics*

Plate: Unpublished

Location and discovery: Rescue excavations. Exposed *in situ*.

Dimensions: None available.

Context: Likely bath house close to the area of discovery of Mosaic 121.

Description: The polychrome tessellated mosaics are geometric in design and date to the third century. The mosaics are likely to belong to a bath house and compare well with some of the Knossos mosaics. In the main field a vault pattern is used to divide up the geometric designs. The central panel contains a lattice pattern of lozenges and squares around a hexagon (**R** 205e), similar to that of the Myrtos bath house mosaic. Also contained is a convoluted wave pattern (**R** 101c) and a checkerboard (**R** 114a), dentilled simple fillet (**R** 2j) and rows of ogives (**R** 49h). Its three types of guilloche are the simple guilloche (**R** 70d), guilloche with a median fillet (**R** 70e) and double guilloche (**R** 74f). The surrounding panels contain stylized plants and rainbow fans.

Materials: Stone and terracotta tesserae.

Date: Third century according to the information sign there.

Bibliography: *K.Estia* 1992–4, 246–9; *AR* 1997–8, 121; Markoulaki 1993, 481.

Stavromenos

74. *Stavromenos Chamaleuriou: Mosaic Traces*

In the area of Stavromenos during the excavation of a bath house, traces of a mosaic were found in the apsidal room (Andreadaki-Vlazaki (1990, 445–6)). The mosaic itself was damaged beyond recognition, but a significant number of tesserae were located.

Sphakaki Pangalochori

75. *Sphakaki Pangalochori (Rethymnon)*

Plate: None available.

Location and discovery: Rescue excavations. Location is unknown.

Dimensions: None available.

Context: Two rooms of a five-roomed seaside house.

Description: None available other than that the floors were not well persevered.

Date: Second century?

Bibliography: *AR* 1997–8, 128; *AR* 1998–9, 124; Andreadaki-Vlazaki 1993; *K.Estia* 1992–4, 251, Markoulaki 1993, 481.

Prefecture of Lasithi

Lato

76. *Lato: Pebble Mosaic*

Plate: None available.

Location and discovery: Identified during excavations.

Dimensions: Not known.

Context: Found in the area of the Prytaneion of the site. In the western room (the Estiatorio) a section of 'mosaic' was discovered below the seat. Another section of 'mosaic' was identified in the area of the stoa.

Description: Described as a 'kind of mosaic', it is made from small pebbles laid in cement. The stoa mosaic is of a similar type with no clear décor.

Date: Hellenistic.

Materials: Pebbles.

Bibliography: Salzmann 1982, cat. no. 67; Apostolakou 2003, 28.

Makrigialos

77–9. *Makrigialos: Three* Domus *Mosaics*

Plate: Papadakis 1979, fig. 2 (for the house plan).

Location and discovery: The *domus* was excavated in 1977. Pendlebury had carried out a small excavation here in the 1930s (unpublished according to Papadakis 1979, 406). While some of the mosaics have been covered *in situ*, some fragments were still visible on site.

Dimensions: Not known. The visible white measures *c.* 1.1 x 1.1 cm.

Context: A large domestic complex with a series of rooms and corridors. Rooms Φ3 and Φ4 both had mosaic floors, now covered (Papadakis 1979, fig. 2). Room H1 also had remains of a mosaic floor in its northern corner. Also discovered in this area was a small marble statue. These rooms were located close to what is believed to have been the principal entrance to the building.

Description: Sparse descriptions of the mosaics were reported. The fragments consisted of small black and white tesserae and included were geometric designs and a border of ivy leaves.

Materials: Exposed on site were parts of the mosaic bedding consisting of a 4-cm thick layer of pink cement on top of an 8-cm thick cobble bedding.

Date: The excavators suggested that the house was occupied from the first to the third century. The mosaics are likely to date from early in this period.

Bibliography: Papadakis 1979, 406–9.

80. *Makrigialos: Bath House*

Plate: None available.

Dimensions: Unknown.

Location and discovery: Excavations of a *domus* (Mosaic 79) with bath house. Current location is unknown.

Context: Bath house. The mosaic is located to the west of the horseshoe-shaped open-air pool.

Description: There is a passing mention by Papadakis (1983, 59) of a mosaic discovered here during his 1970s' excavations. Little description is given other than that it was 'large' and had geometric designs.

Date: According to Papadakis, the construction of the bath house dates to the beginning of the second century.

Bibliography: Papadakis 1983, 59; Papadakis 1980, 524–5; Touchais 1989, 682.

Kouphonisi

81–2. Kouphonisi: Mosaics

Plate: Altamore 2004, fig. 1.

Location and discovery: Several mosaics were discovered on this island, which is situated off the southeast coast of Crete. Many of them were found in very bad condition, mostly due to exposure. An excavation was carried out in the 1970s, but just prior to this Leonard (1972) undertook a one-person survey and recorded the sites, including two small mosaic fragments. The excavated mosaics are covered *in situ*.

Dimensions: Room A: 3.5 x 2.5 m; Room B: 5 x 1 m.

Context: The excavated mosaics were discovered in Rooms A and B of House 1.

Description: The mosaics are simple, mostly plain white, and a couple have some very simple black geometric decoration. The two mentioned by Leonard are so damaged that they can only be described as groups of plain white tesserae.

The mosaics excavated in the 1970s are of simple black geometric decoration on a white background. The mosaic in Room A has a border formed by a line of black with an inner border comprising a diamond and a cross. That in Room B is a rectangular panel formed by a plain black line, inside which is a row of four-armed crosses, each made from poised squares terminating in chevrons.

Date: The house in which the mosaics were discovered has been dated to between the end of the second century B.C.E. and the first century. A coin of Antoninus Pius

(138–161) was discovered in Room D of the house. There is a suggestion on the basis of pottery evidence that Room A could be dated to the second half of the third century. This suggests that the house continued in use for a long period of time. However, none of this information can give reliable dating evidence for the mosaic.

Bibliography: Papadakis 1983, 379–81; Leonard 1972, 361.

83. Kouphonisi: Bath House

Plate: None available.

Location and discovery: The fragments of the mosaics were found in a newly excavated bath house.

Dimensions: Not known.

Context: Bath house.

Description: There is only a passing mention of the mosaics found here in a bath house, and it indicates that the floors consist of only a few fragments of tesserae. There appears to be no geometric pattern.

Date: On the basis of some pottery found in one of the rooms, it is at least possible to say that the bath house was in use in the second century.

Bibliography: Papadakis 1986, 230.

Myrtos

84. Myrtos: Geometric Mosaic

Plate: 22.

Location and discovery: Discovered during trial excavations and conservation work, in the 1970s, the damaged mosaic was cleaned and stabilized and put under cover *in situ*. But it is currently in a perilous state due to erosion, and little of it remains (Pl. 22).

Dimensions: The preserved area was *c.* 5 x 2.2 m at the time of excavation. Loose tesserae measure *c.* 1.1 cm^2.

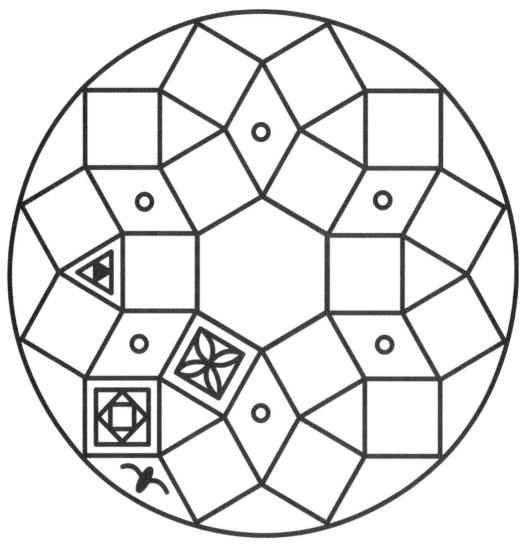

Plate 22 Myrtos, Geometric mosaic, reconstruction drawing (Mosaic 84) (drawing by K. Sweetman).

Context: Situated in the *tepidarium* of a private bath house which apparently dates to the Antonine period.

Description: There are four colours used: black, white, red and yellow (Pl. 22). The grid arrangement is that of two panels on either side of a square. The central square contains a circle which contains a geometric design of squares, triangles and diamonds. More than half of the circle has been damaged so it is impossible to be certain of the design type. However, it is most similar to **R** 205e. From my reconstruction (Pl. 22), it is likely that in this case there would have been only one hexagon. Of the preserved area, the squares are filled with designs of smaller squares containing a pattern of concave squares and four-petalled flowers. The triangles contain smaller triangles, and each diamond contains a small circle. The square is bordered by a band of simple guilloche. An outlined kantharos is found in each of the spandrels. The two panels on either side are made up of **R** 237a intersecting circles forming spindles and concave squares. In this case, there is a single crosslet in each concave square.

Materials: Parts of the mosaic bedding remain and consist of a 4-cm thick layer of clay and pink mortar on top of a 7-cm thick cobble bedding (Pl. 22).

Date: No parallels are found in Greece, but stylistically the mosaic is very like that of the Italian example from Brescello, Room A (Negrioli 1914, fig. 2) which Blake (1930, 113) suggests is likely to be of first-century date. Given the number of elements that these mosaics have in common and the lack of parallels for the design in other areas, it is more likely that the Myrtos mosaic is earlier in date than Antonine (as suggested by the excavators). At the latest, it is likely to be late first to early second century. A second-century geometric mosaic from the House of the Planets in Italica has a similar format but uses rectangles rather than squares.

Bibliography: *AR* 1973–4, 35; Sanders, 138; pers. comm. Sara Paton.

85. *Myrtos: Plain Mosaic Pavement*

Plate: None available.

Location and discovery: Rescue excavation.

Dimensions: Not known.

Context: The mosaic was in a small house which was made out of brick-faced concrete, found a short distance away from the excavated bath house.

Description: Tessellated white mosaic floor.

Date: Not known.

Bibliography: Sanders, 138

Ierapetra

86. *Alykes, Ierapetra: Plain Mosaic Pavement*

Plate: None available.

Location and discovery: Rescue excavations in the Sareidakis Plot in the western part of town to the south of the road to Myrtos.

Dimensions: Not known.

Context: Domestic building? Only the corner of the building was revealed. A well was also excavated in this plot.

Description: Bedding of mosaic floor and tesserae fragments.

Date: Not known.

Bibliography: Apostolakou 2002b, 343–5; *AR* 2002–3, 84.

87. *Viglia, Ierapetra: Plain Mosaic Pavement*

Plate: Apostolakou 1996, pl. 207.

Location & discovery: Rescue excavations in Pavlou Kouper Street in the western part of town to the north of the road to Myrtos. The plan was to conserve and leave the mosaic buried *in situ*.

Dimensions: Not known.

Context: Found in the southern section of a six-roomed Roman house which was not well perserved. The mosaic ran below an eastern wall.

Description: White background with black designs. There were three fields of the same size squares and within are zones of geometric designs; in the central panel, rhomboids with quatrefoils forming a cross and swastikas. Along the width is a zone of intersecting circles forming spindles and concave squares containing crosslets. The east side in black formed a design of semi circles and circles divided in sections and inscribed in a square. In the west is a field of squares with

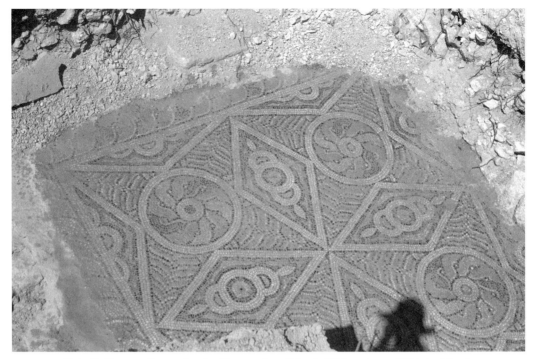

Plate 23 Knossos, Sanatorium Basilica, narthex (Mosaic 88) (courtesy of BSA Archives).

quatrefoils in the corners of the field. In the middle section of the field of rhomboids there was a central panel of polychrome decoration using glass tesserae. The central panel is not well preserved but remains of an inscription, Εἰσίων (Inscription 6), were found at the top (discussed in Chapter 3).

Date: Perhaps late first century on the evidence of the use of black-and-white geometric décor with a central polychrome panel, as with the Lissos (Mosaic 137) and Apollinaris (Mosaic 9) examples.

Bibliography: Apostolakou 1996, 655; *AR* 2001–2, 112.

Recently Reported Mosaics

Agios Nikolaos

Reports of the rescue excavation of a 15-roomed Roman house located in the area of Kastelli in the Bay of Mirabello indicated that some of the floors were made from pebbles bonded in lime cement. Other floors were paved with slabs (Apostolakou 1989, 306–7).

Itanos

Reports in *AR* 1998–9 indicate that pebble floors of both Hellenistic and Roman date have been uncovered during excavations at Itanos.

A1.3 Catalogue: Part 2. Late Antique Mosaic Corpus

Prefecture of Iraklion

Knossos

88–90. *Knossos: Sanatorium Basilica Mosaic*
Plate: 23–4.

Location and discovery: Covered *in situ*. Discovered during research excavations.

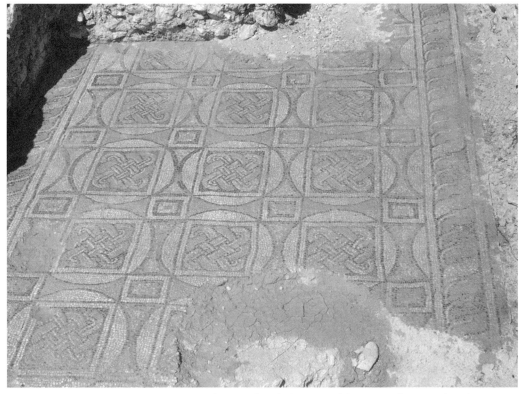

Plate 24 Knossos, Sanatorium Basilica, north aisle (Mosaic 90) (courtesy of BSA Archives).

Dimensions: Narthex: 11.5 x 2.5 m; south aisle: 14 x 2.5 m; north aisle: 10 x 2.5 m (surviving).

Context: The basilica in the north of the Roman city is of a standard plan, with three aisles (Frend & Johnston 1962). Mosaic floors were originally laid in the narthex, the aisles and the sanctuary. It is possible that there are also traces in the nave.

Description: *88–9. The Narthex and the South Aisle* – The narthex and the south aisle have the same mosaic design and are composed of white, red, orange, blue, pink and purple tesserae. A bichrome guilloche border surrounds the mosaic. The main field has a large carpet-like spread of geometric decoration (Pl. 23). The internal part consists of designs of four-pointed stars forming lozenges (**R** 184b). In the Knossos example the

stars contain circles and not squares. The stars are outlined in white with a filler design of multi-coloured zigzags (**R** 199b). Contained within the stars are circles. These are created with a white border and a circular band of bichrome guilloche (**R** 70d). The centre of each circle contains a small circular band of light colour with a dark-coloured dot in the centre. The lozenges are laid out in white containing a central knot design which occurs in each one and is made up of many colours (Pl. 23). Along the edge of the design is a row of half lozenges containing half-knot patterns.

Outside Crete specific parallels for the unusual mosaic iconography are found, for example, at Elis and Gytheion and Eresos basilica (Mytilene). Discussed in Chapter 6.

90. The North Aisle – The north aisle also has a guilloche border, which is the same as the border of the narthex mosaic (Pl. 24). The main field of the mosaic consists of a mat of circles and squares (**R** 144e). The circles and squares are outlined in black. Inside the squares at the intersections is a smaller inscribed square. Contained within the area of the large circles is a guilloche mat. The bobbins are created using the light colour of the circles on the dark background of the bands.

Other Fragments – Sanders (106) mentions other mosaic fragments in the sanctuary area:

(i) 'two wide panels of vari-coloured interlaces divided by a central path of orange and pink scallop shells, all enclosed by a broad frame of elaborate polychrome interlaces'. These mosaics have not yet been published.
(ii) In the nave were pieces of blue and green glass tesserae which may be evidence for wall mosaics.

Materials: Stone and terracotta tesserae.

Date: Mid-fifth century based on the workshop connections as discussed in Chapter 6.

Bibliography: *AR* 1954, 166; Daux 1959, 739; Frend & Johnston 1962, 194; Sanders, 105–7; Volanakis, no. 63; *Byz Corp I*, 109 (no. 86); Sweetman 2003.

91. *Knossos: KMF (Trefoil Sanctuary) Basilica*

Plate: Sweetman 2004b, pls. 42–6.

Location and discovery: Rescue excavations in 1970s in advance of the construction of the new medical faculty. Fragments stored in the Stratigraphic Museum, Knossos.

Dimensions: Only fragments remain. The tesserae vary in size from around 0.68 x 0.68 cm to 0.90 x 0.90 cm.

Context: Bema and nave of a trefoil-sanctuary basilica (Sweetman 2005, fig. 2) located in the north of the Roman city. When the church was excavated only the

substructure of the floor remained: most of the walls had been robbed out to their foundations. Despite this, the plan of the basilica was easily identifiable. The lower courses, at least, had been decorated with encrusted coloured marble with wall or vault mosaics higher up.

Description: No evidence of floor mosaics was found. The fragments can be identified as wall or vault mosaics by their backing and extensive use of glass. Only two sets of wall mosaics survive in Crete to date, and there is a notoriously poor survival rate in Greece anyway (Michaelides 1989b, 198). The mosaics are polychrome and occur in a variety of shades of green, blue, red and pink, black and white and variegated glass. Various fragments show figured, floral and geometric décor. A border of dentilled fillet (**R** 2d) of blue glass and white tesserae was located close to the border area (parts of the marble dado were preserved) (Sweetman 2003). In the northern section of the bema, remains of what could be construed as the letters 'ε' and 'c' (ς) were also recovered. Other fragments from the vicinity and from the bema were reconstructed to illustrate a swastika meander and adjacent circles forming concave squares made from green, red, and blue glass tesserae. In the southern end of the bema, a motif of red and white tangent concentric circles linked by a continuous black spiral is discernible. Additionally, remains of a green elongated triangle pattern could conceivably be a grassy fern design.

In the aisle, sections of green and black tesserae can be reconstructed as intersecting circles forming spindles and concave squares (**R** 237a). Given the colours, they may also be leaves. Sections of a vegetal or floral design can be reconstructed from the remains found in the central aisle, and in general, sections of the mosaic may also represent animals such as a fish or part of a peacock.

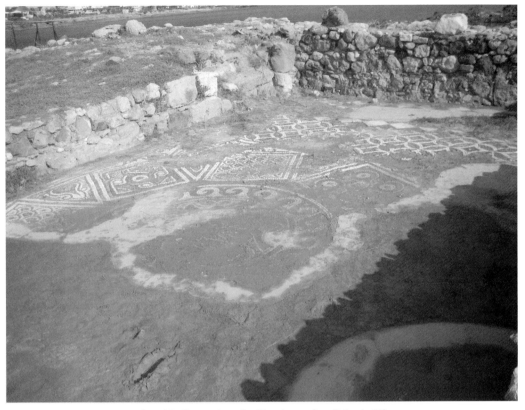

Plate 25 Chersonisos, Basilica A, narthex (Mosaic 92).

Materials: Glass, stone, terracotta, mother of pearl, marble tesserae.

Date: Early fifth century based on the stratigraphy and the date of the church (Sweetman 2004b).

Bibliography: Catling 1978–9 B, 57–8; Megaw 1984; Sweetman 2003; Sweetman 2004b.

Chersonisos

92–3. Chersonisos: Basilica A
Plate: 25–6.

Location and discovery: Discovered during excavations, the mosaics are *in situ*. They are now partially covered, with areas visible, for example, the lion and the deer roundel. There has been considerable damage to the mosaic, especially in the nave area.

The preserved mosaic fragments have been consolidated.

Dimensions: Narthex mosaic: Not known; *c.* 30 tesserae per 10 x 10 cm area. Tesserae 1.2 x 1.2 cm.

Nave mosaic: 24.50 m; *c.* 31 tesserae per 10 x 10 cm area. Tesserae 1.2 x 1.2 cm. The tesserae differ in size depending on where they were used. For example, the tesserae around the border are quite large (*c.* 2 x 2 cm) and regularly cut, whereas those used for the central designs, though regularly cut, are quite a bit smaller in size (*c.* 1.5 x 1.5 cm).

Context: Three-aisled basilica with walls of coarse rubble and occasional use of cut stone (Pl. 25). The mosaics were probably from the first phase of the basilica with its D-shaped construction on the north (Sanders,

98 & fig. 27). Later phases included the patching of the mosaics with tile, the building of the marble tomb in the narthex (no dateable finds were recovered) and the construction of the ambo in the nave. Later tombs of rough stone walling which would appear to date to a third phase were found on top of the mosaics, possibly when the church had gone out of use (Sanders, 98).

A modern church is now built on top of the apse of the original basilica, and some of the original spolia are built into its walls. Around the basilica are various column bases. Some of the marble work is still quite well preserved, for example, the small marble steps which occupy the doorways from the narthex into the nave (Pl. 25).

Description: Colours used are grey, white, black, red, yellow and light blue.

92. *The Narthex Mosaic (Pl. 25)*
The narthex mosaic floor survives only in a few patches, and in some areas it has been repaired with red tile. A small part of a geometric border consisting of interlocking semi-circles forming ogives (**R** 49a) survives in the southwest corner, but most of this area has actually been repaired using large red tiles. Continuing westwards, the border turns into a field of polychrome panels (containing zigzags, a stylized Greek cross, a four-pointed star and a cross ending in an arc shape) which are linked by a Greek key pattern in black and white tesserae. In the north, the roundel of the lion and the deer in polychrome is preserved (Pl. 25). The figures are stylized, with a thin floral scroll intertwining around the two animals. According to Pendlebury's reports (1939, 368), there may have been a similar scene from Basilica B at Suia (Mosaic 159). Directly bordering this circular emblem is a band of wave scroll in

red and white. Radiating from this are eight squares, like spokes but joined together to create a hexagon around the circle. The squares are filled alternately with mats of interlaced bands forming circles and concave squares (**R** 235a) and mats of scale pattern (**R** 217c). The scales themselves contain different colours; the outline is black with an inner border of white, and the main part is in red. This compares with some designs that are used in the Basilica A at Suia (Pl. 50). There are also squares filled with knot-work designs which all differ slightly. Between the squares are triangles and lozenges. The equilateral triangles contain a central heart shape, which is immediately surrounded by a single line with floral decoration emerging from it (Pl. 25). The lozenges and the knot design are discussed in Chapter 6. This is all contained within a square. In each of the four corners were two white triangles, one on either side of the lozenges of the main field. The triangles contain a heart and a floral scroll. Sanders (97) maintains that the heart shapes are ivy tendrils.

In the northern area, the mosaic is partially covered by a tomb. This area consists of joining circles created by four joined spindles. The four spindles form a concave square outlined in white and coloured in black. Each of the spindles is of dark colour with a lighter oval shape inside. The closest parallel for this motif is **R** 46d. Its only difference from the Chersonisos example is that here it is trichrome and has different coloured shapes within each of the darker colours. The colours are made from the use of red, yellow and white tesserae.

93. *The Nave Mosaic (Pl. 26)*
Only the northwest corner of the mosaic in the nave survives. There are two borders. The

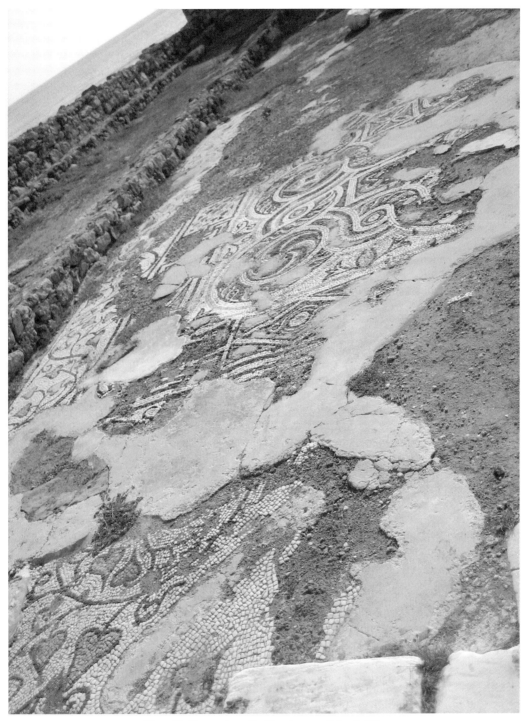

Plate 26 Chersonisos, Basilica A, nave (Mosaic 93).

main outer border is of ivy tendrils (Pl. 26). The scroll is outlined in black on a yellow background with grey filling in the leaves. Standing in the ivy scroll are the remains of a peacock next to the doorway (Pl. 26).[24] This band is wider at the western end and is broken slightly to incorporate the threshold step. On all four sides surrounding the main field and acting as an inner border is a Greek key pattern alternating with rectangular and diamond-shaped panels. These panels contain stylized flowers, adjacent scales (**R** 217c) and short rows of intersecting circles. In one of these panels is a pattern of lozenges. Within the two borders is the main field: interlaced bands forming circles and concave squares (**R** 235a). In this case, alternating guilloche and trichrome bands replace the constant shaded bands. Each of the concave octagons contains a large square. These squares contain designs such as Solomon's knots and intersecting circles forming hollow spindles (similar to **R** 237b). Within the larger circles are wheel designs, stars and Solomon's knots. There are also stylized flowers (Pl. 26), which Sanders terms 'lotus blossom'.

Materials: Terracotta, stone, marble tesserae.

Date: According to Orlandos (1955, 327), the mosaic dates to the end of the fifth/beginning of the sixth century. There are similarities between these mosaics and those from Knossos (Mosaics 89–90), Kera (Mosaics 122–5), Suia Basilica A (Mosaics 156–8) and Chersonisos Basilica B (Mosaics 94–100) making an early sixth-century date possible. It is not possible to date the later architectural constructions with confidence.

Bibliography: Orlandos 1956, 327–55; Sanders, 95–8; Volanakis, no. 75; *Byz Corp I*, 110–11, no. 87.

94–100. *Chersonisos: Basilica B*
Plate: 27; Fig. 8; *Byz Corp I*, pls. 83–4.

Location and discovery: Found during excavation. Much of this mosaic has been preserved *in situ*, though mostly covered over (except where visitors have pulled back the protecting sheets).

Dimensions: Narthex: *c.* 15 x 4.75 m; *c.* 32 tesserae per 10 x 10 cm area. Tesserae 1.1 x 1.1 cm.

Nave: *c.* 29.5 x 7 m; *c.* 28 tesserae per 10 x 10 cm area. Tesserae 1.3 x 1.3 cm.

Apse: *c.* 6 x 3 m (at longest and widest points); *c.* 30 tesserae per 10 x 10 cm area. Tesserae 1.2 x 1.2 cm.

South aisle, north terrace and exo-narthex fragments: *c.* 28 tesserae per 10 x 10 cm area. Tesserae 1.2 x 1.2 cm. Rough cut.

Context: A substantial three-aisled basilica which may have been the episcopal seat (Pl. 27). The walls are limestone-cut blocks mortared together; a small amount of brick is used in the walls and in some areas, unworked stone. Many architectural fragments lie around the area, including marble column bases and fragments of capitals. The finely engraved altar is still in position, but it has been turned upside down. It bears a depiction of a lion facing a deer, reminiscent of the central roundel in the narthex of Basilica A at Chersonisos. In the case of the sculpture, the animals have been converted into sea creatures with the addition of fish tails. The mosaics have been repaired in later times with rough floor tiles, in particular the central aisle. Also in the nave the ambo has been placed in a secondary phase on top of one of the mosaics; the same is true for the tombs which occur on top of the mosaic in the apse.

Description: *94. The Exo-narthex* (Pl. 27): Remains of a floor of rough-cut tesserae

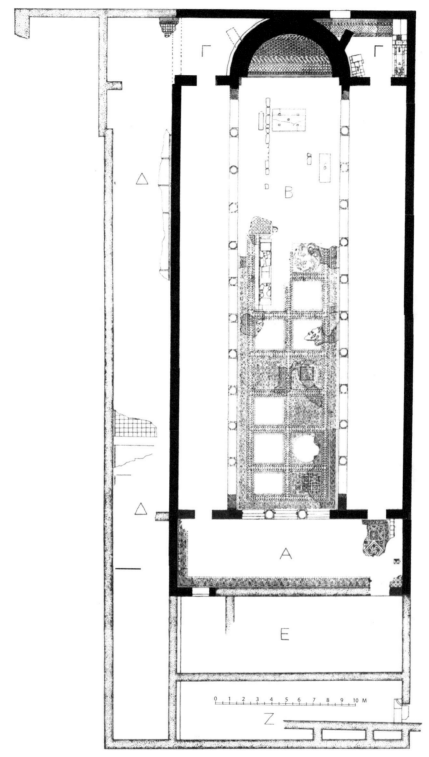

Plate 27 Chersonisos, Basilica B plan (Mosaics 94–100) (Orlandos Archive, courtesy of the
Archaeological Society at Athens).

depicting a geometric field of red-and-white checkerboard outlined in black.

95. *The Narthex* (Pl. 27): Little survives except for the border and a small area in the southeast corner. The border consists of a band of alternating squares in yellow and red on a black background[25] (Pl. 27). Within is a larger border of interlocking semi-circles with a black outline on a yellow background and white ogives within each of the arcs created (**R** 49a). This is the same border as is used in the nave mosaic. The fragment in the southeast of the narthex consists of a square and a lozenge and it is presumed that there was a field of alternating squares and lozenges enclosing a field of smaller and larger squares, the larger ones being recumbent (Pl. 27). In the outer field, the lozenges contain triangles or guilloche knots; the alternating squares contain various geometric designs, including a set of squares in red, yellow and black in one, and in another, a white circle set against a black square containing a five-pointed red star with a yellow centre. Of the internal field of squares, the smaller of these central squares contains a design of a four-petalled flower. The larger recumbent one contains an interlooped circle and square, a single element of strapwork of circles (**R** 82f). The location of the interlooped circle and square is of note as it marks the location of the doorway into the south aisle (Pl. 27). A line of flagstones marks the entrance to the nave. It is unclear if they belong to the original floor or the later patching.

96. *The Nave* (Pl. 27): A border of a band of interlocking semi-circles breaks the main field into a range of panels (Pl. 27). The interlocking semi-circles are created in black outline on a yellow background with white ogives (**R** 49a). Within this band is a band of double guilloche (**R** 74h). This guilloche band

also divides the individual panels in the main field.

Within the border is the main field. It contains square panels of which there were likely to have been 20 (10 on each side) originally. There were at least two figured panels; a fragment of one portraying fish survives (Pl. 27). The panel opposite this contains vine leaves. It is possible that it originally contained a peacock within the scroll. The geometric panels from the south-west side include a mat of circles and squares; the colours used are red, black, white and yellow (**R** 144e). To the east is a panel of a circle within a square and a panel containing a square mat of guilloche. This panel is mirrored in the panel on the northeast side. Returning to the south side is a square within a circle containing a mat of guilloche. To the east are the remains of the two figured panels. A section of a checkerboard panel in blue, black, white and red and the remains of lines are seen below the synthronon. Its layout is unusual, and it may be that this originally held an inscription panel. The most easterly panel of the nave contains wide loops of guilloche surrounding a smaller circle (**R** 68b).

97. *The Apse Mosaic* (Pl. 27; *Byz Corp I*, pl. 83): This mosaic is completely geometric, and much of it was preserved when it was excavated. It consists of, from east to west, a narrow band of guilloche (**R** 70d) and one band of wave-crest design (**R** 101b). This is followed by a broad band of scale pattern (**R** 217c) and then a narrow band of lozenges. The widest band is formed by intersecting circles creating spindles and concave squares (**R** 237a). The final band is a narrow one of lozenges of alternating colours which are really cubes in perspective (**R** 99f).

98. *The Pastophorion Mosaic:* This area of mosaic does not survive well; it was the same

as the apse mosaic but repeated in reverse order, and the final lozenges and circles are omitted (Pl. 27).

99. The South Aisle: Remains of rough-cut tesserae depicting a black frame with red and white tesserae. It has no discernible pattern but could be a checkerboard as in the exo-narthex given that the same materials are used.

100. The North Terrace: Remains of a floor of rough-cut tesserae depicting a geometric field of red-and-white checkerboard outlined in black.

Materials: Stone, marble and terracotta tesserae. A yellow stone is used in the narthex mosaic but nowhere else.

Date: The mosaics belong to the foundation of the basilica. Several building phases followed. Pottery found in the tombs in the pastophorion dated to the late sixth century allows a *terminus ante quem* for the mosaic.

The architecture of the church is similar to that of the church at Lebena, which is considered to have a sixth-century date. There is also a close comparison between this and Basilica A at Chersonisos, for which a late fifth- to early sixth-century date has been proposed.

Bibliography: Platon 1955, 419, no. 10; Orlandos 1956, 241–9; Orlandos 1959, 220–30; Sanders, 98–101; Volanakis, no. 76; *Byz Corp* 1, 111–12 (no. 88).

Note: In his report, Platon (1955, 419) says that there are marble floors as well as mosaics. These are no longer visible.

101. *Chersonisos: Spanoudakis Plot*
Plate: None available.
Location and discovery: Rescue excavations.
Dimensions: Not known.
Context: A Roman and Late Antique building with drains and floor slabs was uncovered. A marble table/altar was found on top of the mosaic, which suggests that the building was a church. The excavators believe it to have been the church referred to by Platon (1955, 419–20).

Description: Comparable designs and craftspersonship to the Chersonisos Basilica B mosaic. No further description.

Date: Late Antique.

Bibliography: Chaniotaki-Starida & Mari 2004, 294; Platon 1955, 419–20 (no. 13).

102–3. *Mallia Basilica Mosaic*
Plate: *Byz Corp I*, 113–14 (no. 92).

Location and discovery: The mosaics, *in situ*, are likely to have been covered over. The basilica is situated in a vast area of marsh and reeds, a short distance from the coast. The area is somewhat inaccessible because of the swampy conditions.[26]

Dimensions: None available.

Context: Only a small area of this three-aisled basilica has been excavated. Its eastern end appears to be unique in Crete because of the annexes attached to it. It is generally considered that there was only one phase and that the mosaics are contemporary with the foundation of the basilica. The walls are constructed of stone and rubble.

Description: There are mosaic fragments in the nave and in the northernmost of the basilica's two annexes.

102. *The Northern Room Mosaic*
Two fragments were preserved near the south and the west walls. The south wall area has a cross design made up of double lines. The arms of the cross consist of large triangles intersecting through the circle and continuing outside it. A fragment of the outer border of ivy leaves on a white background is preserved in this area and is separated from the main area by a black band and a band

of serrated saw tooth pattern **R** 10g. These designs are rendered in black and white. A section of the same border is preserved along the west wall.

103. *The Nave*

Sanders (102) comments that the mosaics here are 'geometric with rose-like designs in three colours'.

Date: Daux reported (1961, 951–2) that there were three main phases of this area of occupation and that the basilica belongs to the third phase, the mid-sixth century. This date would also suit the parallels that the Ionic capitals have with some from the Justinianic Hypsilometopon Basilica in Lesbos (Sanders, 102). Nothing in the mosaic would contradict this.

Bibliography: Daux 1958, 829; Daux 1961, 950–2; Demargne 1974; Sanders, 101–3; Volanakis, no. 68; *Byz Corp I*, 113–14 (no. 92).

104. *Avdhou*

Plate: None available.

Location and discovery: Possibly *in situ*? A visit to the area in 1996 and again in 2008 proved that the mosaic is not currently visible.

Dimensions: Not known.

Context: Likely a basilica. An atrium was still visible in the early 1970s when Sanders visited the site. The peacock on the mosaic led Sanders to identify the building as a basilica.

Description: Sanders (104) reported that a geometric mosaic is recorded from here with peacock motifs.

Date: Not known.

Bibliography: Platon 1956, 419; *BCH* 81 1957, 617; Sanders, 104; Volanakis, no. 46; *Byz Corp I*, P114 (no. 95).

105. *Lyttos*

Plate: None available.

Location and discovery: Mosaics have been found here in association with a church which lies directly below the later Church of the Cross. It is not clear where the mosaics are currently located.

Dimensions: Not known.

Context: Three-aisled basilica. The line of the ancient church can barely be identified below the modern church. Part of the altar of the original church has been reused as a step in the doorway of the modern one. Spolia is widely used in modern buildings in the area.

Description: Limited evidence for these mosaics. Platon (1955, 419) notes that the mosaics were found in the north and west parts of the basilica.

Date: Sanders (104) suggests that the basilica dates to the end of the fifth century on the basis of comparative evidence of the architectural elements.

Bibliography: *K.Khron* 1953, 490; Sanders, 104; Volanakis, nos. 66–7; *Byz Corp I*, P113 (no. 91).

106. *Panagia*

Plate: None available.

Location and discovery: Gerola (1908, 299) said that there were mosaics below the church, but there is no longer any evidence for them now.

Dimensions: None available.

Context: Not known.

Description: None available.

Date: Not known.

Bibliography: Gerola 1908, 299; Sanders, 104; Volanakis, no. 70; *Byz Corp I*, 114 (note 47).

107. *Kastelliana*

Plate: None available.

Location and discovery: When Sanders visited the site in 1973 nothing of either the mosaic or the building was to be seen.

Dimensions: None available.

Context: The function of the building housing the mosaic is uncertain. Because this type of decoration can occur on mosaics in both religious and secular contexts it is difficult be certain that it is Late Antique.

Description: According to Sanders (104), the mosaic had designs incorporating clematis motifs and guilloche borders. The clematis may be similar to that at Suia.

Date: Not known.

Bibliography: Platon 1954, 516; Sanders, 104; Volanakis, no. 61; *Byz Corp I*, P114 (no. 94).

Gortyn

108. *Mitropolis*

Plate: *Byz Corp I*, pls. 77–8.

Location and discovery: Covered *in situ*. The basilica was excavated in the late 1960s.

Dimensions: Not known.

Context: South apse of a triconch church located in the south of the city (Fig. 13). The north apse was paved with a marble floor. The architectural arrangement of the building suggests that it may have functioned as a martyrium (see Sweetman 2004b for further discussion).

Description: Polychrome and tessellated. Three external bands of white and black form the outer border. Within this is a thick band of polychrome guilloche (**R** 72c). Inside this band is another of stepped pyramids, with serrated saw-tooth pattern (**R** 10g). The main field consists of a figured scene of birds and flowers laid out on a white ground. The different bird species, which are found both free-standing and amongst the flowers, are concentrated near the centre of the field, with the flowers forming a further border around the edge.

Two other areas were paved with geometric mosaics. The first consisted of a circle pattern which had twisted decoration and multi-coloured foliage surrounding it. Surrounding the circle were concentric bands with a series of alternating triangles in red and blue; these converged in the centre similar to a shield of triangles in contrasting colours (**R** 327b).

The second section was a central design of a hexagon containing a Solomon's knot. Surrounding the hexagon were six squares, each containing a four-petalled flower. Triangles, each containing a smaller triangle, alternated between the squares. The pattern appears to be continuous, with the base of each square touching another hexagon and the base of each triangle touching another square. Another panel from this area depicts a diamond in a square containing a six-petalled flower.

Date: The mosaic has not been dated securely. Although there are are no close parallels for the mosaic, the birds are depicted in Amphipolis Basilica B (fifth century). The church is believed to date to the mid-fifth century, and Sanders (113) dates the architectural fragments to the mid-fifth century.

Bibliography: Davaras 1960, 460; Daux 1961, 886; Bourboudakis 1968, 139–48; Orlandos 1968, 111; Bourboudakis 1969, 448–50; Sanders, 112–13; Gallas, Wessel & Bourboudakis 1983, 369–71; Volanakis, no. 55; *Byz Corp I*, 108 (no. 85); Lippolis 2005, 173–89.

109. *Gortyn: Basilica in Sector M*

Plate: 28–30; Bourboudakis 2004 figs. 1, 6, 6a, 8, 9, 9a; Farioli Campanati 2004, figs. 5, 6, 7.

Location and discovery: Covered *in situ*. Found during the systematic excavations

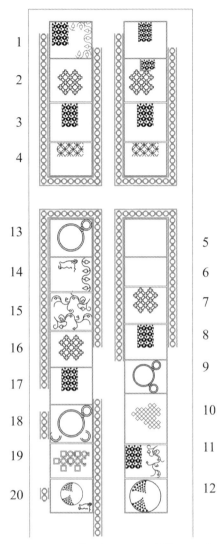

Plate 28 Gortyn, Sector M Basilica (Mosaic 109) (drawing by K. Sweetman).

undertaken by the Italian School and Byzantine Ephorea of Crete. In 1991 trenches originally dug in 1979–80 were extended. Excavations carried out in the south extension of the apse revealed a floor with a polychrome pavement of *opus sectile* (reported in 1993–4).

Dimensions: 11 m long. The basilica measures 60 x 30 m.

Context: Nave of a five-aisled Christian basilica (Pl. 28). The bema contains an *opus sectile* floor. Its size and the presence of the synthronon suggest that the basilica functioned as the episcopal seat. The basilica is located close to the triconch basilica (Mosaic 108) (Fig. 13). The first phase was that of a fourth- to sixth-century building. A black-and-white mosaic floor and two walls were associated with this phase. The second phase was a five-aisled basilica which was destroyed in 618–20. The aisles were paved with slabs, and the nave was paved with polychrome mosaics.

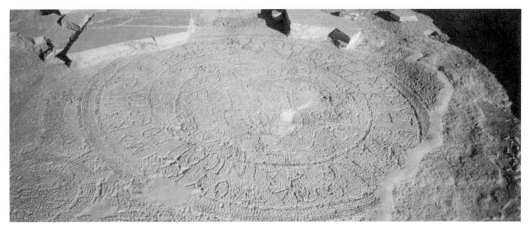

Plate 29 Gortyn, Sector M Basilica, nave (Mosaic 109) (Inscription 9).

The final basilica was likely to have been built and its floors repaired around 620/21 or shortly after, based on the evidence of a coin of Heraclitus, and then destroyed in the 670 earthquake. This basilica was built on a platform which was raised 12 cm above the first. While the line for the *solea* was likely in place (as in the border of the mosaic), a later ambo-*solea* arrangement was placed on top of the mosaic.

Description: Polychrome, tessellated mosaic in two phases. The second phase is the patching of the mosaics, primarily represented by the inscriptions (nos. 9 & 10) inserted in the west on the south side and in the east on the south side. (Follow Pl. 28 for the description.)

The border consists of a band of inter-linking circles (**R** 69f). The larger circles contain stylized flowers. This border divides the mosaic into four areas: two fields of four panels on either side of the *solea* in the western section and two fields of eight panels in the eastern section on either side of the *solea*.

The westernmost panels: Each of the four is mirrored by its opposite on the other side of the *solea*. Starting in the west (Pl. 28):

Panels 1. Scale pattern (**R** 217c); each of the scales contains a small heart-shaped emblem. The panel on the south side contains the much destroyed rectangular donor panel (Inscription 10) (Pl. 30). These panels seem to represent repair work.

Panels 2. Series of hexagons alternating and thus joined by small four-armed crosses.

Panels 3. Scale pattern (**R** 217c); each of the scales contains a small heart-shaped emblem.

Panels 4. Intersecting circles forming concave squares and hollow spindles (**R** 237b); an orthogonal pattern of intersecting circles forming saltires of quasi-tangent hollow spindles and concave squares, the colours counterchanged.

The easternmost panels: The panels may have originally mirrored each other, even if the inclusion of the donor panel in the south at the west end shifted the sequence. The result is that there are at least three panels on the north side which occur on the south.

North starting in the west (Pl. 28):

Panel 5. Destroyed.

Panel 6. Destroyed.

Panel 7. A series of hexagons alternating and thus joined by small four-armed crosses.

❧❧ 223

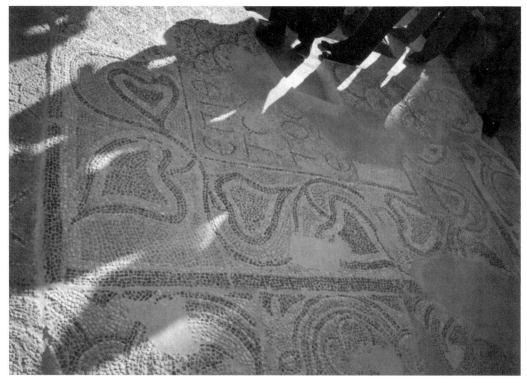

Plate 30 Gortyn, Sector M Basilica, nave (Mosaic 109) (Inscription 10).

Panel 8. Scale pattern (**R** 217c); each of the scales contains a small heart-shaped emblem.

Panel 9. Four-looped circle (largely damaged).

Panel 10. Net pattern.

Panel 11. Scale pattern (**R** 217c); each of the scales contains a small heart-shaped emblem. This may represent patching. Earlier (?) layer of leaf scroll is also preserved.

Panel 12. Circle within a square. The circle contains an outlined triaxial pattern of adjacent equilateral triangles, the colours counterchanged, creating the effect of a chessboard of equilateral triangles (**R** 198e) which, by getting progressively larger from the inside out, creates a swirling pattern (similar to that in Mosaic 5). The spandrels are filled with leaf scroll.

South starting in the west (Pl. 28):

Panel 13. Donor panel (Inscription 9) (Pl. 29). Four-looped circle in a square. The circular-banded border contains the donor inscription discussed in Chapter 6. Enclosed within the band is a kantharos with a peacock on either side. The panel is strikingly similar to that of the basilica at Suia.

Panel 14. Destroyed; remains of leaf scroll and a possible calf or deer.

Panel 15. Destroyed; remains of leaf scroll.

Panel 16. A series of hexagons alternating and thus joined by small four-armed crosses.

Panel 17. Scale pattern (**R** 217c); each of the scales contains a small heart-shaped emblem (this may represent patching).

Panel 18. Four-looped circle. In the loops are leopards, and the space between the circle and the square is decorated with fish.

Panel 19. Row of circles and squares interlooped tangentially (**R** 81b) (similar to that in the nave of the basilica at Almyrida). In this case the design contains fillers such as fish and stylized plants.

Panel 20. Circle within a square. The circle contains a pattern of an outlined triaxial pattern of adjacent equilateral triangles, the colours counterchanged, creating the effect of a chessboard pattern of equilateral triangles (**R** 198e) which, by getting progressively larger from the inside out, creates a swirling pattern (similar to that of Mosaic 5). The space left between the circle and the square is filled with scroll and animals (a calf or a deer?).

Narthex: Remains found during excavations here indicate that the walls were decorated with *opus sectile*.

Atrium and annex: Recent work in the western part of the complex has uncovered a substantial part of the basilica's atrium. In the annex of this area several sections of wall mosaics were recovered (including glass tesserae and inscribed fragments) (*AR* 2004–5, 114).

Materials: Terracotta, stone, marble tesserae.

Date: The mosaic likely dates to the sixth century or possibly early in the Justinianic reign, as the basilica was levelled in 618–20 during the destruction of Gortyn by Heraclitus and is therefore not later than this date.[27] The inscriptions noting the repair of the mosaics are likely to have been around the mid-sixth century, certainly before the 670 destruction.

Bibliography: *ASAtene* 1990–1, fig. 79; *AR* 1991–2, 63; *AR* 1992–3, 60; *AR* 1993–4, 73–4; Italian School 1985; Pariente 1991, 940; Di Vita 1991, 173–7; Pariente 1994, 823; Farioli Campanati 2001, 261–5; Bourboudakis 2004; Farioli Campanati & Bourboudakis, 2005, 165–71.

110. *Matala*

Plate: None available.

Location and discovery: Mosaics were apparently identified in the sixteenth century.

Little has been excavated and current location is not known.

Dimensions: Not known.

Context: It is thought that the Church of the Panagia marks the site of an earlier church, and there are 'early' columns.

Description: No description.

Date: Not known.

Bibliography: Sanders, 114; Spanakis 1972; Volanakis, no. 69; *Byz Corp I*, 114 (no. 93).

Prefecture of Rethymnon

ELEUTHERNA

111–14. *Eleutherna*

Plate: 31–3.

Location and discovery: Excavated as part of the research project on the site of Eleutherna. The mosaics had survived with remarkably little damage, and they are now covered *in situ*.

Dimensions: The basilica measures 14 x 45 m.

Context: North and south aisles and narthex of a triple-aisled basilica on the eastern side of the Acropolis (Pl. 31). A large section of fine polychrome *opus sectile* is preserved in the apse. The nave is paved with slabs.

A small fragment of wall painting is preserved in the narthex and is currently *in situ* behind a glass covering. It depicts red and blue scales similar to the pattern in **R** 217c. This pattern resembles that found on the mosaic in the south aisle. The walls have been preserved to a height of up to 2 m in some places, and many of the columns are still visible. A large complex attached to the south and associated with the church has been excavated. The synthronon indicates that this may have been an episcopal seat.

B

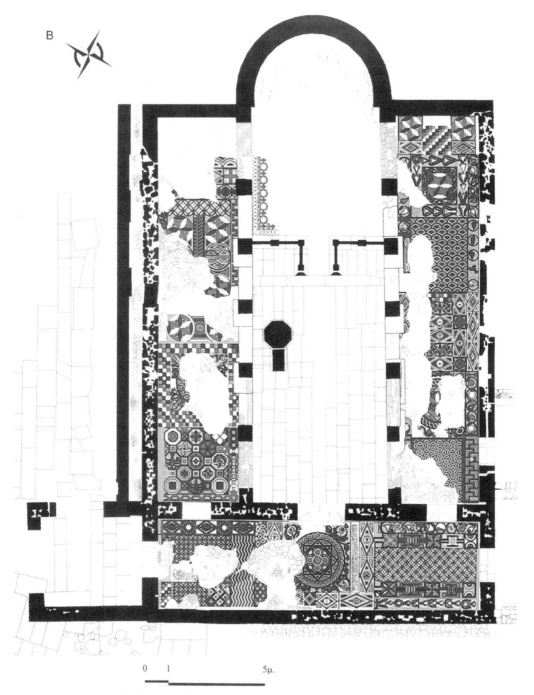

0   1   5μ.

Plate 31 Eleutherna Basilica plan (Mosaics 111–14) (after Themelis 2004c, fig. 35).

There are no mosaics in the church to the west of the Acropolis. However, it is possible that there are mosaics in the basilica at the northern end of the Acropolis. These, however, are damaged and remain at present covered and unpublished. The basilica is referred to by Volanakis 1987, no. 34.

Description: Polychrome mosaic; the tesserae are large and regularly cut (c. 2–3 cm on each side).

111. *The Narthex Mosaic (Pl. 32)*

Divided into three areas, the northernmost section has three main design components, although this part of the mosaic has sustained some considerable damage. Starting from the north, the first panel is of intersecting circles forming hollow spindles (**R** 237b). The colours employed here are yellow for the background with red petals and a central black dot. An inscription, reminding the visitor of the sanctity of the space, is found in the area of intersecting circles (Inscription 12) and is situated directly inside the doorway into the narthex. To the south, a panel contains very thin zigzags in red, blue, black and yellow, all repeated in separate rows; this is similar to multi-coloured zigzags (**R** 199b).

Along the east of these panels is a narrow field which has alternating square and rectangular panels in a single row. In each rectangular panel is a triangle containing a stylized floral design, and in each of the squares are different flowers. To the south of this area is a narrow panel of scallop design, and beyond this is the central panel of the narthex. The mosaic in this area has been patched with tile.

The largest panel in the area is defined on the north and south by a border of two rectangles each containing a lozenge bearing a flower. The western edge consists of a border of squares and rectangles bearing polychrome geometric designs. On the east is the step into the nave. The panel consists of a large circle set within a square (Pl. 32). The circle is formed from an open guilloche border (**R** 68d). The colours used are red and blue with a yellow centre. A design of two intersecting squares containing a further central circle and within that a design of a four-petalled flower is contained within the outer circle. A complex kantharos design with vine scroll coming out from the bottom of it and floral decoration on either side is contained in the spandrels. Immediately to the south of this panel is the inscription panel which provides the name of the founder, Bishop Euphratas of Eleutherna (Inscription 11) (Pl. 33). To the south is the southernmost section of the narthex, which has two borders; the first of which is an ivy scroll (**R** 64d). This area is bordered on the east and west by a row of alternating small and large rectangles linked together by a small rectangular 'tunnel'. Each of the rectangles contains a design: the smaller ones have geometric designs such as swastika meander and the larger ones have floral decoration. The central panel of this section has a field of intersecting circles forming hollow spindles (**R** 237b). The colours are yellow and red with a dot in the centre of the concave square.

112. *The North Aisle (Pl. 31)*

Although the north aisle has suffered some damage there are distinguishable panels. The western section is bordered on one side by a tangled scroll which looks like a stem but has no foliage on it, similar to the **R** 64a pattern. Within is a design of squares and octagons containing different geometric designs, such as Solomon's knots and 6-pointed stars, and other natural designs, such as a bird, a tree and some flowers.

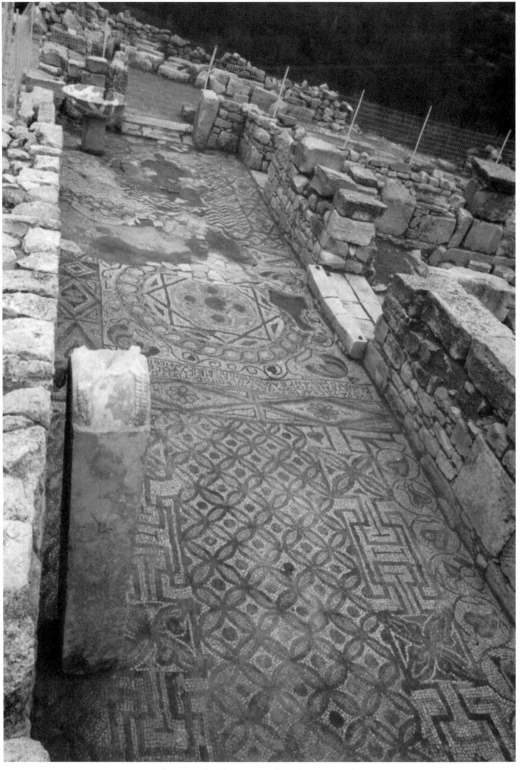

Plate 32 Eleutherna, narthex (Mosaic 111).

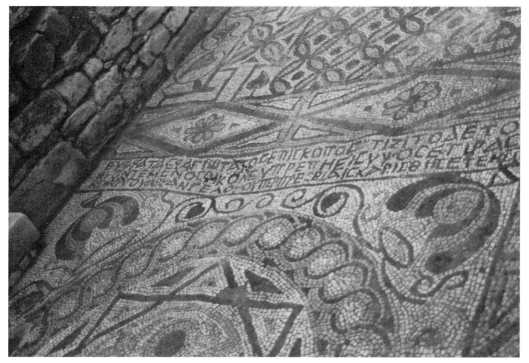

Plate 33 Eleutherna, narthex, detail of inscription and diamond designs (Mosaic 111) (Inscription 11).

The eastern section contains a panel of checkerboard in blue, red and white (**R** 114f). This part of the floor has been quite badly damaged. To the east of this, a swathe of intersecting circles forming hollow spindles (**R** 237b) contains a central design of a six-petalled flower whose terminals are connected by a further six petals, arranged so that they form a circle surrounding the central design (**R** 247e).

113. *The South Aisle (Pl. 31)*

This area of mosaic in the south aisle looks as though it has been constructed in separate parts, since there is no real unity among the panels. The first panel at the western end is that of scallop design similar to **R** 220b. To the east, a damaged area of geometric décor is contained within a border on its north and south sides of floral scroll. Beyond this to the east is a section which seems to break the flow of the floral-scroll border and consists of

rectangles bearing lozenges, some of which are recumbent. Each of the lozenges contains different geometric or floral designs.

To the west is a panel of scale pattern (**R** 217c), but in this case the colours are all the same except for a central dot in each scale. This is bordered on the north by a panel of scroll containing a small bird, and on the south, a leafy and delicate vine scroll (**R** 64d). The section at the eastern end is similar to that at the eastern end of the north aisle. The panel consists of a six-petalled flower, the terminals of some of which are joined together by further petals (**R** 247e). The colours used for the petals are red, blue and yellow. To the south of this panel lies a large one of checkerboard pattern (**R** 114f).

114. *The Bema*

Opus sectile floor is preserved (Pl. 31). The pattern is simple, and the colours used are red, black, white and yellow. The layout consists of squares with small circles in the centre. According to the reports the evidence suggested that this mosaic also covered the inner face of the wall in this area.

Nave: The only evidence for mosaic floors in this area is a small dump of loose tesserae. Tiles here suggest that the floor originally had a tessellated mosaic later replaced with tile.

Materials: Terracotta, stone, marble tesserae.

Date: This mosaic is one of the few Late Antique examples which can be dated accurately. A mid-fifth-century date is suggested on the basis of Inscription 11, which records the bishop Euphratas of Eleutherna, founder of the church. It is known that he attended the Ecumenical Council in 451 as the bishop of Eleutherna. It can be seen therefore, that the basilica cannot have been built any earlier than 430 and not later than 451.

Bibliography: Themelis 1988 298–302; Themelis 1989–90, 266–7; Themelis 1991–3, 252–7; Themelis 1994–6, 272–83; Pariente 1994, 831–2.

115. *Eleutherna:* Domus *Mosaic*
Plate: None available.

Location and discovery: Found during research excavations. Exposed *in situ*.

Dimensions: Not known.

Context: Possible bathroom of a domestic space located to the west of the basilica. The mosaic likely comes from the upper storey.

Description: Black-and-white tessellated mosaic. Black linear décor is preserved, likely from the border area. Another part may be the start of a hexagon-grid decoration. A corner area has a triangle in black outline with a central solid black triangle preserved.

Date: Either third or fourth century?

Bibliography: *AR* 1997–8, 124; Themelis 2003; Themelis 2004c, 64.

Sybrita

116–17. *Sybrita: Thronos Basilica Mosaic*
Plate: 34; *Byz Corp I*, pl. 90.

Location and discovery: Exposed *in situ*. Although it has been conserved the main portion of the mosaic is barely visible (Pl. 34). A large part of the mosaic is cut by a modern house on its north side. Some of the mosaic is visible in the modern church on the site.

Dimensions: The surviving portion measures 8 x 2.70 m. Tesserae: nave, 43 tesserae per 10 x 10 cm area; narthex, 35 tesserae per 10 x 10 cm area.

Context: Nave and narthex of a triple-aisled Christian basilica. A later church has been constructed on top.

Description: Polychrome: primarily, red, black and white. The best-preserved areas are in the narthex (Area 1); in the west of the nave (Area 2); beside the modern church (Area 4) (Pl. 34); and at the southeastern end (Area 5).

116. *The Narthex (Byz Corp I, pl. 90)*
Area 1: The narthex has a border of ivy scroll (R 64d) enclosing undulating bands forming circles of the same size. Enclosed within this border are rows of squares outlined in blue pebbles and within each is a different geometric design. These include a circle which is divided into triangular segments, similar to a wheel design; a circle which contains smaller circles; a square which has smaller circles within it and tiny circles in the space between the larger and smaller square.

117. *The Nave (Pl. 34)*
Area 2: A border fragment of diamonds rendered in white on a blue background is preserved. The diamonds merge with each other even if they are not intersecting, which

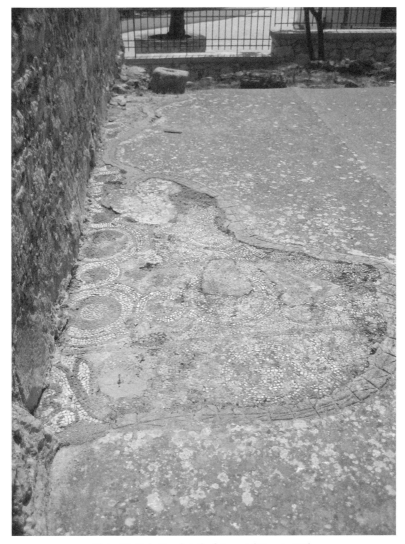

Plate 34 Sybrita, detail of Area 4 (Mosaic 117).

produces an effect similar to a lattice pattern (e.g., **R** 201a). Each diamond contains a circle made up of red-and-blue bands with a white core. The circles also occur outside the diamonds. Within this is a plain blue band and within this is a band of simple acanthus scroll (**R** 69e). Within the central area are panels of geometric decoration, including a panel of intersecting circles forming spindles and concave squares (**R** 237a). In this example, the concave squares contain small circles. There

are also panels depicting circles which are linked by small 'tunnels'.

Area 4: Only fragments are preserved (Pl. 34), and the wall of the modern church runs over this part of the mosaic. Closest to the wall of the church is an outer border of acanthus scroll and a further border of alternating large and small circles (**R** 69e). Within each circle is a design, sometimes of simple geometric patterns such as small circles and concave squares, and sometimes of more complex compositions such as a duck within foliage. Extending out from the corners where the circles meet to form a square are delicate ivy leaves. A vine-and-leaf design is found in other areas. Within this is a panel of scale pattern (**R** 217c).

Area 5: This area consists of a row of alternating large and small circles which is similar to a pair of bands interlooped forming circles (**R** 69f). There are vine leaves extending out from the larger circles. The main band of this design is of white with red and blue tesserae on either side. A fragment at the corner just preserves a bird within a vine scroll. The bird is rendered in blue, white and red and with a distinct red eye.

The mosaic fragment inside the modern church is divided into squares containing different panels of geometric decoration. The motifs are in blue, white and red. The designs consist of a white background with a blue square containing a white circle within which is a further blue circle. Each of these is bordered by a red band. A line of these squares forms a row of diamonds, and above and below each of them are simple squares containing just two circles. To the east of this is the same composition; however, in this instance the colours are used inversely. A guilloche band also borders this panel, and outside of it is a main border of ivy scroll.

Materials: Limestone (?), marble, terracotta tesserae. Tiny pebbles are also used.

Date: Kirsten's second-century date must refer to another mosaic (in Matz 1951, 142f). The fifth-century date in *Byz Corp I* is more appropriate given the context and content of the mosaic (use of birds in scrolls and alternating circles which are typical of Late Antique mosaic designs in Crete).

Bibliography: Gerola 1908, 56; Matz 1951, 142f.; Platon 1955, 415; Sanders, 54, 114–15; Volanakis, no. 44; *Byz Corp I*, no. 97.

Axos

118. *Axos A*

Plate: None available.

Location and discovery: The only evidence for a mosaic is a reference by Pashley (1837, 152). A later church, Agios Ioannis, is now built on top of the earlier one of which all that is visible are some early walls underneath the east apse.

Dimensions: Not known.

Context: Christian basilica which has been covered by a modern church.

Description: None available.

Date: Not known.

Bibliography: Pashley 1837, 152; Sanders, 120; Volanakis, no. 28.

Lappa

119. *Lappa: Phoundana*

Plate: None available.

Location and discovery: This basilica has not yet been excavated. However, traces of mosaics floors were visible in 1959, one of which was either in the shape of a cross or else had cross motifs all over it.

Dimensions: Not known.

Context: The only published detail about the church was that it had a mosaic floor, but there is no record of the position of the floor or of its possible date.

Description: None available.

Date: Not known.

Bibliography: Spanakis 1972, 167; Platon 1959, 391; Sanders, 120; Volanakis, no. 36; *Byz Corp I*, 120 (no. 102).

120. *Lappa: Panochori*

Plate: None available.

Location and discovery: Not known.

Dimensions: Not known.

Context: Not known.

Description: Sanders notes only that there were mosaics reported from this site, and he believes that it may be a third-century church; however, this is an excessively early date for a church in Crete. The information that Volanakis gives is just as limited, and he suggests that the mosaics may be Late Antique in date.

Date: Not known.

Bibliography: Sanders, 120; Volanakis, no. 40; *Byz Corp I*, 118 (no. 100).

121. *Lappa Mosaic (Area Unspecified)*

Plate: *Byz Corp I*, pl. 91.

Location and discovery: The mosaics found here in 1918 are now in storage in the Rethymnon museum. It seems that the mosaic was cut into sections for lifting. During recent work in Lappa the mosaics were re-examined (*AR* 1997–8, 121).

Dimensions: Not known.

Context: Although some scholars suggest the original context was a church, this cannot be confirmed as yet.

Description: In addition to hunt scenes, several sections contain geometric images. It was common to find hunting scenes in Late Antique mosaics outside Crete, but not in church contexts in Crete. From the images available, a panel of swastika meander bearing squares and sandwiched between two bands of wave crest is discernible and this may have served as the main border to the mosaic. Certainly the corner section preserved indicates at least a wave-crest border.

The other published panels consist of hunting scenes, mostly in black and white. Dogs, men and possibly a boar are depicted in one panel, a deer in another. All the figures are in silhouette.

Date: Not known.

Bibliography: Xanthoudidis 1918, 31; Platon 1955 (no. 23); Sanders, 120; Volanakis, no. 39; *Byz Corp I*, 118 (no. 99); *AR* 1997–8, 121.

Kera

122–5. *Kera-Onythe Goulediana (Phalanna)*

Plate: 35–6; *Bzy Corp I*, pls. 92–3.

Location and discovery: Covered over *in situ* (Pl. 35).

Dimensions: Not known. Tesserae: *c.* 35 tesserae per 10 x 10 cm area.

Context: Narthex, nave, bema and north pastophorion of a Christian basilica. There are quite extensive standing remains of the basilica, and it is fortunate that its remoteness has somewhat protected it from regular visitors.

Description: Polychrome using tesserae of red, blue/white and black. The tesserae are small and regularly cut.

122. *The Narthex (Pls. 35–6)*

An outer border of leaf scroll is somewhat damaged. Within this is an inner border of guilloche (**R** 70d) and within this is the main area, which contains two identical rectangular panels. Each of these panels consists of a central octagon with squares radiating out from each side and diamonds from each corner (similar to **R** 205e)[28] (Pl. 35). Within the octagon is a circle bordered by a band of guilloche (**R** 70d). Within this circle is a central design of a four-petalled stylized flower. Within each diamond is a knot-type design consisting of a centre circle with a semi-circle attached on either end of it and a 'tongue' coming out of each semi-circle (similar to the Knossos example) (Pl. 36). There appear to be various designs within the squares, including a guilloche mat and an octagon which is divided into four hexagons around a central square (**R** 169a). There are two of these designs in each of the rectangles.

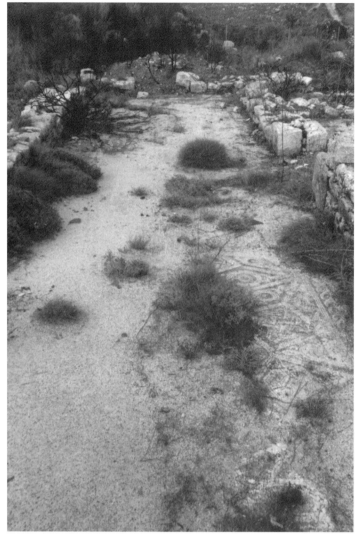

Plate 35 Kera, narthex (Mosaic 122).

The southern part of this mosaic is made up of rows of squares which are divided by lines of smaller squares. These squares contain diamond designs.

123. *The Nave (Byz Corp I, pl. 93)*
This area of mosaic, which is enclosed by a guilloche border (**R** 70d), is divided into three parts. The central one consists of a wheel design, and the two bordering panels have a pattern of squares and rectangles. The squares alternate with rectangles thus forming smaller squares.

124. *The Bema (Byz Corp I, pl. 92)*
The main field consists of a pattern of stars formed by four triangles extending from a central square. Each of the four points contains diamonds, and each of these is joined to three others in the centre of a black square (similar to **R** 186b).

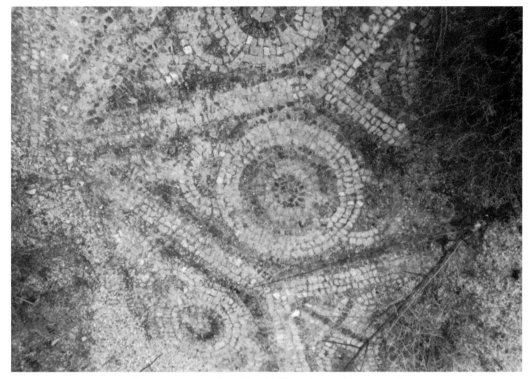

Plate 36 Kera, narthex, detail of knot design (Mosaic 122).

125. *The North Pastophorion*

The motif on the mosaic here is another wheel-based design.

Materials: Blue/black limestone, white marble and red terracotta tesserae.

Date: *Byz Corp I* gives a date of late fifth or early sixth century for the mosaic. This works well in terms of comparative evidence for the geometric décor, which includes examples such as Knossos (Mosaics 98–100) and Basilica A at Chersonisos (Mosaics 92–3). Composite stars are known from Agios Paulos on Kos, dated late fifth–early sixth century. The materials and some of the geometric elements are also found in the Sybrita mosaic.

Bibliography: Platon 1955a, 415; Platon 1955b, 298–305; Platon 1956 (b), 229–31; Sanders, 120–1; Volanakis, no. 33; *Byz Corp I*, 119–20 (no. 101).

Prefecture of Lasithi

126. *Olus*

Plate: 37–8; *Byz Corp I*, pls. 86–9.

Location and discovery: Research excavations. The mosaic is well preserved *in situ* (Pl. 38).

Dimensions: 12.50 x 6.0 m. Tesserae measure *c.* 1.3 cm^2; 30 tesserae per 10 x 10 cm area. Figured elements: 35 tesserae per 10 x 10 cm area.

Context: Nave of a standard three-aisled Christian basilica (Pl. 37). The basilica was constructed out of small blocks of local stone. Apparently some mosaics were also discovered in the narthex, but the excavator indicated that they had been completely destroyed (Pl. 38). The mosaic may have been associated with the earlier of the two phases of church building; there is some patching visible.

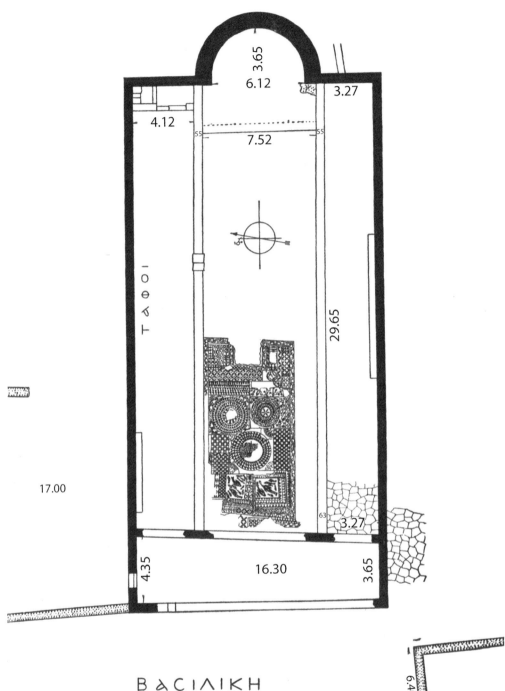

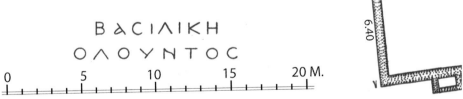

Plate 37 Olus Basilica plan (Mosaic 126) (after Orlandos 1960, fig. 2)
(courtesy of the Archaeological Society at Athens).

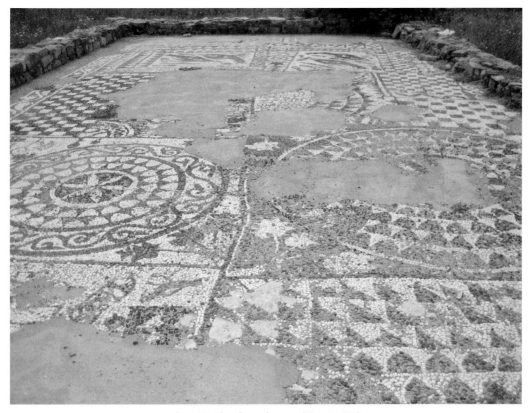

Plate 38 Olus from the east (Mosaic 126).

Description: 'The mosaic in the nave is probably the oddest in Crete', according to Sanders (92). Platon (1955, 420) also remarks on its unusual decoration and says that the mosaic is of unknown form.

The mosaic consists of a series of panels apparently arranged in a random order (Pl. 37). This led Sanders (92) to assume that the mosaic was constructed panel by panel as funding became available. However, this is unlikely given the uniformity of materials and the regularity of construction. The difference in the size of the tesserae used in the figures and used in the geometric decoration is not unusual for other Late Antique mosaics in Crete (e.g., Chersonisos Basilica A). The odd shape of the mosaic is more likely due to the possibility that the mosaics originally belonged to an earlier (smaller) church.

This would account for the mosaic's poor fitting size (Pl. 37). The mosaic consists mostly of panels of black-and-white geometric and floral designs. There is quite extensive use of red tesserae (volcanic?), and in some places yellow is visible, in particular in the two panels of rather stylized dolphins and fish.

From west to east:

At the western end various panels seem to have been inserted to close the gap in the new space. Evidence of two different panels of intersecting circles forming spindles and concave squares and a panel of checkerboard survives. To the east, a short border of ogives lies before the surviving section of the border of ivy scroll begins. This rudimentary border (**R** 64d) encloses part of the mosaic (Pl. 38). On the south side, within the scroll, is a border of rows of diamonds. These diamonds are made up of two rows three tesserae thick. The first uses a red outline, the second a black-and-red one and the third pure black. A central circle in each of the diamonds is also made from these colours. Immediately to the north, the border scroll is not continued; instead, sections of the rows of diamonds and ogives border are in evidence.

To the east of this section lie two figured panels. In the northern one two dolphins have been constructed in red, whereas in the southern panel black is used. These panels have been comparatively skilfully executed with great detail in both the fish and the dolphins (Pl. 38). The southern panel is enclosed by three borders of ogives, and inserted within the border in the east is a donor inscription (Inscription 8) (see Chapter 6) (*Byz Corp I*, pl. 89a). Between the two dolphin and fish panels is a splayed space occupied by a wheel design, a circle containing spindles and two stylized plants. To the north of the northern dolphin panel lies a small section of checkerboard (in red and white) and beyond this a section of diamond checkerboard.

The section to the east consists of two panels of checkerboard on either side of a central square panel which contains a circle which in turn contains an inscription indicating the names of the various donors (Inscriptions 7i & 7ii) (see Chapter 6) (*Byz Corp I*, pl. 89b). The inscription panel is bordered by a checkerboard of triangles. In the spandrels, quarter circles defined by beaded decoration in red and white and with a red-and-white curved-line decoration are found.

To the east again are two large square panels, each containing a circle. The northern one occurs on a square with a black background. Within this, the circle contains a central design of alternating black and white triangles radiating from a central black dot.

This design is enclosed by an outer surround of alternating arcs. In the space left over between the circle and the square itself are some miniature floral decorations.

The southern circle is laid within a white square background. This has a central design of a six-petalled flower, with an arc design surrounding. This arc design is similar to a row of ogives (R 49h). A final border of a simplified leafy scroll surrounds it. Between the circle and within the square is a long leafy and floral scroll covering one side of the square. In each of the other corners is a three-budded plant; one of them, in the northwest corner, is damaged.

Above these panels to the east lies a panel of checkerboard of triangles followed by a panel of ogives (rows of alternate black and white ogives and thorns, which is similar to R 215b). However, in this case they are black and white rows of squares with dots in them, alternating with rows of single circles. On the south side a panel of stylized flowers and the remains of a peacock surrounded by small birds are visible.

The eastern end contains variations of intersecting circles forming hollow spindles (R 237b), rows of lozenges and some scroll panels. The remains of the ivy-scroll border are present here; they outline an architectural feature that no longer survives (Pl. 37).

Materials: Black, red, white and grey stone tesserae. Possibly volcanic stone used for red.

Date: Sanders (92) suggests a fourth-century date for the mosaic based on the lettering and the possible association that the mosaic has with some fourth-century Corinthian-style capitals. This would make it the earliest church mosaic in Crete, but the date is not yet certain.

Bibliography: Orlandos 1955; Orlandos 1960; Platon 1955, 420 (no.14); Sanders, 91–2; Volanakis, no. 84; *Byz Corp I*, P115 (no. 96).

127. *Kolokythia*

Plate: Bourboudakis 1971, pl. 546.

Location and discovery: Only a small fragment of the mosaic was preserved in the basilica. The mosaic is no longer visible, possibly destroyed by coastal erosion which is also affecting the architecture.

Dimensions: Not known.

Context: The pastophorion of a triple-aisled Christian basilica. The mosaic appears to have been partially overlain by the synthronon.

Description: The fragment consisted of a double guilloche (**R** 75a) bordering a wide band of intersecting circles forming spindles and concave squares (**R** 237a).

Date: This mosaic probably belongs to the first phase of the church, that is, late fifth/early sixth century.

Bibliography: Bourboudakis 1971, 529–33; Sanders, 92–4; Volanakis, no. 84.

128. *Itanos*

Plate: None available.

Location and discovery: Discovered during excavations in the basilica in the 1990s.

Dimensions: Unknown.

Context: Found in the apse of Basilica A.

Description: Only a small fragment survives.

Date: Unknown.

Bibliography: Personal observation.

A1.4 CATALOGUE: MOSAICS OF WESTERN CRETE

Published Roman Mosaics of the Prefecture of Chania

Chania

129. *Chania: The Mosaic of Poseidon and Amymone*

Plate: 39; Berti 1972–3, fig. 1.

Location and discovery: Found during a rescue excavation; on display in the archaeological museum, Chania (Pl. 39).

Dimensions: 1.65 x 2.50 m. Figured décor: tesserae *c*. 0.90–0.75 x 0.90–0.75 cm.

Context: *Cubiculum* or small *triclinium* of a Roman *domus* on Odos Korakas (Fig. 14). The off-centre panel of the cocks suggests a *triclinium*, but according to Dunbabin's (1996) estimates it would make quite a small one.

Description: A frieze of intersecting circles forming spindles and concave squares (**R** 237a) forms an outer border on one side. Contained within each of the concave squares, is a small crosslet. The frieze of spindles may have continued at the bottom of the mosaic, but it definitely did not continue around either side of it.

A border of wide guilloche on a black background surrounds the main emblem. The strands are rendered in blue and alternating brown. The design is similar to the **R** 70h shaded guilloche. This is interrupted by a doormat panel of two fighting cocks (Berti 1972–3, fig. 1).

In each of the four corners of the border a black circle contains a blue head with wild black hair (Berti 1972–3, fig. 1). The figures are either winds or Gorgons.

One central panel depicts Amymone being attacked by a satyr at Lerna Spring and the other depicts her being helped by Poseidon. The area of Amymone's face in the first panel is damaged, as is the winged satyr. Amymone sits on a rock, naked save for a cloth draped around her middle and a 'bikini top' which may also be part of the cloak. She holds a hook in her right hand. In the second panel the hook is replaced by a small vessel with water pouring out of it. Amymone still sits but she is facing to the front with the cloak loosely draped but exposing her top half. In

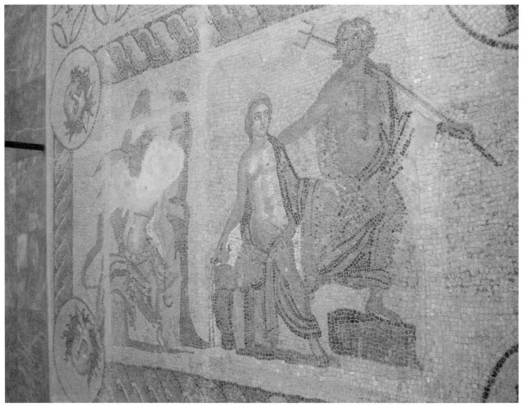

Plate 39 Chania, Poseidon and Amymone mosaic (Mosaic 129).

this panel Poseidon has his hand on her back and stands with one foot on a rock and with a trident in his left hand extended over his shoulder. He is semi-naked, being covered in part by a draped blue cloak.

Materials: Terracotta and stone tesserae.

Date: Mid-third century. Berti (1972–3, 464) dated the mosaic to the late second to early third century on the basis of African parallels such as a mosaic from Tunis Terme di Temetra dated to the beginning of the third century.

Bibliography: Theophanides 1945–7, 37; Berti 1972–3, 451–65; Sanders, 54.

130. *Chania: Plain Mosaic*
Plate: None available.

Location and discovery: Rescue excavation. Current location unknown.

Dimensions: Not known.

Context: Found in the same house as the Poseidon and Amymone mosaic.

Description: Little description is given, except that this is a plain mosaic.

Date: Mid-third century if it is the same date as Mosaic 129.

Bibliography: Platon 1956, 406; Sanders, 54.

131. *Chania: Scatter of Mosaic Fragments*
Plate: None available.

Location and discovery: Rescue excavations in the 1960s close to the Poseidon and Amymone *domus* in the plateia of the Demotikis Agoras. The mosaic pieces are stored in the Chania museum.

Dimensions: Not known.

Context: Roman *domus*?

Description: No description has been published except one that states that there was a scatter of mosaic fragments.

Date: Not known.

Bibliography: Tzedakis 1966, 428; Sanders, 54.

132. *Chania: Cathedral Square, (a) Triton*

Plate: Tzedakis 1970, pl. 409a.

Location and discovery: Rescue excavations in 1969 at Plateia Mitropolis on Halidon (Fig. 14); only a small corner of the mosaic survived. Current location is unknown.

Dimensions: Not known.

Context: Bath house. Three rooms, one of which contained the hypocaust, were excavated. The function of the room with the mosaic is not known. How the three sections of mosaic relate to each other is also not known.

Description: Black-and-white tessellated mosaic. A section of guilloche border survives (**R** 70d). Within is a fine depiction outlined in black, against a white background, of a triton blowing a conch.

Date: First half of the second century according to the excavation report. This date is not secure.

Bibliography: Tzedakis 1970, 467–8; *AR* 1973–4, 40; Michaud 1973, 412; *ILN*, October 1976, p. 91; Sanders, 54; Packard 1980, 326–46.

133. *Chania: Cathedral Square, (b) Inscribed Fragment*

Plate: Tzedakis 1970, pl. 409b.

Location and discovery: Rescue excavations in 1969 at Plateia Mitropolis on Halidon (Fig. 14); only a section of the mosaic survived. Current location is unknown.

Dimensions: Not known.

Context: Bath house. Given the figured décor of this panel it may have been used in a changing area or perhaps a *caldarium* (to protect the feet).[29]

Description: Black-and-white tessellated mosaic. The area preserved depicts a pair of sandals with the letters ΛΑ inscribed on them (Inscription 3) (discussed in Chapter 3) (Tzedakis 1970, pl. 409b). The remainder of the field is taken up with a scroll with pomegranates (?) in the branches.

Date: First half of the second century. This date is not secure.

Bibliography: Tzedakis 1970, 471; Michaud 1973, 412; Sanders, 54.

134. *Chania: Cathedral Square, (c) Scroll Panel*

Plate: Tzedakis 1970, pl. 409c.

Dimensions: Not known.

Context: Bath house. The function of this room is not known though it may be a corridor based on the use of the scroll.

Location and discovery: Rescue excavations in 1969 at Plateia Mitropolis on Halidon (Fig. 14). Current location is unknown.

Description: Black-and-white tessellated mosaic. A small rectangular panel sits in a large field of plain white tesserae. The panel contains a leafy detailed acanthus scroll similar to that of **R** 63e. The Chania example, however, contains a clear stem from which the acanthus leaves spring tendrils.

Date: First half of the second century. This date is not secure.

Bibliography: Tzedakis 1970, 467–8; Michaud 1973, 412.

135. *Chania: Market Square, Dionysus and Ariadne*

Plate: 40–1; Markoulaki 1990, plan.[30]

Location and discovery: Excavated in 1977, the mosaic is now on display in the Chania museum.

Dimensions: The room in which the mosaic was discovered measured 6.30 x 6.25 m. The preserved part of the mosaic

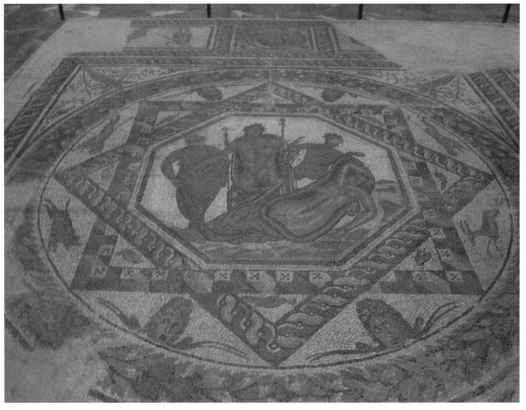

Plate 40 Chania, Dionysus and Ariadne mosaic, detail of central scene (Mosaic 135).

measured just under 4 x 4 m. Tesserae *c.* 0.10–0.50 cm².

Context: Room C of the Villa Dionysus in the Market Square in Chania, on the Vardinoyannis and Anastasakis Plot off Peridou (Fig. 14).

Description: The polychrome mosaic is made up of several figured panels. The main part of the mosaic consists of a central panel of an octagon formed by two intersecting squares (Pl. 40). One of the squares is a guilloche of alternating blue and brown with yellow curves (**R** 70h). The second square is a row of cubes in perspective (**R** 99f) which alternate between blue and brown (Pl. 40). Each square has a yellow top containing five dots on a black background. In each of the corners of the intersecting squares there are

small birds, including a parrot, a partridge, a peacock and some others, some too damaged to identify with sufficient accuracy. Within this octagon is an inner one rendered in blue, and inside this is the scene of the discovery of Ariadne by Dionysus at Naxos (Pl. 40). Dionysus is standing between a Silenus and a satyr. Ariadne is lying outstretched, on what appears to be some rocks in the far right of the scene, with her arm extended over her head. As is typical with Ariadne, she is depicted as mostly naked, with a cloak draped around her. Typical also of this scene is the satyr who is pulling the cloak off of the sleeping Ariadne; his manner is cautious yet curious. Dionysus stands over Ariadne. He wears a cloak outlined in black with blue fill. The cloak is draped around him in much the same manner

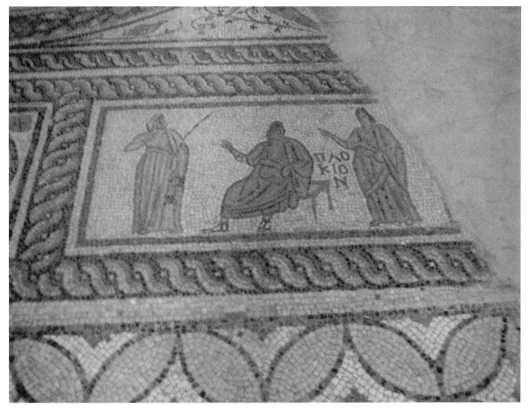

Plate 41 Chania, Dionysus and Ariadne mosaic, detail of Plokion panel (Mosaic 135) (Inscription 4).

as Ariadne's, exposing most of his body. Blue and green glass is used in the illustration of the sea, and blue and grey glass tesserae are used in the rock on which Ariadne sleeps. The Silenus on the left is almost green in colour, with black tesserae marking the curves of his limbs. He wears a dark red cloak and carries a staff made of green glass. Dionysus himself is modelled in red, orange and pale-pink tesserae. He too carries a green glass thyrsus. The figure on the right wears a wreath in his hair and a small wrap of yellow and brown around his waist. Overall the scene is carefully executed, and while not exactly the same as other representations, it still manages to include most of the stock elements for this kind of scene.

Around the octagon is a shadowed circular garland of leaves (similar to **R** 89h). This is very full and is made up of blues, reds, greens and browns (Pl. 40). The garland contains bunches of fruit and some glass tesserae. In the space left over between the octagon and the garland are depictions of four female heads, likely masks (Pl. 40). They all have the typical open mouths and staring eyes of masks, with slight variations so that none of the figures is the same. Also contained are four animals; on one side a lion is chasing a bull, and both are outlined in black and browns. On the opposite side is a big cat, possibly a tiger, chasing a stag.

The circular garland is set within a guilloche square of alternating blue and brown strands on a dark background. In each corner of the square is a very delicate peopled scroll featuring a winged person in the middle of the floral scroll; on either side of the person, within the leaves, are blue birds (Markoulaki 1990, plan). Each of the figures differs slightly from the others, which would suggest that there was not a strict pattern for these particular depictions. A large amount of glass is used in this area of the mosaic as the surrounding foliage is created using green and blue glass. The figures themselves are made using red tesserae with white modelling, and they have beautiful blue-glass wings. A further band of white, three tesserae thick, surrounds the square band of guilloche.

A border of several panels all defined and separated by a continuous band of guilloche encloses the mosaic. The panels contain scenes from a Menander play and also images of the four seasons. Some of the panels have sustained damage. Of the panels on the right-hand side two out of a possible four are complete. One depicts a scene from Menander's play *Plokion* (as identified by the inscription (Πλόκιον)) (Inscription 4) (Pl. 41) (discussed in Chapter 3). The other panel on this side contains a representation of Summer wearing a crown of corn and carrying a sickle. This bust occurs within a circle, and in each of the spandrels is a red circle with a cross running through it. The panel below this at the corner is mostly destroyed, but it has a standing figure wearing a blue garment and a red cloak.

The side at the top of the main area has four panels, of which two are complete. Only a small fragment of a third survives. Two of the panels have scenes from the Menander play.[31] That nearest the corner just has a standing figure wearing a cloak (the rest of it is damaged). Beside this one is a panel containing

a bust of Autumn with his cloak and with vine leaves in his hair. The final panel on this side is mostly preserved and has a standing naked figure holding a rod and stretching out an object to a seated figure. Surrounding the set of panels on the right-hand side is a large band of spindles joined to form alternate concave squares and four-petalled flowers. These are grey in colour with a black outline, set on a white background with a brown square in the middle of the concave squares (**R** 237g).

Materials: Terracotta, stone and glass tesserae.

Date: Second half of the third century, based on the date of the house in which they were found.

Bibliography: Tzedakis 1977, 368; Tzedakis 1978, 364; *AR* 1977–8, 67; *K.Khron* 1984, 326–9; Touchais 1985, 857; *AR* 1985–6, 96; Markoulaki 1990, 449–63.

136. *Chania: Market Square,* Triclinium *of the House of Dionysus*

Plate: 42–3; Markoulaki 1990, plan.

Location and discovery: Excavated in 1977, this mosaic is now on display in the Chania museum. Although conserved, the mosaic had suffered some damage before excavation.

Dimensions: The mosaic is roughly square, and at its longest points the measurements are 5.75 x 5.75 m. Tesserae: *c.* 0.10–0.50 x 0.10–0.50 cm.

Context: The *triclinium* (Room B) of the Villa Dionysus in the Market Square in Chania, on the Vardinoyannis and Anastasakis Plot off Peridou (Fig. 14).

Description: The polychrome tessellated mosaic has two main adjoining sections which would have been enclosed in part by a border or a net pattern; there is a large square panel with the main scene of Dionysus and attached

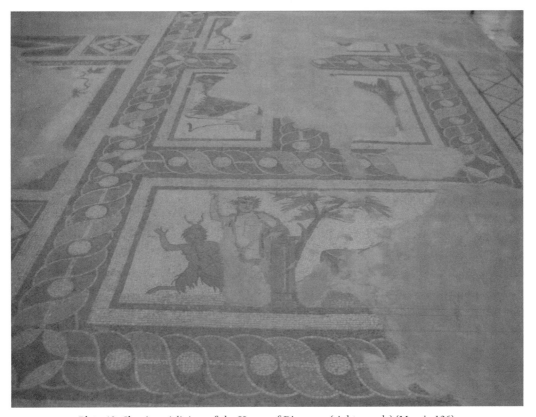

Plate 42 Chania, *triclinium* of the House of Dionysus (right panels) (Mosaic 136).

to this is a long rectangular panel with a border of thick guilloche enclosing four small
panels each facing a different direction.

Section 1 (Pl. 42): Consists of four panels, one which is mostly intact, two which
are only partially damaged and one which is
almost totally destroyed. The best-preserved
panel shows Dionysus leaning on a pillar
with Pan behind him. Dionysus holds a staff
made of glass tesserae. There are also apparently traces of a seated figure in this scene (Pl.
42). The scene is constructed on a white background and is then bordered by a band of
blue and then white. Above this panel are two
smaller panels which face outwards. Each of
them contains a different tragic mask, though
the right-hand one is mostly destroyed. These
panels occur on a white background which is

bordered by a band of blue and then white.
All that remains of the panel at the top end is
a tree and the head of a person on the far side;
a tambourine is also visible. Each of the four
panels is to be viewed from the perspective of
somebody who is moving around the mosaic
as opposed to just standing in the one place
(Markoulaki 1990, plan).

The guilloche border forms a continuous
band surrounding each of the four panels.
It is of a peculiar thick type[32] (discussed in
Chapter 6) with a complex arrangement of
colours and designs (Pl. 42). The first piece is
divided in two by a horizontal band of white
and on either side is blue. The next one has
blue as the upper colour and red as the lower
colour with a central circle of white. The next
piece is the same as the first only instead of

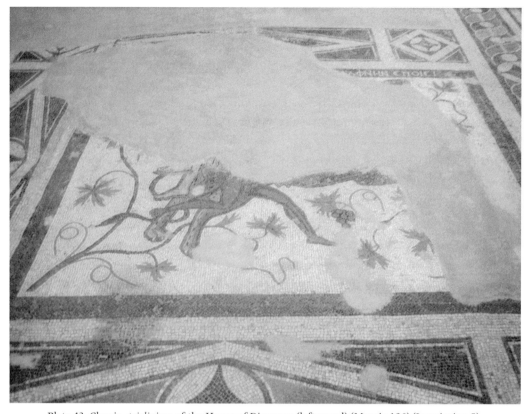

Plate 43 Chania, *triclinium* of the House of Dionysus (left panel) (Mosaic 136) (Inscription 5).

blue on either side of the white band, light blue is used. The fourth section is the same as the second only the colours are in reverse order. This sequence of colours continues right around the mosaic. At each of the four corners of the two large end panels is a circle of white which contains a concave square in blue with a central red dot inside.

Section 2 (Pl. 43): The damaged panel consists of a scene of Dionysus and is laid out as though one was looking at it from the same position as the Dionysus and Pan panel in the first section (Pl. 43). The scene shows a large vine with grapes hanging off it, and the lower legs of a leopard cutting through the vine. Human legs and a pair of feet with sandals, which are positioned as if the person were sitting on the leopard, are preserved. Placed

in a way that suggests that it belongs to the figure on the leopard, a small fragment of a cloak made of green glass is visible. Parts of the wings and a tail of a creature that walks beside the leopard are in evidence. In the top right-hand corner of the mosaic it is just about possible to make out a tambourine in the scene. The surviving remains like the leopard legs, the tambourine and the winged creature suggest that what was originally depicted was a Dionysiac scene, possibly a processional. Although the quality of the mosaic is clear, it is possible to make out a mistake in the rendering of the back leg of the winged creature, its lower part being much thinner than it ought to be. An inscription ([− -]δάφνην ἐποίει) (Inscription 5) is found in the blue-band border of the central scene (for discussion, see Chapter 6) (Pl. 43). Although the inscription is damaged, it may refer to the mosaicist as coming from Daphne, Antioch.

The surrounding panels are all geometric. There were originally seven panels, three at either end of the central scene and one in the middle to the left of the scene. These geometric panels consist of squares within squares; in addition, within the squares are circles containing concave squares. There are three variations, different because of the colours used.

The border of crosslets likely continues around this panel to join the rest of the border around the first panel.

Materials: Terracotta, stone and glass tesserae.

Date: According to the reports, the mosaic was found in a house which is dated to the third century.

Bibliography: Tzedakis 1977, 362–8; *AR* 1977–8, 67; *K.Khron* 1984, 326–9; Touchais 1985, 857; *AR* 1985–6, 96; Markoulaki 1990, 449–63.

Lissos

137. *Lissos: Black-and-White Mosaic with Coloured Panels*

Plate: Sanders, pl. 40.

Location and discovery: Exposed *in situ*.

Dimensions: The mosaic is 6.9 x 5.5 m. Larger tesserae are used in the geometric elements than in the figured, with 80 tesserae per 20 x 20 cm area for the geometric section and 154 tesserae per 20 x 20 cm area for the figured section. The tesserae used measure *c.* 0.85 x 0.85 cm in the geometric elements and 0.70 x 0.70 cm in the figured.

Context: Temple of Asclepius. The temple was refurbished a number of times, and the mosaic is likely to date to the first-century phase. The mosaic is in the room in which the altar and the snake pit are situated. It would have originally covered almost all of the room. Within this room there are also many inscribed architectural blocks which are not *in situ*, and it is unclear if they are reused from an earlier phase or if they were part of the modern reconstruction of the temple.

Description: Black-and-white tessellated mosaic containing polychrome figured panels. A border of delicate leaf scroll is rendered in black on white (**R** 64b); it measures 20 cm in width. Separating this border and the main field is a thin black band. This is used continuously throughout the mosaic to create the different panels of geometric decoration. It also defines the four central panels with the swastika meanders between each of them (**R** 35d).

Within the black band are eight surviving panels of geometric decoration. There appear to have been eighteen geometric panels originally, and these would have surrounded four central panels depicting animals. At the western end, from left to right, the panels include Panel 1, containing a square inside of which is a four-petalled flower with an equal-armed cross running through the centre of it. The flower is in white and the surrounding square in black. A small stepped square is located in each of the corners. Panel 2 is square in shape and contains a design of squares, triangles and diamonds, similar to the design of one of the Villa Dionysus, Knossos, mosaics (7) (**R** 161a). The diamonds bear solid red circles. Panel 3, which is rectangular in shape, contains a mat of intersecting circles forming spindles and concave squares (**R** 237a). Panel 4 contains a design of alternating black and white diamonds within a circle. There are small circles in the corners of this panel. Panel 5 repeats the design of Panel 1. Panel 6 is rectangular in shape and contains a black diamond in which there is a concave square surrounded by a circle. The corners contain L-shapes in red terracotta tesserae. Panel 7 is the same as Panel 6. Panel 8 contains the remains of a floral-scroll design and a feature in the corner which resembles a double axe with an animal (?) on either side. The remains of the panel indicate the same design. The preserved section of Panel 9 contains a red L-shape and a diagonal edge of a lozenge, suggesting that it may be the same as its corresponding panel, Panel 6. Panel 10 is the same as Panels 1 and 5.

Between these outer geometric panels and the central figured one is a rectangular banner containing ovals, two upright and two recumbent. To the north of this panel are the remains of a triangle.

In the centre of the design is a complex of four panels linked together by a swastika meander. Panel 11 contains a duck, Panel 12 a cock and Panel 13 a pig rendered in blue on a black background. Panel 14 is in too poor a condition to identify the subject, but the remains suggest a four-legged animal. These figured panels have all been rendered in polychrome.

Materials: Stone, terracotta and marble (?) tesserae. Also includes small pebbles.

Date: The mosaic covers Hellenistic material and a first-century date is generally regarded as being correct.

Bibliography: Alexiou 1957, 391; Platon 1960, 273; Sanders, 55; *K.Estia* 1992–4, 238.

Suia

138. *Suia: Small Fragment*
Plate: None available.

Location and discovery: A small fragment of a mosaic was found in a pigsty in Suia by Sanders.

Dimensions: Not known.

Context: Not known.

Description: A section of leaf scroll was preserved.

Date: Not known.

Bibliography: Sanders, 171.

Kisamos

139. *Kisamos: Two-Panelled Mosaic*
Plate: Tzedakis 1968, pls. 377–8.

Location and discovery: Discovered in the north of Kisamos in the 1960s during the construction of the national highway. The mosaic had been quite damaged.

Dimensions: 7.60 x 6.80 m

Context: Room A of a Roman town house (Fig. 15). It is likely that because of the T-shape of the mosaic the room functioned as a *triclinium*. Two phases of occupation have been identified (Roman and Late Antique).

Description: Black-and-white tessellated mosaic with polychrome centre. The mosaic consists of two central panels (Tzedakis 1968, pl. 377) surrounded by a swastika meander (**R** 38c) around one panel and a wave pattern (**R** 101b) around the other.

Panel 1: (Tzedakis 1968, pl. 377). This panel consists of a guilloche (**R** 70d), forming a circle set in a square. The interior of the circle is split into a central octagon and radiating out are triangular and oblong panels, each surrounded by the bordering band of guilloche. The panels contain birds in the oblongs and stylized plants in the triangles (Tzedakis 1968, pl. 378). The plants are depicted using light-coloured tesserae on a dark background and the birds, using dark on light. The spandrels contain plain kantharoi. The centre of the mosaic is lost, but enough remains to indicate that it had polychrome tesserae.

Panel 2: (Tzedakis 1968, pl. 377). Only a small fragment survives. It depicts, in black-and-white outline, a dog chasing a goat. Both animals have been carefully rendered with use of shading for anatomical detail. The shadow of the dog has also been depicted.

Surrounding the main mosaic are further panels either of black and white squares or with plain areas of tesserae. There are also areas of net pattern similar to **R** 124a.

Date: The house context dates to the second half of the third century. Hellenkemper Salies (1986, 269) argues convincingly for an earlier date of the mid-second century on the basis of parallels with Italian black-and-white–style mosaics.

Bibliography: Davaras 1967, 498–9; Tzedakis 1968, 416–17; Tzedakis 1969, 431–2; Tzedakis 1970, 471; Michaud 1970, 1161; Michaud 1971, 1067; Sanders, 55; Hellenkemper Salies 1986, 269; Markoulaki et al. 2004, 366.

140. *Kisamos: Centaur and Lion Mosaic*
Plate: Tzedakis 1968, pls. 379–80.

Location and discovery: Discovered in the north of Kisamos during the construction of the national highway. The central panel had been quite damaged.

Dimensions: The room in which the mosaic was found measured 7.50 x 5.70 m.

Context: This mosaic was found in Room B of the same house as Mosaic 139 (Fig. 15). The house is dated to the end of the third century to the beginning of the fourth. In a later season of excavation it was confirmed that there were two building phases: the second half of the third century and the Late Antique period (*AR* 1970–1, 32).

Description: Black-and-white tessellated mosaic with polychrome figured centre (Tzedakis 1968, pl. 379). The field is divided into a nine-panel arrangement, a central panel surrounded by eight others. The figured scene

of a lion attacking a centaur is contained in a square set within an octagon which is set within a further square.

The lion leaps out from behind a tree to attack the centaur (Tzedakis 1968, pl. 380). Only the upper half of the lion is depicted; shading has been employed to illustrate the lion's stretched body, and its mane flies backwards as its head lunges forward. On the right-hand side, the centaur rears with its right hand drawn back as he prepares to aim a spear at the lion. The shadow cast by the centaur is depicted. In the area left over between the square containing the smaller figured design and the octagon there are geometric designs: four Solomon's knots, each contained within a square, and, surrounding the squares, four black and white diamonds, each containing a small white crosslet. The four corners of this square panel have been cut off into triangles, each containing a small white stylized plant.

The eight geometric panels surrounding the main square are rendered in black and white. The central panels on each of the four sides are the same, a white lozenge with black swastika design set on a black square with white cornucopiae in the corners (Tzedakis 1968, pl. 379). There are two of each of the following designs situated at diagonal corners from each other. The first is that of a circle bearing a six-pointed star made up of six diamonds. A small black stylized flower is contained in each diamond. In each spandrel is a black rounded triangle, and in each of these is small white L-shape. The second design consists of an eight-pointed star outlined in black on a white background, which is also made up of eight diamonds. Four of the diamonds contain small black chevrons, and in the other four are different stylized plant designs (Tzedakis 1968, pl. 380). These designs are similar to those found in the Villa Dionysus (Mosaics 2, 4 and 6), the Hutchinson mosaic (17) and the Iraklion mosaic (37). In the space left over between the eight-pointed star and the outer square are four squares and four triangles. Each of the squares contains a black four-petalled flower, and each of the triangles contains a single black pelta.

Surrounding the nine panels on three of its sides is a design of rows of cubes made up of a black and white triangle in each. At the centre of each of the cubes, smaller black and white triangles make up another cube, but here the white is on black and vice versa. On the fourth side of the mosaic, there is a large swathe of plain white tesserae with small black stepped squares (**R** 5a) occurring in rows across the white area.

Date: Hellenkemper Salies argues convincingly for a mid-second-century date on the basis of parallels with Italian black-and-white–style mosaics.

Bibliography: Davaras 1967, 498–9; Tzedakis 1968, 416–17; Tzedakis 1969, 431–2; Tzedakis 1970, 471; *AR* 1969–70, 30; *AR* 1970–1, 32; Michaud 1971, 1059; Sanders, 55; Hellenkemper Salies 1986, 269; Markoulaki et al. 2004, 366.

141. *Kisamos: Paterakis Plot*
Plate: 44; Markoulaki 1987a, pls. 9–20.

Location and discovery: Excavation in the 1960s. Some of the mosaics are now on display in the Kisamos museum.

Dimensions: 1.98 x 2.9 m (e/w) and 5.20 x 2.30 m (n/s). Tesserae: 163 tesserae per 10 x 10 cm area.

Context: Mosaics were uncovered in three of the five rooms of a badly preserved Roman house, located to the north of the town (Fig. 15). The highest walls remaining were 0.65 m and some fragments of wall painting in red

and black were recovered. Room 1, containing this mosaic was the biggest room. Two low (0.10-m high) marble partitions divided the room into three separate parts, creating the T-shape. This is certainly a *triclinium*. It was orientated north to south and entry was from Rooms 2 and 3 (Markoulaki 1987a, plan 2 & pl. 9).

Room 2 was a small room located in the northeast corner and measured 1.50 x 1.70 m.

Room 3 was located directly opposite Room 2, and there was an exit in its western side.

Room 4 was situated east of Room 1. There appear to have been two phases of flooring here, first there was a plain beaten floor and then at a later stage a decorated one was added, which at the time of excavation had been largely destroyed.

A trial trench was dug to see if the mosaic continued on to the north. The floors to the north, however, were paved with stone slabs. A second area of testing was carried out to the west of Room 4 to see if this area had also been mosaic paved, with positive results.

Description: Polychrome tessellated mosaic (white, grey-blue, brown, pink and black). The glass is of yellow, blue, orange, green and light black.

In the east and west areas, forming the T-shape, are simple net-pattern designs (**R** 124a) (Markoulaki 1987a, pl. 9). These areas are joined to the figured mosaic in the south by rows of swastika peltae with a central monogram bichrome knot. There are six of these in a row, and at the end of each is a single circle in a dark colour with a concave square in a lighter colour occupying the centre. A small crosslet is contained in the centre of the concave square. This is all found within a rectangle; the two terminal circles are then separated from the swastika peltae by a dividing black line. The row to

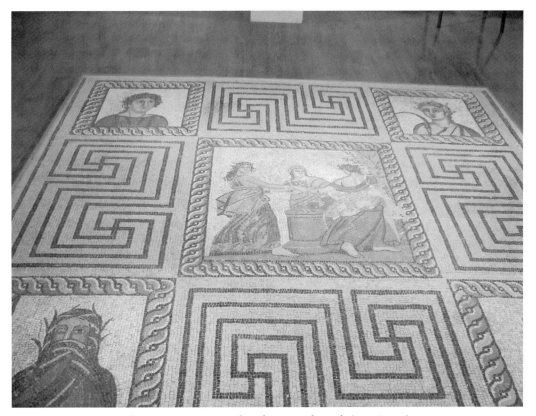

Plate 44 Kisamos, Paterakis Plot, central panels (Mosaic 141).

the right of the main panel of the mosaic has been badly damaged, although it is clearly the same as the left-hand side.

The main area of the figured mosaic is divided into two by a panel depicting a voluted stylized scroll (**R** 64e) (Pl. 44). The upper part of the smaller of the two consists of four panels; three panels directly above one long one. Each of these is bordered by a band of serrated saw-tooth pattern (**R** 10g). The larger panel is a scene of a leopard pursuing a stag, and the other three show scenes of partridges standing among fruit, birds standing by a basket of flowers and, in the panel in the middle, a cock (Markoulaki 1987a, pl. 14). All are orientated the same way.

In the lower panel, three women (the Horae) dance around an altar (Pl. 44). This panel with

a guilloche border is then surrounded by eight other panels. Every second panel is a geometric one of swastika meander (**R** 35f); the adjacent panels depict busts of the four seasons. Each of the four seasons is bordered by a band of simple guilloche on a coloured ground. Below these panels, a single panel of geometric design consists of two parallelograms, each containing a spaced crosslet (**R** 4c).

Room 2 had a mosaic of a square containing a diamond. Room 3 had a net-pattern mosaic, the same as the two panels to the east and west of the main figured mosaic in Room 1.

Materials: Stone, glass, terracotta.

Date: Markoulaki (1987a, 58) suggests a date of the second half of the second century on the basis of the similar depictions of the group of three dancers with the four seasons in mosaics found outside Crete and dated between the second and third century. Coins of Caligula were found in the interior of the house, and other coins dated to c. 286–305. This suggests a long history of occupation of the house.

Bibliography: Tzedakis 1968, 416–17; Tzedakis 1969, 431–2; *AR* 1969–70, 30; *AR* 1970–1, 32; Tzedakis 1972, 637–8; Tzedakis 1979, 397–9; Markoulaki 1987a, 33–59; Markoulaki 1994b, 179–86; press reports 7.3.87; *AR* 1987–8, 76; Touchais 1988, 960.

Phalasarna

142. *Phalasarna*

Plate: None available.

Location and discovery: Exposed *in situ*. Discovered during research excavations.

Dimensions: Not known.

Context: The cistern is attached to the south tower in the area of the northern harbour.

Description: The only reference to the mosaic at Phalasarna is that of a sea pebble floor laid in cement found in a cistern.

Materials: Pebbles.

Date: Hellenistic.

Bibliography: *AR* 1989–90, 81; Frost 1991, 302.

Published Late Antique Mosaics of the Prefecture of Chania

143–6. *Agios Niketas (Frangokastelli Plain)*

Plate: 45–6, Fig. 9.

Dimensions: Nave: c. 13 x 5 m (excl. modern church). Narthex: c. 11.5 x 4.5 m. Exo-narthex: c.12 x 4 m. North aisle: c. 18 x 2 m. Tesserae size: 35 tesserae per 10 x 10 cm area in all areas apart from the exo-narthex, which has c. 38 tesserae per 10 x 10 cm area.

Context: The nave, narthex, exo-narthex and north aisle of the smallest known basilica

in Crete. Although a great deal of it has been destroyed, the central aisle is largely intact (Pl. 45).

Location and discovery: Exposed *in situ* with some conservation.

Description: Polychrome tessellated mosaics consisting of red, white, yellow, light blue and blue tesserae.

143. *The Exo-narthex (Pl. 46)*

At the northern end of the exo-narthex, part of the wall runs over the mosaic. A variety of borders surround this complex of geometric panels. In the north, a leaf scroll has alternating varieties of leaves but is damaged in many places. It surrounds a large rectangular panel within which is a single diamond looped at the corners. Surrounding the diamond are various filler motifs: a pomegranate, stylized flowers, and a small looped circle. To the south of it is a border of wide looped guilloche (**R** 68b). This border encloses panels of scale pattern (**R** 217c), a damaged section of spindles forming circles containing six-petalled flowers made of spindles (**R** 45b). And to the south of this is a band of interlooped alternating circles and squares (**R** 81b). Further south, a panel of diamonds encloses squares and circles, and is bordered by a band of diamonds. The most southerly panel is bordered on its north, east and the west sides by a line with a ribbon running through it. This encloses four diamonds in squares with central circles. In addition to the obvious patching (Pl. 46), the mosaic here is at odds with the others in the church (Pl. 45). The work is shoddy in places (e.g., the stylized flowers in the northern end), and mistakes are apparent in the geometric elements and in the judging of the space needed (e.g., the irregular sizes of the elements within the shield of scales) (Pl. 46).

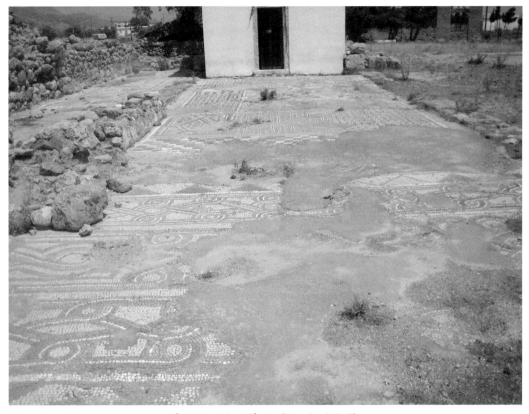

Plate 45 Agios Niketas (Mosaics 143–6).

It is unclear, however, if this represents evidence of an apprentice mosaicist or patching undertaken by an untrained individual.

144. *The Narthex Mosaic (Pl. 45)*

In the narthex, the existing walls in part cover the mosaic, indicating that the mosaics belong to an earlier phase. There are two main borders. The first, at the southern and western sides of the narthex, is an outer scroll (a stylized arcade) (similar to **R** 97a), in this case with the inclusion of alternating hearts and diamonds. The continuation of this border along the western side consists of a band of squares, some in red and some in blue. The northern border has been damaged beyond recognition. Finally, the eastern border consists of a band of trichrome hounds tooth (**R** 10d). The colours throughout appear to have been decided at random. The inner border is an interlaced band of circles and lozenges (similar to **R** 82c), and, in this case, there are alternating colours of red, yellow, blue and white (Pl. 45). These borders enclose two central geometric panels. The first is a triple band of interlooped circles forming small concave squares, similar to **R** 233d. The circles contain a small stepped-square motif. The second panel is similar to the inner border except that it has only the diamonds that interloop with the surrounding rectangle. Evidence of patching of the mosaic is marked by the only use of green tesserae in the entire context.

145. *The Nave Mosaic (Pl. 45)*

Unusual for Cretan examples, no small border such as a scroll or intersecting circles surrounds the nave mosaic, simply a narrow

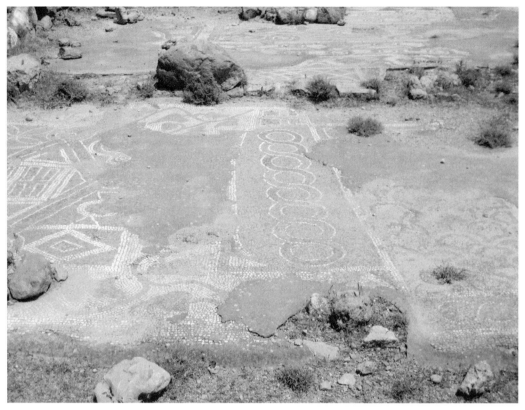

Plate 46 Agios Niketas, exo-narthex from the west (Mosaic 143).

white band on a blue background. At the western end of the nave a panel of checkerboard of all four colours is seen spanning its width. The remainder of the nave mosaic consists of a seven-panel arrangement. The central panel is damaged, but it consisted of two circles linked by intersecting smaller circles. One of the circles contains a square intertwining with a system of loops (Pl. 45). This is similar to the pattern in the nave mosaic at Almyrida (Pl. 47). The other circle contains a system of intertwined loops. In the corners between the circles and the rectangular panel in which they are contained are stylized buds and two triangles of zigzags at the sides (Pl. 45). Surrounding the central panel are the remains of six badly damaged panels, three of which have swastika meander (R 187d).

A section of multi-coloured zigzags (R 199b) and a fragment of an intersecting circle motif are also seen.

Two rectangular panels depict diamonds with knots at the terminal points with small squares in the centres of the looped diamonds. These panels contain depictions of ducks and an eye-like motif. It consists of a circle with a stepped triangle on either side of the circle and has parallels in Crete and beyond (see discussion under the date section).

146. *The North Aisle (Pl. 45)*
The floor in the north aisle is beautifully preserved with the exception of a small area in the west. At the western end, a border band with a ribbon through it is the same as that in the northern end of the exo-narthex. Within

this is a band of stepped squares and moving east is a band of three large squares in a row. Contained within the three large squares is a complex of smaller and larger squares similar to a developed checkerboard design. Three sections of squares increase in size from west to east. The colours alternate between blue and red. To the east is a border of a row of isosceles triangles in alternating colours; this border encloses and separates three main panels within. At the corner points of each panel the border of triangles is broken by a poised square. The western panel has two large diamonds with central squares; the central panel has a design of two large diamonds containing circles; and the final panel (in the east) contains a large scroll with a deer.

Materials: Stone (limestone), marble and terracotta tesserae. Dark grey/blue, white, light grey, red and yellow.

Date: Unknown, partly due to its uniqueness. The 'eye' design of the nave occurs in the narthex mosaic at Almyrida (possibly fifth century). It is also found in the National Gardens in Athens (*Byz Corp II*, pl. 204) and in Aigio (ibid., pl. 106), which are dated to the second half of the fifth century and the first half of the sixth century, respectively. Although this is a striking element, the date range for its occurrence does not help narrow the date of the mosaic.

Bibliography: Lassithiotaki 1971, 118; Sanders, 123; Volanakis, no. 26; *Byz Corp I*, 126 (no. 114).

147. *Tarrha*

Plate: *Byz Corp I*, pl. 97b.

Location and discovery: Below the modern Church of the Panagia the remains of a Late Antique church with a small fragment of mosaic are visible at the west end.

Dimensions: Not known.

Context: South aisle.

Description: Blue, white and red tessellated mosaic.

The fragment consists of a series of intersecting circles forming spindles and concave squares (**R** 237a) (*Byz Corp I*, pl. 97b). Within the centre of the design a square contains a further square with four loops extending out of it, one on each side. These loops are part of the continuing line of the square, which is a single interlooped square. Within this square is a circle and around this is another circle with four petals projecting out of it.

Note: Kirsten (in Matz 1951, 131) mentions a pebble mosaic from a temple in the area, with a depiction of Apollo on it. But since then no trace of the mosaic has been located through excavation, and it is believed to be a mistake on Kirsten's part.

Date: The border design of interlocking semicircles is common in Crete from the middle of the fifth century (e.g., Suia Basilica A or Chersonisos Basilica B) supporting Sanders's (122) date of late fifth to early sixth century. Sanders also states that his date fits in with the style of architecture of the building.

Bibliography: Matz 1951, 131; Weinburg 1960, 99; Sanders, 122; Volanakis, no. 23; *Byz Corp I*, 125–6 (no. 113).

148–51. *Almyrida*

Plate: 47–9; Curuni and Donati 1987, 12.3.

Location and discovery: The mosaic lies exposed *in situ* in the basilica (Pl. 47).[33] Some conservation work has been undertaken on the mosaics and overall they are in good condition. The basilica was partly excavated in 1973 by Bourboudakis, when the positions of the altar and ambo were found *in situ*.

Dimensions: Not known. Tesserae: *c.* 30 per 10 x 10 cm area.

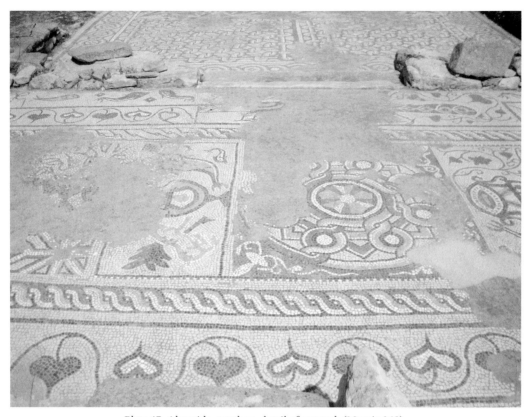

Plate 47   Almyrida, narthex, detail of peacock (Mosaic 149).

Context: Bema, nave, narthex and exo-narthex of a three-aisled, tripartite transept Christian Basilica. The altar base is still in position; an ambo in the middle of the nave evidently belongs to a phase after the mosaics, owing to the fact that it overlies them. The north and south aisles were paved with slabs.

Description: The tesserae in the mosaic are red, black, white and blue/white in colour.

148. *The Exo-narthex*

The area of mosaic in the exo-narthex has sustained considerable damage. The mosaic consists of three different panels, some of which have borders. The southernmost panel is best preserved. It is without a formal border and the central design is a frame of interlooped circles (**R** 82f). In the Almyrida example,

however, there would have been at least twelve of these circles interlooped together. The circles are formed with two main bands of colours, firstly one of blue, white and light blue, and secondly of red, yellow and blue. Both bands also intersect with the surrounding border. Each central circle contains a different design, and three-stemmed flowers, single stepped squares and four rounded triangles are all found within. In the concave squares between the circles are three-stemmed flowers, stepped squares and a four-petalled flower. An open guilloche band (**R** 68d) in red and white on a blue background surrounds the central, most damaged, panel. It consists of an elaborate scroll with abundant leaves and flowers, in blue and red on a white background.

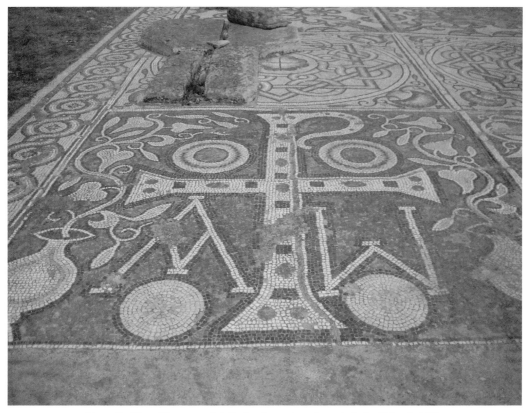

Plate 48 Almyrida, nave, detail of web, cross and semi-circles (Mosaic 150).

At the northern end is a border of vine scroll, similar to that which occurs in the southern end of the narthex. The border only extends around one side of the main panel pattern, similar to the geometric one in the southern end already described, but here the circles do not interloop. Within the concave square are geometric designs.

149. *The Narthex (Pl. 47)*

The narthex has been very elaborately decorated with mosaic, which for the most part is well preserved (Pl. 47). A border of leaf scroll in varying types encloses both geometric and natural panels. In some areas the scroll is of single vine leaves, alternating between red and black; in others it is just a plain triple-sectioned leaf scroll (Pl. 47). Both scrolls show buds coming out of the stems. In the southern half of the narthex mosaic, a scroll of large single leaves with a black outline and alternating white and red fillers is found. The central section is defined on the east by a further border of opposing polychrome fish and, in some areas, dolphins (Pl. 47). These are all rendered as though they occur in a frieze. In the northern part, almost a separate area is defined by an inner border of alternating opposed red and white triangles. Within it is a large carpet design of pairs of white peltae arranged so that free spaces are blue heart shapes with a small red and white decoration (**R** 57f). In the Almyrida example, the two opposed peltae are joined together by a small bar and the central point of the peltae is surrounded by a small bichrome arc.

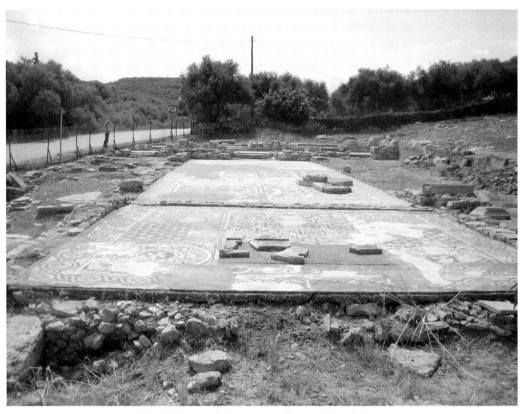

Plate 49 Almyrida, bema from the east (Mosaic 151).

Within this pelta design is a panel filled with red, white and blue checkerboard. To the east of this small panel is another large carpet design of pairs of opposed scales (horizontal and vertical) (**R** 220a). In this case, the outline is in white and the filler in blue, with an added internal design of small red and white squares.

The central section of six panels is contained within the double border. One of the six panels is located in the doorway space from the narthex to the nave. Although the panel has suffered much damage it is clear that it represents two peacocks facing each other (Pl. 47). All that is left is the elaborate tail of one of the peacocks, one of the peacock's legs and some leaf scroll surrounding it. The colours are red, blue and white. This panel is of particular

note because of its position in the doorway of the nave, indicating its function as an apotropaic symbol, or simply to guide worshippers into the holy area. The five other panels in the centre of the narthex are bordered by a tight guilloche (**R** 71a). The colours alternate between pairs of blue and white, and red and white. A central panel within the five depicts a complex geometric design consisting of a central circle interlooped with eight surrounding circles; these in turn are interlooped with a large surrounding circle. All of this is set within two intersecting squares (Pl. 47). The design is similar to that of No. 2 in the nave. A multi-coloured fan design lies in the centre of the inner circle. The spandrels contain a white vegetal scroll. The two panels on either side depict a central kantharos surrounded by fish, dolphins, part of a floral scroll and a four-legged creature (damaged). The north central panel has been damaged although mosaic patching in antiquity is in evidence. To the south, enclosed within the outer scroll, is a panel of intersecting circles forming spindles and concave squares (**R** 237a). In the Almyrida example, however, there is a single white tessera at each point where the spindles meet, and each of the concave squares contains a bichrome circle. The colours used throughout this panel are blue and white. The southernmost panel is that of a central square with a mat of Solomon's knot. From the central square further squares and lozenges radiate out; they contain different geometric mats, including an 'eye' design, a scale design and zigzags. This panel is similar to that in the narthex of Chersonisos Basilica A (Mosaic 92).

Patching is visible in two places on the mosaic: a section in the north and one in the south (Pl. 47).

150. *The Nave Mosaic (Pl. 48; Curuni & Donati 1987, 12.3)*

The nave mosaic consists of six pairs of panels with two further panels, one in the east and one in the west (Curuni & Donati 1987, 12.3), all contained within a border of interlooping circles (**R** 69f). There are stepped squares within the large circles.

The westernmost panel, the largest in the design, is made up of a swathe of alternating large and small circles interlooped tangentially and is similar to the pattern **R** 69f but with concave squares formed through the circles.

The pairs of panels from west to east are:

No. 1: Simple panels of knot-work design (Pl. 48).

No. 2: Squares have been only slightly damaged (i.e., one of the panels to the south) (Curuni & Donati 1987, 12.3). These panels consist of a geometric design of squares, lozenges and triangles. A triangle radiates from each side of a central square. Surrounding each side of each triangle is a lozenge, and the rest of the space is taken up with lozenges and triangles. Within each of the diamonds is a design of either a flower or a cross shape made up of small circles. This could be considered a form of knot design. Within two of the diamonds are stylized flowers. This design overall is similar to **R** 186b.

No. 3: Squares originally contained geometric designs of alternating large and small circles which were also intertwined.

No. 4: Contained a central design of a monogrammatic jewelled cross in each with small circles and rectangles decorating the inside of the cross (Pl. 48). At each terminal of the arms of the cross are two small circles. On either side of the cross at the bottom are the large and very ornate letters A and Ω. The top of the shaft does not terminate in the usual fashion; it winds around to touch the sceptre-like ball. A small kantharos with a large leafy scroll coming out of it is positioned at the outer edges at each side of the cross. This scroll extends to the top of the square and fills in the space between the cross and the square around it. The elaborately decorated ball-like objects on either side of the shaft may represent the tops of sceptres. The second of these panels and the two below have sustained a great deal of damage, but it is possible to work out the original scheme.

No. 5: The middle squares are similar to the easternmost squares in the bema except that in this case the central design is of chevrons. Surrounding the circle within the square is a border design of a kantharos in each corner with two lines of leafy scroll extending out from it (Pl. 48).

No. 6: Within the square, which acts as a border, is a central design of a circle with a web inside it. The web forms eight concave-based triangles and eight semi-circles around the edges. Radiating from this central circle is a complex of circles containing further circles (top of Pl. 48). The circles radiate out in pairs decreasing in size until the band terminates in an oval shape in the corner of the square. Between the four ovals is a row of three peltae running along the side of the square, the central peltae on each side being the biggest. Also near the central circle, separating the pairs of decreasing circles, is a small concave rectangle.

At the eastern end of the nave is a long panel consisting of a carpet design of orthogonal pattern of intersecting circles forming hollow spindles (**R** 237b). Within each of the concave squares is a blue crosslet. The petals are outlined in blue with red centres, while the concave square is white.

151. *The Bema (Pl. 49; Curuni & Donati 1987, 12.3)*

The bema mosaic is bordered by a band of intertwining circles which are small and large alternately (**R** 69f). This border goes right around the central design. It encloses eight panels of various sizes. There are six panels which are arranged in pairs, three on each side of the largest panel and the smallest. The three panels on the northern side are exact images of the three on the southern side.

The easternmost panel is a square one containing a circle. The space between the circle and the square is filled with a leafy scroll with a circle at each corner. Within the large square a complex design of two squares intertwine to create an eight-pointed star (Pl. 49). At each point where the squares cross is a small circle. These look more like knots or

hooks as they have a smaller circle attached which is part of a central circle. Within the main area is a Maltese cross. Below this panel is one of intersecting circles forming hollow spindles (**R** 237b) in red and white. The westernmost panel does not have a border, and the square surrounding it is incorporated into the all-over pattern. The central design consists of rows of sub-rounded squares all interlinked through continuous bands, which also hook onto the outside border, and it is like a section of knot work. All together there are 20 small squares with each containing a different design, either floral and geometric. The two panels in the middle top of the mosaic depict crosses with a small circle on either side of the lower shaft. This in one respect indicates the divinity of the altar which is situated right beside these panels (Pl. 49). Other panels consist of four- and eight-petalled flowers, circles with smaller circles enclosed, stepped squares, a swirly circle and circles intertwined and alternating with squares.

Materials: Stone, terracotta, marble tesserae.

Date: The dates of the basilica are uncertain, and no definite parallels are known for the mosaics. The small stars in the circles occur at Basilica B at Chersonisos and Suia A. The large Latin crosses occur in places such as San Vitale and in the Arian Baptistery at Ravenna. Because of these parallels Sanders (124) suggests a sixth-century date for the mosaic, although *Byz Corp I* indicates that a fifth-century date is more likely. For the most part, the geometric designs in this mosaic are standard types used in Christian basilicas from the fifth to the sixth century. However, the depiction of the cross is unusual on Cretan mosaics, as is the so far unique (in Crete) design of panel No. 1 in the nave. There are also similarities between this and the Episkopi mosaics (161–2), in particular, the panels of intersecting squares (No. 2 in the nave) with the use of kantharoi as filler decorations in the spaces between the circle and the square. The Episkopi mosaic has been dated to the sixth century. A date in the last quarter of the fifth century or the early sixth century would seem appropriate.

Bibliography: Bourboudakis 1973–4, 941–3; Bourboudakis 1973, 505; *AR* 1981–2, 58; Sanders, 123–4; Volanakis, no. 3; *Byz Corp I*, 124 (no. 109).

152. *Armenoi*

Plate: None available.

Location and discovery: Fragments of the mosaic are visible in the church of Ag. Ioannis Theologos.

Dimensions: Not known.

Context: Along with five columns and a capital, the mosaic fragment is the only evidence for a basilica located in the place of the later church.

Description: Of the visible remains it is possible to identify a leaf-scroll border surrounding a panel of peltae. All that is noted in *Byz Corp I* is that it had many colours. Note the architectural remains are not *in situ*.

Date: Not known.

Bibliography: Sanders, 124; Volanakis, no. 6; *Byz Corp I*, 124 (no. 110).

153. *Meskla*

Plate: Orlandos 1955–6, fig. 25.

Location and discovery: In the 1970s, Sanders (124) reported that there was a geometric mosaic in poor condition visible in this area. The mosaic since either has been removed for protection or has completely disintegrated. It is no longer visible.

Dimensions: Not known.

Context: Very little of the Late Antique architecture is visible in the modern whitewashed church. The mosaic was situated in front of the west end of the modern Church of Panagia.

Description: According to Sanders, the mosaic had a border consisting of a series of triangles and this enclosed bands of linked squares. The squares contained various designs of four-rayed flowers, crosses, guilloches, knots and circles with crosses. These geometric designs were in red, blue and white. A very poor photograph of the mosaic was published by Orlandos (1955–6, fig. 25). From it, a pattern of swastika meander containing squares (**R** 195a) can be distinguished. Contained within the squares are guilloche mats and stylized flowers.

Date: Sanders suggests a date of the late fifth to early sixth century.

Bibliography: Platon 1955, 415; Orlandos 1955–6, fig. 25; Sanders, 124; Volanakis, no. 17; *Byz Corp I*, 121 (no. 104).

154. *Kantanos*

Plate: None available.

Location and discovery: Excavated in 1939; no record of where the mosaic may now exist.

Dimensions: None available.

Context: When the site was first excavated by Theophanides he believed that it was a late second- to early third-century *praetorium* on the basis of an inscription now accepted as having been reused in the church from an earlier phase.

Description: All that is available of this mosaic for study is a very poor photograph (I was unable to locate it), but Sanders says that the mosaic resembles closely that in the central aisle of Basilica A at Chersonisos. This cannot be confirmed on the evidence of the publication.

Date: The basilica is likely to date to the late fifth to early sixth century.

Bibliography: Theophanides 1942–4, 31; Sanders, 126; Volanakis, no. 12.

155. *Elyros*

Plate: None available.

Location and discovery: The site of the Christian basilica has never been excavated, and a modern church is now built on top of it. The mosaics are not visible at present but a recent visit to the site identified some tesserae fragments.[34]

Dimensions: Not known.

Context: Christian basilica.

Description: Sanders (126) describes the mosaics as depicting natural scenes of deer, peacocks and flowering tendrils flowing out of kantharoi.

Date: Because of the mosaic's possible similarities to the Suia mosaics and based on some visible architectural fragments, a sixth-century date is suggested for the basilica.

Bibliography: Alexiou 1964, 151; Lassithiotaki 1970, 373; Sanders, 126; Volanakis, no. 9; *Byz Corp I*, 120–1 (no. 103).

156–8. *Suia: Basilica A*

Plate: 50–1.

Location and discovery: *In situ* in a Christian basilica which has been built over by a modern church. The mosaics were removed and re-laid in the modern church (Pl. 51). They are in good condition.

Dimensions: Not known. Tesserae: *c.* 35 per 10 x 10 cm area; figured panel *c.* 42 per 10 x 10 cm area.

Context: Narthex, nave and bema of a Christian basilica.

Description: White, red, yellow and blue-grey tesserae are used throughout.

156. *The Narthex (Pl. 50)*

The mosaics discovered so far in the narthex cover the northern half of the room in three panels (Pl. 50). The panels are bordered by a large band of interlocking semi-circles forming ogives (similar to **R** 49a). On the western and the northern side they are bordered by an inner band of intersecting circles forming hollow spindles (**R** 237b), which is set on a red background.

The northernmost panel consists of a circle within a square. The circle is made of a band of guilloche. Within this is a further square which is filled with a row of adjacent scales (**R** 215c). The next panel consists of a grid of squares and rectangles. Rows of small squares alternate with rectangles, followed by rows of large squares alternating with rectangles. A row of circles is cut by the squares, and within the square space is filling of various motifs, including acanthus leaves, semi-circles and a concave square.

The third panel is very similar to one of the peacock panels in the sanctuary area. It depicts either one or two peacocks on a white background with bright red leaves intertwining around the figure(s) (Sanders, pl. 62).

157. *The Nave (Pl. 50)*

There are three main parts to this mosaic in the nave. The western section consists of three panels each composed of adjacent scales (Pl. 50).

The main part of the middle section is the largest and is bordered on the north and on the south by a band of intersecting semi-circles forming ogives (similar to **R** 49a). Its eastern side is bordered by a band of intersecting circles forming hollow spindles (**R** 237b). Within this part is a central dividing band featuring a shield of scales. On either side of this band are five panels; each one mirrors the panel opposite it. The westernmost panel consists of a mat of a variety of **R** 237b, but in this case a square

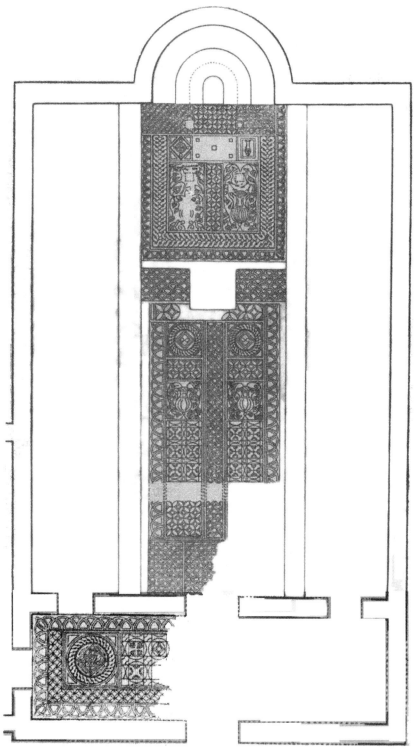

Plate 50 Suia, Basilica A plan (Mosaics 156–8) (after Orlandos 1953, fig. 7) (with permission from *Κρητικά Χρονικά* © Society of Cretan Historical Studies).

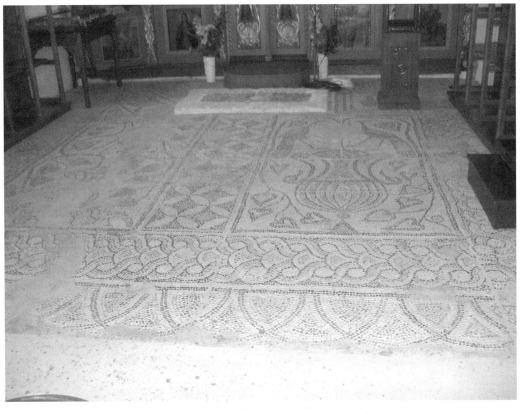

Plate 51 Suia, Basilica A, bema (Mosaic 158).

is enclosed in each of the concave squares. The following panel is similar in layout to Panel 2 of the nave, except that a Greek cross is in each of the circles. Above this panel is one containing a kantharos with ivy leaves coming out of its mouth, and following this panel is a slightly smaller one which is the same as the first. The final part of this section contains a guilloche circle with an enclosed square (Pl. 50).

The third and eastern section in the nave consists of two panels containing adjacent scales.

158. *The Bema (Pl. 51)*

Most of this bema mosaic is bordered by a band of intersecting semi-circles forming ogives (similar to **R** 49a), except for the eastern side and a small portion of the northern side (Pl. 51). There are three panels on the eastern side. The central area is the same as the westernmost panel in the nave (Panel 1), and the two side sections are the same as the panels of the shield of scales.

Below these are four panels bordered on three sides (not on the east) by a variation of double guilloche (**R** 75a). The two larger lower panels are separated by a band of spindles. These two panels depict natural scenes (Pl. 51). The northern one has the remains of a kantharos with ivy leaves coming out of its mouth. At the bottom, on either side of the kantharos, is a different bird (the one on the right is a peacock, the left one is not clear). In the top half, encompassed between the ivy leaves, is a deer.

The southern panel also depicts a kantharos with a large vine scroll spreading out from it. This vine cascades down over two opposed peacocks (Pl. 51). Above these two scenes are two small panels. The southern one is square and encloses a fish, and the northern one encloses a cross in a diamond.

Materials: Stone, marble and terracotta tesserae.

Date: The suggested date for these floors based on various parallels is the mid-sixth century. There are parallels within Crete at Elyros and Alikianos; in both these instances, however, the dates are uncertain because the mosaics are no longer visible. Parallels are also found at Hermione, on mainland Greece. The same use of the semi-circular border can be seen at Basilica A, Chersonisos, which dates to the early sixth century. The scales design can also be seen at the fifth-century basilica in Knossos.

Bibliography: Sanders, 126–7; Volanakis, no. 20; *Byz Corp I*, 121 (no.105); Orlandos 1953, 348.

159. *Suia: Basilica B*

Plate: None available.

Location and discovery: Noted by Pendlebury. It no longer survives.

Dimensions: None available.

Context: Christian basilica.

Description: Pendlebury (1939, 368) describes it as depicting a lion chasing a deer.

Date: Not known.

Bibliography: Pendlebury 1939, 368; Sanders, 127; *Byz Corp I*, 123 (nos. 106 & 107); Volanakis, no. 21.

160. *Lissos Basilica*

Plate: None available.

Location and discovery: Uncovered *in situ*.

Dimensions: Small fragments are visible. Tesserae: *c.* 30 per 10 x 10 cm area.

Context: Two fragments in the churches of the Panagia and Agia Kyriake.[35] The original context may have been the south aisle of the church.

Description: Fragments of the tessellated mosaics in red, black, yellow (?) and white are visible, and the evidence indicates a border of intersecting semi-circles and a field of a shield of scales.

Materials: Stone, marble and terracotta tesserae.

Date: Late Antique.

Bibliography: Sanders, 128; Volanakis, nos. 15 & 16; *Byz Corp I*, 125 (nos. 111, 112).

161–2. *Episkopi*

Plate: *Byz Corp I*, pl. 97a.

Location and discovery: The mosaics are currently *in situ* protected in the later church. Most of the mosaic has been destroyed and only fragments remain.

Dimensions: Not known.

Context: Nave and south aisle of a Christian basilica. A later tenth-century church of the Archangel Michael is constructed on top.

Description: White, blue and red tessellated mosaic.

161. *The Nave Area*

The mosaic in the nave area is circular with a U-shape extending out from it to fit with the rotunda architectural form. A border consists of intersecting semi-circles of red, blue and white tesserae. Within this it is possible to identify seven sections of decoration. Two areas in the east have a scale pattern (**R** 217c). Two surviving fragments of guilloche suggest that they formed as a central division in the floor so that the north and south sides mirrored each other. Surviving on the north side is a square panel containing a circle which further contains two intersecting squares. Within these squares is a circle which is joined to the intersections of the squares by smaller circles.

The area between the intersecting squares and the outer circle contains two fish motifs and a kantharos with vine leaves extending out of it. The rest of this area is damaged. To the west of this square, which is mirrored on the southern side, is a small fragment of leaf scroll (*Byz Corp I*, pl. 97a).

162. *The South Aisle*

In the area of the south aisle there are only small traces of mosaic, but it is possible to establish that there had been a panel of scale pattern (**R** 217c).

Materials: Stone, marble and terracotta tesserae.

Date: Late fifth to early sixth century. Because of the shape of the mosaic it is possible that the original fifth- to sixth-century church had a U-shaped bema. Sanders (129) suggests that it may have been a tetraconch church; if this is so then it would have been one of the few such in Crete. On this basis Sanders compares the church to that of Agios Georgios in Thessaloniki and to the Red Church in Peroushtitsa in Bulgaria, which have been dated to the sixth century. Andreadakis (1988, 365) believes that the rotunda may have been part of the original church. This is likely given the round shape of the mosaic.

There are similarities between one of the panels at Episkopi and that of the intersecting squares in a circle in the nave of the basilica at Almyrida. Unfortunately, not enough of the Episkopi mosaic panel is preserved to say how far the similarities went. The date for the Almyrida mosaic is considered to be late fifth to early sixth century.

Bibliography: Sanders, 128–9; Volanakis, no. 10; *Byz Corp I*, 123 (no. 108); Andreadakis 1988, 365–6.

163. *Alikianos*

Plate: None available.

Location and discovery: Unclear.

Dimensions: None available.

Context: Late Antique church on the site of the Church of Zoodochos Pigi.

Description: Sanders describes the mosaics as being strikingly similar to those of Suia Basilica A. However, this is based on Spanakis's description of them as containing 'deer, peacocks, vases and other geometric designs'. This could refer to any Late Antique church mosaic.

Materials: Not known.

Date: Late Antique.

Bibliography: Sanders 124; Spanakis 1972, 46.

Supplementary Catalogue: Recently Reported Unpublished Mosaics from the Prefecture of Chania

Although the following mosaics are provided with catalogue numbers they are not included in the statistical analysis of date and distribution nor are they included in the main discussion except for purposes of comparison. Their inclusion here is for comparative evidence, and this should not be considered as the final description of the mosaic, its date or even its context until the individual excavators have published their findings in full.

S200. *Aptera*

A mosaic is reported as coming from Bath house I-II, which was discovered during research excavations. According to the report, a date of the first half of the second century is possible but not secure. Now that more of the residential area of the town is being excavated (see, for example, Niniou-Kindeli & Christodoulakos 2004 and the excavation of the peristyle house), it is likely that the finds of mosaics will increase. Niniou-Kindeli & Christodoulakos, 2004, 323.

S201. *Chania: Kydonias Street, Kapetanakis Plot Fragmentary Mosaics*

Badly damaged in antiquity, the mosaics were recovered during rescue excavations of a Roman house. Three rooms were excavated although a definite date has not been proposed. The mosaic contained a guilloche border and a fragment of a female and an animal. Tzedakis 1978, 366; *AR* 1985–6, 96.

S202. *Chania: Plastira Mosaic*

At the junction of Plastira and Apokoronou a bulldozer dug into a large part of a mosaic floor which was constructed of large irregular tesserae. No iconography or discussion of context was reported. A late Hellenistic date was suggested. Markoulaki 1983, 360.

S203. *Chania: Mosaic under the Carpark*

Found during a rescue excavation on Peridou 14. The mosaic was very much damaged, but it was possible to make out in the northwest corner of the room a section which depicted black squares on a white background enclosing kraters. In another section of the room, evidence for geometric patterns includes alternating black and white triangles. Markoulaki suggested a second-century date for the mosaic. Evidence for a stoa and bath house were recovered; however, it is unclear if this mosaic is associated with either. Markoulaki 1990, 435–40; Tzedakis 1979, 391; *AR* 1987–8, 75.

S204. *Chania: Mayrigiannakis House*

At the junction of Peiraios and Mitropolitou Kyrillou, five occupation phases were revealed. In the Roman phase, the remains of a large house were discovered. Three of the rooms had mosaic floors, and the remains of a hypocaust were also revealed. The mosaics are likely to date to the second century. Two of the mosaics were of coarse construction of irregular pebbles in strong cement. The third was a tessellated mosaic of geometric design (much damaged) (*AR* 2004–5, fig. 171). A guilloche border (exactly the same as that surrounding the Medusa mosaic in the Villa Dionysus (Mosaic 5)) surrounded a field of intersecting circles forming spindles and concave squares (**R** 237a) with a poised crosslet included. A large central rectangular panel had a polychrome scene of birds and laurel wreaths. Markoulaki 2002, 244–5; *AR* 2002–3, 86; Markoulaki 1998, 862.

S205. *Chania: El. Venizelou and Archondakis Streets*

A Roman house with a mosaic floor was investigated. There were other mosaic floors which had been located earlier belonging to the same complex. Markoulaki 2002, 245; *AR* 2002–3, 86; *AR* 2006–7, 119.

S206. *Kisamos: Stephanoudakis Plot*

These floors were discovered in a private plot situated near the main cathedral. The mosaic mainly consists of geometric decoration, combined with a section with marble slabs. The geometric décor includes squares which contain checkerboard ornament (**R** 114a) interrupted at the corners by small circles. In the north and south sides a pattern of intersecting hexagons combine to make six-pointed stars. In the squares and rectangles which are created through this design are different geometric patterns, including Solomon's knots, single pelta and some kind of vegetal scroll-type design. A further area of intersecting octagons contains undecorated squares in the middle of the formation. The combination of diamonds and squares in this manner and the use of Solomon's knots and peculiar M-shape which is likely to be some kind of scroll or petalled flower, can be likened to the well-dated late Hadrianic mosaic from Gortyn (Mosaic 46). Markoulaki (2004), dates the mosaic to the middle of the second century. Papapostolou 1975, 347; *AR* 1983–4, 68; Markoulaki et al. 2004.

S207. *Kisamos: Health Centre Mosaics*

Several mosaics have been excavated during the Health Centre excavations. These rescue excavations have uncovered several rooms of a two-phased urban *domus*. The first late second-century phase contained the floors of Mosaic 207a, the Centaur and the Panther (black-and-white mosaic) (Room 2) (Markoulaki 1987b, pl. 324); Mosaic 207b, geometric mosaics which include the inscribed panel Η ΤΥΧΗΣΗ () ΧΗΤΗΣΑΙ ΚΝΩ ΚΘΩΝ ΟΩΥ (this may refer to the artist's having come from Kydonia or Antioch; see Markoulaki et al. 2004, 371); the *Xenia* mosaic, 207c (Room 1) (Markoulaki 1987b, pl. 328); and Mosaic 207d of Medusa and the Masks in medallions (Room 3) (Markoulaki 1987b, pl. 324). In Room 11, Mosaic 207e, the signed mosaic floor depicted a scene of Dionysus, two scenes from Menander comedies (the *Sikyonian(s)* and *Theophoroumene*) and an image of Menander or possibly Homer. The second-phase area (Area 3) contained Mosaic 207f, the Wedding of Dionysus, and the signature Μεροπᾶς ἐψηφοθέτησα (Markoulaki 1987b, pl. 327 & Markoulaki et al. 2004, 372), in what is likely to have been a *triclinium* dated to the third century. Part of the complex had mosaic floors on the second storey (collapsed remains were found) (*AR* 2000–1, 141). These fragments had a bedding of large pebbles and plaster and also a 1-cm thick bed of lime with

a mix of plaster and sherds below. In an earlier phase there may have been a bath building here on the evidence of the pipes (Markoulaki et al. 2004, 372). A number of elements from these mosaics are indicative of workshop production: for example, the 'thick guilloche' used in the mosaic of Medusa and the Masks is found only on the *triclinium* of the House of Dionysus Mosaic, Chania. *AR* 1984–5, 67; *Η Καθημερινή* 11.10.84; *Ακρόπολις* 11.10.84; Markoulaki 1987b, 558–63; Markoulaki et al.1989, 551–80; Markoulaki 1991, 415; Pariente 1994, 839; Markoulaki 1991–3, 222; Markoulaki 1994a, 217–19; Markoulaki Lecture 1998; Markoulaki 1999, 183–97; *AR* 1997–8, 126; Markoulaki et al. 2004.

S208. *Kisamos: Hartzoulakis Plot*

All that was visible of this mosaic were the remains of its matrices. According to the report, the building could be dated to the fourth century and the mosaic may have been removed in antiquity. Tzedakis 1979, 397; *AR* 1987–8, 75.

S209. *Kisamos: I. Farangitakis Plot*

According to the report, there was only one mosaic floor in this rather large mid-third-century Roman house, and there were decorated floors of other types. The mosaic, which was discovered in the main room of the house, had suffered a lot of damage; for example, the central scene may have been dug out. The preserved geometric décor was of ribbons of blue and deep-red creating spirals. Pologiorgi & Markoulaki 1982, 382–3; *AR* 1989–90, 79.

S210. *Kisamos: Kakaournakis Plot*

A badly damaged geometric mosaic was uncovered in a fourth- (?) century Roman house. The geometric décor included small white rectangles on a black background with further geometric themes. A small delicate ribbon border framed the mosaic and rhomboid shapes are repeated in the corners, with three smaller rhomboids in its centre. The report says that the mosaic was obviously made with a great deal of skill, perhaps with master craftspeople working on the centre of the mosaic and apprentices working on the border. Some areas of the mosaic were clearly of a higher standard, whereas those in the northern areas were inferior. The walls were painted with red, yellow, blue and green colours. Tzedakis 1978, 373–4; *AR* 1985–6, 96.

S211. *Kisamos: Grape-Picking Scene*
This well-preserved mosaic depicts a couple embracing and children picking grapes. The main scene has been rendered in polychrome, and it consists of a large vine which takes up almost the entire space with its winding, running branches. In the spaces left over, various people are shown, for example, a couple embracing and a child reaching up to pick grapes. The child, rather fat, holds a special hook for cutting down the grapes. Here the vine winds in behind and around the figure. There may also be a satyr in one section of the mosaic. Also inhabiting the running vine leaves are various small animals and vegetables. The mosaic was discovered in one room of a Roman house dating to the third century. This room had walls with painted plaster, and many fragments of multi-coloured wall paintings were found. This mosaic was found close to the Paterakis Plot and the Skounakis Plot mosaics. Tzedakis 1972, 637–8; *AR* 1976–7, 67; *AR* 1978–9, 65; Touchais 1977, 659; Markoulaki et al. 2004, 366.

S212. *Kisamos: Orpheus Mosaic (Raisakis Plot)*
A section of mosaic depicting Orpheus and the animals was excavated as part of the rescue excavations of a second- to third-century Roman suburban peristyle house. The Orpheus mosaic was found in the *triclinium* in the semi-circle of the mosaic. A stylized scroll surrounded it. The two *cubicula* excavated also had (destroyed) tessellated floors. The later Christian cemetery had damaged many of the other floors including one of birds and geometric décor in the possible *tablinum*. A range of other floor types, such as simple white tessellated mosaic and *opus sectile*, were recovered (see *AR* 1996–7, fig. 128). North and south of the Orpheus mosaic were mosaics damaged in antiquity. The *opus sectile* floor had corners of tessellated mosaic. Part of the main Roman road was also uncovered. Andreadakis 1991, 422–6; ΕΘΝΟΣ 14 December 1992; ΝΙΚΗ 15 December 1992; Pariente 1994, 839; Andreadakis 1991–3, 227–9; Koundi, *Η Καθημερινή* 31 January 1993, 14; *K.Estia* 1994/6, 221; *AR* 1996–7, 122; Markoulaki et al. 2004, fig. 13; Drosinou 1992, 579–81, fig. 6; *AR* 2006–7, 120.

S213. *Kisamos: Mosaic of the Tritons*
An exceptionally fine mosaic was recovered surrounding the *impluvium* (11.10 x 8.80 m) of a Roman house. The four sides of the mosaic depict scenes in red, black and white of tritons, hippocamps, Scylla, dolphins, a sea leopard and other marine creatures. The tesserae size are 2 x 2 cm. A mid-second-century date is reasonable, and Markoulaki argues for this on the basis of the similarities in the style and technique of the mosaic. Furthermore, coins suggest a date of the first half of the second century. Markoulaki also notes that the pottery found is of third century. None of the rooms off the *impluvium* room had any mosaics except for the vestibule which had a plain mosaic (three rows of diamonds). In the same excavations, a destroyed mosaic was also revealed. The modern Mitropolitikos church

lies on top of part of the mosaic. Here is visible a rare use of Western forms on Crete. Markoulaki 1999, 197–9; Markoulaki et al. 2004, fig. 12.

S214. *Kisamos: Nikolakis Plot*

Two mosaics were discovered during excavations of a plot in the north of Kisamos. The mosaics, found in Rooms 8 and 9 of the 10-roomed house, are both geometric. The house had two occupation phases between the first and third centuries. The mosaic in Room 8 has a border of lateral semi-circles, tangent to each other, each linked by a line to the outer border. This encloses a field of running swastikas (**R** 166d). The mosaic in Room 9 has a border of double guilloche (**R** 75a) enclosing a field of squares and triangles similar to **R** 391a. The four corner squares and the central square each contain plants. Both mosaics were damaged. A third mosaic, blue and white, was also found in Room 12. The mosaics date to the first half of the second century as suggested by the coins found in Room 8. Markoulaki 1999, 199–208, figs. 10 & 11; Markoulaki 2004, 368; *AR* 2000–1, 141.

S215. *Kisamos: Eir. Aligizakis Plot*

Two occupation phases were found in the area of the eastern baths in the excavations of this nine-roomed house: Roman and sixth century. The Roman remains were a large house represented by large rooms; Room II contained a mosaic floor. The polychrome mosaic with glass tesserae had a guilloche border which has smaller figured panels within, each framed by a guilloche border. Surrounding this main panel, outside the guilloche frame, were outlined diamonds. Some of the mosaic is still uncovered (under a great deal of earth). Two of the scenes illustrated birds: one, two birds on a bowl and the other, a peacock (?). The style of the mosaic can be dated to the

Severan period (end of the second/beginning of the third century), but pottery associated can be dated to the fourth century. In Room 5 a mosaic with a central scene of Leda and the Swan was located. The Leda and the Swan mosaic has two lower panels which look as though they contain a peacock in one and birds on a bowl in another (possibly *xenia* scenes). Directly surrounding the central panel are smaller panels of masks. A wave scroll surrounds the entire space of the figured panels (i.e., Leda and the mask ones) in addition to a band of adjacent circles linked by a continuous dotted line. Markoulaki 1999, 208–13, figs. 12 & 30; Markoulaki et al. 2004, 368; *AR* 2000–1, 141.

S216. *Kisamos: Skounakis Plot*

Located close to the Paterakis Plot (where the mosaic of the Seasons was discovered), this fine mosaic of the Triumph of Dionysus with surrounding hunt scenes was revealed during excavation. The detailed scroll which acts as a background as well as forming the individual panels is very reminiscent of the North African style of mosaics, as is the choice of the central scene. Another panel contains a scene of grape crushing, and a long panel contains a scene of the return of the hunt with an image of a shrine and cult statue. This mosaic is now in the new museum in Kisamos. It is dated to the second half of the second century. There was another mosaic floor connected with the Paterakis mosaic, but that one was left unexcavated as much of it lay under the road. Together these mosaics make up a substantial insula. Markoulaki et al. 2004, 366 & fig. 11.

S217. *Kisamos: Xirouchakis Plot*

In the south and southeast of the plot a building with mosaic floors was found. Little further information is provided. Andreadaki-Vlazaki 1999, 215–17.

S218. *Kisamos: Late Antique Grave Mosaic*
During the excavations of a Christian cemetery in the Raisakis Plot (see earlier) a mosaic with the Chi-Rho symbol in a border of black tesserae was discovered in the same location as Grave 21. The number of tesserae around Grave 29 may indicate a similar case. The number of examples of the occurrence of mosaics in graves in Greece is very small. Diamandis 2004, 391 & figs. 1 & 11; Drosinou 1992, 579–81, fig. 6.

S219. *Kisamos: Late Antique Church Mosaic*
Markoulaki et al. mention a Late Antique basilica with a mosaic floor which had been found in 1986 as part of the construction of the main road near the Plateia El. Venizelou. The 13th Ephorea had excavated it, and it lay above some Roman graves. Markoulaki, Christodoulakos & Fragkonikolaki 2004, 373 n. 68.

S220. *Kisamos: Late Antique Mosaic*
A Late Antique mosaic located in a plot off the national road on the outskirts of Kisamos may have come from the Theodosakis Plot, which included the excavation of some Late Antique features such as the remains of a house and a drain. The space where the mosaic is looks too small to be part of a church so this may be an uncommon example of a secular Late Antique mosaic in Crete. Drosinou 1994–6, 227.

Addendum: Recent excavations (2010) undertaken by the ephorea on the Episkopi E. Syngelaki Street revealed the remains of a circular building with a sixth-century mosaic floor.

Sphakia: Mosaic Traces
During the Agios Vasilios survey, in the area of Cave Site 5226, a site was revisited and fragments of a mosaic floor (probably Late Antique) were found with large blocks but the material was quickly re-buried by the contractors. Probably came from a substantial Late Antique building. *AR* 1997–8, 120.

R 2d *dentilled simple filet*

R 2j *dentilled simple filet with dentils of squares*

R 4e *row of spaced saltires with serrated arms terminating in a chevron*

R 4c *spaced crosslet of several poised tesserae in each*

R 4j *spaced saltires of tassels*

R 5a *row of spaced and poised serrated squares*

R 10d *trichrome dog's-tooth pattern*

R 10g *serrated saw-tooth pattern*

R 11a *row of superposed isosceles triangles, in counterchanged colours.*

R 27e *bichrome row of tangent poised octagons formed by four hourglasses (forming squares), the colours counterchanged*

Plate 52 Glossary of geometric patterns (**R** 1–**R** 327) (after Balmelle et al. 1985) (drawing by K. Sweetman).

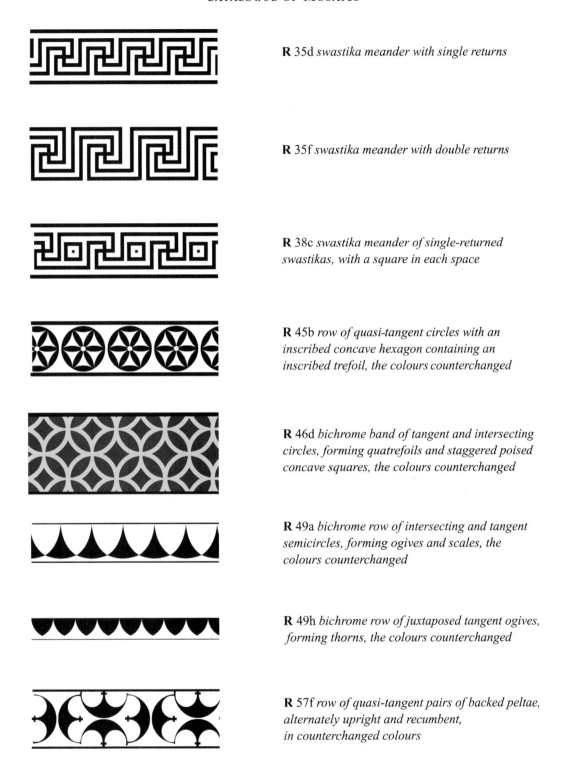

R 35d *swastika meander with single returns*

R 35f *swastika meander with double returns*

R 38c *swastika meander of single-returned swastikas, with a square in each space*

R 45b *row of quasi-tangent circles with an inscribed concave hexagon containing an inscribed trefoil, the colours counterchanged*

R 46d *bichrome band of tangent and intersecting circles, forming quatrefoils and staggered poised concave squares, the colours counterchanged*

R 49a *bichrome row of intersecting and tangent semicircles, forming ogives and scales, the colours counterchanged*

R 49h *bichrome row of juxtaposed tangent ogives, forming thorns, the colours counterchanged*

R 57f *row of quasi-tangent pairs of backed peltae, alternately upright and recumbent, in counterchanged colours*

Plate 52 *Cont.*

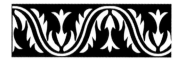

R 63e *polychrome undulating band of acanthus with a lily superimposed on a trifid petal in each undulation*

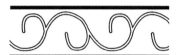

R 64a *stylized scroll*

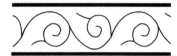

R 64b *voluted stylized scroll*

R 64d *ivy scroll*

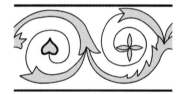

R 64e *simple acanthus scroll*

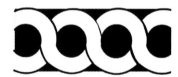

R 68b *bichrome row of undulating interlaced bands forming circles and thorns, the colours counterchanged, in this case the bands are filled with guilloche*

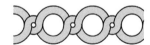

R 69f *pair of undulating asymmetrically shaded bands, interlooped forming circles*

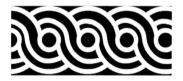

R 68d *bichrome pair of undulating interlaced bands forming circles and thorns, in symmetrically shaded bands, truncated before interlacing*

Plate 52 *Cont.*

R 70d *outlined simple guilloche on a coloured ground*

R 70e *outlined guilloche on a coloured ground with a median filet in the strands*

R 70f *simple guilloche with strands of three repeating colours*

R 70h *asymmetrically shaded simple guilloche on a white ground*

R 70j *asymmetrically shaded simple guilloche on a black ground*

R 71a *tightly braided simple guilloche on a white ground*

R 72c *shaded three strand guilloche on a white ground*

R 74h *straight tongued double guilloche opened to form eyelets*

R 74f *double straight looped guilloche*

R 75a *polychrome tightly braided round-tongued double guilloche, open to form eyelets, on a coloured ground*

Plate 52 *Cont.*

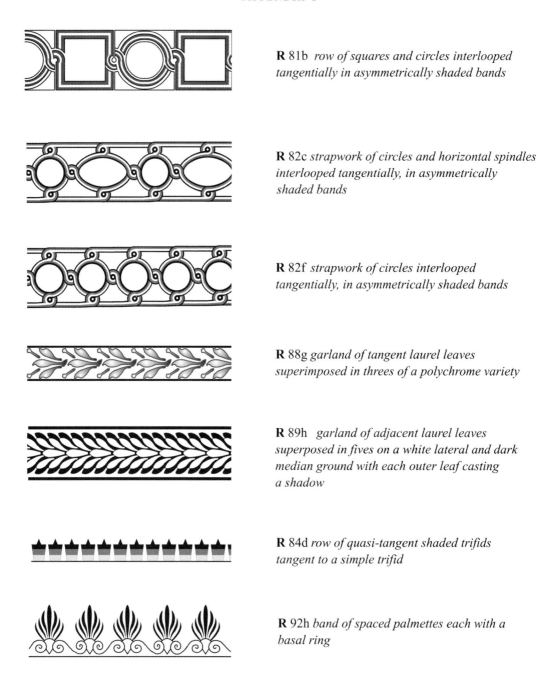

R 81b *row of squares and circles interlooped tangentially in asymmetrically shaded bands*

R 82c *strapwork of circles and horizontal spindles interlooped tangentially, in asymmetrically shaded bands*

R 82f *strapwork of circles interlooped tangentially, in asymmetrically shaded bands*

R 88g *garland of tangent laurel leaves superimposed in threes of a polychrome variety*

R 89h *garland of adjacent laurel leaves superposed in fives on a white lateral and dark median ground with each outer leaf casting a shadow*

R 84d *row of quasi-tangent shaded trifids tangent to a simple trifid*

R 92h *band of spaced palmettes each with a basal ring*

R 97a *bichrome stylised arcade*

Plate 52 *Cont.*

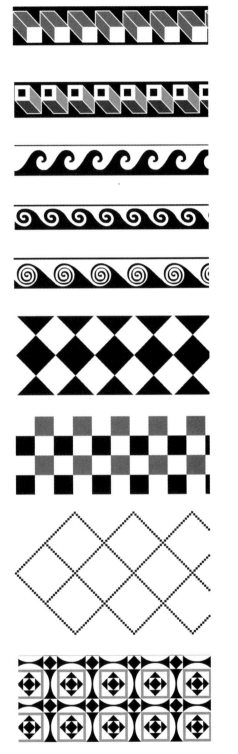

R 99e *row of tangent cuboids*

R 99f *row of tangent cuboids with serrated sides*

R 101a *simple wave pattern*

R 101b *wave pattern (normal)*

R 101c *convoluted wave pattern*

R 114a *checkerboard pattern*

R 114f *trichrome chessboard-pattern, forming for one colour monochrome rows of tangent poised squares*

R 124a *grid of serrated simple filets*

R 144e *grid of bands with a square at the intersections with the compartments inscribed in a circle, creating the effect of bobbins*

Plate 52 *Cont.*

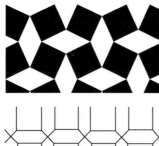

R 161a *orthogonal pattern of adjacent lozenges and squares, the colours counterchanged*

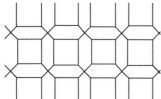

R 169a *outlined orthogonal pattern of irregular octagons adjacent and intersecting on the shorter sides forming squares and oblongs*

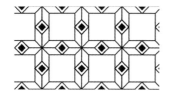

R 173b *outlined orthogonal pattern of tangent eight-lozenge stars forming squares and smaller poised squares*

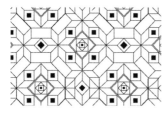

R 176f *bichrome outlined pattern of tangent stellate octagons (consisting of a central square tangent to four smaller poised squares and ensconced in the angles between four pairs of lozenges) creating the effect of eight-pointed stars*

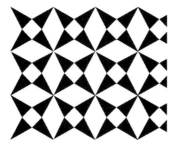

R 184b *orthogonal pattern of tangent four-pointed stars, forming lozenges alternatively recumbent and upright, the stars bearing an axially inscribed square*

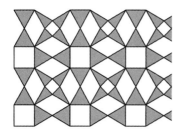

R 186b *bichrome orthogonal pattern of poised tangent octagons forming four pointed stars, with the octagons bearing a four pointed star and the stars bearing an axially inscribed square, the colours counterchanged, creating the effect of an orthogonal pattern of adjacent hexagons*

Plate 52 *Cont.*

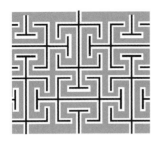

R 187d *orthogonal pattern of swastika meander with recessed reverse returns, the swastikas alternately reversed, with a median simple filet in the interspaces forming Ts*

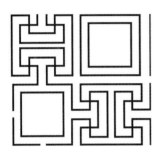

R 195a *outlined orthogonal pattern of spaced latchkey meander of swastikas with single returns, the spaces staggered and containing a square*

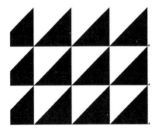

R 197a *chessboard pattern of right-angled isosceles triangles*

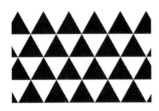

R 198e *outlined triaxial pattern of adjacent equilateral triangles, the colours counter-changed creating the effect of a chessboard pattern of equilateral triangles*

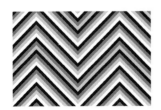

R 199b *zigzag rainbow pattern of simple filet*

Plate 52 *Cont.*

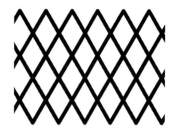

R 201a *bichrome lattice pattern of intersecting double filets*

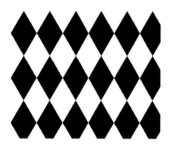

R 202a *chessboard pattern of lozenges*

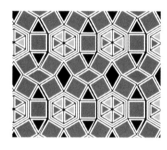

R 205e *lattice pattern of intersecting dodecagons and oblong decagons, forming hexagons and lozenges*

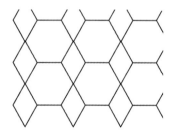

R 213a *outlined pattern of adjacent hexagons and lozenges (creating the effect of adjacent and intersecting large irregular hexagons)*

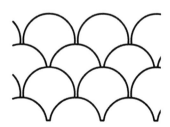

R 215b o*utlined orthogonal pattern of adjacent scales in simple filets*

Plate 52 *Cont.*

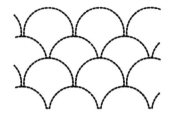

R 215c *bichrome row of tesserae laid in an orthogonal pattern of adjacent scales*

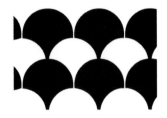

R 217c *orthogonal pattern of adjacent scales, the colours counterchanged*

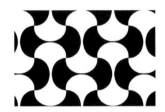

R 220a *bichrome orthogonal pattern of adjacent alternatively vertical and horizontal pairs of opposed scales, the colours counterchanged*

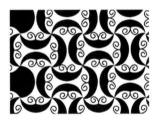

R 222d *orthogonal pattern of tangent peltae in alternating upright and recumbent confronted pairs ('running peltae pattern'), the colours counterchanged, forming cordiform interspaces*

R 229a *trichrome orthogonal pattern of quasi-tangent poised quadrilobes of peltae tangent to a central inscribed saltire of spindles (or quatrefoil) forming concave squares with bi-concave sides, here bearing an inscribed pair or opposed peltae*

Plate 52 *Cont.*

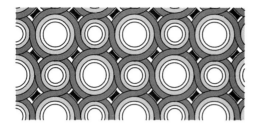

R 233d *grid of interlaced opposed sinusoids in asymmetrically shaded bands alternately spaced and quasi-tangent*

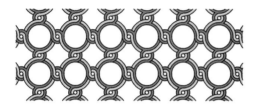

R 235a *polychrome orthogonal pattern of asymmetrically shaded bands interlooped tangentially forming irregular concave octagons (the axial sides shorter)*

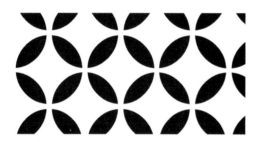

R 237a *orthogonal pattern of intersecting circles, forming saltires of quasi-tangent solid spindles and concave squares, the colours counterchanged*

R 237b *quasi-tangent solid spindles and concave squares (the spindles being hollow)*

R 237g *orthogonal pattern of intersecting circles, forming saltires of quasi-tangent solid spindles and concave squares, the colours counterchanged, with a solid concave square within the centre of each*

Plate 52 *Cont.*

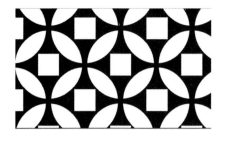

R 238b *bichrome orthogonal pattern of intersecting circles, forming saltires of spindles with the colours counterchanged, here the concave spindles containing an inscribed poised square, the colours counterchanged*

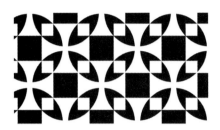

R 239a *bichrome orthogonal pattern of intersecting circles, forming saltires of quasi tangent spindles (here with an inscribed poised square), the colours counterchanged*

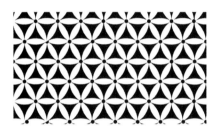

R 247e *triaxial outlined pattern of circles intersecting at six points and spaced forming trefoils and concave hexagons*

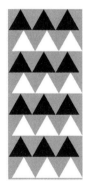

R 327b *shield of triangles in contrasting colours with three triangles per row in eight rows*

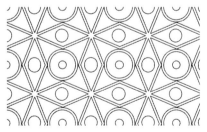

mat of circles and diamonds

Plate 52 *Cont.*

283

@@ @@ @@ @@

APPENDIX 2

CATALOGUE OF MOSAIC INSCRIPTIONS

A2.1 ROMAN MOSAICS

1. Apollinaris mosaic (Mosaic 9) (Pl. 9), ΑΠΟΛΛΙΝΑΡΙϹ ΕΠΟΙΕΙ (Ἀπολλινάρις ἐποίει)
   'Apollinaris made this'

2. The Athlete mosaic (Mosaic 12) (Pl. 10) (http://artsweb.bham.ac.uk/aha/kaw/Knossos/athletes.htm)
   [- – –]ΚΛΟΣ ΣΑΤΟΡΝΙΛΟΣ ([– – –]κλος Σατορνῖλος)
   [- – –]klos and Satornilos probably refer to the names of the athletes

3. Cathedral Square (Mosaic 133), inscribed fragment (Tzedakis 1970, pl. 409b), ΛΑ
   Likely to be an abbreviation of a welcoming sign such as λοῦσαι ἀσφαλῶς (bathe safely).

4. Dionysus and Ariadne (Mosaic 135) (Pl. 41) (Markoulaki 1990, plan), ΠΛΟΚΙΟΝ (Πλόκιον)
   This refers to the title of the Menander play *The Necklace*, which is depicted.

5. *Triclinium* of the House of Dionysus (Mosaic 136) (Pl. 43), [- – –]ΔΑΦΝΗΝ ΕΠΟΙΕΙ ([– -]δάφνην ἐποίει)
   '… from Daphne made it'
   Likely to refer to the ethnikon of the artist who made the mosaic or an aspect of it.

6. Vigila, Ierapetra (Mosaic 87) [- – -]ΕΙΣΙΩΝ[- – -] (Εἰσιών).[1]
   'Goes in'
   The amount of the inscription preserved prohibits a good reconstruction. It is unclear how many letters may be missing from each side or how much room

there may have been for more words. Given that the common words denoting a craftsperson, such as ἐποίει or ἐψηφοθέτησα, ψηφιῶται, κυβευταί, or τεχνῖται, or in Latin, *musearius* or *tesserarius* or even 'donated', ἔδωκεν, do not work well with any of the surviving letters, it is possible that the inscription may have been labelling a figure on the mosaic.

A2.2 Late Antique Mosaics

7i. Olus (Mosaic 126)s
   The inscription is divided into two sections (Pl. 38) (*Byz Corp I*, pl. 89b).
   Θεο|δουλοσ υπερ σω|τηριασ ε||αυτου ε|δωκεν σι|μισιον εν.| Χ[ριστε, Βο|ηθι τω|| δουλω| σου |Ἐπι|φανι.]
   Θεό|δουλος ὑπὲρ σω|τηρίας ἔ||αυτοῦ ἔ|δωκεν σι|μίσιον ἔν. |
   | Χ[ριστέ, Βο|ήθι τῷ|| δούλω| σου | Ἐπι|φάνι].
   'The servant of the Lord for his own salvation gave one semis. O Christ help thy servant Epiphanes'.

7ii. Ἀν[ca.6] υπε[ρ σω]|τη[ριασ ε|αυτου και|| Παντοσ Του οικου| αυτου ε|δωκεν| σιμισι||on εν.]
   Ἀν[ca. 6] ὑπὲ[ρ σω]|τη[ρίας ἑ|αυτοῦ καὶ|| παντὸς τοῦ οἴκου| αὐτοῦ ἔ|δωκεν| σιμίσι||ον ἔν].
   (*IC*.1.XXII 65)
   'Antaxios for his own salvation and of all his own household gave one semis'

8. Olus (Mosaic 126) (Pl. 38) (*Byz Corp I*, pl. 89) [ΗΛΙΟΔΩΡΟΣ ΥΠΕΡ] ΣΩΤΗ|ΡΙΑΣ ΕΑ[ΥΤΟ]Υ ΕΔΩΚΕΝ CIMIC<o>IN
   [Ἡλιόδωρος ὑπὲρ] σωτη|ρίας ἑα[υτο]ῦ ἔδωκεν σ[ιμίσιον ἔν.
   'Heliodoros for his own salvation gave one semis'

9. Gortyn Sector M (Mosaic 109) (Pl. 29)
   ΕΠΙ ΒΕΤΡΑΝΙΟΥ ΤΟΥ ΑΓΙΩΤΑΤΟΥ ΚΑΙ ΜΑΚΑΡΙΩΤΑΤΟΥ ΗΜΩΝ ΑΡΧΙΕΠΙΣΚΟΠΟΥ ΑΝΕΚΑΙΝΙΣΘΗ ΤΟ ΕΡΓΟΝ ΤΗΣ ΨΗΦΩΣΕΩΣ.
   Ἐπὶ Βετρανίου τοῦ ἁγιωτάτου καὶ μακαριωτάτου ἡμῶν
   ἀρχιεπισκόπου ἀνεκαινίσθη τὸ ἔργον τῆς ψηφώσεως[2]
   'In the reign of Vetranios, our most holy and most blessed archbishop, the work of the mosaic was restored'.

10. Gortyn Sector M (Mosaic 109) (Pl. 30)
   ΕΠΙΘ [- — -]
   ΤΟΥ[- — -]
   ΤΟC[- — -]
   E[- — -]
   Not enough of the inscription survives for a confident reconstruction.

11. Eleutherna (Mosaics 111–14) (Pl. 33)
   ΕΥΦΡΑΤΑΣ Ο ΑΓΙΩΤΑΤΟΣ ʽΕΠΙΣΚΟΠΟΣ ΚΤΙΖΙ ΤΟΔΕ ΤΟ

ΘΙΟΝ ΤΕΜΕΝΟΣ, ΟΙΚΟΝ ΕΥΠΡΕΠΗ ΕΙΣ ΥΨΟΣ ΕΓΙΡΑΣ

ΜΙΧΑΗΛ ΤΟΥ ΑΡΧΑΓΓΕΛΟΥ ΟΥΠΕΡ ΠΡΕΣΒΙΑΙΣ ΧΑΡΙΣΘΗΣΕΤΕ

ΥΜΙ(Ν)

Εὐφρατᾶς, ὁ ἁγιώτατος Ἐπισκοπος, κτίζι τόδε τὸ

Θῖον τέμενος, οἶκον εὐπρεπῆ εἰς ὕψος ἐγίρας

Μιχαὴλ τοῦ Ἀρχαγγέλου, οὖπερ πρεσβίαις χαρισθήσετε ἡμῖ(ν)

'His holiness the Bishop Euphratas builds this holy temenos, having erected to its height an appropriate oikos of the Archangel Michael, through whose intercessions the grace (of God) will come upon us'.[3]

12. Eleutherna (Mosaic 111–14)[4]

```
      [- - - ca. 5–7 - - -]
      [. .ὁ]δόν
      [μ]ου εἰς
4     [τ]όπον
      [τ]οῦτον
      ὃν ἔκτι-
      σας· πάλ-
8     .Ο.ΤΟΥ.Α
      ιν ΗΜΙΑΤΩ
      ΝΟΝΕΙΣΩ
      ΣΤΡΣ[. .]
```

Located in the north doorway into the narthex, the inscription reminds the visitor of the sanctity of the space they are entering.[5]

꒰꒰ ꒰꒰ ꒰꒰

APPENDIX 3

MOSAICS AND DATING METHODOLOGY

The following tables are based on the dates which are used throughout the text. The date given is one which has been deduced by the author, rather than the published date. The reasoning behind the deduced date is outlined in the date section for each of the catalogue entries. The method by which each date was achieved is recorded in the table. The mosaics in the tables are arranged by the proposed date, and the undated mosaics are listed at the end. For fuller details on the dating methodologies of the mosaics of Crete, see Appendix 2.

Table A3.1. Mosaic Dates

Mosaic No.	Proposed Date	Area	Method of Dating	Degree of Confidence
55	Early 1st	Gortyn	Stylistically	Possible
43a	Mid-1st	Chersonisos	Stratigraphy?	Possible
15	Late 1st	Knossos	Stylistically & stratigraphy?	Likely
63	Late 1st	Gortyn	Stylistically & stratigraphy?	Possible
9	Late 1st/early 2nd	Knossos	Stylistically	Likely
72	Late 1st/early 2nd	Neos Kournas	Stylistically & stratigraphy?	Possible
84	Late 1st/early 2nd	Myrtos	Stylistically & stratigraphy?	Possible
53	Early 2nd	Gortyn	Stylistically & stratigraphy?	Possible
54	Early 2nd	Gortyn	Stylistically & stratigraphy?	Possible
56	Early 2nd	Gortyn	Stylistically & stratigraphy?	Possible
57	Early 2nd	Gortyn	Stylistically & stratigraphy?	Possible
59	Early 2nd	Gortyn	Stratigraphy	Possible
80	Early 2nd	Makrigialos	Architecture?	Likely
4	1st half 2nd	Knossos	Stratigraphy	Likely
132	1st half 2nd	Chania	Architecture?	Possible
133	1st half 2nd	Chania	Architecture?	Possible

(*continued*)

Table A3.1. (*Continued*)

Mosaic No.	Proposed Date	Area	Method of Dating	Degree of Confidence
134	1st half 2nd	Chania	Architecture?	Possible
1	Mid-2nd	Knossos	Stratigraphy	Likely
2	Mid-2nd	Knossos	Stratigraphy	Likely
3	Mid-2nd	Knossos	Stratigraphy	Likely
5	Mid-2nd	Knossos	Stratigraphy	Likely
6	Mid-2nd	Knossos	Stratigraphy	Likely
7	Mid-2nd	Knossos	Stratigraphy	Likely
13	Mid-2nd	Knossos	Stylistically	Possible
19	Mid-2nd	Knossos	Stylistically & stratigraphy	Possible
25	Mid-2nd	Knossos	Stratigraphy	Possible
32	Mid-2nd	Iraklion	Stratigraphy	Likely
33	Mid-2nd	Iraklion	Stratigraphy	Likely
34	Mid-2nd	Iraklion	Stratigraphy	Likely
35	Mid-2nd	Iraklion	Stratigraphy	Likely
36	Mid-2nd	Iraklion	Stratigraphy	Likely
37	Mid-2nd	Iraklion	Stratigraphy	Likely
60	Mid-2nd	Gortyn	Stratigraphy	Possible
139	Mid-2nd	Kisamos	Stylistically	Possible
140	Mid-2nd	Kisamos	Stylistically	Possible
8	2nd half 2nd	Knossos	Stylistically & stratigraphy	Likely
141	2nd half 2nd	Kisamos	Stylistically & stratigraphy	Sure
11	Late 2nd	Knossos	Stratigraphy	Likely
27	Late 2nd	Knossos	Stylistically & stratigraphy	Possible
38	Late 2nd	Chersonisos	Stylistically	Possible
10	Late 2nd/early 3rd	Knossos	Stratigraphy	Likely
14	Late 2nd/early 3rd	Knossos	Stylistically & stratigraphy	Likely
58	Late 2nd/early 3rd	Gortyn	Stratigraphy	Possible
12	Late 2nd/early 3rd	Knossos	Stratigraphy	Likely
129	1st half 3rd	Chania	Stylistically & stratigraphy	Likely
135	2nd half 3rd	Chania	Stylistically & stratigraphy	Likely
136	2nd half 3rd	Chania	Stylistically & stratigraphy	Likely
17	Late 3rd	Knossos	Stratigraphy & stylistically	Possible
50	Late 3rd	Mallia	Stratigraphy	Possible
47	Early 4th	Chersonisos	Stratigraphy?	Likely
39	Mid-4th	Chersonisos	Stratigraphy?	Possible
40	Late 4th/early 5th	Chersonisos	Stratigraphy?	Possible
43b	Late 4th/early 5th	Chersonisos	Stratigraphy?	Possible
126	Late 4th/early 5th	Olus	Architecture	Possible
91	Early 5th	Knossos KMF	Stylistically	Likely
88–90 (3)	Mid-5th	Knossos	Stylistically & stratigraphy	Likely
108	Mid-5th	Mitropolis	Architecture & stylistically	Likely
111–14 (4)	Mid-5th	Eleutherna	Stratigraphy & inscription	Likely
105	Late 5th	Lyttos	Architecture	Possible
148–51 (4)	Late 5th	Almyrida	Stylistically	Likely
92–3 (2)	Late 5th/early 6th	Chersonisos	Architecture & stylistically	Possible
94–100 (7)	Late 5th/early 6th	Chersonisos	Architecture & stylistically	Possible
109	Late 5th/early 6th	Gortyn, Sector M	Stratigraphy & inscription	Possible
122–5 (4)	Late 5th/early 6th	Kera	Stylistically & stratigraphy	Likely

Mosaic No.	Proposed Date	Area	Method of Dating	Degree of Confidence
127	Late 5th/early 6th	Kolokythia	Stylistically	Possible
147	Late 5th/early 6th	Tarrha	Stylistically & architecture	Likely
153	Late 5th/early 6th	Meskla	Architecture	Possible
154	Late 5th/early 6th	Kantanos	Architecture	Possible
161–2 (2)	Early 6th	Episkopi	Stylistically & architecture	Likely
102–3 (2)	Mid-6th	Mallia	Architecture	Possible
156–8 (3)	Mid-6th	Suia	Stylistically & architecture	Likely

Table A3.2. Mosaics with Wide Date Range

Mosaic No.	Proposed Date	Area	Method of Dating	Degree of Confidence
28	Late 1st C.E.	Knossos	Stratigraphy	Likely
66	Hellenistic	Lebena	Stylistically & stratigraphy	Sure
76	Hellenistic	Lato	Stylistically & stratigraphy	Likely
142	Hellenistic	Phalasarna	Stylistically & stratigraphy	Likely
77–9 (3)	Hellenistic/E. Roman	Makrigialos	Stylistically	Likely
67	Hellenistic/E. Roman	Lebena	Stylistically	Possible
45	1st C.E.	Chersonisos	Stratigraphy? Stylistically	Possible
64	1st C.E.	Gortyn	Stylistically & materials?	Possible
137	1st C.E.	Lissos	Stratigraphy?	Likely
49	2nd C.E.	Chersonisos	Stratigraphy	Likely
29	Pre-2nd or pre–mid-3rd	Knossos	Stratigraphic	Possible
41	3rd	Chersonisos	Stylistically & stratigraphy	Possible
52	3rd	Inatos	Stylistically & stratigraphy	Possible
70	3rd	Vizari	Stylistically	Possible
73	3rd	Lappa	Stylistically & stratigraphy	Possible
42	4th	Chersonisos	Stylistically & stratigraphy	Possible
44	Late Antique?	Chersonisos	Stratigraphy?	Possible
116–17(2)	5th	Sybrita	Stratigraphy & stylistically	Possible
155	6th	Elyros	Stylistically	Possible

Note: No proposed dates: Mosaic nos. 16, 18, 20, 21, 22, 23, 24, 26, 30, 31, 46, 48, 51, 61, 62, 65, 68, 69, 71, 74, 75, 81, 82, 83, 85, 86, 87, 101, 104, 106, 107, 110, 115, 118, 119, 120, 121, 128, 130, 131, 138, 143, 144, 145, 146, 152, 159, 160, 163.

@@ @@ @@ @@

APPENDIX 4

GAZETTEER OF ROMAN AND LATE ANTIQUE ARCHAEOLOGICAL DISCOVERIES IN CRETE SINCE 1980

The sites are listed alphabetically to expedite contextualization of the material. In each entry, the material is discussed by type, and for the larger sites by date of publication. The analysis of the material starts from the 1980 publication of *AR*. This date allows an update of Sanders's gazetteer of sites published in 1982.

Agia Galini

Two domestic complexes of seventh-century date were excavated (*AR* 1989–90, 77).

Agia Photini

New Roman remains were discovered at Agia Photini (Armari) where first-century B.C.E to third-century houses were excavated (*AR* 1994–5, 71 & *AR* 1996–7, 118). Finds included metal and ceramic material. Later, another possible Roman burial was revealed (*AR* 1997–8, 120).

Agios Nikolaos

Rescue excavations have been revealing the remains of what must have been quite a flourishing town. Roman tombs and cemeteries, houses and other occupation evidence have been uncovered (*AR* 1984–5, 64 & *AR* 2002–3, 83). The cemetery at Potamou is discussed below. In the suburban areas of Merambellos and Stavros, Roman cemeteries revealed a range of burial types including cist graves and tile roof-shaped huts (*AR* 1997–8, 117 & *AR* 1998–9, 122). In Kitroplateia area, known Hellenistic and Roman occupation was further extended with the excavation of a first-century Roman house with a hearth and a paved floor. Two more houses were excavated at Mylos (*AR*

1990–1, 70). At Kastelli, a large Roman complex of 15 rooms and two building phases was found. Although the complex was poorly preserved, finds included loom weights, animal bone and pottery from the first to the fifth centuries (*AR* 1991–2, 64).

Alpha (Milopotamos)

Excavations of a bath house furthered the evidence since Sanders (163) identified the cave site (*AR* 1997–8, 123) for the Late Antique occupation of Alpha.

Amphimalla (Georgioupolis)

Sanders (168) had recorded the site of Amphimalla (Georgioupolis) but noted few visible remains. Since then, a third-century domestic building has been excavated (*AR* 1997–8, 126).

Aptera

A systematic programme of excavation, study conservation and presentation has been undertaken at Aptera. The Hellenistic walls were examined and shown to have Roman repairs (*AR* 1995–6, 47). First- to second-century tombs around the site and in the area of Plakalona were investigated, some of which were robbed in Late Antiquity (*AR* 1999–2000, 147 & *AR* 2005–6, 111). It was established that the West Cemetery was in use for most of the occupation of the site (*AR* 2006–7, 117). Parts of a Roman and Late Antique building, as well as a peristyle house, have been excavated (*AR* 1997–8, 121, *AR* 1999–2000, 147 & *AR* 2006–7, 117, respectively). A heroon was uncovered with a series of pillar bases bearing inscriptions which date between the first and second centuries. These may represent reuse or continuation of use of a hero cult shrine. Funerary monuments were also association with the heroon (*AR* 2002–3, 85 & *AR* 2005–6, 111). A first-century temple to Demeter and Persephone was excavated, and baths and cisterns have also been investigated (*AR* 2006–7, 117).

Asimi

North of Asimi, a Roman building was identified, adding to the already known sculpture and sherds (*AR* 2003–4, 83 & Sanders, 150).

Atherinolakkos (Siteia)

A harbour was identified by the finds of a Roman anchor and amphora fragments (*AR* 2000–1, 133).

Axos

The public centre of Axos was tentatively identified, as was a cemetery including tile graves (*AR* 1983–4, 67). Other mortuary remains were found, including a grave which contained a Knossian coin bearing the names Claudius and Messalina (*AR* 1990–1, 77; *AR* 1996–7, 119 & *AR* 2002–3, 85).

Bali

Bali was identified as Astale, the harbour of Axos, and investigations into the Roman storage areas were begun (*AR* 1989–90, 78).

Boutas

A new Roman settlement and cemetery, Daphnes, was identified at Boutas in 1987 (*AR* 1993–4, 84).

Chania

Extensive mortuary and domestic remains have been revealed during rescue excavations in addition to some evidence for civic areas, industries and leisure (Fig. 14).

Mortuary: The majority of the mortuary remains are found around the edge of the urban space, but a few are found within, for example, some from the first and second centuries (*AR* 1994–5, 72). Many of the cemeteries provide a wide diachronic range of use (particularly the Classical cemetery, which contains Roman-built chamber tombs as well as evidence for Late Antique cross-shaped and peribolos burials) (*AR* 2002–3, 86). The Hellenistic and Roman necropolis and a cemetery near the national stadium have been excavated (*AR* 1999–2000, 148–50 & *AR* 2005–6, 111). Other mortuary remains were found at Odos Konstantinopolis (*AR* 1993–4, 84), late second- to early third-century rock-cut tombs and tile burials at the Phortsakis Plot and a late Antique grave at Odos Ypsilandou (*AR* 1997–8, 123–4).

Domestic: Houses have been located at a range of different plots, and many of them have clear evidence for continuation of occupation from Hellenistic to Roman and from Roman to Late Antique. At Patriarchou Kyrillou, three successive phases of a wall, Roman to Late Antique, were identified and in the north there was a Roman house with a kitchen which included a pottery and a Π-shaped hearth (*AR* 1990–1, 77). Many of the houses found also contained mosaics (Kapetanakis Plot (Mosaic S201) (*AR* 1985–6, 96) and Mayrigiannakis Plot (Mosaic S204) (*AR* 2002–3, 86)). On Peridou, part of a Roman building with damaged mosaic floors (Mosaic S203) was found under a horizon containing Ottoman burials (*AR* 1987–8, 75; *AR* 2004–5, 117 & *AR* 2006–7, 117). Some large Roman houses were found, including one at Odos Venizelou and Archondakis junction which had a mosaic floor (Mosaic S205)(*AR* 2006–7, 119). Late Antique material has also been uncovered (e.g., from the Peridou Plot a late fourth-century coin came from the substructure of a paved floor (*AR* 1987–8, 75)). On Boniali, part of the paved courtyard of a Roman complex was found in addition to a fourth-century complex, but its precise function is unclear (*AR* 1987–8, 75 & *AR* 1994–5, 72, respectively).

Public: Evidence for the Hellenistic and Roman agora has been found in part identified by its stoas, rooms and fluted columns (*AR* 1994–5, 72 & *AR* 1995–6, 47).

Baths: A few bath houses were discovered near the Agora, but one seems to have gone out of use in the second century when the Agora was constructed (*AR* 1994–5, 72). Baths ranging in date from the first century to the Late Antique period have been excavated (*AR* 1994–5, 72 & *AR* 1993–4, 84, respectively).

Industrial: Late Antique and Ottoman graves were located over Roman walls and a workshop (Hellenistic) (*AR* 1995–6, 47). Industrial features in the same area were composed of walls and a circular cistern. At Odos Dimokratias, Roman building remains with rubbish pits were found (*AR* 2003–4, 90). Remains of pottery kilns of the first to second centuries contained amphora type AC1a. Such a type has been found in other Cretan sites such as Kastelli, Eleutherna, and Knossos and this suggests that it was used for trading local wine (*AR* 2006–7, 117–18, fig. 139).

Chersonisos

Pockets of the Roman and Late Antique town have been revealed during rescue excavations (Fig. 16).

Mortuary: Excavations in 1985 continued work in the Roman cemetery. Inscriptions indicated that it was a family burial plot (*AR* 1983–4, 60). A square funerary building was located to the east. Three Late Antique box-like tombs were excavated in another area (*AR* 2006–7, 104–5).

Domestic: Four different excavation plots revealed the remains of Roman buildings, some with paved floors and mosaics (*AR* 2000–1, 126) (Mosaics 47 & 48) and also in the Perakis-Papadakis Plot (*AR* 1991–2, 59). Continuation of occupation is seen in some excavations; for example, at the Aspetakis Plot a Hellenistic house with Roman phase was revealed in the area of the presumed Agora. In the south of the plot, a Roman street was uncovered (*AR* 1996–7, 103). At the Sanoudakis Plot, remains of the hypocaust of a bath and also of a Roman road were excavated (*AR* 1997–8, 112).

Late Antique buildings have been revealed in the area of the Creta Maris Hotel and the Kypriotakis Plot (Mosaic 42) as well as a large complex with a good water system (*AR* 1991–2, 59 & *AR* 1992–3, 67). Two further Late Antique buildings were identified at the Sfakianakis (Mosaic 46), Velgerakis-Aspetakis and Mountrakis Plots (*AR* 1997–8, 112 & *AR* 1999–2000, 128–9).

Industrial: A Late Antique potter's workshop, with a late first- to second-century phase, was identified by concentrations of pottery at the Drakopoulou Plot near the theatre (*AR* 1994–95, 60). Storage areas with pithoi and loom-weights indicating workshops were investigated in 1986 (*AR* 1992–3, 67). At the Apostolaki Plot, a large second-century cistern, part of the Roman aqueduct, with vaulted openings was destroyed in the fourth century (*AR* 1999–2000, 128; *AR* 2000–1, 104). A harbour installation was excavated at the Navarchos Nearchos road with a range of associated small finds (*AR* 2006–7, 105).

Public: Extensive excavations throughout the theatre have now taken place, and in one trench first-century material was discovered in the lowest layer (*AR* 1992–3, 67). Other public areas have been revealed in the Apostolaki Plot which may be a Roman temple (*AR* 2006–7, 104–5) with a marble statue of Trajan (*AR* 2000–1, 126). A religious building (possibly a church) was discovered at the Papadakis Plot (*AR* 1998–9, 113 & *AR* 2000–1, 126).

Eleutherna

Extensive work at Eleutherna has revealed a large section of the Roman and Late Antique town (in addition to the early Geometric-Hellenistic material). Roman roads and buildings are known from the hilltop (Prinas) as well as both the east and west flanks of the hill (*AR* 1987–8, 66; *AR* 1988–9, 98–9). Many of the Roman buildings had earlier Hellenistic occupation and some continued into the Late Antique period. On the west side, the early phase of excavations brought to light a Roman building of two phases, second and third centuries. It seems to have been abandoned in 365 after the earthquake. On the east side, the extensive remains of the Christian basilica were excavated (fifth–seventh centuries) with a house occupied from the third to fourth centuries (*AR* 1989–90, 98–9; *AR* 1994–5, 72–3). The mosaic floor came from an upper-storey room (Mosaic 115). The baths to the north of the Roman houses have now been excavated. There is evidence for a Christian community at Eleutherna in the third century (inscribed lintel Νείκην τῶν Κυρείων). The basilica has an earlier predecessor (*AR* 1997–8, 124). Late Antique use of the quarry was identified on the west side of the hill (ibid.).

A Roman lock found in the pottery store of the small Roman bath house (which had collapsed in the 365 earthquake) was studied. The excavators compared it to the Antikythera mechanism (*AR* 2007–8, 111).

Elounda

Although the Late Antique material was quite well known, recently the Roman city is coming to light. Mortuary remains including a fourth-century tomb, a tile grave (*AR* 1985–6, 92) and a cemetery with two inscribed grave stelae were excavated (*AR* 1990–1, 70). Mixtures of grave types, including shaft graves, dating to the first and second centuries have been revealed (*AR* 1998–9, 119; *AR* 2000–1, 133; *AR* 2004–5, 106). A domestic complex, which lay partly in the sea, was excavated to reveal hearths, a paved floor and a circular building with an oven (*AR* 1990–1, 70).

Epanochori Selinou

A second- to third-century Roman tomb with grave goods including a gold ring was excavated (*AR* 1984–5, 67). The nearby shrine also was used in the Hellenistic and Roman periods (*AR* 1987–8, 76; *AR* 1993–4, 84).

Fodele

Excavations revealed that the Church of the Panagia was constructed on an earlier Late Antique church (*AR* 2006–7, 109).

Galatas

The survey showed that Roman settlement was originally in small nucleated clusters and that in the third century small farmsteads were established (*AR* 2006–7, 107 & *AR* 2007–8, 104–5).

Gavdos

Primary historical occupation was during the Hellenistic, Late Antique and Byzantine periods. A Hellenistic or Roman farmstead with an olive press was investigated in more detail (*AR* 2000–1, 141).

Gazi (Suburb of Agios Nikolaos)

Round rock cuttings were investigated and may be storage facilities which were in use from the Minoan to the Roman and possibly to the Late Antique period (*AR* 2008–9, 97).

Gortyn

In the last 30 years much of the work in the city has been focused on the phasing and functions of the areas of the gymnasium (previously known as the praetorium (*AR* 1998–9, 113) (Fig. 7), the Byzantine quarter and the basilica in Sector M (Fig. 13).

Gymnasium: Phases from the first to the eighth century were clarified in the area of the gymnasium. The earliest building was found at the south end of the stoa. Following serious destruction in the second half of the first century the central section was turned into baths. The last restoration of the basilica was made by Heraclius (*AR* 1993–4, 73–4). After the 668 earthquake, the area was taken over by private citizens with houses and oil presses, and the community came to an end in the eighth century (*AR* 1990–1, 68 & *AR* 1993–4, 73–4). Various alterations were undertaken of the gymnasium baths, which were originally a Trajanic addition (*AR* 1998–9, 113 & *AR* 1989–90, 71). After the 365 earthquake, a law court was established in the NW corner of the baths (ibid.), which were abandoned in the late sixth to early seventh century (*AR* 1991–2, 59). Later excavations identified a lavatory (*AR* 1992–3, 65).

Work on the monumental north side of the gymnasium showed that the Hellenistic temple became a public building in the seventh century and then the site of a manufacturing centre in the eighth century (*AR* 2007–8, 105–10). The nymphaeum beside it had a number of phases, including additions in the second and third centuries. At the end of the first century a monumental hall was constructed between the nymphaeum and the temple (*AR* 2008–9, 91–3).

It was clarified that the dromos of the stadium was rebuilt in the Roman period (*AR* 1998–9,113), that part of the gymnasium rested on an earlier wall of the stadium and that stairs linked the two buildings (*AR* 1999–2000, 130).

The road around the gymnasium was dated to the first century (*AR* 1985–6, 89), and further clarification of the network continued (*AR* 1989–90, 71 & *AR* 2003–4, 82).

Temple of Augusti: The Temple of Deified Augustus became part of the original gymnasium in the time of Marcus Aurelius (*AR* 1993–4, 73–4; *AR* 1997–8, 112–4; *AR* 2005–6, 109). Some re-working of it was undertaken, possibly after the 365 earthquake (*AR* 1997–8, 112–14). But the temple clearly continued in use even once the city had been Christianized (*AR* 1999–2000, 130). By the Late Antique period the temple had gone out of use, as tombs and houses (seventh–eighth century) overlay part of it (*AR* 1998–9,113). The altar was dedicated by Tiberius, and excavators suggested that it was used for night-time rites (*AR* 1999–2000, 130). Later, the temple was identified as one to the Egyptian gods rather than to the Augusti, on the basis of the find of a crocodile-headed spout (*AR* 1997–8, 112–14).

Mortuary: At the Mesara Agricultural Research Station part of the Greco-Roman cemetery of Gortyn was investigated. Finds included a jasper ringstone carved with the head of Livy. First- and second-century lamps were also found (*AR* 1981–2, 56–7). Late Antique graves were uncovered in the Roman cemetery, which was defined by its use of hut tombs, south of Mitropolis (*AR* 1991–2, 59). Under the basilica in Sector M, graves of Imperial date were excavated (*AR* 2000–1, 128). In the Agii Deka area, a Roman sarcophagus was found (*AR* 1982–3, 59) and excavations uncovered nine burials: shaft graves, tile graves with single inhumations and one collective burial. Most had been robbed. The intact shaft grave contained jewellery dating to the first–second century. A mausoleum containing first-century material was also excavated (*AR* 1996–7, 103–5).

Domestic: A geophysical survey revealed evidence of Late Roman and Byzantine settlement (*AR* 2001–2, 106). Several areas of houses have been uncovered in the area between the gymnasium and the Temple of Apollo Pythios (the Byzantine quarter), including a multi-period house (fourth, sixth and seventh centuries) (*AR* 1983–4, 62–3;*AR* 1984–5, 61 & *AR* 1988–9, 99). Another area of excavation revealed five phases of occupation from the fifth century, and a potter's kiln was found associated with the latest phase (seventh century). Industrial areas (*AR* 1986–7, 56) and the street network were also revealed (*AR* 1987–8, 66). Sixth- and seventh-century houses were excavated, including a structure which may be a kitchen with ovens and a raised hearth (*AR* 2002–3, 80).

Evidence of significant Justinianic alterations and a final destruction date of 670 were seen in a range of houses (*AR* 1987–8, 66; *AR* 2003–4, 82). The excavators postulated a greater focus on independent rural living and seasonal work in the city, in part because of the reduction in the size of the buildings (*AR* 2005–6, 109). The area was then occupied with burials until the first half of the ninth century (*AR* 2002–3, 80).

Building S: A large multi-phased public building was excavated in the north-west of the area (Building S) (*AR* 2004–5, 113). The main space connected to a series of rooms on the north side. In the second phase (mid-seventh century) the space was downsized, and it may have become a residence. The public building comprised a monumental entrance hall (paved) (Room 52a & 52b) which faced onto the street. A series of rooms led off this hall and gave indirect access to the central room (Room 53). Upper levels were indicated by the remains of collapsed flooring of irregular polychrome marble tiles. Later work revealed the plastered walls and the drainage system (*AR* 2007–8, 105–10, see also plan P107). The area was used in the Venetian period (*AR* 2008–9, 91–3).

Monumental Building at the Pythian Temple: Another monumental building (see plan *AR* 2008–9, 92) built in the sixth/seventh century was excavated in front of the Temple of Pythian Apollo (there may have also been a second- to third-century phase (*AR* 2008–9, 91–3)). The role of the building was uncertain, but the structure maintained a central location in the street network and had wall painting and paved floors (*AR* 2007–8, 106). Several phases of reorganiza-tion of the interior were identified, and it was postulated that the round interior may have been used as a bath building and that the numerous lamps, amphorae jars and necks set into the ground and the burnt animal bone may represent a workshop of some sort (*AR* 2007–8, 106 & *AR* 2008–9, 91–3). There was no trace of collapse, but the building may have been in use in second to third centuries.

Further houses of this period were investigated north of the gymnasium (*AR* 1987–8, 66), in the Odeon/Agora area and West Street (*AR* 2004–5, 112) and in the area of the Pythian Theatre (*AR* 2001–2). Here evidence of a pebble road and its consolidation in the Justinianic period were found.

Aqueduct, Baths, Water, Theatre, Industry: Excavations were undertaken at a number of points around the city, including the hippodrome (*AR* 1986–7, 56). Two reliefs probably dating to the fourth restoration of the baths were found (ibid.). A potters' kiln which produced unusual material was investigated (ibid.).

Work on the Pythian Theatre is ongoing and focused on the clarification of the building, exposing and consolidating it (*AR* 1994–5, 60 & *AR* 2008–9, 92). Excavations here indicated that the building collapsed sometime between the sixth century and the seventh when Gortyn suffered a series of at least three earthquakes (*AR* 2002–3, 80). Further work was undertaken (*AR* 2003–4, 82 & *AR* 2004–5, 113). Many sculptures were found, particularly in the fourth-century destruction debris, including one identified as a Hera Borghese type and one as a Velletri type, the latter identified as Athena by the helmeted head (*AR* 2005–6, 109).

Apsidal Building (Baths South of the Gymnasium): An apsidal building orientated east–west was excavated to the south of the gymnasium. Initial excavations revealed a fourth-century building which had collapsed and was then reused in the seventh century. The apsidal room (*AR* 2004–5, 113) turned out to be a bathroom thereby showing a new bath house. Part of the Byzantine aqueduct was built on this destruction (*AR* 2003–4, 82). Later investigations showed evidence for a second-century reconstruction. The *frigidarium* contained polychrome marble-lined basins. The *caldarium* was not well exposed (*AR* 2007–8, 105–10).

A study of Gortyn's water supply showed that the second century is the earliest certain evidence for the aqueduct. Two aqueducts directed flow to Gortyn and also the Acropolis. Water was distributed across the city through an underground system. Pipes also connected the nymphaeum with the baths. The aqueduct was destroyed in the fourth century and out of use by the fifth. The Byzantine system (late sixth to seventh century) is best understood where the underground pipes were replaced by overground cisterns/fountains (*AR* 2007–8, 105–10).

Acropolis: Work on the Acropolis area focused on the pre-Roman material but did show that many of the buildings were abandoned in the Late Antique period (*AR* 2008–9, 91–3).

Sector M: Joint excavations between the Ephorea and the Italian School were undertaken on the two-phased Late Antique basilica (Mosaic 109). Paved roads were identified on either side of the church (*AR* 1980–1, 42–3). Destruction and reconstruction levels have been identified from the seventh century, and later coins of the Venetian and Palaiologian periods have also been found in the apse (*AR* 1993–4, 73–4). Auxiliary rooms were identified by material dating to the fourth century, and it seems that these rooms were already linked to the apse in the first phase. On the south side of the altar the flooring was of *opus sectile* (*AR* 1993–4, 73–4). The extensive mosaics were consolidated (Mosaic 109) (*AR* 1999–2000, 130), and excavations below revealed a cemetery of Imperial date. One of the donor panels lay directly on top of a tomb (*AR* 2000–1, 128). Most recent work has focused on the baptistery in the building known as the Rotunda (*AR* 2007–8, 105–10).

Other Finds: A headless statue was found while excavators were digging a trench for OTE (the Greek telecommunications company) (*AR* 1983–4, 62–3), and a marble head of a bearded man dating to 150–200 was found by chance (*AR* 1985–6, 89).

Ierapetra

Part of the first- to second-century cemetery was excavated (62 graves) (*AR* 1998–9, 119). At Paramythas (Maliotakis Plot) a series of Roman tile graves were excavated revealing second- to third-century finds. Graves were also investigated at the Lyceum Plot (*AR* 2003–4, 88). Houses and industrial areas have been investigated. At the Pangalos Plot a second-century Roman build-ing with a paved floor was examined. Other buildings dating between the first and third centuries were noted, and at the Alykies site, Roman walls associ-ated with a floor with sections of mosaic were found (Mosaic 86) (*AR* 2002–3, 84). A building with the remains of hydraulic cement was likely to have had industrial use (*AR* 1982–3, 59). Remains of a paved street and associated water system were uncovered during the excavations of a Roman house. Also in the same area, a grave stele used as a base for votive offerings was found (*AR* 1984–5, 64). Other architecture may be related to the town's defences (*AR* 1987–8, 72 & *AR* 1985–6, 94, respectively). Finds of statues, a coin hoard dat-ing to the mid-third century and other industrial features have been revealed (*AR* 1988–9, 102).

Ini

Excavations reveal several buildings including an Episcopal basilica similar to that at Gortyn, a bath and an aqueduct (*AR* 2008–9, 90).

Iraklion

Because of the extensive urban nature of Iraklion, little of the ancient city is known. Some tombs have been excavated and a rubbish dump of the fifth–sixth century architectural pieces was cleared (*AR* 1987–8, 66 & *AR* 1989–90, 71–2). At Agios Ioannis, Apostolakis Plot, a square cistern may indicate an indus-trial installation (*AR* 2001–2, 107). The principal find has been the two-phased Papadakis Plot house with fine mosaic floors (now published) (Ioannidou-Karetsou et al. 2008) (Mosaics 32–37).

Istron

On the small island of Istron, a possible Late Antique or Byzantine monastery was identified (*AR* 2000–1, 134).

Itanos

Excavations on the Itanos necropolis dated the last phase to the first century (*AR* 1997–8, 118 & *AR* 2006–7, 96).

Kampanos

A Roman cist grave dating to the second–third century and a series of robbed Roman tombs were investigated (*AR* 1994–5, 73 & *AR* 1999–2000, 150).

Kantanos

A first- to second-century cist grave was found just southeast of Anisaraki (*AR* 1994–5, 73).

Karnari

A third- to fourth-century cist and tile graves were investigated (*AR* 1993–4, 74).

Kastelli Kisamos

Extensive rescue excavations have revealed substantial sections of the domestic and industrial sections of the city. In terms of public buildings, many bath houses have been excavated and the remains of the Agora with a theatre, stoa and Temple to Dionysus have been investigated. As with other cities in Crete, the Roman cemeteries are known from the suburbs of the town. Furthermore, the evidence of the Late Antique cemeteries is indicative of the change in urban space at this time (Fig. 15).

Mortuary: Several different types of graves and cemeteries have been excavated. Cemeteries have been found at the Kalogridakis Plot dating to the first century (AR 1987–8, 76) and at the Phantakis Plot (second to third century) (AR 1985–6, 96). In another area, vaulted tombs of the second to third century (AR 1989–90, 79–80) and cist graves of the first to second century (AR 1997–8, 126) were investigated.

A tomb on the Polyrrhenia road was investigated (*AR* 1988–9, 108), and at Pano Kamara, the Roman tombs along the main routeway and a Late Antique cemetery were studied (AR 2006–7, 120).

Late Antique cemeteries have been found on earlier Roman buildings (*AR* 1997–8, 126), such as at the Rokakis Plot, the Xerouchakis Plot (AR 2000–1, 141–2) and the Paterakis Plot (*AR* 2002–3, 87). A Late Antique grave mosaic was found during the excavations of the Raisakis Plot cemetery (Mosaic S218) (Diamandis 2004, 391).

Domestic: Roman houses with mosaics have been excavated at the plots of Stephanoudakis (Mosaic S206) (*AR* 1983–4, 68), Kakaournakis (Mosaic S210) (*AR* 1985–6, 96), Paterakis (Mosaic 141) (*AR* 1987–8, 76), Loupsake, Cathedral site and Triton Mosaic (Mosaic S213) (*AR* 1993–4, 84; *AR* 2006–7, 120), Nikolakis (Mosaic S214) (*AR* 2000–1, 141–2), Aligizakis (Mosaic S215) (*AR* 2000–1, 141–2), Skounakis (Mosaic S216) (Markoulaki et al. 2004, 366 & fig. 11) and Xirouchakis (Mosaic S217) (Andreadaki-Vlazaki 1999, 215–17).

At the Theodosakis Plot, a rare example of what appears to be a Late Antique secular mosaic in Crete was revealed (Mosaic S220) (Drosinou, 1994–6, 227).

Farangitakis Plot: A house with mosaic was excavated (Mosaic S209). Multiple phases from the second century were identified with a destruction in the fourth century. Tiled floors and walls were well preserved (*AR* 1990–1, 77; *AR* 1994–5, 73 & *AR* 1996–7, 122).

Raisakis Plot: A large suburban house was excavated at the Raisakis Plot; two of its seven rooms had mosaic floors (Mosaic S212), one of Orpheus and the other of the Wedding of Dionysus (*AR* 1996–7, 121–2). Two Roman and one late Antique building phases were identified. The latter had a semi-circular cistern associated with it. The final building had a hearth, drainage and a well. Part of a road and buildings on the other side of it were revealed (*AR* 1997–8, 126). The mosaics belonged to the earlier phase, and the Orpheus mosaic had a later floor on top of it (ibid.). Two *cubicula* with destroyed mosaic floors and another mosaic with a geometric frame and birds were uncovered in later excavations. Further work also revealed a luxury bath house. Part of the Christian cemetery was built on top of the house (*AR* 2006–7, 120).

Health Centre: Some 20 years of work was undertaken at the Health Centre on the domestic complex (*AR* 1986–7, 60) which became known as the House of Pheidias (*AR* 2006–7, 120) (Mosaic S207). While various excavations revealed industrial features such as kilns (*AR* 1994–5, 73 & *AR* 1994–5, 73), much of the work was focused on clarifying the phasing of the second and third centuries (*AR* 2006–7, 120), lifting and conserving the mosaics (*AR* 1996–7, 121–2) and identifying the evidence for the second storey, particularly the collapsed geometric mosaics (*AR* 1993–4, 84 & *AR* 2000–1, 141–2). Many of the rooms with mosaics did not reveal finds (ibid.), although coins, pottery and architectural fragments were found in others (*AR* 1993–4, 84). The bedding of mosaics from the upper and lower storeys was examined; the bedding from the former consisted of pebbles and plaster and also a 1 cm thick bed of lime with a mix of plaster and sherds below (*AR* 2000–1, 141–2). Further excavations revealed the remains of a kitchen and a private bath (*AR* 2002–3, 87). Overall, this huge complex, which lay along the east–west *decumanus*, was divided by a wall into the east and west wings. The east wing had a peristyle court with a *vivadarium* at the centre and bordered by a stoa (*AR* 2007–8, 112). There was also an auxiliary courtyard which connected to a cooking area (*AR* 2006–7, 120). The west had eight rooms with mosaics, discussed in Appendix 1 (S207). The second phase of the third century was a major extension to the house and showed significant re-modelling with lots of cross walls added to create more rooms and accommodate more people. Some of the mosaic floors were covered by earth floors. The house was destroyed in the 365 earthquake; two bodies were found as part of the destruction (*AR* 2007–8, 112).

Paterakis Plot (Not the Seasons Mosaics): A house which shows occupation from the first century to the fourth was uncovered; in its final phase, there was a workshop installation including kilns and iron slag (AR 1997–8, 126 & AR 2002–3, 87). During the Late Antique period this area became a cemetery (AR 2004–5, 118).

Other houses excavated revealed long occupation, such as that on Plateia Venizeliou with a mid-third-century and Late Antique phase (*AR* 1990–1, 77). Here kitchen vessels, some of them bronze, were found. The Stavroulake Plot house had first and fifth century phases (*AR* 1994–5, 73); at the Plevrakis Plot phases dating to the third, fourth and fifth centuries were identified (*AR* 1997–8, 126) and at the Petromichelakis Plot a Roman paved floor was replaced by a Late Antique earthen floor (*AR* 2000–1, 141–2). Additional houses included those excavated at the plots of Koursounakes, where pottery and frescos were found, and of Skounakis, which had nine pithoi in a row and was destroyed in the third century (*AR* 1990–1, 77). At Plateia Tzanakake walls of a room with an earth-and-pebble floor as well as a piece of plaster dated to the Greco-Roman period were found (*AR* 1994–5, 73). At the Sophoulaki Plot two Roman houses were found (*AR* 1995–6, 47). Near the east road, houses from the second to fourth century were uncovered. A beaten earth floor and architectural fragments were associated (*AR* 1996–7, 121–2).

Baths: A series of baths have been found at various plots including the Apostolakis Plot, which was in use between the first and fifth centuries (AR 1987–8, 76), and a fourth-century example at the Hartzoulakis Plot, which also had the matrices of mosaic floors preserved (Mosaic S208) (*AR* 1987–8, 76). During some rescue excavations in advance of work on the sewage system, parts of two bath houses were revealed, one of the second to fourth century and the other the second to third century (*AR* 1994–5, 73). In the east of the town another excavation exposed what are believed to be the auxiliary rooms of a second- to third-century bath house (*AR* 1996–7, 121–2).

Industrial: At various points throughout the town Roman and Late Antique industrial features have been identified. A long cistern was investigated (*AR* 1989–90, 79–80), and at Vardandanis Street a well-constructed drain was found (*AR* 2002–3, 87) and another workshop containing fine moulds was revealed (*AR* 1999–2000, 150), but their functions were not identified. In other areas, cisterns were identified with metallurgical work (*AR* 1997–8, 126). In the Stratake/ Skoulake Plot a circular structure divided into rooms seemed to be a workshop for glass and faience (*AR* 1993–4, 84). A Late Antique kiln was also revealed during the rescue excavations of the Theodosakis Plot (*AR* 1997–8, 126 & *AR* 2007–8, 112). At the Moraitakis Plot a poorly dated 'Late Roman' watermill was found (*AR* 2000–1, 141–2).

Roads: A portion of the Roman thoroughfare was excavated in the western part of the town. The road (3 m wide) was flagged and had wheel ruts and likely dates between the second and third centuries.

Public Buildings: Other than baths, public buildings are well known from the city, but a large Roman building, possibly public with a central court, was discovered at the Mylonaki Plot and late third- to fourth-century coins were associated (*AR* 1987–8, 76). The first physical evidence for a Late Antique church was revealed near to Museum Square. A mosaic (S219) was also associated (Markoulaki, Christodoulakos & Fragkonikolaki 2004, 373 n. 68).

Other buildings have been found without definite attributions but are likely houses from the plots of Kouphakis-Kalaphatakis (*AR* 1988–9, 108), Apostalakis (ibid.), Kouphake (*AR* 1994–5, 73), Stimadoraki (*AR* 2002–3, 87), Koitsounakis (ibid.) and Fotakis-Chairetakis (ibid.). In the Fotakis-Chairetakis Plot, remains of five architectural phases were found; the best preserved was mid-third to mid-fourth century. The basement was excavated, and the two skeletons found there were probably of individuals killed during the 365 earthquake (ibid.).

Kato Syme

Ongoing work on the Sanctuary of Hermes and Aphrodite revealed Roman phases (*AR* 1991–2, 59).

Knossos

Rescue and some research excavations have brought to light pockets of evidence of the Roman town. A recent study (Sweetman 2010b) has published many of the rescue excavations from the 1970s and 1980s undertaken in the valley (Fig. 12).

Graves: Cemeteries and graves have been identified around the edges of the city. In the north cemetery, four tombs with material dating from eighth century B.C.E. to Roman times (*AR* 1981–2, 51–4), a mausoleum unique to Knossos (*AR* 1989–90, 72) and Augustan Roman tile graves (*AR* 1985–6, 85) were excavated.

The Boboris and Skoulas Plots, also in the north, contained cist and tile graves (*AR* 1996–7, 106 & *AR* 1997–8, 114).

More recent excavations at the Venizelio Hospital have revealed a Roman mausoleum (*AR* 1998–9, 115), pit and cist graves and a built grave with vaulted roof containing gold jewellery and silver pyxis (*AR* 1996–7, 105). A large first-century Roman house tomb with the inscriptions CLUATIUS and CLUATIUS C.f.CONINUS was found (*AR* 2003–4, 77).

Three built tombs (Roman) were found in the location of Monastiraki Kephala (*KS* 168). One tomb (T23) had compartments which were enclosed with tiles, and another tomb had a central elliptical pit. These tombs date to the first–second century (coins), and a third (T7) dates to the Late Antique period (*AR* 1996–7, 105). Also in this area at the Sevastakis Plot, a cist grave with Roman–Late Antique material was excavated (*AR* 1996–7, 106).

At Ambelokipi, Roman tombs were excavated (*AR* 2002–3, 77).

To the south, at Spilia, remains of a Roman tomb with glass, coins and lamps dating to the first century were found (*AR* 1983–4, 61). The Knossos Urban Landscape Project identified Roman rock-cut tombs and mausolea around the valley (*AR* 2007–8, 100).

Houses: Sections of houses have been investigated. Many are without date, such as that in the Vlachakis Plot in Bougada Metochi, where a bronze miniature of Artemis was also found (*AR* 1999–2000, 133–4). Another area of houses had evidence for a first-century destruction (AR 1998–9, 115). At the Kamaritis Plot (*AR* 2002–3, 77) excavations of Roman buildings 100 m to the east of the Villa Dionysus revealed a paved road and drain dating from the second to third century. Other remains may not be so coherent; for example, during the Venizelio excavations part of a Roman wall and a statue of a herm were found (*AR* 1999–2000, 133–4). New excavations at the Little Palace North revealed part of the Roman road and a two-phased house with second-century robber pits (*AR* 2002–3, 77 & *AR* 2006–7, 108).

Houses with Industrial Features: In the Venizelio area a Roman cistern, kilns, a large Roman building and Roman houses were revealed (*AR* 2001–2, 107). At Bougada Metochi a poorly preserved potter's workshop was identified by the clay potter's wheel, plastered pit, clay stands and unbaked pottery. Pottery dating from first century B.C.E. to the first century included amphora, cooking pots, Eastern sigillata B, local pottery imitating terra sigillata A and N Italian Grey ware (*AR* 2002–3, 77).

Baths: The Knossos 2000 excavations focused on three separate areas, two of which likely are bath houses dating between the second and third centuries. One area, containing Mosaic 10, is probably part of a major two-storey building. The other, containing Mosaic 12, is a complex of six rooms with a cistern and a hypo-caust. New buildings with a similar alignment were constructed in the third to fourth century. In the third area, there were walls excavated which seem to be contemporary with the Villa Dionysus (*AR* 1993–4, 74–8 & *AR* 1995–6, 39–42).

Public Buildings: Geophysical survey may have shown up the plan of the Roman Civil Basilica below the surface level but it appears not on the same orientation as the Villa Dionysus (*AR* 1991–2, 59–60).

Kounavi

Ancient Eltyna (Eltynia). A Roman cemetery has been investigated consisting of slab-covered rock-cut tombs. Glass vessels and bronze pins were found (second century) (*AR* 1997–8, 116).

Kouphonisi

A number of buildings have been excavated exposing a considerable range of Roman occupation on the island. Work on the theatre was undertaken, as well as on the main settlement located some 200 m away (*AR* 1984–5, 65). Here, an eight-roomed house was uncovered which was destroyed at the end of the fourth century. Water pipes were also revealed (ibid.). Another large house (15 rooms) was also investigated, uncovering items such as lead fishing weights (*AR* 1988–9, 103). A bath house (Mosaic 83) was found to have been in use from the first to the fifth century (*AR* 1985–6, 95 & *AR* 1992–3, 73). A temple, located some 3 km from the theatre and settlement, was investigated (*AR* 1987–8, 72). Evidence for industrial activity in addition to fishing was found during excavations of a second B.C.E.–first C.E. house where nearby, evidence for the extraction of purple dye from shells and fishing was identified (*AR* 1990–1, 73).

Kritsa

A Roman hut-shaped tomb was discovered (*AR* 1999–2000, 142).

Lappa (Modern Argyroupolis)

Sections of the city's infrastructure as well as domestic remains including a bath house with mosaics have been excavated (Mosaic 73) (*AR* 1994–5, 71; *AR*

1997–8, 121; *AR* 1998–9, 123; *AR* 2000–1, 140). Third-century pottery and a cistern have been excavated (*AR* 1989–90, 77). Indications of a fourth-century destruction were noted at some plots (e.g., Bougioukalakis Plot (*AR* 1994–5, 71)). Work along the Mousellas River revealed the foundations of a large Roman public building (*AR* 2000–1, 141). More recent work has focused on the excavation of a Roman cemetery on the hillslope near Lappa (*AR* 2003–4, 91).

Lasaia

The harbour town (controlled by Gortyn) of Lasaia was recorded by Blackman and Branigan (1975, 28–32) and Sanders (160). Since then, it has been looted quite considerably and the architectural remains, such as the warehouses, graves, temple and basilica, are in a poor state.

Lato

Excavations are ongoing, and a topographic survey has recently been undertaken (*AR* 2006–7, 103).

Lebena

Parts of the Roman domestic quarters of the city were investigated to assess their relationship with the sanctuary. Excavations revealed a large Roman public (?) building, as well as continued occupation in the domestic quarter well into the Late Antique period (*AR* 1994–5, 63; *AR* 2001–2, 108).

Lissos

Work on the harbour area and tombs continued, and many new houses have also been uncovered. One hundred eighteen tombs are visible and mostly single vaulted, often with internal niches. Three examples of two-storied tombs were noted (*AR* 1997–8, 126–7).

Lyttos

During the 1980s excavations at Lyttos, areas of shops and workshops, a large building and a public building (possibly either a prytaneion or a bouleuterion) were revealed (*AR* 1983–4, 64–5). A Roman hut-shaped tomb and a Roman peribolos with inscriptions were excavated (*AR* 2003–4, 79). A dedication to Hadrian was found and taken away for safe keeping (*AR* 1989–90, 72). Epigraphic studies indicated that investment in local festivals continued until at least the late second or third century (*SEG* 1999 (49), 1245).

Makrigialos

Work by Papadakis on the Roman villa which had been identified by Pendlebury. The villa had more than 30 rooms and courtyards (*AR* 1987–8, 72).

Maleme

A Late Antique settlement was discovered (*AR* 1990–1, 77).

Mallia

The survey revealed that occupation in the area was revived from the fourth to sixth century after the Bronze Age use (*AR* 2006–7, 104).

Matala

Evidence for the Roman town at Matala has increased significantly in the last few decades with work on graves, on houses (some with frescos) and on a large complex which included industrial areas. Buildings close to the aqueduct contained Byzantine and Venetian phases, and the houses with the frescos also contained Late Antique phases (*AR* 1987–8, 70 & *AR* 1993–4, 79; *AR* 1993–4, 79). Burials in the caves have been investigated; some individuals appear to have been interred in the 'Late Roman' period, and a cemetery has also been excavated (*AR* 1989–90, 72 & *AR* 2004–5, 116, respectively).

Milatos

Some Roman pottery found (*AR* 2004–5, 106).

Minoa Akroteriou

A Late Antique rock-cut water tank lined with plaster was found by chance (*AR* 1985–6, 95).

Mournes

A Roman tomb was robbed (*AR* 2003–4, 92).

Mylopotamou

At Apladiana, a third-century cist grave was found (*AR* 1996–7, 118). At Alpha, Roman tombs and a Late Antique bath house were investigated (*AR* 1997–8, 121).

Nea Magnesia

Two Roman (fourth century) pit tombs cut into bedrock were excavated (*AR* 1997–8, 127 & *AR* 1998–9, 124).

Neos Kournas (Kavros)

A bath house dating from the first to fourth century was revealed (*AR* 2002–3, 87–8). Further investigation uncovered the remains of an earlier first-century building beneath. The biggest room had an earth floor and tesserae associated with it. An apse produced further plaster floors, mosaics and frescos (Mosaic 72) (*AR* 2006–7, 115).

Panagia Soumbalousa

A Roman tomb was found (*AR* 1999–2000, 140).

Pangalochori

Tombs in a Hellenistic and Roman cemetery were excavated (*AR* 2003–4, 91).

Panormou

Rescue excavations revealed mosaic fragments but little context is known (*AR* 2003–4, 92).

Patsos

At the cave site of Patsos, further investigations of the already identified sanctuary of Hermes provided more evidence for a Hellenistic and Roman date (*AR* 2002–3, 87).

Pediadha Survey

A new survey in the area should help increase our knowledge of the Roman occupation, as well as recording sites which may not survive because of looting or development (*AR* 2008–9, 97).

Pentevi

A Latin inscription naming Nero and the colony at Knossos was found at the site located between Knossos and Iraklion (*AR* 1983–4, 61).

Phaistos

A new survey was begun in the area around Phaistos Palace (*AR* 2007–8, 110).

Plakias

A chance discovery of a Roman bath may belong to the otherwise unidentified Roman town of Lamon (*AR* 1984–5, 67).

Polyrrhenia

Although parts of the Hellenistic city had been excavated, the only evidence of the Roman site had been the epigraphic record, until the investigation of a number of rock-cut houses that were in use in both the Hellenistic and Roman periods (Sanders, 172–3 & *AR* 1997–8, 127).

Potamou (Agios Nikolaos)

A Roman cemetery of the first century was excavated in 1978. A coin of Polyrrhenia with the head of Augustus inscribed Θεὸς Σεβαστὸς ἐπὶ Λάχητος and two coins of Caligula (*AR* 1985–6, 93) were found along with many bronzes and a theatre mask.

Priniatikos Pyrgos Trench II

Excavations took place of an ossuary from the Mid- or Late Byzantine period which may be associated with a church of the Late Antique or Mid-Byzantine period (*AR* 2008–9, 83–4).

Rodavani

A third-century tomb with a male and a female burial was discovered (*AR* 1986–7, 60).

Smarion

Work in the area of Tou Bakalou to Horaphi revealed a Roman farmhouse in which a probable wine press was discovered with storage areas (a room containing pithoi) (*AR* 1984–5, 59).

Sphakakia Pangalachori (Rethymnon)

A seaside house with mosaic floors was excavated (*AR* 1997–8, 128) (Mosaic 75). A cemetery was also located nearby (*AR* 1994–5, 74).

Stavromenos

A Roman bath complex with final use in the fifth century was excavated on the Daphnomele Plot (Mosaic 74) (*AR* 1994–5, 72). Two Roman cist tombs were investigated and a further seven near the beach (*AR* 1997–8, 128). Excavations of a Roman tiled roof tomb were undertaken at Viglia (*AR* 2000–1, 143 & *AR* 2003–4, 91).

Stylos

A rural settlement and some evidence for Roman occupation may represent a first-century farmstead (*AR* 2006–7, 117).

Timbaki

Antiquities looting damaged two Roman burials (*AR* 1999–2000, 140). Cist graves and Roman pottery were then excavated stratigraphically (*AR* 2004–5, 115).

Tsoutsouros (Inatos)

The site of Inatos had been identified but little had been excavated until recently when three 'late Roman' buildings and 25 tombs dating to the second century were discovered. Further excavations revealed 107 tombs, including shaft and hut graves, and later evidence for rock-cut tombs was revealed. It seems to have continued in use until the fourth century (*AR* 1999–2000, 140–1). More recently, a large eight-roomed Roman to Late Antique domestic (?) complex was excavated. It included the remains of Mosaic 52. Nearby, a Roman and Late Antique cemetery was investigated and traces of a Late Antique building were found in the Christakis-Pantelakis Plot (*AR* 2003–4, 80; *AR* 2004–5, 111).

Vasiliki

Two important Roman complexes were investigated at this primarily Minoan site. Initial suggestions were that they were linked with official buildings in Ierapetra, but this is a tenuous connection (*AR* 1992–3, 79–80).

Viannos

A single Roman grave was discovered (*AR* 1985–6, 88). Later, a monumental building associated with the Roman cemetery was dated numismatically to the third century (*AR* 1992–3, 67).

Viglia (Ierapetra)

An extensive cemetery was revealed in the suburbs of Ierapetra at Viglia as well as some damaged houses (*AR* 2000–1, 139). An early Roman apsidal structure with plastered walls was also investigated (*AR* 1992–3, 72). At the Kouper Plot, part of a Roman house was excavated, which included a large rectangular courtyard with three rooms and a circular cistern. Another plot (Lambrakes) revealed four other areas of a Roman building dating to the fourth century. At the Tzoubleka Plot, a Roman house with six rooms dating to the fourth–fifth century was excavated (*AR* 1990–1, 71). At the Maliotakis Plot, a badly preserved 'Late Roman' building revealed a mosaic floor with geometric and floral décor (Mosaic 87). The central panel was not well preserved but had an inscription ΕΙΣΙѠΝ (*AR* 2001–2, 112).

Vizari

At Ellenika, a Roman tomb with two burials was reported (*AR* 1989–90, 78).

Vryses

The shrine was investigated and some Roman material was discovered (*AR* 2006–7, 119–20).

Xerokambos

Rock-cut salt cuttings of Hellenistic-Roman date were investigated (*AR* 1987–8, 74). At Rotsai, a Roman cistern was excavated (*AR* 2001–2, 109).

Zaros

A Roman building at the north end of Lake Votomos was defined as part of the elaborate water system that went to Gortyn (*AR* 1993–4, 80).

NOTES

Preface

1 Florovsky 1969.
2 The mosaics of western Crete are being published by the archaeologist Stavroula Markoulaki and as such do not form part of the primary corpus here.

Chapter One. Introduction

1 Scholars broadly label the medieval period in the east 'Byzantine', but the term is problematic. Like 'Early Christian', it has many cultural connotations. It is commonly applied to varying time periods and is often tied to Eastern theological concepts. Because Crete came under the ecclesiastical jurisdiction, in succession, of both the West and the East, the term 'Byzantine' would be misleading. Given the time span under discussion, the need to be free of cultural connotations and the fact that Crete was tied to both the West and the East, the term 'Late Antique' is most appropriate.

2 Particularly with the work of the Italian School at Gortyn (regular publications in *ASAtene* and in the *Gortina* volumes (I–VI), published in the Monografie della Scuola Archeologica di Atene e delle Missioni Italiane in Oriente series); the excavations by Stavroula Markoulaki (Markoulaki 1983–Markoulaki 2002a & 2002b) and work by the British School at Knossos (regular publications in the *BSA* and also the BSA studies and BSA supplementary volume series).

3 For the trends in the growth of survey projects, see Alcock and Cherry (eds.) 2004, 1–9. See Moody, Nixon, Price and Rackham 1998, 87–95; see p. 88 for an overview of many of the field survey projects in Crete.

4 This trend really began with Sanders's 1982 publication *Roman Crete*. Scholars such as M. Baldwin Bowsky, J. Francis, G. Harrison, A. Kelly, S. Paton and R. Schneider have made significant contributions to the study of imperial Crete since Sanders.

5 When they do, the focus tends to be on craftspeople and workshop production.

6 Creeping determinism was first noted by the psychologist Baruch Fischhoff and has been defined by Florovsky 1969 as 'a bias which leads one to assume that a scenario could not have happened in any other way'. Closely related is the phenomenon of

hindsight bias, which is defined as 'the sense that grows upon us, in retrospect, that what has happened was actually inevitable' (Fischhoff 1975).

7   For definitions, see Section 1.8.

8   A similar issue exists for studies of Roman painting, although recently, scholars such as Leach (2004) are concentrating on the social implications of the art.

9   See Stark (1998, 2) for discussions on issues of style more generally.

10   Baxandall 1985, 58–62. In this chapter, rather than discussing influence, a more detailed approach to the evidence of contact between regions will be endeavoured.

11   Stark 1998, 6.

12   Becker and Kondoleon 2005.

13   See Sparkes 1996.

14   Scott 2000, 12.

15   Dunbabin 1999, 73.

16   Papaioannou 2007, 359–61.

17   Baldwin Bowsky 1994; 1995; 2001a; 2004a; 2004b.

18   Marx 1930, 170.

19   Ingold 1983, 16.

20   All dates are C.E. unless otherwise stated.

21   Cameron 1993, 7.

22   Sanders, 1–9. Tsougarakis (1987a) also provides an analysis of events with less of a focus on written evidence.

23   As also noted by Sonnabend 2004, 25–8.

24   Typically, sources such as Livy (xxxvii.60–xxxviii.39) note the Roman arbitration and issue of pirates (Diodorus Siculus xl.1).

25   Willetts (1965, 156) claims, 'When there was not open war there was only uneasy peace'. The perception continues; see, for example, Sonnabend 2004.

26   For example, Chaniotis 1996, 1999 and 2004; de Souza 1998 and 2000; Alcock 2002; Viviers 2004. There is no doubt that there were Cretan pirates; for example, a decree from Teos (Ionia) records an attack by pirates from Lato in the late third century B.C.E. (*SEG* 2003 (53), 1336 bis).

27   These numbers in bold refer to the mosaics in the catalogue (Appendix 1).

28   The Hellenistic periods at the sites of Aptera, Eleutherna, Gortyn, Knossos, Lato, Lyttos and Prinias have all been the focus of excavation (research or rescue) and/or archaeological survey (see *AR* for up-to-date reports). The 25th Ephorea of Prehistorical and Classical Antiquities are responsible for the excavations at Aptera, and work has been undertaken on three sections of the site of Eleutherna: (a) Katsivelos, (b) Pyrgi and Nissi hills and (c) Orthi Petra, by the Department of Archaeology and Art History of the University of Crete; see P. Themelis (2003). For the on-going work at Gortyn and Prinias, see the excavation publications of the Italian School 'Atti della Scuola' in *ASAtene* and Di Vita 1988 and 1991. For the Knossos material, see Hood and Smyth 1981. The excavations at Lato have been undertaken by the 24th Ephorea of Prehistoric and Classical Antiquities – see Apostolakou 2003 – and at Lyttos, excavations have been undertaken by G. Rethemiotakis of the Iraklion Archaeological Museum.

29   Westgate 2007, 423–57. Alcock's 2002 work provides an excellent account of some of the more contentious issues concerning Hellenistic Crete. More detailed discussion on Hellenistic Crete lies outside the scope of this work.

30   Chaniotis 2005, 109.

31   Westgate 2007, 423–57.

32   Chaniotis 2008, 85.

33   Ibid.

34 De Souza (1998, 113) suggests that the high standard of Cretan silver coins alone is a good indicator of its wealth at the time. As is well accepted, the civil wars in the Late Republic were a significant drain on Rome's resources. The rapid increase in land seizure at this time must have been in part to finance the civil wars and later the Mithridatic wars.

35 See note 8; for example, Livy xxxvi.60.

36 Livy, Ep. XCVII. For the effects of piracy see Rackham and Moody 1997, 197–9.

37 Sources for piracy: Livy, *Ep.* XCVII; Diod. Sic. XL.I; Ps. Ascon, p. 176; Dio Fr.11; Florus 3.7.

38 Livy xxxvii.60.

39 Dio 36.

40 Paton 1994, 142, and Sanders, 14. Baldwin Bowsky (2002, 24) notes that it is possible that Gortyn became the capital because of its support for Octavian whereas Knossos was punished for taking the side of Antony.

41 2001b.

42 Later to become a senatorial province. The joint administration of the two areas is likely to reflect a practical arrangement, perhaps to better control the valuable trade routes between Crete and North Africa.

43 Sanders, 6. Tsougkaraki 1987a, 290.

44 Markoulaki et al. 2004, 357.

45 For a concise summary of Roman administration in Crete, see Sanders, 6–10.

46 See Pautasso 1994–5 (93–102) for an up-to-date list of provincial governors and their recorded activities concerning Crete and Cyrene (75–92).

47 Sanders, 6.

48 Ibid. 7.

49 Sonnabend 2004, 27. Tsougkarakis 1987a, 295. See Baldwin Bowsky, especially 2004a and 2004b, and for commercial connections behind many of the names, see Baldwin Bowsky 2002, 41.

50 Sanders, 5. For a slightly different view, see Baldwin Bowsky 2002, 26.

51 Spyridakis (1999, 68) points out that the fourth–fifth-century inscription which includes a reference to the presbyters and the scholar Theoctistus marks the presence of a Christian community there.

52 *AR* 1998, 124, mentions an inscribed lintel (Νείκην τῶν Κυρείων) from a house which indicates the presence of a third-century Christian community.

53 Eusebius (*Historia Ecclesiastica*) records the presence of a Christian community in Knossos in the second century (discussed by Paton 1994, 148).

54 Tsougarakis 1988, 21.

55 Titus, 1 v. cited in Detorakis 1994, 106. The ten martyred near Gortyn were part of Diocletian's persecutions in 250–1.

56 See earlier for references to the excavation reports from these cities. It should be noted that recent rescue excavations in Chersonisos have revealed fourth-century domestic mosaic floors (Chaniotaki-Starida & Marni 2004, 287–300). Increasingly, there is evidence for Late Antique houses in Eleutherna (Themelis 2002, 275–92); in Rethymnon (Andreadaki-Vlazaki 2000–1b, 279); in Ierapetra (Apostolakou 2002b, 336–42); and in Itanos (*AR* 1997–8, 118) but not necessarily with mosaic floors.

57 Spyridakis 1999, 68.

58 Ibid. 70.

59 Sanders, 6.

60 Tsougarakis 1988, 155.

61 Ibid. 198.

62 Procopius *De Bello Vandalico* v. 23.

63 Sanders, 9.

64 For the topography and environment of Crete, see Rackham and Moody 1997.

65 For example, see Rackham and Moody 1997, 197–9. Additionally, they argue that Crete's landscape has not in fact changed dramatically in two millennia.

66 See Westgate (2007, 423–57) for a fresh study of the Hellenistic houses. For rescue material, see, for example, the five-room house found on Odos Tzanakakis (Chania Andreadaki-Vlazaki 2002, 234–41; 237).

67 Sanders, 30. The survey in the Vrokastro region has shown well the nature of Roman settlement in a fertile region. Hayden 2004b.

68 Sanders, 16–31. See also details from the recent Mesara survey in Watrous et al. 1993.

69 Haggis, Gesell and Preston Day (eds.) 2005, 86–8.

70 Hayden 2004b, 280. For the discussion of the occupation along communication routes, see pp. 272–3.

71 Raab 2001.

72 Hayden 2004b, 274; Sanders, 142.

73 *AR* 2006–7, 107.

74 There may be some evidence for an earlier villa site at Elleniko in the Istron Valley. This has very tentatively been dated to the second century C.E., but not through stratigraphic evidence (Hayden 2004b, 274).

75 Treadgold 2001, 123.

76 Sanders (1982, 30) mentions three possible rural villa sites in Crete: Koleni Kamara in the west, Plaka Kalis in the centre and Pachyammos in the east. However, none of these sites has produced either mosaics or clear evidence to confirm that the architectural remains represent villas.

77 As typified by its marble imports as shown in Paton and Schneider 1999.

78 Marangou 1999, 269–78, and Marangou-Lerat 1995. In the former, she argues that Crete's wine exports flourished after the first century C.E.

79 2001, 14.

80 Sanders, 32.

81 A beautifully preserved olive press in a small industrial area was found on the island of Gavdos (off the south coast of Crete). Drosinou 2004, 415–26; 420–2.

82 Francis 2006, 365–79.

83 Sweetman 2010b.

84 Sanders, 32.

85 1982, 272. Saltpans have been located at Souda, Spinalonga and Elounda (Tsougarakis 1988, 276).

86 Sanders, 33. Weinburg 1960, 90–117, 100, argued that the glass production was probably unable to meet the needs of the whole island.

87 Bekker-Nielsen 2005, 83–97.

88 Marangou-Lerat 1995 and Markoulaki, Empereur and Marangou 1989, 551–80.

89 *AR* 1998–9, 117, notes that there was a Roman potters' workshop of 25 rooms found in Matala.

90 Ibid.

91 Sackett 1992.

92 Sanders, 35.

93 Paton and Schneider 1999. Hadzi-Vallianou 2006, 149, with reference to the import of the granite columns at Lyttos from Asia Minor.

94 Raab 2001, 13; also citing Baldwin Bowsky 1994, 7.

95 Braudel 1972, 103–38.

96 Based on onomastic evidence it is likely that in some cases there were Italian traders who situated themselves in Crete. For example, Baldwin Bowsky lists Roman

names found in places such as Gortyn, Ierapetra and other areas of eastern Crete which have clear associations with Italian traders who were active at Delos (Baldwin Bowsky 1994, 17).

97 Sanders, 35. Although as argued here the trading focus grows to include the northern towns; southern coastal towns such as Lissos and Suia do not seem to have been adversely affected.

98 Sanders, 30.

99 Issues of long-term seismic impacts are discussed in Chapter 3.

100 Even despite the clear impact of the 365 earthquake (see Stiros et al. 2004). For Kisamos, see Markoulaki et al. 2004, and for Chersonisos, see Chaniotaki-Starida and Mari 2004.

101 For example, by the use of Late Antique architecture in later buildings but without a definite ground plan or evidence of the one-time existence of a church from recent historical accounts.

102 See Volanakis, 235–61 for a reasonably up-to-date list of 87 basilicas. He based his data on Sanders's (89) catalogue, which included a range of churches without plan but identifiable by the presence of re-used architectural fragments, the re-use of earlier buildings in later churches, mosaic fragments, or evidence from eighteenth- and early nineteenth-century travellers. Three new ones have been identified since 1987. Early Christian churches are notoriously difficult to date even with stratigraphic evidence, and more often than not, a date range of the late fifth to early sixth century is given.

103 Bowden (2003, 151–4) summarizes the arguments well.

104 The direct threats from Arab invasions and the indirect influence of the overall threat to the empire.

105 The wealth of the church at this time was also diverted to needs more pressing than building projects (Treadgold 2001, 90).

106 Kalokyris 1956, 250–61. It is argued that the church was constructed in the eighth century.

107 Baldwin Bowsky, 1994, 1–45; 1995 41–67; 2001, 97–119; 2004, 95–150.

108 Forster 2001, 137–67. Forster 2004.

109 Sweetman, 2004a, Sweetman, 2004b, Sweetman 2007a and Sweetman 2010b.

110 Moody, Nixon, Price and Rackham 1998; Watrous 1982; Hayden 2004a, 2004b and 2005; Raab 2001, *AR* 2006–7, 107.

111 Ambraseys 2006, 1008. This is also seen following modern seismic disasters such as India's 2001 earthquake, which reduced the town of Bhuj to rubble (http://www.conservationtech.com/india-UNESCO/INDIA-home.htm); the residents began rebuilding almost as soon as it was safe to do so.

112 Stiros and Papageorgiou 2001, 383–6. See specifically Table 1.

113 Sweetman 2007a, 63–5.

114 Sanders, 152; Coldstream 1973, 186; Hood and Smyth 1981, 26; Sackett et al. 1992, 25. Sweetman 2004a and 2007a offer *contra* arguments.

115 Sweetman 2007a.

116 Ambraseys 2006 discusses resettlement after a seismic event. Also see Bourbou 2004 (80) for the rapid resettlement of Eleutherna following the 365 earthquake.

117 Baldwin Bowsky 1995; Sweetman 2007a.

118 Hingley 2005, 10–15.

119 See Hales 2003 and Papaioannou 2007 for approaches to the studies of provinces from the perspective of the local population. Both authors use the term 'Romanization' but with their own definitions for it.

120 Sweetman 2007a.

121 Waters 1995, 3.

122 Alcock (1993, 3–6) in her discussion of the development of Roman Greece in the context of its geographical location within the empire has offered comparative material on world systems analysis from other imperial states.

123 As cited in Sweetman 2007a.

124 Angold and Whitby 2008.

125 Sweetman 2010a.

126 For example, images of Christ and the animals are commonly likened to those of Orpheus and the animals (Mathews 1999, 68–77). The example of the mosaic of the Good Shepherd in the Mausoleum of Galla Placidia in Ravenna is often used. Also see Grabar 1968, 18–19.

127 For comparative examples, see Sweetman 2010a.

128 Sweetman forthcoming.

129 Hingley 1996, 2001 and 2005. Hitchner 2004.

130 Sweetman 2007a, 61–81.

Chapter Two. The Archaeology of Crete

1 For example, some of Sanders's (30–1) conclusions regarding settlement patterns, such as that in the Roman period, Hellenistic occupation shifted from the hilltops to occupy more of the valley floors.

2 Kondoleon 1995 and Muth 1998.

3 These reports come primarily from *Archaeological Reports* (*AR*), although the original Greek documents have been consulted for more detail.

4 In one respect this chapter represents an update and contextualization of *Roman Crete*.

5 In particular, the Akrotiri Peninsula survey (Raab, 2001), Kavousi survey (Haggis 1996a; Haggis, Gesell & Preston Day (eds.) 2005), Lasithi survey (Watrous 1982), Mesara survey (Watrous et al. 1993), Sphakia survey (Moody, Nixon, Price, & Rackham 1989; 1998), Vrokastro survey (Hayden, Moody & Rackham. 1992; Hayden 2004a; 2004b; 2005; 2006), and Ziros survey (Branigan 1998).

6 For example, the same kind of cooking or storage vessel may be common to the Classical, Hellenistic and Roman periods. See Hayden 2005, 57–61, for example.

7 For a detailed example, see Harrison's analysis of the Roman pottery from the Vrokastro survey in Hayden 2005, 57–61.

8 Hayden et al. 1992, 330.

9 For Mochlos, see Soles and Davaras 1992, 416, and for Pseira, see Betancourt and Davaras 1988, 210.

10 Vrokastro survey (Hayden et al. 1992, 332).

11 Ziros survey (Branigan 1998).

12 See Blackman and Branigan 1975, 74.

13 Watrous et al. 1993, 233.

14 Ibid. 232.

15 Sanders, 19.

16 Drosinou 2004 and *AR* 1984–5, 59.

17 Evidence from the Akrotiri survey suggests that this region may be different where agricultural estates around a central villa are found (Raab 2001, 14). See Chapter 1 for further discussion.

18 Recent reports of the Galatas project indicate that in the first and second centuries Roman settlement was in small nucleated clusters and that in the third century C.E. small Roman farmsteads were established (*AR* 2006–7, 107).

19 Branigan 1998, 76–7.

20 Blackman and Branigan 1977, 74. That is not to say that this system did not exist at all. For example, Sanders (23) argues that some of the rural estates around the Mesara must have been controlled by absentee landlords but that this may be the only example on the island (33).

21 See Haggis 1996b, 421, for the issue of rural security, and Haggis, Gesell and Preston Day (eds.) 2005, 86–8, for a more recent interpretation.

22 For the Praisos survey, see Whitley et al. 1999. Branigan 1998, 90.

23 http://sphakia.classics.ox.ac.uk/emccv1990.html

24 Sanders, 16–31.

25 Hayden et al. 1992, 333.

26 2006c.

27 Haggis 1996b, 416. Discussed in more detail in the section on harbours.

28 Haggis 1996a. Sanders also believes them to have been store houses, although A. Kelly (pers. comm.) would argue that these are the remains of a cistern.

29 Blackman and Branigan 1975, Site SC10.

30 *AR* 2000–1, 143.

31 Sanders, 162.

32 Andreadaki-Vlazaki 1991–3, 245–7. *AR* 1996–7, 124.

33 Sanders, 164.

34 *AR* 1997–8, 128.

35 Sanders, 162.

36 *AR* 2003–4, 92.

37 Sanders, 30.

38 Hayden et al. 1992, 333, and Blackman and Branigan 1975, 25.

39 *AR* 1997–8, 125.

40 Blackman and Branigan 1975, Site SC12.

41 http://sphakia.classics.ox.ac.uk/emccv1990.html. Sanders, 31.

42 Haggis in Hayden 2005, 86–8.

43 Raab 2001, 161. She notes that there seems to be evidence of decline also in Gortyn and Knossos which cannot be upheld on current data.

44 The Moni Odigitrias survey revealed only a limited spread of Roman occupation, which, the authors speculate, may in part be due to intensive land use in the period (*AR* 2003–4, 82).

45 *AR* 2006–7, 104.

46 Tsipopoulou 1989, 100.

47 Sanders, 30.

48 For example, see for Chania (*AR* 1997–8, 123) where a Late Antique cist grave was uncovered in a Roman domestic area, and for Kisamos (*AR* 2000–1, 141–2) in Rokakis and Xerouchakis Plots, where Late Antique cemeteries were built on top of Roman houses. This is discussed in more detail in the following section.

49 *AR* 1996–7, 114, and *AR* 1997–8, 118.

50 *AR* 1997–8, 124.

51 *AR* 1985–6, 95.

52 The function of the Late Antique building at Maleme was not identified (*AR* 1990–1, 77).

53 For Chersonisos see *AR* 1991–2, 59, recording the excavations in the area of the Creta Maris hotel, and *AR* 1992–3, 67. At Kisamos, see, for example, the Late Antique house in the Petromichelakis Plot and the cemetery in the Rokakis Plot (*AR* 2000–1, 141–2).

54 *AR* 1989–90, 68.

55 Sanders, 40–2.

56 Wardle and Wardle 2004 (Knossos) and Watrous et al. 1993, 232 (Mesara).

57 For example, in Kritsa Mirabellou (*AR* 1999–2000, 142), south of Mitropolis in Gortyn (*AR* 1991–2, 59), Lyttos (*AR* 2003–4, 79) and Stavros, Agios Nikolaos (*AR* 1998–9, 122).

58 Sanders, 42.

59 Grammatikaki 2004, 471. See also Vasilakis 2004 for a discussion of other mausolea here and at Gortyn.

60 Sanders, 42.

61 *AR* 1997–8, 126–7.

62 Blackman and Branigan 1975, 23–32, Site SC7.

63 For example, at Viannos, a single Roman grave was excavated (*AR* 1985–6, 88). Finds of sarcophagi are often indicative of single inhumations, for example, in Gortyn (*AR* 1982–3, 59). A family burial plot was excavated in Chersonisos within a large Roman cemetery (*AR* 1983–4, 60).

64 *AR* 1996–7, 103–4.

65 Two inscribed grave stelae were found in the excavation of the Elounda cemetery (*AR* 1990–1, 70) and at Knossos (Grammatikaki 2004) and Chersonisos (*AR* 1983–4, 60).

66 2004, 480.

67 *AR* 2006–7, 104–5.

68 See Sweetman 2005.

69 For example, see KS 183, which is located in the southern edge of the Roman domestic area.

70 For example, from Agios Nikolaos (*AR* 1984–5, 64), Elounda (*AR* 1998–9, 119), Kambanos (*AR* 1999–2000, 143) or Timbaki (*AR* 1999–2000, 140).

71 For example, lamps were found in a tile grave in Elounda (*AR* 1985–6, 92).

72 Both found in the excavations of the rock-cut tombs at ancient Eltyna in Pediadha (*AR* 1997–8, 116).

73 Such as the jasper ringstone carved with the head of Livy found in the Hellenistic and Roman cemetery at the Mesara Agricultural Research Station (*AR* 1981–2, 57). A gold ring was also found during the excavation of a second- to third-century Roman tomb in Epanochorio Selinou (*AR* 1984–5, 67).

74 *AR* 1996–7, 195. Grammatikaki 2004.

75 *AR* 1985–6, 92.

76 Coins have been used to date burials, for example, at Potamou (*AR* 1985–6, 93), where two coins of Caligula were found in addition to a coin with the head of Augustus inscribed with Θεός Σεβαστός ἐπὶ Λάχητος. Another Vespasianic coin was found during these excavations (*AR* 1987–8, 71).

77 Lamps have helped to date the cemetery at the Mesara Agricultural Research Station to between the first and second century (*AR* 1981–2, 57) and the Spilia cemetery at Knossos (*AR* 1983–4, 61) to the second half of the first century.

78 *AR* 1990–1, 70, and *AR* 1997–8, 117, respectively.

79 *AR* 1989–90, 72.

80 *AR* 1994–5, 74, and *AR* 1998–9, 119, respectively.

81 Sanders, 39–40.

82 Sanders, 36.

83 Ibid. 37. Other areas include Soulia, Ierapetra and Phoenix on the south coast but also inland areas such as the Idaean Cave and Lappa.

84 Found in inscriptions from Amnisos and Lebena (Sanders, 37).

85 Baldwin Bowsky 2006a, 397 and 403.

86 Sanders, 39.

87 Sanders, 37–9.

88 Sanders, 38.

89 The Ierapetra example is now in the Archaeological Museum in Istanbul (Papadakis, 1986, 51) and the Agios Nikolaos one is in Antalya. Other examples are found at the Athenian Agora, Piraeus and Olympia.

90 Blackman and Branigan 1975, 30 and fig. 8.

91 Hayden et al. 1992, 333.

92 *AR* 2002–3, 85, and *AR* 2005–6, 111 (for the date and identification of the Aptera Heroon). For the Kouphonisi temple, see *AR* 1987–8, 72. The dedication of the Chersonisos temple found in the area northwest of the theatre has not yet been established (*AR* 2006–7, 104–5).

93 *AR* 1997–8, 113; *AR* 1999–2000, 130–1; *AR* 2006–7, 109.

94 *AR* 1997–8, 116.

95 Markoulaki et al. 2004, 373 n. 68 (Kisamos); *AR* 1998–9, 113 (Chersonisos).

96 Sanders, 39.

97 *AR* 1996–7, 123. Note that earlier reports (e.g., *AR* 1991–2, 70) use the name Diktynna instead of Britomartis, but she is essentially the same deity.

98 *AR* 2002–3, 87. See Sanders, 161, who only had one element of evidence from the first century B.C.E. to work on for chronology. *AR* 1991–2, 59, for the Sanctuary of Hermes and Aphrodite at Kato Syme.

99 *AR* 2003–4, 78. *AR* 1997–8, 125.

100 Sackett 1992.

101 See publications by Sidiropoulos 2004 and Oikonomidou 2004 on numismatics.

102 See below for finds, and see the 2004 volume *Creta romana e protobizantina: Atti del convegno internazionale Iraklion, 23–30 settembre 2000*, edited by M. Livadiotti and I. Simiakaki, 1049–1162, for some synthetic sculpture studies.

103 In Gortyn, for example, the headless statue found while a trench was being dug for OTE (*AR* 1983–4, 62–3), and the second-century marble head of a bearded man which was found by accident (*AR* 1985–6, 89). From Chersonisos, a life-size statue and a headless female statue have been recorded (see *AR* 1986–7, 55 & *AR* 1999–2000, 129, respectively).

104 The Ierapetra Museum holds a significant collection of Roman portraiture and sculpture (see Papadakis 1986). For recent finds, see *AR* 1980–1, 46, where two headless female statues are recorded; in *AR* 1984–5, 64, a portrait statue of Demeter which had been painted was discovered during rescue excavations by Davaras in the town. In more recent years marble statue fragments were found in the Mantourakis Plot (*AR* 1988–9). For Iraklion, see *AR* 1989–90, 102, for records of the find of a rubbish dump of architectural fragments dating from the fifth and sixth centuries.

105 *AR* 1999–2000, 133. Furthermore, new light has been shed on imperial sculpture at Knossos in Lagogianni-Georgakarakos's 2004 publication.

106 Sanders, 35.

107 See Chapter 1.

108 1982, 34.

109 Ibid.

110 Ibid. It is unsurprising that Rhodian and Knidian amphorae were of the most common types found on Crete, and it emphasizes the active role the island had along the trade routes between Rome and Alexandria that took in Rhodes or Knidos.

111 Eiring 2001, 91; Forster 2001, 137–8.

112 Hayes 1971.

113 Forster 2001, 138–41.

114 2011.

115 Particularly in the Tholos area. Haggis 1996a, 199.

116 Hayden et al. 1992, 330.

117 Haggis 1996a, 199, for Tholos, and Hayden et al. 1992, 296. Priniatikos Pyrgos also had evidence for kilns and ceramic wasters, one of the few examples of pottery industries being identified through surveys (Hayden et al. 2006,160–5).

118 Raab 2001, 149–56.

119 1975 and 1977, fig. 23.

120 Watrous et al. 1993, 233.

121 Ibid.

122 http://sphakia.classics.ox.ac.uk/emccv1990.html.

123 Ibid.

124 *AR* 1996–7, 114.

125 *AR* 1998–9, 113.

126 Eiring (2000b, 197) noted that 35% of the ceramics at Knossos were represented by locally produced and imitation pottery.

127 *AR* 2003–4, 77.

128 *AR* 2003–4, 77.

129 Markoulaki, Empereur and Marangou 1989.

130 *AR* 2006–7, 117.

131 *AR* 2002–3, 87.

132 *AR* 1998–9, 117.

133 *AR* 1988–9, 99.

134 Ibid., 126.

135 Sanders, 33–4.

136 Sackett 1992. Warren 1987–8.

137 Sweetman 2010b.

138 *AR* 2004–5, 118. Another metallurgical installation which also included a number of water features was uncovered in the south of the town (*AR* 1997–8, 126).

139 *AR* 1999–2000, 150.

140 At the Stratake and Skoulake Plot a circular structure was found divided into rooms with vast quantities of glass and faience and other features indicative of a workshop (*AR* 1993–4, 84).

141 *AR* 2002–03, 86.

142 *AR* 1988–9, 102.

143 *AR* 1987–8, 74.

144 *Natural Histories* 31.81, as noted in Sanders, 33.

145 Haggis 1996b, 421.

146 Pariente 1990, 823.

147 Francis 2006. See also Sweetman 2010b for evidence of beekeeping at Knossos.

148 *AR* 2000–1, 141.

149 Haggis 1996b, 417.

150 Sanders, 141.

151 Branigan 1998, 75.

152 http://webefa.efa.gr/prospection-itanos-/?action=search&objectdefid=5, Site 89.

153 *AR* 1984–5, 59.

154 Hadzi-Vallianou 2006, 195.

155 Haggis 1996a.

156 Ibid., 140.

157 The harbour at Pseira was identified during the Kavousi survey. At Atherinolakkos, Sitia, the remains of an anchor and amphora fragments indicated a harbour (*AR*

2000–1, 133). Thus far investigations of the storage facilities have been undertaken at Astale (*AR* 1989–90, 78).

158 *AR* 2006–7, 105.

159 These range from the works identified at Patella on the west coast (Sanders, 29) to Itanos on the east (ibid., 16) and Tarrha on the southwest (ibid., 29) to Olus on the northeast coast (Sanders, 18).

160 Hayden 2006, 137.

161 Haggis 1996a.

162 Haggis 1996a, 192.

163 Ibid., 205.

164 Haggis 1996a, 190–1.

165 Blackman and Branigan 1975, 28–32.

166 Sanders, 160.

167 *AR* 1997–8, 126–7.

168 Blackman and Branigan 1977, 74.

Chapter Three. Iconography of Cretan Mosaics

1 This refers to mosaic compositions consisting of panels of figured scenes or geometric elements arranged in grids (such as radial compositions or circles or rows of squares, etc.) which often allow multiple views.

2 See discussion in Chapter 6.

3 Balmelle et al. 1985.

4 Parallels for this Late Antique use are also seen in Greece, for example, at Epidauros and the baths at Ipati.

5 Many of the grids discussed in this section only occur on a few mosaics in Crete. They are still valuable for comparative analysis, particularly in terms of date. It is often easier to make comparisons between grid types than between particular elements of decoration, as the latter tend to be more common in many areas over long periods.

6 Markoulaki in Ioannidou-Karetsou et al. 2008, fig. 19.

7 Although rare throughout the empire, another example of the combination is found in Bignor Villa, West Sussex (Toynbee 1964, 262).

8 For example, Room A, Brescello, in Italy (Negrioli 1914, fig. 2), and in the museum at Alessandria (Blake 1930, pl. 22, 2).

9 Here there is a central circle containing a checkerboard pattern of triangles, similar to that in the Medusa mosaic in the Villa Dionysus (10), and there is an outer square border which is framed by a wave scroll and guilloche.

10 This mosaic design is also similar to Mosaic 10 from Knossos. Ramsden 1971, cat. 15, pl. 19b, and Waywell 1979, cats. 14 and 17d, respectively. Ramsden's (now Waywell) Ph.D. thesis (1971) is the most up-to-date corpus of Roman mosaics in Greece. A copy is held in the library of the British School at Athens. I am grateful to Dr Waywell for allowing me access to her work and to the librarians Penny Wilson and Sandra Pepelasis for facilitating it.

11 Campbell 1988, 62, pl. 183.

12 *AMP*, pls. XCVII and LXVIII.

13 Waywell 1979, cats. 25 and 34, respectively.

14 *AMP* 1945, pl. LII. The House of the Calendar mosaic uses a 12-spoke arrangement to accommodate all the months (Campbell 1988, 61, fig. 26 & pl. 183).

15 Smith 1965, 96, 99 and figs. 1 and 2.

16 This arrangement is described by Hellenkemper Salies (1974) as The Web of Interlaced Bands (Bandkreuzgeflecht I). She notes that it is found mostly in Eastern

provinces and is most popular in the Late Antique basilicas. The latter point is not the case for Crete.

17 Sanders, pl. 40.
18 1979, 304. A third-century example comes from the bath house at Philippi (ibid., cat. 41, pl. 50).
19 For example, in Corinth, with Dionysus at the centre (Waywell 1979, cat. 17).
20 For the Antioch examples, see *AMP* XIXa and *AMP* XXIXb, and for the Cypriot one, see Michaelides 1987, pl. 22–3.
21 Hellenkemper Salies 1974, fig. 8.
22 Joyce 1981, pl. 35.
23 Dunbabin 1999, 94.
24 Waywell 1979, cat. 30, pl. 49.
25 1986, 270.
26 *AMP* and Campbell 1988, respectively.
27 Within the main field, not the overall grid.
28 Areopagus House 1, early second century (Waywell 1979, cat. 7).
29 *AMP* XIVa.
30 For example, at Brescello (Negrioli 1914, fig. 2).
31 For example, the second-century geometric mosaic from the House of the Planets at Italica.
32 For example, *in situ* in a *triclinium* of the *domus* at the museum at El Djem.
33 See Chapter 6.
34 These different types of borders include variations of standard types, such as variations of guilloche.
35 They do occur in Roman period mosaics outside Crete.
36 Markoulaki in Ioannidou-Karetsou et al. 2008, fig. 19.
37 Among the Cretan mosaics, there is only one Late Antique example of a wave scroll (Mosaic 92) and it is found as a border to the figured panel of the lion and deer in the narthex (Pl. 25).
38 Dunbabin 1978b, pls. III 6 and XXIV 57, respectively.
39 In mainland Greece a parallel is found in the nave of the basilica at Amfissa (*Byz Corp II*, pl. 320b, cat. 123) dated to the end of the fourth or beginning of the fifth century.
40 *Byz Corp II*, pl. 52.
41 Balty 1977, 93.
42 1974.
43 Hellenkemper Salies 1974, 125.
44 Hellenkemper Salies 1974, cat. 287 and cat. 282, respectively.
45 Ibid., 16.
46 *Byz Corp II*, pl. 193.
47 Markoulaki 1987b, pl. 326. Markoulaki et al. 2004, 372.
48 Panels of Dionysus with subsidiary panels relating to the theatre are found on Mosaics 135 and 136 and on an unpublished example from the Health Centre, Kisamos (Markoulaki 1987b, pl. 324).
49 For example, from Djemila (Dunbabin 1978b, pl. LXX). There are examples of the scene from Antioch (*AMP*, pl. XVI) and from Corinth (Waywell 1979, cat. 20). Triumph scenes were common in other media such as painting and sarcophagi.
50 Other Dionysiac scenes common in the empire are those of Dionysus being handed over at birth to be taken care of by the Maenads, the drunken Dionysus and the Dionysiac orgy.
51 For example, painting from Pompeii (*RPGR* 113) and (*LIMC* Ariadne 129). Sarcophagi with the scene are found, for example, in the Vatican Museum (Turcan 1966, pl. 28),

in the Louvre (Baratte & Metzger 1985, nos. 65 & 66) and in the British Museum (Walker 1990, pl. 16).

52 For example, Socrates Street, Thessaloniki (second to third century) (Waywell 1979, cat. 53, pl. 52). From Antioch, a mosaic dated to 193–235 shows the same theme; however, there is a notable difference in the treatment of the subject matter, not least because of its distinctive architectural setting (*AMP*, pl. XXVIIIb). According to Dunbabin (1978b, 183) Dionysus and Ariadne scenes were less common in North Africa where triumph scenes were favoured (ibid., 174).

53 Dunbabin 1999, pl. 163, and Garcia y Bellido 1972, fig. 1346, for the Merida example and Waywell 1979, cat. 53, pl. 52.

54 Both examples closely reflect a painted medium with carefully modelled drapery and detail, and in the case of the Antioch one, architecture (Ramsden 1971, 250).

55 Goodchild 1971, pl. 47.

56 For the Cypriot example, see Michaelides 1987, pl. XI, and from North Africa, a pavement from Lambaesis (Dunbabin 1978b, 263).

57 The depiction of a Dionysus (?) on a leopard rather than on a tiger suggests a procession rather than a triumph scene. A similar composition is found in Constantine, North Africa (Dunbabin 1978b, pl. 174).

58 A tambourine is preserved in the top right-hand corner of the mosaic.

59 *AMP*, pl. XXXVIIIc.

60 Tzedakis 1972, 637–8. The mosaic has not yet been published in detail.

61 See discussion in Waywell 1979, 316–19. For a North African example, see that from the Maison de Silène (El Djem) dated to 260–80 (Dunbabin 1978b, pl. XLI).

62 For example, the Villa Kolivinou mosaics, Argos (Ramsden 1971, pl. 23), on display in the museum there.

63 Both also have a somewhat distant side-on expression. The represented ages, hairstyles and crowns are the same, but their clothes are slightly different.

64 For example, the central panel of Dionysus and Seasons from the House of Dionysus, Paphos.

65 The mosaic from Room A of the House of the Dionysiac procession at Thysdrus (Dunbabin 1999, fig. 109) is a close example of a non-narrative Dionysiac scene from North Africa.

66 *OCD*, 3rd ed.

67 Darmon 1980, 160.

68 A black-and-white mosaic showing the scene in a single panel. Blake 1936, 169, pl. 35, 2.

69 Aupert 1976, fig. 232.

70 From the House of Dionysus. Daszewski and Michaelides 1988, fig. 10.

71 Daszewski and Michaelides 1988, 27.

72 Aupert 1976, fig. 232.

73 1994, 186 and n. 736.

74 Ibid.

75 Darmon 1980, 158.

76 The lack of chariot is common in Italian versions of the scene (Hellenkemper Salies 1986, 260).

77 *LIMC* Poseidon 110. Here Poseidon is shown with his cloak billowing out behind him and with his arms in a similar position to those in Mosaic 9. Two hippocamps draw the chariot. See also Dunbabin 1978b, 269.

78 This scene is commonly found in Ostia (Becatti 1961, 42–4) and Herculaneum. In these cases there is normally a very crowded scene in black and white and, notably, a chariot is not often depicted.

79 Dunbabin 1978b, 270. Another North African example is from the House of the Triumph of Neptune in Acholla Tunisia (Gozlan 1992, pl. XLVII).

80 Dunbabin 1978b, pl. LXI.

81 Waywell 1979, cat. 34.

82 For painting, see *RPGR* 35, no. 8, and *LIMC* Poseidon 94 and for sculpture see *LIMC* Poseidon 116, 118, 119.

83 Those that do normally involve Perseus, for example, from Bulla Regia, Tunisia (Fantar 1994, 90).

84 This point will be discussed later in the chapter.

85 Markoulaki in Ioannidou-Karetsou et al. 2008, fig. 19.

86 Markoulaki 1987b, pl. 324.

87 1985 and 1978, respectively.

88 From Bepa Armera in Bulgaria (Popova-Moros, 1987, pl. 4).

89 Waywell 1979, cat. 16, pl. 47.

90 Ibid., cat. 47, pl. 51.

91 Ibid., cat. 48. Another well-preserved example is from Piraeus (ibid., cat. 42).

92 *AMP*, pl. XIVa.

93 *RPGR* 208.

94 Dunbabin 1978b, 271.

95 Daszewski 1985, pl. 22. Daszewski (1985, 125) suggests that the Egyptian mosaicists were responsible for the spread in popularity of the Medusa depiction as there is a particularly diverse range of Medusa depictions in Egypt.

96 Pesce 1950, fig 43.

97 1984, 13.

98 Ibid., 19.

99 Ibid., 14.

100 Unlike the gods, the seasons were not commonly associated with a narrative mythological scene.

101 The exact species of bird depicted is not confirmed. Parrish (1984, 28 n.76) has suggested that Autumn is represented by a gallinule and Winter by a wood pigeon (Parrish 1984, 27). If this was the case, and if, as I have suggested, the supposed gallinule is not Winter, then seasons are no longer associated with their respective plants. A more plausible suggestion is that the small bird may be identified as a parrot and therefore has both Dionysiac and autumnal associations. This would mean that the water or marsh bird, perhaps a gallinule, was intended to symbolize Winter.

102 *OCD*, 3rd ed.

103 Waywell 1979, cat. 30.

104 It is fair to assume that this would have been the same for the two sides which have been damaged.

105 Although it is possible that Summer may be female.

106 Commonly, the human personifications carry identifiable attributes. An example from Room 5 of *Villa A* in Ptolemais (Kraeling 1962, pl. LXI) is quite similar to the Kisamos example in that Winter is identified by the cloak, Summer by the hook implement which she is carrying, Autumn by the vine leaves and Spring by the wreath of flowers in her hair. Workshop connections are not likely given the differences in the images of the figures.

107 1984, 69.

108 Parrish 1984, 212 and pl. 73.

109 Markoulaki et al. 2004, fig. 13.

110 Ibid., 368.

111 This includes the North African–style mosaic in the Kisamos Museum.

112 Richter 1960, 49.

113 Waywell 1979, cat. 19, for Corinth, and Dunbabin 1978b, 92, for Tunisia.

114 See Papapostolou 2009.

115 *BSA* Annual Report for the managing committee, 1994–5, 19. It is difficult to define whether the gloves were the *sharp-tong* type or the *caestus*.

116 Waywell 1979, cat. 38, pl. 50.

117 Further examples in other media are found in *RPGR* 278–83.

118 *Byz Corp I*, pl. 91. This mosaic has yet to be published in detail, and it is currently not available to be studied.

119 *Byz Corp I*, pl. 91.

120 Wilson 1983, fig. 11.

121 See, for example, Piazza Armerina in Sicily. Wilson 1983, fig. 12.

122 Dunbabin 1978b, 214.

123 For example, from Greece the most well-known hunting scenes are those of the hunting panels from Argos (Ramsden 1971, pl. 24–6a); although the mosaic is late in date (late fourth century), the scenes of the hunt are still displayed in panels (*Byz Corp I*, no. 6, pl. 28–9).

124 Waywell 1979, 317.

125 Tzedakis 1968, pl. 379.

126 Markoulaki 1987b.

127 Kraeling 1962, pl. LVIII B. A complete contrast is found in Berlin where a centaur attacks a pair of lions because they have just killed the female centaur (*RPGR* 346).

128 As has been discussed, because the dogs wear collars it likely represents a hunt scene. An agrimi is a wild Cretan goat.

129 Markoulaki 1987a, pl. 14.

130 Tzedakis 1968, pl. 377b.

131 Charitonidis et al. 1970, pls. 15–24.

132 Ibid., 101–2.

133 The surviving fragments of the play are frr._K-A and Men. test. _ K-A. (K-A = Kassel and Austin 1998).

134 Markoulaki et al. 2004.

135 Webster 1995. They were associated with Dionysus and are found in his sanctuaries too.

136 Webster 1995, 45. The Chania masks are of young females with their slightly curly hair piled on their heads and curled around their ears.

137 The mask is similar to Webster (1995), Mask No. 8, the brothel keeper.

138 Markoulaki 1987b, pl. 324.

139 Markoulaki et al. 2004.

140 Markoulaki in Ioannidou-Karetsou et al. 2008, fig. 19.

141 Tzedakis 1970, 409a.

142 I would like to thank Hamish Forbes for this suggestion. See Sanders, pl. 40.

143 Tzedakis 1968, pl. 377.

144 Tzedakis 1968, pl. 379.

145 Markoulaki 1987a, pl. 14.

146 *Xenia* is the concept of hospitality; *xenia* scenes often consist of images of a bountiful meal (fruit, bread, fowl, fish, etc.) and are considered to be a welcoming image.

147 Pers. comm.

148 I am very grateful to Sara Paton for bringing this reference to my attention.

149 The most famous example of the doves on a bowl is by Sosos of Pergamon and is now known only from ancient copies such as the mosaic in the Capitoline museum

from Hadrian's Villa in Tivoli (MacDonald and Pinto 1995, fig. 209) (Pliny *Natural Histories* 36.184). Another example is from Casa Del Fauno in Pompeii. A similar scene of parrots drinking is from the Areopagus, Athens (Waywell 1979, cat. 7, pl. 46).

150 Chaniotaki-Starida and Mari 2004, 292.

151 Another two examples of *xenia* scenes are found in the Health Centre excavations; one of these is a subsidiary panel to the mosaic of the Wedding of Dionysus (Mosaic 207f), also likely to be a *triclinium*. Markoulaki et al. 2004.

152 Markoulaki in Ioannidou-Karetsou et al. 2008, fig. 19.

153 Tzedakis 1970, pl. 409a.

154 Although these designs are limited to the corners of the mosaics and are not inhabited running scrolls in the strictest sense (Toynbee & Ward-Perkins 1950, 1–44), they can be considered as sections of peopled scrolls.

155 Markoulaki 1987b, pl. 327, and Markoulaki et al. 2004, 372.

156 The remains of the two wall mosaics from Crete (Gortyn Sector M & Knossos) are not discussed here because of their fragmentary nature. The Knossos one is published in Sweetman 2004b.

157 Milburn 1988, 230.

158 Mathews 1999. Gough 1973. It is also because these were scenes that artists already knew and were easily converted to fit Christian conventions.

159 Gough 1973. This marked a departure from the straight genre scenes such as the hunt and amphitheatre.

160 Kourkoutidou-Nikolaidou and Tourta 1997, pls. 104–7.

161 Dauphin 1980, 128.

162 There is no evidence on Crete for the adaptation of mythological figures such as Orpheus or Asclepius as Christ figures that is common elsewhere, for example, in the Good Shepherd mosaic of the Mausoleum Galla Placidia, Ravenna.

163 They occur in other parts of the empire in Late Antique domestic contexts.

164 The format sometimes occurs in small panels.

165 It may be that these people had no tradition of laying the floors in Crete or knowledge of the Cretan repertoire, or it could have been a greater circulation of ideas or pattern books.

166 Dauphin 1980, 133.

167 Ferguson 1990. For example, Psalm 11:1 refers to the soul fleeing as a bird.

168 Acts 8:36. As seen, for example, in Eleutherna and Olus.

169 There is a chance that they were meant to be peacocks as evidenced by their long tails, but little else would indicate this.

170 Mosaics 92–3, 104, 109, 126, 148–51, 155, 156–8. As it stands, 20% have peacock symbols, although this figure may well have been greater had many of the mosaics not been damaged.

171 Milburn 1988, 36.

172 The feet are just visible in the lower left corner of the plate.

173 Milburn 1988, 50.

174 Sanders, 104.

175 Ibid., 126.

176 For example, the miracle of the loaves and the fish (Mark 6:35–44).

177 Michaelides 1989b, 194.

178 I would like to thank B. MacKay, R. Meenan and D. Sweetman for lively discussion of its identification as a deer.

179 Pendlebury 1939, 368.

180 There are several biblical references to the vine, such as, for example, John 15:1: 'I am the true vine, my father is the vinedresser', and John 15:5: 'I am the vine, you are the branches'.

181 Michaelides 1989b, 194.

182 Olus (108), Basilica A Chersonisos (92–3), Mallia (102–3), Gortyn Sector M (109), Sybrita (116–17) and Almyrida (148–51). A fine example of an ivy-leaf border is found in the narthex of the Eleutherna Basilica, where the leaves are depicted in different stages of development (111–14). A damaged vine-leaf border surrounds two of the geometric panels in the exo-narthex in the basilica at Frangokastelli (143–6). In this area, a later wall was constructed on top of the mosaic and the extent of the vine scroll is therefore unclear.

183 Narthex mosaics at Almyrida (148–51) and Suia (156–8) contain panels of kantharoi with emerging vine leaves, and examples are found in the nave at Almyrida and Bema of Suia. The central motif of the looped circle in the nave of the basilica at Gortyn (109) contains a kantharos with stylized scroll (Pl. 29). Although they are no longer visible, Sanders records that kantharoi with tendrils flowing out of them were depicted on the mosaic from Elyros (155).

184 Small individual panels of stylized flowers such as acanthus are also in the Olus mosaic.

185 Sanders, 104.

186 There are others for which only brief records of the descriptions survive or are possible, such as Avdhou (104), Lyttos (105), Panagia (106), Knossos KMF (91), Matala (110), Axos (118), Lappa (119–20), Armenoi (152), Meskla (153), Kantanos (154), Suia Basilica B (159) and Lissos (160).

187 Bandy 1970, 132–3 and 125, respectively.

188 Ibid., 97.

189 Davis 1962, 19.

190 Milburn 1988, 206.

191 Ramsden 1971, 470. This figure excludes the scores of mosaics that have been found in the last 40 years, particularly through rescue excavation. The figure used here however is still valid for the comparative proportion value.

192 Kondoleon 2000, 64–5.

193 The final one cannot be classified with any security.

194 Bandy 1970, 97b and 103, respectively. The Mount Ida one (fourth–fifth century) is in the Rethymnon Museum.

195 Diamandis 2004, 391 and figs. 1 and 11.

196 For example, see the case of the Eleutherna Basilica Mosaic (111–14), and outside Crete, see the example of the Mas'udiyah mosaic, which is dated to 228 (Kondoleon 1995, 58, quoting Levi 1947, 395, fig. 154).

197 The Satornilos recorded here is not connected with a different athlete, Satorninos from Gortyn, the winner in the stadion race, as suggested by Sweetman (2003, 530) and refuted by Chaniotis in *SEG* 2003 (53–2), 952.

198 Charitonidis et al. 1970, pls. 15–24.

199 2000, 64–5.

200 Dunbabin 1978b, 263. Another example of *venatores* being named is from Smirat (ibid., 268).

201 Ibid., 257. An example of racehorses being named is from Oued Athménia, Room M, of the Baths of Pompeianus (ibid., 267).

202 Yialouris 1967, 206–7, pl. 145b. Ramsden 1971, 472.

203 Tzedakis 1970, pl. 409b.

204 Dunbabin 1989, 41.

205 Ibid., 12.

206 The most common context is the bath house, and they are listed in Dunbabin's catalogue (1990, 107–9); for example: Timgad, Algeria (no. 35), from Sabratha in Libya (no. 28) and from Balazote in Spain (no. 4), all of which have inscriptions accompanying the sandals.

207 Bookidis, 1974, pls. 57–8.

208 Dunbabin 1990, 100.

209 Themelis 2004c, 76.

210 Markoulaki et al. 2004, 371.

211 For example, see that of the House of Dionysos in Paphos (Kondoleon 1995, fig. 46).

212 Ramsden 1971, 481.

213 Kondoleon 1995, figs. 46 and 47.

214 Ibid., 81.

215 In this case, Dunbabin 1999 provides the most comprehensive review of the mosaics of the empire.

216 Ibid., 88.

217 For example, the Amphitheatre mosaic from Nennig. Dunbabin 1999, fig. 84.

218 Dunbabin 1999, 79–81. See, for example, Saint-Romain-en-Gaul, Rustic calendar (ibid., fig. 79). And mythological scenes do occur, for example, the mosaic of the Planetary Deities from Orbe (ibid., fig. 82) or the mosaic of Dionysos from Cologne (ibid., fig. 83).

219 Dunbabin 1999, 100.

220 Ibid., 147.

221 Ibid., pl. 153.

222 Dunbabin 1999, fig. 156.

223 Ibid., 144–5.

224 See, for example, from Thysdrus, House of the Dionysiac Procession, the *triclinium* mosaic (Dunbabin 1999, fig. 108).

225 Dunbabin 1999, 111.

226 For instance, the third-century Hunting mosaic from Althiburus (Dunbabin 1999, fig. 115) or the third-century Amphitheatre mosaic from Smirat (ibid., fig. 118).

227 Ibid., 119–20, figs. 123–4.

228 Ibid., 127. A Late Antique mosaic depicting the hunt is the late fourth-century mosaic of Dominus Julius (Dunbabin 1999, fig. 122).

229 Dunbabin 1999, 168–9.

230 For example, from Antioch the mosaic of Dionysus and Herakles from the House of the Drinking Contest (Dunbabin 1999, 167).

231 See Waywell 1979, cat. 40, pl. 50., with an example from Philippi.

232 It is found at Sami in Kephalonia on the west of the Peloponnese (Waywell 1979, cat. 43, pl. 50).

233 Compare, for instance, the Shahba-Philippopolis mosaic of Tethys (Dunbabin 1999, fig. 173) with that of the Judgement of Paris mosaic from the Atrium house (ibid., fig. 166).

234 Dunbabin 1999, 172.

235 Ibid., 188.

236 Ibid., 225.

237 Ibid., fig. 245.

238 For example, the Constantinian Villa, Room 1 (Dunbabin 1999, fig. 169).

239 Ibid., 177.

240 See Michaelides 1989b, 194.

241 For example from the mosaic of the hunt from Argos (*Byz Corp II*, pl. 28).

242 Kondoleon 1995, 6.

243 Michaelides 1989b, 195. Michaelides also notes the irony of the close artistic connection between Cyprus and Antioch in the Late Antique period because of the religious friction between the two areas that existed until the Church of Cyprus was declared independent in the late fifth century.

244 Michaelides 1989b.

245 Waywell 1979, cats. 28 and 32, respectively.

246 Dunbabin 1999, 212, and Kondoleon 1995, 30.

247 Dunbabin 1999, 211.

248 For example: 'The character of the different regions varied substantially from the highly urbanised south to the military provinces of the Rhine and the much less densely settled West. The use of mosaic in these regions may be seen as one index of Romanisation: immigrant settlers and elements of the indigenous population adopted the Roman way of life, expressed through public building and a certain style of housing, complete with its comforts and ornament' (Dunbabin 1999, 73). Harrison (2004) also argues that dwellings may reflect levels of Romanization.

249 The interpretation of the Poseidon and Amymone scene in two panels may be the nearest to an original figured scene on Cretan mosaics. Geometric elements such as thick guilloche or knot design are Cretan.

250 Dunbabin 1999, 74–6.

251 Brescello (Room A) in Italy (Negrioli 1914, fig. 2).

252 The black-and-white format and the absence of a chariot in the scene are also Western features.

253 Examples of this are from Trier in Germany, the site of the 'Procuratoren' Palast (Parlasca 1959, pl. 16), which has many geometric mosaics; from Hungary, the mosaic from Balàca (Kiss 1973, pl. 11); from Belgium, the mosaic from the site of Téting (Stern 1960, pl. 38); from France, the example at Souzy-la-Briche (Darmon and Lavange 1977, pl. 95); and from Switzerland, examples from Zofingen (von Gonzenbach 1961, pls. 8 and 9).

254 See the mosaic of Artemis bathing from Shahba-Philippopolis (Balty 1977, 20).

255 Parrish 1984, pls. 55 and 79, respectively.

256 Dunbabin, 1978b, pl. 159.

257 For examples of hunting or fishing scenes in Cyrenaica, see Goodchild 1971, fig. 95, and for black-and-white mosaics, see Temple E6 in Cyrene (Stucchi 1975, fig. 236).

258 Kraeling, 1962, fig. 63.

259 The mosaics from Kera have been dated to the late fifth century, whereas the Cyrenaican ones have been dated to the end of the first century (Kraeling 1962, 138).

260 Sanders, pl. 40.

261 The broader relationships of room functions and themes are discussed in Chapter 5.

262 The eight-spoked wheel is not seen in mainland Greece before the late second century, and the vault pattern is rare in the eastern provinces.

Chapter Four. Date and Distribution

1 The analysis does not include recently reported mosaics numbered S200 onwards in the catalogue.

2 Points raised in this chapter will also be discussed in the conclusions regarding the evidence for workshops of mosaicists in Crete.

3 See the publications by Markoulaki 1987b and 1989, and Markoulaki et al. 2004.

4 The mosaics which have been dated by stratigraphic means are listed in Appendix 2.

5   Contextual dating should still be more reliable. See, for example, the chronology proposed for the Panagia Field mosaics in Corinth which has since been refined on the basis of stratigraphic evidence (Sweetman & Sanders 2005).

6   Shelley 1943, pl. 12.

7   Sanders, 112–13.

8   In particular, if they are made from a specific material (pers. comm. Sara Paton). Bowden (2003, 140–50) has shown how different types of capitals and architectural styles can be used to date church architecture.

9   See the work on amphorae from Health Care Centre excavations in Kisamos by Markoulaki, Empereur and Marangou 1989, 551–80.

10 For instance, Hayes's 1983 work on the Villa Dionysus assemblage and Sackett's 1992 work on the Unexplored Mansion and compare them with Forster's later work on the Knossian assemblages in Coldstream, Eiring and Forster 2001 or Forster 2004.

11 Marangou-Lerat 1995, and Markoulaki, Empereur and Marangou 1989.

12 Work by Dr J. Binder has been undertaken but not yet published.

13 This includes two from the Health Centre excavations in Kisamos (Markoulaki et al. 2004).

14 Ramsden 1971, 489a.

15 Sanders, 92.

16 Such as a type of guilloche or figured element, unless the element in question is so exclusive that any parallels are more than likely to be connected. A good example of this is the knot pattern in the Knossos Mosaic 88–90 (Pl. 23).

17 This is discussed in detail later in this chapter.

18 Markoulaki 1999, 197–9, and Markoulaki et al. 2004.

19 Sanders, 51.

20 Volanakis 1987 is the most recent published source for the Late Antique churches of Crete. Platon 1955, Sanders 1982, Pelekanidis and Atzaka 1988 and Sweetman 2011b also deal with chronological issues of the churches.

21 Sweetman 2010a and Avraméa 1997. For Epirus, Bowden 2003, 149–151, argues that the cluster around the first half of the fifth to the first half of the sixth century is not archaeological bias, but his is a wider time span.

22 See, for example, Mosaics 39, 40, 42, 46.

23 This includes mosaics 43a and 43b.

24 This is also the case with Mosaic 9 from Knossos, which contains a polychrome central medallion (Pl. 8).

25 Destruction evidence from the House of the Diamond Frescos (Sackett 1992) and possibly from the Villa Dionysus has prompted scholars to suggest a late second-century earthquake in Knossos. This earthquake is not well attested in other sources. See Stiros and Papageorgiou 2001.

26 Drosinou 1994–6, 227.

27 Sweetman 2004b.

28 In order not to bias the evidence for the purpose of Graph 3 it was necessary to count each group of mosaics from churches as a single entry.

29 That is not to say that surveys cannot identify tesserae or even mosaic traces, for instance, from Sphakia (*AR* 1997–8, 120).

30 Sanders, 30.

31 This figure is based on the data presented by Volanakis, who records 86 churches and one domestic building, with the addition of the recent examples at Chania, Eleutherna, Gortyn Basilica in Sector M, Knossos KMF, Chersonisos, Kisamos, Fodele, Ini and Priniatikos Pyrgos (see Appendix 4).

32 For comparative discussion, see work on the Late Antique Peloponnese (Sweetman 2010a).

33 Now churches have been recognized at the Venetian Church in Chania and near Museum Square in Kisamos.

34 Sanders, 30–1.

35 In many respects this is easily seen in the recent excavations of the Byzantine quarter at Gortyn (see Appendix 4).

Chapter Five. Urban and Architectural Contexts

1 See Allison's introduction to her 1999 edited volume, pp. 3–7, for a discussion of text and domestic space.

2 In particular, Bourdieu 1977.

3 2006, 146.

4 Maca 2006, 144.

5 In both Hodder 1989 and Stark 1998 the focus is on portable material culture, and Stark 1998 includes a focus on technology. Maca 2006, 144, provides a good summary of the development of scholarship.

6 See, in particular Wallace-Hadrill 1988, Locock 1994, Allison 1993 and Scott 1993.

7 As Kondoleon (1995) points out, both Pliny (*Epistles* 2.17.5–10) and Vitruvius (*De Architectura* 6.5.1) refer to the division between the family and visitor sections of the house.

8 'We shape our buildings; thereafter they shape us' (Winston Churchill, *Time* 12 Sept. 1960). 'The architect builds the cell in his mind before he constructs it in wax' (Karl Marx). Cited by Parker Pearson and Richards 1994, 2.

9 Kondoleon 1995, 2, discusses the issue of 'intentional display'.

10 Maca 2006, 146.

11 Bourdieu 1977, 2.

12 Maca 2006, 147.

13 Blake 1930, 101.

14 Kondoleon 1995, 1, notes that domestic art and architecture reflect both the family and business lives of the household and refers to the Roman house as a 'public stage' (ibid., 2).

15 For good wishes on bath house mosaics, see Dunbabin 1989, and for the Pompeii mosaic, see Bergmann 1994, fig. 4.

16 See Allison 1999, 'Introduction', pp. 9–10, for a discussion of the issue of the visibility of different gender roles in houses and a later work (2002) which redresses the masculine bias within discussions of space.

17 Ellis 2000, 5, based on the literary evidence.

18 De Haan (2004, 272) argues that 'if we limit ourselves to elite housing, the debate over the Romanization of housing becomes somewhat clearer. Too often the discussion has been complicated and confused by bringing in middle and lower class living accommodations.' Harrison (2004) suggested that different Cretan houses may reflect different levels of Romanization, but the matter is more complex than this where the context, individuals, social aspirations and issues concerning a definition of Romanization should be taken into account.

19 Maca 2006, 143–56, p. 143. It certainly relates to the residents' desired perception.

20 This is the generally accepted date rather than the secure date. Paton 1994, 143.

21 Sweetman 2007a.

22 Some epigraphic evidence suggests that there may have been a resident population of Campanians; see Sweetman 2007a.

23 Discussed in Chapter 2.

24 http://www.ucl.ac.uk/archaeology/project/knossos/index.htm/.

25 For a full account of Roman Knossos, see Paton 1994 and 2004a, Sweetman 2007a and Sweetman 2010b.

26 Respectively: Sackett et al. 1992, Warren, 1987–8, Paton 1994, Frend and Johnston 1962, Wardle 1998 and Sweetman 2004a and 2004b; 2005.

27 Hood and Smyth 1981.

28 See Sweetman 2004a and 2004b. A more synthetic work on the rescue material has been undertaken (Sweetman 2010b). See also Appendix 4.

29 Vitruvius *De Architectura* 1.7.2.

30 See Callaghan 1978 on the excavations of the Glaukos shrine. Baldwin Bowsky 2006b, 397–403.

31 Baldwin Bowsky 2006b, 410, KN 85.

32 Sackett et al. 1992. More recent excavations in the same area have revealed part of a Roman road and a section of a two-phased Roman building which appears to have gone out of use in the second century. This area is known as the Little Palace North (*AR* 2002–3, 81).

33 *AR* 2001–2, 107–8.

34 *AR* 2003–4, 77.

35 For more detailed discussion, see Sweetman 2010a and 2010b.

36 Sweetman 2004b.

37 For example, rescue excavations at the Venizelio Hospital; see *AR* 1999–2000, 133.

38 Sweetman 2010b. This is particularly seen at the KOP rescue site which is beside *KS* 191 and also *KS* 183.

39 Baldwin Bowsky 2004a. See also Paton 1994 for discussion of the presence of Campanians in Knossos.

40 Grammatikaki 2004. Baldwin Bowsky 2004a.

41 Grammatikaki 2004, 470.

42 See Sweetman 2007a for discussion of issues in identifying these settlers as Campanian.

43 In particular at the Unexplored Mansion.

44 For example, Hood and Smyth 1981, nos. 94, 95, 98, 101 and 102.

45 Given its location on the south coast this would also have been a convenient location for the administrative centre. It seems that after its original inclusion in the empire, Crete was given to Cleopatra by Antonius with Knossos as the political centre (Di Vita 2000b, 6).

46 For example, *IC* IV, 290–1 (Di Vita 2000b, 6).

47 Di Vita 2004.

48 Pernier 1925–6.

49 Formerly known as the Praetorium as discussed in Di Vita 2000b, 7. For the publications of the on-going excavations, see Di Vita 1988, 1997, 2000a, 2001.

50 Regular publications in the *ASAtene* and in the *Gortina* volumes (I–VI) published in the Monografie della Scuola Archeologica di Atene e delle Missioni Italiane in Oriente series. For a recent summary of excavations at Gortyn, see Di Vita 2004, and for the Acropolis at Gortyn see Perna 2004.

51 Di Vita 2000b, 5, notes that the centre of the Forum would have had an open shrine (*sacellum*) which contained statues of the Julio Claudians.

52 The standard range of shaft, tile and hut graves; mausoleums; monumental tombs; and sarcophagi are also found here as in Knossos. Single or multiple inhumations are also found. See, for example, *AR* 1997, 103, for the Agii Deka excavations.

53 Including that found in Area S of the Gymnasium; see *AR* 2004–5, 113–14.

54 A late Antique building was investigated in the early 1970s during excavation of the Roman cemetery to the west of the river; see Lembesis 1971, 298.

55 Now believed to belong to the cult of Egyptian deities (Di Vita 2000b, 10).

56 *AR* 2003–4, 83.

57 See http://www.gortinabizantina.it/index.htm for a well-illustrated summary of the annual excavations. Geophysical survey has revealed much of the settlement (*AR* 2001–2, 106).

58 *AR* 2004–5, 112.

59 *AR* 2002–3, 80.

60 See Volanakis 1987 for the list with the addition of the basilica in Sector M.

61 Spyridakis 1999, 64.

62 Di Vita 2000b, 12.

63 *AR* 2002–3, 80.

64 *AR* 2003–4, 82, and *AR* 2005–6, 112.

65 *AR* 2006–7, 110.

66 *AR* 2002–3, 80.

67 See details in the catalogue of mosaics.

68 Mosaics 105 and 106. See Bourboudakis 2004 and Farioli Campanati 2001 in particular. See *AR* 2003–4, 83, for the workshop.

69 Horden and Purcell 2000, 393.

70 Lappa being the other (Dio 1i.2.).

71 Andreadaki-Vlazaki 1997, fig. 32. It should be noted here that on the current mortuary evidence the size and location of the Hellenistic and Roman towns do not appear to have altered significantly until the Late Antique period (as was the case of Knossos and Gortyn).

72 Markoulaki 1999, 153–8.

73 Sanders, 170.

74 Excavated at the Dagadakis Plot on Peridou and Ipsilandou Streets (Markoulaki 2002, 246–9). The remains of what appears to be a large civic building were uncovered with a *terminus post quem* of the third century (*AR* 2002–3, 86). See Andreadaki-Vlazaki (1997, fig. 32, no. 9) for the theatre.

75 Andreadaki-Vlazaki 2006, 3. *AR* 1994–5, 72.

76 Andreadaki-Vlazaki 2002, 234–43.

77 The larger civic buildings tend to have a better survival rate and are less commonly built on.

78 Markoulaki et al. 2004, pl. III, nos. 56 and 34, respectively.

79 *AR* 1987–8, 76.

80 Markoulaki et al. 2004, pl. III, nos. 21, 56, 16.

81 *AR* 1996–7, 122.

82 Tzedakis 1970, 465–78.

83 Note that there are two Raisakis Plots.

84 *AR* 2004–5, 118.

85 *AR* 1997–8, 126.

86 *AR* 1993–4, 84.

87 *AR* 2000–1, 142.

88 Markoulaki et al. 2004, pl. III, nos. 2, 6, 29, 56, and south of Agios Nikolaos, respectively.

89 *AR* 1987–8, 76.

90 Markoulaki et al. 2004.

91 The bedding was described as being 1 cm thick with a mix of plaster and sherds below (*AR* 2000–1, 141).

92 Markoulaki et al. 2004. pl. III, no. 7. For the amphorae workshop, see Markoulaki, Empereur and Marangou, 1989.

93 For example, the Kalogridakis Plot, with its first-century burials (*AR* 1987–8, 76; Diamandis 2004; Markoulaki et al. 2004, pl. III, no. 9).

94 Markoulaki et al. 2004, 373 n. 68.

95 Ibid., 373.

96 Rescue excavations continue to reveal houses, tombs and water systems (*AR* 2006–7, 104).

97 See Chaniotaki-Starida and Mari 2004.

98 Rethemiotakis 1984, 296.

99 There is a Hellenistic public building known from Kastri.

100 *AR* 2000–1, 126.

101 *AR* 1996–7, 103 (the Sanoudakis Street excavations).

102 *AR* 1997–8, 112.

103 For example, *AR* 2001–2, 104, which records a cistern constructed in the second century and destroyed in the fourth.

104 Extensive fish tanks are still visible to the east of Chersonisos Basilica B on the Kastri.

105 *SEG* 1999 (49), 1218. Chersonisos had the invaluable resource of being able to provide different anchorage depending on the weather.

106 Bishop Andreas of Chersonisos is recorded at the third council of Ephesus in 431 (Hadzi-Vallianou 2006, 257).

107 Although houses have been identified in both, there is as yet little evidence for mosaic floors with the possible exception of Alykes and Viglia, Ierapetra (83 & 84) where the mosaic bedding and some tesserae were found and also in Agios Nikolaos where some pebble floors have been reported.

108 Both towns would have had very good harbour facilities.

109 Baldwin Bowsky 2006c and also Haggis 1996a.

110 For example, see *SEG* 1999 (49), 1231, which records an inscription referring to the restoration of Ierapetra's streets (paid for by Rome) in the middle of the first century. See Hayden 2004a; 2004b; and Haggis 1996b for further discussion on the basis of survey evidence.

111 Sanders, 129.

112 For example, see *AR* 1984–5, 64, and Apostolakou 2002a, 338.

113 *AR* 2002–3, 84 (Alykes), and *AR* 1990–1, 7 (Viglia). See the Tzoubleka Plot for Late Antique evidence.

114 *AR* 1984–5, 64; *AR* 1987–8, 72; *AR* 1992–3, 72; *AR* 2000–1, 134; and *AR* 2002–3, 84.

115 *AR* 1990–1, 70.

116 *AR* 1991–2, 64.

117 Sanders, 13.

118 *AR* 1983–4, 64–5.

119 Andreadaki-Vlazaki 2000–1b, 279. More recent rescue excavations in areas close to Rethymnon such as Panormou (*AR* 2003–4, 92) and Sphakaki Pangalochoriou (*AR* 1998–9, 124) have produced mosaic floors.

120 Connerton 1989. Sweetman forthcoming.

121 See Van Dyke and Alcock (eds.) 2003 for case studies on memory and archaeology and the review of the collection by Ammerman 2004.

122 2005, 1.

123 For example, Pompeii and Corinth. Vitruvius *De Architectura* 1.7.1. He noted that if the town were on the sea the forum should occupy space near the harbour and

if the town were inland the forum should be at the centre of town. Temples to the Capitoline triad and Mercury should be in the forum or main square and temples to Apollo and Dionysus near to the theatre.

124 For Knossos, see Sweetman 2003.

125 Sweetman 2010a and Sweetman forthcoming.

126 Sessa 2007, 175–6.

127 Parker Pearson and Richards 1994a, 9.

128 As Riggsby has discussed regarding *cubicula* (1997, 36, esp. 48). Riggsby equates private space with those who dwell in the house and public with those who are outside the house. *Publicus* would refer to the community.

129 1988.

130 Locock 1994 and Scott 1993, 1994, 1995.

131 Allison 1993.

132 1994. For the application of the evidence to Woodchester Villa, see Scott 1995.

133 Service areas do not commonly have mosaic floors.

134 *De Architectura* VII, iv, 4; VII, v, 2. For example, he recommended a rubbed black surface which gives the appearance of a black pavement, so that when wine is thrown it cannot be seen (VII, vii, 4).

135 Vitruvius *De Architectura* VII, v, 2, for the choice and suitability of different wall paintings

136 Altamore 2004.

137 For Minoa, see Altamore 2004, fig. 6, and Sanders, 169, for a discussion of the architecture. Andreadaki-Vlazaki (1993, 482) reported the new excavations in Rethymnon.

138 Altamore 2004, 257.

139 Sanders, 140.

140 For Eleutherna House 1, see Themelis 2004c, 57–62. See Ellis 2000, 31–3, for discussion of the Peristyle house.

141 Ioannidou-Karetsou et al. 2008, 109–11. See Clarke 1991, 17, for a discussion of the importance of the orientation of the rooms for views.

142 Ioannidou-Karetsou et al. 2008, 111.

143 I am grateful to John Hayes for the suggestion that this house and that of Kouphonisi may have been seaside retreats for Italian visitors.

144 Markoulaki 1999, 197–9; Markoulaki et al. 2004, fig. 12.

145 Altamore 2004, 267. In the original report Hadzi-Vallianou 1990, 409–15, 414, indicates the presence of a small 'cistern' and notes that the pottery was primarily of Roman date with some small numbers of Hellenistic material. A suggestion of a Late Roman date or mid-third century was proposed.

146 See catalogue entry for Mosaic 39 for discussion.

147 See Ellis 2000, 1–6, for a summary of the function of different rooms in Roman houses.

148 Ellis 2000, 6.

149 See Ling 1995, 239–51, for arguments against the connection between motifs and room function.

150 Sweetman 2007b contains a detailed discussion of the Villa Dionysus and its décor.

151 Wallace-Hadrill 1994, 17. I would like to thank one of the anonymous referees for pointing this possibility out to me.

152 Paton 2000.

153 Rooms N3 (4) and S2 (7) both have very simple mosaics and may have been used for more resident-orientated purposes.

154 These areas may be investigated in the future.

155 Ioannidou-Karetsou et al. 2008, 111.

156 See Papadakis 1979, fig. 2, for plan.

157 *Xenia* images often consist of collections of different types of food such as fruit, fish and game.

158 Markoulaki 1987a, 40.

159 Markoulaki et al. 2004.

160 Kankeleit 1994, 36.

161 Sanders, 146, suggested it came from the courtyard of a large building.

162 Nielsen 1993, 42.

163 Particularly in North Africa (Nielsen 1993, 86).

164 See Dunbabin 1989 and Dunbabin 1999 for a range of examples.

165 Nielsen 1993, 42.

166 Nielsen (1993, 141–2) mentions *Bene Laba*, 'have a nice bath', and *Salvom Lavisse*, expressing a hope that the bathers enjoyed their bath.

167 Nielsen 1993, 141.

168 Tzedakis 1970, 471; p. 409b. Another similar example is found in Caldarium in Bath E in Antioch (Campbell 1988, 11, pl. 36). For more discussion, see Dunbabin 1989, 41.

169 Farrington 1999 discusses a couple of baths as 'Romanizing baths' (e.g., the baths north of the Peribolos of Apollo at Corinth and the baths north of the Octagon at Philippi). It seems, however, that they are defined as such first on the basis of their dates (mid-first century B.C.E.) and then as a type. See Farrington 1999, 65, for the types of baths in Greece.

170 The majority of bath house mosaics in Greece use geometric mosaics such as, for example, the first-century East baths at Delphi, the second-century large baths at Argos and the third-century Trikala baths. Those bath house mosaics that have figured decoration are primarily of marine scenes (of a limited variety); examples of these are at the first- to second-century Kronion baths, Poseidon and the Hippocamps and Nereid and a Sea Bull. The third-century mosaics at the Philippi bath display individual scenes of wild beasts such as tigers, lions and bears in octagons.

171 The identification of private bath houses is most commonly based on size. The newly excavated bath house at Knossos is so small that it was likely to have been a private one (12) in contrast to the large public bath houses at Chania (132) or Aptera.

172 Waywell 1979, cat. 31, pl. 49, fig. 28.

173 The Herodes Atticus Odeia at Athens and Corinth, and the Odeia at Epidauros, Patras and Thessaloniki all contain geometric mosaic floors. The odeion at Argos also has mosaic floors and scenes of prize giving, probably appropriate for at least one of the functions of that odeion.

174 For example, Burden 1999, 210, has argued convincingly that the Odeion of Agrippa in the Athenian Agora in part functioned as a means of drawing visitors into the Agora who would have then been able to take account of the Augustan changes, particularly those to the religious topography of the space.

175 Waywell 1979, cat. 4, pl. 45, figs. 5–6.

176 For instance, the late third-century stoa in the Palace of Galerius or the stoas of the Thessaloniki Agora and the mosaics in the area of the northwest shops in Corinth

177 A fourth-century pebble mosaic is located in the treasury of the stoa rather than in the temple itself. Here, the mosaic of a hippocamp is more appropriate to the location of the sanctuary by the sea rather than it is to the god.

178 In this case, the mosaic is a later addition to an earlier Hellenistic temple. See Sanders, pl. 40.

179 Edelstein and Edelstein 1998, 296–9, for sources for the sacrifice of the cock to Asclepius and 300–1 for the pig.

180 Westgate (1997–8) has done some work on the Classical and Hellenistic mosaics in temple contexts and is currently developing this evidence.

181 Ling 1998, 115.

182 Sanders, 31.

183 Clark 2007, 92.

184 Sanders, 118, notes that there are a number of tripartite transepts at Nikopolis. For further discussion, see Bowden 2004.

185 Traditionally preparation rooms and store rooms used by the clergy.

186 Sweetman 2004b.

187 Sanders, 129.

188 Sanders 102, 113 and 122, respectively.

189 The synthronon at Kolokythia is a later addition built on top of the mosaic in the apse (Sanders, 92). For Panormos, see Sanders, 118.

190 *AR* 2008–9, 90.

191 Clark 2007, 92–3.

192 Clark 2007, 92.

193 Similar to Clark's type fig. 1b (2007).

194 Clark 2007, 101–2.

195 This may be indicative of the more revelation elements of the liturgy favoured in the Western church, as opposed to the processional favoured in the East (Mathews 1971, 176).

196 Dauphin (1980, 132–4) argues that the high density of mosaics in areas such as Palestine, Syria and Cilicia are indicative of their wealth. Although Dauphin acknowledges the issues of archaeological bias (ibid., 112–13), the choice of décor is fuelled by a number of factors, including architectural context, and not simply by demand.

197 Ovadiah and Ovadiah 1987.

198 1978b, 26.

199 Wallace-Hadrill 1988, 48.

200 Allison 1993.

201 As discussed in Chapter 7.

202 Dunbabin 1978b, 25.

203 Feld and Basso 1996, 4

Chapter Six. Mosaics of Crete: Craftspeople, Technology and Workshops

1 Dunbabin 1999, 270, discusses one of the few mentions of mosaicists in the historical sources, that is, from Pliny (*Natural Histories* 36.184) describing the mosaics of the Unswept Floor and Doves of the mosaicist Sosos of Pergamon.

2 See Donderer 1989 for a study on the use of inscriptions to allow insight on mosaicists.

3 Dunbabin 1999, 278.

4 In an earlier publication, Dunbabin (1978b, 24) indicated that patrons played a significant role in the development of the North African mosaics mostly through their choice of subjects (ibid., 25). The lack of detailed evidence makes it difficult to argue for or against this case with confidence.

5 These are the only two words to denote the mosaicists' activities found on mosaics in Crete.

6 Dunbabin 1978b, 28.

7 Ibid.

8 Ibid., for example, the bath house mosaic from Sidi Bou Ali.

9 Kankeleit 1994, 82.

10 Ramsden 1971, 497.

11 Another example of such precise detail is the Avenches mosaic which records the donation of the area of the exedra and centre by M. Fl. Marcunus (ibid., 481–2).

12 A detailed example occurs in Italy where the specifics of the area of mosaic paid for are noted (Dunbabin 1999, 325).

13 Ramsden 1971, 497.

14 There are cases where the Roman trianomina are provided (more details follow).

15 Markoulaki 1987b, pl. 327, and Markoulaki et al. 2004, 372.

16 An example from Trikkla in Thrace bears the inscription Τίτος Φλάβιος Ἑρμῆς καὶ [Βά]σσος Ἑρμοῦ [υἱ]οὶ ἑαυτοῖς τ[ῶν γ]ραφομέν[ων ψη]φοθέτ[αι – – -] 'Titus Flavius Hermes and Bassus, sons of Hermes, on their own expense, the mosaicists of the inscription … ' which tells us that there were two craftspeople, sons of Hermes (who was apparently not a Roman citizen). Of the two brothers, one was a citizen (Titus Flavius Hermes), presumably enfranchised by a Titus Flavius. His brother Bassus, however, seems not to have been a citizen (unless T. Flavius, despite the singular, is to be understood with both names). This mosaic provides insight into the nature of working practices, in this case, that work was a family affair, that the craftspeople both designed and laid the floor and that members of the same family may have had different social statuses. Theocharis 1965, 313–16, and pls. 371–2. See Ramsden 1971, 484, for discussion.

17 Fraser and Matthews 1987, 50, and Osborne and Byrne 1994, 42.

18 Fraser and Matthews 1997, 49.

19 See Baldwin Bowsky 2004a, Paton 1994 and Sweetman 2007a for discussion.

20 Kankeleit 1994, 84.

21 Donderer 1989, 55 Nr. A5. This would also fit in with the Campanian link suggested earlier.

22 Sweetman 2003 and 2007b.

23 1997, 299, and 1987, 310.

24 *SEG* 1984 (34), no. 915. Only three tesserae in a curve at the top are preserved.

25 1989, 81 No. A42.

26 Robert 1967, 555.

27 Kankeleit 1994, 83. Markoulaki 1990, 461.

28 Kankeleit 1994, 85.

29 As Kondoleon 2000, 64–5, notes, this is the only example of the signature of an Antiochan mosaicist anywhere in the empire.

30 The exo-narthex of the Frangokastelli mosaic (143–6) is the only clear example of multiple craftspeople at work on one Cretan mosaic.

31 There is little in the ancient sources regarding the possible division of labour among craftspeople, although inscriptions in mosaics are one of the few examples of positive evidence for this (Ramsden 1971, 497).

32 *Byz Corp II*, no. 96.

33 Dunbabin 1978b, 28 n. 59.

34 In the centre of the image.

35 It is possible that the name refers to 'the servant of the Lord' and that there is a mistake in not having the Θεό in the genitive form. However, it is more likely that the name is a personal one. Bandy 1970, 94, and Fraser and Matthews 1987, 214.

36 1970, 95.

37 Bandy 1970.

38 'Demetrios and Epiphanes made this mosaic, Demetrios conceived of the inscription, while Epiphanes was its most skilled executioner, Pavlos is responsible for all good things, a priest and a teacher of divine wisdom' (*Byz Corp II*, no. 96). It should be noted that the use of the name Epiphanes in both cases is coincidental, as the same mosaicist could be responsible for both mosaics. Epiphanes is a common name in Greece in all periods, as can be seen from the number of examples found in the *Lexicon of Greek Personal Names* (Fraser and Matthews 1987; Osborne and Byrne 1994).

39 *IG* ii² 4076, and Bandy 1970, 95.

40 1970, 95.

41 Di Vita 1998–2000, 440–2, fig. 78.

42 *AR* 1999–2000, 132. Additionally, no record of the name was found in *IC*.

43 *SEG* 2001 (51), 1167.

44 Ibid.

45 Di Vita 1996–7, 566, figs. 112 and 113.

46 Ibid. 567, n. 135. From *IC* IV, 460.

47 *AR* 2000–1, 128.

48 S. Stiros and S. Papageorgiou 2001, 383–6. See specifically Table 1. Sweetman forthcoming.

49 Themelis (1994–6, 273); Tzifopoulos 2000, 241–4.

50 A 20-year period is suggested prior to the council meeting as Euphratas was a bishop both on the occasion of the council and at the time of the building of the basilica. It is unlikely that he would have been a bishop for much more than 20 years.

51 Dunbabin 1999, 325.

52 Bandy 1970, 19.

53 Cyprus is an interesting case as it shares both the Eastern preference for labelling scenes and the fashion, not seen in the East, for signing mosaics. See, for example, the Orpheus mosaic from Paphos (Michaelides 1987, 13–14).

54 Becker and Kondoleon 2005. See in particular pp. 32–7 for discussion of the manufacture and placement of the mosaic of the Judgement of Paris.

55 Ibid., 34 and 35.

56 See in particular the Leverhulme project by James and Bjornholt, *The Composition of Byzantine Glass Mosaic Tesserae* (http://www.sussex.ac.uk/arthistory/1–4–13–4.html).

57 Becker and Wypyski in Becker and Kondoleon 2005, 49–61.

58 Newman in Becker and Kondoleon 2005, 62–70. Although not that many mosaics have had petrographic analysis, those that have indicate that the material would have come from local sources (see Dunbabin 1999, 280). Dunbabin notes a range of examples, from North Africa to Switzerland to Britain. She also notes that where good stone sources were limited (such as near Palantia in Hispania Tarraconensis) the mosaicists must have brought their material with them.

59 Becker and Kondoleon 2005, 71.

60 Ibid. This is not a narrow date range.

61 Valuable discussions with Professor Elizabeth James of Sussex University may lead to future collaboration on the scientific analysis of some of the Cretan mosaics. To this end, Nadine Schibille has been working on the KMF tesserae.

62 http://www.sed.manchester.ac.uk/geography/undergraduate/fieldwork/crete/maps/geology.htm, and Becker 1976.

63 *AR* 2003–4, 83.

64 Sweetman 2004b. It is hoped that these fragments may be included for analysis as part of a new project in conjunction with the members of the Network for the Composition of Byzantine Glass Mosaic Tesserae.

65 For example, at Olus (**108**), Kera (**122–5**) and Sybrita (**116–17**) only red, black and white tesserae are used. At Chersonisos Basilica A (**92–3**) and Almyrida (**148–51**) pale grey/blue and also yellow tesserae are added to the basic three. For Roman examples see the Chersonisos Fountain mosaic (**38**) or the *Oecus* Mosaic (**1**) from the Villa Dionysus.

66 *AR* 2000–1, 141.

67 *AR* 1996–97, 121.

68 See Dunbabin 1999, 281–90, for a detailed discussion of the processes involved in laying and finishing a mosaic floor. See fig. 294 for a good example of the use of guidelines.

69 Undertaken by the author in spring 2008 with the invaluable help of Dr R. B. Mackay, R. Meenan and P. D. Sweetman. The fieldwork was generously funded through a grant from the Cotton Foundation and Carnegie Trust.

70 Smith 1965; Sodini 1970 and 1971; Dunbabin 1978b; Campbell 1979; Wilson 1983; Ovadiah and Ovadiah 1987; Assimakopoulou-Atzaka 1984 and 1991; Ling 1991a; Clarke 1994; and Allison 1993.

71 The words can be used somewhat interchangeably, for instance, 'The mosaics of the Baths of Trajan show, right at the beginning of the establishment of schools of mosaicists in Africa, a designer of exceptional originality in charge of a workshop where his assistants were still producing pavements almost in an entirely Italian manner' (Dunbabin 1978b, 19).

72 For discussion, see Ling 1994, and for a range of examples from North Africa, see Dunbabin 1978b, 29. Dunbabin 1999, 281–2, notes that normal practice must have been that mosaics were laid *in situ*.

73 Kondoleon (2000, 65) argues against the idea of pattern books (certainly for figured décor). Dunbabin (1999, 302) and Ling (1991a, 217–19) state that pattern books in some format are likely to have existed for a whole range of Roman artistic media.

74 Ling (1991a, 217) notes the Classical example of the copying of the panels and parchment drawings of Parrhasius as described in sources such as Seneca the Elder (*Controv.* v. 10).

75 Ling, 1991a, pls. 235 and 236, respectively.

76 Ovadiah and Ovadiah (1987, 181) suggest that in the case of the mosaics of Israel the pattern books were passed down from generation to generation. In addition, the use of pattern books may help to account for some of the similarities between mosaics of Christian and non-Christian contexts, for example, those of Orpheus and the animals and Christ as shepherd, respectively (see Mathews 1999).

77 Ling 1991a, 219. Pliny *Natural Histories* xxxv.11.

78 Westgate 1999, 16.

79 Ibid., 16–17.

80 There is little evidence for guidelines in the Cretan mosaics and as yet no direct evidence for the use of templates.

81 For example, Thessaloniki (Waywell 1979, cat. 53, pl. 52).

82 A Syrian example, dated to the third–fourth century, in the Miho Museum (Japan) includes the character labels typical of this period in Syrian mosaics (http://www.miho.or.jp/english/collect/main/image/f1.jpg).

83 From the second- to third-century House of Dionysus and Ariadne. The use of the architectural framework is common in the Antioch mosaics.

84 Reinach 1922, 113 no. 2. A similar range of locations and media are found with scenes of the Triumph of Dionysus as discussed by Kondoleon 1995, 192–221.

85 *LIMC* VII, 616. Rea Silvia 4. Other examples recorded there include Rea Silvia 6 and 7.

86 Huskinson 1996, pl. 9.2. Another close parallel is found in a sarcophagus in the Terme Museum in Rome (no. 214) dating to the second century.

87 Guthrie 1993, 267 and 262–3.

88 Faventinus also closely follows Vitruvius's argument in chapters 18 and 19: On the laying of pavements (Plommer 1973, 99).

89 Dunbabin 1999, 281, fig. 287.

90 Campbell 1979, 288.

91 Lavagne 1977, 61–86.

92 This is the case for the 'thick' guilloche identified on two mosaics in Crete (**136** & **S207d**) and which had not been identified outside of the island.

93 Wilson 1983, 47–8.

94 Ibid., 44.

95 1994, 89.

96 Clarke 1994, 89.

97 In his article Smith (1965, 95), established three schools based in East Yorkshire, Dorset, Somerset and Gloucestershire. In later works he added a further three, including a second-century Colchester-Verulanium School. I would like to thank the anonymous reviewer for bringing this to my attention. Ongoing work, however, does highlight issues of subjectivity in the identification of mosaic schools.

98 Kondoleon 1995, 54–5, 60.

99 Ibid., 28–9.

100 Daszewski 1985, 87.

101 Clarke 1994.

102 By the second century in Africa there were workshops in all the major centres, for example, Sousse, El Djem and Carthage (Dunbabin 1978b, 20).

103 Sweetman 2003, 542.

104 Please note that this is a reconstruction drawing and the stylized flower is not an exact match.

105 Sweetman 2003, 542.

106 Ioannidou-Karetsou et al, 2008; see in particular the section by Markoulaki, pp. 107–47.

107 Ioannidou-Karetsou et al. 2008, 109–47.

108 Tzedakis 1968, pls. 377 and 379.

109 1986, 266–9.

110 There is another example of this style found in a second-century mosaic in Kisamos (Markoulaki in Ioannidou-Karetsou et al. 2008, fig. 41).

111 Markoulaki 1990.

112 Markoulaki 1987b, pl. 324.

113 The closest parallel for this type of 'thick guilloche' (Pl. 42) comes from a mosaic from Avenches in Switzerland (von Gonzenbach 1961, pl. 79).

114 Campbell 1988, 290, and Sodini 1970, 751. For images, see *Byz Corp II*, pls. 126–7 (Elis); Duyuran 1960, pls. 1–8 (Istanbul); Hanfmann 1983, fig. 254 (Sardis); *Byz Corp I*, pl. 101 (Ag. Andreou, Eresos).

115 *Byz Corp II*, pls. 126–7.

116 *Byz Corp II*, pl. 134.

117 Duyuran 1960, pls. 1–8.

118 Hanfmann 1983, fig. 254.

119 *Byz Corp I*, pl. 104.

120 *Byz Corp II*, pls. 126–7.

Chapter Seven. The Provincial View, Globalization and Christianization

1 For example, see Dunbabin 1999, 212.

2 Note Baldwin Bowsky's (2004a & 2004b) evidence for traders on the island.

3 It was generally peaceful save for the notable exception of Judea and flashpoints on the fringes of the empire. This was also the time of the Second Sophistic, so Greek culture was of great interest, encouraging positive forces on the economy. Furthermore, there was no evidence of significant plague or drought and no major earthquakes are recorded in this period as there had been in the first–second century.

4 Alcock 1993.

5 For example, see Sonnabend 2004.

6 Baldwin Bowsky 2002, 26.

7 Ibid., 24. Baldwin Bowsky (2002, 28) also argues *contra* Sanders (1982, 5) that Crete seems to have played a role in Rome's civil wars between Caesar and Pompey in that some Cretan legates were sent to Pompey and archers were sent to both sides. See also discussion in Chapter 1.

8 The route from Puteoli to Alexandria could not be taken without stopping, particularly as travellers would have faced westerly winds and the safest places to stop were Crete or even Rhodes.

9 *IC* IV, 290–1. Di Vita 2000b, 6.

10 Baldwin Bowsky 2002, 38–9.

11 Baldwin Bowsky 2001a, 2001b and especially 2004b.

12 Baldwin Bowsky 2004a and 2006b.

13 See Horden and Purcell 2000, 393, for the importance of what they term places of redistribution.

14 Rackham and Moody 1997, 200.

15 Baldwin Bowsky 2002, 43.

16 Ibid. Sweetman 2007a discusses the lack of impact.

17 Baldwin Bowsky 2002, 41. At Knossos these names appear in coin legends, religious dedications and honorary and sepulchral inscriptions. At Gortyn they appear in religious dedications, sepulchral inscriptions, lists of names and inscriptions granting *proxenia* and *politeia* (ibid., 43).

18 Sweetman 2007a.

19 Grammatikaki 2004.

20 For instance, in the Vrokastro area some of the identifiably Hellenistic settlements continue in use until the middle of the second century and there is some continuity of cult sites (Hayden 2004b, 267).

21 The sanctuary at Lebena is of Hellenistic date, but the temple was modified by the Romans in the late first century B.C.E. or the first century C.E.

22 Other first-century temples are found in the south at Agios Nikolaos in Samaria and at Kato Syme.

23 Sanders, 75. Work on the Acropolis temple was also undertaken in the first century.

24 Baldwin Bowsky (2006b, 403) has tentatively identified evidence for the cult of Isis (possibly at the Demeter Sanctuary) and the cult of Castor and Pollux (possibly at the Glaukos Shrine (ibid., 397)).

25 From Chersonisos, a second-century building inscription (re-used in a Late Antique building) recording the promise of the government official to dedicate a temple during his term (*SEG* 2002 (52), 848).

26 Sanders, 37.

27 For Knossos see Eiring 2000a, 449, and Sackett 1992; for the Vrokastro region, see Harrison 2000, 552.

28 Baldwin Bowsky 2006a, 412.

29 Ibid., 414–15. See particularly the catalogue of inscriptions (pp. 420–6).

30 Hayden et al. 1992, 333, for survey work and Baldwin Bowsky 2006c for inscriptions.

31 Grammatikaki 2004, 465–72, for the Venizelio cemetery.

32 Baldwin Bowsky 2006b, 393.

33 2002, 38–9.

34 In particular, at Kastelli and Chania (Markoulaki, Empereur & Marangou 1989) and Eleutherna (*AR* 2006–7, 117).

35 *AR* 2003–4, 77.

36 Hayden 2005, 58.

37 *SEG* 1999 (49) 1231, *SEG* 2003 (52) 853–4 and *SEG* 2001 (51) 1137–40, respectively.

38 The concentration of excavations in Gortyn, for example, has been on the public area, whereas the cities of the north have been the focus of many more urban rescue excavations discovering domestic areas.

39 Watrous et al. 1993.

40 Watrous 1982.

41 Sanders, 30.

42 Whitley, Prent and Thorne 1999.

43 Marangou-Lerat 1995.

44 Some, such as Elton (2004), would see the imperial cult as an indication of imperial control. It is likely though that in any case much of the inclination for the imperial cult in the East would come from the local population.

45 Kokkinia 2004.

46 Haggis (1996a) is likely correct in his suggestion that the north coast became particularly important as a redistribution centre for the Cyclades.

47 Sonnabend (2004, 25) suggests that perhaps Cretans did not view themselves as either Cretan or Roman but as associated with their own home towns.

48 'From the third to late fifth centuries Crete appears to have been in decline, perhaps accentuated by the series of earthquakes in the 4c' (Sanders, 30). For discussion of memory and Late Antique Knossos, see Sweetman forthcoming.

49 Scott 1994. Even with the concentration on urban centres, evidence can be elusive. For example, until the recent finds from Museum Square, there was little evidence for a Late Antique church in Kisamos, but a seventh/eighth-century inscription from there referred to the servant Andreas of the Church of Kisamos, which meant that a church had to have been there (Spyridakis 1999, 69).

50 For example, many of the southern harbour towns continued to thrive from their location on the west–east trade route until the threat of the Arab invasions.

51 In addition to those noted by Sanders (30), particularly in the Amari and Spili valley, new rural villas have been located, for example, in the northeast during the Agia Photia survey.

52 The same approach as taken by Sweetman 2010a to the Peloponnese is also being applied to Crete.

53 Sweetman 2004b.

54 Spyridakis 1999, 64. Hierocles stated that Gortyn was the most important of the 22 cities of Crete (*Synecd.* 649.5).

55 Sweetman forthcoming.

56 Sweetman 2004b.

57 Sweetman 2010a.

58 Dating between the end of the fourth century and the eighth century (Fig. 6).

59 Themelis 2003.

60 Platon 1956, 229–31.

61 Sanders, 117, 92, 123. See Curuni and Donati 1987, 12.3, for plan.

62 Sanders, 115, 112, 95.

63 Sweetman 2005, fig. 2. Sanders (90) also includes Itanos Basilica C and the Mitropolis martyrium as unusual basilicas, but it is not at all certain that these functioned as churches.

64 See Sweetman 2011b for a more detailed discussion of this point.

65 Ibid.

66 There are multiple churches at Eleutherna and Knossos, but they are likely to have been constructed at different times.

67 Sanders, 108. Some, such as Foschia (2002), would argue that the conversion of temples to churches could be regarded as a second phase of the Christianization of the city.

68 See Sweetman 2010a for comparative discussion.

69 Sanders, 131.

70 Sweetman 2004b.

71 See Michaelides (1989b, 194) for examples from Cyprus.

72 *Byz Corp II*, no. 6, pls. 28–9.

73 Sanders, 30.

74 This is a good example of what Sherratt and Sherratt (1993, 365) describe as 'formalization of commercial links through politicization'.

75 According to Sherratt and Sherratt 1993, 367: 'Westward maritime traffic followed the south Anatolian coast from Cyprus to Rhodes and then could either cycle anti-clockwise around the Mediterranean or continue westwards in two streams: either along the southward margin through Crete and up the west coast of Greece to cross to southern Italy and Sicily, or through the Cyclades to Euboea and Attica'.

76 Haggis 1996a, 204.

77 Hayden (2004a, 277) and Haggis (1996a) both refer to this possibility.

78 Marangou-Lerat 1995.

79 Sanders, 34. Crete also may have exported herbs and spices.

80 Marangou 1999, 278.

81 This is also supported by the Chersonisos ostraca (see *SEG* 1999 (49), 1218) recording everyday transactions. There are two groups, one occurring in months between March and April or November/December and the other between June and July. Litinas believes that the first group refer to slaves and small shopkeepers and the second to importers or wholesalers. The amounts indicated are substantial, indicating large-scale transactions.

82 Raab 2001, 44, suggests that the presence of imported pottery on rural sites is indicative of the production of an agricultural surplus. Although this may be the case for some sites, the additional wealth is more likely to have been generated through handling goods for trade, as discussed in the conclusion.

83 Sanders, 70. Although the date of the bath house is uncertain, Sanders believes that a date in the early part of the Roman period is likely.

84 Sanders, 87–8.

85 Baldwin Bowsky 2002, 31.

86 Castells 1996, 5.

Appendix 1. Catalogue of Mosaics

1 *Décor*, and Balmelle et al. 2002.

2 Although the traditional label of villa as given by Hutchinson (1934–5, 164) has been retained here, the house is more properly a town house or *domus* (Fig. 18).

3 Please note that further images of the mosaics of Knossos can be found in Sweetman 2003, pls. 73–89.

4 Paton 1998 provides a detailed discussion of the history of excavations.

5 This idea is highly unlikely. It seems that Gough's religious nature got the better of him, and he assumed that the large number of lamps with erotic decoration found in the Villa Dionysus must have indicated a cult centre (pers. comm., Sara Paton).

6 Paton's architectural study of the Villa Dionysus also suggests that this room is earlier than the rest of the *domus* (pers. comm.).

7 I would like to thank one of the reviewers for identifying this.

8 K2K = Knossos 2000 excavations.

9 I would like to thank Todd Whitelaw for bringing this reference to my attention.

10 The Knossos (KN) Logbook is a record of chance finds and minor rescue excavations undertaken in the Knossos Valley by archaeologists at the British School at Knossos. It is now housed in the Archive of the BSA in Athens.

11 Held in the Archive of the British School at Athens.

12 The only available record of the mosaic consists of three black-and-white photographs in the Archive of the British School at Athens. I am grateful to Dr Whitelaw for bringing to my attention the third photograph in the Archive, which identified the mosaic as that from Hutchinson's 1938 excavation.

13 Although this band probably functions as a border, it is also possible that it starts a second field of design. No conclusive evidence either way has come to light.

14 This is a record of some rescue excavations in the Knossos Valley. The book is currently housed in the Archive of the British School at Athens.

15 It is possible that only one mosaic existed and that Sanders identified the mosaic bedding in the section as a second mosaic.

16 The pottery was examined by D. Grigoropoulos.

17 This is the code given to the rescue excavations in Knossos: K = Knossos KE = abbreviation of the name of the plot.

18 There is some doubt about the dating of the geometric mosaic from the Villa Dionysus. Therefore, perhaps the similarities with the Iraklion pavement means that the mosaic is not as early as believed.

19 This is very similar to that of the design occurring in the central emblem of the Medusa mosaic from the Villa Dionysus (Mosaic 5).

20 I am extremely grateful to Dr Hadzi-Vallianou, the excavator of this plot, who very generously gave me her original excavation plans, photographs and accounts so that I could research this mosaic. This entry is based on her excavation archive for the site.

21 The only other place where this pattern is seen is in Mosaic 8 at the Villa Dionysus.

22 Excavations and historical sources suggest that the site was occupied in the fourth century B.C.E.; the temple is dated to the late second/early first century B.C.E. through epigraphic evidence.

23 I am very grateful to Mrs Ninou, the archivist of the Archaeological Society of Athens, for generously allowing me access to the Kalokyris Archive for use in this publication.

24 It is possible to see the outline of the tail of the peacock in the lower left corner of the plate.

25 It is now more of a blue colour which is likely faded from the original black.

26 The archivist of the French School at Athens kindly searched the archives, but no records of the excavation seem to be there.

27 Note that Di Vita 2000b, 12, suggests that the first wave of damage may have been due to an earthquake.

28 This is very similar to the design in the narthex of Basilica A, Chersonisos (92–3).

29 I would like to thank one of the anonymous readers for this suggestion.

30 This refers to the scaled pull-out drawings in the publication.

31 Another mosaic with Menander scenes was found during the Health Centre excavations in Kisamos (S207e).

32 The only parallel for this particular type of guilloche comes from the mosaic of the masks at the Health Centre excavations in Kisamos (S207d).

33 More of the mosaic is now visible since this plan was published.

34 Expertly located by K. A. MacKay and R. Meenan.

35 Thanks to B. MacKay and D. Sweetman for finding this.

Appendix 2. Catalogue of Mosaic Inscriptions

1 Apostolakou 1996, 655, and SEG 1999 (49), 1232. I would like to thank B. Millis for useful discussions of this inscription and others that follow.

2 SEG 2000 (50), 904.

3 Translation from Themelis 2004c, 76.

4 *SEG* 2000 (50), 889. I would like to thank B. Millis for all his help with this.

5 See Tzifopoulos in Themelis 2000, 237–59.

BIBLIOGRAPHY

Aguilar, M. 2005. 'The Archaeology of Memory and the Issue of Colonialism: Mimesis and the Controversial Tribute to Caesar in Mark 12:13–17'. *Biblical Theology Bulletin*, Summer, 1–12.

Alcock, S. E. 1993. *Graecia Capta: The Landscapes of Roman Greece* (Cambridge).

Alcock, S. E., ed. 1997. *The Early Roman Empire in the East*. Oxbow Monographs 95 (Oxford).

Alcock, S. E. 2002. *Archaeologies of the Greek Past: Landscape, Monuments and Memories* (Cambridge).

Alcock, S., and J. Cherry, eds. 2004. *Side-by-Side Survey: Comparative Regional Studies in the Mediterranean World* (Oxford).

Alexander, M., and M. Ennaifer. 1973. *Corpus des Mosaïques de Tunisie*. Institut National d'Archéologie et d'Arts. Vol. I, fasc. I (Tunis).

Alexiou, S. 1957. 'Χρονικά', *K.Khron*, 382–394.

  1964. 'Κάτω Ασίτες', *A.Delt*. 19 B3, 444.

  1973. 'Χρονικά', *K.Khron*, 457–78.

Alföldi-Rosenbaum, E., and J. Ward-Perkins. 1980. *Justinianic Mosaic Pavements in Cyrenaican Churches*. [Monografie di Archeologia Libyca XIV.] (Rome).

Allegro, N. 2004. 'Gortina al momento della conquista romana: Il dato archeologico'. In Livadiotti and Simiakaki (eds.), *Creta romana e protobizantina*, 531–8.

Allison, P. 1993. 'How Do We Identify the Use of Space in Roman Housing?' In E. Moorman (ed.), *Functional and Spatial Analysis of Wall Painting*, 1–8.

Allison, P., ed. 1999. *The Archaeology of Household Activities* (London).

Allison, P. 1999. 'Introduction'. In Allison (ed.), *The Archaeology of Household Activities*, 1–18.

  2002. 'Engendering Roman Spaces'. In Robertson, Seibert, Fernandez and Zender (eds.), *Space and Spatial Analysis in Archaeology*, 343–54.

Altamore, G. 2004. 'Ville e edifice-laboratorio sui litorali cretesi: Architettura, paesaggio e attività produttive'. In Livadiotti and Simiakaki (eds.), *Creta romana e protobizantina*, 257–68.

Ambraseys, N. N. 2006. 'Earthquakes and Archaeology'. *Journal of Archaeological Science* 33.7, July 2006, 1008–16.

Ammerman, A. J. 2004. 'Reviewed Work(s): *Archaeologies of Memory* by Ruth M. Van Dyke and Susan E. Alcock'. *Journal of Field Archaeology* 29.3/4, 474–7.

Andreadakis, M. 1984. ʽΟ ναός του Μιχαήλ Αρχαγγέλου Επισκοπής Κισάμου΄, in Δ΄ Συμπόσιο Βυζαντινής και Μεταβυζαντινής Αρχαιολογίας και Τέχνης, Περιλήψεις, 6–7 (Αθήνα).

1988. ʽΑρχαιολογικές ειδήσεις 1987΄. K.Estia 2, 351–72.

1991. ʽΟικόπεδο Αντ. και Ευαγγ. Βεστάκη΄. A.Delt. 46 B2, 422–6.

1991–3. ʽΟικόπεδο Αντ. και Ευαγγ. Βεστάκη΄. K.Estia 4, 227–9.

Andreadaki-Vlazaki, M. 1990. ʽΟικόπεδο Δαφνομήλη΄. A.Delt. 45 B2, 445–6.

1991–3. ʽΣταυρομένος Χαμαλευρίου΄. K.Estia 4, 245–7.

1993. ʽΟικόπεδο αδελφών Μυτιληναίου΄. A.Delt. 48 B2, 482.

1997. *The County of Khania through Its Monuments from the Prehistoric Period to Roman Times* (Athens).

1999. ʽΟικόπεδο Ετ. Ε. Ξηρουχάκη΄. K.Estia 7, 215–17.

2000–1a. ʽΠάνορμο΄. K.Estia 8, 315.

2000–1b. ʽΡέθυμνο΄. K.Estia 8, 279.

2002. ʽΟδός Τζανακάκη΄. K.Estia 9, 234–43.

2006. *Αρχαίοι τόποι και μνημεία, Νομός Χανίων* (Chania).

Angold, M., and M. Whitby. 2008. ʽThe Church: Structures and Administration΄, chapter III.11.1. In Jeffreys, Haldon and Cormack (eds.), *The Oxford Handbook of Byzantine Studies*, 571–82.

Apostolakou, S. 1989. ʼʼΑγιος Νικόλαος Μιραμπέλλο΄. A.Delt. 38 B2, 306–7.

1996. ʽΒιγλιά Ιεράπετρας΄. A.Delt. 51 B2, 655.

2002a. ʽΟικόπεδο Κωννου Παγκάλου΄. K.Estia 9, 336–42.

2002b. ʽΑλυκές΄. K.Estia 9, 343–5.

Apostolakou, V. 2003. *Λατώ* (Athens).

AR 1935 = Payne, H. 1935. ʽArchaeology in Greece, 1934–5΄. *Journal of Hellenic Studies: Archaeological Reports* 55, 135.

1938 = Young, G. M. 1938. ʽArchaeology in Greece, 1937–38΄. *Journal of Hellenic Studies: Archaeological Reports* 58, 232–33.

1951 = Cook, J. M. 1951. ʽArchaeology in Greece, 1951΄. *Journal of Hellenic Studies: Archaeological Reports*, 27–49.

1954 = Cook, J. M., and Boardman, J. 1954. ʽArchaeology in Greece, 1953΄. *Journal of Hellenic Studies: Archaeological Reports* 1, 26–45.

1957 = Hood, M. S. F. 1957. ʽArchaeology in Greece, 1956΄. *Journal of Hellenic Studies: Archaeological Reports* 5, 3–23.

1958 = Hood, M. S. F. 1958. ʽArchaeology in Greece, 1957΄. *Journal of Hellenic Studies: Archaeological Reports* 5, 3–24.

1959 = Hood, M. S. F. 1959. ʽArchaeology in Greece, 1958΄. *Journal of Hellenic Studies: Archaeological Reports* 6, 3–26.

1961 = Hood, M. S. F. 1961. ʽArchaeology in Greece, 1960–1΄. *Journal of Hellenic Studies: Archaeological Reports* 8, 3–31.

1964 = Megaw, A. H. S. 1963–1964. ʽArchaeology in Greece, 1963–64΄. *Journal of Hellenic Studies: Archaeological Reports* 10, 3–30.

1969–70 = Fraser, P. M. 1969–1970. ʽArchaeology in Greece, 1969–70΄. *Journal of Hellenic Studies: Archaeological Reports* 16, 3–31.

1970–1 = Fraser, P. M. 1970–1971. ʽArchaeology in Greece, 1970–71΄. *Journal of Hellenic Studies: Archaeological Reports* 17, 3–32.

1971–2 = Catling, H. W. 1971–1972. ʽArchaeology in Greece, 1971–72΄. *Journal of Hellenic Studies: Archaeological Reports* 18, 3–26.

1973–4 = Catling, H. W. 1973–1974. ʽArchaeology in Greece, 1973–74΄. *Journal of Hellenic Studies: Archaeological Reports* 20, 3–41.

1977–8 = Catling, H. W. 1977–1978. ʽArchaeology in Greece, 1976–77΄. *Journal of Hellenic Studies: Archaeological Reports* 24, 3–69.

1978–9 = Catling, H. W. 1978–1979. 'Archaeology in Greece, 1978–79'. *Journal of Hellenic Studies: Archaeological Reports* 25, 3–42.

1979–80 = Catling, H. W. 1979–1980. 'Archaeology in Greece, 1979–80'. *Journal of Hellenic Studies: Archaeological Reports* 26, 3–54.

1980–1 = Catling, H. W. 1980–1981. 'Archaeology in Greece, 1980–81'. *Journal of Hellenic Studies: Archaeological Reports* 27, 3–48.

1981–2 = Catling, H. W. 1981–1982. 'Archaeology in Greece, 1981–82'. *Journal of Hellenic Studies: Archaeological Reports* 28, 3–62.

1982–3 = Catling, H. W. 1982–1983. 'Archaeology in Greece, 1982–83'. *Journal of Hellenic Studies: Archaeological Reports* 29, 3–62.

1983–4 = Catling, H. W. 1983–1984. 'Archaeology in Greece, 1983–84'. *Journal of Hellenic Studies: Archaeological Reports* 30, 3–70.

1984–5 = Catling, H. W. 1984–1985. 'Archaeology in Greece, 1984–85'. *Journal of Hellenic Studies: Archaeological Reports* 31, 3–69.

1985–6 = Catling, H. W. 1985–1986. 'Archaeology in Greece, 1985–86'. *Journal of Hellenic Studies: Archaeological Reports* 32, 3–101.

1986–7 = Catling, H. W. 1986–1987. 'Archaeology in Greece, 1986–87'. *Journal of Hellenic Studies: Archaeological Reports* 33, 3–61.

1987–8 = Catling, H. W. 1987–1988. 'Archaeology in Greece, 1987–88'. *Journal of Hellenic Studies: Archaeological Reports* 34, 1–85.

1988–9 = Catling, H. W. 1988–1989. 'Archaeology in Greece, 1988–89'. *Journal of Hellenic Studies: Archaeological Reports* 35, 3–116.

1989–90 = French, E. B. F. 1989–1990. 'Archaeology in Greece, 1989–90'. *Journal of Hellenic Studies: Archaeological Reports* 36, 3–82.

1990–1 = French, E. B. F. 1990–1991. 'Archaeology in Greece, 1990–91'. *Journal of Hellenic Studies: Archaeological Reports* 37, 3–78.

1991–2 = French, E. B. F. 1991–1992. 'Archaeology in Greece, 1991–92'. *Journal of Hellenic Studies: Archaeological Reports* 38, 3–70.

1992–3 = French, E. B. F. 1992–1993. 'Archaeology in Greece, 1992–93'. *Journal of Hellenic Studies: Archaeological Reports* 39, 3–81.

1993–4 = French, E. B. F. 1993–1994. 'Archaeology in Greece, 1993–94'. *Journal of Hellenic Studies: Archaeological Reports* 40, 3–83.

1994–5 = Tomlinson, R. A. 1994–1995. 'Archaeology in Greece, 1994–95'. *Journal of Hellenic Studies: Archaeological Reports* 41, 1–47.

1995–6 = Tomlinson, R. A. 1995–1996. 'Archaeology in Greece, 1995–96'. *Journal of Hellenic Studies: Archaeological Reports* 42, 1–47.

1996–7 = Blackman, D. 1996–1997. 'Archaeology in Greece, 1996–97'. *Journal of Hellenic Studies: Archaeological Reports* 43, 1–126.

1997–8 = Blackman, D. 1997–1998. 'Archaeology in Greece, 1997–98'. *Journal of Hellenic Studies: Archaeological Reports* 44, 1–129.

1998–9 = Blackman, D. 1998–1999. 'Archaeology in Greece, 1998–99'. *Journal of Hellenic Studies: Archaeological Reports* 45, 1–124.

1999–2000 = Blackman, D. 1999–2000. 'Archaeology in Greece, 1999–2000'. *Journal of Hellenic Studies: Archaeological Reports* 46, 1–152.

2000–1 = Blackman, D. 2000–2001. 'Archaeology in Greece, 2000–01'. *Journal of Hellenic Studies: Archaeological Reports* 47, 1–145.

2001–2 = Blackman, D. 2001–2002. 'Archaeology in Greece, 2001–02'. *Journal of Hellenic Studies: Archaeological Reports* 48, 1–115.

2002–3 = Whitley, J. 2002–2003. 'Archaeology in Greece, 2002–03'. *Journal of Hellenic Studies: Archaeological Reports* 49, 1–88.

2003–4 = Whitley, J. 2003–2004. 'Archaeology in Greece, 2003–04'. *Journal of Hellenic Studies: Archaeological Reports* 50, 1–92.

2004–5 = Whitley, J. et al. 2004–2005. 'Archaeology in Greece, 2004–05'. *Journal of Hellenic Studies: Archaeological Reports* 51, 1–118.

2005–6 = Whitley, J. et al. 2005–2006. 'Archaeology in Greece, 2005–06'. *Journal of Hellenic Studies: Archaeological Reports* 52, 1–112.

2006–7 = Whitley, J. et al. 2006–2007. 'Archaeology in Greece, 2006–07'. *Journal of Hellenic Studies: Archaeological Reports* 53, 1–121.

2007–8 = Morgan, C. et al. 2007–2008. 'Archaeology in Greece, 2007–08'. *Journal of Hellenic Studies: Archaeological Reports* 54, 1–113.

2008–9 = Morgan, C. et al. 2008–2009. 'Archaeology in Greece, 2008–09'. *Journal of Hellenic Studies: Archaeological Reports* 55, 1–101.

Archibald, Z., J. Davies and V. Gabrielsen, eds. 2005. *Making, Moving and Managing: The New World of Ancient Economics, 323–31 BC* (Oxford).

Assimakopoulou-Atzaka, P. 1984. 'Τα Παλαιοχριστιανικά Ψηφιδωτά Δάπεδα του Ανατολικού Ιλλυρικού', *Actes du Xe congrès international d'archéologie Chrétienne* (II) (Thessaloniki, 28th September–4th October 1980), 361–444 (Thessaloniki).

1987. *Σύνταγμα των Παλαιοχριστιανικών Ψηφιδωτών Δαπέδων της Ελλάδος ΙΙ: Πελοπόννησος – Στερεά Ελλάδα* (Κέντρο Βυζαντινών Ερευνών Θεσσαλονίκη) (Thessaloniki).

1991. 'The Mosaic Pavements of the Aegean Islands during the Early Christian Period'. In Farioli Campanati (ed), *XXXVIII Corso di Cultura sull'Arte Ravennate e Bizsantina*, 33–65.

Aupert, P. 1976. 'Chronique des Fouilles et Découvertes en Grèce en 1975'. *BCH* 100, 591–745.

Baldwin Bowsky, M. W. 1994. 'Cretan Connections: The Transformation of Hierapytna'. *Cretan Studies* 4, 1–45.

1995. 'Roman Crete: No Provincial Backwater'. In Πεπραγμένα του 7ου Διεθνούς Κρητολογικού Συνεδρίου 1.1, 41–67 (Rethymno).

2001a. 'Gortynians and Others: The Case of the Antonii'. *Eulimene* 2, 97–119.

2001b. 'When the Flag Follows Trade: Metellus, Pompey and Crete'. *Electrum* 5, 31–72.

2002. 'Reasons to Reorganize: Antony, Augustus and Central Crete'. In Dabrowa (ed.), *Tradition and Innovation in the Ancient World*, 25–65.

2004a. 'Of Two Tongues: Acculturation at Roman Knossos'. In Salmeri, Raggi and Baroni (eds.), *Colonie Romane Nel Mondo Greco*, 95–150.

2004b. 'From Traders to Landowners: Acculturation in Roman Gortyn'. In Livadiotti and Simiakaki (eds.), *Creta romana e protobizantina*, 33–47.

2006a. 'Roman Patronage, Greek Identity: How Lyttos Finally Won the War against Knossos'. In Πεπραγμένα του 8ου Διεθνούς Κρητολογικού Συνεδρίου, Elounda 1–6 October, A5, 407–20 (Iraklion).

2006b. 'From Capital to Colony: Five New Inscriptions from Roman Crete'. *ABSA* 101, 385–426.

2006c. 'Highways and Byways of Roman Hierapytna (Crete): Four New Claudian Road Inscriptions'. *ASAtene* 84.1, 551–80.

2011. 'Colonia Iulia Nobilis Cnosus, the First 100 Years: The Evidence of Italian Sigillata Stamps'. In Sweetman (ed.), *Roman Colonies in the First Century of Their Foundation*, 117–34.

Balmelle, C., et al. 1985. *Le Décor géometrique de la mosaïque gréco-romaine I: Répertoire graphique et descriptif des compositions linéaires et isotropes* (Paris).

Balmelle, C., et al. 2002a. *Le Décor géometrique de la mosaïque gréco-romaine I: Répertoire graphique et descriptif des compositions linéaires et isotropes*, 2nd ed. (Paris).

Balmelle, C., et al. 2002b. *Le Décor géometrique de la mosaïque gréco-romaine II: Répertoire graphique et descriptif des décors centrés* (Paris).

Balty, J. 1977. *Mosaïques de Syrie* (Brussels).

Bandy, A. C. 1963. 'Early Christian Inscriptions of Crete'. *Hesperia* 32, 227–47.

1970. *The Greek Christian Inscriptions of Crete.* Χριστιανική Αρχαιολογική Εταιρεία Χ (Athens).

Baratte, F., and C. Metzger. 1985. *Catalogue des sarcophages en pierre d'époques romaine et paléochrétienne. Musée de Louvre* (Paris).

Barrett, J. C. 1997. 'Romanization: A Critical Comment'. In Mattingly and Alcock (eds.), *Dialogues in Roman Imperialism*, 51–64.

Batalla, C. M. 1994, ed. VI Coloquio Internacional sobre Mosaico Antiguo, Palencia-Mérida, Octubre 1990 (Guadalajara).

Baxandall, M. 1985. *Patterns of Intention: On the Historical Explanation of Pictures* (Yale).

BCH (no author). 1957. 'Chronique des fouilles et découvertes en Grèce en 1956'. *BCH* 81, 496–713.

Becatti, G. 1961. *Scavi di Ostia. Vol. IV, Mosaici e pavimenti marmorei* (Rome).

Becker, L., and C. Kondoleon. 2005. *The Arts of Antioch: Art Historical and Scientific Approaches to Roman Mosaics and a Catalogue of the Worcester Art Museum Antioch Collection* (Princeton).

Becker, M. 1976. 'Soft-Stone Sources on Crete'. *Journal of Field Archaeology* 3.4, 361–74.

Bekker-Nielsen. T., ed. 2005a. *Ancient Fishing and Processing in the Black Sea Region* (Aarhus).

Bekker-Nielsen, T. 2005b. 'The Technology and Productivity of Ancient Sea Fishing'. In Bekker-Nielsen. T. 2005. *Ancient Fishing and Processing in the Black Sea Region*, 83–97.

Bergmann, B. 1994. 'The Roman House as Memory Theatre: The House of the Tragic Poet in Pompeii'. *Art Bulletin* 76.2, 225–56.

Berti, F. 1972–3. 'Poseidon ed Amymone. Un mosaico romano di Chania'. *ASAtene* 50–1, 451–65.

Betancourt, P. B., and C. Davaras. 'Excavations at Pseira, 1985 and 1986'. *Hesperia*, 57.3, 207–25.

Bingöl, O. 1997. *Malerei und Mosaik der Antike in der Türkei* (Mainz am Rhein).

Blackman, D., and K. Branigan. 1975. 'An Archaeological Survey on the South Coast of Crete between the Agiofarango and Chrisostomos'. *ABSA* 70, 17–36.

1977. 'An Archaeological Survey of the Lower Catchment Area of the Agiofarango Valley'. *ABSA* 72, 30–84.

Blake, M. E. 1930. 'The Pavements of the Roman Buildings of the Republic and Early Empire'. *MAAR* VIII, 7–161.

1936. 'Roman Mosaics of the Second Century in Italy'. *MAAR* XIII, 69–214.

1940. 'Mosaics of the Late Empire in Rome and Vacinity'. *MAAR* XVII, 81–130.

Bookidis, N. 1974. 'Sanctuary of Demeter and Kore on Acrocorinth. Preliminary Report V: 1971–73'. *Hesperia* 43, 278–85.

Bourbou, C. 2004. *The People of Early Byzantine Eleutherna and Messene (6–7th Centuries A.D.): A Bioarchaeological Approach.* (Athens).

Bourboudakis, E. 1968. 'Ἀνασκαφὴ Μητροπόλεως Μεσαρᾶς Κρήτης'. *PAE*, 139–48.

1969. 'Μεσαιωνικὰ μνημεῖα Κρήτης'. *A.Delt.* 24 B2, 437–50.

1971. 'Μεσαιωνικὰ μνημεῖα Κρήτης'. *A.Delt.* 26 B2, 520–33.

1973. 'Χρονικά'. *K.Khron* 478–511.

1973–74. 'Βυζαντινὰ καὶ μεσαιωνικὰ μνημεῖα Κρήτης'. *A.Delt.* 29 B3, 935–43.

2004. 'Ἀνασκαφή Μητρόπολης'. In Livadiotti and Simiakaki (eds.), *Creta romana e protobizantina*, 617–37.

Bourdieu, P. 1977. *Outline of a Theory of Practice.* Cambridge Studies in Social and Cultural Anthropology 16 (Cambridge).

Bowden, W. 2003. *Epirus Vetus: The Archaeology of a Late Antique Province* (London).

Bowden, W. 2004. 'Epirus and Crete: Architectural Interaction in Late Antiquity'. In Livadiotti and Simiakaki (eds.) *Creta romana e protobizantina*, 787–800.

Branigan, K. 1998. 'Prehistoric and Early Historic Settlement in the Ziros Region, Eastern Crete'. *ABSA* 93, 23–90.

Braudel, F. 1972. *The Mediterranean and the Mediterranean World in the Age of Philip II* (London).

Bruneau, P., and J. Ducat. 1965. *Guide de Délos* (Paris).

Burden, J. 1999. 'Athens Remade in the Age of Augustus: A Study of the Architects and Craftsmen at Work'. Ph.D. diss. (Berkeley).

Burnett, A. M., M. Amandry and P. Ripollés. 1992. *Roman Provincial Coinage. Vol.1, From the Death of Caesar to the Death of Vitellius (44BC–AD69)* (London).

Cadogan, G., E. Hatzaki and A. Vasilakis, eds. 2004. *Knossos: Palace, City, State. Proceedings of the Symposium*. Iraklion, November 2000. BSA Studies 12 (London).

Callaghan, P. 1978. 'KRS 1976: Excavations at a Shrine of Glaukos, Knossos'. *ABSA* 73, 1–30.

—— 1994. 'Archaic, Classical and Hellenistic Knossos: A Historical Summary'. In Evely, Hughes-Brock and Momigliano (eds.), *Knossos*, 135–40.

Cameron, A. 1993. *The Mediterranean World in Late Antiquity, AD 395–600* (London).

Campbell, S. D. 1979. 'Roman Workshops in Turkey'. *AJA* 83, 287–92.

—— 1980. 'Antioch and the Corpus of Mosaics in Southern Turkey'. In Farioli Campanati (ed.), *Il Mosaico Antico*, 143–8.

—— 1988. *The Mosaics of Antioch* (Toronto).

—— 1991. *The Mosaics of Aphrodisias in Caria* (Toronto).

Carando, E., and A. G. Benvenuti. 2006. *Patrasso colonia di Augusto e le trasformazioni culturali, politiche ed economiche della Provincia di Acaia agli inizi dell'età imperiale romana. Atti del Convegno internazionale Patrasso 23–24 marzo 2006* (Athens).

Carington Smith, J. 1982. 'A Roman Chamber Tomb on the South East Slopes of Monasteriaki Kephala, Knossos'. *ABSA* 77, 255–93.

Castells, M. 1996. *The Rise of the Network Society, the Information Age: Economy, Society and Culture*. Vol. I (Oxford) (2nd ed., 2000).

Catling, H. W. 1976–7. 'The Knossos Area, 1974–76'. *Journal of Hellenic Studies: Archaeological Reports* 23, 3–24.

—— 1978–9. 'Knossos, 1978'. *Journal of Hellenic Studies: Archaeological Reports* 25, 43–58.

Catling, H. W., and G. B. Waywell. 1977. 'A Find of Roman Marble Statuettes at Knossos'. *ABSA* 72, 85–106.

Cavanagh, W. G., and M. Curtis, eds. 1998. *Post Minoan Crete. Proceedings of the First Colloquium* (10–11 November 1995). BSA Studies Series 2 (London).

Chaniotaki-Starida, L., and M. Mari. 2004. 'Παλαιοχριστιανική Χερρόνησος (4ος-7ος αι μ.Χ.)'. In Livadiotti and Simiakaki (eds.), *Creta romana e protobizantina*, 287–300.

Chaniotis, A. 1996. *Die Verträge zwischen kretischen Poleis in der hellenistischen Zeit. Heidelberger althistorische Beiträge und epigraphische Studien* 24 (Stuttgart).

Chaniotis, A., ed. 1999a. *From Minoan Farmers to Roman Traders: Sidelights on the Economy of Ancient Crete. Heidelberger Althistorische Beiträge und Epigraphische Studien* 29 (Stuttgart).

Chaniotis, A. 1999b. 'Milking the Mountains: Economic Activities on the Cretan Uplands in the Classical and Hellenistic Period'. In Chaniotis (ed.), *From Minoan Farmers to Roman Traders*, 181–220.

—— 2004. 'From Communal Spirit to Individuality: The Epigraphic Habit in Hellenistic and Roman Crete'. In Livadiotti and Simiakaki (eds.), *Creta romana e protobizantina*, 75–88.

—— 2005. 'Inscribed Instrumenta Domestica and the Economy of Hellenistic and Roman Crete'. In Archibald, Davies and Gabrielsen (eds.), *Making, Moving and Managing*, 92–116.

—— 2008. 'What Difference Did Rome Make? The Cretans and the Roman Empire'. In Forsen and Salmeri (eds.), *The Province Strikes Back*, 83–105.

Charitonidis, S., L. Kahill and R. Ginouèvs. 1970. *Les Mosaïques de la Maison de Mènandre à Mytilène* (Bern).

Chehab, M. 1965. 'Les charactéristiques de la mosaïque au Liban'. In Picard and Stern (eds.), *La Mosaïque Gréco Romaine I*, 330–40.

Christie, N., ed. Forthcoming. *Vrbes Extinctae: Archaeologies of Abandoned Classical Towns* (Surrey).

Clark, D. L. C. 2007. 'Viewing the Liturgy: A Space Syntax Study of Changing Visibility and Accessibility in the Development of the Byzantine Church in Jordan'. *World Archaeology* 39:1, 84–104.

Clarke, J. R. 1979. *Roman Black-and-White Figural Mosaics* (New York).

    1991. *The Houses of Roman Italy, 100 B.C.–A.D. 250* (Berkeley).

    1994. 'Mosaic Workshops at Pompeii and Ostia Antica'. In Johnson, Ling and Smith (eds.), *5th International Colloquium on Ancient Mosaics*, 89–103.

Coldstream, J. N. 1973. *Knossos: The Sanctuary of Demeter*. BSA Suppl. 8 (London).

Coldstream, J. N., and H. W. Catling, eds. 1996. *Knossos North Cemetery: Early Greek Tombs*. BSA Suppl. 28 (London).

Coldstream, J. N., L. J. Eiring and G. Forster, eds. 2001. *Knossos Pottery Handbook: Greek and Roman*. BSA Studies 7 (London).

Connerton, P. 1989. *How Societies Remember* (Cambridge).

Curuni, S. A. 1991. 'Monumenti di Creta Paleocristiana indagine sulla consistenza del patrimonio architettonico'. In Farioli Campanati (ed.), *XXXVIII Corso di Cultura sull'Arte Ravennate e Bizsantina*, 131–67.

Curuni, S. A., and L. Donati. 1987. *Creta bizantina: Rilievi e note critiche su ventisei edifici du culto in relazione all'opera di Giuseppe Gerola* (Rome).

Dabrowa, E., ed. 2002. *Tradition and Innovation in the Ancient World. Electrum: Studies in Ancient History*, vol. 6 (Cracow).

Darmon, J. P. 1980. *Nympharum Domus. Les Pavements de la maison des Nymphes à Néapolis (Nabeul, Tunisie) et leur lecture* (Leiden).

Darmon, J. P., and H. Lavagne. 1977. *Recueil des mosaïques de la Gaule II/3. Lyonnaise* (Paris).

Darmon, J. P., and A. Rebourg, eds. 1994. *La Mosaïque Gréco-Romaine IV*. Actes du Colloque Internationale sur La Mosaïque Gréco-Romaine (Trèves, 8th–14th August 1984). (Paris).

Daszewski, W. A. 1985. *Corpus of Mosaics from Egypt I* (Mainz am Rhein).

Daszewski, W. A., and D. Michaelides. 1988. *Mosaic Floors in Cyprus* (Rome).

Dauphin, C. 1980. 'Mosaic Pavements as an Index of Prosperity and Fashion'. *Levant* 12, 112–34.

Daux, G. 1958. 'Chronique des fouilles et découvertes en Grèce en 1957'. *BCH* 82, 664–830.

    1959. 'Chronique des fouilles et découvertes en Grèce en 1958'. *BCH* 83, 567–793.

    1961. 'Chronique des fouilles et découvertes en Grèce en 1960'. *BCH* 85, 601–954.

Davis, J. G. 1962. *The Architectural Setting of Baptism* (London).

Davaras, K. 1960. Ἐπιγραφαὶ ἐκ Κρήτης Ι'. *K.Khron*, 457–65.

    1967. 'Νομός Χανίων'. *A.Delt*. 22, Β2, 498–501.

de Almrida, F. 1975. 'Sur quelques mosaïques du Portugal: Torre de Palma et autres'. In Stern and Le Glay (eds.), *La Mosaïque Gréco-Romaine II*, 219–20.

de Haan, N. 2004. 'Living like the Romans? Some Remarks on Domestic Architecture in North Africa and Britain'. In de Ligt, Hemelrijk and Singor (eds.), *Roman Rule and Civic Life*, 261–73.

de Ligt, L., E. A. Hemelrijk and H. W. Singor, eds. 2004. *Roman Rule and Civic Life: Local and Regional Perspectives. Proceedings of the Fourth Workshop of the International Network. Impact of Empire (Roman Empire, C. 200 B.C.–A.D. 476), Leiden, June 25–28, 2003* (Amsterdam).

de Souza, P. 1998. 'Late Hellenistic Crete and the Roman Conquest'. In Cavanagh and Curtis (eds.), *Post Minoan Crete*. 112–16.

    2000. *Piracy in the Graeco-Roman World* (Cambridge).

DeLaine, J. 1988. 'Recent Research on Roman Baths'. *JRA* 1, 19–30.

DeLaine, J., and D. E. Johnston, eds. 1999. *Roman Baths and Bathing*. Proceedings of the First International Conference on Roman Baths, Vol. 1, Bathing and Society; Vol. 2, Design and Construction, *JRA* Suppl. 37 (Portsmouth, RI).

Demargne, P. 1974. *Malia. Plan du site. Plans du Palais. Indices*. Études Crétoise XIX (Paris).

Detorakis, T. E. 1994. *History of Crete*. Translated by J. C. Davis. (Iraklion).

Di Vita, A. 1988. *Gortina I*. Monografie della Scuola Archeologica di Atene e delle Missioni Italiane in Oriente, III (Rome).

1990–1. 'Atti della scuola, 1990–91'. *ASAtene* 68–9, 405–500.

1991. 'I Recenti scavi della *S.A.I.A.* a Gortina: Un contributo alla conoscenza di Creta tardo-antico e protobizantina'. In Farioli Campanati (ed.), *XXXVIII Corso di Cultura sull'Arte Ravennate e Bizsantina*, 169–83.

1996–7. 'Atti della scuola, 1996–97'. *ASAtene* 74–5, 467–584.

1997. *Gortina II. Pretorio il materiale degli scavi Colini, 1970–1977*. Monografie della Scuola Archeologica di Atene e delle Missioni Italiane in Oriente 7 (Padua).

1998–2000. 'Atti della scuola, 1998–2000'. *ASAtene* 76–8, 357–466.

2000a. *Gortina V.1:1 Lo scavo del Pretorio (1989–1995)*. Monografie della Scuola Archeologica di Atene e delle Missioni Italiane in Oriente XII (Padua).

Gortina V.1:2 Lo scavo del Pretorio (1989–1995). Monografie della Scuola Archeologica di Atene e delle Missioni Italiane in Oriente XII (Padua).

Gortina V.1:3 Lo scavo del Pretorio (1989–1995). Tavole. Monografie della Scuola Archeologica di Atene e delle Missioni Italiane in Oriente XII (Padua).

Gortina V.2 Lo scavo del Pretorio (1989–1995). Tabulati delle unita stratigrafiche. Monografie della Scuola Archeologica di Atene e delle Missioni Italiane in Oriente XII (Padua).

Gortina V.3 Lo scavo del Pretorio (1989–1995). Monografie della Scuola Archeologica di Atene e delle Missioni Italiane in Oriente XII (Padua).

2000b. *Gortyn in Crete: Archaeology and History of an Ancient City*. Translated by K. Axelos (Athens).

2000c. 'Settore B Appendice: L'area a Sud della basilica giudiziaria'. In Di Vita 2000a. *Gortina V.1:2 Lo scavo del Pretorio (1989–1995)*, 767–81.

2001. *Gortina V.3:1 t.1 and t. II. Lo scavo del Pretorio (1989–1995). I Materiali. Monografie della Scuola Archeologica di Atene e delle Missioni Italiane in Oriente XII* (Padua).

Gortina V. 3:2 Lo scavo del Pretorio (1989–1995). I Materiali – Tavole. Monografie della Scuola Archeologica di Atene e delle Missioni Italiane in Oriente XII (Padua).

2004. 'Gortina. Archeologia e storia di una città antica'. In Livadiotti and Simiakaki (eds.), *Creta romana e protobizantina: Atti del convegno internazionale Iraklion, 23–30 settembre 2000*, 459–76 (Padua).

Diamandis, N. 2004. 'Το παλαιοχριστιανικό νεκροταφείο της Κισάμου'. In Livadiotti and Simiakaki (eds.), *Creta romana e protobizantina*, 383–96.

Donderer, M. 1989. *Die Mosaizisten der Antike und ihre Wirtschaftliche und Soziale Stellung: Eine Quellenstudie* (Erlangen).

Drosinou, P. 1992. ''Οικόπεδο Αλεξ. και Γεωργίου Ραϊσάκη'. *A.Delt* 47, 579–81.

1994–6. ''Οικόπεδο Εμμ. Θεοδοσάκη'. *K.Estia* 5, 227.

2004. 'Εγκατάσταση ελαιοπιεστηρίου των ρωμαϊκών χρόνων στη νήσο Γαύδο'. In Livadiotti and Simiakaki (eds.), *Creta romana e protobizantina: Atti del convegno internazionale Iraklion, 23–30 settembre 2000*, 415–26 (Padua).

Dunbabin, K. M. D. 1978a. *Excavations at Carthage, 1976* IV (Ann Arbor).

1978b. *The Mosaics of Roman North Africa: Studies in Iconography and Patronage* (Oxford).

1979. 'Technique and Material of Hellenistic Mosaics'. *AJA* 83, 269–92.

1982. 'The Victorious Charioteer on Mosaics and Related Monuments'. *AJA* 86, 65–89.

1989. 'Boiarum Grata Voluptas: Pleasures and Dangers of the Baths'. *PBSR*, n.s. 44, 7–46.

1990. 'Ipsa Deae Vestigia … Footprints Divine and Human on Graeco-Roman Monuments'. *JRA* 3, 85–110.

1994a. 'Trampling upon the Envious: A Mosaic from Ostia with an Apotropaic Inscription and Image'. In Darmon and Rebourg (eds.), *La Mosaïque Gréco Romaine IV*, 67–8.

1994b. 'Early Pavement Types in the West and the Invention of Tessellation'. In Johnson, Ling and Smith (eds.), *5th International Colloquium on Ancient Mosaics*, 26–41.

1996. 'Convivial Spaces: Dining and Entertainment in the Roman Villa'. *JRA* 9, 66–81.

1999. *Mosaics of the Greek and Roman World* (Cambridge).

Duyuran, R. 1960. 'Istanbul'. *Annual of the Archaeological Museums of Istanbul* 9, 18–21.

Edelstein, E. J., and L. Edelstein. 1998. *Asclepius. Collection and Interpretation of the Testimonies*. Vols. I and II (Baltimore).

Eiring, J. 2000a. 'KS178 – An Industrial Area in the Greek City of Knossos'. In Πεπραγμένα του Η'Διεθνούς Κρητολογικού Συνεδρίου Ηράκλειο, 9–14 Σεπτεμβρίου 1996, A1, 443–56 (Iraklion).

2000b. 'Knossos at the Turn of the Millennium: *Romanitas* and Pottery'. *Rei Cretariae Romanae Factorum Acta* 26, 197–203.

2001. 'The Hellenistic Period'. In Coldstream, Eiring and Forster (eds.), *Knossos Pottery Handbook*, 91–136.

Ellis, S. P. 2000. *Roman Housing* (London).

Elsner, J. 1995. *Art and the Roman Viewer: The Transformation of Art from the Pagan World to Christianity* (Cambridge).

Elton, H. 2004. 'Romanization and Some Cilician Cults'. In de Ligt, Hemelrijk and Singor (eds.), *Roman Rule and Civic Life*, 231–41.

Ennaïfer, M., and A. Rebourg, eds. 1999. *VIIème colloque international pour l'étude de la mosaïque antique* (Tunis, 3–7 octobre 1994) (Tunis).

ΕΘΝΟΣ. 14 December 1992. 'Kastelli Kisamos'.

Eusebius. *Historia Ecclesiastica*. Loeb Edition (K. Lake and J. Oulton, eds., 1926).

Evans, A. 1902–3. 'Knossos Excavation'. *ABSA* 9, 1–154.

1928. *The Palace of Minos at Knossos*. Vol. II (London).

Evely, D., H. Hughes-Brock and N. Momigliano, eds. 1994. *Knossos: A Labyrinth of History. Papers in Honour of Sinclair Hood* (Oxford).

Falkener, E. 1852–3. *On the Antiquities of Candia No.1* (London).

1854. *Theatres and Other Remains in Crete. From a MS History of Candia by Onorio Belli in 1586* (London).

1860. *Museum of Classical Antiquities II* (London).

Fantar, M. H., et al. 1994. *La Mosaïque en Tunisie* (Paris).

Farioli Campanati, R., ed. 1983. *Il Mosaico Antico* [III Colloquio Internazionale Sul Mosaico Antico (Ravenna 6th–10th September, 1980)] (Ravenna).

(ed.) 1991. *XXXVIII Corso di Cultura sull'Arte Ravennate e Bizsantina. Seminario Internazionale di Studi sul tema: 'La Grecia insulare tra Tardoantico e Medioevo'* (Ravenna).

2001. 'I mosaici pavimentali della basilica di Mitropolis a Gortyna'. In Paunier and Schmidt (eds.), *La Mosaïque Gréco-Romaine VIII*, 261–5.

2004a. 'La basilica di Mitropolis a Gortina: Tipologia e articolazione degli spazi liturgici'. In Livadiotti and Simiakaki (eds.), *Creta romana e protobizantina*, 637–51.

2004b. 'Per la lista episcopale di Gortyna in età protobizantina nella documentazione archeologica. Precisazioni e nuovi dati da iscrizioni musive'. *Νέα Ῥώμη / Nea Rhome. Rivista di studi bizantinistici* 3, 115–30.

Farioli Campanati, R., and M. Bourboudakis. 2005. 'La Decorazione pavimentale e parietale della cattedrale di Gortyna (Creta)'. In Morlier (ed.), *La mosaïque gréco-romaine IX*, 165–71.

Farrington, A. 1999. 'The Introduction and Spread of Roman Bathing in Greece'. In DeLaine and Johnston (eds.), *Roman Baths and Bathing*, 57–66.

Feld, S., and K. Basso, eds. 1996. *Senses of Place*. School of American Research Advanced Series Seminar (Santa Fe).

Ferguson, E., ed. 1990. *Encyclopaedia of Early Christianity* (London).

Finney, P., ed. 1993. *Art, Archaeology and Architecture of Early Christianity* (New York).

Fischhoff, B. 1975. 'Hindsight-Foresight: The Effect of Outcome Knowledge on Judgment under Uncertainty'. *Journal of Experimental Psychology: Human Perception and Performance* 1, 288–99.

Florovsky, G. 1969. *The Study of the Past*. In Nash (ed.), *Ideas of History*. Vol. 2, 364.

Forsen, B., and G. Salmeri, (eds.). 2008. *The Province Strikes Back: Imperial Dynamics in the Eastern Mediterranean* (Helsinki).

Forster, G. 2001. 'The Roman Period'. In Coldstream, Eiring and Forster (eds.), *Knossos Pottery Handbook*, 137–67.

2004. 'Shadow of a City? A Review of Late Roman Knossos'. In Cadogan, Hatzaki and Vasiliakis (eds.), *Knossos*, 489–92. *BSA Studies* 12, 489–91.

Foschia, L. 2002. 'Shifting Pagan and Christian Cult Places in Late Antiquity: From Monumentalization to Cryptocult and Vice Versa'. In G. Muskett et al. (eds.), 2002, *Acts of the Symposium on Mediterranean Archaeology (SOMA), Fifth Annual Meeting of Postgraduate Researchers. University of Liverpool, 23–25 February 2001*. BAR International Series 1048, 105–11 (Oxford).

2009. 'The Preservation, Restoration and Re(construction) of Pagan Cult Places in Late Antiquity, with Particular Attention to Mainland Greece'. *Journal of Late Antiquity* 2.2, 209–33.

Francis, J. 2006. 'Beehives and Beekeeping in Graeco-Roman Sphakia'. In *Πεπραγμένα του 8ου Διεθνούς Κρητολογικού Συνεδρίου Elounda 1–6 October* A5, 365–79 (Iraklion).

Fraser, P. M., and E. Matthews. 1987. *A Lexicon of Greek Personal Names*. Vol. I (Oxford).

1997. *A Lexicon of Greek Personal Names*. Vol. IIIA (Oxford).

Frend, W. H. C., and D. E. Johnston. 1962. 'The Byzantine Basilica Church at Knossos'. *ABSA* 57, 168–238.

Frost, F. J. 1991. 'Excavations at Phalasarna, Western Crete'. *AJA* 95, 302.

Gallas, K., K. Wessel and M. Bourboudakis, 1983. *Byzantinisches Kreta* (Munich).

Garcia Y Bellido, A. 1972. *Arte Romano* (Madrid).

Gerola, G. 1905. *Monumenti veneti nell'isola di Creta*, I.1 (Venice).

1906. *Monumenti veneti nell'isola di Creta*, I.2 (Venice).

1908. *Monumenti veneti nell'isola di Creta*, II (Venice).

1917. *Monumenti veneti nell'isola di Creta*, III (Venice).

1932–40. *Monumenti veneti nell'isola di Creta*, IV (Venice).

Goodchild, R. G. 1971. *Kyrene und Apollonia* (Zurich).

Gosden, C. 2004. *Archaeology and Colonialism. Cultural Contact from 5000 BC to the Present* (Cambridge).

Gough, M. 1973. *The Origins of Early Christian Art* (Geneva).

Gozlan, S. 1992. *La Maison du Triomphe de Neptune à Acholla (Botria, Tunisia)* [École Française de Rome] (Rome).

Grabar, A. 1968. *Christian Iconography* (Princeton).

Grammatikaki, E. 1992. 'Μπουγάδα Μετόχι Κνωσού (οικόπεδο Α. Βλαχάκη)'. *A.Delt*. 47 B2, 558.

1996. 'Κνωσός. Βενιζέλειο Νοσοκομείο'. *A.Delt*. 51 B2, 624–30.

2004. 'Ταφικά μνημεία Κνωσού'. In Cadogan, Hatzaki, and Vasiliakis (eds.), *Knossos*, 481–88. *BSA Studies* 12, 465–72.

Granger, F., trans. 1934. *Vitruvius De Architectura* (London).

Greco, E., ed. 2009. *Patrasso colonia di Augusto e le trasformazioni culturali, politiche ed economiche della Provincia di Acaia agli inizi dell' eta imperiale romana: Atti del Convegno Internazionale, Patrasso 23–24 marzo 2006* (Athens).

Greene, K. 1986. *The Archaeology of the Roman Economy* (London).

Gregory, T. E., ed. 1993. *The Corinthia in the Roman Period. Including the Papers Given at a Symposium Held at The Ohio State University on 7–9 March, 1991*. *JRA* Suppl. Series 8 (Portsmouth, RI).

Guarducci, M. 1935. *Inscriptiones Creticae Opera at Consilio Frederici Halbherr Collectae*. Vols. I–IV (Rome).

1978. *Epigrafia Greca*. Vol. IV (Rome).

Guimier-Sorbets, A. 1980. 'Une banque de données sur la mosaïque dans le monde grec, des origines à la fin de l'époque hellénistique'. In Farioli Campanati (ed.), *Il Mosaico Antico*, 515–24.

Guizzi, F. 1999. 'Private Economic Activities in Hellenistic Crete: The Evidence of the Isopoliteia Treaties'. In Chaniotis (ed), *From Minoan Farmers to Roman Traders*, 235–47.

Guthrie, W. K. C. 1993. *Orpheus and Greek Religion* (Princeton).

Hadzi-Vallianou, D. 1989. *Lebena: The Ancient City and the Shrine of Asclepius* (Athens).

    1990. 'Νομός Ηρακλείου'. *A.Delt* 45, B2, 409–28.

    2006. *Crete, Province of Pediada, Kastelli, Gouves, Chersonisos Municipalities. Natural Environment, Settlements, Antiquities and Monuments. 5000 Years History* (Heraklion).

Haggis, D. 1996a. 'The Port of Tholos in Eastern Crete and the Role of a Roman Horreum along the Egyptian 'Corn Route'. *Oxford Journal of Archaeology* 15.2, 183–209.

    1996b. 'Archaeological Survey at Kavousi, East Crete: Preliminary Report'. *Hesperia* 65.4, 373–432.

Haggis, D., G. Gesell and L. Preston Day, eds., 2005. *Kavousi I. The Archaeological Survey of the Kavousi Region* (Philadelphia).

Halbherr, F. 1893. 'Researches in Crete'. *The Antiquary* 28, 110–12.

Hales, S. 2003. *The Roman House and Social Identity* (Cambridge).

Hanfmann, G. M. A. 1983. *Sardis, from Prehistoric to Roman Times: Results of the Archaeological Exploration of Sardis, 1958–1975* (London).

Harrison, G. W. M. 1985. 'The Joining of Cyrenaica to Crete'. In Barker, Lloyd and Reynolds (eds.), *Cyrenaica in Antiquity*. BAR International Series 236, *Society for Libyan Studies Occassional Papers* 1, 365–73.

    1988. 'Background to the First Century of Roman Rule in Crete'. *Cretan Studies* I, 125–55.

    1993. *The Romans and Crete* (Amsterdam).

    1994. 'Old (and False) Perceptions Die Hard'. *Cretan Studies* 4, 137–47.

    2000. 'A Roman's View from Vrocastro: Prosperity and Romanisation of Eastern Crete'. In *Πεπραγμένα του Η΄Διεθνούς Κρητολογικού Συνεδρίου Ηράκλειο, 9–14 Σεπτεμβρίου 1996* A1, 545–52 (Iraklion).

    2004. 'Organization of Dwelling Space in Roman Crete: The *Disiecta Membra* of Cities'. In Livadiotti and Simiakaki (eds.), *Creta romana e protobizantina*, 751–57.

    2006. 'Model for the Longevity of Paganism in Roman Crete: Aesculapius'. In *Πεπραγμένα του 8ου Διεθνούς Κρητολογικού Συνεδρίου Elounda 1–6 October* A5, 449–59 (Iraklion).

Harrison, R. M. 1962. 'An Orpheus Mosaic at Ptolemais in Cyrenica'. *JRS* 52, 11–18.

Harrison, R. M., and G. R. J. Lawson. 1965. 'The Mosaics in Front of the Vilayet Building in Istanbul'. *Annual of the Archaeological Museums of Istanbul 13–14*, 216–18 (Oxford).

Hawkins, S., and R. Hastie. 1990. 'Hindsight Biased Judgments of Past Events after the Outcomes Are Known'. *Psychological Bulletin* 107.3, 311–27.

Hayden, B. 2004a. 'The Roman Period in the Vrokastro Area, Eastern Crete: Settlement Patterns, Sites and Subsistence'. In Livadiotti and Simiakaki (eds.), *Creta romana e protobizantina*, 269–81.

    2004b. *Reports on the Vrokastro Area, Eastern Crete: The Settlement History of the Vrokastro Area and Related Studies*. Monograph 119, vol. 2 (Philadelphia).

    2005. *Reports on the Vrokastro Area, Eastern Crete. Vol. III, The Vrokastro Regional Survey Project Sites and Pottery*. University Museum Monograph 123 (Philadelphia).

Hayden, B., J. A. Moody and O. Rackham. 1992 'The Vrokastro Survey Project, 1986–1989: Research Design and Preliminary Results'. *Hesperia* 61.3, 293–353.

Hayden, B. et al. 2006. 'Preliminary Results of the Istron, Mirabello, Geophysical and Geoarchaeological Project, 2002–2004'. *ABSA* 101, 135–81.

Hayes, J. W. 1971. 'Four Early Roman Groups from Knossos'. *ABSA* 66, 249–75.

    1983. 'The Villa Dionysos Excavations, Knossos: The Pottery'. *ABSA* 78, 97–169.

2001. 'Early Christian Pottery from Knossos: The 1978–81 Finds from the Knossos Medical Faculty Site'. *ABSA* 96, 431–54.

Hellenkemper Salies, G. 1974. 'Untersuchungen zu den geometrischen Gliederungsschemata römischer Mosaiken'. *Bonner Jahrbücher* 174, 1–176.

1986. 'Römische Mosaiken in Griechenland'. *Bonner Jahrbücher* 186, 241–85.

Hingley, R. 1996. 'The Legacy of Rome: The Rise, Decline and Fall of the Theory of Romanization'. In Webster and Cooper (eds.), *Roman Imperialism*, 35–38.

Hingley, R., ed. 2001. *Images of Rome: Perceptions of Ancient Rome in Europe and the United States in the Modern Age*. *JRA* Suppl. Series 44 (Portsmouth, RI).

Hingley, R. 2005. *Globalizing Roman Culture: Unity, Diversity and Empire*. (London).

Hitchner, R. 2004. 'Roman Globalization and Longevity of Empire'. *Archaeological Institute of America 105th Annual Meeting Abstracts*, January 2–5, 2004, San Francisco, 83 (Boston).

Hobsbawm, E., and T. Ranger, eds. 1992. *The Invention of Tradition* (Cambridge).

Hodder, I., ed. 1989. *The Meaning of Things: Material Culture and Symbolic Expression* (London).

Hoddinott, R. F. 1975. *Bulgaria in Antiquity: An Archaeological Introduction* (London).

Hogarth, D. G. 1899–1900. 'Early Town and Cemeteries'. *ABSA* 6, 70–85.

Hood, M. S. F., P. M. Warren and G. Cadogan. 1964. 'Travels in Crete in 1962'. *ABSA* 59, 50–99.

Hood, S., and D. Smyth. 1981. *Archaeological Survey of the Knossos Area*. *BSA* Suppl. Vol. 14 (London).

Horden, P., and N. Purcell. 2000. *The Corrupting Sea: A Study of Mediterranean History* (Oxford).

Hornblower, S., and A. Spawforth, eds. 1996. *The Oxford Classical Dictionary*, 3rd ed. (Oxford).

Huskinson, J. 1996. *Roman Children's Sarcophagi* (Oxford).

Hutchinson, R. W. 1934–35. 'Knossos'. *British School at Athens: Report for the Session 1934–35*, 5–7.

Ingold, T. 1983. 'The Architect and the Bee: Reflections on the Work of Animals and Men'. *Man*, n.s., 18.1 (March), 1–20.

Ioannidou-Karetsou, A., S. Markoulaki, N. Poulou-Papadimitriou and B. Penna. 2008. *Ηράκλειο. Η άγνωστη ιστορία της αρχαίας πόλης* (Iraklion).

Italian School, 1985. *Ancient Crete: A Hundred Years of Italian Archaeology, 1884–1984* (Rome).

Jeffreys, E., J, Haldon and R. Cormack. 2008. *The Oxford Handbook of Byzantine Studies*. (Oxford).

Jobst, W. 1982. *Römische Mosaiken in Salzburg* (Wien).

Johnson, P., R. Ling and D. J. Smith, eds. 1994 and 1995. *5th International Colloquium on Ancient Mosaics* (Bath 5th–12th September 1987) JRA Suppl. Series 9 (Ann Arbor).

Johnston, D. E. 1994. 'Some Possible North African Influences on Romano-British Mosaics'. In Johnson, Ling and Smith (eds.), *5th International Colloquium on Ancient Mosiacs*, 295–307.

Jones, A. H. M. 1963. 'The Greeks under the Roman Empire'. *DOP* 17, 3–19.

1964. *The Later Roman Empire, 284–602* (Oxford).

1969. 'Church Finance in the Fifth and Sixth Centuries'. *Journal of Theological Studies* 11, 84–94.

Joyce, H. 1981. *The Decoration of Halls, Ceilings and Floors in Italy in the Second and Third Centuries A.D. Archaeologia 17* (Rome).

Kalokyris, K. A. 1955. 'Συμπληρωματικὴ ανασκαφὴ τῆς ἐν Πανόρμῳ Κρήτης παλαιοχριστιανικῆς βασιλικῆς'. *PAE*, 321–6.

1956. ''Ανασκαφὴ βυζαντινῆς βασιλικῆς ἐν Βυζαρίῳ Κρήτης'. *PAE*, 250–61.

Kankeleit, A. 1994. *Kaiserzeitliche Mosaiken in Griechenland Band I and II* (Munich).

1997. 'Symposion mit Menander und Dionysos, Römische Mosaiken aus Griechenland'. *Antike Welt* 28, 309–18.

1999. 'Der Amymonemythos auf Mosaiken in Griechenland'. *Zeitschrift für klassische Archäologie* 12 / IX / 1999 (http://farch.tsx.org/forum0999/12mosgr.htm).

Karamalaki, N. 1999. 'Νέος Κουρνάς (Καβρός)'. *A.Delt* 54, B2, 863–5.

2002. 'Νέος Κουρνάς (Καβρός)'. *K.Estia* 9, 259–61.

Kassel, R., and C. Austin, eds. 1998. *Poetae Comici Graeci*. Vol. VI. 2 *Menander* (Berlin).

Kazhdan, A., and G. Constable. 1982. *People and Power in Byzantium* (Columbia).

Kenner, H. 1965. 'Römische mosaiken aus Österreich'. In Picard and Stern (eds.), *La Mosaïque Gréco-Romaine I*, 85–94.

Keppie, L. J. F. 1991. *Understanding Roman Inscriptions* (London).

Khader, A. B. 2006. *Tunisian Mosaics: Treasures from Roman Africa*. Translated from the French by S. Grevet (Los Angeles).

Kiss, A. 1973. *Roman Mosaics in Hungary* (Budapest).

Kitzinger, E. 1965. 'Stylistic Developments in Pavement Mosaics in the Greek East from the Age of Constantine to the Age of Justinian'. In Picard and Stern (eds.), *La Mosaïque Gréco-Romaine I*, 341–52.

1970. 'The Threshold of the Holy Shrine: Observations on Floor Mosaics at Antioch and Bethlehem Kyriakon'. *Festschrift Johannes Quasten*, 639–47.

1977. *Byzantine Art in the Making* (London).

Kokkinia, C. 2004. 'Ruling, Inducing, Arguing: How to Govern (and Survive) a Greek Province'. In de Ligt, Hemelrijk and Singor (eds.), *Roman Rule and Civic Life*, 39–58.

Kolarik, R. C. 1994. 'Tetrarchic Floor Mosaics in the Balkans'. In Darmon and Rebourg (eds.), *La Mosaïque Gréco-Romaine IV*, 171–83.

Kondoleon, C. 1995. *Domestic and Divine: Roman Mosaics in the House of Dionysos*. (Ithaca).

2000. *Antioch: The Lost Ancient City* (Princeton).

Kosouva, A., G. Moschovi and A. Giagkaki, 2004. 'Επιφανειακή έρευνα στη Γαύδο. Ενδείξεις για τη ρωμαϊκή και την πρωτοβυζαντινή κατάληψη του χώρου'. In Livadiotti and Simiakaki (eds.), *Creta romana e protobizantina*, 397–414.

Koundi, D. 1993. 'Καστέλλι Κισάμου'. *Καθήμερινη* 31st January, 14.

Kourkoutidou-Nikolaidou, E., and A.Tourta. 1997. *Wandering in Byzantine Thessaloniki* (Athens).

Kraeling, C. H. 1962. *Ptolemais, City of the Libyan Pentapolis* [University of Chicago Oriental Institute Publications, vol. XC] (Chicago).

La Rosa, V., and E. Portale. 2004. 'Per La Festòs di età Romana e Protobizantina'. In Livadiotti and Simiakaki (eds.), *Creta romana e protobizantina*, 477–514.

Lagogianni-Georgakarakos, M. 2004. 'Divus Augustus: νέα στοιχεία αυτοκρατορικής λατρείας στη ρωμαϊκή Κνωσό'. In Cadogan, Hatzaki and Vasilakis (eds.), *Knossos*, 489–92. *BSA Studies* 12, 457–63.

Lake, M. 2007. 'Viewing Space'. *World Archaeology* 39.1, 1–3.

Lancha, J. 1981. *Recueil général des mosaïques de la Gaule III: Narbonnaise 2* [Xe Supplement à Gallia] (Paris).

Larfeld, W. 1898. *Handbuch der griechischen Epigraphik*. Vol. II (Leipzig).

1907. *Handbuch der griechischen Epigraphik*. Vol. I (Leipzig).

Lassithiotaki, K. 1970. 'Ἐκκλησίες τῆς δυτικῆς Κρήτης, D. Ἐπαρχία Σελίνου'. *K.Khron KB* 133–210, 347–88.

1971. 'Ἐκκλησίες τῆς δυτικῆς Κρήτης'. *K.Khron KB*, 95–177.

Lavagne, H. 1977. 'Deux mosaïques de style orientalisant'. *Monpiot* 61, 61–86.

1979. *Recueil général des mosaïques de la Gaule III: Narbonnaise-I* [Xe Supplement à Gallia] (Paris).

Lavin, I. 1963. 'Antioch Hunting Mosaics and Their Sources'. *DOP* 17, 181–268.

Le Roux, P. 2004. 'La romanisation en question'. *Annales HSS* 59.2, 287–311.

Leach, L. 2004. *The Social Life of Painting in Ancient Rome and on the Bay of Naples.* (Cambridge).

Leader-Newby, R. 2007. 'Inscribed Mosaics in the Late Roman Empire: Perspectives from East and West'. In Newby and Leader-Newby (eds.), *Art and Inscriptions in the Ancient World*, 179–99.

Leatham, J., and S. Hood. 1958–9. 'Sub-Marine Exploration in Crete'. *ABSA* 53–4, 263–80.

Lechner, F. J., and J. Boli, eds. 2004. *The Globalization Reader* (Oxford).

Leekley, D., and R. Noyes. 1975. *Archaeological Excavations in the Greek Islands* (Park Ridge, NJ).

Lembesis, A. 1971. 'Ἀνασκαφικαὶ ἔρευναι εἰς κεντρικὴν Κρήτην'. *PAE* 284–300.

1972. 'Νομὸς Ηρακλείου'. *A.Delt.*, B2, 624–5.

Leonard, A. 1972. 'Kouphonisi Revisited'. *Archeologica Classica* 24, 353–63.

Levi, D. 1941. 'The Allegories of the Months in Classical Art'. *Art Bulletin* 23.4, 251–92.

1947. *Antioch Mosaic Pavements.* Vols. I and II (Princeton).

1959. 'The Religion of the Earliest Hellenes: Votives from a Post-Mycenaean Shrine. Excavations at Gortyna in Crete – Part I'. *ILN*, December 26, 946–8.

Levick, B. M. 1967. *Roman Colonies in Southern Asia Minor* (Oxford).

Liddell, H. G., and R. Scott. 1925. *A Greek-English Lexicon* (Oxford).

Ling, R. 1991a. *Roman Painting* (Cambridge).

1991b. 'Brading, Brantingham and Your: A New Look at Some Fourth-Century Mosaics'. *Britannia* 22, 147–57.

1994. 'Against the Reverse Technique'. In Johnson, Ling and Smith (eds.), *5th International Colloquium on Ancient Mosaics*, 77–89.

1995. 'The Decoration of Roman Triclinia'. In Murray and Tecusan (eds), *In Vino Veritas*, 239–51.

1998. *Ancient Mosaics* (London).

Lippolis, E. 2000. 'Il Settore C'. In Di Vita, *Gortina V.1:2 Lo scavo del Pretorio (1989–1995)*, 389–513.

Lippolis, I. 2005. 'Mosaici di etá tardoantiac a Gortina (Creta)'. In Morlier (ed.), *La mosaïque gréco-romaine IX*, 173–89.

Livadiotti, M., and I. Simiakaki, eds. 2004. *Creta romana e protobizantina: Atti del convegno internazionale Iraklion, 23–30 settembre 2000* (Padua).

Locock, M. 1994. 'Meaningful Architecture'. In M. Locock (ed.), *Meaningful Architecture: Social Interpretations of Buildings*. Worldwide Archaeology Series 9, 1–13 (Avebury).

L'Orange, H. P., and P. J. Nordhagen. 1966. *Mosaics* (London).

Maca, M. 2006. 'Body, Boundaries and "Lived" Urban Space: A Research Model for the Eighth-Century City at Copan, Honduras'. In Robertson, Seibert, Fernandez and Zender (eds.), *Space and Spatial Analysis in Archaeology*, 143–56.

MacDonald, W. L. 1965. *The Architecture of the Roman Empire* (Yale).

MacDonald, W. L., and J. A. Pinto. 1995. *Hadrian's Villa and Its Legacy* (Yale).

MacEachern, S. 1998. 'Scale, Style, and Cultural Variation: Technological Traditions in the Northern Mandara Mountains'. In Stark (ed.), *The Archaeology of Social Boundaries*, 107–31.

Mandalaki, S. 1997. 'Τσούτσουρος'. *A.Delt.* 52, 995–8.

Mango, C. 1972. *The Art of the Byzantine Empire, 312–1453 (Sources and Documents)* (Englewood Cliffs, NJ).

Mano-Zissi, D. 1965. 'La question des différentes écoles de mosaïques gréco-romaines de Yougoslavie et Essai d'une esquisse de leur évolution'. In Picard and Stern (eds.), *La Mosaïque Gréco-Romaine I*, 287–96.

Marangou, A. 1999. 'Wine in the Cretan Economy'. In Chaniotis (ed.), *From Minoan Farmers to Roman Traders*, 269–78.

Marangou-Lerat, A. 1995. 'Le vin et les amphores de Crète, de l'epoque classique à l'epoque impériale'. *Études Crétoise* 30 (Paris).

Markoulaki, S. 1983. ʿΟδός Πλαστήραʾ. *A.Delt.* 38, 360–1.

1987a. ʿΟἱ Ὧρες καὶ οἱ Ἐποχὲς σὲ Ψηφιδωτὸ ἀπὸ τὸ Καστέλλι Κισάμουʾ. *K.Estia* 1, 3–58.

1987b. ʿΚαστέλλι Κισάμουʾ. *A.Delt.* 42 B2, 558–66.

1988. ʿΠροϊστορικὲς καὶ κλασσικὲς ἀρχαιότητεςʾ. *K.Estia* 2, 283–4.

1989/90. ʿΑρχαιολογικές ειδήσεις 1987ʾ. *K.Estia* 3, 252–4.

1990. ʿΨηφιδωτά "Οἰκίας Διονύσου" Στο Μουσείο Χανίωνʾ [*Πεπραγμένα του Στ´ Διεθνούς Κρητολογικού Συνεδρίου᾿ Τομός ΑΙ (Χανιά 424–430 Αύγουστος 1986)*], 449–63 (Χανιά).

1991. ʿΚαστέλλι Κισάμουʾ. *A.Delt.* 46 B2, 415.

1991–3. ʿΚίσαμος Κέντρο Υγείαςʾ. *K.Estia* 4, 222.

1993. ʿΚοινοτικό οικόπεδοʾ. *A.Delt.* 48 B2, 481.

1994. ʿΚίσαμος Κέντρο Υγείαςʾ. *K.Estia* 5, 217–20.

1994. ʿA Season Mosaic in West Creteʾ. In Batalla (ed.), VI Coloquio Internacional sobre Mosaico Antiguo,179–86.

1998. ʿΟδός Σκαλίδη, Πειραιώς και Μητροπολίτου (οικόπεδο Μαυριγιαννάκη)ʾ. *A.Delt.* 53 B3, 862–4.

1999a. ʿΚίσαμος Κέντρο Υγείαςʾ. *K.Estia* 7, 183–97.

1999b. ʿΑκαλύπτος Χώρος Ιερού Μητροπολιτικού Ναού Κισάμουʾ. *K.Estia* 7, 197–9.

1999c. ʿΟικόπεδο Νικολακάκηʾ. *K.Estia* 7, 199–208.

1999d. ʿΟικόπεδο Ειρ. Αλυγιζάκηʾ. *K.Estia* 7, 208–13.

2002a. ʿΟικόπεδο Μαυριγιαννάκηʾ. *K.Estia* 9, 244–5.

2002b. ʿΟικόπεδο Δαγαδάκηʾ. *K.Estia* 9, 246–9.

Markoulaki, S., G. Christodoulakos and C. Fragkonikolaki. 2004. ʿΗ αρχαία Κίσαμος και η πολεδομική της οργάνωσηʾ. In Livadiotti and Simiakaki (eds.), *Creta romana e protobizantina*, 355–74.

Markoulaki, S., J-Y. Empereur and A. Marangou. 1989. ʿRecherches sur les centres de fabrication d'amphores de Crète occidentaleʾ. *BCH* 113, 551–80.

Marx, K. 1930. *Capital* (London).

Mastino, A., ed. *L'Africa romana: Atti del VI convegno di studio Sassari 16–18 dicembre 1988* (Sassari).

Mathews, T. F. 1971. *The Early Churches of Constantinople: Architecture and Liturgy* (University Park, PA).

1999. *The Clash of the Gods: A Reinterpretation of Early Christian Art* (Princeton).

Mattingly, D. 2004. ʿBeing Roman: Expressing Identity in a Provincial Settingʾ. *JRA* 17, 5–25.

Mattingly, D. J., and S. E. Alcock, eds. 1997. *Dialogues in Roman Imperialism: Power, Discourse, and Discrepant Experience in the Roman Empire. JRA Suppl.* Series 23 (Portsmouth, RI).

Matz, F. 1951. *Forschungen auf Kreta 1942* (Berlin).

McKay, A. G. 1975. *Houses, Villas and Palaces in the Roman World* (Southampton).

Megaw, A. H. S. 1984. ʿA Cemetery Church with Trefoil Sanctuary in Crete.ʾ *Actes du Xe Congrès International d'Archéologie Chrétienne* (II) (Thessaloniki, 28th September–4th October 1980) (Thessaloniki).

Melfi, M. 2004. ʿIl santuario di Lebena e la rinascita del culto di Asclepio nel II sec d.Cʾ. In Livadiotti and Simiakaki (eds.), *Creta romana e protobizantina*, 515–30.

2006. ʿThe Topography of Lebena According to the Description of A. Taramelli (1894)ʾ. In *Πεπραγμένα του 8ου Διεθνούς Κρητολογικού Συνεδρίου Elounda 1–6 October* A5: 435–48 (Iraklion).

2007. *Il Santuario di Asclepio a Lebena*. Monografie della scuola archeologica di Atene e delle missioni Italiane in Oriente XIX (Athens).

Michaelides, D. 1987. *Cypriot Mosaics* (Nicosia).

1989a. ʿBerenice and the Mosaics of Roman Cyrenaicaʾ. In Mastino (ed.), *L'Africa romana*, 357–72.

1989b. 'The Early Christian Mosaics of Cyprus'. *Biblical Archaeologist* 52: 4, 192–202.

Michaud, J. P. 1970. 'Chronique des fouilles et découvertes en Grèce en 1968 and 69'. *BCH* 94, 883–1164.

1971. 'Chronique des fouilles et découvertes en Grèce en 1970'. *BCH* 95, 803–1067.

1972. 'Chronique des fouilles et découvertes en Grèce en 1971'. *BCH* 96, 593–816.

1973. 'Chronique des fouilles et découvertes en Grèce en 1972'. *BCH* 97, 253–412.

Milburn, R. 1988. *Early Christian Art and Architecture* (Aldershot).

Millet, M. 1990. *The Romanization of Britain: An Essay in Archaeological Interpretation* (Cambridge).

Mintzberg, H., J. Lampel, J. Quinn and S. Ghoshal. 2003. *The Strategy Process: Concepts, Contexts, Cases* (Englewood Cliffs, NJ).

Moody, J., L. Nixon, S. Price and O. Rackham. 1989. 'Archaeological Survey in Sphakia, Crete'. *EMC/CV* 33, n.s. 8, 201–15. See http://sphakia.classics.ox.ac.uk/publications.html

1998. 'Surveying Poleis and Larger Sites in Sphakia'. In Cavanagh and Curtis (eds.), *Post Minoan Crete*, 87–95.

Moody, J., L. Nixon, S. Price, O. Rackham and V. Niniou-Kindeli. 1990. 'Archaeological Survey in Sphakia, Crete'. *EMC/CV* 34, n.s. 9, 213–20. See http://sphakia.classics.ox.ac.uk/publications.html

Morgan, C. 2009, 'Federico Halbherr and Knossos'. *ASAtene LXXXVII, serie III, 9, Tomo I*, 43–69.

Morlier, H., ed. 2005. *La mosaïque gréco-romaine IX. Collection de l'École Française de Rome 352* (Paris).

Moorman, E., ed. 1992. *Functional and Spatial Analysis of Wall Painting. Proceedings of the Fifth International Congress on Ancient Wall Painting* (Amsterdam, 8–12 September 1992) (Leiden).

Müller, S. 1990. 'Prospection de la plaine de Mallia'. *BCH* 114, 921–30.

1992. 'Prospection de la plaine de Mallia'. *BCH* 116, 724–52.

Murray, C. 1993. 'Art and the Early Church'. In Finney (ed.), *Art, Archaeology and Architecture of Early Christianity*, 215–58.

Murray, O., and M. Tecusan, eds. 1991. *In Vino Veritas*. A four-day International Conference on Wine and Society in the Ancient World, held in Rome from 19th to 22nd March, 1991 (London).

Muth, S. 1998. *Erleben von Raum, Leben im Raum: Zur Funktion mythologischer Mosaikbilder in der römisch-kaiserzeitlichen Wohnarchitektur.* Archäologie und Geschichte 10 (Heidelberg).

Nash, R. H., ed. 1969. *Ideas of History.* Vol. 2 (New York).

Neal, D. S. 1981. *Roman Mosaics in Britain.* [Britannia Monograph Series No. 1] (London).

Negrioli, A. 1914. *Notizie degli Scavi di Antichitá.* Vol. XI.

Nevett, L. C. 1995. 'Gender Relations in the Classical House'. *ABSA* 90, 363–81.

Newby, Z., and R. Leader-Newby 2007. *Art and Inscriptions in the Ancient World* (Cambridge).

Nielsen, I. 1993. *Thermae et Balnea: The Architecture and Cultural History of Roman Public Baths.* I and II (Text and Plates) (Aarhus).

NIKH. 15th December 1992. 'Kastelli Kisamos'.

Niniou-Kindeli, B., and G. Christodoulakos. 2004. 'Ρωμαϊκή Άπτερα. Μια πρώτη προσέγγιση'. In Livadiotti and Simiakaki (eds.), *Creta romana e protobizantina*, 313–34.

Oikonomidou M. 2004. 'Η Κρητική νομισματοκοπία στα ρωμαϊκά χρόνια. Τύποι –συμβολισμός'. In Livadiotti and Simiakaki (eds.), *Creta romana e protobizantina*, 165–70.

Orlandos, A. K. 1927. 'Η Κρήνη τῆς Φιγαλείας'. *A.Delt.* 11, 1–7.

1929. 'Αἱ παλαιοχριστιανικαὶ βασιλικαὶ τῆς Λέσβου'. *A.Delt.* 12, 1–72.

1953. 'Η παλαιοχριστιανικὴ Βασιλικὴ τῆς Συίας'. *K.Khron* 1953, 338–59.

1955. 'Ἀνασκαφὴ Χερσονήσου Κρήτης'. *PAE*, 327–35.

1955–6. ʿΔύο βυζαντινὰ μνημεῖα τῆς δυτικῆς Κρήτης'. *Ἀρχεῖον τῶν Βυζαντινῶν Μνημείων τῆς Ελλάδος*, 126–205.

1956. Ἀνασκαφὴ τῆς βασιλικῆς Καστρίου Χερσονήσου'. *PAE*, 241–9.

1959. Ἀνασκαφὴ Χερσονήσου Κρήτης'. *PAE*, 220–9.

1960. Ἐξερεύνησις τῆς βασιλικῆς Ὀλοῦντος'. *PAE*, 308–16.

1964. Περισυλλογὴ ἀρχαίων καὶ ελάσσονες ἀνασκαφαὶ εἰς Κρήτην'. *Ergon*, 147–51.

1968. Κρήτη Μητρόπολις Μεσαρᾶς'. *Ergon*, 95–202.

1975. Περισυλλογὴ ἀρχαίων καὶ ἐλάσσονες ἀνασκαφαὶ εἰς Κρήτην'. *Ergon*, 195–202.

Osborne, M. J., and S. G. Byrne. 1994. *A Lexicon of Greek Personal Names*. Vol. II (Oxford).

Ovadiah, A. 1980. 'Mosaic Pavements Discovered in the Last Decade in Israel (1970–1980)'. In Farioli Campanati (ed.), *Il Mosaico Antico*, 309–20.

1994. 'Mosaic Pavements of the Herodian Period in Israel'. In Johnson, Ling and Smith (eds.), *5th International Colloquium on Ancient Mosaics*, 67–77.

Ovadiah, A., and R. Ovadiah. 1987. *Mosaic Pavements in Israel* (Rome).

Packard, P. M. 1980. 'A Monochrome Mosaic at Isthmia'. *Hesperia* 49, 326–46.

Panayiotakis, N., ed. 1988. Κρήτη Ιστορία και Πολιτισμός τ. Α' (Iraklion).

Papadakis, N. 1979. 'Μακρύ Γιαλός Σητείας'. *A.Delt*. 34 Β2, 406–9.

1980. 'Μακρύ Γιαλός'. *A.Delt*. 35 Β2, 524–5.

1983a. 'Κουφονήσι Σητείας'. *A.Delt*. 39 Β2, 379–81.

1983b. *Sitia: Fatherland of Myson and Kornaros. A Historical, Archaeological and Cultural Guide* (Sitia).

1986a. *Ierapetra: Bride of the Libyan Sea. A Historical, Archaeological and Cultural Guide* (Ierapetra).

Papadakis, N. 1986b. 'Κουφονήσι Σητείας'. *A.Delt*. 41 Β2, 228–31.

Papaioannou, M. 2007. 'The Roman *Domus* in the Greek World'. In Westgate, Fisher and Whitley (eds.), *Proceedings of the Conference 'Building Communities'*, 351–62.

Papapostolou I. A. 1975. 'Νομὸς Χανίων'. *A.Delt*. 30 Β2, 347–8.

Papapostolou I. 2009. 'Παρατηρήσεις σε ψηφιδωτά των Πατρών'. In Carando, E. & A. G. Benvenuti, *Patrasso colonia di Augusto e le trasformazioni culturali, politiche ed economiche della Provincia di Acaia agli inizi dell'età imperiale romana. Atti del Convegno internazionale Patrasso 23–24 marzo 2006* (Athens), 211–256.

Pariente, A. 1990. 'Chronique des fouilles et découvertes en Grèce en 1989'. *BCH* 114, 703–837.

1991. 'Chronique des fouilles et découvertes en Grèce en 1990'. *BCH* 115, 835–957.

1994. 'Chronique des fouilles et découvertes en Grèce en 1993'. *BCH* 118, 695–866.

Parker Pearson, M., and C. Richards (eds.), 1994a. *Architecture and Order: Approaches to Social Space* (London).

Parker Pearson, M., and C. Richards. 1994b. 'Ordering the World: Perceptions of Architecture, Space and Time'. In Parker Pearson and Richards (eds.), *Architecture and Order*, 1–37.

Parlasca, K. 1959. *Die römischen Mosaiken in Deutschland* (Berlin).

Parrish, D. 1979. 'The Mosaics from Roman Tunisia: An African Variation of the Seasons Theme'. *AJA* 83, 279–85.

1984. *The Seasons Mosaics of Roman North Africa* (Rome).

1994. 'Variations on the Iconography of the Winter Season in Roman Mosaics'. In Darmon and Rebourg (eds.), *La Mosaïque Gréco-Romaine IV*, 39–47.

Pashley, R. 1837. *Travels in Crete* (London).

Paton, S. 1991. 'A Roman Corinthian Building at Knossos'. *ABSA* 86, 297–318.

1994. 'Roman Knossos and the Colonia Julia Nobilis Cnosus'. In Evely, Hughes-Brock and Momigliano (eds.), *Knossos*, 141–53.

1998. 'The Villa Dionysos at Knossos and Its Predecessors'. In Cavanagh and Curtis (eds.), *Post Minoan Crete*, 123–8.

2000. 'The Villa Dionysos at Knossos: A *Domus* and Its Décor'. In *Πεπραγμένα του Η΄ Διεθνούς Κρητολογικού Συνεδρίου Ηράκλειο, 9–14 Σεπτεμβρίου 1996* Α2, 553–62 (Iraklion).

2004a. 'Knossos: An Imperial Renaissance'. In Cadogan, Hatzaki and Vasiliakis (eds.), *Knossos. BSA Studies* 12, 451–7.

2004b. 'The Villa Dionysos, Knossos: Recent Work'. In Livadiotti and Simiakaki (eds.), *Creta romana e protobizantina*, 281–6.

Paton, S., and R. M. Schneider. 1999. 'Imperial Splendour in the Province: Imported Marble on Roman Crete'. In Chaniotis (ed.), *From Minoan Farmers to Roman Traders*, 279–304.

Paunier, D., and C. Schmidt, eds. 2001. *La Mosaïque Gréco-Romaine VIII* [Actes du VIIIème Colloque International pour l'étude de la Mosaïque Antique et Médiévale (Lausanne, 6–11 octobre 1997)]. *Cahiers d'archéologie romande* (Lausanne.).

Pautasso, A. 1994–5. Ἀνθύπατοι Κρήτης και Κυρήνης. Osservazioni sull'attività dei proconsoli nella provincia nei primi secoli dell'impero'. *ASAtene* 1994–5, 72–3, 75–108.

Pelekanidis, S., and P. Atzaka. 1988. *Σύνταγμα των παλαιοχριστιανικών ψηφιδωτών δαπέδων της Ελλάδος I; Νησιωτική Ελλάς (Κέντρον Βυζαντινών Ερευνών Θεσσαλονίκη)* (Thessaloniki).

Pendlebury, J. D. S. 1939. *The Archaeology of Crete* (London).

Perna, R. 2004. 'Acropoli di Gortina in età romana e protobizantina'. In Livadiotti and Simiakaki (eds.), *Creta romana e protobizantina*, 545–56.

Pernier, L. 1915. 'Gortina, capitale della "Provincia Cretae et Cyrenarum"'. *Bullettino della Società Italiana per la diffusione e l'incoraggiamento degli studi classici (Atene e Roma)* **18**, 49–65.

1925–6. 'L'Odeum', nell' 'Agora', di Gortina presso il Leteo'. *ASAtene* 8–9, 1–69.

Pernier, L., and Banti, L. 1947. *Guida Degli Scavi Italiani in Creta* (Rome).

Pesce, G. 1950. 'Il "Palazzo Della Colonne"'. In *'Tolemaide Di Cirenaica'* [Monografie di Archeologia Libica, vol. ii] (Rome).

Petsas, P. 1964. 'Ten Years at Pella'. *Archaeology* 17, 74–84.

1965. 'Mosaics from Pella'. In Picard and Stern (eds.), *La Mosaïque Gréco-Romaine I*, 41–56.

Phillips, K. M. 1960. 'Subject and Technique in Hellenistic-Roman Mosaics from Sicily'. *Art Bulletin*, December, 244–62.

Picard, G. 1965. 'Un thème du style fleuri dans la mosaïque africaine'. In Picard and Stern (eds.), *La Mosaïque Gréco-Romaine I*, 125–36.

1994. 'Tradition iconographique et représentation de l'actualité dans la mosaique antique'. In Darmon and Rebourg (eds.), *La Mosaïque Gréco-Romaine IV*, 47–55.

Picard, M. G., and H. Stern (eds.) 1965. *La Mosaïque Gréco-Romaine I* [Actes du Colloque Internationale sur la Mosaïque Gréco-Romaine (Paris, 29th August–3rd September, 1963)] (Paris).

Piccirillo, M. 1993. *The Mosaics of Jordan* (Amman).

Platon, N. 1951. Χρονικά'. *K.Khron* 434–49.

1954. Χρονικά'. *K.Khron* 499–517.

1955a. 'Αἱ ξυλόστεγαι παλαιοχριστιανικαὶ βασιλικαὶ τῆς Κρήτης'. [Πεπραγμένα Θ΄Διεθνούς Βυζαντινολογικού Συνεδρίου I (Θεσσαλονίκη 12–19 Απριλίου 1953)] *Ελληνικά* Supplement 7 (Athens).

1955b. Ἀνασκαφὴ Ὀνυθὲ Γουλεδιανῶν Ρεθύμνης'. *PAE,* 298–305.

1956a. Χρονικά'. *K.Khron* 405–42.

1956b. Ἀνασκαφὴ παλαιοχριστιανικῆς βασιλικῆς Κερᾶς Ὀνυθὲ Γουλεδιανῶν'. *PAE,* 229–31.

1959. Χρονικά'. *K.Khron* 359–93.

1960. Ἀνασκαφαὶ εἰς Χανιά, Ρόκκαν καὶ Λισόν'. *A.Delt.* 27 Β2, 272–3.

Plommer, H. 1973. *Vitruvius and Later Roman Building Manuals* (Cambridge).

Poinssot, C. 1964. 'Quelques remarques sur les mosaïques de la maison de Dionysos et d'Ulysse à Thugga (Tunisie)'. In Picard and Stern (eds.), *La Mosaïque Gréco-Romaine I*, 219–32.

Pollitt, J. J. 1986. *Art in the Hellenistic Age* (Cambridge).

1990. *The Art of Ancient Greece: Sources and Documents* (Cambridge).

Pologiorgi, M., and S. Markoulaki. 1982 ʾΚαστέλλι Κισάμου'. *A.Delt.* 37, 382–3.

Popova-Moros, B. 1987. 24 ДРЕВНИ МОЗАЙКИ ОТ БЪЛГАРИЯ (Sofia).

Raab, H. A. 2001. *Rural Settlement in Hellenistic and Roman Crete: The Akrotiri Peninsula.* BAR International Series 984 (Oxford).

Rackham, O., and J. Moody. 1997. *The Making of the Cretan Landscape* (Manchester).

Ramsden, S. E. 1971. 'Roman Mosaics in Greece, the Mainland and the Ionian Islands'. Ph.D. diss., Institute of Archaeology (London).

Reinach, S. 1922. *Répertoire de peintures grecques et romaines* (Paris).

Rendini, P. 1988. 'Elementi di pavimentazione e decorazione'. In Di Vita, *Gortina I*, 317–19.

Rethemiotakis, G. 1984. ʾΝομός Ηρακλείου'. *A.Delt.* 39B, 296–8.

Richter, G. M. A. 1960. *A Handbook of Greek Art* (London).

Riggsby, A. M. 1997. '"Public" and "Private" in Roman Culture: The Case of the *Cubiculum'.* *JRA* 10, 36–57.

Rizakis, A. D. 1997. 'Roman Colonies in the Province of Achaia: Territories, Land and Population'. In Alcock (ed.), *The Early Roman Empire in the East*, 15–36.

Robert, L., and J. Robert. 1967. 'Bulletin épigraphique'. *Revue d'Études Greques* 80, 543–73.

Robertson, C. M. 1965. 'Greek Mosaics'. *JHS* 85, 72–90.

    1975. *A History of Greek Art* (Cambridge).

    1981. *A Shorter History of Greek Art* (Cambridge).

Robertson, E. C., J. D. Seibert, D. C. Fernandez and M. U. Zender, eds. 2006. *Space and Spatial Analysis in Archaeology* (Calgary).

Robertson, R. 1992. *Globalization* (London).

Robinson, D. M. 1934. 'The Villa of Good Fortune at Olynthos'. *AJA* 38, 501–10.

Romano, D. G. 1993. 'Post-146 B.C. Corinth, and Planning of the Roman Colony of 44 B.C.'. In Gregory (ed.), *The Corinthia in the Roman Period*, 9–30.

Rossiter, J. J. 1989. 'Roman Villas of the Greek East and the Villa in Gregory of Nyssa Ep. 20'. *JRA* 2, 101–10.

Rugman, A. M., and R. M. Hodgetts, 2003. *International Business* (Indianapolis).

Rush, P. (ed.) 1995. *Theoretical Roman Archaeology: Second Conference Proceedings.* World Archaeology Series (Aldershot).

Sackett, L. H. 1972. 'Knossos – The Unexplored Mansion'. *A.Delt.* 27, 265–6.

Sackett, L. H., ed. 1992. *Knossos from Greek City to Roman Colony: Excavations at the Unexplored Mansion.* BSA Suppl. 12 (London).

Salmeri, G., A. Raggi, and A. Baroni, eds. 2004. *Colonie Romane Nel Mondo Greco. Conference Proceedings, Pisa, November 2000. Minima epigraphica et Papyrologica-Separata III* (Rome).

Salzmann, D. 1982. *Untersuchungen zu den antiken Kieselmosaiken* (Berlin).

Sanders, I. F. 1976. 'Settlement on the Plain of the Messera Crete'. *ABSA* 71, 131–7.

    1982. *Roman Crete* (Warminster).

Scheibelreiter, V. 2006. 'Stifterinschriften auf Mosaiken Westkleinasiens'. *Tyche Supplement 5* (Vienna).

Scott, E., ed. 1993. *Theoretical Roman Archaeology: First Conference Proceedings.* World Archaeology Series (Aldershot).

Scott, S. 1993. 'A Theoretical Framework for the Study of Romano-British Villa Mosaics'. In Scott (ed.), *Theoretical Roman Archaeology*, 103–13.

    1994. 'Patterns of Movement: Architectural Design and Visual Planning in the Romano-British Villa'. In Locock (ed.), *Meaningful Architecture,* 86–98.

    1995. 'Symbols of Power and Nature: The Orpheus Mosaics of Fourth-Century Britainnia and Their Architectural Contexts'. In Rush (ed.), *Theoretical Roman Archaeology*, 105–23.

    2000. *Art and Society in Fourth-Century Britain: Villa Mosaics in Context.* Oxford University School of Archaeology Monograph No. 53 (Oxford).

Scuola Archeologica Italiana di Atene. 1984. *Creta Antica* (Rome).

Sear, F. B. 1977. *Roman Wall and Vault Mosaics* (Heidelberg).

Sen, A. 2004. 'How to Judge Globalism'. In Lechner and Boli (eds.), *The Globalization Reader*, 16–22.

Sessa, K. 2007. 'Christianity and the *Cubiculum*: Spiritual Politics and Domestic Space in Late Antique Rome'. *Journal of Early Christian Studies* 15.2, 171–204.

Shelley, J. M. 1943. 'The Christian Basilica near the Cenchrean Gate at Corinth'. *Hesperia* 12, 166–89.

Sherratt, S., and A. Sherratt. 1993. 'The Growth of the Mediterranean Economy in the Early First Millennium BC'. *World Archaeology* 24, 361–78.

Sidiropoulos, K. 2004. 'Νομισματική ιστορία της ρωμαϊκής και πρωτοβυζαντινής Κρήτης (67 π.Χ. – 827 μ.Χ.): Testimonia et desiderata. In Livadiotti and Simiakaki (eds.), *Creta romana e protobizantina*, 193–224.

Slane, K. 1989. 'Corinthian Ceramic Imports: The Changing Pattern of Provincial Trade in the First and Second Centuries CE'. In Walker and Cameron (eds.), *The Greek Renaissance in the Roman Empire*, 219–25.

    2003. 'Corinth's Roman Pottery: Quantification and Meaning'. In Williams and Bookidis (eds.), *Corinth, the Centenary, 1896–1996*, 321–49.

Smith, D. J. 1965. 'Three Fourth-Century Schools of Mosaic in Roman Britain'. In Picard and Stern (eds.), *La Mosaïque Gréco-Romaine I*, 95–156.

    1983. 'Mosaics'. In Henig (ed.), *A Handbook of Roman Art* (London).

Smith, W., ed. 1880. *Dictionary of Greek and Roman Biography and Mythology* (London).

Sodini, J. P. 1970. 'Mosaïques paléochrétiennes de Grèce'. *BCH* 94, 699–753.

    1971. 'Mosaïques paléochrétiennes de Grèce: Compléments'. *BCH* 95, 581–4.

Soles, J. S., and C. Davaras. 'Excavations at Mochlos'. *Hesperia* 61.4, 413–45.

Sonnabend, H. 2004. 'Roman Rule and Cretan Identity. The Impact on Society and Culture'. In Livadiotti and Simiakaki (eds.), *Creta romana e protobizantina*, 25–8.

Spanakis, S. 1972. *Crete: A Guide* (Iraklion).

Sparkes, B. 1996. *The Red and the Black: Studies in Greek Pottery* (London).

Spawforth, A. J. S. 1984. 'Notes on the Third Century A.D. in Spartan Epigraphy'. *ABSA* 79, 263–88.

    1985. 'Families at Roman Sparta and Epidaurus: Some Prosopographical Notes'. *ABSA* 80, 191–258.

    1994. 'Excavations at Sparta: The Roman Stoa, 1988–1991: The Inscriptions'. *ABSA* 89, 433–41.

Spawforth, T. 1995. 'Buthrotum'. *Anglo-Hellenic Review* 12, 7.

Spyridakis, S. 1999. 'Cretan Ecclesiastical Inscriptions: Notes and Observations'. *K.Khron* Λ', 62–76.

Stampolidis, N., ed. 2004. *Eleutherna: Polis. Acropolis. Necropolis* (Athens).

Stark, M. T. 1998. 'Technical Choices and Social Boundaries in Material Culture Patterning: An Introduction'. In Stark (ed.), *The Archaeology of Social Boundaries*, 1–11.

Stark, M. T., ed. 1998. *The Archaeology of Social Boundaries* (Washington, D.C.).

Stefanakis, M. I. 1999. 'The Introduction of Coinage in Crete and the Beginning of Local Minting'. In Chaniotis (ed.), *From Minoan Farmers to Roman Traders*, 247–68.

Stern, H. 1957. *Recueil des mosaïques de la Gaule I/1 Belgique* (Paris).

    1960. *Recueil des mosaïques de la Gaule I/2 Belgique* (Paris).

    1963. *Recueil des mosaïques de la Gaule I/3 Belgique* (Paris).

    1967. *Recueil des mosaïques de la Gaule II/1 Lyonnaise* (Paris).

Stern, H., and Blanchard-Lemée, M. 1975. *Recueil des mosaïques de la Gaule II/2 Lyonnaise* (Paris).

Stern, H., and M. Le Glay, eds. 1975. *La Mosaïque Gréco-Romaine II* [Actes du Colloque Internationale sur La Mosaïque Gréco-Romaine (Paris, 30th August–4th September, 1971)] (Paris).

Stiros, S. C., and S. Papageorgiou, 2001. 'Seismicity of Western Crete and the Destruction of the Town of Kisamos at CE 365: Archaeological Evidence'. *Journal of Seismology* 5, 381–97.

Stiros, S., S. Papageorgiou and S. Markoulaki. 2004. 'Καταστροφή των κρητικών πόλεων το 365 μ.Χ.'. In Livadiotti and Simiakaki (eds.), *Creta romana e protobizantina*, 427–44.

Strong, D. 1976. *Roman Art* (Harmondsworth).

Stucchi, S. 1975. *Architettura Cirenaica*. [Monografie di Archeologia Libica IX.] (Rome)

Sweetman, R. J. 1999. *'The Roman and Early Christian Mosaics of Crete'*. Ph.D. diss., University of Nottingham.

    2001. 'The Evidence of Itinerant Craftspeople from the Mosaics of Roman Crete'. In Paunier and Schmidt (eds.), *La Mosaïque Gréco-Romaine VIII*, 249–60.

    2003. 'The Roman Mosaics of the Knossos Valley'. *ABSA* 98, 517–47.

    2004a. 'The Changing Nature of Knossos: Roman to Late Antique – Some Problems'. In Cadogan, Hatzaki and Vasilakis (eds.), *Knossos*, 481–8. *BSA Studies* 12, 480–8.

    2004b. 'Late Antique Knossos. Understanding the Development of the City: Evidence of Mosaics and Religious Architecture'. *ABSA* 99, 315–54.

    2004c. 'The Mosaics of Roman and Early Christian Knossos: Interpreting Their Contexts and Workshop Production'. In Livadiotti and Simiakaki (eds.), *Creta romana e protobizantina*, 1173–85.

    2005. 'Knossos Medical Faculty Site: Late Antique Graves and Other Remains'. *ABSA* 100, 331–86.

    2006. 'The Romanization of Knossos: A Study of Mosaics and Other Material Culture'. In *Πεπραγμένα του 8ου Διεθνούς Κρητολογικού Συνεδρίου Elounda 1–6 October* A5, 421–34 (Iraklion).

    2007a. 'Roman Knossos, the Nature of a Globalized City'. *AJA* 111.1, 61–82.

    2007b. 'Identification of Space through a Study of Mosaics: A Case Study, Knossos, Crete'. In Westgate, Fisher and Whitley (eds.), *Proceedings of the Conference 'Building Communities'*, 363–71.

    2010a. 'Christianization of the Peloponnese: The Topography and Function of Late Antique Churches'. *Journal of Late Antiquity* 3.2 (Fall), 203–61.

    2010b. 'Roman Knossos: Discovering the City through the Evidence of Rescue Excavations'. *BSA* 105, 339–69.

Sweetman, R. J., ed. 2011a. *Roman Colonies in the First Century of Their Foundation* (Oxford).

Sweetman, R. J. 2011b. 'The Knossos Medical Faculty Basilica in Its Cretan Context'. In *Proceedings of the Cretelogical Congress, Chania 2006, B2*, 49–61 (Chania).

    Forthcoming. 'Knossos and Sparta: Lost Late Antique Cities'. In Christie (ed.), *Vrbes Extinctae*.

Sweetman, R. J., and G. Sanders. 2005. 'A New Group of Mosaics from Corinth, in the Domestic Context and the Context of the Colony'. In Morlier (ed.), *La mosaïque gréco-romaine IX*, 359–69.

Tammisto, A. 1997. *Birds in Mosaics: A Study on the Representation of Birds in Hellenistic and Romano-Campanian Tessellated Mosaics to the Early Augustan Age*. [Acta Instituti Romani Finlandiae 12.] (Rome).

Themelis, P. 1988. Ελεύθερνα, νομός Ρεθύμνης'. *K.Estia* 2, 298–302.

    1989–90. Ελεύθερνα, νομός Ρεθύμνης'. *K.Estia* 3, 266–7.

    1991–3. Ελεύθερνα, νομός Ρεθύμνης'. *K.Estia* 4, 252–7.

    1994–6. 'Βασιλική και προσκτίσματα, Ελεύθερνα, Νομός Ρεθύμνης'. *K.Estia* 5, 272–83.

Themelis, P., ed. 2000. *Πρωτοβυζαντινή Ελεύθερνα: Τομέας 1* (Rethymnon).

Themelis, P. 2002. 'Ελεύθερνα'. *K.Estia* 9, 275–92.

    2003. *Ancient Eleutherna: East Sector* (Athens).

    2004a. 'Υστερορωμαϊκή-Πρωτοβυζαντινή Ελεύθερνα, τομέας I'. In Livadiotti and Simiakaki (eds.), *Creta romana e protobizantina*, 445–59.

Themelis, P., ed. 2004b. *Πρωτοβυζαντινή Ελεύθερνα: Τομέας 2* (Rethymnon).

Themelis, P. 2004c. 'The Polis Sector I'. In Stampolidis (ed.), *Eleutherna*, 46–81.

Theocharis, D. 1965. ''Ασκληπιε ον Τρίκκης (Τρίκαλα)'. *A.Delt.* 20 B2, 313–16.

Theophanides, B. 1942–4. 'Κανδανός'. *AE*, 37–46.

    1945–7. 'Ψηφιδωτὸν ἐν Χανίοις'. *AE*, 37–46.

Tommaso, G. 2000. 'Il Settore B: La Basilica del Pretorio'. In Di Vita, *Gortina V.1:1 Lo scavo del Pretorio (1989–1995)*, 284–383.

Touchais, G. 1977. 'Chronique des fouilles et découvertes en Grèce en 1976'. *BCH* 101, 513–666.

    1985. 'Chronique des fouilles et découvertes en Grèce en 1984'. *BCH* 109, 759–862.

    1988. 'Chronique des fouilles et découvertes en Grèce en 1987'. *BCH* 112, 611–96.

    1989. 'Chronique des fouilles et découvertes en Grèce en 1988'. *BCH* 113, 581–700.

Toynbee, J. M. C. 1948. 'Beasts and Their Names in the Roman Empire'. *PBSR* 16, 24–37.

    1964. *Art in Britain under the Romans* (Oxford).

    1965. *The Art of the Romans* (London).

Toynbee, J. M. C., and J. B. Ward-Perkins. 1950. 'Peopled Scrolls: A Hellenistic Motif in Imperial Art'. *PBSR* 5, 1–44.

Treadgold, W. 2001. *A Concise History of Byzantium* (Hampshire).

Trimble, J. 2001. 'Rethinking "Romanization" in Early Imperial Greece: Butrint, Corinth and Nicopolis'. Review of *Die Römische Kolonie von Butrint und die Romanisierung Griechelands* by J. Bergemann. *JRA* 14, 625–8.

Turcan, R. 1966. *Les sarcophages Romains Dionysiaques* (Paris).

Tsipopoulou, M. 1989. *Archaeological Survey at Aghia Photia, Siteia* (Partille).

Tsougarakis, D. 1987a. 'Ρωμαϊκή Κρήτη'. In Papaiotakis (ed.), *Κρήτη Ιστορία και Πολιτισμός τ. Α'* 287–336 (Iraklion).

    1987b. 'Η Βυζαντινή Κρήτη'. In Papaiotakis (ed.), *Κρήτη Ιστορία και Πολιτισμός τ. Α'*, 340–404 (Iraklion).

    1988. *Byzantine Crete: From the 5th Century to the Venetian Conquest*. Historical Monographs 4. (Athens).

Tzedakis, G. 1966. 'Νομὸς Χανίων'. *A.Delt.* 21 B2, 425–9.

    1968. 'Νομὸς Χανίων'. *A.Delt.* 23 B2, 413–20.

    1969. 'Νομὸς Χανίων'. *A.Delt.* 24 B2, 428–36.

    1970. 'Νομὸς Χανίων'. *A.Delt.* 25 B2, 465–78.

    1972. 'Νομὸς Χανίων'. *A.Delt.* 27 B2, 635–44.

    1977. 'Νομὸς Χανίων'. *A.Delt.* 32 B2, 322–33.

    1978. 'Νομὸς Χανίων'. *A.Delt.* 33 B2, 364–84.

    1979. 'Νομὸς Χανίων'. *A.Delt.* 35 B2, 390–401.

Tzifopoulos, Y. Z. 2000. 'The Inscriptions'. In Themelis (ed.), *Πρωτοβυζαντινή Ελεύθερνα*, 237–59.

van der Mijnsbrugge, M. 1931. *The Cretan Konion* (London).

Van Dijk, J. 2005. *The Network Society: Social Aspects of New Media* (London).

Van Dyke, R., and S. E. Alcock, eds. 2003. *Archaeologies of Memory* (London).

van Effenterre, H. 1988. 'La Crete serait-elle une terre de colonisation?' *Cretan Studies* 1, 73–82.

Vasilakis, A. S. 1989–90. 'Λέβηνα'. *K.Estia* 3, 286.

    1996. 'Λέντας'. *A.Delt.* 51 B2, 642–3.

Vasilakis, fl. S. 2004. 'Ρωμαϊκά Μαυσλεία Κνωσού και Γόρτυνας'. In Livadiotti and Simiakaki (eds.), *Creta romana e protobizantina*, 699–708.

Vassal, V. 2006. *Les pavements d'opus signinum: Technique, décor, function architecturale*. BAR International Series 1472 (Oxford).

Vermeule C. 1968. *Roman Imperial Art in Greece and Asia Minor* (Harvard).

Vickers, M., and J. M. Reynolds. 1971–2. 'Cyrenaica, 1962–1972'. *Archaeological Reports for 1971–1972*, 27–45.

Ville, G. 1965. 'Essai de datation de la mosaïque des gladiateurs de Zliten'. In Picard and Stern (eds.), *La Mosaïque Gréco-Romaine I*, 147–56.

Viviers, D. 1999. 'Economy and Territorial Dynamics in Crete from the Archaic to the Hellenistic Period'. In Chaniotis (ed.), *From Minoan Farmers to Roman Traders*, 221–34.

2004. 'La conquête romaine de l'île et plus particulièrement ses liens avec l'organisation des traffics crétois à l'époque hellénistique'. In Livadiotti and Simiakaki (eds.), *Creta romana e protobizantina*, 17–24.

Volanakis, I. H. 1987. 'Τα παλαιοχριστιανικά μνημεία της Κρήτης'. *K.Khron, KZ*, 235–61.

von Gonzenbach, V. 1961. *Die römischen Mosaiken der Schweiz* (Basel).

Walbank, M. E. H. 2002. 'What's in a Name? Corinth under the Flavians'. *ZPE* 139, 251–65.

Walker, S. 1990. *Catalogue of Roman Sarcophagi in the British Museum*. Corpus Signorum Imperii Romani, Great Britain. Vol. 2, fasc. 2 (London).

Walker, S., and A. Cameron, eds. 1993. *The Greek Renaissance in the Roman Empire. Papers from the Tenth British Museum Classical Colloquium*. BICS Suppl. 55 (London).

Wallace-Hadrill, A. 1988. 'The Social Structure of the Roman House'. *PBSR* 56, 43–97.

1994. *Houses and Society in Pompeii and Herculaneum* (Princeton).

Wallerstein, I. 1974. *The Modern World-System* (New York).

1980. *The Modern World-System II* (New York).

Wardle, K. A. 1996. 'Roman Knossos'. In *AR* 1995–6, 41–2.

1997. 'Η Καθημερινή Επτά ημέρες'. 30.4.97, 29–30.

Wardle, K.A. 1998. 'Knossos 2000: Report on Excavation and Study from 1993–9' (unpublished).

Wardle, K. A., and D. Wardle. 2004. 'Glimpses of Private Life: Roman Rock Cut Tombs of the First and Second Centuries CE at Knossos'. In Cadogan, Hatzaki and Vasilakis (eds.), *Knossos*, 473–80. BSA Studies 12, 471–80.

Ward-Perkins, J. B. 1981. *Roman Imperial Architecture* (London).

Warren, P., and G. C. Miles. 1972. 'An Arab Building at Knossos'. *ABSA* 67, 285–96.

Warren, P. M. 1984–5. 'Knossos: Stratigraphical Museum Excavations, 1978–82, Part III'. *AR* 31, 124–9.

1987–8. 'Knossos: Stratigraphical Museum Excavations, 1978–82, Part IV'. *AR* 34, 86–104.

Waterhouse, H. 1994. 'The Knossos "Town Mosaic" Reconsidered'. *Cretan Studies* 4, 165–74.

Waters, M. 1995. *Globalization* (London).

Watrous, L. V. 1982. *Lasithi: A History of Settlement on a Highland Plain in Crete*. Hesperia Supplement 18 (Princeton).

Watrous, L. V., D. Xatzi-Vallianou, K. Pope, N. Mourtzas, J. Shay, C. T. Shay, J. Bennet, D. Tsoungarakis, E. Angelomati-Tsoungarakis, C. Vallianos and H. Blitzer. 1993. 'A Survey of the Western Mesara Plain in Crete: Preliminary Report of the 1984, 1986, and 1987 Field Seasons'. *Hesperia*, 62.2, 191–248.

Wattel-de Croizant, O. 1995. *Les Mosaïques représentant le mythe d'Europe: Évolution et interprétation des modèles grecs en milieu romain* (Paris).

Waywell, G. B. 1973. 'A Roman Portrait Bust from Knossos'. *ABSA* 68, 295–6.

Waywell, S. E. 1979. 'Roman Mosaics in Greece'. *AJA* 83, 239–321.

Webb, R. 1999. 'The Aesthetics of Sacred Space: Narrative, Metaphor, and Motion in *Ekphraseis* of Church Buildings'. *Dunbarton Oaks Papers* 53, 59–74.

Webster, J. 2001. 'Creolizing the Roman Provinces'. *AJA* 105, 209–55.

Webster, J., and N. J. Cooper, eds. 1996. *Roman Imperialism: Post-colonial Perspectives. Proceedings of a Symposium Held at Leicester University in November 1994*. Leicester Archaeology Monographs 3 (Leicester).

Webster, T. B. L. 1967. *Hellenistic Art* (London).

1995. *Monuments Illustrating New Comedy*. Vols. 1 and 2. Institute of Classical Studies London Suppl. Series 50 (London).

Weinburg, G. 1960. 'Excavations at Tarrha, 1959'. *Hesperia* XXIX, 90–117.

Westgate, R. 1997–8. 'Greek Mosaics in Their Architectural and Social Context'. *BICS* 42, 93–115.

— 1999. 'Genre and Originality in Hellenistic Mosaics'. *Mosaic* 26, 16–25.

— 2007. 'House and Society in Classical and Hellenistic Crete: A Case Study in Regional Variation'. *AJA* 111, 423–57.

Westgate, R., N. Fisher and J. Whitley, eds. 2007. *Proceedings of the Conference 'Building Communities: House Settlement and Society in the Aegean and Beyond'*. *BSA* Studies 15 (London).

Whitley, D. 1998. *Reader in Archaeological Theory* (London).

Whitley, J. 1991. *Style and Society in Dark Age Greece: The Changing Face of a Pre-literate Society, 1100–700 BC* (Cambridge).

Whitley, J., M. Prent and S. Thorne. 1999. 'Praisos IV: A Preliminary Report on the 1993 and 1994 Survey Seasons'. *BSA* 94, 215–64.

Wiles, D. 1991. *The Masks of Menander: Sign and Meaning in Greek and Roman Performance* (Cambridge).

Willetts, R. F. 1955. *Aristocratic Society in Ancient Crete* (London).

— 1965. *Ancient Crete* (London).

— 1969. *Everyday Life in Ancient Crete* (London).

— 1977. *The Civilisation of Ancient Crete* (London).

Williams, C. K. 1993. 'Roman Corinth as a Commercial Center'. In Gregory (ed.), *The Corinthia in the Roman Period*, 31–46.

Williams, C. K., and N. Bookidis, eds. 2003. *Corinth, the Centenary, 1896–1996*. Corinth Vol. XX (Princeton).

Wilson, R. J. A. 1981. 'Mosaics, Mosaicists and Patrons'. *JRS* 71, 173–7.

— 1982. 'Roman Mosaics in Sicily: The African Connection'. *AJA* 86, 413–28.

— 1983. *Piazza Armerina* (London).

— 1990. *Sicily under the Roman Empire: The Archaeology of a Roman Province, 36BC–AD535* (Warminster).

Wiseman, J. 1979. 'Corinth and Rome 1: 228 B.C.–A.D. 267'. *ANRW* II.7, 438–538.

Woodhead, A. G. 1981. *The Study of Greek Inscriptions*, 2nd ed. (Cambridge).

Woolf, G. 1992. 'Imperialism, Empire and the Integration of the Roman Economy'. *World Archaeology* 23.3, 283–93.

— 1998. *Becoming Roman: The Origins of Provincial Civilization in Gaul* (Cambridge).

Wroth, W. 1886. *Catalogue of the Greek Coins of Crete and the Aegean Islands* (London).

Xanthoudidis, S. 1918. 'Χερσόνησος: παράρτημα τοῦ Ἀρχαιολογικοῦ Δελτίου'. *A.Delt.* 4, 30–2.

INDEX

Achaea, 5
Actium, Battle of, 95
Aegean and islands, 35, 73, 143, 148
Aguilar, M., 102
Alcock, S.E., 138, 312 n. 29, 316 n. 122
Alföldi-Rosenbaum, E. and J. Ward-Perkins
    Justinianic Mosaic Pavements in Cyrenaican Churches, xv
Allison, P., 103–4
Altamore, G., 105
Ambraseys, N.N., 15
Andreadakis, M., 266
Antikythera mechanism, 294
Aphrodisias, 16
Arabs, 13, 89; *see also* Crete
Archaeological Society, 203
art, 19
Asia Minor, 29, 73, 74, 76, 134, 148
    Ephesus, 16
    Sardis, 134, 135
Avars, 10

Baldwin Bowsky, M.W., 8, 12, 14, 21, 26, 29, 139, 140, 141,
    313 n. 40, 314 n. 96, 342 n. 7
Balmelle, C., 157
Bandy, A.C., 120, 122
Baxandall, M., 4
Bekker-Nielsen, T., 12
Belgium, 76
Berti, F., 240
bias, 4, 5, 7, 20, 79, 80, 101, 311 n. 6, 330 n. 28, 331 n. 16
    archaeological, 29, 86, 87, 93, 143, 330 n. 21, 337 n. 196
    creeping determinism, xvi, 1, 15, 75, 311 n. 6
    hindsight, 1, 15, 312 n. 6
biblical references
    Isaiah 11:6–7, 66
    John 15:1, 67, 327 n. 180
    John 15:5, 327 n. 180
    Mark 6:35–44, 326 n. 176
    Psalms 11:1, 326 n. 167
    Psalms 42:1, 66

Blackman, D. and K. Branigan, 20, 21, 22, 24, 29, 305
Blake, M.E., 209
Bourboudakis, E., 255
Bourdieu, P., 90, 91
Bowden, W., 330 n. 8
Britain, 72, 130, 339 n. 58
Bruneau, P., 50
Bulgaria, 51, 266
Burden, J., 336 n. 174

Campbell, S.D., 41
  and J.P. Sodini, 134
    Mosaics of Aphrodisias in Caria, xv
Carington Smith, J., 175
Castells, M., 150, 151
Chaniotaki-Starida, L., and M. Mari, 191, 193
Chaniotis, A., 7
Christ, Christianity and Christianization, 2, 16, 25, 43, 46,
    60, 61–2, 63, 64, 65, 68, 69, 79, 88, 94, 115, 120,
    128, 139, 144–8, 269, 294, 296, 301, 313 n. 51,
    316 n. 126, 326 n. 157 and n. 161, 334 n. 67,
    340 n. 76; *see also* Crete
  archangel Michael, 122, 265, 286
  archbishops, archpriests and bishops, 81, 121, 122, 123
    names of
      Andreas of Chersonisos, 334 n. 106
      Andreas of Kisamos, 343 n. 49
      Dometios, 122
      Euphratas of Eleutherna, 122, 227, 230, 286, 339 n. 50
      Theodoros of Gortyn, 121
      Vetranios, 121, 285
    seats of, 147, 216, 222, 225, 299
  churches, 6, 9, 10, 11, 13–14, 17, 22, 23 (fig), 25, 27, 37,
    43, 45, 56, 61–2, 63, 64, 65, 68, 71, 74, 76, 80, 82,
    85, 86, 88, 94, 96, 97, 98, 99, 100, 112–15, 117,
    119–22, 133, 135, 136, 138, 144, 145, 146–7, 195,
    201, 212, 213–20, 221, 222, 225–32, 233–8, 239,
    252–5, 256–61, 262–4, 265–6, 269, 271, 294, 295,
    298, 302, 307, 315 n. 101 and n. 102,
    330 n. 8, 344 n. 66